D0498626

Psychotherapists in Clinical Practice

PSYCHOTHERAPISTS IN CLINICAL PRACTICE

COGNITIVE AND BEHAVIORAL PERSPECTIVES

EDITED BY

Neil S. Jacobson

University of Washington

THE GUILFORD PRESS
New York   London

© 1987 The Guilford Press
A Division of Guilford Publications, Inc.
200 Park Avenue South, New York, N.Y. 10003
All rights reserved

No part of this book may be reproduced, stored in a retrieval system, or transmitted,
in any form or by any means, electronic, mechanical, photocopying, microfilming,
recording, or otherwise, without written permission from the Publisher

Printed in the United States of America

Last digit is print number: 9 8 7 6 5 4 3 2 1

Library of Congress Cataloging in Publication Data

Psychotherapists in clinical practice.

Includes bibliographies and index.
1. Cognitive therapy. 2. Behavior therapy.
I. Jacobson, Neil S., 1949-   [DNLM: 1. Behavior
Therapy—methods. 2. Cognition. WM 425 P974]
RC489.C63P78 1987   616.89′142   86-18474
ISBN 0-89862-690-0

CONTRIBUTORS

LAUREN BRASWELL, PhD, North Memorial Medical Center, Minneapolis, Minnesota

EDNA B. FOA, PhD, Department of Psychiatry, Medical College of Pennsylvania, Philadelphia, Pennsylvania

IRIS GOLDSTEIN FODOR, PhD, School Psychology Program, New York University, New York, New York

STEVEN C. HAYES, PhD, Department of Psychology, University of Nevada, Reno, Nevada

STEVEN D. HOLLON, PhD, Department of Psychology, Vanderbilt University, Nashville, Tennessee

NEIL S. JACOBSON, PhD, Department of Psychology, University of Washington, Seattle, Washington

FREDERICK H. KANFER, PhD, Department of Psychology, University of Illinois, Champaign, Illinois

PHILIP C. KENDALL, PhD, Department of Psychology, Temple University, Philadelphia, Pennsylvania

ROBERT J. KOHLENBERG, PhD, Department of Psychology, University of Washington, Seattle, Washington

ARNOLD A. LAZARUS, PhD, Rutgers–The State University of New Jersey, New Brunswick, NJ; Private Practice, Princeton, New Jersey

GAYLA MARGOLIN, PhD, Department of Psychology, University of Southern California, Los Angeles, California

JOAN PIASECKI, BA, Department of Psychology, University of Colorado, Boulder, Colorado

BRUCE K. SCHEFFT, PhD, Department of Psychology, Northern Illinois University, DeKalb, Illinois

GAIL STEKETEE, PhD, Department of Psychiatry, Medical College of Pennsylvania, Philadelphia, Pennsylvania

MAVIS TSAI, PhD, Private Practice, Seattle, Washington

CONTENTS

Psychotherapists in Clinical Practice

CHAPTER 1

Cognitive and Behavior Therapists in Clinical Practice: An Introduction

Neil S. Jacobson
University of Washington

THE GROWTH OF BEHAVIOR THERAPY

It is easy to forget that behavior therapy is still a relatively young treatment modality. Despite occasional clinical applications of a learning theory as early as the 1920s (Kazdin, 1978), behavior therapy really burst upon the psychotherapeutic scene in the late 1950s. In just a quarter of a century, behavior therapy has evolved from a peripheral fringe movement to part of the mainstream. Although its influence in the disciplines of psychiatry and social work remains marginal, the impact of behavior therapy on clinical psychology has been remarkable: Within clinical psychology, behavior therapy is widely taught in graduate programs, increasingly well-represented at internship sites, and bolstered by a substantial proportion of practicing clinical psychologists who identify themselves as behavior therapists (Norcross & Prochaska, 1982; O'Leary, 1984; Smith, 1982, Tuma & Pratt, 1982; Wilson, 1984).

In addition to its popularity, behavior therapy has, despite its short history, accumulated the most impressive track record of any psychotherapeutic modality for rigorous, controlled outcome research (Kazdin & Wilson, 1978). As a result, more is known about the efficacy of behavior therapies than about all other theoretical perspectives in the field of psychotherapeutic research combined. The commitment to controlled research has enabled investigators to document legitimate and in some cases remarkable breakthroughs (e.g., flooding and response prevention as a treatment for obsessive–compulsives: Foa, Steketee, & Ozarow, 1985; behavioral family therapy with schizophrenic families: Falloon, Boyd, & McGill, 1984; and cognitive-behavioral treatments for depression: Beck, Rush, Shaw, & Emery, 1979). It has also exposed limited or weak treatments that might otherwise have hung around for decades (e.g., covert conditioning: Mahoney, 1974; or systematic [imaginal] desensitization with severe anxiety disorders: Barlow & Wolfe, 1981). This empirical

1

focus has resulted in a great deal of clinical innovation and technique development, and has allowed behavior therapy to escape the shackles of rigid orthodoxy.

PROBLEMS IN THE LITERATURE

Yet despite the growth, the popularity, and the legitimate accomplishments of behavior therapy over the past 25 years, it is still perceived by a substantial portion of the mental health community as a technology that is useful only as an adjunct treatment, and even then for only a few specific target populations. Behavior therapy has never caught the imagination of the mental health masses (Norcross & Prochaska, 1982; Smith, 1982). Even a surprising percentage of self-described behavior therapists label themselves as eclectic or integrative in their approach to therapy, and very few insist that they never use techniques that are typically thought of as nonbehavioral (Norcross & Wogan, 1983; Wilson, 1984).

Of course, this phenomenon that I am noting is by no means unique to behavior therapy; indeed, eclecticism and integrationism have become growing trends within the psychotherapeutic community, and the purists from any school are swamped by a substantial plurality of self-described eclectics (Norcross & Prochaska, 1982; Smith, 1982; Wilson, 1984). However, it seems clear that behavior therapy as it is written about in the literature often only scratches the surfaces of what transpires in clinical practice (cf. Goldfried & Davison, 1976), even in the clinical practice of self-described behavior therapists. It is my belief that a number of factors have conspired to cloud these clinical realities.

Perhaps the most important of these obfuscating factors has been, ironically enough, the research context in which most behavior therapy techniques were developed. The clinical research laboratory brings with it demands for carefully specified client populations, with restrictions that maximize statistical power through sample homogeneity. Research also gravitates toward clinical problems that are relatively easy to specify, measure, and manipulate, and environments over which the experimenter has as much control as possible.

The implications of these research demands are that behavior therapy has tended to develop and flourish around certain types of clinical problems as opposed to others. Moreover, the targets of behavior therapy research do not always correspond to those commonly faced by practicing clinicians. There are numerous examples of this bifurcation between the research literature and clinical practice. In the early days of desensitization research, investigators tended to focus on analogue phobic populations that bore little resemblance to anxiety-disordered clients seeking therapy (e.g., Paul, 1969). As research has gradually shifted to clinically phobic populations, it is becoming increasingly evident that early technologies built upon the analogue populations have to be altered considerably in the clinical setting (see Foa & Steketee, Chapter 3, this volume). And even when these alterations occur, significant portions of clients remain either unimproved or somewhat dysfunctional following treatment (Barlow & Wolfe, 1981; Jacobson, Wilson & Tupper, 1986).

As a second example, the vast literature in the treatment of severely disturbed institutionalized adults can be used to illustrate these points. A substantial portion of that literature is devoted to modifying isolated behaviors that are not an essential part of the disorder (cf. Davison, 1969). Although teaching a schizophrenic subject to make his or her bed might demonstrate that reinforcement principles can be used to modify behavior, it does not demonstrate that reinforcement principles can be used to eliminate or even reduce schizophrenic behavior to a clinically significant degree. Despite some dramatic isolated success stories (Paul & Lentz, 1977), much of this literature is of dubious clinical significance and has precious little application to clinicians working in hospital settings with acutely psychotic patients.

As a final example, consider the once voluminous and now largely moribund literature on assertiveness training. There is no doubt that unassertive behavior is a common phenomenon in our culture, especially among women. Moreover, it may even be related to some behavior disorders. But my contention is that this literature proliferated because unassertive subjects were easy to find, assertiveness was easy to measure, and thus research programs could be easily built via assertion training. How else would one explain the popularity of this literature in contrast to the dearth of studies on severe clinical disorders such as depression? It was a literature that took on a life of its own, but which shed little light on the treatment of the kinds of clinical problems that come to the attention of practicing clinicians.

This is the essential point: Much of the behavior therapy literature has failed to speak to the practicing clinician. These points are made implicitly in many of the chapters composing this volume, but most explicitly by Fodor (Chapter 6), Hayes (Chapter 9), and Kohlenberg and Tsai (Chapter 10). This has been particularly true with adult outpatient populations. There is no literature on how to treat many of the clients confronting clinicians on a day-to-day basis. The long and the short of it is that, in our quest for internal validity, we have evaluated the efficacy of our treatments on such restrictive client populations that behavior therapy technology has not been extended to cover many of those who sit in our outpatient waiting rooms hoping for our help.

There is another problem: The behavior therapy literature has not tended to be explicit about the context in which behavioral techniques are delivered. Even though isolated contributions have been made to the role of the therapist–client relationship in behavior therapy (Wilson & Evans,

1977), most of the behavior therapy literature tends to be silent on questions relating to the formation of a therapeutic alliance, strategies for dealing with noncompliance and termination, and ways to provide a context that facilitates the effective implementation of behavior therapy technology.

A number of books have been written over the past 10 years that try to add clinical material to the technological skeleton. Prominent examples are the edited volumes by Goldstein and Foa (1978) and the recent volume by Barlow (1985). However, even these outstanding volumes do not adequately address all of the issues mentioned above, because they tend to be organized according to disorders, the very disorders that have received the most attention in the behavior therapy literature that, as I have just argued, leaves out much of what the clinician must deal with in clinical practice.

FILLING IN THE GAPS

The impetus for this book is the belief that there is not enough material in the behavior therapy literature to support a practicing clinician working in settings where outpatients must be treated. Yet there are thousands of clinicians working in outpatient settings who think of themselves as behavior therapists. These apparently contradictory statements lead to a variety of questions. What is it that makes someone a behavior therapist? What goes on behind the closed doors of the consulting room that bridges the gap between the literature and clinical practice? To what extent can the variables that bridge this gap be isolated, specified, and studied in their own right?

This book provides information relevant to all of the above questions. All of the contributors are people who identify themselves either as behavior or cognitive-behavior therapists. All of them are teachers and clinical supervisors, leaders in the field who have made significant contributions to the "behavior therapy" literature. They were asked to write personal accounts describing in clinical depth how they treat clients, including the clinical tidbits that are typically heard only by their own trainees. In order to increase the likelihood that all authors would address a common set of core issues, they were all asked to follow an outline that specified particular areas of focus (see Table 1-1).

As the reader will note upon reading the chapters, there is a great deal of clinical innovation going on incognito in the cognitive-behavior therapy field. What is equally striking is the heterogeneity of directions in which these innovations are heading. Some of the most striking trends can be summarized as follows:

Cognitive connection. The incorporation of cognitive theory and therapy into behavior therapy has been so total that it is difficult to find pure

TABLE 1-1. Outline of Areas of Focus for Each Chapter

I. Theoretical model
II. Theory of therapeutic change
   1. Diagnostic and assessment procedures
   2. Typical treatment goals
   3. Division of ideal or typical stages of treatment
   4. Typical structure of therapy sessions
   5. Hypothesized active ingredients of treatment approach
III. Specific techniques
   1. Case material
   2. Transcripts if appropriate
   3. How and when are cognitive techniques used?
   4. How and when are techniques traditionally thought of as nonbehavioral and/or noncognitive used?
   5. Limitations and contraindications of your approach
IV. Role of the therapist
   1. What are the clinical skills and other therapist attributes most essential to successful therapy?
   2. Give some examples of treatment errors ("bad therapy")
V. Common clinical issues
   1. Forming a therapeutic alliance
   2. Resistance and noncompliance
   3. Termination
   4. Influence of therapist's values
   5. Etc.
VI. How successful is this approach?
   1. Data from outcome research
   2. For whom is your approach indicated and contraindicated?
   3. What are the major needs for future development?

behavior therapists working with outpatients. Hence the title of this book! Despite the obvious paradigm problems inherent in incorporating mediational concepts into a behavioristic view of the clinical world (see Hayes, Chapter 9, and Kohlenberg & Tsai, Chapter 10), the cognitive connection has flourished in the behavior therapy world. It is probably no coincidence that cognitive therapy began to become acceptable to behavior therapists as their work moved into uncharted outpatient domains such as depression (e.g., Piasecki & Hollon, Chapter 4). Cognitive therapy provided a vehicle for behavior therapists to conceptualize and attempt to modify internal events without resorting to psychodynamic concepts. Since the reality of the outpatient clinical world is such that thoughts and feelings are often the presenting problems, behavior therapists needed some way to handle these clinical phenomena; for many therapists behaviorism did not, in and of itself, provide the answers. Moreover, standard functional analytic solutions involving the translation of internal events into overt behavioral concomitants has often been problematic (cf. Jacobson, 1985a, 1985b).

Cognitive therapy has been relatively easy to integrate with behavior therapy, despite the theoretical tension between mediational and nonmediational models. Like traditional behavior therapy, cognitive therapies are very explicit, well-delineated, and therefore easily replicable. Moreover, they usually include many types of interventions that are not only compatible but at times indistinguishable from standard behavioral interventions (Deck et al., 1979). Finally, cognitive therapies have shared the commitment of behavior therapists to systematic technique development and controlled evaluation of therapeutic outcome. Seven of the nine remaining chapters incorporate cognitive concepts and/or techniques at least to some degree.

Other forms of integration/eclecticism. In order to increase the range and applicability of behavior therapy, many of the authors contributing to this book have expanded the model to incorporate intervention strategies that are commonly viewed as nonbehavioral. The most well-known and systematic model built upon such expansionism is the "multimodal" framework developed by Arnold Lazarus and summarized by him in Chapter 8. But the movement is also reflected in more focused attempts at intergration such as Fodor's (Chapter 6) incorporation of Gestalt therapy principles, and to some extent Margolin's (Chapter 7) embracing of systems theory. Finally, there is a different sort of integration reflected in the work of Kanfer and his associates (Chapter 2). In Kanfer's "self-management" therapy, a wide variety of techniques and interventions are used, but they are all incorporated within a broad-based theoretical framework oriented towards social learning, following from Kanfer's earlier pioneering work in the area of self-control.

Back to basics. The two final chapters represent a third solution to the inadequacies of the traditional behavior therapy literature in addressing the problems faced by adult outpatients. Both Hayes (Chapter 9) and Kohlenberg and Tsai (Chapter 10) argue that there is no need to expand upon, add to, or deviate from behaviorism; in fact, the problem, according to these authors, is that behavior therapy researchers have not payed close enough attention to behaviorism. These two chapters are fascinating because, while they both look to Skinner and radical behaviorism for their answers in devising treatments for adult outpatients, they find very different answers. Indeed, neither of them derive from radical behaviorism a system that looks much like traditional behavior therapy at all. At a technical level, these two chapters are as eclectic as any in the book, despite the adherence to orthodox Skinnerian principles at the theoretical level. Hayes's approach is reminiscent in many ways of strategic therapy (e.g., Haley, 1965), while Kohlenberg and Tsai describe an approach that closely resembles psychoanalytic psychotherapy.

ESTABLISHING A COMMON GROUND

What unites all of these approachs and makes them cognitive and behavior therapies? Perhaps nothing. It may be simply an illusion to suggest that a school of therapy is represented in this book. It may be that people who call themselves behavior therapists, just like other clinicians in the mental health field, end up almost inevitably becoming at least technically eclectic, because no model of therapy adequately deals with the gamut of clinical problems requiring the services of a therapist.

However, I do believe that all of the contributors to this book can legitimately claim to be cognitive and/or behavior therapists. They share common elements that in some ways can, when taken together, serve as a definition of contemporary behavior therapy.

First, all of the approaches to therapy described in this book owe great allegiance to conceptual and theoretical principles from general psychology. In addition to the learning theory connection, which remains visible to varying degrees in all chapters, clinical techniques have been enriched by social psychology (Chapter 2), cognitive psychology (Chapter 4), and developmental psychology (Chapter 5). In many ways, it appears that the application of principles established in the laboratories of general psychology remains a distinguishing characteristic of contemporary behavior therapy.

Second, all of the chapters emphasize contingencies in the current environment as central to both understanding and successfully treating the client. Besides the corresponding de-emphasis on historical insight as a precursor to change, this linking of both adaptive and maladaptive behavior to current environmental antecedents and consequences manifests itself in a number of different ways. One is a systematic assessment process where the therapist seeks to elucidate these behavior–environment connections. Another is the intervention strategies that usually follow directly from the hypothesized links between behavior and the current environment. A third is the tendency toward rigorous, empirical evaluation of outcome.

The emphasis on establishing and modifying current contingencies is more obvious in some chapters than in others, but it is present in all. Even in the chapters where cognitive events are at the forefront of case conceptualization and intervention, they are linked to overt behavioral and environmental events. Moreover, Piasecki and Hollon (Chapter 4), despite a causal model that clearly emphasizes internal events, teach their depressed clients to be applied behavior analysts: The clients are trained to test their beliefs empirically through systematic observation and hypothesis testing, and the ability to master this process is viewed as a major change mechanism in the cognitive treatment for depression.

Third, virtually all authors make extensive use of a technology that has been traditionally associated with behavior therapy. These so-called behavioral techniques are not emphasized in all chapters, because authors were requested to elaborate on other aspects of their work. But intervention strategies, which could be considered a core battery for outpatient behavior therapy, were alluded to and integated into all approaches. Even though few clinicians would adhere to a technique-oriented definition of behavior therapy today, it is significant that exposure techniques, progressive muscle relaxation, self-monitoring, behavior rehearsal, and other contingency management procedures remain central to clinicians' self identification as behavior therapists.

In the final analysis, these chapters collectively comprise a provocative, clinically rich set of treatises about the practice of psychotherapy. They are not necessarily easy to assimilate. But they do testify to the fact that the cognitive and behavior therapies are alive and well.

REFERENCES

Barlow, D. H. (Ed.). (1985). *Clinical handbook of psychological disorders*. New York: Guilford.

Barlow, D. H., & Wolfe, E. (1981). Behavioral approaches to anxiety disorders: A report on the NIMH–SUNY Albany Research Conference. *Journal of Consulting and Clinical Psychology, 49*, 448–454.

Beck, A. T., Rush, A. J., Shaw, B. F., & Emery, G. (1979). *Cognitive therapy of depression*. New York: Guilford.

Davison, G. C. (1969). Appraisal of behavior modification techniques with adults in institutional settings. In C. M. Franks (Ed.), *Behavior therapy: Appraisal and status* (pp. 220–278). New York: McGraw-Hill.

Falloon, R. H., Boyd, J. L., & McGill, C. W. (1984). *Family care of schizophrenia: A problem-solving approach to the treatment of mental illness*. New York: Guilford.

Foa, E. B., Steketee, G. S., & Ozarow, B. J. (1985). Behavior therapy with obsessive compulsives: From theory to treatment. In M. Mavissakalian, S. M. Turner, & L. Michelson (Eds.), *Obsessive compulsive disorders: Psychological and pharmacological treatments*. Plenum: New York.

Goldfried, M. R., & Davison, G. C. (1976). *Clinical behavior therapy*. New York: Wiley.

Goldstein, A., & Foa, E. (Eds.). (1978). *Handbook of behavioral interventions*. New York: Wiley.

Haley, J. (1965). *Uncommon therapy: The psychiatric techniques of Milton A. Erickson, M.D.* New York: Norton.

Jacobson, N. S. (1985a). The role of observational measures in behavior therapy outcome research. *Behavioral Assessment, 7*, 297–308.

Jacobson, N. S. (1985b). Uses versus abuses of observational measures. *Behavioral Assessment, 7*, 323–330.

Jacobson, N. S., Wilson, L., & Tupper, C. (1986). *The clinical significance of treatment gains resulting from exposure-based interventions for agoraphobia: A reanalysis of outcome data*. Unpublished manuscript, University of Washington.

Kazdin, A. E. (1978). *History of behavior modification: Experimental foundations of contemporary research*. Baltimore, MD: University Park Press.

Kazdin, A. E., & Wilson, G. T. (1978). *Evaluation of behavior therapy: Issues, evidence, and research strategies*. Cambridge, MA: Ballinger.

Mahoney, M. J. (1974). *Cognition and behavior modification*. Cambridge, MA: Ballinger.

Norcross, J. C., & Prochaska, J. O. (1982). A national survey of clinical psychologists' affiliations and orientations. *Clinical Psychologist, 35*, 1–8.

Norcross, J. C., & Wogan, N. (1983). Relationship of behavior therapists' characteristics, activities and clients to reported practices in therapy. *Professional Psychology: Research and Practice, 14*, 44–56.

O'Leary, K. D. (1984). The image of behavior therapy: It is time to take a stand. *Behavior Therapy, 15*, 219–233.

Paul, G. L. (1969). Outcome of systematic desensitization. II: Controlled investigations of individual treatment, technique variations, and current status. In C. M. Franks (Ed.), *Behavior therapy: Appraisal and status* (pp. 105–159). New York: McGraw-Hill.

Paul, G. L., & Lentz, R. J. (1977). *Psychosocial treatment of chronic mental patients: Milieu vs. social-learning programs.* Cambridge, MA: Harvard University Press.

Smith, D. (1982). Trends in counseling and psychotherapy. *American Psychologist, 37*, 802–810.

Tuma, J. M., & Pratt, J. M. (1982). Clinical child psychology practice and training: A survey. *Journal of Clinical Child Psychology, 11*, 27–34.

Wilson, G. T. (1984). Clinical issues and strategies in the practice of behavior therapy. In C. M. Franks, G. T. Wilson, Philip C. Kendall, & K. D. Brownell, *Annual review of behavior therapy: Theory and practice* (Vol. 10, pp. 291–320). New York: Guilford.

Wilson, G. T., & Evans, I. N. (1977). The therapist–client relationship in behavior therapy. In A. S. Gurman & A. M. Razin (Eds.), *The therapist's contributions to effective psychotherapy: An empirical approach* (pp. 544–565). New York: Pergamon.

CHAPTER 2

Self-Management Therapy in Clinical Practice

Frederick H. Kanfer
University of Illinois

Bruce K. Schefft
Northern Illinois University

INTRODUCTION

The clinical practice of self-management therapy has as its central theme the model of self-regulation developed by Kanfer (1970) and his colleagues (Kanfer & Hagerman, 1981; Kanfer & Karoly, 1972) and the more recent model on managing the clinical change process (Kanfer & Grimm, 1980) as a problem solving task (Kanfer & Busemeyer, 1982). The clinical approach also emphasizes the utilization of laboratory-based research and behavior theory from various areas of psychology, predominantly learning psychology (Dollard & Miller, 1950; Kanfer, 1961; Kanfer & Phillips, 1970; Rotter, 1954; Skinner, 1953) but also from social psychology (Brehm, 1976; Goldstein, Heller, & Sechrest, 1966; Kanfer, 1984) and information processing (Kanfer & Hagerman, 1985; Lachman, Lachman, & Butterfield, 1979; Merluzzi, Rudy, & Glass, 1981). Recognizing the limitations of the utility of laboratory research and basic theory in daily operation, the approach nevertheless stresses the importance of empirical verification of ideas and observations and recourse to the body of scientific knowledge as a source of hypotheses. Although behavioristic in its origin, it emphasizes the significance of environmental and biological determinants. It views the social and cultural setting of therapy, the interactions between therapists and clients, and between the psychological and biological systems of the participants as factors that strongly influence therapeutic goals and strategies. With increasing research and a body of knowledge organized by microtheories in such areas as motivation, health psychology, information processing, social psychology, and biopsychology, the attempt to account for the complexity of clinical prac-

10

tices has increasingly expanded. Self-management therapy is best viewed as a metatheoretical framework that draws on different subareas of psychology for heuristic and explanatory concepts. Thus it is pluralistic in its recourse to scientific theory.

The clinical application of this approach differs from various nonbehaviorally oriented schools of therapy and from some variants of behavior therapy in several ways. First, it highlights the requirement that the client actively participate throughout the entire therapeutic process. Although the therapist "instigates" changes in motivation, goals, and behaviors in the client (Kanfer & Phillips, 1966), the therapeutic process requires alteration in client's self-generated processes, such as thinking, planning, problem solving, and decision making. It demands active involvement in treatment to facilitate learning and, later, maintenance of targeted changes in behavior. Thus it includes cognitive or mediational variables in its treatment focus. A variety of techniques, including environmental control or psychopharmacological interventions may be used, but the ultimate criterion of successful outcome of therapy is a change in the client's interactions with his or her environment and his or her self-reactions in a manner that relieves personal distress and improves the client's relationships in his or her daily living situation (Kanfer & Schefft, in press).

Second, by emphasizing the importance of client motivation to change, our approach gives close attention to assisting clients in the development of specific goals, in clarifying the potential benefits of therapy, and in answering for the client the general question "How will I be better off after treatment?" in a very specific way. Only a person who has a clear image of the benefits of change is motivated to undertake the demanding tasks of a therapeutic process.

Third, self-management therapy centers on preparation for the future, rather than on reconstruction of the past. The main focus of this problem-solving orientation is on facilitating movement toward the therapeutic objective rather than on understanding the causes of the present dysfunction.

To enhance the active role played by the client throughout therapy, he or she is taught to assume some of the functions of the therapist in examining behaviors, setting goals, solving problems, reinforcing progress, and applying learned skills to new situations. Over the course of treatment, the client is helped to become increasingly self-reliant within the therapeutic setting and in the natural environment. Self-management therapy therefore concentrates on training effective self-regulatory behaviors, and strengthening the motivational resources intrinsic to self-regulation. The clinical approach not only highlights active client involvement. It also provides a framework for enhancing client effort and participation throughout all phases of the therapy process. The model which guides clinical application attempts to anticipate and minimize common difficulties encountered in treatment and to reduce client opposition to the change process from the beginning.

The conceptual framework assists the clinician in identifying issues that are commonly encountered as the client passes through various phases of therapy. It also helps the clinician to use tactics and operations at any given moment in therapy that follow directly from the translation of the theoretical model into clinical operations. The strong tie between conceptual guidelines, research, and clinical operations is one of the distinguishing features of the self-management approach. Therefore, preference for tactics or methods, whenever possible, is given on the basis of relevant data from any subarea of psychology or empirical findings from other sources.

THEORETICAL MODEL OF BEHAVIOR DISORDERS

The underlying model of psychopathology (Kanfer, 1971, 1977; Kanfer & Phillips, 1970; Kanfer & Saslow, 1969), views all behavior as a result of the impact of three classes of variables. *Alpha* variables consist of all inputs from the external environment. They include reinforcement-contingencies, stimulus control, discriminative cues, models, social, and cultural infrastructures. *Beta* variables include inputs and reactions that are initiated and maintained primarily by the person. In this class of events all internal and self-generated processes, such as thinking, planning, decision making, problem solving, and other self-reactions are considered. Although most of these behaviors are the result of socialization processes and interactions with the physical and social environments, self-generated processes can initiate and direct behavior over long periods of time, and contribute to a decreased dependence on environmental and biological factors. The third class of behavior determinants are called *gamma* variables. They encompass the contributions of the genetic and biological system, including the characteristics of information processing, the physiology and the biological predispositions of the individual.

This metamodel fits a general system approach in which alpha, beta, and gamma inputs and outputs constantly affect each other and shape the development and behavior of the person. For example, in the development of an anxiety disorder, the person's sensitivity to physical and somatosensory cues, the self-regulatory system, the reciprocal interaction with the social environment as well as the availability of various coping responses set the stage for the course of events from an initial anxiety-arousing episode to the eventual display of intensive anxiety reactions, avoidance behaviors, and detrimental self-reactions (Schefft, Moses, & Schmidt, 1985). Our model of therapy is based on the assumption that there are multiple pathways by which persons can display similar syndromes. Therefore we stress a careful analysis of the contributing factors as a precursor to the selection of target behaviors and therapeutic goals (Kanfer, 1985). While a lack of social skills may be critical for one chronic anxiety patient, lack of social support, or self-defeating self-reactions or overwhelming inability to deal with intense fear reactions may represent the central issues in the therapy of another patient. Similarities among clients may be based either on the universality of biological and psychological mechanisms or on the resemblance of the requirements and reactions of shared cultural settings. Thus, therapeutic interventions with standardized programs are possible for some problems. Long-term effectiveness of therapy nevertheless requires attention to remediation of the specific factor that contributed most to the problem in an individual patient.

The present model implies that assignment of a patient to diagnostic categories, such a depression or schizophrenia, does not yield clues for specific therapy strategies (Kanfer, 1985; Kanfer & Nay, 1982; Kanfer & Saslow, 1965). For example, under prolonged stress, one person may develop headaches, another backaches, another gastrointestinal problems. Different symptoms develop in persons with different genetic susceptibility, particular learning experiences, and sociocultural settings. However, these different symptoms may be the result of the operation of similar processes.

Self-regulatory variables play a special moderating effect on the net impact of the biological, environmental, and personal variables which may lead to behavior disorders. This reasoning suggests that dysfunction in a person's self-regulatory skills may precipitate the development of pathological symptoms. Deficits in self-monitoring, inappropriate or excessive criteria, based on either internal or external events (e.g., standards for professional work, personally relevant criteria, or criteria for health/physical states), deficits in self-evaluation, or impaired self-corrective feedback can lead to ineffective self-regulation. Particular constellations of physiological and affective cues, along with sensory stimulation, can constitute reference points against which behavior is compared during the self-regulatory process. For example, in the absence of adaptive responses to changes in physiological and affective cues, self-regulatory behavior may become dysfunctional, or when nonadaptive responses to fear-arousing situations, self-reactions, or social situations are repeated and over-learned, behaviors become automatic, stereotypic and habitual. Situations are then no longer evaluated on their particular characteristics and the response tends to generalize. Such automatic reactions are difficult to change since they bypass the controlled processing of self-regulatory sequences and are evoked as conditioned responses, regardless of their appropriateness in a given context (Schneider & Shiffrin, 1977).

Effective self-regulation requires attention to a variety of internal and external cues and the evaluation of one's reaction against some criterion. In many clients with long-standing maladaptive behaviors, self-regulatory processes no longer interpose between cues and reactions. Clients often report being unaware of the circumstances that trigger symptomatic behaviors or their effects. Reinstatement of intervening self-regulatory processes, together with the training of new and more effective behaviors, constitutes the first task of therapy, followed by the later focus on building up the endurance of the newly acquired behavior. In some cases, the initial focus is on modifying the behavior first, with subsequent changes in self-regulatory responses. In others, response modification can be achieved only after self-regulatory processes are altered.

THEORY OF THERAPEUTIC CHANGE

In its simplest form we view therapy as a process of change in which problematic behaviors that have become highly stereotyped and difficult to control by the client are modified or supplanted by more effective action patterns that are initially under high control by the person, but later become automatic and integrated into his or her daily life. In addition to the reduction of distress and symptoms, the change implies a movement toward a way of life that is more personally satisfying and socially acceptable. To accomplish these goals, therapy is viewed as an intervention using a combination of alpha, beta, and gamma variables within a self-management framework.

It is often said that therapy is "hard work." Our model suggests that this is true not only for the therapist but also for the client. As we have indicated, controlled processing demands most of the client's attention, since it deals with changing content. It involves novel situations and requires the integration of information in a new way. In contrast, automatic processing demands little of the client's cognitive capacities. The critical task of the clinician, early in therapy, is to use various interventions to assist the client in discontinuing the problematic behaviors that are well-established and resistant to change, while at the same time instigating the client to develop behaviors that have the characteristic of controlled processing. As Kanfer and Hagerman (1985) have stated:

> If a universal rule of therapy can be stated at all, it is that during the change process the client must be aided to produce verbal and motor behaviors in interactions and self-reactions that are predominantly nonstereotyped, relatively novel, of initial low frequency of occurrence, and that have the characteristics of controlled processing. Control of cognitive and verbal responses is then shifted so that the behavior becomes rule-governed, rather than elicited by specific stimuli. Put in common language, the client must learn to think and act differently, more flexibly and more daringly during the transition process. (p. 22)

Our theoretical model yields several principles for effective change. The therapist acts as an instigator of change, and the shift from automatic to controlled processing characterizes the initial phase of instigation therapy (Kanfer & Phillips, 1969). The clinician guides the client through a process which activates self-regulatory behaviors, with the ultimate goal of finding more effective behavior patterns, which can again become well-learned and stabilized.

The style of the therapist in self-management interventions follows from these guidelines. Therapist responses must guide the client away from habitual responses, and engage the client in the purposeful use of self-regulatory behaviors such as self-monitoring, goal setting, self-evaluation, and goal-oriented problem solving. For example, the clinician does not begin sessions by using such common and familiar phrases as "How are things going?" or "How are you feeling?" These phrases tend to elicit well-learned, repetitive and stereotypic responses in the client. By phrasing the question in a way that is unlikely to elicit oft-repeated stock phrases, the client is obligated to shift to a controlled processing mode. For example, one could begin, "What have you done differently this week than previously?"

Another rule which follows from our model is that active participation requires incentives, as well as a clear definition of the end-state (i.e., the therapeutic objective). The client must be motivated to work toward goals that are acceptable and clear. This requires a thorough goal and value clarification in which desired and potential outcomes of therapy are brought into a relationship with the client's life goals, desires, hopes, and expectations. For some clients new goals may have to be developed before the motivation for change can occur.

It is our belief that setting the conditions that favor change is a *primary* task of therapy. Several central goals must be accomplished toward this end. In addition to the acceptance of the utility of change in the context of his or her life expectations, the client must also be helped to gain the confidence that he or she can solve the current problem(s) and future difficulties, with decreasing assistance from the therapist. The client must develop skill in arranging his or her own affairs, analyzing and resolving problems, anticipating difficulties, and using newly learned therapeutic strategies to plan future directions. Finally, the client must be helped to learn "rules of conduct," that is, strategies that assist in the recognition and management of future problem situations.

The therapist's role is to help the client by providing methods and training that make the change as simple and attractive to the client as possible. Toward this end, Kanfer and Grimm (1980) have developed a process model of clinical change which assists in the creation of favorable conditions for therapeutic change. The central premise of the model is that therapeutic intervention will often prove fruitless unless such factors as client motivation, resistance (i.e., fear of change, negativism, reactance, and countercontrol) and commitment to change are given proper attention. Motivation to engage in a change process is required not only for the above reasons, but also for more pragmatic reasons. Client attendance and adherence to treatment procedures depend on it.

Commitment to change is a precondition for later execution of specific therapeutic activities. Completion of assignments and tasks outside sessions serves not only as a substantive goal but facilitates (and is an index of) commitment. Finally, resistance, broadly understood as opposition to change, is a pervasive problem for all forms of therapy. Dealing with it is essential for treatment progress. As Marks (1978) has so aptly stated, "Both motivating and executing factors (treatment methods) are crucial. An effective treatment is of little use if patients cannot be motivated to carry it out" (p. 497).

Our emphasis on motivation has led to a detailed consideration of those variables that influence the level of client involvement both within and between sessions. We conceptualize the implementation of "treatment techniques" as a later phase in therapy. It is preceded by a systematic attention to the process and the contextual factors required to help the client recognize the benefits of a change and, later, to carry out the demanding tasks of specific therapy procedures. Administration of treatment techniques involving the acquisition of new behaviors constitutes only one component of therapy. These methods are combined with the systematic utilization of variables that influence the therapy process per se.

We structure the treatment process so that a major responsibility for change is shifted to the client from the onset of therapy. To maintain active client involvement and build skills in effective self-regulatory behavior, we utilize a number of features that constitute the core of self-management therapy. These features derive from the convergent findings in several research areas. In general, many experiments and their associated theories (e.g., Bem, 1972; Kanfer & Grimm, 1978; Kopel & Arkowitz, 1975; Langer, 1983; Perlmuter & Monty, 1979) suggest that perceived freedom of action, responsibility for decisions, and opportunity for choices tend to motivate and improve learning and to reduce opposition to change. From these laboratory data the following general prescriptions can be extended to the clinical setting.

1. *Self-generation of behavior.* Plans, ideas, goals, and specified behaviors are enacted more readily when originated and voiced by the client.

2. *Negotiation of objectives.* Greater commitment is expected when therapy subgoals and end-states result from negotiations in which clients perceive themselves to be equal partners.

3. *Pacing progress to permit success and mastery experiences.* When the client participates in determining the rate of progress and the difficulty of

therapeutic program steps and he or she gradually experiences success in mastering each step, increasing commitment, cooperation, and assumption of responsibility can be expected.

4. *Perceived control.* The application of the foregoing guidelines, combined with restructuring or reorienting client perceptions and experimenting to gain feedback about the impact of one's behavior on the social and physical environment and on one's own body, can yield increased perception of control. Perceived control enhances self-efficacy, and beliefs in one's competence. It increases willingness to risk change and may heighten the attractiveness of therapy.

5. *Self-attribution.* Causal self-attributions following a successful outcome can favor commitment, motivate new learning and improve affective tone. In practice, clear credit to clients for even minor achievements and stress on the therapist's supportive rather than directive role can enhance self-attribution.

The most important reasons for our stress on self-management therefore lie in the beneficial effects not only of speeding up new learning, but also of encouraging the client toward deep personal involvement in therapy and a greater readiness to overcome the aversion to change, and to the emotional and cognitively taxing demands of the therapy process. Of particular note also is the incompatibility of client "resistant" behaviors, such as counter-control, reactance noncompliance or poor attendance, when the client perceives him- or herself as freely executing choices, controlling some facets of therapy and thereby shouldering responsibility for therapeutic improvement.

Our treatment model describes a step-by-step sequence of phases in order to assist the client in reaching various subgoals throughout the course of treatment. The model is recursive. It guides the therapist in returning to earlier phases of the treatment process, when it is necessary to deal with issues that remain unresolved or recur later and impede the progress of therapy. Outside influences, such as collateral effects of changes in target behaviors or intervention by others, or encountering unexpected failures or deficits, may necessitate such a retracing of steps.

A PROCESS MODEL OF THERAPY

Central issues that require careful attention throughout treatment include motivating the client to maintain contact with the therapist, activating controlled processing, assisting the client in dealing with distress and symptoms directly, and building a repertoire to cope with variations of the central complaint that may occur in the future. The process model is designed to maximize the client's attainment of these goals by sequencing the order in which they are highlighted throughout the therapy program. The focus of our approach is therefore first on setting the context within which change occurs. This includes (1) establishing a working therapeutic relationship; (2) creating a belief by the client that change is possible and desirable; and (3) facilitating the client's active involvement in the therapy program. The last point implies helping the client to recognize that decisions regarding important issues, along with shared control over the direction of treatment, are to a large extent his or her responsibility. Techniques are used to help the client to assume this task, even if for some clients this is only possible in small ways at first. For example, we recently saw a client who sought therapy because he found himself feeling angry most of the time. The initial assignment was structured to be easily accomplished. It was designed to help him assume responsibility for learning about events and interactions that precipitated his emotional arousal. A negotiation format in therapy was used to provide the client with perceived control over the specific nature of the task. This permitted him to choose the particular situations he would observe, as well as the mechanics by which he would record them. The client decided to use a daily log and describe situations in which he found himself emotionally aroused, together with his thoughts prior to and during such situations.

The seven phases of our model (Kanfer & Grimm, 1980) are summarized in Table 2-1. The deliberate structure of the treatment model emphasizes that one cannot take for granted that the client will be enthusiastic about participating in and complying with treatment, even when the therapist is confident about the effectiveness of his treatment methods and skills.

The first four phases focus on preparing the client to become an active participant in therapy. The fifth phase represents the point at which most systematic behavior therapy programs are presumed to begin. It is the segment of therapy on which most textbooks, case reports, research studies and training manuals focus most of their effort and attention.

The rationale underlying an emphasis on the importance of the initial phases is based on our clinical experience that, for example, neurotic clients rarely see the need for altering their self-view or their social-interactional patterns as the goal of therapy, nor do they anticipate the implications of a change for their routines of daily living. Addictive clients are not motivated by their desire to give up the temporary relief found in alcohol or drug consumption. Their goal, like the goal of anorexics or clients with marital problems or antisocial behaviors, is often to alter only the consequences of their actions rather than the behaviors themselves. Psychosomatic clients do not readily see the need to discuss their personal lives with a therapist. They are usually primarily concerned with getting rid of their pain and discomfort, preferably without any changes in their behaviors, emotional reactions, or thought patterns.

TABLE 2-1. Primary Goals of Each Phase of Therapy

Phase	Primary goals
1. Role Structuring and Creating a Therapeutic Alliance	1. Facilitate the person's entry to the role of client 2. Form a working relationship 3. Establish motivation to work with therapist
2. Developing a Commitment to Change	1. Motivate client to consider positive consequences of change 2. Activate client toward change of status quo 3. Reduce demoralization
3. The Behavioral Analysis	1. Refine client's problem definition 2. Identify relevant functional relationships 3. Motivate client toward specific changes
4. Negotiating Treatment	1. Seek agreement of target areas 2. Establish priorities for change program and initiate specific procedures 3. Accept responsibility for engaging in planned therapy program
5. Treatment Execution and Motivation Maintenance	1. Conduct treatment program 2. Assess collateral and radiating effects of change in target behaviors 3. Evaluate and, if necessary, enhance motivation to change and comply with treatment requirements
6. Monitoring and Evaluating Progress	1. Assess behavior change 2. Assess client's use of general coping skills 3. Introduce new therapy objectives, if necessary
7. Treatment Generalization and Termination	1. Evaluate and foster self-management skills for meeting future problems 2. Phase out contact with client

Note. From: Kanfer, F. H., & Grimm, L. G. (1980). Managing clinical change: A process model of therapy. *Behavior Modification, 4*(4), 419–444.

Unless the preconditions for change are carefully prepared in Phases I through IV, the clinician is likely to encounter client behaviors that have been variously termed "reactance," "resistance," or "counter-control." For example, with most phobic clients, systematic desensitization works very effectively (Klepac, 1975; Weissberg, 1977). However, unless issues specified in Phases I through IV are addressed prior to practicing desensitization, clients may return after the first week, reporting that they "can't visualize the scenes," "can't relax," or "forgot to do the assignment." It is an ideal client who is able to benefit from treatment when it begins directly at Phase V. We are all familiar with the rare yet satisfying clients who are highly motivated, know exactly what they want, present themselves enthusiastically for treatment, and can be helped very effectively in two or three therapy sessions by the direct application of established treatment techniques. Under these conditions, the preconditions for change in our model have already been met or can be dealt with in a very short time.

Phase I. Creating a Therapeutic Alliance

The Client's Definition of the Problem

Most clients view therapy as a process in which they describe their problems freely to an attentively listening therapist, who then offers the best solution, on the basis of his professional knowledge (Kanfer & Marston, 1964). But problem description and analysis requires a context of trust and openness and a skill in observation and information-gathering; and treatment requires adoption of specified roles. Therefore, initial interviews are devoted to structuring therapy roles and creating a therapeutic alliance. The ease with which this is done often depends on the way in which the person was labeled (or labeled him- or herself) as a patient, who and what identified the presenting complaint as a problem, who referred the client for treatment and for what purpose. Clients often seek treatment not because they are distressed, but because someone else is bothered by their behavior, for example, a parent, a spouse, policeman, or judge. In less extreme cases, a clinician may face a client who is ambivalent about being in treatment, yet verbalizes his or her expectations for change. The definition of how a person becomes a patient is important, since it is likely to influence the degree of participation during early treatment sessions. Sociocultural variables are among those factors that contribute to the individual's perception of the client role, as well as the nature of the behaviors that are labeled as problematic and the manner in which they are labeled, the client's health-belief model, and the relative weight of situational versus personal attributions about the source of the problems. The client's view of his or her problem as temporary, as an accident, as a personal characteristic, or as no problem at all influences the way in which therapy is structured.

The effects of a client's definition of his or her problem on role structuring are aptly illustrated by a case we recently treated. The patient presented himself for biofeedback treatment, stating that he wanted relief from extreme feelings of stress, including headaches, backaches, and generalized muscle tension. He attributed these complaints to working too hard as an insurance salesman. As treatment progressed, it became clear that factors involving other life areas were significant in producing his stress. One day the patient appeared wearing a bandage and explained that his wife had struck him on the nose and broken it. Further questioning revealed that the patient's wife had struck him repeatedly and had broken his nose last year. His perception of his problem as being related to physical exhaustion due to overwork required considerable restructuring. His view that biofeedback was the solution to his problem indicated the primary need for changing his perceptions about the nature of therapy and the requirement for his active engagement in the process. We recommended and negotiated couples therapy. Biofeedback was not used, since the couple made good progress.

Structuring the Client's Role

Another important issue in the first phase of treatment is the extent to which the therapist's expectations for the structure of treatment is congruent with that of the client. The client's expectations are often colored by his or her implicit goals and the nature of his or her past experiences in therapy or in other helping relationships (Wilkins, 1979). Creating a therapeutic alliance can become particularly difficult with clients who have had repeatedly unsuccessful experiences in therapy (Bootzin & Lick, 1979). Poor expectations of outcome, and the assumption of the passive client role that is demanded by some therapies, can thus lead to special needs for redefining the nature of the client's role.

Clients who expect therapists to solve their problems without a need for the clients to change their behaviors present another common difficulty for therapists. We have called this the "drive-in syndrome." Clients with this perception of therapy act as if they could bring in their problems at 8:00 am, drop them off, and come back at 5:00 pm, expecting to have everything cleaned up. Rather than deal directly with this issue early in therapy, the therapist focuses at first on presenting the therapeutic relationship as an opportunity for something positive to be done. At this point, therapy is heavily oriented toward little more than creating a therapeutic alliance. Only after later work, when it is clear what goals are appropriate for the client, can full efforts be devoted to implementing a change.

After the first several interviews, marking the attainment of the objective of Phase I, the client should walk out of the office and say to him- or herself "Here is someone with whom I can work and who can help me to improve things." Creating the context for therapy by forming a positive therapeutic alliance is necessary not only to establish a trusting atmosphere but also to enhance the client's desire to return for further treatment. Obviously, one cannot do therapy with a client who does not come back. From various statistics, it is apparent that over one third of clients do not return after the second interview, often perhaps due to prematurely focusing on solving their problems rather than devoting time to structuring the setting.

Activating Client Involvement

Motivating the client to continue therapy is a critical feature, but we simultaneously try to prepare the client, through various interview strategies, to assume an active role and to accept the fact that the client has to help him- or herself, though with the help of the therapist. We encourage the client's self-activation by communicating the attitude that implies "I believe you can handle it, but if you can't, I'll help you. But first we have to be clear about what bothers you, and what you could do about this problem." As clients describe their complaints, we communicate empathy but simultaneously encourage clients to assume as much responsibility as possible. For example, with one client with marital problems, we conveyed concern but also prepared him for taking action between sessions. The client had repeatedly suffered disastrous defeats during marital quarrels. The initial objective was to help him feel understood by the therapist and yet to begin to generate alternatives. This idea was communicated by saying, "Things are rough, but how could they get better? What do you think you could do to avoid these quarrels or to make them less upsetting next time?" The attempt was made to help the client start thinking on his own, begin to identify specific factors, and engage in initial efforts at problem solving. During this process, the concept of responsibility must be sensitively paced, since the premature introduction of these notions may be perceived as excessive and frightening demands, leading the client to escape from therapy. To illustrate a very clear error in implementing these objectives, it would have been very threatening to say, "Nobody can help you with that except yourself. You're going to have to do it on your own." The therapist should never communicate an unwillingness to offer support, help, or understanding. Rather, he or she should convey a willingness to provide assistance with the implicit contract that the client will also work with him or her.

The process of activating client involvement early in therapy is illustrated by our work with a 21-year-old white single female who presented herself for outpatient therapy following inpatient hospitalization for a suicidal gesture. While hospitalized, therapeutic issues concerned her depressed mood in the context of chronic low self-esteem, interpersonal passivity, and social withdrawal. Although she had completed 3 years of college with good grades, her work history was limited to brief periods of employment at fast-food restaurants. Due to a long-term conflict with her parents, she had been living with her grandparents for several years. She was discharged from inpatient care following some reduction of dysphoria. She came to the clinic on the recommendation of her psychiatrist. The following transcript is from an early therapy session. It demonstrates the instigating style for activating the involvement of the client in therapy.

Client Statement	*Self-Management Therapist Response*
I just feel like what I have to say to people isn't very important, and I freeze up inside when someone comes up and talks to me.	That must be a very uncomfortable feeling; I wonder what you could do about that?
I don't know . . . I've tried so hard to feel better, but nothing seems to work.	What have you done to try to feel better?
I don't know . . . I guess I've tried to convince myself that I'm a good person but I never really believe it.	If you were really a good person, what kind of things would you be doing during the day, and how would you be different than you are now?
I'm not sure. I never thought about it.	Well, take a minute to think about it now, (*7-second pause*). Try to imagine feeling good about yourself, and what kind of things would be different in your life.
For one thing, when people at school come up to me, I would not freeze up inside and want to run away.	What would you do instead?
I'd have a conversation with them.	What would you talk about?
Well, I guess, maybe about our classes and how things are going.	How can one start a conversation? What could you say to start off?
I suppose I could ask them how they are doing.	Fine, and after that, what could you say?
I don't know, that's where I always get stuck and start to freeze up.	Before you mentioned that maybe you could talk about your classes.
Oh, well, I don't know what to say about them.	If you wanted to know how their classes were going for them, how could you find out?
I guess I would ask them.	Exactly how would you do that?
"How are your classes going?"	Okay, that's a start. And what would you say after that?
I'm not sure.	Well, let's pretend that I've just come up to you at school and I'm in one of your classes. Let's run through what you might say.

A brief role-play followed during which a combination of modeling, feedback, and review was used to help the client identify and rehearse open-ended questions for initiating and maintaining a short conversation. Dialogue continued following the role-play.

Client Statement	Self-Management Therapist Response
	Well, how do you think you did?
I guess okay, but you were helping me.	So, you don't deserve any credit at all?
Well, a little bit.	As you say that, you look pleased with yourself.
Yeah, I guess I did all right.	I think you did too. You've done it once now. Do you think you could do it again this afternoon at school?
It's easier here with you—it's safe. It's a lot harder to do it all alone.	Yes, it is. But that's what you said earlier about getting depressed as soon as you left the hospital. How was it? Were you able to manage? You don't appear to be very depressed today.
Yeah . . . (5-second pause). I guess so. I suppose I did something on my own.	So maybe there is hope for you?
(Laughing slightly.) Yeah.	Good! Now, tell me about what you're going to do today to start a conversation at school, and show me how you're going to do it.

The therapist went on to help the client specify the exact goal for her exercise and how she would attain it, outlining in detail what she might say, whom she might address, and when and where she might carry out the exercise each day for the rest of the week.

As can be seen from this example, the style of the therapist is characterized by empathy combined with a heavy reliance on activating statements. Rather than providing answers and solutions for the client in a directive manner, self-activation is encouraged by assisting the client to provide statements and ideas, with only as little prompting and mild encouragement from the therapist as is necessary. In this manner, client involvement and responsibility are fostered from the very start of therapy, with increasing demands for responsibility as skills are developed.

We conceptualize the early process as a stage during which the therapist's actions and words acquire some control over the client's behavior. It is inconceivable that therapeutic change can be mediated by interview exchanges unless the therapist's verbal behavior has some influence on the client (Ferster, 1979). Gradually this influence extends from control in sessions to between-session activities. This extension must be mediated by the client's increased self-regulation in the use of his or her own cognitive and behavioral skills.

As these subgoals are obtained, there is increasing attention to enhancing the client's responsibility for decision making, problem solving, and involvement in his or her own therapeutic change. This process is often begun by an early tentative exploration of goals and values. This can be accomplished in many cases by activating the client's self-attention, using such statements as "I don't yet know what kind of a person you'd like to be. Can you help me by describing how you might like to behave (in a specific circumstance), and how you would be different if you changed for the better?" These verbal interactions are followed up with assignments to self-monitor or to observe others, or by an appropriate task. As the client responds, he or she is beginning to assume some responsibility, setting up objectives and actively participating.

The early involvement of the client in orienting the direction of therapy is important for other reasons as well. It is critical to have the client's cooperation since emotions, memories and perceptions are rarely observed and related by passive or reluctant clients. The report of events that are not accessible to the therapist is often important for diagnostic purposes. This issue becomes particularly important when clients are not self-referred.

Defining the Therapeutic Relationship

The therapist's role is that of a catalyst. By his or her actions and questions, he or she engages clients in formulating hypotheses and activates them toward changing conditions from an unacceptable to a more acceptable state. The boundaries of the therapeutic relationship are set up in such a way that the relationship does not extend beyond a professional but sincerely empathic and concerned interaction. The therapeutic conduct is contrary to the popular image of behavior therapists as mechanistic, impersonal, and emotionally detached. However, our structure of the relationship is also unlike other therapies that hold that the therapeutic relationship must be an intense, personal, and emotional relationship, and that consider it to be the major mechanism for therapeutic change. The self-management approach is a clearly defined *professional* relationship (Kanfer, 1980), in which the focus is on the *client's* problems and behaviors, and its goal the modification of those problems and behaviors for the client's benefit. The therapist communicates respect for the client essentially by conveying the message: "I accept you as a client because I am very concerned with helping you alleviate your distress and move toward becoming the kind of person that you would like to be, within realistic bounds and with your cooperation." The development of a personal relationship with the client, along any other than professional lines, is outside the scope of therapy and should be avoided. Personal relationships reduce the therapist's objectivity, lessen his or her effectiveness as instigator of change and blur the focus on the client's problems.

Disrupting Automatic Responses

To facilitate the client's adoption of a new role, it is first necessary to break up the pattern of well-learned responses, including self-reactions. A task-oriented attitude by the therapist communicates to the client that therapy consists of an intense analysis of various actions, including their antecedents and consequences. Consequently, habitual, well-rehearsed verbal explanations or vague, general statements are challenged, and the client is encouraged to develop a questioning attitude about his or her "clichés" and automatic reactions. The shift to a controlled processing mode (Shiffrin & Schneider, 1977) implies greater attention to one's behavior and internal processes, increasing self-awareness. The disruption of automatic response chains also prepares clients for a later reexamination of those perceptions and responses that obstruct progress by opposition and resistance to change. Explicit strategies for disrupting automatic responses are described in detail on page 46 in the section "Specific Techniques." They are applied to disrupt interactional behaviors or nonverbal symptomatic responses as well.

Phase II. Developing a Commitment to Change

Anticipation of a Favorable Outcome

The second phase of our process model concerns the development of a commitment to change. Critical subgoals of this phase include motivating the client to consider the positive consequences of change, activating the client toward changing the status quo, and working to reduce demoralization. The first issue to be considered is the helping of clients to anticipate a favorable outcome. To accomplish this task, a relatively simple and concrete assignment—one that the client cannot possibly fail, given reasonable effort—may be negotiated for the first week. Although completion of this assignment may not be of great importance *per se*, the successful completion of even the smallest behavioral task can be used effectively. The use of small and simple behavioral tasks as confirmatory evidence that clients are capable of changing serves not only to increase self-confidence but also to undermine old negative self-evaluations and hopelessness. The therapeutic style helps clients to view their beliefs about themselves as testable hypotheses rather than as facts. The therapist then works with them to confirm or reject these hypotheses and to develop an expectation of improvement.

The building of positive client expectations in therapy is frequently impeded by demoralization. Frank (1973) used this term to refer to combinations of self-reactions and attitudes that foster debilitating hopelessness and despair in clients with histories of unsuccessful experiences. In addressing this problem, the client is instructed in using self-monitoring, effective self-evaluative behaviors, and positive feedback. The objective is to enhance the client's internalization of positive confirmatory feedback. The therapist capitalizes on any small success in the everyday experiences of the client. Sometimes it is useful to provide a good deal of reinforcement to clients for having the courage and ambition to begin the first step of change, that is, coming to therapy. The changeability of behavior and the gradual nature of the change process are emphasized simultaneously. To increase the client's confidence that improvement is possible, the therapist conveys a repeated expression of belief in the client's ability to change. Supporting actions, expressing the therapist's confidence in the client's ability, are particularly helpful in bolstering the client's belief that he can make at least small changes during the early phases of treatment.

Change of the Status Quo

Continuing the focus on active involvement from Phase I, the client's role is further structured by the communication of an implicit contract and the concept of the mutual responsibility of both client and therapist. The therapist assumes responsibility for providing ample assistance in helping clients change their own behavior. The client's obligation is to follow through on between-session activities and tasks that are negotiated and agreed upon from session to session. This idea is strengthened by conveying to the client the message that therapeutic changes happen between sessions, not during sessions.

To enhance the enactment of new behaviors between sessions, negotiations and discussions do not deal with whether a given task will be attempted, but with how, when, where, with whom, and how often clients would like to perform the task. Choice over the parameters of the task and control over its criteria are thus essentially handed to the client. Whenever possible, instigation is used to engage the client in planning for extra-session tasks. For example, we often say, "Given what we have just said, what is it that you can try to do in the coming week?" Similarly, "So you're going to monitor your blood pressure twice a day, when could you do that? At 9:00 am and what other times?" These interactions serve not only to help clients to shape and refine their tasks but also to commit themselves definitely to do them.

The initial task for a client may not be a specific attempt to change. A client may be hesitant to specify problems or tasks. Nevertheless, for diagnostic purposes the interview should always reveal some area in which client activity can be fruitful. For example, if a client is unsure about exactly what bothers him or her, the therapist may make this the basis of the assignment, perhaps by saying, "This might be a good thing to think about and spend some time on this week. Could you keep track of just when you feel uncomfortable?" The details, definitions of discomfort, time of observation, method of recording are then worked out (see Kanfer, 1980, for rules on contracting). Rather than attempting to "overcome resistance," the client's ambivalence or doubts are accepted. At the same time, efforts are made to engage him or her in nonthreatening yet new and different behaviors between sessions.

Consistent with the emphasis on the importance of action as opposed to intentions alone, it is critical to provide positive reinforcement contingent upon the execution of assigned tasks, but to avoid giving immediate reinforcement simply for the stating of an intention (Kanfer, Cox, Greiner, & Karoly, 1974).

In activating clients to change the status quo, it is useful to help them to become accurate observers of their own behavior, particularly with regard to responses that appear most relevant to the focal complaint. Emphasis is placed on their ability to identify the positive aspects of their thinking, feeling, and behavior in specific situations. The therapist also guides clients' attention to areas in which changes are needed and helps them to evaluate the outcome of their efforts in relationship to the goals that they have set. For each therapy session, client and therapist need to deal with such issues as defining the client's self-directed questions: "What are my goals for this week?" "What can and will I do to work toward those goals?" "How will I know when I do it?" "How will I give myself credit when I obtain my goals?" "What plans can I make for the future in dealing with similar people or situations?" (See also Shelton & Levy, 1981). To further the application of such self-regulatory skills, we typically engage the client in answering these questions at the close of each session: "What is the most important thing that you have learned in this session?" and "How can you apply that during the day [during the week]?" or, "What can you do differently now, as a result of what we have dealt with today?"

Enhancing Self-Regulatory Skills

To facilitate the learning of self-regulatory skills early in therapy, we have used six mottos that summarize in simple, common form the essential features of our approach. These "think rules" have been used widely by therapists as criteria for their own orientation in interviews. The rules have also been communicated to both individual clients and groups in explaining desirable standards for communication in therapy.

The early introduction and teaching of these rules in therapy provides clients with specific skills for initiating and maintaining new behaviors. In turn, the enhancement of self-regulatory skills results in the client's increased awareness of his or her potential for change, and a heightened self-confidence in new situations. In brief the "think rules" are:

1. *Think behavior.* The formulation of problems and their resolutions is couched in terms of action. Since it is primarily behavior that is the target of change in therapy, action should be the main dimension on which the therapeutic interchanges focus. Our use of the term "behavior" includes self-reactions, emotional responses, cognitive events, and the various combinations of these that are often described as attitudes, beliefs or experiences of feeling. This emphasis urges both therapist and client to avoid concentrating their attention on personal characteristics or traits, on by-products of events, or on constructing causal explanations as the target for change. Consistent with the focus on action, clients are discouraged from thinking about the "why" of a problem. Instead, they are helped to concentrate on "what" and "how."

2. *Think solution.* The emphasis in interaction lies on behaviors designed to change situations and/or the client's satisfactions. Even slight contributions that promise to solve at least a component of a defined problem are preferable to a prolonged discussion of problematic states. Alternative actions and environmental changes, or any options that reduce the total problematic situation are of central concern, both in therapy sessions and in the client's daily activities between sessions.

3. *Think positive.* Despite its apparent triteness this rule can assist the client if it is translated into specific operations. Clients, as well as therapists, are encouraged to seek positive outcomes and to reinforce any plans, strategies, or actions that achieve them. It is critical that clients assess and develop their strengths and assets rather than focus only on their weaknesses and disabilities. Behavioral criteria are set in relation to the client's past performances rather than in terms of ideal norms or idealized persons.

4. *Think small steps.* This common rule in behavior therapy refers to the importance in breaking down tasks into immediately manageable units. Clients are urged to set standards for progressive steps in a sequence, even though a distant outcome may be used as an objective to which the various small steps and subgoals could eventually lead. The client is helped to consider alternatives for branching out or changing directions after each small step, depending on the outcome of that step. Translated into daily therapy operations, this often takes the form of the therapist challenging the client to consider what is the least he or she can do to alter the situation.

5. *Think flexible.* A person's life experiences do not depend on his or her own actions alone. A changeable and inconsistent environment, the

behavior of others and the ever-changing opportunities and limitations caused by a person's progress along a given path can alter goals. For these reasons, clients are encouraged to make commitments tentatively, on a trial and error basis; they are helped to recognize that there may be many different paths to reach a goal, and to prepare backup plans for important action sequences. Further, the enhancement of flexibility is intended to contribute to the client's self-confidence and self-efficacy.

6. *Think future.* In balancing popular concern with understanding causes of behavior, the client is encouraged to shift toward preparing for and coping with future events. Planning, the systematic anticipation of outcomes, rehearsal, the utilization of available information, and the acquisition of skills needed in these anticipated situations dominate the interview exchange. While this exchange does not exclude discussion, role play, or the reassessment of past events and behaviors, their use is clearly subordinated to the major goal of helping the client to prepare for the future.

The reader will note that the sequences of these "think rules" is not accidental. Each lays the ground work for the next one. The development of even minimal skill in the use of these rules, better prepares clients to set small goals, take action, engage in positive self-evaluations, and plan self-corrective behaviors.

Building Incentives for Change

Following efforts to change the status quo and the enhancement of self-regulatory skills, attention is turned to the primary goal of the second phase. Developing commitment and assisting clients to follow through involves three issues. The first is the development of intentions. This construct refers to cognitive events that include plans, the anticipation of consequences, and the positive emotional correlates of such planning. Secondly, clients are assisted in moving from intentions to action by attempts to create favorable conditions for the transition, including training the skills necessary for the development of commitments and the movement toward their implementation. Finally, the execution of intended action requires skills, positive and corrective feedback during initial steps, the self-correction of goal-directed behaviors, and the recognition that the goal has been attained.

According to our conceptualization, a major task of therapy is to enhance motivation by guiding the client toward the attainment of clearly specified objectives. A variety of techniques are used for the purpose of developing new incentives or altering current ones. In general, a sequence of goal states that becomes increasingly demanding as the client moves through the seven phases of therapy is developed. However, motivation should increase as the client progresses through the goal states. According to the process model, motivation for change by specific actions may at first be primarily extrinsic, depending heavily on reinforcement by the therapist. As therapy moves through the attainment of subgoals specified in the seven phases, motivation should become more intrinsic. The client learns more effective self-regulatory behaviors, develops new incentives, obtains confirmatory evidence of his capacity from having attained self-selected goals, and, hopefully, experiences a reduction in distress. The intrinsic motivation includes the satisfaction which accrues due to mastery and to the client's increasing sense of control and perceived competence that accompanies achievement of personally relevant incentives. As has been described by various theorists (Bandura, 1977; Kanfer, 1977), the development of effective self-management skills serves also to provide the client with a sense of generalized mastery and autonomy.

The clinical translation of these conceptual issues begins by helping the client to answer the question "Why should I participate in this change program?" The focus is on assisting the client to consider different possible goals, to become concerned with the positive aspects of change, and essentially to "dream new dreams." It may be necessary to train clients to consider alternatives and to imagine possible consequences of change. At the same time, the therapist must remain sensitive to the ambivalence that most clients have about their ability to do what is needed in order to change.

Indeed, the fear of changing is one of the major obstacles to initial participation and involvement in therapy. Clients are often willing to submit passively to procedures but are less enthusiastic about changing well-learned behaviors and self-reactions that have become parts of their lifestyles. As a familiar and common example in the area of weight management, obese clients frequently state that they would prefer to have their jaws wired shut rather than change their eating habits. To reduce these fears, clients must be helped to understand that change can present a positive alternative. Often even the repeated imagery of a different lifestyle can reduce the fear of the unknown. By use of goal and value clarification methods and strategies, clients are helped to develop a picture of what life would be like if they were to be successful in attaining their goal.

The therapist's implicit promise that a client will benefit from therapy, though often given, is not enough to motivate change. More specifically, if full commitment is expected, the client must have clear answers to such questions as the following: "What positive things can I get out of therapy?"; "Where am I going and what will it cost in effort, money, or time to get there?"; "Will I like it when I get there?" In developing the client's commitment to change, the task is to increase his or her motivation to want to reach the self-selected goal. A motivated client is one who is willing to spend effort, energy, money, and whatever it takes to achieve a goal. To be thus willing, the client has to know what the goal-state is like, to be confident that he or she can approach it and that it is consistent with his or her other goals and values. In cases when the client has a goal that is ethically objectionable to the therapist or is part of the client's problem (e.g., to become more comfortable about seeking sexual contact with minors), the task is to motivate him or her to develop a life pattern in which the basic need is met in socially acceptable ways.

Goal and Value Clarification

This process plays a useful role in channeling client motivation toward specific objectives. An important issue in goal and value clarification is to determine how the therapeutic objectives can be made to be consistent with the client's value system, thereby minimizing later obstacles to treatment. For example, in working with severely subassertive patients, failure to devote attention to value clarification may result in passive opposition to treatment. After reaching a minimally proficient skill level in asserting opinions and beliefs, the patient may fail to show further gains. Detailed questioning often reveals that the patient's value system is inconsistent with an expression of assertiveness and that he or she highly values docility, fatalism and passivity. Clearly, the target of therapy would have to be redirected for such patients.

Value clarification procedures are not used to uncover the intrinsic values and beliefs of clients, but to help set up tentative goals toward which they can strive. These goals may be modified over time, but it is important that they are consistent with both the clients' current needs and enduring self-characterizations and values. Used in this manner, value clarification can best be conceptualized as a process rather than a treatment method. It is designed to lead to new behaviors through the building of intentions and the preparation for action. Clients are guided through a series of procedures over time, beginning with the first session, in which the focus is on planning and on the anticipation of behavior change consequences. Clients are helped to identify how they wish to and could change, and to consider the associated personal costs and benefits. To illustrate this process, during the beginning of treatment we often say, "I'd like to take some time to explore with you your thoughts about what you would like to get from therapy. As we have said already, there are a lot of things that you could choose to work on, but I'd like to find out more about the way *you* would like to be different, and what that would change in your life." As clients identify increasingly specific treatment objectives, therapists work to explore the consistency between personal values and stated goals, and to clarify benefits as well as costs of treatment.

During this process, clients can be given innumerable tasks, such as (1) describing at least three ways in which he or she might be different;

(2) considering what effects these changes would have on others; (3) exploring the personal benefits of changing; (4) describing some potentially negative outcomes and how they would interfere with attaining the client's goals; (5) exploring how the changes would be consistent with the client's view of the kind of person he or she would like to be; (6) imagining how he or she wants to be thought of in old age. Numerous examples and behavioral assignments are described in a book by Kobery and Bagnall (1976).

The process of goal and value clarification creates a fundamental incentive for the client throughout therapy. It is continued over several sessions with appropriate assignments between sessions. Goal-attainment scaling forms are often used to monitor changes.

After goal and value clarification is completed, clients should have considered several of the following questions:

1. What are my (realistic) goals?
2. How can I reach these goals, including alternative solutions?
3. What does it take for me to attain these goals, including such issues as:
   a. What do the goals mean to me in terms of specific steps;
   b. What requirements and prerequisites are necessary for these steps;
   c. What can I do currently that will help me realize these steps?
4. What are the goals worth to me?
5. How will the goals benefit me and others?
6. What are the potential positive and negative outcomes?

Inconsistencies in goals and values are examined in order to assist clients in determining how they can work toward objectives that are personally valued *and* therapeutically useful.

The instigative therapist style is continued throughout the goal and value clarification. Probes, prompts, and half sentences are used to help the client generate observations and hypotheses. A statement that illustrates this is "You tell me that you want to be able to relax and remain free of tension at all times. But on the other hand, you say that you should never stop working and pushing yourself hard because if you did you would feel like a lazy person. Can you help me understand how you put those two things together?" In addition to instigating self-examination, the therapist assists clients in questioning values and beliefs that might undermine attempts toward any therapeutic change. It is important to note that at no point does the therapist attempt to suggest to clients a proper way to view themselves. He or she also avoids judging their values. The therapist may, however, help clients to generate re-evaluative statements or doubts on their own, avoiding what has been variously termed as reactance (Brehm, 1976) or resistance (Wachtel, 1982).

The use of goal and value clarification early in therapy should lead the client to spend time and energy between sessions considering the ways in which he or she would like to be different, and the implications of these goals. For example, clients in a stress-management program are instructed to observe other people during the week, noticing how they relax and experimenting with similar strategies. These behaviors reflect our therapeutic purpose in that they motivate clients to become concerned with issues discussed during the interview and to enact new behaviors in their daily living situations. Given the attainment of a positive therapeutic alliance, the procedures during this phase should lead the client to ask him- or herself, "How is what is happening [in a specific situation] relevant to what I am doing in therapy?", "How does [a given situation] lend itself to try out something new?", and ideally, "How can I find opportunities to practice or try out this new behavior?"

Consolidating a Commitment to Change

Throughout Phase II, as clients report the attainment of small therapeutic subgoals, they are helped to recognize and be proud of their accomplishments, and encouraged to continue similar change efforts with relatively modest goals. The successful outcome is used to reduce demoralization and strengthen self-confidence. It also assists clients in preparing for future situations.

Throughout this phase, issues relevant to the therapeutic alliance continue to be carefully monitored. The clients' level of active involvement, their belief in their ability to change, and their assumed responsibility for change are closely observed. If problems arise, a return to these earlier issues is made. For example, the emergence of noncompliant behaviors, efforts to control the therapist's behavior, or loss of confidence in the utility of therapy signal the need to redirect the focus of treatment sessions until these issues are resolved.

The strategies for enhancing commitment generally share several common elements: (1) reducing the shock value of change; (2) planning, developing, and enacting acquisition of specific skills; (3) increasing self-confidence through the covert rehearsal of mastery experiences and creating some success experiences; (4) strengthening the acceptance of treatment goals as being expected personal benefits rather than an imposed necessity.

Imagery and role-play procedures are particularly useful in overcoming inertia about change. These methods can give the client a vivid picture of what it would be like to be different, and how a different life would benefit him or her. Through the experiential clarification of the positive consequences of change, the client gets into closer contact with the goal-state of the change program and its incentive values become more salient.

A central assumption of therapeutic efforts is that everyone is motivated. The main question is "Motivated for what?" During the initial two phases, the therapist attempts to strengthen the incentive value of the therapy context and to lay the foundation for later, more intense therapy efforts. Thus a series of successive and overlapping incentives are developed, facilitating the client's difficult task of making changes—often radical changes—in his or her behavior or lifestyle.

Phase III. The Behavioral Analysis

A detailed diagnostic process is delayed until the third phase because it is only then that a client is likely to participate fully in providing the information required for a functional analysis. Information about the client is of course gathered and processed for therapeutic purposes from the beginning of therapy, but the assessment is more sharply focused in this phase. Only after successful attainment of the issues described during Phases I and II can the client accept the reasons for active involvement in treatment. It is then clearer and easier for the client to share the task of a behavior analysis with the therapist. With an increased sense of commitment, the client can devote attention to observing his or her behavioral, emotional, and cognitive responses and their contexts, as a foundation for the choice of specific intervention targets and methods.

This view implies that early screening and psychological assessment, often routine at the time of intake in many clinical settings, may be premature. In fact, it may interfere with the therapeutic process. Early assessment supports a passive client role, signaling the professional's role as a healer who requires diagnostic information so that he or she can then prescribe proper treatment.

Finally, early use of formal assessment procedures tend to be "fishing expeditions" because the clinician does not yet know what questions the procedure should answer (Kanfer, 1985; Kanfer & Nay, 1982). It is only after structuring therapy and obtaining a general commitment for change that the clinician can effectively focus on selecting a *specific* target behavior. The behavioral analysis is not an assessment of all aspects of the client's life. It is an indepth assessment of those specific areas of the client's life in which the therapeutic program will be targeted.

During the behavioral analysis, antecedent, response, and consequence dimensions of various behaviors are identified. Clients thereby also learn to identify, anticipate, and change antecedents and consequences in order to bring behavior under their own control. An additional objective involves assisting clients in refining the problem definition and specifying clear behavioral goals. Throughout this phase, the question is focused not only on what is wrong, but also on what aspects of the client's behavior and life situation can be improved.

The behavioral analysis phase has two essential goals: (1) to help clients recognize the connection between their own behaviors and external or self-generated stimuli and reinforcers, and (2) to demonstrate to the clients that they have it within their power to influence others by their actions and by the situations they set up. This training helps the client and therapist to pinpoint targets. It also enhances the client's capacity to predict and control behavior and bolster related positive self-reactions.

Behavioral analysis is seen as a continuous activity (Kanfer, 1985). From the first interview on, clients learn to identify the differences between their current state of affairs and the desirable goal state. Gradually they also learn to formulate a functional analysis that specifies initial goals. As therapy progresses, continuing re-evaluation of goals occurs (Kanfer & Busemeyer, 1982).

The skills that the client learns in the earlier phases aid him or her later in collecting the data for the analysis. For example, self-monitoring, role-playing, or testing the effects of one's behavior on others can be put to use to specify information needed for developing precise treatment objectives. Proper handling of the first two phases enables the client to be more attentive to the antecedents and consequences of his or her behavior. At this time the client should also feel more comfortable in sharing intimate information that may be salient for the analysis of his or her problem. While the therapist listens to vague descriptions of the client's complaints during initial interviews in order to establish a working relationship, he or she works with the client in Phase III to obtain descriptions of events and behaviors (and the temporal relationships among them) in terms of verifiable events and with the greatest precision possible. For example, an earlier statement about "getting angry with my partner" now is phrased in terms of the specific situation, actions of the partner that preceded it, the thoughts and events that triggered specific self-reactions and emotional cues, and the consequences of feeling angry. This practice results in an indepth exploration of a focal theme and may limit the topics covered in a particular session.

The assessment phase yields a general plan to guide later therapy sessions. Consequently, there is a tentative plan for sessions that permits a systematic approach toward the immediate objectives to be accomplished during a session. Although these plans always give way to issues that the client may bring up or to occurrences of unexpected events, they do afford a directional structure for the interviews, in contrast to the practice of following the client's lead as he or she responds to the inquiry "What would you like to talk about today?"

Assessment questions arise out of the context of treatment objectives. A question guiding the therapist is "What information is needed to determine whether the stated goals are realistic, and to help the client achieve those stated goals?" The behavioral analysis provides a problem-solving description of the client's current state in relation to a desirable state. From this analysis, treatment strategies and techniques are derived for later use. If a client's overall level of psychological functioning is tenuous, the therapeutic objectives may differ from those of a person who is well-integrated, even though the presenting complaints may be very similar. Delineation of the precise nature of the problem and of the client's personal resources thus provides guidance for both setting goals and selecting the type of intervention for that particular client.

Once a core problem has been clearly identified, the behavioral analysis shifts to defining the variables that may limit or facilitate a client's benefits from a specific intervention. Intellectual abilities, self-expectations, family expectations, socioeconomic patterns and standards, and cultural norms are variables to be considered during the analysis (see Kanfer & Grimm, 1977; Kanfer & Saslow, 1969). But even though, in principle, innumerable factors may influence the client at the moment and thus shape the change process, only a few can be selected for detailed consideration. For practical reasons, analysis stops when several factors are noted that appear to have an overriding influence on the client. Their choice is determined by their relevance to the clinician's decisions about shared objectives, treatment methods, and probable ease of modification. The therapist must ask: "Why do I want to ask about this variable? What will it tell me? What decisions must I make now and how would information about this event or variable give me better documentation for our decision?"

A final aspect of the assessment phase concerns the evaluation of the client's motivational level. The client's completion of between-session assignments, participation and investment during sessions as well as the involvement shown by using self-management strategies reflect his or her motivation for a given course in therapy. Any indication of a low level of concern, effort, or cooperation may require recursion to achieve the subgoals of Phase II.

Phase IV: Negotiating Treatment Objectives

After the client's commitment for change has been assured and the problematic dimensions have been clarified, specific objectives and their priorities are negotiated. During this phase, we attempt to accomplish the following subgoals: (1) seek agreement on target areas; (2) establish priorities for the change program, specify change methods, and design the program sequence; (3) help the client accept responsibility for engaging in the planned therapeutic program; and (4) negotiate a contract for the initiation of the change procedures. Throughout this phase, the therapist makes sure that the client perceives him- or herself as having some choices and control over the objectives and their associated treatments. While maintaining the prerogatives of the expert in selecting techniques for changing behavior, the therapist collaborates with clients in clarifying and selecting particular treatment objectives. The attitude to be fostered is conveyed by the statement "What outcomes would satisfy you and be worth the effort of being involved in therapy?" Although the therapist represents the perspective of society as far as what range of goals would be acceptable or have high priority, he or she attempts to help the client to generate such goals.

Much of this phase is devoted to selecting the target behaviors and ordering their priorities and sequence (Kanfer, 1985). In collaboration with the client, the clinician defines a goal-state and proposes the intervention steps needed to move the client toward the goal. This approach suggests that target behaviors are selected on the basis of their expected utility for improving the client's problematic situation rather than on the basis of theoretically derived cause–effect inferences.

As we have suggested earlier, changes at any level, whether interactional or interpersonal, will alter other behaviors in the client's repertoire (Kazdin, 1982). Change in any target behavior therefore produces a new behavioral pattern. As a result, target behaviors cannot be chosen in isolation from the relationship between them and other responses that may co-vary (Kanfer, 1985). These interrelationships are likely to affect the attainment of the goal, as well as the later maintenance of therapeutic change (Schefft & Lehr, 1985). Priority in the selection of specific target behaviors is given to those that yield the widest range of overall changes in all behaviors and consequences defined for the goal state. For example, in the modification of excessive drinking, target behaviors may include dealing with work or family problems, assertiveness, and self-reactions that reduce stress or strengthen the client's future ability to cope with the cues that precede drinking. Regardless of the focal complaint and specific content of a therapy program, the potential collateral and the radiating effects of a targeted change require careful evaluation.

Following the establishment of initial targets, the client's expectations from therapy are explored further. In addressing this topic, the objective is to help the client to understand the relationship between the specific program procedures and their purpose. To enhance the client's involvement and participation, he or she must perceive the relevancy between the procedures and objectives. This assists the client in providing an answer to the important question: "Why should I do this?"

During the negotiation of treatment objectives, a therapeutic contract is prepared. However, it is important to note that it is the process of developing the contract, and not the resulting product that represents the important therapeutic contribution. A contract means clarifying the goals, the procedures used, and the specific roles and responsibilities of the therapist and the client, as well as defining a plan of action which prepares for execution of the program. In negotiating specific objectives and related between-session tasks, clients are assisted in arranging conditions that facilitate their adherence to various aspects of the program. For example, in negotiating a specific assignment, clients are helped to decide when to do the task, in what settings it is easiest for them to do it, how they can remember to do it, and what are the consequences of doing the task.

The process of contracting is illustrated during this phase with a 37-year old divorced black school teacher. She sought outpatient therapy for anxiety related to increasing performance demands on the job. The following transcript is from a session during which related goals in three areas were negotiated. The goals included increasing assertive behavior, building relaxation and stress coping skills, and increasing self-esteem. After instruction and rehearsal in the use of calming self-statements and tension-release techniques, the interview focused on clarifying a plan of action and a specific assignment for the week.

Client Statement	*Self-Management Therapist Response*
	So it seems that we've agreed that the first thing for you to work on is to learn how to relax yourself.
Yes, I think so. And I think the deep breathing and positive statements are going to help a lot.	What would you do this week to apply these new strategies often?
Well, I can do deep breathing and talk to myself positively every time I feel like I'm getting uptight.	Do you think you want to wait until you're already uptight to work on relaxing, or do you want to practice relaxing before you get uptight?
I want to do it before I feel stressed.	So, I think you may want to practice it a while every day until you are so good at it that you can just slide into it as soon as you notice an upset coming on. How often do you think you could do your practice?
I'll practice at least twice a day.	What might be the best times for you to do that during the day?
I guess before I go to work in the morning, and maybe one other time.	Would that be before breakfast or after?
After, because I always feel better after I eat something.	Ok, so after breakfast. And about what time would that be?
Well, it would have to be before 7:30, because I leave for work then.	How many minutes can you practice?
I think 20 minutes would be good.	That would be fine. So from 7:10 to 7:30 you would practice relaxation every day.
Yes, I can do that.	That's great. Say, will you have enough time, I mean do you get up pretty regularly to get ready each morning?

Client Statement	*Self-Management Therapist Response*
Yeah, I suppose I better set my alarm earlier.	That's a good idea. When will you have to set it for?
Well, I get up at 6:15 now, but I just barely get out of the house on time.	I suppose you'll have to get up 20 minutes earlier then to do the relaxation.
Oh, yeah, about 6:00 would be right; I can cut down on reading the paper.	So, you'll set your alarm for 6:00 this week?
Yeah.	And to remember to do the relaxation exercises, how are we going to remind you as you have your breakfast to do it next?
Well, let's see. . . . I could ask my sister to remind me.	That's okay. Is she always around, and will she remember it?
I guess you're right. Maybe I better do it myself. . . . I could write myself a note and pin it over the breakfast table.	Hey, that's a great idea! Couldn't miss seeing it when you eat. Okay. Now let's go over again just what you'll do. Now what's the first thing? You better get up at 6:00?
I'm going to set my alarm earlier tonight. Then I'll pin a reminder over the table.	Gee, that's fine. Now let's make believe you just finished your breakfast. What do you do next?

At this point client and therapist role-played the sequence, including the relaxation exercise steps. Both then made notes of the key steps, including a record of the time and duration of the practice, and set up a similar routine for afternoon sessions. The therapist then continued.

Client Statement	*Self-Management Therapist Response*
	Well, we got that down pretty fast. But that's a lot of things to do, let's talk about what it will get you and why you would want to do it. . . .
Well, I get so uptight all the time . . . and the deep-breathing we did was real good. It sure would be nice not to get so tense so I can talk sense with people. . . . If I could only be relaxed more. . . .	And these exercises will help you do just that.
Yeah, I really need to do that. I felt more relaxed just now when we did it. . . .	

After agreement was reached on this assignment, the interview shifted to a discussion of issues related to the client's poor interpersonal interactions. It was emphasized that the client's exercise experiences would be reviewed in the next session.

As seen in the above example, the elements described as part of the contract process require only little time but their inclusion greatly enhances the compliance with negotiated goals. It is particularly important that any contracted behavior be defined clearly, role-played, and discussed to avoid misunderstanding and assure the client's capability to carry out the necessary steps.

In negotiating particular treatment goals, the approach is characterized by a great deal of flexibility. During the negotiation process, the therapist can specify, in a collaborative fashion, the nature of the client's responsibilities and tasks. Negotiation does not imply that we "advocate a cafeteria-style therapy in which clients pick problems and select treatment methods. . . . The outcome of negotiating target behaviors and treatment plans ideally leads both parties to accept the target behaviors as worthy of change and to believe the treatment methods are the most expeditious for the defined problem and client characteristics" (Kanfer & Grimm, 1980, p. 431). This process also prepares for achieving the specificity of the procedures required for the execution of the program.

Phase V: Treatment Execution and Motivation Maintenance

After preparing the conditions under which a change program can most easily and effectively be carried out, the therapist can focus on the use of the change methods and techniques that most textbooks heavily emphasize. This phase is spent mainly in utilizing specific techniques to help the client move toward the attainment of the selected therapy targets. The techniques span the entire range of procedures described in the cognitive–behavioral literature (cf. Hersen, Kazdin, & Bellack, 1983; Kanfer & Goldstein, 1980; Meichenbaum & Jaremko, 1983). Consequently, the treatment of an anxiety patient may involve desensitization or anxiety management, work with a marital problem may involve couples communication skills training, and work with a psychosomatic patient may involve biofeedback or other stress-management techniques.

Concomitant with the conduct of the treatment program, the therapist carefully monitors the following subgoals: (1) assessing the collateral and radiating effects of change in target behaviors, including the impact on nontargeted responses; (2) teaching the use of behavior change techniques to facilitate the learning of new responses, gradually fading out the use of these techniques as well as therapist support, as new behaviors become more automatic; (3) assessing and, if necessary, enhancing the motivation of the client to comply with the treatment program.

In assessing the collateral and the radiating effects of the targeted behavior change, the therapist needs to consider several issues which were described earlier. An example of one such issue is illustrated by considering therapy with a pain patient. Elimination of a pain problem will have multiple effects on various aspects of the person's life. An obvious consequence of the change is the availability of the free time that results when the pain problem is eliminated, since the client no longer spends time dealing with the pain, its prevention, and remedies. Since medications, physical therapy, and other activities related to the physical condition are no longer required, demands on the pain-free client are increased. He or she often requires assistance in developing alternative behaviors to carry out the functions previously served by the illness behavior.

Because the successful treatment of focal complaints can have a significant impact on the entire life pattern of the client, renegotiation for new goals and new therapeutic contracts may be needed as treatment progresses. At each stage of progress during therapy, either the client successfully integrates newly learned behaviors into his or her life pattern or new problems arise because the new attitudes, actions, or plans conflict with other often unchangeable aspects of his or her life situation.

Modes of Learning

Conduct of the treatment program in the fifth phase involves selection from a wide variety of well-established techniques of behavior therapy. Regardless of the specific content and procedural steps, the following structure is used to ensure that learning can occur at several levels: (1) *instruction*, with the focus on giving information and engaging the client in the cognitive rehearsal of various strategies; (2) *modeling*, with an emphasis on vicarious learning, observation of social models, and the use of visual, verbal, and kinesthetic modalities; (3) *direct experience*, with the use of instrumental/operant, autonomic, *in vivo* learning, including various conditioning procedures in the life context in which the acts ultimately need to be carried out; (4) *review*, with an emphasis on the verbal–symbolic and on rules and encoding of the experience to provide easy retrieval, transfer, and generalization to new situations. Integration of these four modes of learning is also combined with a shift in the focus of the learning process from breaking up maladaptive behavior at the beginning of therapy to introducing new behaviors that are at first under cognitive control and deliberately practiced, replacing the earlier automatic responses. As therapy progresses and positive outcomes strengthen these new acts and cognitive events, they, in turn, become more stereotyped and habitual, with decreasing components of controlled processing. The cycle is parallel to Kimble and Perlmuter's (1970) description of the shift in human learning from involuntary to voluntary and then again to involuntary behavior.

Throughout the implementation of the fifth phase, the therapist utilizes every small gain by the client to reinforce the act, and to confirm the client's ability to change and attain therapeutic goals. This feeling of mastery (White, 1959) or self-efficacy (Bandura, 1977) has been widely viewed as essential in therapy. Small gains also serve to assist the client in building rules of conduct and self-statements for use in future situations. The preparation for generalization is illustrated by the case of a 24-year-old male with whom we worked in an inpatient ward. He was admitted following a series of hallucinatory experiences and suicidal attempts, with the diagnosis of paranoid schizophrenia. The patient responded well to a behavioral self-management approach and was transferred to a day-treatment program. A highly valued goal for him was to develop the skills necessary to sit through several 3-hour classes at the university he was attending. Subgoals included reducing distractability, managing psychomotor agitation and arousal, and building coping self-statements to minimize debilitating self-reactions. Following the client's first successful experience in sitting through 1½ hours of classroom time, he was assisted in describing his accomplishments and crediting himself for having attained an important personal goal. Simultaneously, in sessions he verbally identified the coping self-statements and relaxation strategies he had successfully used. He identified self-statement strategies, such as attending to the reasons for staying through the class, instead of focusing on fear-related responses, rehearsing positive self-statements such as "I can do it," and using deep-breathing and attention-diverting relaxation strategies, as he had learned in therapy. He was then encouraged to discuss how he could apply these same techniques in mastering similar situations in which impatience, anxiety, and subsequent agitation had previously interfered with his functioning.

Phase VI: Monitoring and Evaluating Progress

During the sixth phase of therapy, the subgoals include: (1) evaluating changes in the client and his or her environment; (2) assessing increases in coping skills as well as related effects on the client and significant others; (3) utilizing accumulated data such as monitoring logs to review progress and strengthen gains; (4) negotiating new therapy objectives if necessary; (5) motivating completion of therapy with gradual withdrawal of the therapist's support.

By the sixth phase in treatment, self-management strategies and behavior change techniques should be well established. Consequently, the primary emphasis is on the review of the behaviors that have been learned and the enhancement of their application to future similar situations. The following message is conveyed by the therapist: "How could you use what you did in that situation to help you again in the future?" As clients become increasingly responsible for therapeutic decisions, the therapist decreases his or her activity level and overall responsibility. With an emphasis on fostering the future application of strategies that have furthered the client's progress, and enhancing self-attributions of behavior change, clients are assisted in extending their effectiveness to other parts of their lives, essentially becoming effective agents as their own therapists (see Goldstein & Kanfer, 1979).

In building the clients' feelings of confidence and self-efficacy, the therapist systematically draws attention to changes that have been made throughout the course of treatment. Records or tapes from early sessions can be reviewed and contrasted with the clients' current status to help them identify their gains.

By handling concrete problems the client learns a series of skills that can be generalized and used in the future. Consequently, the therapeutic focus shifts. It is no longer on how to overcome a specific situation, but on how to recognize, prevent or reduce the intensity of future problem situations. Rehearsal strategies are central to the therapeutic response style during the sixth phase in treatment. Whenever the client reports a positive experience or an attempt to apply a new behavior resulting in a positive gain, the therapist conveys the following message: "That's great that you did that, and I bet that there are other situations that you could handle like that." This response style facilitates the articulation of "rules of conduct" that can guide effective future coping (Kanfer, 1979).

Monitoring and evaluating progress during the sixth phase represents a continuation of some of the subgoals and activities from the fifth phase. An important activity is the monitoring of collateral effects of a change in targeted behaviors. Successful change in targeted behavior can sometimes be accompanied by deterioration in ancillary areas of functioning. To illustrate the importance of working with nontargeted changes during therapy, consider a case in which problems arose after a patient successfully mastered reduction of severe back pains. After being nearly symptom-free for 3 weeks, his back pains recurred. Examination of nontargeted areas revealed that the recurrence of his pain coincided with increasing emotional demands by his wife. The focus of treatment shifted to a re-examination of his marital relationship, and the client was able to identify and develop skills required for changes in the marriage. In later sessions goal and value clarification procedures were used to clarify the level of interpersonal involvement that he desired with his spouse. With assistance from the therapist, he prioritized a series of marriage-related goals and worked on them, concomitant with his continued practice of and improvement in pain-control.

This phase in treatment thus serves to obtain feedback on the effectiveness of the proposed program and on the appropriateness of the selected target behavior. It is a time at which both client and therapist may introduce problem areas and goals that previously had not been apparent or were not acceptable to the client for therapeutic attention. It is also a transitional stage prior to termination. Monitoring and evaluating progress yields information about the extent of work that may be required during the next phase.

Phase VII: Treatment Generalization and Termination

The last phase deals with the following key issues: (1) fostering self-management skills for the application to new and future problem situations; (2) preparing for therapy termination and arranging for transient support, if needed; (3) gradually dismantling the supportive therapeutic structure; (4) encouraging the client's acceptance of the termination of the therapeutic change process.

Although a variety of different strategies are used to approach the termination process, the general rule is to avoid abrupt termination. Increased interview focus on future events, a reduction in the frequency of meetings, and a gradual reduction of the therapist's activity level mark the phasing-out process. This combination of techniques capitalizes on the client's earlier acquisition of self-management skills and his or her enhanced self-efficacy. The gradual withdrawal of the "therapeutic umbrella" is illustrated by a procedure in which clients are given tentative appointment times that must be confirmed 24 hours in advance. Thus clients are reassured that they can fall back on the therapist's help, if it is needed. This gradual withdrawal can extend over 4 or 5 weeks with outpatients. In our use of this procedure, we have noted that most clients do not call but feel reassured that the opportunity exists. An alternative procedure is to offer the client limited telephone "talk-time" for minor issues they need to address. It is important to limit the allotted time to no more than about 15 minutes. In all of these procedures, the client's perception of choice and continued availability of therapeutic assistance for crises is maximized by the therapist. Consistent with the participation model of the self-management approach, the client is included in deciding the timing and form of termination procedures. For some clients, the ability to initiate and handle termination is a critical test of the effectiveness of therapy. For example, for a client whose complaint involved the inability to make decisions, the decision of whether or not to call to schedule an appointment is in itself a therapeutic experience. The approach to termination in such a case is to use it both to test and to strengthen the client's newly acquired skill in decision-making.

To further future coping and to develop cognitive strategies and "rules of conduct," clients are asked to summarize the most important things they have learned at the close of each session. Increased proficiency in these reviews is expected as treatment moves toward the end of therapy. During the final phase of treatment, this review can be conducted in a termination interview. In addition, the termination interview can be used to obtain feedback on the therapist's effectiveness and an evaluation of the treatment that was offered. Suggestions for change can be elicited to help the therapist to serve clients better in the future. The session also offers the client the opportunity to feel truly a participant in the process, someone who can influence the therapist's work, thus further enhancing the client's perceived control and related positive self-reactions.

The seventh phase of our model is relatively short because very early in treatment the therapist begins to prepare the client for autonomy and generalization. It usually is marked more by a treatment focus on ending than on changes in behavior.

SPECIFIC TECHNIQUES

Introduction

The preceding section outlined the conceptual level of the self-management approach. The model suggests strategies and procedures that are particularly helpful in developing the therapeutic context and in creating favorable conditions that further the change process. The use of these procedures is deliberate and planned. The clinician must ask him- or herself at each phase of treatment what purpose a technique would serve at that moment, what effects it is likely to have, and how it would further the overall course of treatment. This point is worthy of emphasis because a variety of elegant and effective treatment methods and programs have been widely used, without consideration of their appropriateness at a given time nor of their utility in facilitating the change process toward a specified outcome for an individual client. Since the questions about the function of a technique form the major criteria for the decision to use it, a variety of tactics and methods derived from different theoretical orientations can be employed. The primary consideration is whether a method, appropriately used, will have the desired and expected effect on client behaviors. Neither the popularity nor the theoretical rationale of a technique is sufficient to warrant its application or its rejection.

We can distinguish two categories of techniques that have been used in self-management therapy. The first group relates to the structure of the therapeutic process. It includes tactics to communicate to the client his or her responsibility for active participation, methods for developing and maintaining client motivation, and techniques to strengthen self-regulatory activities in coping with fears or conflicts. A second category of techniques deals with the substantive aspects of the client's problem. Any of the prevailing treatment techniques for obtaining the reduction of specific symptoms, for the development of skills, or for the attainment of any other therapeutic objective can be utilized in the target-oriented treatment (Phase V). In this section we deal only with the first category, since the methods in the second category comprise the well-known and widely described programs of behavioral and cognitive-behavioral therapies (e.g., those described in Hersen *et al.*, 1983; Kanfer & Goldstein, 1980; Kendall & Hollon, 1979; Turner, Calhoun, & Adams, 1981; Walker, Hedberg, Clement, & Wright, 1981).

Interview Structure

In practice, the initial interviews have a dual function. The first is to facilitate communication, enabling the client to be comfortable about discussing personal topics and to perceive the therapist as a potential helper. The second function is to structure the therapist role as that of a person who takes the client seriously and who responds to the ostensible interest of the client to engage in a change process. A variety of techniques are used that differentiate the therapeutic interaction from the usual social encounters that the client has previously experienced. The highlights of the structure consist of the therapist's gentle insistence that clients communicate unambiguously, with reference to specific incidents or behaviors, and that the interaction center on material relevant to the therapeutic task. Meaningless polite phrases, general opinions, or well-rehearsed, automatic verbal sequences are therefore discouraged. In contrast to social conversation, difficult or sensitive topics are not eschewed, nor are reassuring or comforting responses used when they would circumvent a thorough analysis of a client's emotional reactions or thoughts. Clearly, the therapist's sensitivity to the client's momentary needs dictates the degree to which strict adherence to dealing with the problem at hand is pursued. The acceptance of the client as a person is not equivalent to the acceptance of everything that person says or does. The therapist operates on the implicit assumption that every client can assume at least some degree of responsibility for his or her own actions or thoughts. Such an assumption is communicated by encouraging the client to elaborate on allusions and expressions of vague feelings or attitudes. Illustrations are solicited to clarify and specify just what it is that the client means to convey.

An additional element in the early interview structure lies in the establishment of an implicit three-part agreement: (1) the client will attend to the therapist's communications; (2) the client will gradually increase efforts to employ the therapist's statements in daily living; (3) his or her behavior, both outside as well as in therapy sessions, will come under control of the verbal exchange during the interview. For example, the interview should serve to motivate the client to think about the content of the interview between sessions, to attend to new dimensions in his or her daily environment, to raise questions about his or her own behavioral potentials, and to enact new behaviors between sessions, even if only in tentative form.

As sessions progress, the flow of the interview should be increasingly characterized by the client's greater participation, and by the introduction of more planning, decision-making, and evaluating of new behaviors. These activities should take the place of the client's earlier stereotyped recitations of difficulties. In addition, following a focus derived from research on information processing and memory (Ericsson & Simon, 1980), the interviewer should attempt to shift the client's interview behavior along three dimensions in order to enhance a correspondence between the interview reports and actual behavior. First, there is an emphasis on discussing present behaviors and situations and relating them to future situations, rather than on reviewing past experiences. Second, interview material is shifted from general to specific statements. Third, the content is switched from the verbal mode to the experiential mode. Essentially, the research on the structure of memory and recall suggest that a client who talks about a recent specific event, thought, or behavior, and who is prompted to reexperience or reintegrate this event in the therapy session is likely to give more accurate information, to have better recall of what happens during the interview, and to be more fully involved in attempts to analyze and understand his or her own actions. In contrast to common therapy practices, questions concerning metacognitive processes such as describing a feeling (without a specific referent) or characterizing oneself or others in general terms is viewed as relatively nonproductive.

Interviewer Style

The specific way in which an interviewer utilizes various strategies depends upon the individual therapist and the client. Nevertheless, a broad sketch of the interview style can be given by highlighting some of the characteristics of a technique that we have developed for conducting an approach oriented to self-management. Perhaps this orientation can be best characterized by comparing it to the style of inquiry of the television detective in the "Columbo" series. While therapeutic interviews are not at all like detective work in that they do not look for causes or attempt to discover hidden secrets, Columbo's interviewing style shares with our approach the persistent effort to become specific, to encourage clarification by the subject, to involve the subject in attempting to understand the issue at hand and to engage controlled processing in these efforts. We can briefly summarize the key elements of this style.

1. The interviewer assumes the role of a naive person with respect to the information given by the client. This role is not difficult to play, since

in fact therapists are indeed naive regarding knowledge about a client's social environment, behavior patterns, autonomic responses and cognitive events.

2. Although the interviewer takes blame for lack of understanding the sequence of events, he or she gently confronts the client with inconsistencies and asks for clarification. This probing about the client's life events can be communicated as a strong interest on the part of the therapist rather than as a sign of ignorance. In our experience, most clients have reported positive reactions to this tactic.

3. The interviewer challenges the client to increase the clarity of his or her responses. Attempting to clarify a series of events and their related circumstances not only yields a clear picture for the therapist but also obliges the client to make such clarifications for him- or herself. The challenge can often be made by carrying through a somewhat exaggerated implication of the client's statements. For example, when a client states, "I never want to see my father again," the therapist, within the context of the session may say, "You mean, even if he were to stop criticizing you and would accept your marriage, you would never want to see him, under *any* circumstances?"

4. The interviewer insists on specific information to help the client reevaluate generalized judgments. For example, when a client says, "Sometimes I feel so anxious I can't do anything," the therapist might reply, "You know, everyone feels anxious in a different way; please tell me what happens where, and how you notice things in your body when you are anxious." And later the inquiry might continue as follows: "What thoughts go through your mind at that time?" and then, "Can you think of a specific incident that recently happened, and then describe to me what you thought and did?"

5. The therapist attempts to focus on introducing change into a person's behavior or environment, or calls attention to features that are changeable. For example, when a client says, "I just can't control my drinking once I get into a bad mood," the therapist might work toward some limiting factors that are under the client's control by asking, "Have there been situations in which this urge is less strong and you can suppress it for awhile?"

6. To facilitate the self-generation of behaviors, the therapist sets up partially complete sentences and waits for the client to finish them. For example the therapist might say, "Now let's see, you said that you can sometimes distract yourself from worrying about your job by . . . (pause). If the client doesn't answer, then the therapist can prompt a reply: "Tell me again just how you did that."

7. By developing a hypothesis and beginning to draw implications, the therapist can help the client to note implications for a change in his or her behavior. For example, the therapist reviews by saying, "So, your

partner gets real angry whenever you are depressed, and you shut him off or turn away. I wonder how he knows what you are trying to tell him by your behavior?"

Although these and other related procedures appear to be mainly cognitively oriented, they are also used to elicit or moderate client emotions, and they can be used with direct reference to the in-session exchanges between therapist and client. Both the interview structure and its related style represent techniques for combining affective elements with verbal symbolic or cognitive interchanges and, most importantly, attempt to activate novel behaviors or initiate behavior changes outside the therapy session.

Relating Cognitive, Behavioral, and Affective Components

In our approach, continuing emphasis is put on interrelating thoughts, actions, and emotions. Attempts are made to supplement verbal interchanges with direct experiences in the session and in the client's natural environment. Samples of interactional behaviors, emotions, and thoughts can serve as a basis for the analysis of an episode to provide feedback about the experience to the client, and to develop specific cues to which newly acquired responses can be attached. For these reasons the therapist often shifts from verbal interchange to a brief role play or behavioral rehearsal in order to bring the referred experience into the sessions in a more vivid fashion. This approach is based on the belief that verbal-symbolic or cognitive behavior sequences are also subject to modification and that they form an integral part of behavioral chains, both as antecedents and consequences of overt actions. The interview methods stress the close linkage between actions and plans—between intentions and decisions on the one hand, and between actions and their feedback and cognitive evaluations on the other hand. Further, the clinician seeks to establish a bridge between affective and other biological inputs and actions by helping the client to attend to and learn to categorize these stimulations and reactions in relation to both interpersonal and cognitive behaviors.

A most critical aspect during the later treatment phases is that of helping the client recognize not only *how* to behave differently but also *when*. To this end, problematic episodes are role-played, discussed, and rehearsed in detail. A starting point can then be found that is discriminable and that can serve as an alerting stimulus to the client for interposing self-regulatory mechanisms and disrupting an automatic and disturbing behavioral sequence. For example, in training a client to recognize clearly any internal or environmental cue, all early signals that elicit an anxiety reaction, or the cues associated with an urge to overeat or to act abusively toward a child are first defined. Elaboration of the cues and, if possible, some immediate tangible reminder associated with their occurrence can then be used for training alternate behavior chains.

Dealing with Client Reluctance to Assume Responsibility

In our experience, the following five problems were most common in efforts to motivate the client to assume responsibility in the change process. While they differ in the degree to which they interfere with therapy, the understanding of these sources of reluctance suggests possible techniques for dealing with them.

1. Fear of the unknown, of taking risks, or of changing is the most common obstacle to active client participation. The prospect of changing a life-long behavioral pattern represents a threat to everyone. Many situations and behavior patterns may be distressing and problematic to a client, but ultimately their tolerance is preferred to undertaking a change that may lead to unforeseeable consequences and may even worsen difficulties and distress. Clients who have long found solace in adhering conservatively, and sometimes rigidly, to well-known routines are particularly threatened. They are reluctant to give up a well-established behavior when faced with the potential for anxiety that may be associated with an expectation of loss of control and an inability to meet new demands. To reduce the fear of the unknown, we include extensive preparation for each step of the change process, strengthen the client's belief in his or her own capability to handle new situations, and gradually introduce new behavior patterns or situational changes. In extreme cases, exercises in risk-taking with deliberate exposure to new and unknown situations, beginning with unimportant outcomes and relatively nonthreatening situations, can be used to prepare clients for the assumption of responsibility in more critical life situations.

2. Clients who have had long experiences in which helplessness, learned incompetence, and similar interpersonal maneuvers were effective in shifting to other people responsibilities for actions can be expected to show the same pattern in a therapeutic relationship. Such clients often show initial mild and superficial compliance, and collaboration without commitment. Undermining the effectiveness of such techniques in therapy is a necessary strategy for extinguishing this approach. Nevertheless, continued support from other persons in the client's social setting may work against the therapist's efforts by maintaining the effectiveness of passive and helpless behaviors. The inclusion of these persons in therapy may, in some cases, help to reduce their obstructive influence.

3. Habitual dependency patterns differ from the above in the emotional components of the pattern. While helplessness and learned incompetence often are accompanied by negative self-attitudes and elaborate displays of ineptitude, clients who have a habitual dependency pattern

simply have learned to select a lifestyle in which others can be maneuvered to take responsibility. Consequently, decision making is often avoided, passivity is maintained and partners are found who are willing to assume responsibility for the clients. Once this pattern is established, these clients also tend to blame others for failures and simply seek new caretakers to work with them. In therapy these persons are often clients who switch from therapist to therapist in the futile expectation that someone will know what to do for them, avoiding active participation throughout. As in the previous group, the first intervention target in therapy lies in altering the dependency pattern and its positive consequences. In both groups the presented complaint is often closely related to these long-standing dependency patterns. Increases in autonomy, positive self-reactions, and confidence in one's own ability may in fact represent the most critical goal not only for facilitation of a change process but for therapy itself.

4. The lack of specific skills to initiate needed changes is found in many clients. These persons may make a genuine effort and be seriously motivated to alter their behavior pattern or life situation. Training in decision making, planning instrumental or interpersonal behaviors, and assistance in the gradual development of the required skills are common strategies for this group. In most cases these clients present the least difficulties to therapists.

5. The conflict between desiring change and maintaining some elements of the status quo may be a source of low motivation and reluctance to participate. Strong positive outcomes of the dysfunctional behavior itself (e.g., in addictions) or the support by social networks (partners, agencies, or others) for maintaining the present situation or active opposition to change present serious obstacles. In these clients, a most frequent initial therapeutic intervention lies in enhancing the client's motivation toward a change or intervening in the supporting relationships that prevent such a change. Consistent with our earlier belief that therapy cannot be undertaken without some cooperation and interest by the client, it should be clear that the above sources of difficulties may vary in clients from a degree of severity that makes therapy futile at one point in time to mild cases that may necessitate only brief therapeutic strategies to establish client involvement in the therapeutic process.

Techniques Employed Primarily in Specific Phases

Although the following techniques illustrate some of the approaches that we have used to attain a goal that is specific to one of the seven phases in our model, the recursive nature of the model suggests that their use may be necessary in any phase.

In the preceding section, we have described techniques that are frequently applied throughout therapy even though they are usually initiated at the beginning. During the *second* phase, when the development of a commitment for change is the primary goal, motivational issues are most heavily highlighted. The general assumption we hold is that clients, jointly with therapists, need to work toward establishing individual goals for the course of therapy and to establish the relationship between these goals and the client's broader values. The techniques in goal and value clarification serve to instigate the client's participation in selecting treatment objectives that are consistent with his or her general life theme and to increase motivation toward achieving them. The approach emphasizes the importance of the client's self-perception, his or her participatory role in goal setting and the possibility of selecting differing goals and subgoals. The specific techniques used here are similar to those described in a number of publications on this area. We have drawn most heavily on our own experience and on the publications of Koberg and Bagnall (1976), Lee (1978), and Bolles (1977) to help clients explore, recognize, and work with goal-states that are of importance to them. The therapist continually emphasizes that these techniques are not designed to discover the "true" value system or goals that a person holds. Specific goals and desired end-states may change over time or as a result of therapeutic exercises. The function of the techniques is to provide the client with an acceptable incentive for change at this time.

Exercises range from the observation of the effort and energy expended in daily actions for a desired outcome to the assignment of sketching in detail the conditions that would make the client's life more satisfying at the present or 5 years later. Other assignments include planning idealized scenes in which the client describes what he or she would wish a partner or children to say about the client when he or she has reached old age. The reader is referred to Koberg and Bagnall (1976) for the wide range of specific exercises.

The use of goal and value clarification procedures is illustrated in our work with a 25-year-old single male with a history of hyperkinetic behavior, difficulties in intimate relationships and anger control. After a therapeutic alliance had been established, the critical issue became his commitment to the change program. Influenced by several years of unsuccessful treatment, the client's perceptions about the efficacy of therapy were negative, and feelings of hopelessness were a central theme of his clinical presentation. The dissolution of the relationship with his girlfriend precipitated his seeking therapy, and seemed to reinforce his belief that he was a "loser" incapable of change. His response to relationship-related emotional distress was one of great anger and self-punitive behavior, both of which removed him further from the social support and companionship he so badly wanted.

Goal and value clarification strategies were used at this early point in therapy to build incentives for the client to participate in the change program. The following transcript illustrates an attempt to help the client to explore and sample different goal states, as well as establish some objectives toward which he was willing to work in subsequent sessions.

Client Statement	*Self-Management Therapist Response*
What's the use of trying? Every time I open myself up to someone, I end up getting shafted. I'm just a loser and I might as well face it now.	I wonder if you are a loser. Maybe you just keep acting the same way and repeating the same mistakes.
What's the difference? I don't know what else to do, and doctors haven't been able to help me.	Okay, let's try something with me. I'd like you to take a few minutes to imagine what it would be like if you liked yourself. . . . How you would be different from the way you are now?
I'd be a lot different!	How would you be different? What would be different in your life from the way things are now?
For starters, I wouldn't feel like nobody cares about me, and I wouldn't be angry all the time, losing my cool and taking it out on myself.	What would you be doing instead?
I would have people to talk to when I was feeling down or lonely.	So, what would you be doing differently?
I wouldn't scream and yell at people. I would tell them how I really felt inside.	If you were able to tell them how you really felt inside, what do you think might happen?
Well, they'd either reject me or tell me how they felt inside too and be a friend.	So if you learned to talk to people to tell them how you think and feel, you might not feel so alone and misunderstood.
Yeah, but I don't know how to do that even though I keep trying real hard to be friendly. I always end up getting scared of being rejected and I guess I get angry then.	If you did know how to initiate and maintain close relationships, would you be more of the kind of person you really want to be?
Yes, definitely, but that's where I get stuck.	You've already said that there are always several specific things you would be doing differently. Instead of screaming and yelling at people, you would be doing what?
Talking in a calm voice.	Instead of criticizing yourself and being hard on yourself, you would . . . ?
Like myself better and be more positive.	And instead of ruffling your feathers and looking and sounding angry, you'd . . .

Client Statement	*Self-Management Therapist Response*
Talk about my feelings inside and be a little more open to people.	Okay. So what would be some of the benefits of doing that?
I suppose people might get to know me better and maybe I would have some friends.	What else would be good about changing in that way?
I wouldn't have all that anger inside all the time. I would feel like I'm a good person and that some people liked me.	Anything else that might be positive if you changed?
I would probably begin to feel more confident—like I'm okay and I can do some things right.	Ok, now, close your eyes. Imagine what that would feel like. . . . How you would feel inside, if you just really had an open talk with someone and she tells you she likes you and you feel accepted. . . . What's going through your mind? . . . Sort of think aloud. . . .

A brief guided imagery exercise followed in which the client was assisted in creating a vivid picture of what it would be like if he changed. Details of daily life situations were elicited to make the goal state more concrete and real to him, and to assist in identifying specific behaviors to be targeted later in the treatment program. Dialogue then continued:

Client Statement	*Self-Management Therapist Response*
(*Looking pleased as he opens his eyes.*)	You have a smile on your face for the first time that I've seen.
Yeah. Well, that sure would be nice if things were that way.	But it wouldn't be easy to get there. It would take a lot of hard work. What could be some of the negative things about changing in that direction?
Like you say, it would be a lot of hard work.	Would you be willing to try it? I mean is it really worth it?
I'm pretty sure, yeah. It's better than what I have now, which is nothing.	And what else could it cost you?
I'd have to take some risks, and maybe get rejected a few times.	Could you handle that?
I have so far, not too well, but I've handled it.	Okay, what else could it cost you?
I might fail at it and be a loser just like I always am.	You mean, you'd be back where you are now. Do you think it would be worth the effort?
I really have nothing to lose, and maybe there's something to gain.	Okay, well let's talk about where and how we can get started.

Following this dialogue, the session focused on clarifying and negotiating specific tasks that would result in the client spending increasing time and energy during the week considering how he would be different and the implications of these changes for his daily life. The purpose was to enhance his incentive for change by increasing his involvement with various potential goal-states. The example illustrates the role of goal and value clarification in creating a fundamental need for the remainder of the therapeutic program, and in building the client's commitment to the therapeutic tasks.

The role of goal and value clarification varies according to the client. For some, observing and defining current goals and values may be the major task of therapy. Clients who complain of alienation, loss of personal identity, vague and general depression or apathy often have failed to develop appropriate and attainable goals and objectives for themselves. The reduction of discomfort and a clearer focus in their life activities may present major goals. Resolution can be facilitated by helping clients examine, try out, and adopt a range of attainable goals and acceptable values. For many of these clients, the second phase of treatment, with its emphasis on enhancing a commitment for change, may extend for much of the course of therapy and represent the major focus of treatment. When clients with these problems have previously acquired experience and skill in handling difficult situations but lack direction, the later phases of treatment may be brief. For others who are seriously committed to a change and who have formulated their desires and goals for a satisfactory life situation prior to coming to therapy, the strategies associated with the second phase of treatment may be very brief and in some cases not necessary.

The therapist often encounters persons who have conflicting goals and values and who require assistance to resolve these conflicts. Finally, some clients hold goals and values that are unrealistic, unattainable, or in strong conflict with social norms. With these clients, the therapist is faced with the difficult task of developing new incentives or helping clients at least interpose subgoals or rearrange their hierarchy of potential goals in a manner that is satisfying to clients and acceptable to society.

Techniques for Problem Definition

During the *third* phase, often overlapping with previous ones, the client is helped to specify the particular conditions, behaviors, and consequences that are problematic in his or her present life situation. Detailed analysis of critical incidents is then coupled with efforts to consider alteration in any of these factors and relate them to the therapeutic objectives established during the prior phase. A variety of behavioral assessment techniques, including self-observation and didactic procedures for problem solving and decision making, are used during this phase.

In completing a behavioral analysis, we find it helpful to use a graphic model that represents various life sectors in the form of slices of a pie. The sectors include the following areas: work; family; health; social; self-care; moral–religious; economic; and the pursuits of educational, sexual, recreational, and personal achievements. Clients are asked to allot portions of the entire pie to these sectors, first according to the amount of attention, energy, and effort *currently* invested in them, and then in accordance with their wishes for an *ideal* distribution of them. The allotment is made not only in terms of the time actually spent in a sector but also in terms of the amount of time spent in fantasizing and worrying about that sector. An activity may be assigned to several sectors, for example, a job that permits personal achievement or social interactions may be divided up among each of these sectors. The frequencies and types of problems that distress the client are also assigned to various sectors. A variety of exercises, observations, and plans can be designed, with different functions for various clients. In all cases, it helps to clarify, for both client and therapist, in which life sector problems occur most frequently, whether they are limited to specific life sectors or are general, and what changes and redistributions of energy and time may be desirable and feasible for the client. The entire analysis is related to the earlier goal and value clarification and represents a refinement of it. As in the goal and value clarification, it is made clear that it is *not* the absolute distribution of time, energy, concern, or precision that is sought. The analysis is designed primarily as a "scanning device" to permit the best selection of a target area and to focus on some behaviors as a starting point for the change program. Space permits only a brief overview of this technique. In practice it may be used as a background and rationale for a series of assignments, both for helping the client define therapeutic goals and for motivating the initiation of a change.

Contracts

In the *fourth* phase, treatment objectives are developed and procedures are contracted. Although the interviewer's style, which incorporates a negotiating framework throughout therapy, involves a constant use of explicit and implicit contracts, specific contracts for treatment objectives and for particular methods are developed jointly by the therapist and client only fully in the fourth phase. The specific techniques for contracting have been described in detail elsewhere (Kanfer, 1980). In general, the contracts are made only for short periods (for example, for two to three sessions, reviewed and revised as therapy progresses). It is important to note that it is not the contract as a product that is critical but the contract as a process that involves defining goals, specific activities to be carried out, and clear consequences for these activities.

Problem-Specific Techniques

The preceding strategies and methods are used to prepare the client for an intensive target-focused program. During the *fifth* phase, various techniques, described extensively in textbooks on cognitive behavior therapy and behavior therapy, are utilized to alter the selected target behaviors. Throughout this process, constant emphasis is placed on preparing for generalization by asking clients to try the therapeutic technique (e.g., desensitization, coping strategies, self-instruction, etc.) in new situations, including those that do not present serious problems at the moment. During the fifth and in subsequent phases, clients are also asked to recapitulate their progress. Verbal–symbolic review of the changes that have occurred in the preceding portion of therapy is conducted repeatedly because it provides semantic descriptions for new experiences and coping techniques that can be more easily transferred to different settings. Therapists also help clients to prepare for increased stress or difficulties by using the various techniques that have been associated with relapse prevention (Marlatt & Parks, 1982).

The *sixth* phase includes no specific techniques or strategies. It overlaps with the fifth phase, but places greater emphasis on monitoring and evaluating progress and on encouraging clients to try out new skills in their daily routines.

Preparation for Termination

The *seventh* and last phase is devoted to paving the way for the transition from one's status as a client to a return to the natural life setting. In institutional settings, the focus lies on the gradual reduction of the "therapeutic umbrella" by encouraging leaves, supporting client contacts with various agencies, employers, family members, and other community settings, and preparing resources for "life after discharge." In outpatient treatment, clients are encouraged to assume increasing responsibility for solving daily problems and for planning the continued utilization of information and skills gained in therapy past termination. If necessary, clients are helped to make arrangements for seeking entry into a supportive network that would assist them in coping with future difficulties.

We are aware of the difficulties involved in termination, both from the client's and therapist's perspectives. Following our concept of minimal intervention, the therapist's task is essentially completed when the client achieves a stable status that is acceptable both to him or her and to society, and the problem or distress that resulted in the need for treatment has been eliminated or reduced to a tolerable level. To assure that treatment does not continue beyond this point, the therapist attends to indicators of the client's readiness for termination. Decreased richness of material brought into therapy sessions, improved functioning in daily activities, decreased discomfort in daily living, and achievement of therapeutic goals exemplify such signs. A gradual decrease in the frequency of sessions, brief phone contacts, and "open appointments" can be used to ease the termination of therapy. During this phase, the therapist communicates his or her readiness to assist a client when a specific need arises and yet supports the client in any attempt to revert to an autonomous role and give up the comforting, dependent, and supportive relationship that constitutes the therapeutic contacts.

Limitations on the Use of This Approach

In research on the effectiveness of various schools of psychotherapy, primary emphasis has been placed on the underlying conceptual model and the particular techniques derived from it. Both empirical evidence and clinical experience have suggested however that other factors may also be important in determining the outcome of therapy. No model operates without implementation by a therapist on a particular client in a specified setting. Various personal characteristics of therapists and their skill and sensitivity in translating a particular model into practical operation play an important role in achieving therapeutic success. The complex matrix of interactions between theory, therapist skills and experience, patient characteristics and clinical settings has created serious difficulties in any attempts to evaluate a major factor to which success or failure can be attributed. In this section we describe some patient and therapist characteristics that we consider important prerequisites for the effective application of the self-management approach. Many of these characteristics would be proposed also for other schools of therapy. The following recitation of criteria for effective therapy interactions toward successful outcome should not be interpreted as a prescription for inevitable success. Numerous variables, not under control of either participant in the change process, can and do affect therapeutic effectiveness. An understanding of the requirements and limitations of our approach therefore simply represents guidelines toward optimizing the clinical application of our theoretical model for therapy.

SOME REQUIREMENTS OF AN EFFECTIVE SELF-MANAGEMENT THERAPIST

The personal requirements for self-management therapy fall into three clusters: knowledge; technical and social skills; and beliefs, motives and values. In common with all mental health workers, a therapist must be a person who is genuinely concerned with improving the welfare of others and the society in which we live. For face-to-face contacts, the additional requirements shared with all schools of therapy are the capacity for empathic behaviors, the sensitivity needed to judge appropriate timing of various tactics or actions in consistency with the client's momentary need, and the ability to observe human behavior with some degree of detachment. In addition to these esteemed personal characteristics, the self-management approach, like many other forms of therapy, requires some distinctive skills to achieve the translation from the conceptual basis to daily operations.

Interview tactics and specific procedures are used not in a lock-step fashion, but rather as tools to achieve a particular purpose. Their proper use requires training to translate general tactics into specific operations and to consider in advance their purpose and their potential impact on the client. In training novice therapists, we emphasize that a question, comment, or therapeutic procedure should always be preceded by a brief moment of reflection about the purpose of the operation. What effects might it have on the client, and how would both the client and the therapist handle the next step? The ability to formulate and test specific hypotheses, usually of minor scope in moment-to-moment interviewing, requires training and experience in selecting useful hypotheses and in couching them in terms of the specifics of the client and the momentary content of the interview.

Most clients in therapy are there because they are unhappy; they lack confidence and hope. They also have acted, verbalized, fantasized, and felt ineffectively and frequently stereotypically though often in ways that appear logical to them. Therapists need training to shed their common social and conversational patterns and to react to clients in ways that modify their cognitive, behavioral, and emotional sequences. For these reasons, therapists must be able to modulate their own expression of emotions and their thinking, in a manner somewhat similar to the behavior of good actors on stage, to clearly communicate support and encouragement, surprise, dissatisfaction or mild confusion caused by a client's vague or contradictory statements or actions. As we noted in our discussion of the interview style we use, there must be a continuous effort by the therapist to keep the client working at the problem at hand. In training therapists, we have used modifications of the microcounseling procedure, practice in role play and in self-correcting feedback from videotapes to help new therapists acquire these skills. To some degree, the therapist must be skillful in communicating and managing the impression that he or she wishes to make on the client for the purpose of advancing movement in the therapeutic process.

In addition to familiarity with the conceptual framework that guides case management, the empirical evidence that supports it, and the technical instruments available to put it into operation, another type of knowledge is required. Numerous differences exist in the developmental histories, subcultural patterns, personal and social norms, and environmental demands and pressures in the real world in which our clients operate. It is impossible to be familiar with all of these factors. However, some awareness is needed of broad differences in subcultural patterns, varying demands by different environmental milieus and by age, sex, community, and socioeconomic status to work effectively with a client. No hypothesis about factors influencing the client's problem nor about useful therapeutic objectives can be made without such differentiated knowledge in each case. Although it is helpful if the therapist has had a wide range of life experiences, this does not obviate the need for understanding the conditions under which the individual client lives, the social and biological factors that influence clients of different ages, sex, and cultural backgrounds, and the particular demands made in the client's personal setting. In fact, we believe that there are limits to the effectiveness of a therapist whose cultural, social, and moral–religious backgrounds differ widely from those of the client. For most clients, it is possible to obtain this information directly from them and thus "educate" the therapist with regard to the parameters that need to be taken into account in the individual case. But there are limits to a therapist's capacity to treat certain patients. For example, in our own experience we have found it necessary to consult with female colleagues in order to gain a better understanding of the range of biological and social influences that affect a female client with regard to such issues as childbearing and abortion, and the integration of a female role that combines homemaking with a career. We have consulted with colleagues from minority groups in order to have a better understanding of problems facing clients from some orthodox religious sects, from the black population, or from geographic areas in which distinct sociocultural patterns prevail. While we do not expect all therapists to be fully aware of the developmental, cultural, and living patterns of each person in our pluralistic society, it is critical that the therapist recognize his or her limitations in dealing with clients for whom these particular factors represent significant determinants of the behavior problem under scrutiny.

In addition to knowledge about the client's background, we also believe that it is essential that the therapist have some understanding of his or her own personal limitation with regard to biases and expectations associated with his or her own history. In training novice therapists, we have found it helpful to use a variety of devices such as videotapes, feedback in role play, and mirror exercises to demonstrate the impact of mannerisms, gestures, facial expressions, and voice inflections on an interview partner. For example, unusual body postures, speech patterns, and idiosyncratic mannerisms can be pointed out and modified for enhancing the effectiveness of the therapist. These comments are not intended to convey a need for extensive personal analysis as a prerequisite for therapists, but we believe that in interview therapy, the therapist as a person is part of the instrument in the change process. Therapists simply need to know the characteristics of the instruments they use, which includes their own persons.

Therapists hold a wide range of different attitudes, values, and beliefs. In their professional role, however, it is desirable that they share the common belief that there are a variety of possible lifestyles for clients, other than those chosen by the therapist or fantasized as the therapist's ideal. We consider essential a strong belief that most human beings have positive qualities that can be developed and utilized in therapy, as well as a willingness to forego personal gains from client contacts in order to offer the best service to clients. The primary motivation for the therapist must not be to receive praise, subservience, flattering dependency by the client, or even the attainment of the therapeutic goals set by the client. The effective and skillful utilization of therapeutic strategies and techniques to help the client to improve his or her own welfare should be the personal goal of the therapist. Thus, the most important source of positive reinforcement ought not to come from the client in session but from the therapist's own evaluation of his or her intervention procedures and the reinforcement and constructive suggestions offered by colleagues in the discussion of cases.

Recognizing that therapists are, after all, human beings with weaknesses, limitations, and peculiarities, we have noted in training novice therapists some of the temptations that the young therapist encounters. We have designated these as the "three devils sitting on the shoulder of the therapist." These self-oriented motives or "devils" can lead therapists to commit errors at all stages of treatment. They are the following:

1. *Voyeurism.* Most human beings are driven by an inherent curiosity about the private lives of others. Therapy presents an ideal opportunity to satisfy such curiosity. But soliciting information from a client about specific situations or thoughts *must not* be motivated by the therapist's curiosity but only by the relevance of the information for the strategy pursued at the moment.

2. *The power motive.* By nature of the therapeutic relationship, the client is seeking help, advice, or support from the therapist. On the surface, it would appear that this is an asymmetric relationship in which the therapist has the powers to heal, to judge, or to manipulate the client, not only in sessions but also along the path of life. Therapeutic tactics that serve mainly to affirm or enhance the therapist's power vis-a-vis the client lapse into an unethical use of the therapeutic relationship by serving the therapist's self-interests. Indeed, with some clients power struggles do occur in the interview setting. We believe that it is critical for the therapist to recognize the degree to which such maneuvers are attempts by the client to control the therapist's behavior or efforts by the therapist to control the client's behavior. Some tactics *clearly* and *solely* aim to attain a

therapeutic objective to which the client has agreed. There must be clearly differentiated interpretations of what has been called "resistance," as opposed to those used primarily as justification for therapist control.

3. *Self-therapy.* Many persons enter mental health fields in the hope of finding solutions for their own problems. Indeed, all interpersonal experiences, and particularly therapeutic interactions, have much to offer in the growth and development of both therapist and client. But, as in the struggles noted with the preceding "devils," these motives must remain secondary, lest they interfere with the therapist's primary and sole obligation, namely, to help the client.

Even though therapists are generally motivated in their work by their desire to help clients, direct personal involvement that exceeds the professional structure of the relationship can cause difficulty both for the therapeutic process and for the therapist in the long run. Excessive concern, emotional involvement, or the taking of an argumentative or persuasive position often handicaps the therapist in conducting effective treatment. If carried out for a long period of time, it also tends to lead to "burn out" or the development of antagonistic attitudes both toward clients, who may be perceived as failing to appreciate the therapist's intense efforts, and toward a society that seems to constantly block the execution of the therapist's wise counsel.

The therapist's obligations, as described in the ethics manual of the American Psychological Association, are to both the client and society. Perhaps the most difficult task for a therapist in many cases is to recognize the need to limit encouragement and support of clients whose behaviors jeopardize the welfare of other persons. In individual therapy, but particularly in family or group therapy, the therapist must be constantly aware of the consequences of the therapeutic objective, not only for the client but also for the welfare of other people. Other ethical considerations (Kanfer & Goldstein, 1980) include recognition of the limitations of the therapist's own competence and the obligation to refer the client to other professionals when needed. Deceptive practices and direct exploitation for the therapist's social, sexual, or financial gains are clearly unethical. A somewhat less obvious principle, which we consider to be inherent in the therapist role, is the obligation to intervene in the client's life only to the extent that the client desires a change or that the social environment insists on it. Proprietary interests coupled with the universal dictum that a person's growth process is never complete are poor and insufficient reasons for extending therapy beyond the attainment of the objectives jointly agreed upon by therapist and client.

TREATMENT POPULATIONS

Although the conceptual model is based on the assumption that self-regulatory processes are central to the actions of human beings, accessibility to clients, willingness to engage in therapeutic interactions (or even social contact), and the opportunity for some autonomy in the environment to try out new skills are factors that limit the suitability of the approach. Creating a therapeutic alliance may be difficult in settings in which the therapist's integrity and confidentiality is in doubt. For example, with severely disturbed psychotic patients, the approach may be most appropriate only after medication, operant conditioning methods, or other techniques have been used, and the person is responsive to social inputs. Although several segments of our conceptual model imply a heavy reliance on cognitive skills, self-control techniques, and other tactics, our approach has been used with retarded children and adults (Litrownik, 1982), with psychotic patients (Breier & Strauss, 1983), with psychosomatic patients (Sturm, 1982), and with geriatric patients (Rom-Rymer, 1986). To apply the model for these populations, special techniques are adapted for the interview interactions and for the training and practice of various behaviors. These modifications assist the therapist in attaining the goals of various therapy segments without a change in the overall conceptual framework or in the sequencing of the phases described in our model. Clearly, extensive neurological damage, severe retardation, or special conditions that make it difficult or impossible for the client to fantasize, test, and experience new ways of acting and thinking can impede or completely defeat the therapeutic effort.

In working with a wide range of clients, we have found that the most serious constraint indications for treatment lie not in the psychological or biological limitations of the client but in the context and setting in which therapy is embedded. Clear and *realistic* expectations by the client that the intervention will aggravate his or her life status is a serious obstacle to treatment. While all human beings are motivated toward new goals, special circumstances may produce a situation in which the greatest benefit to a client is the continuance of his or her current status. For example, for some terminally ill patients, the psychological cost of engaging in a change effort may be too high in relation to the potential benefits to be derived. In less extreme situations, continued and powerful support by the social environment for maintaining the problem situation, for example, when substantial disability payments are continued, or when stability in a familial setting hinges exclusively on the client's current adjustment pattern, the therapist's efforts to instigate a change may be undermined or totally defeated. When a therapist cannot offer an incentive that is sufficient to overcome the advantages of the current problem situation, adaptation to present living conditions and tolerance of an unalterable setting may be best for the client. In this case, a self-management approach would be counterproductive.

These limitations should be clearly understood as defining extreme conditions. The tasks of helping dependent or resistant clients to develop the motivation for change is, as we have indicated above, a responsibility of the therapist in the early stages of treatment. Client resistance or strong dependence on the therapist or demands that the therapist offer solutions and assume responsibility for treatment are in themselves not *prima facie* arguments against utilization of our approach. They represent challenges to the therapist to help the client develop motivation for a change. With such a client, early focus is primarily on any tactic that increases the probability that the client will return for therapy. We have postulated this clinical dictum in the form of our first law of therapy: You cannot do effective therapy with a client who does not return. Consequently, an initial focus on creating a therapeutic alliance may be necessary before judgments can be made, even with clients for whom a later joint decision is reached that therapy is not feasible at the present time.

The factors mentioned above and others must be taken as moderating factors rather than absolute criteria. The younger the client (until middle adolescence), the more difficult it is to carry out the self-management approach as fully as is described above. Similarly, the degree of the development of self-regulatory skills, of autonomy and freedom of movement in the client's environment, and of personal assets and talents for different life patterns, attitudes, and skill development all determine the ease with which a self-management approach can be effective in short-term interventions.

The approach we have proposed has been developed for and applied to clients in the United States and Western Europe. Although we have not studied cross-cultural differences in controlled experiments, we have noted the requirement that the client's subculture agree with the major assumption that each person can, at least to some extent, guide his or her own destiny and influence his or her future life. We have had several clinical experiences in which basic religious or cultural standards and beliefs of clients have represented insurmountable obstacles to treatment. These clients' philosophical assumptions of fatalism or divine control of human conduct and their belief in the inevitability of the course of individual life have seriously counteracted their capacity for and interest in assuming responsibility for planning and executing changes. Thus, diametrically opposed philosophical or religious beliefs that deny a person's capability to participate in shaping his or her own future are serious counterindications for treatment by self-management therapy.

Experimental Basis

The self-management approach was developed (Kanfer, 1961, 1965, 1970, 1971, 1977, 1980; Kanfer & Grimm, 1980) in order to extend the behavioral model from exclusive reliance on environmental control to outpatient settings in which "instigation therapy" by means of self-control and self-regulation is the major tool. Following early studies on verbal conditioning (Kanfer, 1958; 1968) and self-reinforcement (Kanfer, 1964; Kanfer & Marston, 1963a,b), research focused on self-evaluation (Kanfer & Duer-feldt, 1967, 1968), self-monitoring (Kanfer, 1970), and self-control (Kanfer, 1971). Subsequently, research progressed to the study of contracts and goal setting (e.g., Kanfer & Karoly, 1972) through the investigation of the relationships between these self-generated processes (e.g., Kanfer et al., 1974; Spates & Kanfer, 1977). This program of research led to the development of the self-regulation model. The self-management therapy approach (Kanfer, 1980; Kanfer & Busemeyer, 1982; Karoly & Kanfer, 1982) is derived from the theoretical model of self-regulation; refinement of the model as well as its supporting research is continuing.

Despite the large and growing literature on self-management, relatively little research has been done to evaluate the efficacy of the complete self-management approach described in this chapter. Most of the research in the area has focused on individual components of the therapy approach, such as self-monitoring (e.g., Kanfer & Gaelick, 1986; Kirschenbaum & Karoly, 1977), self-control (e.g., Goldfried & Trier, 1974; Suinn & Bloom, 1978) and self-reinforcement (e.g., Rehm, 1977; Rodin, 1980).

Several ancillary research literatures have investigated the clinical utility of separate concepts on which the self-management approach is based. Generally, research has suggested that these self-management components enhance motivation as well as the learning and maintenance of new behaviors. These components include perceived choice and control, the self-generation of behavior, self-attribution, and the active client-participation model.

Research on Self-Management Components

Empirical support for component parts of self-management therapy is abundant, particularly as a result of laboratory and analogue studies. For example, consistent support has been found for the utility of components of the self-regulation model in dealing with self-control problems, resistance to temptation, delay of gratification, and tolerance of aversive stimulation. Extensive summaries of these studies are found in Kanfer (1979, 1980); Watson and Tharp (1977); Thoresen and Mahoney (1974); and most current texts in counseling and clinical psychology. A review of research and methods based on the approach is also found in Karoly (1977) for use with children. Kirschenbaum and his co-workers report and review work on self-monitoring and self-evaluation (Kirschenbaum & Tomarken, 1982), on the application of self-management methods in sports (Kirschenbaum, 1984), and on contracting (Kirschenbaum & Flanery, 1983). A book on self-management and behavior change (Karoly & Kanfer, 1982) reports research and practical applications for various types of clinical problems. The theories, research, and their treatment applications have been summarized in a National Institute of Mental Health Science Report on behavioral self-control (Runck, 1982).

Perceived choice has received considerable empirical attention. Investigations on the study performance of college students (Liem, 1975), the psychological and physical well-being of the elderly (Langer & Rodin, 1976; Schulz, 1976), the reduction of anxiety reactions (Corah & Boffa, 1970), the tolerance of aversive stimulation (Kanfer & Seidner, 1973), and performance levels on learning tasks (Kanfer & Grimm, 1978) have supported the utility of perceived choice in enhancing motivation, increasing self-satisfaction, and improving effort. The clinical literature further indicates that perceived choice reduces countercontrol and resistance in therapeutic situations (Goldfried, 1982; Karoly & Kanfer, 1982; Perlmuter & Monty, 1979).

Perceived control is a related concept equally well embedded in the self-management framework. Data on a variety of populations with numerous classes of behaviors support the idea that perceived control increases positive self-reactions (Curtis, 1984; Langer, 1983; Rodin, 1980), improves personal and task performance (Harter, 1982; Heiman, LoPiccolo & LoPiccolo, 1981), and enhances motivation and effort (Marlatt & Parks, 1982). Other individual components of the self-management approach have been equally well supported in the literature. Among the findings that lend empirical support to the clinical utility of self-management concepts are the following: (1) the self-generation of behavior produces effects that are superior to those obtained when the source of behavior is external to the individual (Johnson & Raye, 1981; Raye, Johnson, & Taylor, 1980; Slamecka & Graf, 1978); (2) the self-attribution of behavior change enhances commitment (Harvey, Ickes, & Kidd, 1978; Kanfer & Karoly, 1972) and post-treatment maintenance (Colletti & Kopel, 1979; Kanfer, 1979); (3) the self-generation of goals increases client participation in treatment (Karoly & Kanfer, 1982; Shelton & Levy, 1981); (4) the negotiation of consistency between therapist and client goals reduces opposition to treatment (Cameron, 1978; Wachtel, 1977, 1982); (5) the pacing of treatment to the client's skill level and needs maximizes success and mastery experiences (Bandura, 1977; Kanfer, 1980); (6) the enhancement of perceived competence is related to positive therapeutic gains (Bandura, Adams, & Bayer, 1977; Kanfer, 1979); (7) coping-skill training that emphasizes the flexible response to a category of situations instead of a stimulus-specific response sequence improves generalizations of behavior change (Deffenbacher & Suinn, 1982; Goldstein & Kanfer, 1979; Karoly & Steffen, 1980); and finally, (8) active participation and effort in therapy is highly associated with positive treatment outcome (Curtis, 1984; Gomez-Schwartz, 1978; Keithly, Samples, & Strupp, 1980; Sifneos, 1971).

Studies on Self-Management Therapy

The self-management model of therapy, as presented in this chapter, was applied in the treatment of addictive behaviors in a residential program for alcoholics. The program was developed by R. Schneider and his colleagues, in collaboration with the senior author, at the Furth Clinic in Germany. The treatment package employed self-control methods and relapse training, relaxation therapy, problem solving, and social skills training, but the key feature of the approach was the organization and context of these methods in accordance with the present model (Schneider, 1982). Based on an extensive system for data collection, a 1-year follow-up on approximately 500 patients indicated an 80% abstinence rate for those who returned the mail questionnaires. Approximately 35% of the patients did not return the questionnaires. Of these 120 persons, a sample of 65 was visited in person by a psychologist. On the basis of this information, it was established that 40% of this group had remained abstinent. A 4-year follow-up revealed essentially the same findings.

In another field study with over 300 long-term unemployed persons, Kanfer (1984) examined the efficacy of the self-management approach in enhancing various self-regulatory skills needed for greater employability. As a result of the 8-week program, persons trained in self-management were able to find employment much more easily than those in control groups. Relative to no-treatment and refusal control groups, self-management participants reentered the work force at a ratio of nearly 2 to 1 at a 2-month follow-up. In addition, the self-management group showed a significantly higher employment rate at 6-month follow-up, with a ratio of 2 to 1 employed.

In a recent study, Schefft (1983) compared the self-management therapy to standard cognitive-behavioral therapy and to relationship psychotherapy. In this experiment 55 non-assertive college females showing moderate levels of overall psychopathology were matched on levels of psychological adjustment, assertiveness and motivation. Detailed treatment manuals were prepared to guide the therapist's conduct of the three approaches. Two replications were completed, each over nine weekly 2-hour sessions per treatment group. Assessment included behavioral and self-report measures of process and outcome, obtained every 3 weeks during treatment and at 6-week and 3-month follow-ups. Procedural checks verified that each of the treatment procedures closely resembled the therapeutic approach it was designed to represent, and that all were unequivocally distinguishable from each other.

All therapies were effective in altering some self-reactions and interpersonal behaviors, but the self-management group was superior on a majority of behavior change indices, equal on others and inferior on none. Self-management was also most effective in enhancing perceived control, perceived competence, interpersonal comfort level and assertiveness, both on behavioral measures and self-reports. Measures of rate and durability of change further indicated that self-management therapy led to the most rapid rate of change in positive self-reactions, resistance level, and active involvement in therapy, and resulted in the greatest maintenance of therapeutic gains. Cognitive-behavioral therapy was found to be more effective than relationship therapy in increasing positive self-views and assertive behavior. These findings demonstrate the clinical utility of the process model as a systematic context for treatment administration.

Using concepts and strategies from the self-management approach, Fuchs and Rehm (1977) showed the superiority of a self-control program in producing and maintaining therapeutic change in depression. Rehm, Fuchs, Ross, Kornblith, & Romano (1979) replicated these findings. Rodin (1980) demonstrated the efficacy of self-management coping skill training on both the production and maintenance of therapeutic change in elderly persons.

Kirschenbaum and his co-workers (e.g., Kirschenbaum, Humphrey, Malett, 1981; Kirschenbaum & Karoly, 1977) used the self-management model as a basis for a series of studies exploring the efficacy of self-regulatory training on improving academic skills. Kirschenbaum and Karoly (1977) investigated the effects of self-monitoring in a group of college students. Consistent with predictions from the model, negative self-monitoring relative to other conditions led to lower self-evaluation, increased self-punishment, and lowered performance levels. In another study, Kirschenbaum et al. (1981) trained groups of college students in self-control skills and varied specificity of planning (daily vs. monthly vs. none) to investigate effects on study time, study skills, and grades. Results indicated the following: (1) establishing explicit performance standards facilitated effective self-regulation; (2) the setting of excessively high performance standards led to ineffective self-regulation; (3) training in planning, goal-setting, and self-control improved persistence of studying and grades. Kirschenbaum, Tomarken, and Ordman (1982) replicated these results.

The self-management therapy model has also resulted in the development of various programs of self-control therapy in the treatment of various complaints. For example, the approach has been found to be effective in reducing social evaluation anxiety (Kanter & Goldfried, 1979); in managing eating disorders (Mahoney, Maura, & Wade, 1973); and in developing self-instructional approaches for general clinical problems (Meichenbaum, 1977). Goldfried and Trier (1974) showed that relative to a control treatment receiving a counterconditioning rationale for speech anxiety, a self-control procedure produced the greatest reduction of both targeted and nontargeted anxiety. It was the only treatment to show posttreatment maintenance of change. Denny and Rupert (1977) found that a self-control procedure was superior to traditional desensitization in reducing test anxiety and improving grades. Finally, Kanter and Goldfried (1979) showed that in comparison to wait-list control, self-control treatment significantly reduced social anxiety and nontargeted anxiety.

Overall, the research on self-management supports the utility of the approach in producing and maintaining effective behavior change with a diversity of populations. Numerous studies suggest that the separate components of the approach (e.g., self-instructional training within a self-control framework) or individual combinations of components (e.g., self-monitoring plus self-evaluation) can also contribute to therapeutic change. Although controlled investigations of the complete self-management therapy framework are few, they do offer encouraging support for the efficacy of this model for managing the clinical change process. Based on the available research, it is expected that clinical groups showing motivational deficits and conflicts (as in addictive behaviors) may be particularly well suited to the self-management approach, due to the emphasis on client participation in goal setting, and the focus on reducing resistance, enhancing commitment, and preparing for future coping.

EPILOGUE

We have presented a therapeutic approach that has its roots in Skinner's operant approach to behavior modification, Rotter's social-learning theory, Kantor's interbehavioral system, and our own research and clinical experience. The approach grew out of an attempt to supplement earlier behavior modification methods with techniques appropriate for interview therapy and for clients for whom environmental control was impossible or undesirable. Since its earliest formulation (Kanfer, 1961), it has become clear that a single mechanism of change is insufficient to explain the variety and richness of the flow of interchanges between a client and a therapist and between the therapy dyad and the social systems in which they operate. Our approach has begun to incorporate implications for treatment methods from research in cognitive and social psychology, and more recently from various other system approaches particularly as applied to behavioral medicine. But there is still an insufficient base in psychological theory and knowledge, and a lack of heuristics or guidelines for the operational translation of theory and research findings for all of clinical practice. The moment-to-moment interactions of clinicians, especially in interviews, therefore still rest heavily on clinical folklore, supervisor-transmitted experiences and common knowledge.

The scope of clinical work has broadened to the extent that it ranges from short-term counseling for a variety of problems in every day living to extensive and prolonged interactions to rehabilitate severely disturbed, biologically deficient, or socially deviant persons. Clinicians also consult on problems in daily living, health, personal relationships, sports, leisure and recreational activities, and many other areas. In light of the extended range of populations, target problems, and situations for which clinicians offer their services, it is doubtful that a comprehensive theory of behavior change can be developed to encompass all of these different situations. Nevertheless, the common task in therapeutic interventions almost always involves the facilitation of a change in the affected person or group. For these reasons, the psychology of learning, of both behavior and cognitive events, remains an essential core. However, the conditions under which such learning takes place have not been given sufficient attention until recently. Research in information processing and on the interface between biological, social, and psychological domains, as well as research on the biological substratum of learning and an awareness of the critical role that the clinician's own psychological processes play in therapy all have pointed to the need for basing a theory of psychotherapy on a wider foundation than a single change mechanism or even a single subdomain of psychology such as learning or motivation. Research that seems to point to similarities in therapist operations among many schools of therapy, and to the importance of the client's preconceptions about treatment, have added impetus to the development of the model that we have presented here. It can best be viewed as a metatheoretical model that, like others (e.g., Prochaska & DiClemente, 1982), attempts to pull together a variety of data on change processes for which both research and clinical experience provide some support. These conceptualizations of therapy suggest the need for continued attention to the results of research and microtheories in various areas of psychology to strengthen or modify the conceptual clinical framework and its operations.

In addition to the need for incorporating more available psychological data in our formulation of therapy processes, there is also a need for evaluating long-term effects of treatment, not only with regard to specific symptoms or target behaviors but also with regard to changes in nontargeted actions, life satisfactions, and the level of psychological and biological well-being.

Ultimately, the interaction between client and clinician represents a microcosm in which many of the same variables operate as those that affect human beings from day to day in other settings and situations. Future research toward the increased effectiveness of therapy will face many major decisions. Which phenomena require study and how these are to be conceptualized must be considered. Necessary in this process will be determining how to select out of the large mass of information about human functioning those microtheories and research bodies—in psychology as well as all other sciences—that are most relevant to the treatment process, and how to pare down their number so they can be handled by the clinician in daily routines.

REFERENCES

Bandura, A. (1977). Self-efficacy: Toward a unifying theory of behavioral change. *Psychological Review, 84,* 191–215.

Bandura, A., Adams, N. E., & Bayer, J. (1977). Cognitive processes mediating behavioral change. *Journal of Personality and Social Psychology, 35,* 125–139.

Bem, D. J. (1972). Self-perception theory. In L. Berkowitz (Ed.), *Advances in experimental social psychology* (Vol. 6, pp. 2–62). New York: Academic Press.

Bolles, R. N. (1977). *What color is your parachute: A practical manual for job hunters and career changers.* Berkeley, CA: Ten Speed Press.

Bootzin, R. R., & Lick, J. R. (1979). Expectancies in therapy research: Interpretative artifact or mediating mechanism? *Journal of Consulting and Clinical Psychology, 47,* 852–855.

Brehm, S. S. (1976). *The application of social psychology to clinical practice.* Washington, DC: Hemisphere Publishing.

Breier, A., & Strauss, J. S. (1983). Self-control and psychotic disorders. *Archives of General Psychiatry, 40,* 1141–1145.

Cameron, R. (1978). The clinical implementation of behavior change techniques: A cognitively oriented conceptualization of therapeutic "compliance" and "resistance." In J. P. Foreyt & D. P. Rathjen (Eds.), *Cognitive behavior therapy: Research and application* (pp. 223–250). New York: Plenum.

Colletti, G., & Kopel, S. A. (1979). Maintaining behavior change: An investigation of three maintenance strategies and the relationship of self-attribution to the long-term reduction of cigarette smoking. *Journal of Consulting and Clinical Psychology, 47,* 614–617.

Corah, N., & Boffa, J. (1970). Perceived control, self-observation, and response to aversive stimulation. *Journal of Personality and Social Psychology, 16,* 1–4.

Curtis, J. M. (1984). Motivational techniques for individual and group psychotherapy. *Psychological Reports, 54,* 271–277.

Deffenbacher, J. L., & Suinn, R. N. (1982). The self-control of anxiety. In P. Karoly & F. H. Kanfer (Eds.), *Self-management and behavior change: From theory to practice* (pp. 393–442). New York: Pergamon.

Denny, D. R., & Rupert, P. A. (1977). Desensitization and self-control in the treatment of test anxiety. *Journal of Counseling Psychology, 24,* 272–280.

Dollard, J., & Miller, N. E. (1950). *Personality and psychotherapy.* New York: McGraw-Hill.

Ericsson, K. S., & Simon, H. A. (1980). Verbal reports as data. *Psychological Review, 87,* 215–251.

Ferster, C. B. (1979). *A laboratory model of psychotherapy: The boundary between clinical practice and experimental psychology.* Unpublished manuscript, The American University.

Frank, J. B. (1973). *Persuasion and healing: A comparative study of psychotherapy* (2nd ed.). Baltimore, MD: Johns Hopkins University Press.

Fuchs, C. Z., & Rehm, L. P. (1977). A self-control behavior therapy program for depression. *Journal of Consulting and Clinical Psychology, 45,* 206–215.

Goldfried, M. R. (1982). Resistance and clinical behavior therapy. In P. L. Wachtel (Ed.), *Resistance: Psychodynamic and behavioral approaches* (pp. 95–114). New York: Plenum.

Goldfried, M. R., & Trier, C. S. (1974). The effectiveness of relaxation as an active coping skill. *Journal of Abnormal Psychology, 83,* 348–355.

Goldstein, A. P., Heller, K., & Sechrest, L. B. (1966). *Psychotherapy and the psychology of behavior change.* New York: Wiley.

Goldstein, A. P., & Kanfer, F. H. (Eds.). (1979). *Maximizing treatment gains: Transfer enhancement in psychotherapy.* New York: Academic Press.

Gomez-Schwartz, B. (1978). Effective ingredients in psychotherapy: Prediction of outcome from process variables. *Journal of Consulting and Clinical Psychology, 46,* 1023–1035.

Harter, S. (1982). A developmental perspective on some parameters of self-regulation in children. In P. Karoly & F. H. Kanfer (Eds.), *Self-management and behavior change: From theory to practice* (pp. 165–206). New York: Pergamon.

Harvey, J. H., Ickes, W. J., & Kidd, R. F. (Eds.). (1978). *New directions in attribution research* (Vol. 2). New York: Erlbaum.

Heiman, J. R., LoPiccolo, L., & LoPiccolo, J. (1981). The treatment of sexual dysfunction. In A. S. Gurman & D. P. Kniskern (Eds.), *Handbook of family therapy* (pp. 592–627). New York: Brunner/Mazel.

Hersen, M., Kazdin, A. E., & Bellack, A. S. (Eds.). (1983). *The clinical psychology handbook.* New York: Pergamon.

Johnson, M. K., & Raye, C. L. (1981). Reality monitoring. *Psychological Review, 88,* 67–85.

Kanfer, F. H. (1958). Verbal conditioning: Reinforcement schedules and experimenter influence. *Psychological Reports, 4,* 443–452.

Kanfer, F. H. (1961). Comments on learning in psychotherapy. *Psychological Reports, 9,* 681–699.

Kanfer, F. H. (1964). Control of communication in dyads by reinforcement. *Psychological Reports, 15,* 131–138.

Kanfer, F. H. (1965). Structure of psychotherapy: Role playing as a variable in dyadic communication. *Journal of Consulting Psychology, 29,* 325–332.

Kanfer, F. H. (1968). Verbal conditioning: A review of its current status. In T. R. Dixon & D. L. Horton (Eds.), *Verbal behavior and its relation to general S-R theory* (pp. 254–290). Englewood Cliffs, NJ: Prentice-Hall.

Kanfer, F. H. (1970). Self-regulation: Research, issues and speculation. In C. Neuringer & J. L. Michael (Eds.), *Behavior modification and clinical psychology* (pp. 178–220). New York: Appleton-Century-Crofts.

Kanfer, F. H. (1971). The maintenance of behavior by self-generated stimuli and reinforcement. In A. Jacobs & L. B. Sachs (Eds.), *The psychology of private events* (pp. 39–57). New York: Academic Press.

Kanfer, F. H. (1977). The many faces of self-control, or behavior modification changes its focus. In R. B. Stuart (Ed.), *Behavioral self-management* (pp. 1–48). New York: Brunner/Mazel.

Kanfer, F. H. (1979). Self-management: Strategies and tactics. In A. P. Goldstein & F. H. Kanfer (Eds.), *Maximizing treatment gains: Transfer-enhancement in psychotherapy* (pp. 185–224). New York: Academic Press.

Kanfer, F. H. (1980). Self-management methods. In F. H. Kanfer & A. P. Goldstein (Eds.), *Helping people change: A textbook of methods* (Rev. 2nd ed., pp. 334–389). New York: Pergamon.

Kanfer, F. H. (1984). Self-management in clinical and social interventions. In J. H. Harvey, J. E. Maddox, R. P. McGlynn, & C. D. Stoltenberg (Eds.), *Interfaces in psychology* (Vol. 2 pp. 141–165). Lubbock, TX: Texas Tech University Press.

Kanfer, F. H. (1985). Target selection for clinical change programs. *Behavioral Assessment, 7,* 7–20.

Kanfer, F. H., & Busemeyer, J. P. (1982). The use of problem-solving and decision-making in behavior therapy. *Clinical Psychology Review, 2,* 239–266.

Kanfer, F. H., Cox, L. E., Greiner, J. M., & Karoly, P. (1974). Contract, demand characteristics and self-control. *Journal of Personality and Social Psychology, 30,* 605–619.

Kanfer, F. H., & Duerfeldt, P. H. (1967). Effect of pretraining on self-evaluation and self-reinforcement. *Journal of Personality and Social Psychology, 7,* 164–168.

Kanfer, F. H., & Duerfeldt, P. H. (1968). A comparison of self-rewards and self-criticism as a function of types of prior external reinforcement. *Journal of Personality and Social Psychology, 8,* 261–268.

Kanfer, F. H., & Gaelick, L. (1986). Self-management methods. In F. H. Kanfer & A. P. Goldstein (Eds.), *Helping people change: A textbook of methods.* (Rev. 3rd ed.) New York: Pergamon.

Kanfer, F. H., & Goldstein, A. P. (Eds.). (1980). *Helping people change: A textbook of methods* (Rev. 2nd ed.). New York: Pergamon.

Kanfer, F. H., & Grimm, L. G. (1977). Behavioral analysis: Selecting target behaviors in interview. *Behavior Modification, 1,* 7–28.

Kanfer, F. H., & Grimm, L. G. (1978). Freedom of choice and behavioral change. *Journal of Consulting and Clinical Psychology, 46,* 873–878.

Kanfer, F. H., & Grimm, L. G. (1980). Managing clinical change: A process model of therapy. *Behavior Modification, 4,* 419–444.

Kanfer, F. H., & Hagerman, S. M. (1981). The role of self-regulation. In L. P. Rehm (Ed.), *Behavior therapy for depression: Present status and future directions* (pp. 143–179). New York: Academic Press.

Kanfer, F. H., & Hagerman, S. M. (1985). Behavior therapy and the information processing paradigm. In S. Reiss & R. R. Bootzin (Eds.), *Theoretical issues in behavior therapy* (pp. 3–33). New York: Academic Press.

Kanfer, F. H., & Karoly, P. (1972). Self-control: A behavioristic excursion into the lion's den. *Behavior Therapy, 3,* 398–416.

Kanfer, F. H., & Seidner, M. L. (1973). Self-control: Factors enhancing tolerance of noxious stimulation. *Journal of Personality and Social Psychology, 25,* 381–389.

Kanfer, F. H., & Marston, A. R. (1963a). Condition of self-reinforcing responses: An analogue to self-confidence training. *Psychological Reports, 13,* 63–70.

Kanfer, F. H., & Marston, A. R. (1963b). Determinants of self-reinforcement in human learning. *Journal of Experimental Psychology, 66,* 245–254.

Kanfer, F. H., & Nay, W. R. (1982). Behavioral assessment. In G. T. Wilson & C. M. Franks (Eds.), *Contemporary behavior therapy: Conceptual and empirical foundations of clinical practice* (pp. 367–402). New York: Guilford.

Kanfer, F. H., & Phillips, J. S. (1966). Behavior therapy: A panacea for all ills or a passing fancy? *Archives of General Psychiatry, 15,* 114–128.

Kanfer, F. H., & Phillips, J. S. (1969). A survey of current behavior therapies and a proposal for classification. In C. Franks (Ed.), *Behavior therapy: Appraisal and status* (pp. 445–475). New York: McGraw-Hill.

Kanfer, F. H., & Phillips, J. S. (1970). *Learning foundations of behavior therapy.* New York: Wiley.

Kanfer, F. H., & Saslow, G. (1965). Behavioral analysis: An alternative to diagnostic classification. *Archives of General Psychiatry, 12,* 529–538.

Kanfer, F. H., & Saslow, G. (1969). Behavioral diagnosis. In C. Franks (Ed.), *Behavior therapy: Appraisal and status* (pp. 417–444). New York: McGraw-Hill.

Kanfer, F. H., & Schefft, B. K. (in press). *Guiding the process of therapeutic change.* Champaign, IL: Research Press.

Kanter, M. J., & Goldfried, M. R. (1979). Relative effectiveness of rational restructuring, self-control, and desensitization in the reduction of interpersonal anxiety. *Behavior Therapy, 10,* 472–490.

Kantor, J. R. (1924). *Principles of psychology.* 2 volumes. New York: Knopf.

Kantor, J. R. (1953). *The logic of modern science.* Bloomington, IN.: Principia Press.

Karoly, P. (1977). Behavioral self-management in children: Concepts, methods, issues, and directions. In M. Hersen, R. M. Eisler, & P. M. Miller (Eds.), *Progress in behavior modification* (Vol. 5, pp. 197–263). New York: Academic Press.

Karoly, P., & Kanfer, F. H. (Eds.). (1982). *Self-management and behavior change: From theory to practice.* New York: Pergamon.

Karoly, P., & Steffen, J. J. (Eds.). (1980). *Improving the long-term effects of psychotherapy: Models of durable outcome.* New York: Gardner Press.

Kazdin, A. E. (1982). Symptom substitution, generalization and response covariation: Implications for psychotherapy outcome. *Psychological Bulletin, 91,* 349–365.

Keithly, L., Samples, S., & Strupp, H. (1980). Patient motivation as a predictor of process and outcome in psychotherapy. *Psychotherapy and Psychosomatics, 33,* 87–97.

Kendall, P. C., & Hollon, S. D. (Eds.). (1979). *Cognitive behavioral interventions*. New York: Academic Press.

Kimble, G. A., & Perlmuter, L. C. (1970). The problem of volition. *Psychological Review, 77,* 361–384.

Kirschenbaum, D. S. (1984). Self-regulation and sports psychology: Nurturing an emerging symbiosis. *Journal of Sport Psychology, 6,* 159–183.

Kirschenbaum, D. S., & Flanery, R. C. (1983). Behavioral contracting: Outcomes and elements. In M. Hersen, P. Eisler, & P. M. Miller (Eds.), *Progress in behavior modification* (Vol. 15, pp. 217–275). New York: Academic Press.

Kirschenbaum, D. S., Humphrey, C. C., & Malett, S. T. (1981). Specificity of planning in adult self-control: An applied investigation. *Journal of Personality and Social Psychology, 40,* 941–950.

Kirschenbaum, D. S., & Karoly, P. (1977). When self-regulation fails: A test of some preliminary hypotheses. *Journal of Consulting and Clinical Psychology, 45,* 1116–1125.

Kirschenbaum, D. S., & Tomarken, A. J. (1982). On facing the generalization problem: The study of self-regulatory failure. In P. C. Kendall (Ed.), *Advances in cognitive behavioral research and therapy* (Vol. 1, pp. 121–200). New York: Academic Press.

Kirschenbaum, D. S., Tomarken, A. J., & Ordman, A. N. (1982). Specificity of planning and choice applied to adult self-control. *Journal of Personality and Social Psychology, 43,* 576–585.

Klepac, R. (1975). Successful treatment of avoidance of dentistry by desensitization or by increasing pain tolerance. *Journal of Behavior Therapy and Experimental Psychiatry, 6,* 307–310.

Koberg, D., & Bagnall, J. (1976). *The all-new universal traveller: A soft-system guide to creativity, problem-solving, and the process of reaching goals*. Los Altos, CA: Kantmann.

Kopel, S., & Arkowitz, H. (1975). The role of attribution and self-perception in behavior change: Implications for behavior therapy. *Genetic Psychology Monographs, 92,* 175–212.

Lachman, R., Lachman, J. L., & Butterfield, E. C. (1979). *Cognitive psychology and information processing: An introduction*. Hillsdale, NJ: Erlbaum.

Langer, E. J. (1983). *The psychology of control*. Beverly Hills, CA: Sage.

Langer, E. J., & Rodin, J. (1976). The effects of choice on enhanced personal responsibility for the aged. *Journal of Personality and Social Psychology, 34,* 191–198.

Lee, M. J. (1978). *An analysis and evaluation of structured decision systems*. Doctoral dissertation, Ohio State University.

Liem, G. R. (1975). Performance and satisfaction as affected by personal control over salient decisions. *Journal of Personality and Social Psychology, 31,* 232–240.

Litrownik, A. J. (1982). Special considerations in the self-management training of the developmentally disabled. In P. Karoly & F. H. Kanfer (Eds.), *Self-management and behavior change: From theory to practice* (pp. 315–352). New York: Pergamon.

Mahoney, M. J., Moura, N. G. M., & Wade, T. C. (1973). The relative efficacy of self-reward, self-punishment, and self-monitoring techniques for weight loss. *Journal of Consulting and Clinical Psychology, 40,* 404–407.

Marks, I. M. (1978). Behavioral psychotherapy of adult neurosis. In S. L. Garfield & A. E. Bergin (Eds.), *Handbook of psychotherapy and behavior change* (pp. 493–547). New York: Wiley.

Marlatt, G. A., & Parks, G. A. (1982). Self-management of addictive disorders. In P. Karoly & F. H. Kanfer (Eds.), *Self-management and behavior change: From theory to practice* (pp. 443–488). New York: Pergamon.

Merluzzi, T. Z., Rudy, T. E., & Glass, C. R. (1981). The information-processing paradigm: Implications for clinical science. In T. Z. Merluzzi, C. R. Glass, & M. Genest (Eds.), *Cognitive assessment* (pp. 77–124). New York: Guilford.

Meichenbaum, D. (1977). *Cognitive behavior modification*. New York: Plenum.

Meichenbaum, D., & Jaremko, M. E. (Eds.). (1983). *Stress reduction and prevention*. New York: Plenum.

Perlmuter, L. C., & Monty, R. A. (Eds.). (1979). *Choice and perceived control* (pp. 131–142). Hillsdale, NJ: Erlbaum.

Prochaska, J. O., & DiClemente, C. C. (1982). Transtheoretical therapy: Toward a more integral model of change. *Psychotherapy: Theory, Research and Practice, 19,* 276–288.

Raye, C. L., Johnson, M. K., & Taylor, T. H. (1980). Is there something special about memory for internally-generated information? *Memory and Cognition, 8,* 141–148.

Rehm, L. P. (1977). A self-control model of depression. *Behavior Therapy, 8,* 787–804.

Rehm, L. P., Fuchs, C. Z., Roth, D. M., Kornblith, S. J., & Romano, J. M. (1979). A comparison of self-control and assertion skill treatment of depression. *Behavior Therapy, 10,* 429–442.

Rodin, J. (1980). Managing the stress of aging: The role of control and coping. In S. Levine & H. Ursin (Eds.), *Coping and health* (pp. 172–202). New York: Plenum.

Rom-Rymer, D. N. (1986). *Aging and our community's nursing homes: An experimental clinical intervention.* Doctoral dissertation: University of Illinois at Urbana-Champaign.

Rotter, J. B. (1954). *Social learning and clinical psychology.* Englewood Cliffs, NJ: Prentice-Hall.

Runck, B. (1982). *Behavioral self-control.* (NIMH Science Reports, pub. no. (ADM) 82-1207). Washington, DC: U.S. Government Printing Office.

Schefft, B. K. (1983). *Self-management therapy vs. cognitive restructuring plus behavior rehearsal vs. relationship psychotherapy: A controlled study of process and outcome.* Doctoral dissertation, University of Wisconsin–Milwaukee. (University Microfilms No. 84-09364)

Schefft, B. K., & Lehr, B. K. (1985). A self-regulatory model of adjunctive behavior change. *Behavior Modification, 9,* 458–476.

Schefft, B. K., Moses, J. A., & Schmidt, G. L. (1985). Neuropsychology and emotion: A self-regulatory model. *International Journal of Clinical Neuropsychology, 7,* 207–213.

Schneider, R. (Ed.). (1982). *Stationäre Behandlung von Alkoholabhängigen.* Munich: Gerhard Rotteger.

Schneider, W., & Shiffrin, R. M. (1977). Controlled and automatic human information processing: I. Detection, search and attention. *Psychological Review, 84,* 1–66.

Schulz, R. (1976). Effects of control and predictability on the psychological well-being of the institutionalized aged. *Journal of Personality and Social Psychology, 33,* 563–573.

Shelton, J. L., & Levy, R. L. (1981). *Behavioral assignments and treatment compliance.* Champaign, IL: Research Press.

Shiffrin, R. M., & Schneider, W. (1977). Controlled and automatic human information processing: II. Perceptual learning, automatic attending, and a general theory. *Psychological Review, 84,* 127–150.

Sifneos, P. E. (1971). Changing patients' motivation for psychotherapy. *American Journal of Psychiatry, 128,* 74–77.

Skinner, B. F. (1953). *Science and human behavior.* New York: Macmillan.

Slamecka, N. J., & Graf, P. (1978). The generation effect: Delineation of a phenomenon. *Journal of Experimental Psychology: Human Learning and Memory, 4,* 592–604.

Spates, C. R., & Kanfer, F. H. (1977). Self-monitoring, self-evaluation and self-reinforcement in children's learning: A test of a multi-stage self-regulation model. *Behavior Therapy, 8,* 17–24.

Sturm, J. (1982). Verhaltenstherapie im Landeskrankenhaus. In H. Helmsagn, N. Linden, & V. Reuger (Eds.), *Psychotherapie in der Psychiatrie* (pp. 330–335). Berlin: Springer.

Suinn, R. M., & Bloom, L. J. (1978). Anxiety management training for Type A persons. *Journal of Behavioral Medicine, 1,* 25–35.

Thoreson, C. E., & Mahoney, M. J. (1974). *Behavioral self-control.* New York: Holt, Rinehart, & Winston.

Turner, S. M., Calhoun, K. S., & Adams, H. E. (1981). *Future perspectives in behavior therapy.* New York: Plenum.

Wachtel, P. L. (1977). *Psychoanalysis and behavior therapy: Toward an integration.* New York: Basic Books.

Wachtel, P. L. (Ed.). (1982). *Resistance: Psychodynamic and behavioral approaches.* New York: Plenum.

Walker, C. E., Hedberg, A., Clement, P. W., & Wright, L. (1981). *Clinical procedures for behavior therapy*. Englewood Cliffs, NJ: Prentice-Hall.

Watson, D. L., & Tharp, R. G. (1977). *Self-directed behavior: Self-modification for personal adjustment* (2nd ed.). Monterey, CA: Brooks/Cole.

Weissberg, M. (1977). A comparison of direct and vicarious treatments of speech anxiety: Desensitization, desensitization with coping imagery, and cognition modification. *Behavior Therapy, 8*, 606–620.

White, R. W. (1959). Motivation reconsidered: The concept of competence. *Psychological Review, 66*, 297–333.

Wilkins, W. (1979). Expectancies in therapy research: Discriminating among heterogeneous nonspecifics. *Journal of Consulting and Clinical Psychology, 47*, 837–845.

CHAPTER 3

Behavioral Treatment of Phobics and Obsessive-Compulsives

Edna B. Foa
Gail Steketee
Medical College of Pennsylvania

The purpose of this chapter is to describe our treatment for anxiety disorders and to discuss the processes that take place during such treatment. Among the anxiety disorders, we have elected to focus on phobics and obsessive-compulsives because much is known about how to treat them successfully. In contrast, research on the treatment of generalized anxiety disorder and posttraumatic stress disorder is still in its infancy.

The processes by which treatment produces change should be explicated in order to develop and implement effective therapy. Therefore, we shall first describe the nature of phobias and obsessive-compulsive disorders, and specify the impairments that are targeted for therapeutic change. We shall then delineate techniques and procedures that have been used in altering these pathological features, and describe the processes underlying these treatments. In this way, we hope to provide the clinician with the ability to identify the specific impairments presented by a given patient in order to arrive at specific treatment goals and devise treatment programs that are tailored to meet these goals.

The treatment procedures described here should be viewed as *examples* of programs that have been found effective to date with the majority of phobics and obsessive-compulsives. New and better treatment methods will undoubtedly be generated in the future as our understanding of anxiety disorders increases and knowledge of treatment processes accumulates. We hope that the reader will use the theoretical knowledge provided in this chapter as a guideline for devising treatment programs rather than as procedures to be rigidly applied.

Exposure-based procedures have proven to be the treatment of choice for phobics and obsessive-compulsives. However, mere exposure to feared stimuli is by no means sufficient to alleviate fear—nor may such a procedure be necessary for all patients. In this chapter, therefore, we shall also discuss the characteristics of those who fail to benefit from exposure treatment, as well as considering variables other than exposure that seem to affect treatment outcome, such as therapist attitude and the verbal information transmitted during exposure sessions. In discussing the mechanisms and outcome of treatment, we have drawn from experimental work and from our own experience as clinicians in an effort to provide not only formal knowledge about therapeutic procedures but also an intuitive understanding of the therapeutic process.

BEHAVIORAL AND COGNITIVE MODELS OF ANXIETY DISORDERS

Two types of theoretical models have guided the development of behavioral-cognitive procedures in the treatment of anxiety disorders: stimulus–response (S–R) models, which emphasize automatic associative processes, and cognitive models, which implicate thoughts and beliefs as causative of anxious states.

Stimulus–Response Theories

To explain phobic and obsessive–compulsive disorders, Mowrer's (1939) two-stage theory for the acquisition and maintenance of fear and avoidance has been commonly adopted. Further developed by Dollard and Miller in 1950 and again by Mowrer in 1960, this theory proposes that a neutral event becomes associated with fear by being paired with a stimulus that innately provokes discomfort. Through an associative process, concrete objects as well as thoughts and images acquire the potential to produce anxiety. In the second stage of symptom development, escape or avoidance responses are developed to reduce the discomfort provoked by the conditioned stimuli. These responses are maintained because of their success in reducing such discomfort. Phobics develop passive avoidance patterns of behavior in order to minimize encounters with feared situations (e.g., refraining from entering a shopping center). Because of an extensive generalization of their fear to other situations, obsessive–compulsives find passive avoidance ineffective in controlling anxiety/discomfort. They therefore resort to active avoidance patterns, that is, ritualistic behaviors such as washing and checking.

Several authors have pointed to the inadequacy of Mowrer's theory as an etiological model of pathological fear (e.g., Rachman & Wilson, 1980). Many phobic patients cannot recall conditioning events associated with symptom onset (McNally & Steketee, 1985; Murray & Foote, 1979; Ost & Hugdahl, 1981). Onset does, however, often follow stressful life events, which Watts (1979) has suggested may serve to sensitize the individual to cues that have an innate tendency to elicit fear. Extending this hypothesis, Teasdale (1974) proposed that anxiety responses learned during early experiences may be exaggerated by stress. In the same vein, Rachman (1971) posited that for obsessive–compulsives, a state of heightened arousal could lead to the sensitization of certain thoughts that have special significance for the individual. Related to these notions is Eysenck's (1979) theory that brief exposure to upsetting events that are above the tolerance threshold of an individual will produce sensitization; under such circumstances, a phobia will be developed.

Accordingly, individuals who are more highly aroused physiologically (i.e., whose threshold is low) may be more susceptible to developing an anxiety disorder. There is evidence to suggest that obsessive–compulsives (Boulougouris, 1977) and complex phobics such as agoraphobics or social phobics (Lader, 1967) are more physiologically aroused than normals, and that individuals who are more highly aroused are more likely to become phobic (Hugdahl, Fredriksen, & Ohman, 1977). It is possible, then, that heightened physiological arousal in combination with a general stressor and fear experiences associated with specific objects or situations may play an important role in the genesis of anxiety disorders.

Whereas the way in which one acquires phobias and obsessive–compulsive disorders is still largely unclear, the maintenance of such disorders seems to be satisfactorily accounted for by S–R theories. Indeed, there is evidence to support the contention that avoidance and compulsions are maintained at least in part by their ability to decrease anxiety. Experiments have demonstrated that a confrontation with certain situations gives rise to anxiety/discomfort and that the removal of these feared circumstances reduces it (Hodgson & Rachman, 1972; Hornsveld, Kraaimaat, & Van Dam-Baggen, 1979; Roper & Rachman, 1976; Roper, Rachman, & Hodgson, 1973).

Cognitive Theories

Cognitive psychotherapies are founded on the assumption that thoughts and beliefs have a causal role in emotions and behavior. Although the emphasis on cognitions refers primarily to conscious processes, cognitive theorists have also attempted to identify unconscious automatic processes that are hypothesized to contribute to pathology (e.g., Beck, Rush, Shaw, & Emery, 1979). Accordingly, cognitive therapies attempt to modify automatic thoughts, belief systems, and irrational ideas. The therapist tries to produce cognitive changes in the patient by what is verbally communicated during therapy sessions. Some cognitive approaches such as Ellis's rational–emotive therapy (RET) do not address etiological factors specific to anxiety disorders. Rather, they assume that there are causative mechanisms common to all neurotic behavior and emotions. According to Ellis

(1980), emotional disturbance is caused by a specific set of cognitive structures involving mistaken ideas about how one views others and the conditions of life in general. RET is based on a philosophy of life which emphasizes rational thinking, tolerance of self and others, acceptance of uncertainty, and self-direction. By vigorously disputing clients' irrational ideas, the therapist promotes the adoption of a desirable set of values and attitudes and thereby facilitates the formation of new cognitive structures that, in turn, facilitate adaptive emotions and behavior.

In contrast to these general cognitive explanations of psychopathology, Beck and his colleagues have attempted to formulate a theory about cognitive deficits that are specific to pathological anxiety (Beck & Emery, 1979). According to this view, anxiety-disordered individuals distort reality with regard to danger through misinterpretation, overgeneralization, catastrophic predictions of the future, and arbitrary inferences. "The anxious patient differs from the normal in that his judgement of danger is likely to be unrealistic: he systematically misconstrues innocuous situations as dangerous; he exaggerates the probability of harm in specific situations; and he perseveres in having thoughts or visual images about being physically or psychologically harmed" (Beck & Emery, 1979, p. 11).

Advancing a theoretical view that integrated S–R notions and cognitive concepts, Foa and Kozak (1985) conceptualize anxiety disorders as specific impairments in fear memory-networks. A starting point for this approach was Lang's (1979) bioinformational theory, which states that fear exists as an information network in memory that includes feared *stimuli*, fear *responses*, and their *meanings*. This memory structure is conceived of as a program for fear behavior that occurs when a fear network is accessed or activated. Neurotic fears, propose Foa and Kozak, differ structurally from normal fears. Like Beck and Emery (1979), they posit that pathological anxiety is characterized by the presence of erroneous estimates of threat. In addition, they note that anxiety disordered individuals exhibit unusually high negative valence for the threatening events, as well as excessive responding (e.g., physiological responses, avoidance, etc.).

Pathological fears are also distinguished by their resistance to change, suggest Foa and Kozak. This inflexibility may reflect a failure to activate the fear network (i.e., to experience fear), either because of successful avoidance or because the feared situation is rarely encountered spontaneously in everyday life (e.g., snakes in an urban setting). Additionally, anxiety may persist because of some impairment in the mechanisms of change. To summarize this view, excessive cognitive defenses (e.g., denial), high arousal with failure to habituate, faulty premises (e.g., "If John didn't smile at me in the corridor, it means he doesn't like me"), and erroneous rules of inference (concluding that the lack of evidence that a situation is not dangerous means that it is dangerous), are all impairments that hinder the processing of information necessary for changing the fear structure.

THEORY OF THERAPEUTIC CHANGE

The foregoing discussion suggests that a theory regarding the therapeutic change of pathological anxiety should account for the mechanisms mediating changes in beliefs and attitudes, arousal and behavior. Before discussing such mechanisms, we shall first consider the psychopathology of anxiety disorders.

Classification and Description of Anxiety Disorders

The DSM-III description of anxiety disorders (American Psychiatric Association, 1980) is a natural starting point. It lists seven anxiety disorders that seem to be divisible into three categories: (1) phobic disorders, which include agoraphobia, social phobia, and simple phobia (e.g., acrophobia); (2) anxiety states, including panic disorder, generalized anxiety disorders (GAD), and obsessive–compulsive disorder (OCD); and (3) posttraumatic stress disorder (PTSD), which is characterized by the presence of excessive anxiety and distress following a traumatic event. Unlike DSM-III, the classification system that we shall present here focuses on the descriptive aspects of each disorder rather than on theoretical notions about their etiology.

In the DSM-III, agoraphobia is defined as fear and avoidance of being alone or in public places without help or escape. Simple phobia is defined as irrational fear and avoidance of a situation or object other than social situations and public places. Persistent fear of social situations and the desire to avoid those situations in which the individual is afraid of scrutiny and embarrassment characterizes social phobia. Some identified external source of anxiety (e.g., social situation, supermarket, snake) and its avoidance is common to all phobias. In addition, descriptions of both social phobia and agoraphobia include a fear of anticipated loss or catastrophe. The agoraphobic expects incapacitation from, for example, a heart attack or fainting, and avoids situations from which escape is difficult or help unavailable. The social phobic seeks to avoid public humiliation and embarrassment. On the other hand, preoccupation with future harm is not a diagnostic requirement for simple phobia.

The second class of anxiety disorders, anxiety states, is distinguished in the DSM-III by the absence of avoidance behavior as a diagnostic requirement. Panic disorder and generalized anxiety disorder are characterized by heightened physiological responding and the absence of a circumscribed external source of anxiety. Criteria for an obsessive–compulsive disorder are recurring unwanted thoughts or repetitive stereotypic behaviors that are recognized as senseless. Re-experiences of the stress of a specific traumatic event from the past and numbness or withdrawal from the external world following such an event are the hallmarks of posttraumatic stress disorder.

While providing clear descriptions of the anxiety disorders, the DSM-III offers no theoretical framework by which these disorders can be organized. Several dimensions are proposed by Foa, Steketee, and Young (1984). These include the presence or absence of *avoidance behaviors,* of *external fear cues,* and of thoughts about *anticipated harm.* Internal cues for fear (e.g., thoughts, physiological responses, impulses) occur in every anxiety disorder. Agoraphobics, for example, fear their own physiological responses (internal cues), since they signal anticipated harm. To protect themselves, they avoid situations that are deemed likely to provoke physiological arousal (eternal cues). All three types of fear cues are thus contained in the agoraphobic's fear structure.

Some obsessive–compulsives' fear structures also include all three types of fear cues. A patient with washing rituals, for example, avoids external situations that provoke an internal feeling of contamination that is, in turn, accompanied by concern about illness. Unlike phobics, however, obsessive–compulsives are rarely successful in passively avoiding their feared situation and therefore develop active avoidance in the form of ritualistic behavior. Obsessive–compulsives without overt rituals (obsessionals) may fear external cues (e.g., knives) that are associated with anticipated harm (such as stabbing one's child). They may or may not avoid contact with such cues.

Panic disorder is characterized by the presence of internal fear cues (e.g., physiological arousal) that patients often associate with some harmful consequence. This arousal, however, is not triggered by identifiable external cues; therefore, no avoidance patterns develop in panic disorder. Typically, in generalized anxiety-disordered (GAD) individuals, external cues, anticipated harm, and avoidance patterns are absent; only internal cues are in evidence. For posttraumatic stress disordered (PTSD) individuals, thoughts and images provoke anxiety. For some, these are generated by external cues that may or may not be avoided. For others, flashbacks and feared images appear spontaneously and therefore external cues and avoidance behaviors are absent. Neither GAD nor PTSD patients fear harmful consequences other than the persistent experience of high anxiety.

The treatment of anxiety disorders aims at reducing the anxiety produced by the fear cues and eliminating avoidance behavior that reinforces the fear. There is ample evidence to suggest that treatment procedures that involve exposing patients to their feared objects, situations, or thoughts are effective in ameliorating their symptomatology (Emmelkamp, 1982b; Marks, 1978). Through what mechansims does exposure reduce anxiety?

Mechanisms for Fear Reduction

Foa and Kozak (1985) suggest that for the successful treatment of pathological anxiety, two conditions should be present: (1) the fear network must be activated, as indicated by some fear response (e.g., heart rate increase, muscle tension, verbal report of anxiety); and (2) the treatment should provide information incompatible with the faulty aspects of the fear network. Treatment, then, is aimed at dissociating fear responses from the feared objects or situations, at reducing the patient's estimated probabilities of harm and its valence, and at changing faulty beliefs and attitudes.

Dissociation of Responses to Stimulus Situations

It has been repeatedly observed that when patients are exposed to feared situations, either in imagery or in reality, a gradual reduction in fear responses takes place. Such habituation in the fear context provides the information that physiological responses associated with fear decrease despite the presence of the feared cue. This new information about the absence of arousal weakens the response–stimulus associations in the fear structure. Systematic desensitization (Wolpe, 1958) is a deliberate attempt to provide such information via associating relaxation with the feared situation. In flooding (Stampfl & Levis, 1967), exposure is prolonged to allow spontaneous anxiety reduction and the consequent weakening of the link between representations of feared stimuli and fear responses.

Evaluation of Threat

As we noted in discussing the categorization of anxiety disorders, anticipated threat constitutes a particular focus in some individuals. Accordingly, the patient's estimates of the danger inherent in both stimuli and responses may require modification. Several types of evaluations can characterize the fear structures of those who manifest anxiety disorders. First, there is a reluctance to engage in fear-provoking experiences because of one's presumption that anxiety will persist until escape occurs. Second, the fear stimuli and/or fear responses are associated with an unrealistically high potential for causing either psychological (e.g., going crazy, losing control) or physical (e.g., dying, being ill) harm. For example, the agoraphobic who feels his or her heart pounding believes that heart failure is imminent. Third, the feared consequences often have an unusually high negative valence, that is, they are viewed as extremely aversive.

For example, for a social phobic, criticism is felt to be a major catastrophe, whereas it is only mildly or moderately aversive for most people. The first evaluation is corrected when habituation during the feared situation occurs (short-term habituation). The patient who observes that his or her anxiety gradually declines during exposure changes his or her belief that anxiety will stay forever. Correction of patients' inaccurate estimates of eventual harm often requires repeated exposures; such changes are reflected in long-term habituation when exposure to a feared cue ceases to provoke fear. Valence is altered through repeated exposures and the consequent habituation of anxiety responses. The social phobic who faces criticism with little manifestation of fear (after habituation has occurred) is likely to modify his or her judgment of how terrible it is to be criticized.

Individuals may differ with respect to the recalcitrance of their mistaken evaluations. Several factors may account for their resistance to change. First, the nature of the belief may preclude its disconfirmation during the course of treatment. For example, a patient who fears contaminating his daughter with "leukemia germs" (acquired via contact with leukemia patients or hospital cancer wards) believed that visiting a hospital would result in the development of cancer in his child sometime within the next several years. The absence of cancer in the daughter following a series of exposures to hospitals and cancer patients will not constitute adequate evidence to contradict this belief. Second, the patient's theory of potential harm may have so many qualifications that any disconfirming information is readily discounted; information incompatible with his beliefs is thus difficult to provide. An agoraphobic who failed to experience the expected panic during a series of exposures to a supermarket dismissed the information about the absence of panic on the ground that the conditions that cause her to panic were not presented there. She asserted, "I felt exceptionally well this morning and I knew this would be a good day, so I didn't get a panic." On a later occasion, she explained the absence of panic as a consequence of the good weather. On the third occasion, she thought the supermarket was not crowded enough to provoke panic.

In proposing that fear reduction occurs through changes in stimulus–response links and in associated meanings, Foa and Kozak (1985) do not imply that a person is aware of all the processes that take place during exposure. As noted by Nisbett and Wilson (1977), cognitive processes are not always amenable to accurate assessment via introspection. Indeed, only a minority of phobics reported catastrophic thoughts during imagery of their feared situations (Rimm, Janda, Lancaster, Nahl, & Dittman, 1977). Nor do Foa and Kozak imply that modification of mistaken beliefs was best accomplished via discussion with the patient. In fact, techniques that relied heavily on self-reports of cognitive processes seem to have had limited effectiveness in treating anxiety disorders.

The process of anxiety reduction might thus be viewed as involving a series of changes in a fear structure of which only certain elements may be available for introspection. Unconscious processes, such as stimulus-response dissociations, may effect changes in beliefs and attitudes that are in the realm of awareness and are more closely related to overt actions. For example, habituation of autonomic nervous system responses (e.g., heart rate) in the presence of feared stimuli may lead to a change in evaluating the endurance of anxiety, and thereby alter the attitude that anxiety should be avoided at all costs. This could lead to more general changes in one's perception of self-efficacy and to accompanying behavioral changes.

In summary, Foa and Kozak (1985) suggest that once a fear has been evoked by information that adequately matches an individual's fear structure, several mechanisms come into play. The information that short-term physiological habituation has occurred may sever bonds between stimulus elements and response elements in the fear memory structure. The resulting lower arousal facilitates the processing of information embedded in the exposure situation that is incompatible with pre-existing unrealistic beliefs. Indeed, high levels of arousal are known to interfere with information processing (Yerkes & Dodson, 1908). The reduction in estimation of how harmful the feared situation is, as well as the decrease in negative valence associated with anticipated harm, obviate the tendency to avoid the feared situation, thereby further reducing the physiological activity associated with preparation for escape or avoidance. Habituation between sessions is then evident; this long-term absence of anxiety constitutes additional information that modifies more general beliefs and attitudes about one's ability to cope with feared situations in general.

BEHAVIORAL AND COGNITIVE TREATMENTS FOR ANXIETY

As apparent from the theoretical discussion above, a major goal of treatment for phobic disorders is to sever associations between fear responses and stimuli that do not merit fear by altering erroneous cognitions. Accordingly, assessment procedures are designed to identify the cues that elicit fear, the associated cognitions, and the avoidance or escape behaviors that are aimed at the reduction of fear/discomfort. The behavioral treatments that have been developed for anxiety disorders all encourage a confrontation of the feared cues. After delineating the processes for assessing the fear structure, we will briefly describe several treatment procedures that are currently applied to phobics and obsessive-compulsives. We shall not discuss here guidelines for a standard psychological assessment, which includes the collecting of information regarding family background, history of the problem, factors associated with its onset, general mood state, treatment history, and so on. Rather, we will focus on how to solicit material necessary to plan a treatment program for phobics and obsessive-compulsives.

Assessment

The major vehicle for assessing anxiety symptoms is the clinical interview in which the nature of the external cues (e.g., tangible objects), internal cues (e.g., images, impulses, and physiological sensations), and worries about future consequences are elucidated. In addition, the patterns of escape and avoidance of the feared cues are explored. For obsessive-compulsives, information about active avoidance patterns (i.e., ritualistic behavior) is also collected. The identification of the type of cues that elicit discomfort in the anxiety disordered patient constitutes the basis for planning his or her treatment program.

External Cues

The majority of phobics and obsessive-compulsives experience fear when confronted with certain external cues. The therapist should solicit highly specific information about such cues in an attempt to identify the major sources of concern. Simple phobics are often concerned with only one type of feared cue, such as dogs, thunder, or heights. Agoraphobics typically fear a multitude of situations including supermarkets, theaters, churches, elevators, or driving on expressways. Social phobics also present with a variety of circumstances that provoke discomfort, such as entering a crowded room, speaking in public, eating in front of others, or attending a social gathering.

Obsessive-compulsives with washing rituals, like agoraphobics, have a panoply of disturbing external cues. Contamination "travels" and, there-fore, objects become contaminated through even remote contact with the source of contamination. It is impossible to understand the patient who fears walking in the woods, sitting near people who have just returned from a visit to the zoo, and sitting near her fireplace (where a bat was found 2 years ago) without knowing that these situations were all asso-ciated with potential contact with rabies, the patient's main concern. When a multitude of situations are reported to evoke fear, an underlying dimension often exists. To ascertain that the exposure treatment includes a representative sample of feared situations, identification of such a di-mension is essential.

Internal Cues

Anxiety/discomfort may be generated by internal cues, that is, thoughts, images, or impulses that are fearful, shameful, or disgusting. For an obsessive-compulsive, such cues may include impulses to stab one's child, (which may be triggered, in turn, by external cues such as knives or scissors), or thoughts that one's spouse may have an auto accident on the way home. Agoraphobics typically fear bodily sensations such as heart palpitations, sweating, dizziness, or warm flushes, which are interpreted to signal danger. Concern about physical sensations such as blushing or hand tremors is common for social phobics who fear that their discomfort will be noticed by others who will then disrespect them. Simple phobics, while going to considerable lengths to avoid the physical sensations of anxiety, usually do not report fears of internal sensations. Identification of internal cues is important since treatment should in part be aimed at reducing the fear associated with them.

Anticipated Harm

Often the external and internal cues that arouse anxiety are related to anticipated harm, which for some may be the primary source of discomfort. For example, many obsessive–compulsives with washing rituals fear disease, physical debilitation, or the death of themselves or others. Those who check repeatedly seek to prevent an error that will lead to harm (e.g., looking in the rearview mirror after driving over a bump to ensure that one has not run over a pedestrian). Social phobics worry about being scrutinized, criticized, and rejected; in the main, their expression of concern about offending others reflects a fear of being rejected. Many specific phobics are alarmed that the situation they fear will lead to personal physical danger (e.g., being bitten by a dog, falling). Others avoid objects or situations because they dislike the intense unpleasant sensations associated with anxiety rather than because the situation is perceived as dangerous. Agoraphobics also avoid the bodily sensations associated with fear, not only because they are connected with anxiety, but also because, unlike simple phobics, they associate anxiety symptoms with impending catastrophe. For example, the agoraphobics for whom heart palpitations signal a heart attack avoid situations that might increase their heart rate. Similarly, situations that may cause dizziness may be avoided because this sensation is interpreted to signify that one is going crazy.

Beliefs and Attitudes

Patients differ with respect to the estimated probability that their feared consequence will occur, and the negative valence they associate with that consequence. The prominence of these two cognitive aspects of fear vary across anxiety disorders. Simple phobics mainly exaggerate the probability that their feared consequence will occur. The suburbanite who avoids her backyard for fear of encountering a venomous snake and being bitten by it overestimates the likelihood of such an event. Whereas social phobics may also overestimate the risk of their feared disaster (e.g., being criticized or rejected), the main impairment in their fear structure is the strong negative valence they attach to being rejected. The agoraphobic who fears that panic attacks will cause her physical harm (e.g., heart attack) suffers from a pathological overestimation of the likelihood that panic will lead to permanent harm. Those who fear the social/psychological consequences of a panic attack (e.g., criticism for disturbing a religious ceremony if a panic attack occurs) evidence both an erroneous probability estimation and exaggerated valence. This latter pattern is also characteristic of obsessive–compulsives. The obsessive washer who fears getting an infection from using a public toilet overestimates the likelihood of contracting such an infection; he or she also overreacts to the possibility of contracting an infection.

Another psychopathological feature that distinguishes anxious individuals from normals is the high negative valence they attack to discomfort itself. The simple phobic who employs elaborate avoidance tactics to prevent contact with cockroaches, from which he fears no real harm, exhibits an exaggerated sensitivity to discomfort. The obsessive–compulsive refrains from touching doorknobs (which produce only mild to moderate anxiety) also manifests such oversensitivity.

Avoidance Patterns

Having identified the patient's fear cues, the therapist should inquire about escape and avoidance patterns. By definition, all phobics attempt to avoid situations that lead to discomfort or, if such situations are unavoidable, they try to escape them. A snake phobic avoids the backyard; a dog phobic may play only indoor rather than outdoor tennis lest a dog wander onto the courts. Agoraphobics avoid situations that they believe are likely to elicit intense anxiety sensations and the catastrophes associated with them. Their avoidance can range from shunning a few places when alone and enjoying unrestricted movement when accompanied by a trusted person to completely refusing to leave home and insisting on the continuous presence of designated trusted individuals. In general, the avoidance behaviors of agoraphobics are designed to minimize the chance of finding themselves in a situation in which a panic attack (or intense anxiety) occurs, immediate escape is impossible, and consequently physical harm or embarrassment is likely to result. Examples of avoidance include: shopping at unpopular hours to avoid lines; driving routes that do not involve one-way streets, bridges, expressways, or tunnels; and sitting near the exit in theaters and churches.

The avoidance patterns of obsessive–compulsives sometimes resemble those of phobics, for example, refraining from using public restrooms to ensure that they do not contract venereal disease or refusing to drive to avoid injuring people. Avoidance often becomes extremely debilitating: In order to avoid the contamination of her home, one patient required all family members to remove their clothes upon entering, to shower, and to dress in "uncontaminated" clothing. Another patient who had obsessive thoughts that he might attack his wife, refrained from watching television or reading the newspaper for fear he would encounter references to violence that would trigger his obsessions. He also avoided the kitchen, where he feared the sight of knives or forks would elicit impulses to stab his wife.

When passive avoidance fails and the patient finds him- or herself in anxiety arousing circumstances, the phobic and agoraphobic simply escape. Obsessive compulsives, on the other hand, need to develop different methods to remove themselves from discomfort or danger. For washers, mere escape from a contaminating object is ineffective because contamination continues, even after the removal of the object. Washing or cleaning is then necessary to restore a state of comfort. For checkers who fear that overlooking an error will result in a catastrophe, escaping the circumstance where the "error" was committed is again ineffective. Such patients seek to insure that the feared error is detected and corrected via repeatedly checking their actions. The ritualistic behavior of an obsessive-compulsive, then, serves the same function as the escape behavior of a phobic.

Treatment

Exposure-Based Treatment

Several procedures for ameliorating pathological fear have been developed in the last 25 years. Early conceptualizations of neurotic anxiety based on learning theory emphasized external fear cues and overt avoidance. This focus on external cues might explain why behaviorists have developed treatments that focused on the exposure to such cues. More recently, the emphasis has shifted to nonexternal fear cues (e.g., autonomic arousal, thoughts of impending catastrophies) with the resultant development of cognitive techniques (Beck, 1976; Meichenbaum, 1977).

Exposure treatment is a set of techniques whose common denominator is confronting patients with their feared cues. These techniques can be divided according to the medium of exposure (imaginal vs. *in vivo*), the length of exposure (short vs. long) and the level of arousal (low vs. high). If the various exposure procedures are ordered along these dimensions, then systematic desensitization in which exposure is imaginal, brief, and minimally arousing occupies an extreme position on each dimension. In direct contrast, *in vivo* flooding exposes patients to actual life events for prolonged periods and under conditions designed to elicit high levels of anxiety. In reviewing the efficacy of exposure treatment, we shall first consider procedures in which confrontation with the feared cue was introduced in imagery, and then proceed to discuss the efficacy of *in vivo* procedures.

The first imaginal technique is *systematic desensitization*, which is composed of three ingredients: (1) a graded anxiety hierarchy of relevant external situations; (2) a response incompatible with anxiety such as relaxation; and (3) the pairing of brief imaginal exposures to these stimuli with the anxiety-reducing response. Many studies have demonstrated the efficacy of systematic desensitization with simple phobics (e.g., Cooper, Gelder, & Marks, 1965; Marks & Gelder, 1965). When compared with other therapeutic procedures such as hospitalization or group and individual insight psychotherapy, systematic desensitization was found superior (Gelder, Marks, & Wolfe, 1967). In contrast, agoraphobics have been poor responders to this procedure (Jansson & Ost, 1982). Gelder *et al.* (1967) treated 44 outpatients, of whom approximately half were agoraphobics and the remainder were simple phobics. Patients were divided into three groups: One group received 25 sessions of systematic desensitization; the second group had 50 sessions of individual psychotherapy; and the third was given 75 sessions of group psychotherapy. Of the three treatments, systematic desensitization produced greater and faster improvement at the 6-month mark. However, agoraphobics tended to be poor responders to systematic desensitization. Despite the good response of socially anxious volunteers to systematic desensitization, social phobic patients achieved limited improvement at best (for review, see Emmelkamp, 1982).

No controlled prospective studies have been conducted to evaluate the effects of desensitization with obsessive–compulsives. The available case reports, however, suggest that it is ineffective with most of these patients. In a retrospective study conducted by Cooper *et al.* (1965), of ten obsessive–compulsive subjects, only three improved with systematic desensitization. A control group treated with psychotherapy and drugs improved more. Beech and Vaughn (1978) summarized the single cases that used systematic desensitization with obsessive–compulsives; only four of ten patients improved.

Imaginal flooding is a procedure by which a patient is asked to fantasize for a prolonged period encountering situations that are extremely anxiety producing. As noted above, flooding and desensitization occupy opposing positions on several procedural parameters and are derived from different theoretical viewpoints. These differences have prompted interest in comparing the relative efficacy of the two procedures. In a study by Marks, Boulougouris, and Marset (1971), 16 patients (7 phobics and 9 agoraphobics) received six 50-minute sessions each of systematic desensitization and of flooding in a crossover design. On the whole, flooding was found to be more effective than systematic desensitization. However, when agoraphobics and simple phobics were examined separately, the latter showed equal benefit from the two techniques. Agoraphobics, on the other hand, improved significantly more with flooding. It should be noted, though, that patients received 70 minutes of *in vivo* exposure, either gradual or abrupt, during the last two sessions of each type of treatment. Therefore, the results may not represent the pure effects of the two imaginal procedures alone.

The efficacy of imaginal flooding and of systematic desensitization with agoraphobics and with simple phobics was studied in a prospective study utilizing a control group which received treatment using nonfear imagery and free association (Gelder *et al.*, 1973). All received eight 90-minute sessions of imaginal desensitization or flooding followed by four sessions of *in vivo* practice that was gradual in the desensitization condition and abrupt in the flooding group. The two behavior therapy procedures were superior to the control treatment on psychiatric ratings, but did not differ from each other, for either agoraphobics or simple phobics. On the behavioral measure, flooding was superior to systematic desensitization for all patients; the breakdown for agoraphobics and simple phobics was not available on this measure. Unfortunately, the design of this study again confounded the effect of imaginal exposure with *in vivo* exposure.

The relatively poor results of systematic desensitization with agoraphobics can be explained by the relative absence of high arousal in this procedure. The experience of arousal for agoraphobics may be an important therapeutic ingredient if indeed they fear physiological arousal. Support for this explanation is derived from Chambless, Foa, Groves, and Goldstein's (1979) findings that imaginal flooding in conjunction with an intravenously administered barbiturate was less effective than flooding alone. Since the drug led to lower anxiety during flooding, its hindrance to improvement suggests that the experiencing of physiological anxiety may be therapeutic for agoraphobics. However, a reanalysis of the data at follow-up with a smaller sample found only a trend in this direction (Chambless, Foa, Groves, & Goldstein, 1982). Additional support for the therapeutic role of anxiety for agoraphobics comes from the finding that only agoraphobics who experienced intense anxiety during the first few sessions of *in vivo* exposure benefitted from treatment (Hand, personal communication, 1985). With simple phobics, Lang, Melamed, and Hart (1970) and Borkovec, and Sides (1979) reported that the greater the initial arousal (as measured by heart rate response), the better the outcome.

When imaginal flooding was employed with obsessive–compulsives, results were quite disappointing (Emmelkamp & Kwee, 1977; Stern, 1978). However, the procedure was moderately helpful in relieving the symptoms of obsessive–compulsives with checking rituals (Foa, Steketee, & Grayson, 1985). Only one study has examined the effect of flooding in imagination with socially anxious patients. Shaw (1979) compared flooding with systematic desensitization and social skills training and found no differences among treatments.

In vivo exposure refers to any treatment that focuses on confronting patients in reality (as opposed to fantasy) with their feared objects or situations. In recent years, imaginal procedures have fallen out of favor as evidence favoring in vivo exposure has accumulated. As is noted by Mathews (1978), "the available evidence suggests that direct exposure is always superior with simple phobics" (p. 399). Indeed, the anxiety reduction achieved during imaginal exposure procedures has frequently failed to generalize to real stimuli (Barlow, Leitenberg, Agras, & Wincze 1969; Watson, Gaind, & Marks, 1972). With agoraphobics, the picture is more ambiguous. In two studies with this population, actual contact with feared stimuli yielded greater improvement than did contact via imaginal exposure. Using a crossover design, Stern and Marks (1973) compared two sessions each of long and short exposure in fantasy and in practice; long in vivo exposure proved the most effective. However, the use of a tape recorder rather than a therapist to present imaginal scenes and the constant order of the treatments (imaginal always preceded in vivo exposure) renders interpretation of these findings difficult. These shortcomings were remedied by Emmelkamp and Wessels (1975), who employed a factorial design in four sessions each, comparing prolonged in vivo exposure with imaginal exposure delivered by a therapist. Again, on most variables, in vivo exposure produced a superior outcome.

In contrast, equivalent effects of these two exposure media were reported by Mathews, Johnston, Lancashire, Munby, Shaw, and Gelder (1976), who compared eight weekly sessions each of imaginal flooding, in vivo exposure, and a combination of the two. In an attempt to reconcile the discrepancy between their results and those of Emmelkamp and Wessels (1975), Mathews et al. suggest that their instructions to practice between sessions might have washed out group differences. This interpretation was not supported by the results obtained by Chambless, et al., (1982), who contrasted eight bi-weekly sessions of imaginal flooding followed by 4 months of supportive psychotherapy with an attention control condition followed by four months of weekly in vivo exposure. Although their patients were not instructed to practice between sessions, imaginal exposure was as effective as in vivo exposure.

The Chambless et al. results must be interpreted with caution because of the time confound (the imaginal flooding and the in vivo flooding were not conducted in parallel). This study, however, did allow investigation of the long-term effects of imaginal and in vivo exposure; all of the preceding studies reported only short-term findings, which may have obscured the picture. Mathews (1978) suggested that the effects of imaginal treatment may be delayed whereas in vivo exposure produces immediate effects.

Indeed, only in the shorter trials was exposure *in vivo* found superior to exposure in fantasy. Long term follow-up, then, may be required to adequately assess the relative efficacy of the two exposure modalities.

The application of *in vivo* exposure to obsessive–compulsives is complicated by the nature of their fears. As noted earlier, for an obsessive–compulsive, the physical removal of a feared object or situation does not necessarily constitute escape and hence he or she needs to perform compulsive actions. In 1966, Victor Meyer described a treatment program for obsessive–compulsives that was composed of *in vivo* exposure and response prevention, that is, the blocking of ritualistic behavior. Through the use of these two procedures, exposure was prolonged and avoidance or escape blocked. Rabavilas, Boulougouris, and Stefanis (1976) compared two sessions each of short and long fantasy and short and long practice. On target symptoms no differences between fantasy and practice emerged. Foa, Steketee, Turner, and Fisher (1980) found that the combination of imaginal and *in vivo* exposure was as effective as *in vivo* exposure at posttreatment. However, at follow-up, the former was more effective in maintaining the gains of obsessive–compulsive checkers. In a later study, again with obsessive–compulsive checkers, the effect of each exposure media alone was examined without the addition of response prevention (Foa *et al.*, 1985). No differences were observed either at posttreatment or at follow-up; both procedures were moderately effective. In an attempt to identify the relative contributions of exposure and response prevention to treatment outcome with obsessive–compulsives, several studies have been conducted. They indicated that *in vivo* exposure mainly affected anxiety directed toward contaminants, whereas response prevention influenced ritualistic behavior. A combination of the two procedures was superior, both at posttreatment and follow-up. (Foa, Steketee, & Milby, 1979; Foa, Steketee, Grayson, Turner, & Latimer, 1984)

In summary, prolonged exposure either in imagination or *in vivo* is the treatment of choice for agoraphobics and obsessive–compulsives. For simple phobics, either brief or long exposure is equally effective, with *in vivo* procedures producing the greatest gains. With the development of these treatments, the prognosis of refractory conditions such as agoraphobia and obsessive–compulsive disorders has vastly improved. Seventy percent of agoraphobics (Emmelkamp & Kuipers, 1979; Munby & Johnston, 1980) and 75% of obsessive–compulsives (Foa, Grayson, Steketee, Doppelt, Turner, & Latimer, 1983; Marks, Hodgson, & Rachman, 1975) benefitted from exposure programs. *In vivo* exposure produced lasting benefits for the majority of social phobics; 55% to 60% of patients were satisfied with the number of social contacts that they had after exposure treatment (Butler, Cullington, Munby, Amies, & Gelder, 1984). It should also be noted that social skills training, which can be construed as *in vivo* exposure to contrived social situations, generally yielded more satisfactory results than did imaginal procedures for socially anxious individuals. It should be noted that few patients with anxiety disorders leave therapy with no trace of their fears. However, as mentioned above, the majority benefit to a clinically significant degree.

Cognitive Procedures

Cognitive therapists, as Ledwidge (1978) notes, "attempt to change behavior by influencing the client's pattern of thought and rely chiefly on speech as the instrument of change" (p. 356). These techniques have developed from the assumption that cognitions play a causative role in behavior (e.g. Beck, Rush, Shaw, & Emery, 1979; Ellis, 1970). The many studies that have employed a variety of cognitive procedures with fearful student volunteers have shown them to be effective but not more so than exposure techniques (Ledwidge, 1978). Only a few controlled studies have investigated the outcome of cognitive therapies with anxiety disordered patients. At posttreatment, exposure *in vivo* was found superior to cognitive restructuring with simple phobics (Biran & Wilson, 1981) and with agoraphobics (Emmelkamp, Kuipers, & Eggeraat, 1978; Emmelkamp & Mersch, 1982). At a 1-month follow-up, the results are more equivocal. Exposure *in vivo* remained the superior treatment for simple phobics. But in the Emmelkamp and Mersch study, agoraphobics treated with cognitive methods improved further after treatment, whereas those treated with *in vivo* exposure showed some relapse, so that both treatments were equally effective at that time. When *in vivo* exposure was compared with problem-solving treatment for agoraphobics, the former proved superior both at posttreatment and at a 6-month follow-up (Jannoun, Munby, Catalan, & Gelder, 1980). The addition of cognitive techniques to *in vivo* exposure did not enhance outcome at posttreatment or at follow-up for agoraphobics (Emmelkamp & Mersch, 1982), for obsessive–compulsives (Emmelkamp, Van der Helm, Van Zanten, & Plochg, 1980), or for a mixed group of driving phobics and agoraphobics who were treated for their driving fears (Williams & Rappoport, 1983).

When different treatment procedures are compared, it is desirable to insure that they do not share the same elements. However, instructions for confrontation with feared objects is an integral part of many cognitive treatment programs. Similarly, most exposure therapists discuss, albeit unsystematically, the erroneous beliefs associated with their patients' fears. Instead of studying the dichotomy between the procedures, the separate effects of the two components should be explored, with the goal of working toward complementarity, rather than contradiction. The focus of investigations of cognitive and exposure therapies should be to identify the specific beliefs and behaviors targeted for change and to develop the most efficient and effective means for altering them.

IMPLEMENTATION OF TREATMENT

Obviously, the first phase of any treatment should focus on diagnosis and assessment. The information collected during this phase constitutes the basis for selecting the appropriate treatment procedures and for generating a treatment plan tailored to the patient's problems. The therapist seeks information about the situations, thoughts, or images that are feared, avoided, or escaped and about the erroneous beliefs and attitudes that require modification. For most patients, three to six 1 hour sessions are sufficient for the collecting of such information. In planning the treatment, the therapist must judge whether the therapy sessions will be primarily devoted to exposing the patient to his or her feared cues or to directing and advising the patient in self-exposure. The research findings are equivocal regarding the importance of the therapist's presence during the actual exposure. Clinical observations indicate that individuals who are severely impaired by their fears require the aid of their therapist and of significant others to enter and remain in feared circumstances. On the other hand, patients with moderate fear who are otherwise functional are likely to gain most from treatment that concentrates on guiding the exposure homework. In addition to instructions for exposure, such sessions should also include demonstration and practice of coping skills, when indicated (e.g., relaxation for phobics, appropriate breathing instructions for agoraphobics). Whether self- or therapist-aided exposure is selected, treatment should also address the patient's erroneous beliefs and negative attitudes.

With severe obsessive–compulsives and agoraphobics, clinical impression and research findings suggest that treatment by exposure is more effective when conducted several times per week for a few weeks rather than on a weekly basis for a longer period. A time-limited intensive treatment program seems to maximize the patient's motivation and compliance with treatment procedures that generate considerable discomfort. If an obsessive–compulsive is asked to refrain from washing his or her hands for a period of three weeks, he or she can mobilize inner resources to tolerate the resultant discomfort. It is doubtful whether this patient would be willing to comply with such a regimen for a period of three months. With a short but intensive program, the treatment becomes the focus of a patient's life and therefore has a greater impact upon his or her daily behaviors and cognitions than a less frequent and prolonged therapy.

To maintain treatment gains, it is desirable to conduct several additional sessions on a weekly basis. For obsessive–compulsives, we have developed a 4-week program in which patients are seen daily (excluding weekends) for 1½ to 2 hours during the first 3 weeks, and are visited at home for 8 hours during the 4th week. A typical therapy session proceeds as follows: The first few minutes are spent in a discussion of the patient's current mood, urges to ritualize, and prior homework assignment. Unexpected upsetting events are also attended to at the beginning of the session. In the remaining time, procedures directed at anxiety reduction are implemented. First, the patient is exposed in fantasy to descriptions of the situations, objects, or thoughts (including thoughts of future harm) that provoke fear and discomfort. Patients are instructed to imagine the content of the verbal description as vividly as possible and to allow themselves to feel as if they were actually in these situations. Typically, subjective anxiety increases gradually and then decreases. Imaginal exposure is terminated when a substantial reduction in discomfort is observed.

Following imaginal exposure, the therapist confronts the patient, in a graded sequence, with items or situations that provoke discomfort. Whenever possible, the objects or situations are selected to correspond to those presented imaginally in the same session. Exposure *in vivo* should continue until a substantial reduction in anxiety is achieved. In successive sessions, more disturbing items are added to previous ones; the most anxiety-provoking situations are typically presented by the 6th session. When a patient shows extreme difficulty in confronting a feared situation, it may be helpful for the therapist to model contact with the feared item.

For washers, all nonessential washing and cleaning is eliminated except for one 10-minute shower every 5th day. Checkers are permitted one check only of items that are normally checked after use, such as stoves and door locks. Other objects judged not to require routine checking (e.g., unused electrical appliances, discarded envelopes) may not be checked. In the last few sessions of treatment, the patient should be introduced to the rules of "normal" washing, cleaning, or checking. Response prevention requirements are relaxed to enable the patient to return to what is considered to be a normal routine.

Other centers have developed similar intensive exposure programs for agoraphobics (Chambless & Goldstein, 1982). We are unaware of intensive treatment programs for socially phobic individuals; it seems likely, however, that they also will benefit more from frequent rather than weekly sessions. The intensive therapy programs may yield better results because they increase the likelihood of frequent "successful" exposures and at the same time reduce the probability of unplanned exposures (between sessions) that may be terminated by escape or followed by unpleasant consequences (e.g., a panic attack, social rejection). Because simple phobics are for the most part successful in avoiding incidental exposures and are therefore less likely to experience negative consequences, they may not require frequent sessions. For them, intensive treatment may be more efficient but not more effective.

The implementation of exposure treatment will be illustrated using the following case example:

Case Description

Peggy was a 47-year-old upper-class white Protestant woman, married to a businessman. The couple had two children, aged 25 and 22. Peggy sought treatment to rid herself of worries about cancer, rabies, and AIDS which led to excessive cleaning and washing. The onset of her obsessive-compulsive symptoms had occurred 15 years earlier when she was attending her mother who had terminal cancer. Peggy began to fear that unless she washed or cleaned excessively, her contact with her mother and the oncology department in which her mother was hospitalized would lead to her contracting the disease. After her mother's death, Peggy inherited jewelry and other valuables which she regarded as contaminated but did not want to discard. She brought them home and stored them separately with other contaminated objects. Her fear of cancer led to avoidance of people with cancer, places they visited, their relatives, and hospitals in general. Two years later, Peggy developed a fear of rabies after discovering a bat in her chimney. Having been advised that bats carried rabies and were dangerous, she began to fear contracting rabies from bats, as well as from other animals, including raccoons and squirrels. Peggy began to avoid going to woods and parks, refraining from walking under tall trees for fear that a rabid squirrel's saliva might drip on her. She also avoided people who had recently visited zoos, as well as objects and areas in her home that she felt might have been in contact with the bat. She gave away her dog for fear that he had been contaminated by the bat and consequently would develop rabies.

A year prior to seeking treatment, Peggy began to fear contracting AIDS after reading about this illness in the newspapers. To protect herself, she avoided places that she expected homosexuals to frequent (e.g., certain restaurants, beauty parlors, etc.). Since her son-in-law, a physician, had discussed an AIDS patient whom he had treated, she shunned physical contact with him and places he sat.

When her efforts to avoid feared places associated with cancer, rabies, and AIDS failed, Peggy resorted to excessive washing and cleaning. Her maid was instructed to clean contaminated places repeatedly. Peggy bathed herself for up to 45 minutes a day and washed her hands excessively for a total of 2 hours per day. Her extensive avoidance behavior was the most debilitating aspect of her disorder.

Rationale for Exposure Treatment

In presenting the treatment rationale to Peggy, the targets for cognitive changes were spelled out as follows:

THERAPIST: Well, I understand you're afraid that if you walk under a tree you could get rabies from a squirrel that spit on you. What do you believe is the actual likelihood that a squirrel will spit on you and that if it does, you'll get rabies? What is the percentage of that likelihood?

PATIENT: Oh, probably about 40%.

THERAPIST: You mean that 40% of the people who walk in the woods will die of rabies?

PATIENT: Well, I guess that doesn't really make sense. Not that many people die of rabies.

THERAPIST: It also means that four out of every ten times you walk under a tree, you'll get rabies.

PATIENT: That's possible. I do think I could get it.

THERAPIST: The goal of treatment then, should be to convince you that it's very unlikely that a squirrel will spit on you and that even if it did, it's very improbable that you'd get rabies. After walking under trees many times without getting rabies, you will find out that you were mistaken in thinking that it's highly likely that you would get rabies.

In this case, it is not expected that exposure will influence the valence of Peggy's fears, since rabies is a serious disease. Rather her estimated likelihood of contracting rabies is the target of change.

The following example illustrates the rationale provided when exposure is used to modify valence with a social phobic.

THERAPIST: I understand that you avoid going to social gatherings. For example, you don't join your co-workers for lunch. What are you afraid will happen in these situations?

PATIENT: People might start talking to me and when I answer I'll blush, my voice will quiver, and I won't be able to think of the right words. Everybody will notice I'm nervous.

THERAPIST: What if they see that you're nervous?

PATIENT: I don't want people to think that something is wrong with me. If they see me act nervous, they won't respect me.

THERAPIST: Well, most people are anxious in certain situations and may show signs of nervousness. But they care much less than you about the possibility that people might criticize them because they are somewhat anxious. It would be better for you if you cared less about people's response to your anxiety. Therefore, during treatment, I'll ask you to repeatedly imagine the worst things that people might say about you.

PATIENT: How will that help?

THERAPIST: You'll get used to being criticized for your anxious response and consequently will care less about it if it should happen to you in reality. I'll also ask you to *actually* go into social situations you've been avoiding. This way you'll find out that the harsh criticism that you are afraid of is unlikely to happen.

Treatment Planning

Prior to the implementation of exposure, the therapist introduces the treatment plan to Peggy, the obsessive–compulsive washer.

THERAPIST: I would like to discuss our plan for the first week of therapy. As you know, treatment will take place daily and each session will last about 1½ hours. It's clear that we need to expose you both in imagination and in reality to the things that bother you, which we talked about in previous sessions. As I already indicated, we'll also limit your washing. The scenes you will imagine will focus on the harm that you fear can happen if you don't wash and the actual exposures will focus on the things that contaminate you. Restricting your washing will teach you how to live without rituals. In imagination, you will picture yourself touching something you're afraid of, like the grass under the trees, without washing and then becoming ill with rabies-like symptoms. We will have you imagine going to a doctor who can't figure out what's wrong with you and orders a series of tests.

PATIENT: Yes, this is exactly what I am afraid of.

THERAPIST: Okay, now let's plan the treatment. On the 1st day, we'll start with things that you fear but will not overwhelm you. That would include walking on the grass where squirrels might have been playing, and sitting in the general waiting area of a hospital. On the 2nd day, we'll sit on the grass under the trees and then walk to 13th Street where there are gay bars. On the 3rd day, we'll sit in the oncology waiting room, touch the chairs there and eat a chocolate bar from the hospital gift shop. [The therapist continues to detail the next sessions in the manner described above.] In the second week, we will repeat the worst situations, like feeding the squirrels in the park and going to the zoo to touch the wires of the raccoon's cage.

Treatment Sessions

As discussed above, treatment begins with exposure to moderately difficult items, progressing to the most disturbing ones by the beginning of the 2nd week. The major feared items are repeated during the remainder of the 2nd and 3rd week. The following sequence, which occurred on the 6th day of treatment, is exemplary of this process:

THERAPIST: How was your weekend?

PATIENT: Not that great. I suppose it was as good as I could expect. I took my shower Friday night and I was so nervous about finishing in time that I don't even know if I washed right. I hope I did it the way I was supposed to.

THERAPIST: Most people feel the same way the first time they do it. But you aren't supposed to wash "right," just to wash quickly. How did you do with your homework?

PATIENT: I walked outside in my yard and picked up one of the acorns. On Saturday, I went to my hairdresser and used the toilet there. Then, I stopped at the florist and ordered some flowers. I haven't done that for over a year.

THERAPIST: Very good, you did a lot of work. That's great! Now let's drive to the zoo like we planned.

At the zoo, the goal for that day's session was first to touch the wire of the raccoon's cage and then to come into direct contact with the animal's saliva. The following verbatim material exemplifies the therapy process:

THERAPIST: Now, before we leave for the zoo, let's go over what we're going to do there. We'll go to the children's zoo and we'll feed the raccoon. They told me he likes pretzels! First, I'll have him bite a piece of the pretzel and then ask you to touch the spot that he bit.

PATIENT: I don't think I'm ready to do that yet.

THERAPIST: Well, I'm certain you can do all that. Will it help if I do it first?

PATIENT: Well maybe if I see you do it. . . . You don't think it's dangerous? You would really touch it?

THERAPIST: I am certain it isn't dangerous. I assume that any animal in the children's zoo is healthy. In general, I figure that any animal which doesn't look or behave in a sick way is healthy. Of course I'll touch it.

PATIENT: If you will do it first, I suppose I could do it.

Peggy and the therapist then drove to the zoo where the treatment session continued. En route to the children's section, Peggy displayed avoidance patterns such as refraining from touching the railings in front of the bird's cage for fear of contracting germs. Such avoidance was discouraged and she was asked to touch railings and cages and enter into the monkey house, which she preferred to avoid. At the children's zoo, the therapist steered Peggy toward the raccoon's cage.

THERAPIST: Okay Peggy, I'd like you to first touch the wires with both hands like this (therapist models) and then touch your face and hair, like so.

PATIENT: Yech, I don't believe you're doing that. You really aren't afraid?

THERAPIST: No, there's no reason to be afraid. I know it's hard for you to do it, but everything we've done so far, like sitting on the grass, was also difficult at first and now you can do them more easily.

PATIENT: Okay. (*She touches the wires with two fingers.*)

THERAPIST: Touch it with your entire palm.
(*Peggy does so hesitantly and removes her hands quickly.*)

THERAPIST: Now, I'd like you to keep your hands on the wires.

PATIENT: What if the raccoon touches my hands?

THERAPIST: That's exactly what our goal is today, to touch the raccoon's nose and saliva. He couldn't bite you through the wire mesh anyway. (*Peggy holds her hands against the cage and then touches her face and hair.*)

THERAPIST: That's great. Okay now let's give the raccoon the pretzel to bite so we can touch the part that his teeth touched. (*The therapist holds the pretzel out to the animal who bites off a piece.*)

THERAPIST: Here I want you to touch this part here.

PATIENT: I really don't think this is wise.

THERAPIST: Peggy, we went over the rationale for this treatment several times. I want to remind you that when you're not very fearful you know that touching this pretzel is not dangerous. (*The therapist hands her the pretzel. Peggy looks resigned and accepts it. After a few silent minutes, she reports:*)

PATIENT: Well, it's not quite as bad as I thought but I still don't like it very much.

THERAPIST: As in previous sessions, within an hour you'll probably feel much more comfortable. Now, put this piece of pretzel in your pocket and carry it around with you for homework. Later today, I'd like you to hold it in your hands for two hours.

The remainder of the session was spent in the zoo observing and touching other animals. With each successive session, Peggy became increasingly more comfortable and showed less hesitance to be in contact with the raccoon's saliva. Homework during this time included walking under trees, going to places where she might encounter homosexuals and contaminating her possessions with the pretzel touched by the raccoon.

The Role of Cognitive Procedures

As mentioned earlier, the addition of cognitive techniques, such as cognitive restructuring and positive self-statements, to exposure has not enhanced treatment efficacy with phobics and obsessive–compulsives. When employed alone, for the most part cognitive procedures yielded results inferior to those achieved by exposure. However, it is obvious from the above description of the application of exposure procedures that informal attempts to change cognitions are employed throughout the sessions. The rationale provided to the patient for why exposure treatment is helpful includes change in the patient's attitudes and beliefs. The therapist asserts that "by exposing you again and again to situations you're afraid of, you will find out that the harm you've anticipated won't happen. You'll also learn that confrontation with fearful situations eventually leads to reduction of discomfort, whereas avoidance tends to actually strengthen your fear."

Frequently during exposure sessions, we ask patients to note the fact that their feared consequences have not materialized and that anxiety does decrease with exposure. An agoraphobic would be reminded that the heart attack she feared has not happened, nor has she behaved in a crazy fashion despite her initial high anxiety in the supermarket. Moreover, the therapist points out to her that she was less anxious at the end of the exposure than she was in the beginning, even though she has not used her customary method of reducing fear, that is, escape.

The change in the valence of the patient's concerns is also pointed out as in the following example:

THERAPIST: Do you still feel your heart beating fast?

PATIENT: Yeah, I can still feel it, but it scares me less than it used to.

THERAPIST: Good, so you have learned that even if your heart races, it's hardly a sign of disaster and therefore you care less when it happens.

The effectiveness of comments noting the absence of disasters is often enhanced by the use of humor. For example, a patient who spent hours making sure he was dressed and groomed perfectly for fear of criticism and rejection was asked to walk in a shopping mall with part of his shirt tail untucked and with his hair uncombed. On his return from the mall, the therapist greeted him as follows: "You look terrible today! I certainly wouldn't want to be seen walking with you. What sort of snide remarks have you gotten about your appearance today?" It is important that the therapist laugh *with* and not *at* the patient and avoid the use of humor with those who are not capable of participating in it.

The informal application of cognitive strategies is so embedded in the behavior of the sensitive therapist that it is difficult, if not impossible, to estimate the extent to which cognitive methods are required. Only a study in which comments addressing cognitive issues are systematically excluded from exposure sessions will permit adequate assessment of their efficacy.

The Role of Other Strategies

Many anxiety-disordered individuals exhibit difficulties other than their presenting complaint. Obsessive–compulsives are often socially isolated and require social skills training. Many agoraphobics lack the ability to assert themselves appropriately and can benefit from assertiveness training. Family therapy may be needed for families that have been stressed by the demands that the patient's anxiety symptoms have placed on members in order to resolve the anger and resentment that has accumulated. Improvement in the patient's symptomatology following behavioral treatment may alter the family dynamics; family therapy may be needed to reestablish new, more normative patterns of interaction.

When short-term treatment programs are employed, the anxiety symptoms are addressed first. Other interventions, such as family therapy or social skills training, are usually employed after the anxiety symptoms have subsided. With patients who are not treated in an intensive program, interventions aimed at fear reduction can be interwoven with procedures directed at other changes.

THE ROLE OF THE THERAPIST

Presence of the Therapist

A study of obsessive–compulsives by Emmelkamp and Van Kraanen (1977) compared exposure treatment planned by a therapist but carried out in his or her absence to exposure with the therapist present. Results showed that both were equally effective. Such findings should not be taken to indicate that the therapist is superfluous to the treatment process; they merely suggest that some patients can carry out assignments given by their therapist without him or her being present. Many obsessive–compulsives find themselves unable to implement exposure and/or response prevention on their own. A very articulate obsessive–compulsive patient provided the following insight on this issue: "It is very difficult to stick with an object when you feel contaminated, are sick inside, and your panic keeps increasing, if you do not know that the feeling will pass. There must be a depth of trust in the therapist the patient can feel that will permeate the barrier of doubt and fear as the treatment moves along." It seems that the therapist is important during the high anxiety periods, helping prevent a return to usual habits of dealing with anxiety and avoidance.

With agoraphobics, treatment programs have been developed to minimize the therapist's time. A home-based exposure treatment was developed in Oxford, England (Mathews, Gelder, & Johnston, 1981). This program enlisted friends and relatives to help the patient carry out a treatment composed mainly of exposure to feared situations. The therapist's role was merely to provide supervision and guidance throughout the program. The results of this treatment plan were equal to those obtained when the therapist was present during exposure.

In a study aimed at investigating the effects of imipramine and exposure on agoraphobics (Marks, Gray, Cohen, Hill, Mawson, Ramm, &

Stern, 1983), half of the patients received 1-hour sessions, held every other week, of therapist-aided exposure; the other half received relaxation training. All patients were instructed in self-exposure homework. After the third session, therapists rapidly cut down on accompanying patients during exposure or being with them during relaxation. Patients who received the 3 hours of therapist-aided exposure showed a slight superiority up to 28 weeks; at later follow-ups (up to 2 years) this difference disappeared (Cohen, Monteiro, & Marks, 1984). It is important to note that this study does not permit conclusions about the effects of therapist-aided exposure because of the almost negligible amount of therapist time spent with the patient, the brevity of the exposure session, and the infrequent visits to the therapist. It does, however, indicate the potency of therapist's exposure instructions. Another study (Ghosh, Marks, & Carr, 1984) showed that exposure instructions are equally effective when delivered via a computer, a book, or a therapist. In the latter study, 69% of the patients were agoraphobics, 14% social phobics, and 17% were simple phobics. In contrast to the above studies, Williams, Dooseman, and Kleifield (1984) found that therapist presence during exposure sessions enhanced treatment efficacy.

Clinical Skills Necessary for Successful Therapy

An investigation of the effect of therapist behavior during exposure on treatment outcome for height phobics revealed that the encouragement of patients to confront increasingly difficult situations proved more beneficial than permitting patients to progress at their own rate (Williams, Turner, & Peer, 1985). These results concur with those found regarding obsessive–compulsives and phobics: Respectful, understanding, encouraging, explicit, and challenging therapists achieve better outcomes than permissive and tolerant ones (Rabavilas, Boulougouris, & Perissaki, 1979).

Intensive treatment via exposure to feared situations and prevention of avoidance behavior provokes considerable stress for patients. Their willingness to undergo such treatment attests to their strong motivation. This treatment regimen requires that the therapist maintain a careful balance between pressuring the patient to proceed and sympathizing with his or her discomfort. The behavior of anxiety-disordered patients during treatment ranges from willing cooperation to blatant manipulation. To some extent, knowing when to push, when to confront and when to be flexible is a matter of good theraputic skills and judgment based on experience. As much as possible, however, the therapist should exhibit warmth and empathy to counteract the discomfort embedded in exposure treatment programs, while still insisting that the patient confront feared circumstances as agreed upon at the outset of therapy.

The following verbatim material, taken from the third treatment session with an agoraphobic illustrates this point. The patient has been asked to stay in a supermarket alone for 20 minutes.

PATIENT: I'm afraid I won't be able to stay. I haven't been alone in a store as big as this in years.

THERAPIST: I know how upset you must feel. On the other hand, the tactic of avoiding for all these years has not helped you get over your fear. I'm sure that you'll be able to stay that long. I'll come to pick you up in exactly 20 minutes

PATIENT: I won't like it, but if I have to, I'll try.

THERAPIST: Remember you had similar doubts two days ago when I left you in Wanamaker's [department store] for 10 minutes. You ended up feeling less concerned about it after a while. I want you to use this memory now and wander around with a grocery cart.

PATIENT: But this is so much more difficult than being in Wanamaker's.

THERAPIST: Remember, at the beginning of treatment we agreed that you would follow instructions, even when it's difficult. It's important that you remain alone here in the supermarket because tomorrow it won't be any easier. Now go ahead, take a cart and I will see you in 20 minutes back at the deli counter. (*Patient hesitates.*) Go ahead, you can do it.

Given the difficulty that many obsessive–compulsives exhibit when first prevented from ritualizing after being exposed to feared situations, the therapist's presence during the first few exposure sessions seems strongly advisable. Homework assignments between sessions are usually sufficient to provide patients with the needed sense of self-mastery, thus enabling them to attribute their gains to *their own* ability to control their actions. Emmelkamp and Van Kraanen (1977) noted that self-exposure tended to enhance the maintenance of gains better than did therapist-aided exposure. Therefore, a reduction of the therapist's participation toward the end of the treatment program may facilitate changes in the patient's self-efficacy and thus improve long-term outcome.

Common Errors during Exposure Treatment

Motivational Issues

As noted earlier, exposure treatment requires a strong motivation on the part of the patient. An expectation that treatment will benefit them is, of course, essential. It can be enhanced by a clear explanation of the mechanisms by which such treatment operates. Failure of the patient to understand the rationale for exposure may reduce the motivation to follow the treatment regimen. For an obsessive–compulsive, after ascertaining that treatment by exposure and response prevention is indicated, the following rationale is provided:

THERAPIST: During treatment I will ask you to touch things that are disturbing to you, such as toilet seats in public bathrooms, and you won't be allowed to wash or clean yourself. I know that this will be very hard for you, but there is a good reason for asking you to do it. In a way, I'm asking you to do the opposite of what you have been doing. So far you've done your best to avoid contamination and when that didn't work you washed. As a result, you were never able to find out that nothing would have happened if you hadn't washed. If I expose you to toilet seats and don't let you wash, you will find out that your beliefs about the negative consequences of touching toilet seats are wrong. Also, you'll find out that even when you don't wash, in time you'll feel less upset and the feeling of dirtiness will decrease. For these reasons it is important that we reverse your habits, although it will be very difficult for you. I'll try to help you through treatment in whatever way is needed.

The Absence of a Clear Therapeutic Contract

At the outset of treatment, it is essential to clarify the roles of the therapist and of the patient during the exposure treatment program. The therapist should secure the patient's agreement that he or she will follow the therapist's instructions without arguments and attempts to bargain:

THERAPIST: Before we start, I am going to ask you that even though you feel very uncomfortable and quite upset at times, you won't avoid situations that you were assigned to confront and you won't leave them before your anxiety has decreased considerably. This treatment is very demanding. I'll try to help you as much as I can by planning the treatment with you so you know what to expect each day and by supporting you whenever you need it. Between sessions you can always call me here or at home if a problem comes up. You should also enlist the help of your family and friends, as we discussed. I'll always tell you ahead of time what tasks you will be asked to do during a session and what your homework will be. I will never surprise you by asking you to do things we didn't discuss beforehand. In return, you must not refuse to carry out assignments even though they might produce a lot of fear at first.

The absence of such a contract often leads to arguments and to attempts on the patient's part to bargain for an easier assignment. Such arguments are disruptive to the process of treatment. If the therapist refuses to attend to them, he or she is perceived as rigid and indifferent to the patient's feelings. A power struggle may then ensue. On the other hand, if the therapist complies with the patient's request, he or she cannot execute the treatment program effectively. In either case, treatment is disrupted. Obviously, the establishment of a clear contract does not ensure that a patient will not try to bargain. However, it enables the therapist to curtail the process, as exemplified in the following discussion with an agoraphobic:

PATIENT: I don't feel well today. I barely slept because I was worrying about driving and I have a headache. I don't think today is a good day for me to try to drive on the highway

THERAPIST: I'd like to remind you of our agreement that we would follow the program with minimal arguments. I understand that you are upset and nervous, but you are likely to be just as upset before the next session. Delay is not a good strategy.

PATIENT: But I don't see how it will affect my progress if we delay it just until next Wednesday.

THERAPIST: I'm afraid we'll have to stay with the program that you and I agreed upon before.

When patients resist exposure consistantly, the therapist may elect to terminate treatment and invite them to return when they feel prepared to endure the discomfort generated by exposure. Alternatively, if the therapist feels that a noncompliant patient requires a continuing therapeutic relationship, the stated goal of therapy may be changed from reduction of phobic symptoms to support and counseling for other issues such as marital discord or interpersonal difficulties.

Inflexibility

In the above example, the patient's refusal to follow instructions resulted from her phobic concern. The amelioration of this phobia, however, requires continued exposure. The therapist, therefore, did not accede to her request. However, in some instances, a more flexible approach is indicated. When patients appear emotionally overwhelmed, (i.e., crying, shaking) either because of an upsetting life event or as a result of confrontation with the feared situation, they are unlikely to benefit from the therapist's insistence that they come into contact with a situation that is even more frightening. In a state of terror, an individual is unlikely to process the new information embedded in exposure. If such is the case, the therapist is advised to repeat exposure to the items presented in the previous session and support the patient as much as possible. The exposure should be aborted for a session in rare cases, in order to address intervening issues of concern. Insensitivity to the presence of overwhelming anxiety that interferes with the patient's normal responses, and inattention to exceptional life events may jeopardize the treatment and increase the probability of premature termination by the patient.

COMMON CLINICAL ISSUES

Forming a Therapeutic Relationship

Hadley and Strupp (1976) have found the therapist to be an oft-cited source of negative effects in psychotherapy. However, it appears that the personal qualities of the therapist, which ostensibly are central to the outcome of psychotherapy, have less impact on the more precisely formulated techniques of behavioral therapy (Mathews, Johnston, Shaw, & Gelder, 1973). It is likely that the more powerful the therapeutic procedure employed, the less pronounced will be the effect of the therapist. Nevertheless, during the preliminary stages of information gathering, (which are more similar to traditional psychotherapeutic interventions), the interaction between the therapist and the patient may determine whether or not the patient will give the therapist the opportunity to provide him or her with proper treatment by continuing therapy.

The symptoms of anxiety-disordered patients, particularly agoraphobics and obsessive–compulsives, permeate nearly all facets of their lives. When they first meet the therapist, they want to discuss their symptoms in detail. It is, therefore, important to devote the first and sometimes second session to collecting information concerning their symptoms and to delay life-history taking until later. Periodically during the session, it is advisable that the therapist summarize verbally what he or she has learned in order to confirm that he or she has understood the patient. The patient's perception that he or she is understood forms a basis for trust and cooperation. Another way to validate the therapist's conceptualization of the problem is to form predictions about the patient's behavior in situations that have not been discussed and to present them to the patient, as the following example illustrates:

THERAPIST: Let me summarize here. I understand that every object or person that was in some contact with your mother is frightening and contaminating to you. So you told me that your husband's workplace is contaminated because one of the workers lives near your mother. I suppose that you would also avoid going to your sister's home since your mother visits there.

PATIENT: Yes that's right. I haven't seen them for six years and I feel really bad about that. Isn't it crazy?

THERAPIST: Not at all. If contact with your mother contaminates you, then it makes sense that you would avoid your sister. It seems quite logical, given your basic premise.

PATIENT: You're the first one who really understands me.

The patient felt reassured that her problem was familiar to the therapist. By being told that her behavior followed logical rules, she also felt she was not "crazy." Once information about the fears and avoidance patterns has been collected, the rationale for avoidance and compulsive behavior should be presented.

THERAPIST: You see, every time you touch something that you think came into direct or indirect contact with your mother, you feel contaminated and extremely uncomfortable. You've learned that you can gain at least some degree of comfort by washing or cleaning. So, by now, you believe that the only manner in which you can become comfortable is by washing repeatedly. Judging by your past experience, this belief is quite reasonable. And, in fact, everytime you wash and feel better, you strengthen this belief as well as your habit of washing excessively.

When patients are informed of the exposure treatment, they invariably become quite anxious. It is important that the therapist express an attitude of warmth and empathy to counteract the fact that he or she proposes a harsh and emotionally painful therapy.

THERAPIST: I know how afraid you must be at the thought of spending two hours in the supermarket alone since this is exactly what you've been avoiding all these years. If I knew of a treatment that could help you with your fears with less suffering, I would use it. But, unfortunately, exposing you to feared situations is the most effective way to help you get over your fears. I'll try to make it as easy as possible for you by supporting you when you're anxious and by being available when you need to talk to me. But I will not help you continue to avoid.

Focusing on the symptoms in the first sessions, conveying an understanding of the dynamics of the symptoms, and having a warm, empathic attitude toward the patient facilitate a good therapeutic relationship.

Resistance and Noncompliance

As was noted above, establishing and adhering to a clear verbal contract between the patient and therapist reduces resistance and noncompliance considerably. Patients who doubt their ability to adhere to the treatment program are encouraged to contact former patients who have recently completed treatment. Such contact increases the patients' expectancy for a positive outcome and their belief in their ability to comply with the demands.

Despite a clear contract, however, some patients attempt to strike bargains with the therapist to delay or omit difficult tasks. The therapist may first remind them of the rationale for completing the task, and of their agreement not to argue about preplanned exposures. For some patients, modelling by the therapist helps overcome initial resistance. The following dialogue with a patient who feared contracting venereal disease from public toilets was illustrative of this point.

PATIENT: I don't want to touch the toilet seat! You are asking me to do things that other people don't do!

THERAPIST: If I thought this were dangerous, I wouldn't ask you to do it.

PATIENT: You wouldn't touch it, would you?

THERAPIST: Oh yes, I would. I've done this many times. Here, let me show you. (*Therapist rubs both hands over the seat and rubs his face, hair, and clothing.*) You see, this is what I want you to do now. Go ahead.

PATIENT: Okay, but it's still disgusting.

THERAPIST: Some people feel it's disgusting and that's okay. But it's not okay to be afraid to touch the toilet seat.

In the face of resistance and noncompliance, the therapist should insist that the patient follow the agreed-upon treatment plan. However, it is important that he or she refrain from giving orders and arguing repeatedly that they be followed. Resistant patients should be reminded that the therapist is merely an expert who guides them in the application of procedures that have proven effective in ameliorating their type of disorder. Yet, it is the *patient's responsibility* to make use of the therapist's expertise. The following example illustrates how this attitude is conveyed to the patient.

THERAPIST: As I explained to you in the beginning, we do not know of any better way to reduce fear then repeatedly confronting situations one is afraid of for a long period of time. This requires some courage on your part and you may decide that you do not wish to exert the effort needed to expose yourself. At this point, you know what the options are and it is up to you to decide what you'd like to do. I'm sure you already know what will probably happen if you don't comply with the treatment program. If you feel that now is not the right time for you to go through this treatment, you might prefer to stop and contact us at a later point. Or you might prefer for now to work in therapy on issues other than your fears. You might want to think about this and let me know the next time we meet what you'd like to do.

Generalization and Maintenance of Therapeutic Gains

Common to most phobics and obsessive–compulsives is the multiplicity of the situations and objects they fear and avoid. We discussed earlier the importance of identifying the common denominator that underlies the phobic situations, to ensure that the treatment includes exposure to a representative sample of these situations. Exposure to a large variety of feared circumstances (some during treatment sessions and the remainder through homework assignments) is essential for achieving generalization. An example is provided by a 35-year-old woman who had a severe dog phobia that sharply restricted her daily activities. She avoided virtually all outdoor activities, including walking short distances in her neighborhood and using her car to travel one block to visit a friend for fear of encountering a dog. She refrained from visiting the homes of dog owners, played only indoor tennis, and so on. Treatment sessions involved gradual exposure to a large docile leashed dog until by the fifth session she could permit him to jump on her with little reservation. Homework assignments were comprised of approaching dogs owned by various friends and acquaintances to ensure the generalization of her reduced fear to other dogs. Similarly, an agoraphobic would be asked to visit a variety of supermarkets, theaters, and shopping centers; an obsessive–compulsive washer would be confronted with many different doorknobs, public bathrooms, and floors.

If several different sources of fear are detected in a patient, each should be treated separately in the manner described above. The treatment literature (e.g., Williams & Kleifeld, 1985) suggests that there is no reason to expect that the reduction in a fear of heights will extend to the reduction of a fear of dogs in a person who is phobic of both. Likewise, an obsessive–compulsive who manifests both washing and checking rituals will not transfer his or her gains from treatment for contamination fears to concerns about the safety of his or her home.

At the end of exposure treatment, the therapist should prescribe a self-exposure maintenance regimen to ensure periodic contact with previously avoided situations and to prevent a return to former phobic avoidance patterns. This is especially critical when the feared situations are not encountered in normal daily routines. For example, an obsessive–compulsive who feared contamination from death-related objects and situations had few occasions in her daily routine to come into contact with her main contaminants, such as funeral homes, cemeteries, and hearses. After treatment, she was instructed to visit cemeteries twice weekly for one month, once weekly for an additional two months, and once monthly for three months. A man who avoided visiting doctors for fear that the visits would produce severe anxiety leading to a heart attack was asked to schedule regular appointments with a variety of specialists within the 2-month period after therapy.

Termination of Treatment

In time-limited intensive treatment programs, the termination date is established at the outset of therapy. Many patients who enter such programs express concern in anticipation of the date of termination. Some fear that they will cease to make progress after the intensive stage terminates and therefore are doomed to retain forever whatever remains of their symptoms. Others are concerned that, left on their own without therapeutic support, they will be unable to retain their gains and will relapse into their initial state. Such concerns are addressed by reminding patients that they will continue to be in contact with their therapist throughout the maintenance period.

PATIENT: There are only three more days left before the program ends, and I was still anxious yesterday when I spread lime in my garden.

THERAPIST: Was it as bad as in the beginning of treatment?

PATIENT: No, of course not, but I still worry about it. I'm afraid that when I'm done with the program it will get worse.

THERAPIST: You've had these fears for so many years that one can hardly expect that they will disappear completely after only 3 weeks. But remember, I'll continue to see you weekly for a while, and that will give us an opportunity to deal with difficulties you may encounter.

Patients who perceive that their treatment goals have been achieved and their improvement has been stable during the maintenance period do not usually require special procedures for termination. Reassurance that, if necessary, the therapist will be available for consultation or booster sessions is usually sufficient to put such patients at ease. In fact, these individuals often propose termination themselves. There are, however, patients who develop a dependency on the therapist. They seem to assign a magic power to him or her and attribute the maintenance of their improvement to the continuation of therapy. For such patients, the interval between sessions can be gradually increased, initially by 2 weeks, then 1 month, and so on. A third category of patients consists of those who *actually* require continued contact to maintain their gains since, when left unmonitored, they revert to former avoidance and escape patterns. For these patients, once-a-month maintenance sessions may continue, sometimes for years.

Treatment Efficacy: Success and Failure

The evidence for the efficacy of exposure and cognitive procedures has been summarized earlier. In this section we shall describe the factors that are associated with treatment outcome.

Inadequate Treatment

Most critical to successful outcome is the appropriate implementation of treatment. As noted earlier, failure to apply both exposure and response prevention for obsessive-compulsives will lead to inferior results, as will brief exposures for agoraphobics. Intermittent sessions may also impede success, especially for agoraphobics and obsessive-compulsives. Premature termination of the exposure treatment, whether instigated by the therapist or by the patient, is likely to result in failure or relapse. Another evident reason for failure is noncompliance, which has been discussed in detail earlier. Clearly, if patients do not follow the treatment regimen, they undergo, in effect, an inadequate therapy trial.

Familial Patterns

With agoraphobics, complaints about partners and marital conflicts were found to be associated with negative outcome (Bland & Hallam, 1981; Emmelkamp & Van der Hout, 1983; Milton & Hafner, 1979). Typically, family members have experienced years of frustration with the patient's symptomatology. It is thus not surprising that some are impatient, expecting treatment to result in total symptom remission and being disappointed and angry when that doesn't happen. Conversely, some family members continue to protect the patient from formerly upsetting situations. Years of accomodation to the patient's peculiar requests have established habits that are hard to break. For example, the husband who was accustomed to accompanying his agoraphobic wife on all of her out-of-home activities may find it disconcerting to call home and find that she is out. Additionally, he may experience difficulty in handing over to his wife household activities that he has come to regard as his responsibility. The familial patterns above can offset progress during treatment and/or interfere with the maintenance of gains, and therefore may call for the application of family therapy. Conversely, a positive relationship with family members and flexible familial patterns seem to facilitate the necessary adjustments and thereby foster the maintenance of gains.

Functioning without Symptoms

Many obsessive-compulsives and agoraphobics, as well as some social phobics, have become nonfunctional as their symptomatology has increasingly dominated their everyday lives. Successful treatment often leaves a considerable void in their daily routine. Assistance in the development of new skills and the planning of both social and occupational activities should be the focus of follow-up therapy in these cases. A complicating factor is the patient's concern that the new ventures may fail, which often prevents him or her from acquiring the necessary skills or making needed overtures. Failure to attend to the rehabilitation needs of patients may lead to relapse.

Patient Characteristics

The search for patient variables associated with responsiveness to exposure treatment has not yielded much success. For agoraphobics, higher initial physiological arousal was found in patients who responded poorly to treatment (Stern & Marks, 1973), as was long duration of symptoms (Mathews et al., 1976) and negative expectations of outcome (Emmelkamp & Emmelkamp-Benner, 1975).

The duration of obsessive–compulsive symptoms, unlike agoraphobic symptoms, did not predict outcome. On the other hand, several authors have noted that the presence of severe depression hampers the effectiveness of treatment by exposure and response prevention (e.g., Boulougouris, 1977; Foa, Grayson, & Steketee, 1982). Studies employing pharmacological intervention provide further support for the proposition that depression impedes the effectiveness of behavioral treatment with obsessive-compulsives. In comparing the effects of clomipramine and placebo, Marks (1980) found that the drug effected improvement and facilitated the effects of behavioral treatment only in severely depressed patients. With agoraphobics, however, the presence of depression did not predict the response to treatment (Emmelkamp & Van der Hout, 1983).

Habituation of anxiety, both within and between sessions, has been observed during exposure treatment. Both types of habituation have been found to be related to successful outcome with obsessive-compulsives. Depressed patients habituate less than nondepressed ones. The former were also more anxious than the latter when confronted with feared situations (Foa, Steketee, Grayson, & Doppelt, 1983). Lack of habituation during treatment sessions was also associated with failure in agoraphobics (Emmelkamp & Van der Hout, 1983).

In summary, therapists should implement treatment in a manner that has been found likely to maximize its efficacy. With severely depressed obsessive-compulsives, efforts should be made to reduce depression before proceeding with a behavioral program. For patients who react to exposure with high levels of anxiety and do not show a gradual decline in discomfort over sessions, a more gradual approach may be called for. Proper attention should be given to familial relationships and their interaction with the effects of treatment. When indicated, interventions should be implemented to facilitate adjustment to the changes in intra- and interpersonal equilibrium that often follow improvement in the patient's symptomatology.

CONCLUSIONS

In this chapter we have described the use of exposure with phobics and obsessive-compulsives, and attempted to provide an explanation for its effectiveness. We have devoted considerably less space to the use of cognitive techniques with these disorders. Only a few studies have investigated the value of such methods with anxiety disorders; as we have pointed out, cognitive procedures have not produced as many positive results as exposure treatment has, and when added to the latter, have not led to much increase in its efficacy. The failure of cognitive procedures to generate change in symptomatology does not necessarily mean that they are intrinsically inappropriate for anxiety disorders. Rather, the available cognitive methods may not address the specific cognitive deficits of pho bics and obsessive–compulsives. If, as is suggested by Foa and Kozak (1985), anxiety-disordered individuals are impaired in the manner in which they process certain information, the application of procedures that correct these impairments should reduce symptomatology. Future research efforts should be directed at identifying specific "cognitive pathologies" and developing techniques that directly alter them.

ACKNOWLEDGMENT

The preparation of this chapter was supported by Grant No. 31634 from the National Institute of Mental Health awarded to Edna B. Foa.

REFERENCES

Agras, W. S. (1967). Transfer during systematic desensitization therapy. *Behaviour Research and Therapy, 5,* 193–199.

American Psychiatric Association (1980). *Diagnostic and statistical manual of mental disorders* (3rd ed., DSM-III). Washington, DC: Author.

Barlow, D. H., Leitenberg, H., Agras, W. S., & Wincze, J. P. (1969). The transfer gap in systematic desensitization: An analogue study. *Behaviour Research and Therapy, 7,* 191–196.

Beck, A. T. (1976). *Cognitive therapy and the emotional disorders.* New York: International Universities Press.

Beck, A. T., & Emery, G. (1979). *Cognitive therapy of anxiety and phobic disorders.* Philadelphia: Center for Cognitive Therapy.

Beck, A. T., Rush, A. J., Shaw, B. F., & Emery, G. (1979). *Cognitive therapy of depression.* New York: Guilford.

Beech, H. R., & Vaughan, M. (1978). *Behavioral treatment of obsessional states.* New York: Wiley.

Biran, M., & Wilson, G. T. (1981). Treatment of phobic disorders using cognitive and exposure methods: A self-efficacy analysis. *Journal of Consulting and Clinical Psychology, 49,* 886–899.

Bland, K., & Hallam, R. S. (1981). Relationship between response to graded exposure and marital satisfaction in agoraphobics. *Behaviour Research and Therapy, 19,* 335–338.

Borkovec, T. D., & Sides, J. (1979). The contribution of relaxation and expectance to fear reduction via graded imaginal exposure to feared stimuli. *Behaviour Research and Therapy, 17,* 529–540.

Boulougouris, J. C. (1977). Variables affecting the behavior modification of obsessive–compulsive patients treated by flooding. In J. C. Boulougouris & A. D. Rabavilas (Eds.), *The treatment of phobic and obsessive–compulsive disorders.* Oxford, England: Pergamon.

Butler, G., Cullington, A., Munby, M., Amies, P., & Gelder, M. (1984). Exposure and anxiety management in the treatment of social phobia. *Journal of Consulting and Clinical Psychology, 52,* 642–650.

Chambless, D. L., Foa, E. B., Groves, G. A., & Goldstein, A. J. (1979). Flooding with brevital in the treatment of agoraphobia: Countereffective? *Behaviour Research and Therapy, 17,* 243–251.

Chambless, D. L., Foa, E. B., Groves, G. A., & Goldstein, A. J. (1982). Exposure and communications training in the treatment of agoraphobia. *Behaviour Research and Therapy, 20,* 219–231.

Chambless, D. L., & Goldstein, A. J. (Eds.). (1982). *Agoraphobia: Multiple perspectives on theory and treatment.* New York: Wiley.

Cohen, D., Monteiro, M., & Marks, I. M. (1984). Two-year follow-up of agoraphobics after exposure and imipramine. *British Journal of Psychiatry, 144,* 276–281.

Cooper, J. E., Gelder, M. G., & Marks, I. M. (1965). Results of behaviour therapy in 77 psychiatric patients. *British Medical Journal, 1,* 1222–1225.

Dollard, J., & Miller, N. E. (1950). *Personality and psychotherapy: An analysis in terms of learning, thinking and culture.* New York: McGraw-Hill.

Ellis, A. (1970). *The essence of rational psychotherapy: A comprehensive approach to treatment.* New York: Institute for Rational Living.

Ellis, A. (1980). Rational–emotive therapy and cognitive–behavior therapy: Similarities and differences. *Cognitive Therapy and Research, 4,* 325–340.

Emmelkamp, P. M. G. (1982). *Phobic and obsessive–compulsive disorders: Theory, research, and practice.* New York: Plenum.

Emmelkamp, P. M. G., & Emmelkamp-Benner, A. (1975). Effects of historically portrayed modeling and group treatment on self-observation: A comparison with agoraphobics. *Behaviour Research and Therapy, 13,* 135–139.

Emmelkamp, P. M. G., & Kuipers, A. C. M. (1979). Agoraphobia: A follow-up study four years after treatment. *British Journal of Psychiatry, 134,* 352–355.

Emmelkamp, P. M. G., Kuipers, A. C. M., & Eggeraat, J. B. (1978). Cognitive modification versus prolonged exposure *in vivo:* A comparison with agoraphobics as subjects. *Behaviour Research and Therapy, 16,* 33–41.

Emmelkamp, P. M. G., & Kwee, K. G. (1977). Obsessional ruminations: A comparison between thought-stopping and prolonged exposure in imagination. *Behaviour Research and Therapy, 15,* 441–444.

Emmelkamp, P. M. G., & Mersch, P. P. (1982). Cognition and exposure *in vivo* in the treatment of agoraphobia: Short-term and delayed effects. *Cognitive Research and Therapy, 6,* 77–90.

Emmelkamp, P. M. G., Van der Helm, H., Van Zanten, B., & Plochg, I. (1980). Contributions of self-instructional training to the effectiveness of exposure *in vivo:* A comparison with obsessive–compulsive patients. *Behaviour Research and Therapy, 18,* 61–66.

Emmelkamp, P. M. G., & Van der Hout, A. (1983). Failures in treating agoraphobia. In E. B. Foa and P. M. G. Emmelkamp (Eds.), *Failures in behavior therapy.* New York: Wiley.

Emmelkamp, P., & Van Kraanen, J. (1977). Therapist-controlled exposure *in vivo* vs. self-controlled exposure *in vivo:* A comparison with obsessive–compulsive patients. *Behaviour Research and Therapy, 15,* 491–496.

Emmelkamp, P. M. G., & Wessels, H. (1975). Flooding in imagination vs. flooding *in vivo.* A comparison with agoraphobics. *Behaviour Research and Therapy, 13,* 7–16.

Eysenck, H. J. (1979). The conditioning model of neurosis. *The Behavioral and Brain Sciences, 2,* 155–199.

Foa, E. B., Grayson, J. B., & Steketee, G. S. (1982). Depression, habituation, and treatment outcome in obsessive–compulsives. In J. Boulougouris (Ed.), *Learning theory approaches to psychiatry*. New York: Wiley.

Foa, E. B., Grayson, J. B., Steketee, G., Doppelt, H. G., Turner, R. M., & Latimer, P. R. (1983). Success and failure in the behavioral treatment of obsessive compulsives. *Journal of Consulting and Clinical Psychology, 39*, 933–938.

Foa, E. B., & Kozak, M. J. (1985). Treatment of anxiety disorders: Implications for psychopathology. In A. H. Tuma & J. D. Maser (Eds.), *Anxiety and the anxiety disorders*. Hillsdale, NJ: Erlbaum.

Foa, E. B., Steketee, G., & Grayson, J. B. (1985). Imaginal and *in vivo* exposure: A comparison with obsessive compulsive checkers. *Behavior Therapy, 16*, 292–302.

Foa, E. B., Steketee, G., Grayson, J. B., & Doppelt, H. G. (1983). Treatment of obsessive–compulsives: When do we fail? In E. B. Foa & P. M. G. Emmelkamp (Eds.), *Failures in behavior therapy*. New York: Wiley.

Foa, E. B., Steketee, G., Grayson, J., Turner, R. M., & Latimer, P. R. (1984). Deliberate exposure and blocking of obsessive–compulsive rituals: Immediate and long term effects. *Behavior Therapy, 15*, 450–472.

Foa, E. B., Steketee, G., & Milby, J. B. (1980). Differential effects of exposure and response prevention in obsessive–compulsive washers. *Journal of Consulting and Clinical Psychology, 48*, 71–79.

Foa, E. B., Steketee, G., Turner, R. M., & Fischer, S. C. (1980). Effects of imaginal exposure to feared disasters in obsessive–compulsive checkers. *Behaviour Research and Therapy, 18*, 449–455.

Foa, E. B., Steketee, G., & Young, M. (1984). Agoraphobia: Phenomenological aspects, associated characteristics and theoretical considerations. *Clinical Psychology Review, 4*, 431–457.

Gelder, M. G., Bancroft, J. H., Gath, D. H., Johnston, B. W., Mathews, A. W., & Shaw, P. M. (1973). Specific and non-specific factors in behaviour therapy. *British Journal of Psychiatry, 123*, 445–462.

Gelder, M. G., Marks, I. M., & Wolfe, H. H. (1967). Desensitization and psychotherapy in the treatment of phobic states: A controlled enquiry. *British Journal of Psychiatry, 113*, 53–73.

Ghosh, A., Marks, I. M., & Carr, A. C. (1984). Controlled study of self-exposure treatment for phobics: Preliminary communication. *Journal of the Royal Society of Medicine, 77*, 483–487.

Hadley, S. W., & Strupp, H. H. (1976). Contemporary views of negative effects in psychotherapy: An integrated account. *Archives of General Psychiatry, 33*, 1291–1302.

Hodgson, R., & Rachman, S. (1972). The effects of contamination and washing in obsessional patients. *Behaviour Research and Therapy, 10*, 111–117.

Hornsveld, R. H. J., Kraaimaat, F. W., & Van Dam-Baggen, R. M. J. (1979). Anxiety discomfort and handwashing in obsessive–compulsive and psychiatric control patients. *Behaviour Research and Therapy, 17*, 223–228.

Hugdahl, K., Fredrikson, M., & Ohman, A. (1977). "Preparedness" and "arousability" as determinants of electrodermal conditioning. *Behaviour Research and Therapy, 15*, 345–353.

Jannoun, L., Munby, M., Catalan, J., & Gelder, M. (1980). A home-based treatment program for agoraphobia: Replication and controlled evaluation. *Behavior Therapy, 11*, 294–305.

Jansson, L., & Ost, L. (1982). Behavioral treatment for agoraphobia: An evaluative review. *Clinical Psychology Review, 2*, 311–336.

Lader, M. H. (1967). Palmer skin conductance measures in anxiety and phobic states. *Journal of Psychosomatic Research, 11*, 271–281.

Lang, P. J. (1979). A bio-informational theory of emotional imagery. *Psychophysiology, 6*, 495–511.

Lang, P. J., Melamed, B. G., & Hart, J. (1970). A psychophysiological analysis of fear modification using an automated desensitization procedure. *Journal of Abnormal Psychology, 76,* 220–234.

Ledwidge, B. (1978). Cognitive behavior modification: A step in the wrong direction? *Psychological Bulletin, 85,* 353–375.

Marks, I. M. (1978). Behavioral psychotherapy of adult neurosis. In S. L. Garfield & A. E. Bergin (Eds.), *Handbook of Psychotherapy and Behavior Change.* New York: Wiley.

Marks, I. M. (1980, March). *Pharmacological and behavioral treatment of obsessive–compulsive disorder.* Paper presented at the Annual Meeting of the American Psychopathological Association, Washington, D.C.

Marks, I. M., Boulougouris, J., & Marset, P. (1971). Flooding versus desensitization in the treatment of phobic patients. *British Journal of Psychiatry, 119,* 353–375.

Marks, I. M., & Gelder, M. G. (1965). A controlled retrospective study of behaviour therapy in phobic patients. *British Journal of Psychiatry, 111,* 571–573.

Marks, I. M., Gray, S., Cohen, D., Hill, R., Mawson, D., Ramm, E., & Stern, R. S. (1983). Imipramine and brief therapist-aided exposure in agoraphobics having self-exposure homework. *Archives of General Psychiatry, 40,* 153–162.

Marks, I. M., Hodgson, R., & Rachman, S. (1975). Treatment of chronic obsessive–compulsive neurosis by *in vivo* exposure: A two-year follow-up and issues in treatment. *British Journal of Psychiatry, 197,* 349–364.

Mathews, A. M. (1978). Fear-reduction research and clinical phobias. *Psychological Bulletin, 85,* 390–404.

Mathews, A. M., Gelder, M. G., & Johnston, D. W. (1981). *Agoraphobia: Nature and Treatment.* New York: Guilford.

Mathews, A. M., Johnston, D. W., Lancashire, M., Munby, D., Shaw, P. M., & Gelder, M. G. (1976). Imaginal flooding and exposure to real phobic situations: Treatment outcome with agoraphobic patients. *British Journal of Psychiatry, 129,* 362–371.

Mathews, A. M., Johnston, D. W., Shaw, P. M., & Gelder, M. G. (1973). Process variables and the prediction of outcome in behavior therapy. *British Journal of Psychiatry, 123,* 445–462.

McNally, R. J., & Steketee, G. (1985). The etiology and maintenance of severe animal phobias. *Behaviour Research and Therapy, 23,* 431–436.

Meichenbaum, D. (1977). *Cognitive-Behavior Modification: An Integrative Approach.* New York: Plenum.

Meyer, V. (1966). Modification of expectancies in cases with obsessional rituals. *Behaviour Research and Therapy, 4,* 273–280.

Milton, F., & Hafner, J. (1979). The outcome of behavior therapy for agoraphobia in relation to marital adjustment. *Archives of General Psychiatry, 36,* 807–811.

Mowrer, O. H. (1939). A stimulus–response analysis of anxiety and its role as a reinforcing agent. *Psychological Review, 46,* 553–565.

Mowrer, O. H. (1960). *Learning theory and behavior.* New York: Wiley.

Munby, M., & Johnston, D. W. (1980). Agoraphobia: Long term follow-up of behavioral treatment. *British Journal of Psychiatry, 137,* 418–427.

Murray, E. J., & Foote, F. (1979). The origins of fear of snakes. *Behaviour Research and Therapy, 17,* 489–493.

Nisbett, R. E., & Wilson, T. P. (1977). Telling more than we know: Verbal reports on mental processes. *Psychological Review, 84,* 231–279.

Ost, L. G., & Hugdahl, K. (1981). Acquisition of phobias and anxiety response patterns in clinical patients. *Behaviour Research and Therapy, 19,* 439–447.

Rabavilas, A. D., Boulougouris, J. C., & Perissaki, C. (1979). Therapist qualities related to outcome with exposure *in vivo* in neurotic patients. *Journal of Behavior Therapy and Experimental Psychiatry, 10,* 293–299.

Rabavilas, A. D., Boulougouris, J. C., & Stefanis, C. (1976). Duration of flooding sessions in the treatment of obsessive-compulsive patients. *Behaviour Research and Therapy, 14,* 349–355.

Rachman, S. (1971). Obsessional ruminations. *Behaviour Research and Therapy, 9,* 229–235.

Rachman, S. J., & Wilson, G. T. (1980). *The effects of psychological therapy.* Oxford, England: Pergamon.

Rimm, D. C., Janda, L. H., Lancaster, D. W., Nahl, M., & Dittman, K. (1977). An exploratory investigation of the origin and maintenance of phobias. *Behaviour Research and Therapy, 15,* 231–238.

Roper, G., & Rachman, S. (1976). Obsessional-compulsive checking: Experimental replication and development. *Behaviour Research and Therapy, 14,* 25–32.

Roper, G., Rachman, S., & Hodgson, R. (1973). An experiment on obsessional checking. *Behaviour Research and Therapy, 11,* 271–277.

Shaw, P. (1979). A comparison of three behaviour therapies in the treatment of social phobia. *British Journal of Psychiatry, 134,* 620–623.

Stampfl, T. G., & Levis, D. J. (1967). Essentials of implosive therapy: A learning-theory-based psychodynamic behavioral therapy. *Journal of Abnormal Psychology, 72,* 496–503.

Stern, R. S. (1978). Obsessive thoughts: The problem of therapy. *British Journal of Psychiatry, 132,* 200–205.

Stern, R. S., & Marks, I. M. (1973). Brief and prolonged flooding: A comparison in agoraphobic patients. *Archives of General Psychiatry, 28,* 270–276.

Teasdale, Y. D. (1974). Learning models of obsessional-compulsive disorder. In H. R. Beech (Ed.), *Obsessional states.* London: Methuen.

Watson, J. P., Gaind, R., & Marks, I. M. (1972). Physiological habituation to continuous phobic stimulation. *Behaviour Research and Therapy, 10,* 269–278.

Watts, F. N. (1979). Habituation model of systematic desensitization. *Psychological Bulletin, 86,* 627–637.

Williams, S. L., Dooseman, G., & Kleifield, E. (1984). Comparative effectiveness of guided mastery and exposure treatments for intractable phobias. *Journal of Consulting and Clinical Psychology, 52,* 505–518.

Williams, S. L., & Kleifield, E. (1985). Transfer of behavioral change from treated to untreated phobias in multiply phobic clients. *Behavior Modification, 9,* 22–31.

Williams, S. L., & Rappoport, A. (1983). Cognitive treatment in the natural environment for agoraphobics. *Behavior Therapy, 14,* 299–313.

Williams, S. L., Turner, S. M., & Peer, D. F. (1985). Guided mastery and performance desensitization treatments for severe agoraphobia. *Journal of Consulting and Clinical Psychology, 53,* 237–247.

Wolpe, J. (1958). *Psychotherapy by reciprocal inhibition.* Stanford, CA: Stanford University Press.

Yerkes, R. M., & Dodson, J. D. (1908). The relation of strength of stimulus to rapidity of habit-formation. *Journal of Comparative Neurology, 18,* 459–482.

CHAPTER 4

Cognitive Therapy for Depression: Unexplicated Schemata and Scripts

Joan Piasecki
University of Colorado, Boulder

Steven D. Hollon
Vanderbilt University

The last 2 decades have seen a major burst of interest in cognitive and cognitive-behavioral therapies for the emotional disorders (see Hollon & Beck, 1986, for a review). Fueled by an interest in the role of beliefs, attitudes, and information processes in the etiology and maintenance of the major psychopathological disorders, these approaches have generally adopted a model of change that holds that modifying or compensating for these cognitive processes can produce major alterations in the disorder of interest (Mahoney, 1977).

While there are a variety of cognitive and cognitive-behavioral interventions, we have had our predominant experience with Beck's cognitive therapy (Beck, 1964, 1967, 1970; Beck, Rush, Shaw, & Emery, 1979). In particular, our experience has been concentrated in the treatment of depression—the primary, but certainly not the only, disorder to which cognitive therapy has been applied (see, for example, Beck, 1976; Beck & Emery, 1985; Emery, Hollon, & Bedrosian, 1981; or Freeman, 1983, for extensions to other problem areas).

Cognitive therapy for depression has been well supported in a series of controlled clinical trials (Beck, Hollon, Young, Bedrosian, & Budenz, 1985; Blackburn, Bishop, Glen, Whalley, & Christie, 1981; Covi, Lipman, Roth, Pattison, Smith, & Lasseter, in press; Hollon, DeRubeis, Evans, Tuason, Wiemer, & Garvey, 1986; Murphy, Simons, Wetzel, & Lustman, 1984; Rush, Beck, Kovacs, & Hollon, 1977; Teasdale, Fennell, Hibbert, & Amies, 1984) and may provide prophylaxis against symptomatic recurrence or relapse (Blackburn, Eunson, & Bishop, in press; Evans, Hollon, DeRubeis, Piasecki, Tuason, & Garvey, 1986; Kovacs, Rush, Beck, & Hollon, 1981). A detailed treatment manual is available as a training resource (Beck et al., 1979), as are instruments for ascertaining the fidelity

121

(DeRubeis, Hollon, Evans, & Bemis, 1982; Evans, Hollon, DeRubeis, Auerbach, Tuason, & Wiemer, 1983; Hollon, Evans, Elkin, & Lowery, 1984) and competence (Young, 1980) of therapy execution.

Despite this rather rich array of clinical training materials, the actual practice of cognitive therapy involves a variety of strategies, conceptualizations, and procedures that are rarely explicated outside of the idiosyncratic supervision session (e.g., Hollon, 1984). In the language of social cognitive processes (Neisser, 1976; Nisbett & Ross, 1980), we would posit that cognitive therapists possess only partially articulated schemata concerning the nature of depression and people in general, but utilize knowledge-behavior sequences, or scripts (Abelson, 1981), in directing efforts to produce change. In conjunction with our research and teaching over the last decade, we have provided clinical workshops, didactic training, and individual and group supervision for scores of therapists, ranging from neophytes to experienced clinicians. We have particularly emphasized the use of audiotaped or videotaped sessions in the supervision process, augmented by the role playing of specific maneuvers and discussions of relevant conceptualizations. In this chapter, we attempt to articulate some of the conceptualizations that have guided those efforts and the techniques and strategies that have sprung from those conceptualizations. In short, we shall attempt to make explicit the schemata and scripts that have guided our clinical practice of cognitive therapy for depression.

COGNITIVE THEORY OF DEPRESSION

Cognitive therapy for depression is based upon a cognitive model which suggests that the thinking of depressed individuals is characteristically negative and dysfunctional (Beck, 1963, 1967). Beck has described the operation of a negative cognitive triad; negative views of the self, the world, and the future, as representative of thought content in depression. Others, such as Abramson, Seligman, and Teasdale (1978), have stressed the role of depressotypic causal attributions in the etiology of depression. Further, Beck has argued that the information processing of depressed individuals can be characterized as systematically biased in a negative direction. Examples include *selective abstraction*, the tendency to attend only to the one negative instance in an array of positive ones; *arbitrary inference*, drawing a negative inference in the absence of any negative input; *magnification*, perceiving a minor negative event to be more important than it actually is; and *all-or-none thinking*, the tendency to see events only in absolutes, typically absolute negatives. It has been well established that nondepressed individuals also process information in a nonnormative fashion, utilizing certain heuristics that yield systematically positive biases (cf. Kahneman, Slovic, & Tversky, 1982; Nisbett & Ross, 1980). Evans and Hollon (in press) have suggested that depressed and nondepressed individuals may differ more in the nature of the initial content of their schemata (negative vs. positive), than in the operation of nonnormative biasing heuristics.

Cognitive models of depression hold that the negative affect and dysfunctional behavioral passivity typical of depression are the products of the negative cognitive content and systematic bias in information processing. This model is typically presented as a diathesis-stress model, in which predisposing attitudes and inactive schemata (the diathesis) are triggered by distressing life events. Other factors such as biochemical abnormalities or behavioral skills deficits are also seen as potentially contributory causal mechanisms in some individuals, but, by and large, major emphasis is placed upon the role of negative beliefs and dysfunctional information processing in the etiology and maintenance of depression.

COGNITIVE THEORY OF THERAPY

A cognitive theory of change would posit that modification of the negative beliefs and/or dysfunctional information processing noted above should result in an amelioration of the negative affect and behavioral passivity common to depression (Beck, 1967, 1970). These cognitive changes can be brought about in a variety of ways; via reasoning and persuasion, as in rational–emotive therapy (RET) (Ellis, 1962); via self-statement modification approaches based largely on repetition, as in self-instructional training (Meichenbaum, 1977); or via empirical hypothesis testing (Hollon & Beck, 1979). While each of these methods is utilized in cognitive therapy, there is a particular emphasis on the last. In essence, the therapist is always alert to opportunities to use the client's own behaviors to test that client's beliefs. Thus, a change in beliefs depends not so much on therapist credibility or persuasiveness as on the consequences of that client's own behaviors. The working assumption is that an actual demonstration of a belief's invalidity will go further to change a belief than will a discussion with the therapist.

PROCEDURES OF COGNITIVE THERAPY:
STRATEGIES AND SEQUENCES

The sequence of cognitive therapy can be divided into rough stages, including (1) providing a *rationale*, (2) training in *self-monitoring*, (3) *behavioral activation strategies*, (4) training in *identifying cognitions*, (5) *evaluating beliefs*, (6) exploring *underlying assumptions*, and (7) preparing for *termination and relapse prevention*. We will discuss each in turn. Before proceding with that discussion, however, there are several points that need to be made. First, it is important to note that these sequential elements are not discreet and self-contained, either temporally or conceptually. It is common practice to include elements of several in any given session. For example, while one of the main goals of the initial session may be to provide a rationale for a cognitive approach to therapy, the therapist will also typically want to provide some training in basic self-monitoring, often combining that with an instance of behavioral activation (presented as an experiment), and frequently tying the whole package to the identification and evaluation of one or more beliefs. Similarly, the therapist will typically want to begin talking about termination in the initial session. Given that cognitive therapy is frequently, but not invariably (Hollon, 1984), practiced as a short-term therapy, the issue of termination will arise rapidly. It can either be handled actively and early, or ignored and avoided. We clearly prefer the former. As we shall discuss in the section on termination and relapse prevention, the issue itself can be turned to therapeutic advantage by using it to motivate an accelerated pace within the therapy sessions.

The second major point is that cognitive therapy is, we believe, most effective in the long run when practiced as a skills-training approach. Our ultimate goal is always to try to make ourselves obsolete as therapists by virtue of training the client to do our job. This gives therapy a heavily pedagogical flavor. Rather than being an enterprise in which one person (the therapist) "operates" on another (the client), our goal is to teach the client how to be his or her own cognitive therapist. The relevance of this stance for the sequence of therapy is that specific topics unfold as the main unit to be taught across the given sessions. The therapist may use any or all of the various procedures at any point in therapy, but the order in which topics are presented as the main topic for didactic discussion corresponds roughly to the order listed above.

Finally, it should be noted that although there is no antipathy between either the theory or practice of cognitive therapy and formal clinical assessment, there is also no particular tie. Careful diagnostic evaluation is more nearly the rule than the exception, but there currently exists no methodologically sound evaluation of cognitive therapy in populations other than primary unipolar depressives. We would be reluctant to assume that cognitive therapy would be a sufficient intervention in the bipolar affective disorders or the schizophrenias, and would invariably want to have such clients evaluated with regard to medications. Its utility for other nonpsychotic disorders remains to be evaluated. What is clear is that there is little emphasis placed on nondiagnostic assessment; elaborate life history or anamnestic interviews are rarely pursued. Nor is there much emphasis placed on determining the underlying nature of the client's personal intrapsychic or interpersonal dynamics. The operating assumption is that any such relevant information will come to light in the process of attempting to produce symptomatic change, rather than being a necessary precursor to such efforts. It is unusual to spend more than one session deciding to do cognitive therapy or preparing to begin. In many instances in actual clinical practice, intervention may be initiated at the first contact between client and therapist.

Providing a Rationale

The first stage in cognitive therapy is to present a cognitive model of depression and a cognitive theory of change and to provide the client with an understanding of how the therapy will proceed. We typically like to provide the client with a copy of a small pamphlet called "*Coping with Depression*" (Beck & Greenberg, 1974) at the earliest possible time, preferably prior to the first therapy session. The pamphlet, which describes depression, presents a cognitive model, and previews the major elements of cognitive therapy, can serve as a useful point of departure for the initial session.

It is always important to be aware of the client's understanding of his or her distress and his or her expectations for therapy. By providing the pamphlet and directing the discussion to its contents in the opening session, it is frequently possible to elicit the client's own idiosyncratic understanding of his or her problems and expectations regarding therapy.

Several problems can arise that can be turned to therapeutic advantage. For example, many clients may simply not read the pamphlet. Some may feel overwhelmed and put upon, others simply may not allot sufficient time and begin to feel guilty, while still others may have the expectation that it is the therapist's job to do therapy and not theirs to do "homework." Whatever the difficulty, it provides an opportunity for discussion, education, and problem solving.

We typically like to draw the client out about his or her experience of depression and his or her understanding as to why he or she is currently depressed. Typically, the client will discuss perceived inadequacies or overwhelming life events, material consistent with Beck's cognitive triad. The information uncovered in this process can then be used to illustrate a cognitive theory of depression, typically presented in a A-B-C framework in which the beliefs at point B are seen to mediate the consequences (affects or behavior) at point C in response to a given situation or circumstance at point A. By presenting this model in the context of the client's own experience, the therapist can establish its immediate relevance.

We have found it useful to then provide an additional illustration of the cognitive model by asking the client to imagine what his or her affect or behavior (point C) would have been in response to the antecedent situation (point A) had he or she known that a different evaluation or belief than the one he or she initially experienced were true (point B). For example, in the course of presenting her understanding of why she was depressed, one client revealed that she felt guilty about having divorced her paraplegic husband and uncomfortable around her grown children, leading her to avoid contact with them, because she was convinced that they shared her view that she had "quit" on the marriage. While the therapist did not have all of the relevant facts pertaining to the situation, she asked the client to simply imagine what her affect would be if she were able to reach the conclusion that her initiation of divorce proceedings had been justified by the husband's postillness behavior change (she would feel less guilt) and what her actions would be toward her children if she were to learn that she was wrong in her estimation of their evaluations of her (she would initiate greater contact). At this point, the therapist was not seeking to detect errors in the client's thinking, merely to demonstrate that mood and behavior are frequently tied to that thinking. Further, this process illustrated that if such errors did exist and if they could be corrected, then her affect should become less depressed and her behavior more adaptive.

We try to avoid presenting cognitive theory as a proven fact (it is not; see, for example Coyne & Gotlib, 1983). Similarly, we try not to make claims for the effectiveness of cognitive therapy that cannot be substantiated. Clients frequently want to know if they can be helped by the approach (fearful, of course, that they cannot). Our typical reply is that we don't know what the specific outcome will be for them (which we don't), but that about three persons in four usually do benefit. What we can't guarantee is that the specific approach will work for the specific client, and we tell them so. We can promise a clear way of determining early in treatment if the therapy is working, and our assistance in either changing the nature of the therapy and/or the therapist if the present therapy does not provide rapid relief. (Our experience has been that for unipolar depression, 90% of the response is typically obtained within the first 6 weeks; Hollon *et al.*, 1985).

Frequently, the client has a long list of personal failures and negative life experiences to recount, all suggesting that the problem is not his or her beliefs, but in his or her actual limitations and/or life experiences. While we would not want to overlook the possible existence of skill deficiencies or real life problems, we typically find it useful to educate the client about the nature of self-fulfilling prophecies (Darley & Fazio, 1980). In brief, negative beliefs and expectations can lead the individual to act in a less than fully adaptive fashion, producing exactly the kind of negative outcomes later cited as proof of personal incompetence or the barrenness of one's own surrounding environment. For example, one client who had been out of work for 3 years expressed the belief that he was incompetent and unemployable and cited his experience over the preceding years as evidence. On closer examination, it turned out that he had spent his first several months looking for employment in only the specific area for which he had been trained (teaching art in a small liberal arts college) and in which few jobs existed, and the last 2½ years not actively seeking suitable employment. He had become so sure that he could not succeed that he had stopped engaging in the appropriate behaviors, and was now interpreting his continued lack of success as evidence supporting his beliefs.

In most cases, the client's private formulation as to the cause of his or her distress falls into one of two major categories, the first being the more prevalent. Most clients attribute their distress to some major, trait-like failing in themselves; that is, they appear to have an active, depressotypic negative self-schema (Markus, 1977). In a smaller percentage of cases, the client's view of self may not be so negative, but his or her view of the world is quite bleak. These individuals are often quite angry and resentful. This distinction may correspond to Arieti's classic differentiation of "self-blaming" from "claiming" depressions (1959). In either case, the client's expectations for securing the kinds of things from life that would be satisfying and fulfilling are quite negative. Our belief is that the therapist should, in the initial sessions, offer an alternative conceptualization of how the client has reached the point of needing therapy, which makes as much sense as the "personal flaw" or the "unfriendly world" hypothesis. This alternative conceptualization would typically stress the remedial nature of the difficulties by emphasizing the role of malleable states (e.g., that the client has simply selected the wrong strategies, a problem that can be rectified by experience and corrective feedback) over permanent traits and attributes, thus permitting a broader, more hopeful perspective. This reconceptualization is not presented as a fact, but merely as a hypothesis. Such a conditional presentation is predicated on: (1) the fact that we really don't know if it is accurate, since some clients may be truly too incompetent or unable to do what they want; and (2) our desire to start the client thinking in terms of multiple models to be evaluated, rather than in terms of a single model to be accepted as reality.

The provision of an alternative model is, we believe, an underrecognized aspect of cognitive therapy. Ross (1977) has suggested that there are at least three ways of changing existing beliefs: (1) via explicit evidentiary-based disconfirmation of existing beliefs; (2) by providing an alternative reconceptualization of existing evidence; and (3) by providing insight into the aberrant processes that led to a belief. All three, and especially the first, are used throughout cognitive therapy, but the provision of an explicit alternative conceptualization early in therapy can greatly facilitate organizing the process for the client as therapy proceeds.

It is often important to be clear as to what cognitive therapy is not (or should not be allowed to become). Frequently, clients perceive (and neophyte therapists presume) that what is being suggested is that the client think *positively*. The goal of cognitive therapy is to have the client think accurately, regardless of the outcome. The covert implication is that greater accuracy will offset existing negative biases. The goal is not to help clients feel better temporarily by believing something that may not be true (e.g., "Every day, in every way, I am getting better and better"), rather, the goal is to assist them in learning how to engage more powerfully in reality testing, relying increasingly on controlled empiricism rather than passive supposition, and how to deal with the actual obstacles that are uncovered in a more effective way.

Similarly, it is important to stress that, with only a few exceptions, it is not what a client *thinks* (in the narrow sense of what passes through the oonoorium), but what he or she *believes* that is determinative of what he or she feels and does, if a cognitive model can be said to apply. Thus, simply repeating some form of cognitive "catechism," without having some reason to actually believe those "positive" self-statements, is seen as being a shallow approach to a change of belief(s).

Finally, it is presumed that existing beliefs have a history and a rationale of their own, and that change requires more than a simple act of faith. The presumption is made that the client has probably followed some semblance of reason and experience to arrive at a belief, and that those same processes will doubtless need to be invoked to change that belief. For example, we recently observed a neophyte cognitive therapist working with a client who held unrealistically high performance standards in her job as the manager of a fast-food restaurant. After establishing with the client that these standards existed and were rigorous, the therapist simply exhorted the client to "tell yourself that it's alright not to be perfect, then you'll feel better." Our preference would have been for the therapist to have asked the client what she expected to happen if she could, indeed, meet her own standards, what she expected it would cost her if she did not, or worse, did not even try to meet those standards, and then to have experimented with various levels of behavioral "perfection" to observe what the actual consequences were. Simple exhortations, repetitions, or motivationally based appeals ("If you just think this way you will feel better") are rarely sufficient to change beliefs.

Training in Self-Monitoring

We typically like to introduce training in systematic self-monitoring in the first therapy session. The interested reader can consult any of the standard cognitive-behavioral manuals for a more thorough discussion of the various methods and procedures of self-monitoring (e.g., Beck *et al.*, 1979; Hollon & Beck, 1979). For our present purpose, we will simply note that we like to begin by having the client self-monitor phenomena that are readily attended to and most relevant to the client's distress, (e.g., affects, events, and/or behaviors), saving cognitive self-monitoring for later in therapy.

A typical first homework assignment might be to have the client record his or her mood on an hourly basis between sessions, noting briefly major activities engaged in or the situations experienced in those intervals. We have learned to begin such monitoring in the actual session by having the client record retrospectively the affects or events experienced for the several hours prior to treatment. This insures that the client knows precisely what he or she is being asked to do and how to do it. This can prove invaluable if, as often happens, some type of problem arises in completing the assignment. Both therapist and client have seen the client engage in the specific behavior required and both know that it is in the client's behavioral repertoire. In practice, we typically start by recording the client's first response or two ourselves, then politely pass the paper and pen to the client with the request that they continue the recording themselves. We also often invite the client to imagine what kinds of problems might arise as he or she tries to continue such recording between sessions.

Our rationale for the self-monitoring, which we try to make explicit for the client, is that we have learned not to try to rely on memory in our search for clues to the factors controlling the client's moods and behaviors. If cognitive biases exist, they will influence recall even more strongly than immediate experience. Furthermore, the molecular self-monitoring may provide clues to the key processes controlling the client's moods that would have escaped recognition and/or recall. Thus, self-monitoring is presented both as a particularly careful means of inquiry and as a source of data for testing the applicability of the cognitive model to the particular client.

As therapists, we explicitly take on the role of detective, and invite the client to join us in the sleuthing process. The self-monitoring is then presented as an exercise in evidence gathering, often begun before we even know precisely what theories we will ultimately be testing. It is an exercise requiring only enthusiasm in its execution, rather than certainty in its outcome. In this fashion, we can often involve the frequently pessimistic client in a fairly concrete activity that is relatively simple to perform, yet an activity with potentially important implications that can only be guessed at until its completion. This stance usually helps mobilize the client to gather "facts" for subsequent hypothesis testing, committing them behaviorally to the process even before we can realistically hope to shake their belief in their typically negative self- and/or world view. In this way, we are launching the client in the process of self-investigation, even in the face of pessimistic and negativistic beliefs that would otherwise block movement.

It is important to remember to review homework assigned earlier in the following session. In our experience, the leading cause of patient noncompliance is therapist inattention to what clients have already been assigned (we are pleased if we get about a 50% return rate on activities assigned with depressed patients, and that only if we touch all the bases noted). We usually like to ask the client to extract what he or she has learned from the exercise, in an effort to ensure that the client is thinking about the material that he or she did not cover. We then ask the client to "walk us through" the record, providing details as they go. This frees up the therapist to look for connections or patterns in the material that might not otherwise be noticed. Such patterns or themes can then become the basis of subsequent hypotheses to test.

Behavioral Activation

Despite its name, cognitive therapy is, in essence, an integrated combination of cognitive and behavioral procedures. Extensive use is made of various behavioral activation strategies, particularly in the early sessions, but always in the context of explicit hypothesis testing. For example, it might prove useful to encourage a client unable to initiate a complex task consisting of many components to break that task into several smaller, more manageable parts and to concentrate on completing only the initial component before moving on to the next. This procedure, called "chunking," is a strategy common to many behavioral interventions. In cognitive therapy, however, it is not presented solely as a strategy to facilitate reaching a goal, but more fundamentally as a way of testing whether or not tasks can be more successfully executed with a more adaptive plan. Thus, the utilization of a behavioral activation strategy is presented in such a fashion that the strategy itself becomes the manipulation in an experiment designed to test the belief that "I can't accomplish important things." Success via "chunking" (or other behavioral activation strategies) not only meets the immediate performance goal, but also disconfirms a specific expectation in a manner that points to the validity of our earlier reconceptualization of the client's situation; namely, that the client has the capacity to be effective if only he or she selects more effective performance strategies. Even very concrete behavioral routines can, if presented in this context, facilitate the shift from a depressotypic, trait-like, and "personal failing" schema to one in which causal weight is ascribed to the behaviors selected, not to some trait in the person.

There are numerous behavioral activation strategies that could be discussed. The interested reader is again directed to the extant treatment manuals (e.g., Beck et al., 1979; Hollon & Beck, 1979). The key point is that behavioral components play a vital role in the execution of cognitive therapy, but not as separate and discrete strategies. Rather, they often form the primary method for testing the beliefs held by the client in the service of promoting generalized change in the client's larger cognitive network. In this manner, it is usually possible to increase the likelihood that the client will comply with the request. Oftentimes, pessimistic or negativistic clients will engage in a behavioral task, presented as a test between competing models, simply to prove to the therapist that the alternative, less pessimistic model is in error. Furthermore, behavioral activation increases the impact of the outcome in terms of generalization to other times and situations by virtue of its facilitating belief change.

Identifying Cognitions

Clients frequently have trouble gaining access to their own beliefs in a given situation. In some instances, this is probably just a reflection of lack of practice in introspection, while in other instances it appears that the operative meanings are simply not passing through the "stream-of-consciousness." We usually begin training in cognitive self-assessment in the first session with the introduction of the *A-B-C* model and the concept of automatic thoughts, but may not really emphasize this material (in the sense of making it the major topic for discussion) until several sessions into therapy.

The notion of automatic thoughts is a critical concept in cognitive therapy. Automatic thoughts are defined as seemingly reflexive cognitions occurring in various situations. They are typically linked to affect (i.e., they typically make sense given the client's affective experience) and they often seem to arise unbidden. Frequently, the client experiences these thoughts as occurring in a "back-channel" of the stream-of-consciousness. For example, the client may be sitting in the initial session trying to focus on the therapist's discussion of the nature of cognitive-behavioral therapy, but be experiencing nagging doubts about whether he or she can really benefit from the approach. The assumption is that such automatic thoughts are typically, but not invariably, governed by the processes controlling automatic, nonvolitional parallel thinking, in Schiffrin and Schneider's classic distinction (Schneider & Shiffrin, 1977; Shiffrin & Schneider, 1977), rather than sequential deliberate trains of thought.

We attempt to facilitate the identification of these automatic thoughts in a variety of ways, such as by discussing their nature, by providing analogies (e.g., few of us need to consciously self-instruct while driving a manual transmission car, although many of us did when first learning), and by stopping the session at the advent of any abrupt shift in mood or demeanor on the part of the client to inquire about whatever was just passing through the client's stream-of-consciousness. Similarly, the process of having the client reconstruct his or her self-monitoring records can serve as a useful point of departure for inquiring about automatic thoughts, as can an imaginal, role-play, or *in vivo* performance acts.

We have sometimes found that verbalizing our own automatic thoughts can both facilitate recognition of the phenomenon and model appropriate self-disclosure. For example, divulging that even while attending to the flow of the session, we, as the therapist, sometimes catch ourselves wondering if we are being coherent, looking foolish, or can actually help, both demonstrates what we mean and communicates an openness that transcends concerns about self-presentation.

It is important not to insist that thoughts precede emotions, since the client will often experience the temporal sequence in precisely the reverse order (see Zajonc, 1980, for the argument that such a temporal ordering obviates the cognitive model). We would not be surprised if the processes resulting in a thought passing through the sensorium took longer to be recounted than the processes resulting in the experience of affective change. All the cognitive model would claim is that some type of information processing is going on that leads to both phenomena and that is, itself, subject to modification on the basis of subsequent experience.

Similarly, it is also important not to insist that the client always experience one or more automatic thoughts in the context of any abrupt affective change. In many instances, such does not appear to be the case. It is important in such cases to inquire about the meaning of the context to the client and what expectations they can generate regarding that situation, regardless of whether or not those meanings or situations were recognizably present in the cognitive sensorium during the affective shift. Too often, clients and neophyte therapists adopt a shallow view of the cognitive model, assuming that it is the actual occurrence of a discrete event, the occurrence of a particular thought in the stream-of-consciousness," rather than the ascription of meaning, that is linked to affect and behavior.

Evaluating Beliefs

We essentially divide the process of evaluating beliefs into three main steps: (1) exploring their meaning; (2) evaluating their validity in a rational fashion, using only the evidence currently available; and (3) testing their validity in a prospective, empirical fashion. We discuss each process in turn.

Exploring Meaning

There are two questions that should be virtually automatic for a cognitive therapist. The first is "Can you give me an example?" and the second, "What does that mean to you?" The former can be useful at any point in therapy, particularly when trying to make sure that we know precisely what phenomena the client has in mind. The latter is essential to the process of exploring the meaning system surrounding a specific automatic thought.

Labeled the "downward arrow" technique by Burns (1980), this process is one of eliciting from the client the idiosyncratic connotations in which a given thought or belief is embedded. For example, if a client reported an abrupt shift in affect associated with the thought "I'm a failure in my job," it is important to know whether that perceived failure is seen as indicating a major flaw in the self (e.g., "I fail because I'm stupid," or "lazy," or "unworthy," etc.), or as predicting a major danger in another life sphere (e.g., "Since I'm a failure, my wife will hold me in contempt and my children will no longer look up to me"). In our experience, the most common error made by beginning cognitive therapists with a behavioral background is to jump too rapidly into an evaluation of a given belief without a sufficient exploration of its subtle nuances. Conversely, beginning cognitive therapists with a dynamic background tend to stay far too long at this stage, as if explorations alone will accomplish the goals of therapy.

While there are not firm guidelines, we have typically found that about four or five "And what does that mean to you?" prompts will allow the therapist and client to gain some insight into the full connotative context. One additional rule of thumb that we have found useful is to sit back, close our eyes, and imagine what affects we would feel *if we believed what the client believes.* If we cannot imagine ourselves experiencing the affects the client reports in that situation, then there is something in the client's idiosyncratic meaning system that we still do not fully comprehend.

Evaluating Beliefs Rationally

There are three questions that we try to remember to raise and impart to our clients. The first is "What's the evidence for this belief?", typically labelled the *evidence* question. With this prompt, we ask the client to evaluate, in an even-handed fashion, the evidence both for and against a specific cognition. For example, the previously discussed client who had been unemployed for 3 years, had allowed his personal papers (including tax returns) to accumulate unattended in a large box in his basement. Early one Sunday morning, in the early stages of therapy, buoyed by some initial successes in putting together his portfolio, he decided to go to the basement and put his financial affairs in order. Within minutes, he had pitched into a markedly dysphoric mood, sitting and staring at the box, thinking "I never get anything done. I'm a failure, a bad person."

In the next session, we evaluated whether or not it was true that he "never [got] anything done." He had at least some specific pieces of evidence; the box full of 3 years' worth of tax receipts and personal papers remained untouched and there were several other tasks over the preceding week that he had intended to complete but had not. However, there were other pieces of evidence, many of them noted in his self-monitoring records, that argued against the validity of his belief. He had, for example, completed the aforementioned portfolio. He had also taken his family to the museum the preceding weekend, a task he had assigned himself in the face of having largely ignored his family during his depression. He had also completed several tasks at work and had submitted a proposal to teach a studio arts course in the evening at a local technical college. In short, his belief that he never got anything done was in error, clearly shown to be so via his own records, rather than the therapist's persuasiveness.

The second question, "Is there another way of looking at this?," is typically labelled the *alternative explanations* question. Recall that the client just discussed had first attributed his belief that he never got anything done (since shown to be erroneous, in its starkest form) to his being a "failure" and a "bad person." While he was clearly not a total "failure," or a thoroughly "bad" person given even his own criteria, since he did have some evident accomplishments, he also had some notable incidents of nonaccomplishment. If some stable, trait-like flaw in his person did not account for these instances, what did?

After a review of the accomplishments and nonaccomplishments of the preceding week, it became clear that the times that he met his goals were the times that he "chunked" up the task and approached it in a step-by-step fashion. Conversely, those times in which he did not meet his goals were typically those instances when, as with the task of sorting out his personal papers, he approached a task in an "all-or-nothing" fashion, became overwhelmed, and failed to initiate the necessary behavior. The reconceptualization then became one in which "success" or "failure" was less a result of the inherent trait-like "badness" that he ascribed to himself than of the nature of the performance strategy he adopted.

The third and final question involves the client asking him- or herself "Even if my beliefs are true, what are the real implications [or consequences] for me?", also referred to as the *implications* question. In some instances, the specific initial belief of the client turns out to be in part or wholly accurate, but the implications attached are still in error. In a widely available videotape, called the "Mia" tape, Aaron Beck (1977) worked with a client who was depressed and suicidal because she feared her husband was having an affair. Pursuing the "downward arrow" technique, Beck elicited from her the associated concerns: (1) that the husband was engaged in the affair because she, the wife, had gotten "big and fat and sloppy;" (2) that if she confronted him, he would leave her; and (3) that she would then be unable to care for herself or her two children. In the session, Beck focused in part on what she would have to do to deal with life if her husband did indeed leave her, that is, if her worst fears were realized. Over subsequent months it turned out that the husband was indeed having an affair and that he did indeed leave her for the other woman. However, she had grossly underestimated her own ability to cope with this event. By the time Beck saw her for a follow-up interview (about 9 months later), she had gone back to work, begun paying greater attention to her personal appearance, and had gained a sense of pride in her ability to relearn to do the things she had done while single, such as balancing a checkbook and making payments on bills. While her life had clearly been complicated by a painful separation, she was far from crushed by the event and, if anything, rebounded in a fashion that represented a higher level of functioning than she had exhibited during her marriage.

These three questions are, of course, interrelated. Frequently, raising the *implications* questions leads directly back to the *evidence* question (e.g., "What evidence do you have that you could not survive living without your husband?"). Similarly, the *alternative explanations* question logically leads to a review of the available evidence in order to choose between the two or more competing models.

Finally, we have learned to try to verbalize orally for the client the processes we go through as therapists, labelling as best we can the factors weighed in our decisions and the principles to which we adhere. Initially, that may take the form of working with the client to evaluate a belief without commenting on the process, then returning at a later point to that example and walking the client through the processes we followed. Later, we try to verbalize the processes we follow as we go, subsequently encouraging the client to identify those same steps in his or her covert behavior. In this fashion, we both model the process of change and insure some repetition in the service of committing those steps to memory.

Prospective Empirical Hypothesis Testing

If there is anything that sets cognitive therapy apart from other cognitive interventions (and there may not be, since our failure to recognize this component in those other approaches may simply be a function of our lack of intimate familiarity with them), it is the key role accorded to the process of prospective hypothesis testing (Hollon & Beck, 1979, 1986). Our contention is that the single most powerful way to induce people to change their beliefs is to help them show themselves that those beliefs are in error by testing their own behavior. We alluded to this process in our discussion of behavioral activation strategies. By the middle stage of therapy, it has become, along with the rational validity evaluation procedures just described, the main focus of the therapeutic session.

Several examples can best illustrate this process. In the aforementioned example of the out-of-work artist, identifying two contrasting models to explain his 3-year history of vocational disappointment ("bad person failure" vs. "inappropriate behavioral strategy selection") led directly to such a prospective test. The client decided to attempt again to work on bringing order to his personal papers, but this time doing so by taking only a handful of papers at a time. Within a week of applying this "chunking" strategy, he had largely brought his financial records under control.

In a second example already briefly alluded to, a middle-aged divorcée, concerned that her grown children resented her for divorcing their paraplegic father and certain that they regarded her to be a bad mother, was encouraged to approach her children directly about these issues. She had always avoided such discussions because she was convinced that she knew what their responses would be. Rather than risk a "hurtful" confrontation with them, she elected to write a letter to each. Although the responses that she received were not uniformly benign, they were far more supportive than she had imagined. Her youngest child, a boy, did resent her actions, while the three oldest children, all girls, felt she had acted appropriately or, if anything, had waited too long. She further learned that her three older children generally regarded her as a loving parent and a good role model, albeit one who was a little too distant emotionally and avoidant of intimate disclosure.

In a final example, yet another recent client of a colleague had largely avoided any major intimate relationships since being rendered infertile due to surgery in her early 20s. Although she greatly desired those relationships and would have valued starting a family, she had developed a pattern of ending any relationship as soon as it showed signs of developing in order to avoid the pain of rejection when her condition became known. Her belief was that no eligible male would want to have a relationship with a woman who could not bear children. At her therapist's urging, she agreed to conduct a "disguised" survey in which she raised the issue with male coworkers as if it were the plot of a soap opera. While three of her twelve respondents agreed with her prediction and indicated that they would terminate such a relationship, nine of the twelve did not, stressing the importance to them of quality of the relationship over any desire to sire children.

In each of these cases, the client was explicitly encouraged to collect information in a prospective, empirical fashion that spoke to the validity of one or more of their beliefs. In each case (but not in all instances of each case) the consequences were at variance with the client's predictions and contributed to a change in both beliefs and behavior.

Several points need to be made about this kind of prospective hypothesis testing. First, in keeping with our theme of cognitive therapy as a didactic, skills-training approach, we think it is quite important to involve the client in the process of designing the experiments to be run, much like working with a new graduate student. This does not mean that the therapist (like the advisor) needs to be passive in the process; rather the therapist should try to draw the client (like the student) into the process, shaping and refining (and sometimes suggesting) the proposal, but always working within a context of *collaborative empiricism* (Hollon & Beck, 1979).

Second, the therapist would be well advised to remember that the goal is to collect evidence that, depending upon its nature, would be compelling to the client. It does little good to collect evidence that the client would consider to be fatally flawed before the experiment is even begun. For example, before the mother in the second example mailed her letters to her children, much care went into deciding exactly how to word each in order to maximize the likelihood of securing an honest, even if distressing, response.

Finally, the therapist would also be well advised to remember that such experimentation may sometimes set the client up for personal embarrassment or actual harm, at least as far as the expectations of the client are concerned. It is usually possible to consider real or fantasized risks in advance and to design the experiment so as to reduce their likelihood. Having the unmarried client in the third example disguise her inquiry as a casual discussion of the plot of a television show both facilitated frankness on the part of her respondents and protected her confidentiality.

Underlying Assumptions

Most depressed clients will have begun to experience considerable symptomatic relief by the time they are about two-thirds through therapy. We typically like to work twice weekly over the first 4 to 8 weeks, and once weekly through the last 4 weeks of a 12-week, 20-session course of cognitive therapy. At that point, we find ourselves increasingly looking for the broader themes that may emerge from the multiple specific situations dealt with earlier in therapy. In cognitive therapy, such themes are seen as reflecting the operation of certain generic, abstract beliefs referred to as *underlying assumptions*.

Unlike automatic thoughts, underlying assumptions rarely emerge spontaneously in the "stream-of-consciousness." Rather, they appear to represent abstract principles that can be inferred on the basis of consistencies in the client's specific cognitions, affects, and behaviors. They sometimes emerge in the process of exploring the meaning systems surrounding specific automatic thoughts and can often be noted in the early weeks of therapy for later discussion.

In the example of the out-of-work academic, during his initial effort to organize his personal papers, he ended up labelling himself a "bad person" in response to his inability to perform. Over the first several weeks of therapy, the client frequently labelled himself a "bad person" or "bad boy" in a variety of situations. In an effort to pursue this theme, we set aside a later therapy session for the exploration of this construct, including its connotations, consistencies, affective relationships, and historical origins. It became apparent that he labelled himself a "bad person" in situations in which there was something he greatly wished to accomplish (e.g., filing personal papers, visiting his aging mother, joining his wife at a social occasion), but which, for any of a variety of reasons (some quite legitimate), he did not.

A pattern emerged in which any instance of failure to accomplish some task elicited the construct, along with an affective mixture of sadness and anger. Asking him to recall the earliest time he could remember in which he experienced that same mix of emotions, he reported being forced to compete with his younger brother for his father's approval by stuffing envelopes on weekends for the family mail order business. While sad about being repeatedly out-performed by his more able younger brother, he was also angry about being forced to compete at all, and soon came to be labelled the "bad one" for the disinterested, resigned way in which he came to perform.

In general, a theme became evident in which the client believed that he had to perform, even if he wasn't sure he wanted to, and that, if he failed to do so, there was something wrong with his basic character. This theme appeared to make sense out of his reactions in a variety of disparate situations and seemed consistent with the particular idiosyncratic blend of affects he experienced at those times.

Uncovering this broad theme and some possible etiological basis for it served several purposes. First, it helped organize a rather varied array of specific vignettes that had been worked on over the previous ten weeks. Second, it helped normalize the client's experience by providing a plausible (if unprovable) explanation for how he had developed the beliefs that he held. From the client's newfound perspective, any normal child growing up in the environment he had encountered would likely have developed the complex of beliefs and affective reactions he had developed—a reassuring "insight." Finally, articulation of this theme facilitated even more powerful subsequent hypothesis testing by allowing the client to generate specific predictions that he could then subject to additional tests.

Cognitive therapy is not adverse to historical reconstruction, but it does argue that symptomatic change can, and typically should, precede such efforts. Similarly, there is a strong preference in cognitive therapy for working inductively, focusing concretely on specific thought–affect sequences early in treatment before moving on to more general themes, which stands in sharp contrast to related approaches such as RET (Ellis, 1962). It is our belief that both historical reconstruction leading to insight and the articulation of general themes can facilitate the consolidation of change, but that neither is a particularly efficient strategy for producing that change initially.

Preparing for Termination and Preventing Relapse

As noted earlier, we think it is quite useful to begin preparing for termination from the first session on. The therapist can do this by clearly communicating that cognitive therapy for depression is typically a short-term intervention. This does not mean that therapy *must* terminate after 10 to 12 weeks, only that it often can. In some instances, other problems may emerge (e.g., stable personality disorders that transcend the depression) that merit additional therapy (Hollon, 1984). Similarly, we try to make it clear that if the client has not shown evidence of response within a reasonable period of time (i.e., 4 to 6 weeks), it is the therapy that is suspect, not the client.

The accelerated pace of therapy and the didactic, collaborative stance adopted by the therapist are both predicated on the notion that therapy will not continue indefinitely. We repeatedly raise the issue of termination throughout therapy in an effort to keep motivation and involvement high, saying things like "I realize that these assignments are time-consuming, but in a couple of weeks, assuming that you're doing better by then, we'll be discontinuing therapy, and I want to be sure that you really have a good feel for this kind of strategy." Similarly, we emphasize the more time-consuming process of teaching the methods to the client rather than simply practicing them on the client by saying, for example, "Let me ask you to review what we've just been doing in evaluating that belief, and tell me what steps we've followed. We'll be terminating in just a few weeks and I want to be sure that you can repeat the process on your own."

As noted earlier, we usually prefer seeing depressed clients at least twice weekly at the outset, reducing sessions to once weekly somewhere between 4 and 8 weeks. This reduction in session frequency can be treated as a "dress-rehearsal" for eventual termination, since the decline in actual frequency is as great from twice-a-week to once-a-week sessions as it is from once-a-week to no sessions. We encourage clients to treat this period as a practice period for termination, noting carefully what thoughts and affects are stimulated, and bringing them in for subsequent discussion. Not infrequently, clients experience more anticipatory distress before the reduction than they do once it has begun. This "pseudo-experiment" either serves to directly relieve distress about termination prior to the actual occurrence, or, in a minority of cases, highlights the issues that need to be dealt with before termination can comfortably occur.

Relapse prevention is, in our opinion, facilitated by many of the same stances and strategies described above. Continually reminding the client that therapy is not expected to last forever, mobilizing greater active client participation via stressing the short-term nature of therapy, and slowing the treatment process down to teach theory and procedure to the client, rather than simply applying those aspects, all, we believe, facilitate the acquisition of specific skills that contribute to the apparent prophylactic effect of cognitive therapy.

Discussing and role playing what the client can try to do if he or she becomes depressed in the future is a major aspect of our relapse prevention strategy. We start by noting that our client is at greater risk for subsequent episodes of depression than most other people. We also note that that does not mean that they *will* become depressed again, only that they might. We ask the client to imagine what could happen to induce renewed dysphoria, how they would recognize its early stages, and what they would do in that event. If the client replies, "Come back and see you again" we reply, "Fine, I'd like to see you again too, but I would just as soon that visit involved your telling me what you had done to forestall your depression, rather than how depressed you had become." We then lead the client into a concrete discussion of the actual self-management strategies he or she could utilize—for the most part the things he or she has been learning to do in therapy—before resuming treatment.

It is important to assess what a client thinks it would mean if he or she relapsed. We've seen clients infer that such a relapse meant that treatment had not worked, leading them to reject any reinitiation of contacts and, in at least one instance, inducing an acute suicidal crisis. We like to use an analogy that likens depression to "getting dirty" and cognitive therapy to "taking a shower." In this analogy, the fact that someone gets "dirty" again after taking one shower doesn't mean that the original shower didn't work, it simply means that it may be time to take another. Moreover, after someone knows how to take showers, getting "dirty" will never again seem to be as big an ordeal as it once did. We further like to point out that subsequent episodes, unpleasant though they may be, provide an opportunity to solidify learning. Anecdotal reports from the follow-ups of clients observed over the span of several years suggests that while subsequent episodes may not be noticeably less severe when they do occur, their frequency of recurrence and their length are both reduced, apparently by the application of the client's growing skills in cognitive-behavioral self-management.

We have been treating depressed patients longer than we have been practicing cognitive therapy, and have been struck by how likely our clients are to attribute change to our personal characteristics rather than to the therapeutic procedures. It is not clear that our personal characteristics have changed that markedly over time, but our success in therapy clearly has, at least given our own anecdotal records. One of the things we have learned to do is to welcome and capitalize on relapses that occur spontaneously during the course of therapy. In many instances, those relapses are associated with a decrease in effort on the client's or therapist's part after some initial relief was evident. Such variation in the clinical course, especially if tied to a variation in specific procedure, can help highlight the causal role of the specific therapeutic activities. When no relapse occurs spontaneously, it is often useful to discuss instigating a "planned relapse" in the middle-to-late phases of treatment (e.g., the client could agree to discontinue all active hypothesis testing and rational reevaluations, and schedule time to ruminate about his or her presumed failings). After the client becomes somewhat more dysphoric, he or she can reinvigorate applicable self-management efforts, usually leading to a second remission. Clients often appear impressed that we are so sure that it is the therapy procedure that is the actual agent of change, deriving considerable reassurance from this perception—although, in all honesty, we must say that while we have often talked about instigating a therapeutic relapse, we have never actually had a client agree to let us do so.

We have also learned to encourage clients to try to teach some of these newly acquired cognitive skills to a friend or family member; running open-ended group therapy sessions also facilitates this process. One of the best ways to facilitate the acquisition of knowledge in a way that stays with the client over time is to urge them to take on the role of a teacher with someone else.

Finally, we prefer to schedule one or more follow-up contacts with the client after therapy terminates, and make it clear that *the client does not need to be symptomatic to see us again.* Our experience has been that such sessions typically became boring to both participants after about twenty minutes, but they probably have a useful role to play in reducing anxiety at the time of termination.

THE ROLE OF THE THERAPIST

In general, the therapist in cognitive therapy takes on the role of a teacher—not in a pedantic or authoritarian way, but in a way similar to a clinical researcher working with a bright graduate student or an established professional supervising a promising protegé. The goal is to impart skills, many of them developed in collaboration with earlier clients, that go beyond the normal coping skills that most people develop to deal with life's typical frustrations. Elsewhere (Evans & Hollon, in press), we have speculated that much of what we do focuses on to training clients to apply more careful, deliberate information-processing tactics to the process of change than most of us are prone to use most of the time. In a sense, we teach people these nonnormative, atypically purposeful reality-testing strategies for short-term use in the service of combatting depression.

We also consider it quite important that the therapist be able to take an open, flexible stance in the pursuit of information. Cognitive therapy is predicated on the notion that all beliefs are open to challenge—both the client's and the therapist's—and a real committment is made to a methodology (i.e., collaborative empiricism), rather than to an existing body of presumed knowledge. This spirit is embodied in our reluctance to present cognitive theory as a fact to be accepted; rather, we present it as a theory that may or may not apply to the particular client. Similarly, we try not to assume that we know how any given experiment will turn out; since we are so often in error, it behooves us to be humble. Our stance is that of an expert, with specific and delimited areas of competence closely related to a methodology, rather than that of an authority, someone presumed to know the answers. As cognitive therapists, our goal is to ask questions in a productive way, seeking empirically verifiable answers, rather than to provide those answers.

One of our favorite role models was the character of Detective Columbo, portrayed by Peter Falk in a recent television series. Columbo would approach each case in a state of apparent naiveté, asking a series of simple questions until he was able to make sense out of what happened. He avoided rushing to judgment prematurely, and pursued "loose ends" doggedly, even in the absence of any clear thread. We like this analogy precisely because it presumes so little prior knowledge on the part of the therapist. If you have a good procedure for getting at the facts, you can start from a state of relative ignorance, thrash about in the data for a period of time, and still have reason to be confident of closing in on the truth. Cognitive therapy is a comfortable therapy for those who like to leap before they look, in that it presumes that you can start anywhere in a process and rapidly zero in on what you need to know.

Traditionally valued therapist characteristics (e.g., warmth, genuineness, and empathy) are probably useful, but we see them as being far from sufficient. In early writings and demonstrations, Beck appeared almost indifferent to such considerations (see, e.g., the original "Mia" tape by Beck, 1977), although later writings began to reflect a greater valuation of these attributes. It is probably not necessary for a person to particularly like or feel comfortable with a teacher in order to learn from him or her, but the nature of the self-doubts and sensitivities that bring most people into therapy render them particularly vulnerable to interpersonal slights and embarrassments. Studies are currently under way to tease out the relative contributions of nonspecific relationship aspects versus specific techniques. In their absence, it seems wise to assume that both solid nonspecific relationship skills and specific cognitive strategies require attention.

There are some ways in which even nonspecific aspects of the relationship need to be shaped to fit the cognitive approach. For example, empathy—the ability to understand and be sensitive to the client's experience—has been frequently targeted as an important clinical attribute (Rogers, 1957). In cognitive therapy, it is important to be empathic without appearing to endorse the reality of the client's perceptions. Thus, rather than saying, "That's really awful, no wonder you feel so badly," a cognitive therapist might say, "That's a really difficult situation. If I were faced with that situation, *and if I interpreted it the way that you're interpreting it*, I would feel badly too." The key here is to achieve and communicate an understanding of the client's affective experience, without unintentionally signalling agreement with the premises that that affective experience may be based upon. We always want to "validate" the client's affective experience, since, in the cognitive model, affects are seen as invariant consequences of the client's beliefs, and not as something that has been chosen or that is either appropriate or inappropriate. Nevertheless, we feel that a recognition of the client's experiences must be conveyed in a way that is consistent with the notion that the client's prior beliefs and attitudes are very much open to question.

We also tend to be advocates of "leveling" strategies in therapy, that is, we prefer engaging clients in an egalitarian relationship, particularly with regard to what we each know about the world. We do not presume that we have any special characteristics that set us apart from others, or any special insight into the nature of the world. What we do have to offer are some technologies that may be useful in combating depression and an approach (i.e., collaborative empiricism) that may be particularly useful in separating fact from fiction. Our goal is not to impart wisdom to our clients, since we have no special wisdom to impart, nor to transmit any special solutions to life's many problems. Rather, our goal is to engage our clients in a collaborative process of discovery, in which no beliefs are sacred (including any the therapist may hold) and in which carefully reasoned trial and frequently committed error, with subsequent corrections based on feedback from those trials, are the order of the day. We strive to form a "therapeutic alliance" (Luborsky, 1976) that most nearly approximates a shared adventure, in which neither client nor therapist know precisely how events will proceed, but in which each can plunge ahead, with a reasonable expectation that the process will be self-corrective.

Control is frequently a key issue in depression, particularly for a depressed client who feels generally ineffectual and unable to deal with life's current demands. What we want to model for clients is an openness to the process of discovery, rather than a presumption of knowledge (and thus power). Our goal is to serve as a consultant who is prepared to provide special skills, rather than an authority who can provide certain answers.

SPECIAL CLINICAL ISSUES

Resistance and Noncompliance

We define the terms "resistance" and "noncompliance" in a fashion that highlights the distinctions between the two (Hollon, 1983). For us, resistance is an active process in which some mechanism or motivation prevents the client from agreeing to or carrying out an agreed-upon activity. Noncompliance, conventionally defined in somewhat broader terms, is, for us, a passive process in which the client simply fails to put into affect an agreed-upon plan of action.

Passive noncompliance is, we think, a nearly universal phenomenon in depression. It is, we believe, close to the essence of the disorder, and we are never surprised to see it in evidence in therapy. Such passive noncompliance often reflects a basic expectation of failure; the client does not do because the client does not think that he or she can do, or can succeed in reaching some goal even if he or she does do.

Our strategies for dealing with passive noncompliance are straightforward. First, we expect it to occur, not condoning or encouraging it, but simply anticipating that any time one deals with a depressed client, one is likely to encounter passive noncompliance. Second, we try to structure requests and assignments in such a way that its likelihood is reduced. Many of the core techniques in cognitive therapy are targeted at this process, (e.g., "chunking," role playing potential difficulties with an assignment before sending the client out, or beginning an assignment in a session for completion outside the session, etc.). Third, we define the task in such a way that completion is not the only goal. Thus, if a client encounters difficulty initiating some agreed-upon task, the assignment switches from task completion to the observation of the factors that make task completion difficult. In this way, it is possible to break the cycle of negative expectation leading to behavioral passivity, the common theme in passive noncompliance. Finally, we analyze the "problems" noted to result in passive noncompliance, applying standard cognitive-behavioral strategies to this analysis and resolution.

In short, passive noncompliance is not viewed merely as a disruptor of therapy. Rather, it is viewed as an expected, contributory aspect of therapy. It is less a reason for moving away from a cognitive-behavioral strategy than it is the target of that strategy. Passive noncompliance with the activities requested in therapy then becomes a mini-laboratory for the cognitive therapy process, with the corollary assumption that any problems related to noncompliance with therapeutic tasks are likely to be related to the processes retarding the pursuit of major life tasks.

Active resistance is approached from a similar stance, although it is typically a more complex, if less frequent, process. Whenever apparently simple requests mysteriously don't get acted upon, and the conventional cognitive-behavioral response of breaking the task down and practicing it with the client doesn't suffice to resolve the issue, one should suspect the presence of some type of active resistance. As with passive noncompliance, we view this less as a time to jettison the cognitive model than as a time to apply that model to the problem. In particular, we would point out our dilemma to the client, saying something like, "I can't help but notice that you don't seem to be able to fill out the Dysfunctional Thoughts Records between sessions, and that puzzles me, since you seem to have no problem in our meetings. I wonder if we can try to explore what lies behind that." We routinely first ask clients directly if they have any sense as to what that underlying reason might be, inviting them to feel free to be perfectly frank. If that does not suffice, we may bring up examples from other clients, involving such issues as power struggles, fears of change, different implicit agendas, and so on. For example, we might say, "Now, I don't know if this is going on for you or not, but I've sometimes had clients who later told me that they found my manner too overbearing and directive and that they sometimes just 'dug in their heels' and refused to do what I was asking. Is anything like that going on for you?" The appendix of the Beck *et al.* (1979) treatment manual contains a list of various reasons for not doing homework. Clients can sometimes identify issues more readily when given such a list than they can when asked to provide them without a prompt. It can also be useful to identify the affects experienced when about to attempt a task, with a subsequent search for the beliefs related to those affects. Finally, we sometimes find it expedient to have the client fantasize about what it would be like to complete such a task, or to have the changes that such completion might yield occur. We have, for example, seen clients who have been unable to initiate simple tasks discover that, in their fantasies, the successful completion of such a task would produce a state of affairs that they view as being overwhelming.

In short, neither passive noncompliance nor active resistance are viewed as reasons to move away from a cognitive-behavioral approach. Rather, both are seen as potential targets for analysis and modification using precisely those procedures. And far from being mysterious anomalies that only disrupt the progress of therapy, both are looked upon as likely involving the same kinds of beliefs and affective reactions that led the client into therapy in the first place. By providing a clear depiction of those cognitive-affective patterns, as well as providing a mini-laboratory in which to practice, it is often the case that such "problems" in therapy can be turned to therapeutic advantage. Our experience has been that noncompliance with and resistance to the various tasks and assignments in cognitive therapy can play the same curiously facilitative role ascribed to the occurrence and resolution of the transference phenomenon in the dynamic approaches.

Suicidal Ideation

An assessment of suicidal ideation is requisite whenever treatment is initiated with a person who is depressed. Although a discussion of how to assess the intensity of suicidal ideation is not within the scope of this paper, it is important to mention that this intensity does vary among clients on a wide continuum from mild, passive ideation (e.g., "Life is not worth living") to severe suicidal preoccupation including a specific suicide plan. The therapist must determine that the client's level of suicidal ideation can be effectively dealt with in a therapy session. From a cognitive-behavioral perspective, the focus is on the client's thoughts about why he or she wants to kill him- or herself. Often the thoughts center around hopelessness, guilt, inadequacy, and helplessness. They are, like other cognitions of the depressed person, usually overly general and inaccurate. Once identified, suicidal thoughts and the cognitions behind them are amenable to standard cognitive strategies. Therapist and client can examine the evidence for thoughts that reflect the client's feelings of hopelessness, guilt, or inadequacy. Tasks, decisions, or events that are overwhelming for the client can be broken down into smaller, more manageable components. Alternative ways of thinking about the client's problems can be generated, as well as solutions other than suicide. The interested reader is directed to the discussion of "alternative therapy" in the Beck, et al. (1979) treatment manual. The key point for our current discussion is that the vocalizing of suicidal ideation should always be taken seriously in cognitive therapy, its presence actively inquired about, especially in initial sessions, and priority given to dealing with it when it is present.

Working with Low-Income Clients

There are two areas that may be especially important when working with clients who are coping with an inadequate income. The first is that individuals from lower socioeconomic groups may be less familiar with therapy in general and so may not know what to expect from the therapist or from the therapeutic interaction overall. Time should be taken in this case to "socialize" the client for therapy prior to introducing the cognitive-behavioral approach. This socialization for therapy includes providing explicit information about what the client can expect from the therapist in terms of crisis intervention, how problems appropriate for work in therapy are identified, how often sessions are held and how long they last, a description of the problems people come to therapy for, how to cancel or reschedule appointments, and what to do if there are problems with fees. The therapist should also provide the client the opportunity to ask questions and should be particularly attentive to eliciting the client's reactions to questions that the therapist asks and to the sessions overall. The second area that may be important with low-income clients is that of practical problems. It will be difficult for the client to focus on the cognitive and emotional aspects of being depressed, for example, if he or she is worried about supporting his or her children but does not know how to utilize the social welfare system. In short, the therapist and client may spend more session time, especially initially, in dealing with practical issues concerning money, food, contacting lawyers, finding doctors, calling social workers, and so on. It is important for the therapist to recognize and attend to issues that are relevant to the client. Because sufficient finances are so tied to power, both personal and societal, the therapist should also be alert to the client's feelings of powerlessness. While some of the client's thoughts around such issues are likely to be accurate, it will be important to pursue personal meanings and to discuss the adaptive or maladaptive function of such thoughts.

In general, our strategy is to help prepare the client to deal with these practical issues, rather than to get directly involved ourselves. We might, therefore, help a client rehearse a phone call to a key social welfare agency (or a landlord, civil authority, bank manager, etc.), perhaps even encouraging the client to make a call (or write a letter) during the therapy session. Our goal, as always, is not to do for the client, but rather to help the client develop the strategies required to gain control over his or her life.

Cognitive Therapy with Women

There has been considerable discussion in the past 15 to 20 years about women's roles and the passive position women have tended to occupy both personally and societally. In the depression literature, researchers have proposed societal variables as possible reasons for the preponderance of women in the depression statistics. Because powerlessness has long been reinforced as a characteristic of women and because it is also a common target symptom in the cognitive-behavioral approach to treating depression, special issues arise in the treating of depressed women with cognitive–behavioral techniques.

There are two areas of particular concern: (1) how to help a woman adaptively challenge her own thoughts and beliefs while providing her the tools to recognize and value her own perceptions; and (2) how to be an active, directive therapist without stripping away the client's sense of power (this latter concern, of course, is one that also affects relationships with male clients).

Traditionally, although certainly not always explicitly, women have been taught to doubt their own perceptions of events, other people, and even themselves. The viewpoints, values, and thought patterns of women have been undervalued and misunderstood. This chronic self-questioning and self-doubt sometimes results in a feeling of being crazy, which is exacerbated when a woman becomes depressed. As we have stated previously, one of the underpinnings of the cognitive-behavioral approach is the challenging of thoughts and beliefs. This systematic challenging can potentially reinforce a woman's implicit notions that she "thinks wrong," is inadequate, or is dependent on others to help her think about the world. Given these possibilities, there are several tactics that the therapist can be attentive to in order to work more effectively with female clients. It is important for the therapist to pay particular attention to affirming beliefs as well as disaffirming them. The way in which thoughts are challenged will also be important. For example, saying, "Let's both of us take a look at what you just said, so that we can check it out" is much less threatening than, "How do you know that?" Attending to the presence of double messages in the client's communications or interactions with other people will often be very fruitful with respect to sorting out evidence for beliefs on two sides of an important issue. Careful attention to how and with whom the client checks out thoughts and beliefs is also helpful. For example, the woman who describes herself as the "black sheep" of the family, probably cannot rely on her family to provide her with useful feedback on issues of self worth, even if the client's evidence for her belief that she is the "black sheep" is not the concrete, specific evidence that is so desirable in cognitive therapy. The therapist should also make an effort to elicit and concretize thoughts having to do with powerlessness: The client's own efforts to gather evidence, experiment with activities, or make changes that have had the desired results or have provided useful information should be emphasized.

The second issue that arises in working with women is related to power in the therapeutic relationship. The cognitive-behavioral treatment approach is explicitly collaborative and as such should facilitate a power-sharing situation. Two factors mediate against this. One is that it is very easy for some women to hand over power in a relationship, especially to "authority figures." The second is that the cognitive therapist is expected to be particularly active in the sessions. Again, special attention to several ameliorative strategies will be helpful in confronting these issues. Emphasizing the client's ability to decide what is important to focus on will be helpful in agenda setting. If the client does not bring in an agenda, the therapist might suggest that she take a few minutes at the beginning of the session to think about her week and jot down some highlights. As opposed to the therapist reading through the client's homework, the dyad might share responsibility by having the client summarize her observations about the assignments and indicate to the therapist which aspects of the homework were most significant. Making changes in the direction of the session explicit, and negotiating those shifts with the client, can also be important in facilitating a sense of control and power for the client. Carefully assessing the client's attributions, particularly with respect to her successes, should also provide helpful information and an opportunity to highlight the client's contribution to her own well-being.

Clearly, the issues delineated above are not necessarily specific to women. They are also not an exhaustive description of the issues that come up in the practice of cognitive-behavior therapy for depression with women. These issues and the strategies recommended for addressing them may also be relevant to individuals or to members of minority groups who have confronted or do confront societally reinforced powerlessness.

SUMMARY

Cognitive therapy is, despite its name, a cognitive–behavioral intervention best understood as an approach that attempts to apply a strategy of empirical hypothesis testing to the task of changing beliefs. There is a growing body of literature which suggests that it is at least as effective as any major alternative in treating the acute episode for nonbipolar, nonpsychotic depressed clients and, perhaps, uniquely successful in preventing the subsequent return of symptoms.

Throughout this chapter, we have attempted to describe not so much the main procedures of cognitive therapy (these are well described in texts such as the Beck et al., 1979 treatment manual) as the more personalized, idiosyncratic "twists" that we incorporate in actually putting the approach into practice. Many of those "twists" involve slowing down the process in order to facilitate teaching the procedure to the client. This emphasis on teaching within therapy—which, in essence, turns the therapy session into something more nearly resembling a two-person "research seminar" than a typical therapy session—is, we believe, to a great extent responsible for the apparent prophylactic effect noted by, for example, Blackburn et al. (in press), Evans et al. (1986), and Kovacs et al. (1981). Similarly, we have tried to highlight our efforts to be collaborative, open, and nonauthoritative to offset the sense of powerlessness and ineffectualness so often experienced by depressed clients. Finally, we have attempted to verbalize our reliance on a brand of reasoned empiricism, stressing that what we have to offer clients is not so much the "answers" to life's questions, as a methodology for pursuing those "answers."

In short, we have undertaken to enunciate the idiosyncratic "scripts" that we follow in putting cognitive therapy into actual practice. Other experienced cognitive therapists may well have described other "scripts;" we make no claim for universality. Similarly, most of what we have described is drawn purely from subjective opinion and anecdotal experience. As always, if any of these musings are seen as having merit, they then should properly fuel more systematic inquiry that may disconfirm our findings and be itself open to disconfirmation, rather than those findings being accepted as truths merely on the basis of their apparent worth.

ACKNOWLEDGMENTS

Preparation of this chapter was supported, in part, by a grant from the National Institute of Mental Health (RO1-MH33209) to the Department of Psychology, University of Minnesota, and the Department of Psychiatry at the St. Paul–Ramsey Medical Center, St. Paul, Minnesota. We would like to express our appreciation to Bonnie Arant Ertelt, for her secretarial assistance in the preparation of the manuscript. We would particularly like to thank the four experienced cognitive therapists, Dave Coats, ACSW, Virginia Jacobson, ACSW, Frank Spoden, ACSW, and Marlin Wiemer, PhD, all study therapists in our empirical trials over the last eight years, who so generously shared their insights into the clinical process with us as we prepared the manuscript.

REFERENCES

Abelson, R. P. (1981). Psychological status of the script concept. *American Psychologist, 36,* 715–729.

Abramson, L. Y., Seligman, M. E. P., & Teasdale, J. D. (1978). Learned helplessness in humans: Critique and reformulation. *Journal of Abnormal Psychology, 87,* 49–74.

Arieti, S. (1959). Manic–depression. In S. Arieti (Ed.), *Handbook of clinical psychiatry* (Vol. 1, pp. 419–454). New York: Random House.

Beck, A. T. (1963). Thinking and depression: I. Idiosyncratic content and cognitive distortions. *Archives of General Psychiatry, 9,* 324–333.

Beck, A. T. (1964). Thinking and depression: II. Theory and therapy. *Archives of General Psychiatry, 10,* 561–571.

Beck, A. T. (1967). *Depression: Clinical, experimental, and theoretical aspects.* New York: Hoeber.

Beck, A. T. (1970). Cognitive therapy: Nature and relation to behavior therapy. *Behavior Therapy, 1,* 184–200.

Beck, A. T. (1976). *Cognitive therapy and the emotional disorders.* New York: International Universities Press.

Beck, A. T. (1977). *A demonstration of cognitive therapy of depression: Mia I.* Center for Cognitive Therapy, Philadelphia, PA.

Beck, A. T., & Emery, G. (1985). *Anxiety disorders and phobias.* New York: Basic Books.

Beck, A. T., & Greenberg, R. L. (1974). *Coping with depression.* New York: Institute for Rational Living.

Beck, A. T., Hollon, S. D., Young, J., Bedrosian, R. C., & Budenz, D. (1985). Treatment of depression with cognitive therapy and amitriptyline. *Archives of General Psychiatry, 42*, 142–148.

Beck, A. T., Rush, A. J., Shaw, B. F., & Emery, G. (1979). *Cognitive therapy of depression.* New York: Guilford.

Blackburn, I. M., Bishop, S., Glen, A. I. M., Whalley, L. J., & Christie, J. E. (1981). The efficacy of cognitive therapy in depression: A treatment trial using cognitive therapy and pharmacotherapy, each alone and in combination. *British Journal of Psychiatry, 139*, 181–189.

Blackburn, I. M., Eunson, K. M., & Bishop, S. (in press). A two-year naturalistic follow-up of depressed patients treated with cognitive therapy, pharmacotherapy and a combination of both. *British Journal of Psychiatry.*

Burns, D. D. (1980). *Feeling good: The new mood therapy.* New York: William Morrow.

Covi, L., Lipman, R. S., Roth, D., Pattison, J. H., Smith, J. E., & Lasseter, V. K. (in press). Cognitive group psychotherapy in depression: A pilot study. *American Journal of Psychiatry.*

Coyne, J. C., & Gotlib, I. H. (1983). The role of cognition in depression: A critical appraisal. *Psychological Bulletin, 94*, 472–505.

Darley, J. M., & Fazio, R. (1980). Expectancy confirmation processes arising in the social interaction sequence. *American Psychologist, 35*, 867–881.

DeRubeis, R. J., Hollon, S. D., Evans, M. D., & Bemis, K. M. (1982). Can psychotherapies for depression be discriminated? A systematic investigation of cognitive therapy and interpersonal therapy. *Journal of Consulting and Clinical Psychology, 50*, 744–756.

Ellis, A. (1962). *Reason and emotion in psychotherapy.* New York: Stuart.

Emery, G., Hollon, S. D., & Bedrosian, R. C. (Eds.). (1981). *New directions in cognitive therapy.* New York: Guilford.

Evans, M. D., & Hollon, S. D. (in press). Cognitive information processing in clinical depression. In L. B. Alloy (Ed.), *Depression: An experimental perspective.* New York: Guilford.

Evans, M. D., Hollon, S. D., DeRubeis, R. J., Auerbach, A., Tuason, V. B., & Wiemer, M. J. (1983, July). *Development of a system for rating psychotherapies for depression.* Paper presented at the Annual Meeting of the Society for Psychotherapy Research, Sheffield, England.

Evans, M. D., Hollon, S. D., DeRubeis, R. J., Piasecki, J., Tuason, V. B., & Garvey, M. J. (1986). *Relapse/recurrence following cognitive therapy and pharmacotherapy for depression: IV. Two-year follow-up in the cognitive-pharmacotherapy project.* Unpublished manuscript, University of Minnesota and the St. Paul–Ramsey Medical Center, Minneapolis–St. Paul, MN.

Freeman, A. (1983). *Cognitive therapy with couples and groups.* New York: Plenum.

Hollon, S. D. (1983, December). *Resistance and noncompliance in cognitive behavior therapy for depression.* Paper presented at the Annual Convention of the Association for the Advancement of Behavior Therapy, Washington, DC.

Hollon, S. D. (1984). Cognitive therapy for depression: Translating research into practice. *the Behavior Therapist, 7*, 125–127.

Hollon, S. D., & Beck, A. T. (1979). Cognitive therapy of depression. In P. C. Kendall & S. D. Hollon (Eds.), *Cognitive–behavioral interventions: Theory, research, and procedures* (pp. 153–203). New York: Academic Press.

Hollon, S. D., & Beck, A. T. (1986). Cognitive and cognitive–behavioral therapies. In S. L. Garfield & A. E. Bergin (Eds.), *Handbook of psychotherapy and behavior change* (3rd ed., pp. 443–482). New York: Wiley.

Hollon, S. D., DeRubeis, R. J., Evans, M. D., Tuason, V. B., Wiemer, M. J., & Garvey, M. J. (1986). *Cognitive therapy, pharmacotherapy, and combined cognitive-pharmacotherapy in the treatment of depression: I. Differential outcome.* Unpublished manuscript, University of Minnesota and the St. Paul-Ramsey Medical Center, Minneapolis–St. Paul, MN.

Hollon, S. D., Evans, M. D., Elkin, I., & Lowery, A. (1984, May). *System for rating therapies for depression*. Paper presented at the Annual Meeting of the American Psychiatric Association, Los Angeles, CA.

Kahneman, D., Slovic, P., & Tversky, A. (Eds.). (1982). *Judgment under uncertainty: Heuristics and biases*. New York: Cambridge University Press.

Kovacs, M., Rush, A. T., Beck, A. T., & Hollon, S. D. (1981). Depressed outpatients treated with cognitive therapy or pharmacotherapy: A one-year follow-up. *Archives of General Psychiatry, 38*, 33–39.

Luborsky, L. (1976). Helping alliances in psychotherapy: The groundwork for a study of their relationship to its outcome. In J. L. Claghorn (Ed.), *Successful psychotherapy* (pp. 92–111). New York: Brunner/Mazel.

Mahoney, M. J. (1977). Reflections on the cognitive learning trend in psychotherapy. *American Psychologist, 32*, 5–13.

Markus, H. (1977). Self-schemata and processing information about the self. *Journal of Personality and Social Psychology, 35*, 63–78.

Meichenbaum, D. (1977). *Cognitive–behavior modification: An integrative approach*. New York: Plenum.

Murphy, G. E., Simons, A. D., Wetzel, R. D., & Lustman, P. J. (1984). Cognitive therapy and pharmacotherapy, singly and together, in the treatment of depression. *Archives of General Psychiatry, 41*, 33–41.

Neisser, U. (1976). *Cognition and reality: Principles and implications of cognitive psychology*. San Francisco: Freeman.

Nisbett, R. E., & Ross, L. (1980). *Human inference: Strategies and shortcomings of social judgment*. Englewood Cliffs, NJ: Prentice-Hall.

Rogers, C. R. (1957). The necessary and sufficient conditions of therapeutic personality change. *Journal of Consulting Psychology, 21*, 95–103.

Ross, L. (1977). The intuitive psychologist and his shortcomings. In L. Berkowitz (Ed.), *Advances in experimental social psychology* (Vol. 10, pp. 173–220). New York: Academic Press.

Rush, A. J., Beck, A. T., Kovacs, M., & Hollon, S. D. (1977). Comparative efficacy of cognitive therapy versus pharmacotherapy in outpatient depressives. *Cognitive Therapy and Research, 1*, 17–37.

Schneider, R. M., & Shiffrin, W. (1977). Controlled and automatic human information processing: I. Detection, search and attention. *Psychological Review, 84*, 1–66.

Shiffrin, R. M., & Schneider, W. (1977). Controlled and automatic human information processing: II. Perceptual learning, automatic attending, and a general theory. *Psychological Review, 84*, 127–190.

Teasdale, J. D., Fennell, M. J. V., Hibbert, G. A., & Amies, P. L. (1984). Cognitive therapy for major depressive disorder in primary care. *British Journal of Psychiatry, 144*, 400–406.

Young, J. (1980). *The development of the Cognitive Therapy Scale*. Unpublished manuscript, Center for Cognitive Therapy, Philadelphia, PA.

Zajonc, R. B. (1980). Feeling and thinking: Preferences need no inferences. *American Psychologist, 35*, 151–175.

CHAPTER 5

Treating Impulsive Children via Cognitive-Behavioral Therapy

Lauren Braswell
North Memorial Medical Center
Minneapolis, Minnesota

Philip C. Kendall
Temple University

A cognitive-behavioral system operates on the following basic principles. These points are based on Mahoney (1977) and are adopted from Kendall and Bemis (1983).

1. The human organism responds primarily to cognitive representations of and experiences in its environment rather than to the environments and experiences per se.
2. Most human learning is cognitively mediated.
3. Thoughts, feelings, and behaviors are causally interrelated.
4. Cognitive events, processes, products, and structures (e.g., self-talk, expectancies, attributions, schemata) (see Ingram & Kendall, 1986) are important in understanding and predicting psychopathological behavior and the effects of therapeutic interventions.
5. Cognitive events, processes, products, and structures can be cast into testable formulations that can be integrated with behavioral paradigms, and it is possible and desirable to combine cognitive treatment strategies with enactive techniques and behavioral contingency management.
6. The task of the cognitive-behavioral therapist is to act as a diagnostician, educator, and consultant who assesses distorted or deficient cognitive activities and dysfunctional behavior patterns and works with the client to design learning experiences that remediate dysfunctional cognition, behavior, and affective patterns.

A major emphasis within a cognitive-behavioral model of child psychopathology and psychotherapy (Kendall, 1985) is placed on (1) both the learning process and the influence of the contingencies and models in the environment while (2) underscoring the centrality of mediating/information-processing factors in both the development and remediation of child-hood disorders. Cognitive-behavioral analyses of childhood disorders in-volve considerations of numerous features of the child's internal and external environment and represent an integrationist perspective. Cogni-tive, affective, social, and developmental processes are given meaningful roles alongside behavioral processes in understanding etiology and pre-scribing remediation.

Cognitive-behavioral therapy for children is a class of interventions including self-instructional and social problem-solving training, coping modeling, affective education, role playing, and the management of be-havioral contingencies. To various degrees, these interventions have been integrated and utilized in the treatment of children displaying problems with hyperactivity (e.g., Hinshaw, Henker, & Whalen, 1984), aggression (e.g., Camp, Blom, Herbert, & van Doornick, 1977; Kettlewell & Kausch, 1983), social isolation (e.g., Gottman, Gonso, & Schuler, 1976), and night-time fears (e.g., Graziano & Mooney, 1980; Kanfer, Karoly, & Newman, 1975). Our version of cognitive-behavioral therapy is for the treatment of children with deficits in self-control (Kendall & Braswell, 1985). Much of our discussion will be related to this expertise, but our comments on this therapy are relevant to the larger class of cognitive-behavioral interven-tions, since these inteventions sometimes differ more in emphasis than in content.

NATURE OF THE TARGET SAMPLE AND
THE FOCUS OF THE INTERVENTION

As stated above, our cognitive-behavioral procedures were developed for use with impulsive children. Children within this group are described as attention-disordered, overactive, disobedient to adult authorities, exter-nalizing (Achenbach, 1966), or undercontrolled and/or aggressive toward others. They may carry formal DSM-III diagnoses of attention deficit disorder with or without hyperactivity or conduct disorder.

Why is a cognitive-behavioral intervention, including an elaborated version of self-instructional training, an appropriate treatment for this group? Several lines of research suggest that one could understand these children's deficits in self-control as the result of some anomaly in the development of internal control and the verbal control over behavior. The most frequently cited theories addressing the functional relationship be-tween language and behavior are those of Soviet psychologists Luria (1959, 1961) and Vygotsky (1962). Vygotsky proposed that internalization of verbal commands is the crucial step in a child's establishment of volun-tary control over his or her behavior. Luria suggested a three-stage sequence in which the child's behavior is initially controlled by the verbalizations of others, usually adults (other–external). In the next stage, the child's own overt verbalizations direct his or her behavior (self–external), and finally, by age five or six, the child's behavior is controlled by his or her own covert self-verbalizations (self–internal). Luria also theorized that during the other–external and self–external phases, verbal control is primarily impulsive rather than semantic, with speech functioning as a physical stimulus that can inhibit or disinhibit responses. As the child develops, verbal control shifts to a semantic orientation, for the child learns to respond to speech as a carrier of specific symbolic meaning. As a result of these two shifts, by approximately age 6, the normally developing child acquires self–internal regulating speech and is responsive to the content of verbalizations. Copeland (1983) provides a further review of the developmental significance of children's self-directed speech.

The work of Mischel and Patterson (1975, 1976) on the delay of gratification also provides support for the role of self-verbalization in regulating impulsive behavior. Mischel (1974) summarized evidence that self-generated strategies, such as self-instructions and self-praise, helped children reduce frustration during delay of gratification tasks. In this type of research, the "training" in self-instruction was very brief; in fact, it usually involved the experimenter simply instructing the child to say a particular sentence or think a particular thought. Patterson and Mischel also examined verbal self-control in a series of studies on verbal strategies for resisting distraction (Mischel & Patterson 1976; Patterson & Mischel, 1975, 1976). The findings suggested that preschoolers did not spontaneously produce self-instructions to help them cope with highly distracting stimuli but when provided with a specific cognitive plan, the children were able to work longer in the distracting situation. Very similar research strategies have also been utilized in studies of rule-following behavior (Monohan & O'Leary, 1971; O'Leary, 1968), with results suggesting verbalization of simple self-instructions can reduce rule breaking in children.

Self-instructional training is also considered an appropriate intervention with children who act out because it can address difficulties in social problem solving and perspective taking. The notion that externalizing children may differ from normals in some of their social cognitive processes has received support. In a series of studies, Dodge and his colleagues (Dodge & Frame, 1982; Dodge, Murphy, & Buchsbaum, 1984; Richard & Dodge, 1982) have observed that aggressive boys do display social cognitive biases and deficits that distinguish them from normals. In comparing delinquents and nondelinquents at ages 10 to 11 and 14 to 15, Hains and Ryan (1983) found that while these two groups were similar on certain dimensions of social problem solving, the delinquent subjects were less exhaustive in their consideration of different aspects of the social problem-solving process. These findings led Hains and Ryan to conclude

that acting-out behavior may result from incomplete or inaccurate inferences made in social situations. Their conclusions regarding delinquents
are highly similar to those of Dodge and colleagues with school-aged
acting-out children who have not yet been identified as delinquent. Hudson, Forman, and Brion-Meisels (1982) found that 7-year-olds rated as
high in role-taking ability could be distinguished from those classified as
low in this ability on a number of behavioral dimensions, including social
problem solving and helping behaviors. In addition, in a longitudinal
comparison of emotionally disturbed versus normal boys, Guracharri,
Phelps, and Selman (1984) observed that while the progression through
levels of interpersonal understanding appeared to be the same for both
groups, the disturbed youths lagged behind the normals in their rate of
progression through these levels.

In addition to focusing on self-instructions that address the child's
deficits in verbal mediation, social problem solving, and perspective taking,
this intervention program directs and reinforces the child's behavior. As
will be elaborated in the following section, the child is exposed to extensive formal and informal modeling of reflective behavior. The child is
given numerous opportunities to practice being a reflective problem
solver. Some of these opportunities focus on academic problems while
others focus on social problems and involve the use of role playing. These
new behaviors are reinforced within the sessions by concrete and social
contingencies. Despite the fact that the self-instructions (cognitive training) get top billing in the name of this intervention, we wish to be clear
that we believe the child becomes capable of implementing the self-instructions (e.g., learns to stop and think) via the repetitious modeling and
practice of thoughtful procedures in a context providing incentive manipulation and social support.

COMPONENTS OF THERAPY

This section describes the major components in our cognitive-behavioral
therapy for non-self-controlled children. These components include (1) a
problem-solving approach, (2) self-instructional training, (3) modeling,
(4) affective education, (5) behavioral contingencies, and (6) role-play exercises. Many of these components are common to other types of cognitive-behavioral interventions. If one wished to classify the components, 1,
2, and 4 could be described as primarily cognitive strategies, while 3, 5 and
6 are primarily behavioral strategies. After describing these components,
we shall discuss the integration of these strategies that occurs when the
components are applied as an organized treatment package. Readers interested in a more detailed description of the program are referred to the
treatment manual by Kendall, Padawer, Zupan, and Braswell (1985) presented in Kendall and Braswell (1985).

Problem-Solving Approach

A problem-solving orientation towards difficult situations is basic to this and most other cognitive-behavioral interventions. While it would be more accurate to term this an "attitude" rather than a "component," we feel it is so central to the conduct of this therapy that it must be listed prior to the other components or techniques. Since D'Zurilla and Goldfried (1971) presented problem solving, most behavior therapists and cognitive therapists have found heuristic value in the adoption of a problem-solving approach to interpersonal problems.

From a developmental perspective, it is interesting to ponder at what age children are able to truly adopt a problem-solving orientation in their interpersonal dilemmas. We believe that whether or not children grasp the full philosophical implications of this perspective, they can benefit from a problem-solving approach. One sign of its efficacy is that children do seem to grasp at least some aspects of this model. For example, with training, even preschool children can learn to generate alternative problem solutions (Shure & Spivack, 1978; Spivack & Shure, 1974). On a more speculative note, a nonspecific benefit of the model may be it's power to decrease the emotionalism surrounding some family difficulties. For example, to approach a child's misbehavior as a problem to be solved rather than as the inevitable outcome of having a "bad" kid or being "bad" parents may diffuse some of family's negative feelings and allow them to address the issue with hope rather than guilt and despair.

It seems reasonable to assert that, since there exists an indefinite number of potential problem situations and an infinite list of discrete solutions, interventions are best focused not on teaching specific responses but on *training the cognitive processes* involved in problem solving. The ability to achieve successful solutions to problems across various situations is the desired therapeutic outcome.

Self-Instructional Training

Self-instructions are self-directed statements that provide a thinking strategy for children with deficits in this area and serve as a guide for the child to follow through the process of problem solving. As originally implemented by Meichenbaum and Goodman (1971) self-instructions reflect the desire of the therapist to break down the process into discrete steps. Accordingly, each self-instruction represents one step of solving a problem.

As illustrated in Table 5-1, these self-directed statements proceed from the generation of a definition of the problem, to stating the approach to the problem, focusing of attention, and self-rewarding for correct responses or using a coping statement following incorrect solutions.

TABLE 5-1. Content of Self-Instructional Procedures

Problem definition	"What's the problem? What do I need to figure out?"
Problem approach	"I need to think about the different choices."
Focusing of attention	"Now I need to concentrate and think of the consequences of each choice."
Choosing an answer	"O.K. I've thought about it and I think this one is best."
Self-reinforcement or	"I did it right! I'm doing a good job."
Coping statement	"I got this one wrong. On the next one I'll slow it down and really concentrate. I can ask for help if I need it. Next time I'll try and go more slowly and concentrate more and maybe I'll get the right answer."

The problem-solving self-instructions are designed to help the child (1) recognize that there is a problem and identify its features, (2) initiate a strategy that will help him or her move toward a problem solution, (3) consider the options, and (4) take action on the chosen plan. Importantly, the self-rewarding self-instruction is included to strengthen the child's "thinking" habit.

The coping statements are designed to avoid overly negative self-talk. We do not want children to try, to make a mistake, and to tell themselves, "That was really stupid; I'm dumb," or have an overly emotional reaction. What we do want is an effort, and if the effort proves incorrect, a comparatively neutral self-stated reaction such as "Oops, I made a mistake; I'll have to think it over again" would be much preferred. This is a concrete example of how maintaining a problem-solving approach may be able to diffuse the child's tendency to attribute failure to his or her own ineptitude.

One of the most important aspects of the self-instructional procedure is the meaningfulness of the actual sentences for the individual child. That is, saying the self-instructions the way we therapists would is *not* as crucial as having the child say them in his or her own words. Individualizing the self-directed statements far surpasses "saying what we say" as the goal of the therapist.

Support for the individualizing of the self-instructions has been demonstrated in the research of Meyers, Cohen, Schlesser, and colleagues (Cohen, Meyers, Schlesser, & Rodnick, 1982; Schlesser, Meyers, & Cohen, 1981). In a study examining both the Piagetian stage of the child (preoperational vs. concrete operations) and the type of training, Cohen *et al.* (1982) found that only the concrete operational children who received a "directed discovery" type of training demonstrated significant generalization of this training to other cognitive tasks. Children in the directed discovery training were led by their therapists to "discover" the self-instructional statements that would guide problem-solving through a Socratic dialogue. The therapists used a series of prepared questions to guide this dialogue.

In our effort to imitate the developmental sequence outlined by Luria (1959, 1961), the training procedures are designed to aid the child's internalization of the self-instructions. Toward this end, the therapist uses the following sequence of training. First, the therapist models task performance and talks out loud while the child observes. The child then performs the task him- or herself while saying the self-instructions out loud (initially with some prompting from the therapist). The therapist then models the task while whispering the self-instructions and the child imitates this action. Finally, the therapist models task performance using covert self-instructions and modeling visual cues of reflective behavior, (e.g., pausing, silently counting the steps on his or her fingers, stroking the chin or beard, etc.), and the child imitates this behavior. The speed at which the therapist moves from overt to covert self-instructions should be entirely determined by the child's readiness to master each phase. For example, if the therapist has questions about the child's basic grasp of the self-instructions, then self-instructing should continue at an overt level.

At this point, we should make a brief comment about the tasks employed in training self-instruction. We cannot overemphasize that the actual activities are of little importance as long as they require the child to select one or more choices from an array of alternatives. In our program we have a definite sequence of the types of tasks that we believe enhances the child's acquisition of the self-instructions (see Table 5-1). It may be that this sequence is of some importance even if the specific tasks are not. The initial tasks are psychoeducational and are similar to tasks required in the classroom. As the central purpose of these tasks is to foster the acquisition of the self-instructions, they are designed to be simple and nonstressful. Gradually, the sessions shift emphasis to interpersonal play situations (solving puzzles or playing checkers together) and the appropriate use of self-instructions in these cases. These sessions are followed by tasks that require the child to generate affective labels and behavioral alternatives and consequences that fit with presented problem situations. The final series of sessions deal with the child's particular problem behaviors and involve the role playing of specific situations. This gradual building to the role playing of difficult interactions is designed to assure that the child understands the use of self-instructions before having to apply them in emotionally arousing situations.

Modeling

The therapeutic use of modeling entails the exposure of a client to an individual who actually demonstrates the behaviors to be learned by the client. In our intervention, the therapist models self-instructions in both a formal and an informal manner. Formal modeling occurs during task instruction as the therapist performs the tasks out loud, verbalizing the steps and modeling the behaviors associated with successful task performance. The tutor and child then alternate performing the tasks. Initially the therapist prompts the child in the use of the steps and helps the child develop his or her own memory aids, such as cue cards. Gradually, the therapist fades the self-instructions to a whisper and then to a completely covert event. Whenever a new task is being learned or when the child makes a mistake, the therapist returns to modeling overt self-instructions and has the child do the same with the next few problems.

The therapists are also informal models in the use of self-instructions with a variety of real-life problem situations that can be encountered during the course of the intervention. Some of these "real-life problems" are planned. For example, during the first session the therapist comments on how disorganized his or her briefcase of training materials is and then softly talks him- or herself through a plan for organizing the situation ("Hmm . . . I could keep the pencils in this side container and all of the loose papers in this folder). In subsequent sessions, the therapist then reminds him- or herself of the previously made plan while getting out or putting up materials. When possible, the therapist attempts to present him- or herself as a *coping model* rather than a *mastery model*. For example, when confronted with a real-life problem the tutor might display some initial difficulty or concern but would eventually be able to cope with the problem situation. This style is in contrast to presenting a mastery model in which the tutor would overcome each problem situation easily and without concern or anxiety. The following transcript demonstrates the therapist being a coping model around a minor problem situation that arose in the therapy.

THERAPIST: Let's see. Now that we've finished for today we can add up your chips. I guess we'll need a pencil for that. Where did I put that pencil? (*Looks in briefcase hurriedly.*) Hmmm . . . I thought I put it in here but I guess not.

CHILD: Maybe it's in your purse.

THERAPIST: Yes, maybe I put it there (*Looks in purse.*) . . . but I don't see it. I really get irritated with myself when I misplace things, but I guess getting mad doesn't really help me find my pencil.

CHILD: You don't look mad.

THERAPIST: I'm mad on the inside . . . I'm saying angry things to myself.

CHILD: Oh! Like "You dummy, where's that pencil?"

THERAPIST: Yeah, like that. I need to tell myself to calm down and look carefully in each of the places the pencil might be. Maybe I'll look in the briefcase again. (*Looks in briefcase while carefully rearranging the contents.*) Would you look at this! My pencil was in between two folders. The first time I looked I was in such a hurry I didn't see it there. I guess I need to slow down and stop and think.

CHILD: Yeah!

This brief moment in therapy allowed the therapist to model how one copes with frustration and how one is eventually able to attain the desired goal.

Affective Education

In addition to modeling a self-instructional approach to problem solving, the content of some of the sessions is specifically designed to help the child develop his or her ability to accurately label personal emotional experiences, as well as the emotions of others. It is hypothesized that this ability contributes to one's effectiveness in solving interpersonal problems. In research applications of this program, we typically devote the ninth and tenth sessions to the presentation of pictures of individuals with various expressions and postures or who are in different problematic situations. The child's task is to use the self-instructional steps to come up with different emotions that could fit the stimulus materials, as well as different solutions for the problem situations. The specific materials are not important. One could use specifically prepared materials for affective education or pictures from magazines. The point is to have materials that can generate discussion about a range of different emotions. To help the child avoid using just "mad," "sad," and "glad" as descriptors, the therapist and child sometimes begin this type of session by preparing a "feelings dictionary" that lists a number of different positive, negative, and neutral emotions. As will be discussed in the next section, feelings can also be identified and discussed during the role-playing activities that occur in the sessions following those more specifically focused on affective education.

Role Playing

While discussing problem situations and generating alternatives are valuable parts of this program, we believe it is also important to behaviorally act out these situations and various alternatives for action. We typically introduce role playing only after the child has mastered the verbal self-instructions or not before the tenth or eleventh session. This gives the child an opportunity to be somewhat proficient with the self-instructions prior to applying them with more emotionally charged material.

To describe our rather structured approach to role playing, we begin with a set of cards listing common interpersonal problem situations. In order to maximize the relevance of the situations for the individual child, the therapist can use the original intake concerns or consult with the parents or teacher to generate items. The child and therapist alternate randomly selecting the cards to be used. After reading the problem situation together to be sure it is understood by the child, the therapist and child generate alternatives. Initially the therapist takes the lead in generating alternatives but this task should be turned over to the child as soon as he or she grasps the nature of the activity. After alternatives have been suggested, the therapist and child then consider the emotional and behavioral consequences of each alternative from the perspective of the child and others in the situation. This discussion essentially creates the script that can then be used for acting out each possible resolution of the situation.

In setting up the role play, the child's *active involvement* is to be encouraged. For example, let the child help select props that will be used or, if the therapist is to play the role of a significant person in the child's life, he or she can ask the child what types of things this person would say and do in response to each alternative. With the first few role plays, it is often valuable to have the therapist assume the role of the child, but over time the child can be increasingly asked to "play him- or herself." After acting out the various alternatives for a given problem, the therapist and child should discuss their thoughts and feelings about each possibility. Then the child can select the alternative he or she views as the best. This type of discussion is illustrated in the following transcript. This exchange occurred after the therapist and child had acted out different possibilities for dealing with the situation in which a child was trying to retrieve a pencil he had lent but the borrower was refusing to give it up.

CHILD: It was sort of fun in there where the mean kid got hit.

THERAPIST: It was fun to show how mad you were, but what do you think would happen if you really did that?

CHILD: The teacher would get mad.

THERAPIST: And then what?

CHILD: Then I'd get sent to the principal's office.

THERAPIST: And then what?

CHILD: Then they would call my folks!

THERAPIST: Would you get your pencil back?

CHILD: No.

THERAPIST: And it sounds like you would get in trouble.

CHILD: Yeah, I think the last one was good because then if you just ask for the pencil back nicely and tell him you won't give him your stuff anymore if he doesn't give it back . . . like . . . maybe he'll give it to you.

THERAPIST: Yes, how would you feel then?

CHILD: Happy because I got the pencil back . . . and happy because I wasn't a tattletale.

THERAPIST: How do you think the other kid felt?

CHILD: Well, maybe, okay because he could feel honest that he gave it back.

THERAPIST: What about the teacher?

CHILD: She wouldn't even know what was going on so I guess she'd be okay.

THERAPIST: What about the second choice, when you could tell the teacher?

CHILD: No, I don't like to be a tattletale.

THERAPIST: So that's not a choice that feels right for you?

CHILD: No.

THERAPIST: Which choice do you think was best?

CHILD: The last one.

THERAPIST: Because?

CHILD: I got the pencil back, and me and the other kid didn't get in trouble.

As you can see from this example, discussion of the emotional impact of different choices is strongly encouraged. In this way, the affective education component initiated in earlier sessions is maintained and elaborated.

When it is the therapist's turn to declare what he or she thinks is the best choice, a general guideline of selecting the most appropriately assertive response is utilized. The therapist must be mindful, however, that in some situations, for good and bad reasons, it is not generally acceptable for a child to be as assertive as would be appropriate for an adult, so the therapist needs to be realistic in discussing possible consequences of such behavior with the child. Also the therapist can communicate that some problems have more than one good solution while with other difficulties one may have no truly attractive choices.

Despite the gradual progression toward role-playing activities, some children express resistance to acting-out activities. In these cases, it is helpful for the therapist to share his or her own reluctance or sense of awkwardness about play acting and the thoughts she or he is having (e.g., "Maybe I'll look stupid and you'll laugh at me," "I'm not a very good actor," "What if someone walks by and sees us? I'll feel silly"). Then the therapist can discuss how she or he is coping with these thoughts and feelings. On a more optimistic note, we should add that the role-playing activities are greatly enjoyed by most children.

Behavioral Contingencies

Specific behavioral contingencies are a component of this intervention. These contingencies are designed to motivate the child to learn and rehearse the self-instructional problem-solving methods. A review of the literature in this area (Kendall & Braswell, 1985; Urbain & Kendall, 1980) suggests that programs vary tremendously in the extent to which they include explicit behavioral contingencies. It is our sense that the inclusion of these contingencies is extremely important, particularly when working with more externalizing types of children. The contingencies included in the current program include response-cost, self-reward, and self-evaluating rewards for completed homework assignments, and social reward.

Response Cost

A response-cost contingency operates throughout each session. The child receives a given number of reward tokens at the beginning of each session, and he or she is instructed that he or she can lose a token for the commission of certain specified behaviors. In the program utilized in treatment outcome studies, the three reasons a child can lose chips include failing to use the self-instructions, going too fast, or getting the wrong answer on the task problem or question. Thus, the response cost serves as a cue to help the child slow him- or herself down and use the self-instructions appropriately. When the therapist enacts a response cost, the reason for the token loss is clearly and calmly stated, so the child knows exactly what he or she must do to improve performance on the next task. The rationale for using response-cost procedures springs from the nature of the target sample. Non-self-controlled children tend to respond quickly without evaluating all of the possible alternatives to a problem, so that they make many "careless" mistakes. When presented with a choice of alternative answers, impulsive children will sometimes answer correctly, conceivably obtaining the right answer by chance or because the problem was so easy that the answer was immediately apparent. If one *only* reinforces an impulsive child for right answers, which can be a matter of luck or fast guessing, one in effect spuriously rewards the child for being quick and less than fully thoughtful. In order to circumvent this problem, the cognitive-behavioral strategy uses a response-cost contingency. Most children seem to grasp the nature of this contingency; however, as will be described in a subsequent section, some children do react to this contingency with distress. In such cases, modifications can be made.

Self-Reward and Self-Evaluation

To balance the response-cost procedures, the program includes several types of reward contingencies. As described in the section on self-instructions, one of the steps or statements taught to the child is "I did a good job." The exact wording does not concern us as much as the need for self-reward following successful task performance. In addition to the formalized self-reward that is included in the self-instructions, therapists are encouraged to foster the child's use of self-instructions in any appropriate instance.

To aid the child in knowing when he or she merits self-reward, self-evaluation skills are taught. At the end of each session, the therapist shows the child a "How I did today" chart, which is actually just a 5-point rating scale, with 1 indicating "not so hot" and 5 indicating "super extra-special." The therapist then tells the child that she or he (the therapist) will pick a number that she or he thinks best describes the child's behavior during the session. The child is then asked to pick a number also, and if his or her number equals or is within one point of the therapist's rating, then the child earns a bonus token or chip. The therapist typically describes this rating procedure in the first session and provides an elaborate explanation of why she or he picked a particular number. Then the child actually engages in the self-evaluation in subsequent sessions.

Homework Assignments

Children also have an opportunity to earn bonus tokens by completing the "homework assignments." In the early sessions, homework involves thinking of a situation when he or she might have been able to use the self-instructions and remembering to describe this situation to the therapist at the beginning of the next session. As therapy progresses, the child's homework becomes remembering an opportunity when he or she used the self-instructions outside of therapy and informing the therapist of this incident. The therapist may have to prompt the child to help him or her elaborate on how the self-instructions were employed. It is, of course, possible for the child to tell a story about using the self-instructions that isn't true. The therapist has no way to ascertain the validity of the story, so if the child's response seems plausible and appropriately elaborated it should be rewarded. Ideally, the process of doing the homework or even just thinking about it aids in the generalization of the self-instructions from therapy to the home or school.

Social Reward

In an effort to create a rewarding environment for the child, therapists are also urged to be liberal in their use of smiles, comments such as "Good," "Fine," and "Nice job" and any of the generally socially rewarding messages appropriate for children. Research by Braswell, Kendall, Braith, Cary, and Vye (1985) suggests that encouraging phrases, such as "I can see you're trying," "Keep it up," and so on, may be particularly valuable. These socially rewarding messages set the tone for the sessions: positive, rewarding, and encouraging.

Integration of Cognitive and Behavioral Components

The major components of this intervention represent a range of cognitive and behavioral strategies. At the emphatically cognitive end of the continuum, there is the notion of maintaining a problem-solving approach. This element could be perceived as a cognitive set. In addition, the affective education component attempts to teach the child about the role of emotions as they are related to thoughts and behavior. While dealing with affect, it is a cognitive event in that it involves helping the child comprehend the connection between certain observable signs and specific emotional states. At the behavioral end of the continuum there are the response-cost and reward contingencies that are enacted to encourage the learning and practice of the other therapy elements. The verbal self-instructions are basic examples of cognitive self-statements. While initially they are overt and observable, it is the goal for these statements to become covert. In the context of this particular training, however, these self-instructions are also firmly tied to specific behaviors to be used when approaching a problem. Thus even this most emphatically cognitive component has explicit behavioral correlates. The phenomenon of modeling is a behavioral event that is presumably having significant impact on the child's cognitive *and* behavioral grasp of the specific events being modeled. Finally, role playing, as it is employed in this intervention, involves both the cognitive exercise of preparing a script of alternatives and consequences for various situations and the behavioral exercise of enacting these alternatives and consequences.

INTERVENTION OVERVIEW

Assessment

Effective intervention cannot occur without a careful evaluation of the client. Children who are homogeneous in terms of a lack of self-control will nevertheless vary in levels of self-esteem, intellectual ability, and many other features. A child who is impulsive but has high self-esteem and good peer relations is different from one who is equally impulsive but has low self-esteem and poor peer relations. An impulsive child with documented neurological impairments will require very different treatment from an impulsive child who is without neurological signs but has parents who have never set firm and consistent limits. The following comments are offered as brief guides to assessment. The reader is referred to Kendall and Braswell (1985) for further details.

The intake interview can be used to gather information of particular relevance in implementing cognitive-behavioral interventions. More specifically, the parents should be encouraged to translate terms such as "out of control" or "hyper" into specific behavioral examples. In keeping with behavioral tradition, one would also want to establish the antecedents and consequences for these specific behaviors. Obtaining a developmental history from the parents is valuable for detecting factors suggestive of neurological impairment (e.g., anoxia at birth or prolonged high fevers at an early age) and/or indications of the parents' involvement in the child's self-management problems (e.g., when the parents allow virtually no opportunities for experiments in independent functioning). Interview time with the child could address the child's awareness or level of understanding of his or her difficulties.

Behavior rating scales are useful for obtaining a global view of the child's behavior from the perspective of his or her parents and teachers. While "broad spectrum" rating scales such as the Child Behavior Checklist (CBCL; Achenbach, 1978; Achenbach & Edelbrock, 1978) or the Conners Teacher and Parent Questionnaires (Conners, 1969) may provide valuable information, other scales, such as the Self-Control Rating Scale (SCRS; Kendall & Wilcox, 1979) could be more relevant in preparation for a cognitive-behavioral intervention. The SCRS was specifically developed to assess self-control in elementary school children as rated by their classroom teacher and/or parents (as in Kendall & Braswell, 1982). This 33-item measure is based on a cognitive-behavioral conceptualization of self-control, wherein self-controlled children are said to possess the cognitive skills necessary to generate and evaluate alternatives and the behavioral skills needed to inhibit unwanted behavior and engage in desired action.

Task performance measures such as the Porteus Maze Test (Porteus, 1955) and the Matching Familiar Figures Test (MFF; Kagan, 1966) allow the clinician to observe the child's potential to be impulsive on cognitive tasks. Chandler's bystander cartoons (Chandler, 1973) and Selman's measure of interpersonal awareness (Selman, 1980) permit the assessment of the child's ability to recognize the thoughts and feelings of others and take the perspective of another. Still other measures such as the Purdue Elementary Problem-Solving Inventory (PEPSI; Feldhusen & Houtz, 1975); and the Means–Ends Problem-Solving task (MEPS; Shure & Spivack, 1972) enable the therapist to assess the child's cognitive skills for solving interpersonal dilemmas. All of these measures have some problematic features, yet they provide the therapist with an "in the office" opportunity to observe how the child negotiates a problem-solving situation. Beyond yielding a certain score, the evaluator can observe what, if any, problem-solving strategies the child possesses. Role playing is one method of eliciting these strategies. The therapist could assume the role of a teacher, parent, or peer in various hypothetical problem situations and see what solutions the child is able to create.

Self-report assessment of the child's expectancies, attributions, and self-concept can be quite valuable in preparation for a cognitive-behavioral intervention. Many therapists have emphasized the impact of expectancies upon behavior. This relationship is addressed in Bandura's concept of self-efficacy expectations (Bandura, 1977). According to this view, a child's self-efficacy is the extent to which the child expects that he or she can successfully execute the behaviors that lead to desired outcomes. Change in self-efficacy has been posited as the common underlying cognitive process that accounts for changes in behavior. Brief assessments of self-efficacy expectations could be incorporated into traditional testing sessions by simply asking children how confident they are that they will complete the task at hand and then evaluating the fit between the child's expectations and the actual outcome of the task. The concept of attributions is closely related to that of expectations, but attributions concern how we explain an event *after* it has occurred. The attributions children offer to explain their own task behavior can be quite interesting. Children who attribute task success to their personal effort may be more likely to show improvement following cognitive-behavioral intervention than those who attribute their success to luck, fate, or other factors external to themselves (Braswell, Koehler, & Kendall, 1985). A self-report assessment of the child's self-concept could be inferred from interview data, but can also be assessed via objective scales such as the Piers–Harris Children's Self-Concept Scale (PH; Piers & Harris, 1969) and the Perceived Competence Scale for Children (Harter, 1982). These various types of self-report measures can help the therapist understand what the child expects of him- or herself, how he or she explains personal success or failure, and the extent to which the child has a generally positive or negative self-view.

When circumstances permit more extensive assessment, behavioral observations at home or school, sociometric data, and archival data (grades, number of trips to the principal's office, number of skipped classes, etc.) can help the therapist have an even clearer understanding of the specific problems the child is experiencing. One notion that is helpful in guiding our assessment choices is the distinction between general *impact* level and *specifying* level assessments (Kendall, Pellegrini, & Urbain, 1981). Testing at the specifying level attempts to clarify exactly what thoughts and behaviors the child is displaying and provides specific targets for intervention. Behavioral observations, task performance measures, and self-report assessments yield specifying level information. Evaluation at the general impact level addresses how the child's behavior impacts on others in his or her environment. Ratings provided by parents, teachers, or peers are examples of impact level assessments, as is archival information.

Throughout the assessment phase, the therapist faces a series of questions or decisions that determine what actions should follow. Is this child actually lacking in self-control? If so, is he or she in need of other treatments in addition to self-instructional training, such as a pharmacotherapy or family therapy? Is the problem the result of the parents' inappropriate expectations rather than the child's impulsivity? If so, would they benefit most from parent education or family therapy? It is these questions that must ultimately guide the choice of assessment tools and subsequent treatment strategy.

Typical Stages of Treatment

For the purpose of a general overview, it may be most helpful to conceptualize our cognitive-behavioral training as having four phases: (1) introduction; (2) skill building; (3) skill expansion; and (4) skill consolidation and termination. This view derives from our experience with a highly structured 12-session protocol of self-instructional training. We believe, however, that these phases also apply to more extended clinical applications and tend to be true for other types of cognitive-behavioral interventions.

Introductory Phase

After the child has completed the assessment process and has been judged as a suitable candidate for self-instructional training, he or she enters the introductory phase of treatment. This phase encompasses two to four sessions depending on the rate at which the child assimilates the information presented. The key task of this phase is to introduce the child to the therapist and to the structure of the intervention. In the first session, the therapist explains all the elements of the therapy—the self-instructions, the response-cost contingency, the reward menu, methods of earning bonus chips, and so on. This represents a great deal of information and the therapist must constantly be judging the extent to which the child is comprehending the program and making allowances for that child's particular rate of understanding. The emphasis at this point is on helping the child learn the ground rules for sessions and establishing a positive affective tone to the working relationship.

In addition to the concrete details, the therapist strives to be extremely clear about what she or he expects of the child. For example, the therapist expects the child to work at mastering the self-instructions. The therapist does *not* expect that the child will get every problem correct, but is encouraged to tell the child that they will (both) go as slowly as they need to in order to do a good job. By the manner in which the therapist conducts the sessions, he or she establishes that there will be collaborative action between the therapist and child, with the therapist doing some teaching of the method of problem-solving while both the child and therapist work on examples.

Another important task of the introductory phase, especially in the first session, is learning the child's view of why he or she is in treatment. If the child states "My mom (teacher) says I'm hyper" or some similar assessment of his or her behavior by an adult, the therapist can help the child come up with descriptions of more specific problematic behaviors that get him or her into trouble with adults or other kids. If the child has no idea why he or she is in treatment and/or denies having any difficulties, the therapist does not need to press the issue at this point and can state that the child will be learning a special way to solve problems that can help with homework and also with people problems at home or school.

Skill-Building Phase

After the child has mastered the session format and has practiced the self-instructions with simple psychoeducational materials, he or she becomes capable of working out more problems with fewer examples from the therapist. In this phase the therapist introduces homework assignments and fades the self-instructions from overt to covert. One challenge of this phase is to help the child understand the primacy of the problem-solving methods over the details of the particular problems being solved. In other words, the therapist can communicate that he or she sees the child is really trying to be a careful problem-solver even if the child has trouble with math problems or puzzle problems. Conversely, with some children the therapist may need to praise the child for his or her good math or puzzle skills but remind him or her to use the self-instructions while working. In our particular program, the use of behavioral contingencies is extremely effective in reminding kids to persist with the self-instructions, but verbal reminders are also valuable and help to clarify in-session expectations.

In the second phase, the therapist also encourages the child to share more of him- or herself in terms of likes and dislikes about school and home. The goal of these discussions is to obtain a more elaborated picture of how the child views him or herself and how he or she perceives problematic situations.

Skill Expansion

In this phase, there is a shift toward applying the self-instructional methods in interpersonal problem situations. In our research programs this phase begins at the eighth or ninth session. By this time many children are proficient in applying the self-instructions with games and impersonal tasks; however, most children need help making the cognitive shift to applying these methods for the solution of interpersonal problems. As discussed in a subsequent section, this phase includes affective educational tasks, discussion of behavioral alternatives and consequences, and role playing of problematic situations.

Skill Consolidation and Termination

This final phase includes helping the child apply self-instructional methods to problems that child has experienced. In this phase there may be a "loosening" of the behavioral contingencies and more discussion about how the child could use these methods to cope with future problems. At some point during this phase, it is helpful to have the therapist and child reverse roles, with the child teaching the therapist the self-instructional methods.

General elements of conducting a good termination are also relevant. Specifically, the child should be told of the ending several sessions in advance and be involved in planning some special activity for the final session. The therapist should communicate his or her feelings about working with the child and feelings about ending and provide the child with an opportunity to express his or her feelings and reactions. The therapist and child can also discuss how one goes about deciding if he or she should re-enter therapy. Ideally, case discussions of how one decides when it is time to stop therapy or re-enter therapy are conducted with the child and his or her parents.

Structure within Sessions

There is an order to events within each session that is fairly consistent across sessions. All sessions (other than the first) begin with a review of the self-instructions and inquiry about whether the child remembers an example of when he or she could have or did use the self-instructions. The therapist then introduces the task for that session and models how the self-instructions are applied to that task. The therapist verbalizes the self-instructions with the child while the child performs the task, and finally, the child completes the task while self-instructing. The therapist and child alternate solving problems, with the therapist doing fewer as the session progresses. Typically, by the second (i.e., the skill-building) phase, the therapist is modeling how the child can fade the self-instructions from overt to covert. Whenever a response cost is enacted, however, the therapist reverts to overt verbalization of the self-instructions for the next few problems. At the end of the session the self-evaluation is conducted and bonus chips are awarded. Finally the therapist and child "bank" the earned chips and the child selects a reward from the reward menu. There is a general tendency for early sessions to be more highly structured than later sessions; however, even the final sessions roughly conform to this outline.

Active Ingredients

We believe strongly that it is the combination of cognitive and behavioral elements that produces the most effective outcomes. This belief is supported by our research (Kendall & Braswell, 1982) in which it was found that change on the greatest number of outcome measures following cognitive-behavioral treatment. The fact that some positive changes were observed for both the behavioral and attention control conditions reminds us, however, of the presence of other active ingredients. As we shall discuss, we feel the therapist enthusiasm and ability to encourage the child's emotional involvement in the sessions are crucial elements that go beyond the specific theoretical model of treatment.

THE ROLE OF THE THERAPIST

Desirable Attributes

We would like to highlight the positive elements of the therapist attitude, the ability to establish trust, and the skill at enhancing the child's involvement in therapy as central desirable attributes. (Of course, it's quite helpful if the therapist is already in the habit of talking to him- or herself out loud!) We should also note that the task of exercising good clinical skills is made more complex with an intervention of this type because it is training as well as therapy. Training calls for a didactic stance that is not necessarily consistent with a traditional therapeutic stance. Thus, the therapist faces the very real challenge of presenting the information the client needs to do the required tasks while still attempting to create a warm and receptive environment that encourages the client's open discussion of his or her problems. Inevitably, the more the therapist must talk in a session, the less the client can talk.

With this caution in mind, some therapist attributes assume special importance. Certain therapist attitudes and affects are such attributes: From our personal experience and observation of other therapists, it seems particularly efficacious for the therapist to be quite positive and enthusiastic, but not at the cost of being too frenetic or impulsive. Someone who is enthusiastic but has relatively even personal pacing meets this criterion. In addition, the most effective therapists seem to bring a sense of personal structure to the therapy and yet to be able to be flexible in how they attain their goals within this structure. They seem to sense when it is appropriate to "bend" the intervention rules or standards in the pursuit of higher therapeutic goals.

The importance of trust in the therapeutic relationship goes without saying, but there are some specific aspects of establishing trust with child clients and specific behavioral correlates of trust in this intervention that merit discussion. Working with a child client presents certain complexities in that the child rarely seeks help for him- or herself. Rather, some adult, usually a parent or teacher, is the motivating force behind the child's contact with a mental health professional. Given this situation and the fact that parents have legal responsibility for the child, the therapist is likely to have involvement with these adults, even though the child is officially the client. Both the adults and the child will benefit from the therapist's efforts to clarify his or her role. Thus, at the outset of therapy, the therapist can explain that he or she will be communicating with parents and/or teachers about issues relevant to the child, but the specifics of what the child says and does in therapy are confidential, except in those circumstances outlined by law and ethical standards. At this point the therapist can also explain the nature of the therapeutic relationship to the child, pointing out how it is like and unlike being close friends. These items are mentioned in our discussion of trust because we think that it is crucial for the development of trust that the therapist consistently act in accordance with the guidelines he or she has established. Presenting certain guidelines at the beginning gives the therapist something to refer to when the child begins to ask questions about contact with parents and teachers, or begins to make requests that fall outside the boundaries of the relationship. Beyond fostering trust via the management of these relationship issues, trust is also developed by the therapist's consistency in the handling of many details of the therapy. This includes having the appropriate therapy materials (e.g., tokens, the reward menu, pencils, etc.), and promptness and reliability regarding the appointment time. Communicating the sense that the therapist has adequately planned and prepared for the therapy session may not only enhance the therapeutic relationship; it provides another subtle model of reflective behavior. The therapist could even share with the child the way in which the therapist had to "stop and think" in order to be prepared for the session.

Finally, we would like to emphasize the importance of the therapist's ability to nurture and encourage the child's involvement in therapy. By "involvement" we mean both the extent to which the child is attentive to session activities and the degree to which the child is actively contributing to these activities by providing suggestions for role-playing situations or bringing in tasks or materials to use in the training. Braswell *et al.* (1984) found that the extent to which the child offered suggestions in the session was significantly and meaningfully related to the child's improvement, as judged by teacher ratings. The therapist can facilitate the child's involvement by giving him or her the right to decide how certain role-play situations are structured or what rules to use in certain game situations. The child's involvement is also facilitated by the therapist's ability to be quiet when it is not crucial that he or she be talking. As indicated above, although this intervention is didactic in nature, the therapist must work at keeping the child from becoming a passive student.

Common Pitfalls

The structure of any intervention produces certain inherent dangers or pitfalls that must be avoided if the therapy is to be truly effective. There are also pitfalls that cut across different types of therapy. In this section, we shall highlight the following three difficulties that are directly related to certain components of this particular therapy and that the therapist must strive to minimize or avoid: (1) intensive task focus; (2) mechanized self-instructions; and (3) rigid behavioral contingencies. We shall reserve the discussion of issues common to many types of interventions for consideration in the following section.

Intensive Task Focus

In order to train the self-instructional methods, one must train the child on some type of task. The therapist must be clear, however, that the goal is that the child learn the self-instructions, not necessarily that the child becomes proficient in performing the particular tasks. The therapist should feel free to select the tasks he or she believes will be useful for the particular child rather than being bound by task examples presented in journal articles or books, since, other than the affective education and role-playing exercises that were selected for their content, the tasks were selected because they were functional for training self-instructions. Gradually changing the self-instructions one uses from task-specific statements to more general, conceptual statements that could be applied to any type of problem also helps keep the focus on the method rather than the task. The results of Kendall and Wilcox (1980) suggest that the use of conceptual self-instructions may enhance treatment generalization.

Mechanized Self-Instructions

When one has a standard set of statements to be used in problem solving, there is the risk that, with repeated use, one will begin to say the statements without attaching any meaning to them. One must avoid having either the therapist or the child begin to sound like a robot. The therapist can emphasize how the statements can be varied yet have the same meaning, and the child can be encouraged to produce various ways of stating the self-instructions in his or her own words. On occasion the therapist may wish to model "catching himself" sounding like a robot and consciously introduce new phrases that can be used. It may be impossible to completely avoid this pitfall, but the alert therapist can use the opportunity of detecting the mindless use of statements to model the desired change and variation in the self-instructions.

Rigid Behavioral Contingencies

While we encourage the therapist to be consistent about established rules and guidelines, this consistency must be balanced with an awareness of how the child is responding to the particular contingencies being used. The goal is for the contingencies to function as an aid, not a deterrent, to the child's learning. As an explanation of this point, we offer the following examples.

During the course of one treatment-outcome study (Braswell, 1984), three subjects in the cognitive-behavioral condition were observed to have very adverse reactions to enactment of the response-cost contingencies. In order to be sensitive to the child's emotional status and yet remain within a cognitive-behavioral model of treatment, the following modifications were made. With two cases, the children were given additional opportunities to earn bonus chips at the beginning of each session for correctly responding to a series of simple questions on the self-instructions. With one of the two children, this modification greatly improved his enjoyment of the sessions. With the other child an additional technique of giving the tutor chips and having the child apply the response-cost contingency with the tutor for her mistakes was also utilized. This modification provided the tutor with opportunities to model how one copes with mistakes. The third case involved a fifth-grade girl who seemed quite disinterested in the reward menu, which seemed like "kids' stuff" to her. However, she became more involved in treatment when the menu was expanded to include some pre-adolescent-oriented grooming items. Following these alterations, all three subjects were able to actively participate in the training sessions without emotional distress.

In addition to being flexible in order to avoid the child's distress, one can also alter the system to minimize the therapist's distress. For example, if a child has great difficulty sitting in his or her chair during the session and this is interfering with learning the material, the therapist could decide to create a new rule so that the response cost process would be enacted for unauthorized movement out of the chair. With this type of situation the therapist can usually involve the child in creating a reasonable rule, as depicted in the following example.

THERAPIST: It looks like it's hard for you to sit in your chair today.

CHILD: Yeah, I guess.

THERAPIST: I think that getting up and down is making it hard for you to do the tasks at your best, so what could we do about this?

CHILD: I don't know. . . . Say I can't do it?

THERAPIST: I could say that. Do you think it would help?

CHILD: No. . . . Well . . . I don't know.

THERAPIST: Can you think of a way we could use the chips?

CHILD: Oh . . . you could take a chip when I get up. . . . Ugh!

THERAPIST: But what if you have a good reason to get up?

CHILD: Well . . . I could tell you that.

THERAPIST: Yes, maybe if you need to get up you can ask me about it first.

CHILD: Yeah! Then I wouldn't lose a chip.

THERAPIST: What if you don't ask?

CHILD: Then you'd take one.

THERAPIST: Oh . . . so what is the new rule?

CHILD: If I get up without asking, I lose a chip.

THERAPIST: And?

CHILD: If I ask first I don't lose a chip.

THERAPIST: O.K. let's try that and see if it helps you do your best work.

In this example, the therapist was able to take a problem that was occurring in the session and use it as an opportunity for problem solving and negotiation, with the contingency system used to enforce the new rule.

COMMON CLINICAL ISSUES

Certain types of difficulties or dilemmas are present in virtually every form of therapy. In this section we shall address how we attempt to prevent acting-out, resistant behavior on the part of the child client, how we handle it when it occurs, what methods are used to program for generalization, how termination is managed, and how treatment is modified for a child of lower socioeconomic status or non-majority culture background.

Prevention of Acting-Out Behavior

Given that this cognitive-behavioral intervention is designed for use with externalizing children, one might expect that great energy goes into the prevention or handling of acting-out behavior. We must say, however, that while we have some additional suggestions to offer, the actual structure of the intervention seems to have a significant preventative effect on acting out within sessions. We attribute this to the power of one-to-one attention and the ongoing behavioral contingencies. So the incidence of acting out *in* the session is actually much less than one might expect with an externalizing patient population.

Beyond the factors inherent in the program a valuable method preventing resistance and acting out is to avoid scheduling sessions at times that are unnecessarily aversive for the child. For example, if the highlight of the child's school day is gym class, sessions at that time should be avoided. In school-based intervention programs, there must be negotiation with the child's teacher about an appropriate time, but the goal is to avoid cutting the child off from the few activities he or she views as particularly reinforcing. Thus, the child's frustrations about having to be in therapy may be reduced. One can also reduce the probability of experiencing resistance if one is attentive to subject variables such as age and cognitive level, and then selects tasks and reward materials appropriate for that age and stage. An example discussed in the previous section illustrated this point. The experimenter had failed to realize that one of the fifth-grade girls perceived herself as a preteen, and accordingly she shunned the "school kid" rewards we offered. Changing the reward menu to match her perceived age greatly reduced the resistance she displayed. In a similar vein, if a task or activity is too boring or too demanding for a child, this may increase his or her frustrations, and therefore, the probability that he or she will act out.

Coping with Acting-Out Behavior

When acting-out behavior is occurring in the session, the therapist has a number of strategies he or she can use that are consistent with the treatment model. The use of any one strategy can be determined by the therapist's judgment of what the child is able to do to examine his or her own behavior at that moment. A guiding principal might be to rely on more cognitive methods when possible but apply more purely behavioral strategies when the cognitive methods are not immediately effective. To elaborate, one could ask the child to stop and think and treat the behavior he or she just exhibited (e.g., tearing up his or her paper because the answer was incorrect) as an example of a problem to be solved. The therapist and child could generate and then role play alternative methods the child could have used to cope with the frustrations of having made a mistake. In other words, problems in the session can be turned into opportunities for applying the self-instructional methods. Some externalizing children may display difficulty getting "settled down" at the beginning of the session or sometimes become overexcited and silly in the middle of a session. In these situations the therapist may wish to train the child in the use of simple imagery and/or relaxation procedures. If one is working with a child whose impulsivity seems to be mediated by anxiety more than lack of self-control, the relaxation procedures could be incorporated into the beginning of each session. In cases where the child cannot yet problem solve about his or her own in-session behavior and/or when the acting out is more destructive or manipulative, then one may wish to enact behavioral consequences, such as the loss of tokens, in addition to attempts to problem solve about the behavior. In very extreme examples, the therapist may need to impose in-session time-outs or end the session early.

Fostering Maintenance and Generalization

Perhaps the most crucial and complex task the therapist faces is working toward the maintenance and generalization of treatment gains. All interventions, including the current program, struggle with this issue. Evidence for the generalization of behavioral gains to the classroom setting has been good (see Kendall & Braswell, 1982; Kendall & Wilcox, 1980; Kendall & Zupan, 1981; and the section on research support in this chapter), but the tests of the long-term maintenance of therapeutic gains have yielded mixed results (Kendall, 1981; Kendall, 1982). Also, the positive effects of a school-based intervention program did not seem to generalize to the home in a treatment-specific manner, for parents of children in cognitive-behavioral, behavioral, and attention-control conditions, all rated their children as improved following the intervention phase (Kendall & Braswell, 1982). Thus, we have a way to go in our programming for generalization, but there are some existing components that may be responsible for the positive findings that have been achieved at this point.

Some components designed to enhance generalizations are incorporated in the self-instructions themselves. For example, the explicit training of self-reinforcing statements following task completion and self-evaluation at the end of the session are included in an attempt to help the child develop his or her own methods of self-reward that can be utilized outside the structure of this particular program. The fading of the self-instructions from overt to covert use enables the child to engage in self-talk in the classroom or home. Generalization is also encouraged by the use of problematic situations that are real for the child in the discussion of behavioral alternatives and consequences and as the material for active role-play. The use of homework assignments requires the child to report on opportunities where he or she could have or did use the self-instructional steps in school or at home.

In clinical practice, generalization can be enhanced by educating the parents to the basic concepts of the program and giving them ideas about what new reflective behaviors to look for and reinforce. As part of this education, parents should be introduced to the concept of shaping. The therapist can communicate that the development of reflective behavior is a slow, gradual process, and the parents can play a key role in nurturing the child's fledgling attempts at careful problem-solving. For example, the parent can be taught to reframe situations in which the child is slow to make a decision, such as selecting what clothes to wear for school or picking a treat at the grocery store, as examples of reflective behavior. Parents could respond to these incidents by labeling them for the child with statements such as "I see you're going slow and trying to make the best decision." The parent can also be trained to help the child generate behavioral alternatives to problem situations at home or school. Including the parents is also valuable because an uninformed parent might be detracting from the training by inadvertantly encouraging "beat the clock" behaviors. Thus, providing parents (and teachers) with information about the content of training and the need for their support can increase their positive and decrease their negative impact on the child. Further suggestions for working with parents and teachers are provided in Kendall and Braswell (1985) and in an unpublished parent guide prepared by Braswell, Shapiro, and Kendall (1983).

Working with Low-Socioeconomic-Status and Minority Clients

Our cognitive-behavioral approach has been examined with economically diverse (Braswell, Kendall, & Urbain, 1982) and ethnically diverse samples (Braswell, 1984). Variations in income within majority culture samples do not seem to influence how readily the children are able to accept the type of intervention. High- and low-socioeconomic-status (SES) children tend to achieve different scores on the outcome measures we have utilized, but they show equivalent amounts of change from pretest to posttest or pretest to follow-up when these scores are covaried with a measure of verbal IQ. Thus, in the context of this program, economic differences in subjects can be coped with in the same manner one must cope with differences in cognitive level, (e.g., selecting tasks of an appropriate difficulty level and using self-instructions that are understandable to the child).

The findings of Braswell (1984) are relevant to work with children who are both low SES and nonwhite. While the standard procedures were effective with some of these children, there was a notable subgroup of black, low income children who displayed significant emotional reactance to the response-cost procedures. Variations in the contingencies that proved to be effective with these children have been described earlier in this chapter. The point to be emphasized is that one must be flexible in the application of both the cognitive and behavioral components of the intervention. It may also be the case that the racial match of the child and therapist becomes increasingly important as the child's relationship to the majority culture decreases on other variables, such as income, IQ, or locus of control.

Much of what we have said in this section could be summarized by the concept of callibrating the intervention to match the abilities and needs of the client. In the case of this particular therapy, this process involves a balancing of the cognitive and behavioral elements of the program. For example, to prevent or cope with resistance, some children respond best to distinctly behavioral methods, such as concrete rewards. Other children are more amenable to an emphasis on the cognitive aspects of the program and can problem solve about their in-session behavioral difficulties. This callibration process also applies to planning for generalizations, with some children requiring the use of explicit behavioral contingencies in the home or classroom while other children may be able to maintain the use of more reflective strategies with only verbal reminders and cognitive modeling provided by parents or teachers.

INDICATIONS OF TREATMENT EFFICACY

The effectiveness of cognitive-behavioral therapy with impulsive children has been examined in a series of studies by Kendall and his colleagues.

Program Research

Following a successful preliminary case study (Kendall & Finch, 1976) and group outcome study (Kendall & Finch, 1978), Kendall and Wilcox (1980) examined the contribution of different types of self-instructional training with behavioral contingencies to the attainment of generalized change. Self-instructional training that focused on the specific training task (concrete labeling) was compared with training that was relevant to the task but was also general and could thus be applied to other situations (conceptual labeling). The 33 8- to 12-year-old subjects were referred by teachers for a problematic lack of self-control that interfered with both academic performance and classroom deportment. Using a randomized block procedure, with teacher ratings on the Self-Control Rating Scale (SCRS; Kendall & Wilcox, 1979) as the blocking factor, the subjects were assigned to one of the two treatment conditions or an attention-control group. All subjects were seen for six 30- to 40-minute sessions but only the two treatment groups received self-instructional training with coping modeling and a response-cost contingency. At posttest and one-month followup, teachers' blind ratings of self-control and hyperactivity evidenced significant change due to treatment, with the treatment effects stronger for the conceptual labeling group. Thus, a generalization of treatment effects to the classroom was found. A self-report measure of impulsivity showed no change, and all three groups improved on the MFF and Porteus

Mazes. In addition, Kendall and Wilcox provided date on the self-control ratings of nonreferred children to give some guidelines or norms for assessing treatment impact. At both posttreatment and follow-up, the mean ratings of the conceptual treatment group fell just within one standard deviation of the mean for the nonreferred children.

At one-year follow-up (Kendall, 1981) numerous improvements were found for subjects in all treatment groups—perhaps due to increased age. Teacher ratings showed differences favoring the conceptually trained children, but with the small number of children available, the differences did not reach statistical significance. It was observed that conceptually trained children showed significantly better recall of the material they had learned when compared with the concretely trained and control groups. Conceptually trained children were rated by their new classroom teachers as not sufficiently lacking in self-control to warrant referral.

In a study of the relative effectiveness of individual and group application of the self-instructions with response-cost contingencies, Kendall and Zupan (1981) employed twice as many treatment sessions (12) as had Kendall and Wilcox (1980). Thirty teacher-referred, non-self-controlled children from grades 3 to 5 who were problems in the classroom were assigned according to a randomized block procedure to either the individual treatment condition, the group treatment condition, or a nonspecified group treatment (control) condition. All children received 12 45- to 55-minute sessions, averaging twice a week for 6 weeks. Except for the instructions relating to the self-instructions and contingencies, children in all three conditions were given similar tasks, task instructions, and performance feedback.

Multiple assessments were used to evaluate the treatment procedures, including measures of children's task performance and cognitive skills and two teacher ratings of classroom behavior. In addition to children's performance (latencies and errors) on the MFF, the MEPS task (Shure & Spivack, 1972), and Chandler's (1973) bystander cartoons (a measure of social perspective taking) were utilized. Teachers who were blind to subjects' conditions completed the SCRS and Conners hyperactivity ratings. Each of these assessment measures was administered pretreatment, posttreatment, and at a two-month follow-up. The Peabody Picture Vocabulary Test (PPVT; Dunn, 1965) was administered pretreatment to acquire a general index of each child's verbal abilities. At posttreatment the group and individual treatment conditions demonstrated significant improvements on the self-control ratings. The changes in teachers' ratings of hyperactivity paralleled the self-control ratings; however, the changes were significant for all three conditions. Analysis of maintenance effects indicated that both self-control and hyperactivity ratings showed significant improvements, but that the improvement at follow-up was independent of the child's treatment conditions. Improvements that were independent of the child's treatment condition were also seen in performance on the MFF. Changes in perspective taking at follow-up were positive. Both individual and group treatments produced lasting improvements; the nonspecific control condition did not. Changes in test performance for means–ends problem solving were in the opposite direction than would be expected. This trend appeared to be the result of the use of the same test material for repeated administration and the tendency of the children to tell shorter stories on each administration. Shorter stories resulted in lower MEPS scores.

In terms of normative comparisons, using the teachers' blind ratings data, the mean SCRS scores of the cognitive-behavioral treatment conditions at posttreatment were within one standard deviation from the normative mean. Similarly, the hyperactivity ratings for the cognitive-behavioral treatment conditions were brought within normative range. These normative comparisons suggest that the children receiving the cognitive-behavioral treatment (individually or in groups) evidenced improvements that brought them (at posttreatment) within a normal range of self-control and hyperactivity. These improvements, resulting from lengthier treatments, were greater than those reported in Kendall and Wilcox (1980).

At one year follow-up (Kendall, 1982), improvements were found for subjects across treatment conditions. Only the children receiving group treatment were not significantly different from nonproblem children on ratings of self-control; only the children receiving individual treatment were not significantly different from nonproblem children on hyperactivity ratings. Structured interviews indicated that individually treated children showed significantly better recall of the ideas they had learned and produced significantly more illustrations of use of the ideas than either the group treatment or the nonspecific treatment conditions. Apparently, there is evidence for generalization to the classroom (as observed in the teachers' ratings) but an absence of compelling evidence for long-term maintenance.

Kendall and Braswell (1982) conducted a components analysis of the Kendall treatment package. As in the previous Kendall studies, the 27 8- to 12-year-old subjects were selected via teacher referral for the exhibition of non-self-controlled behavior that interfered with academic and social performance in the classroom. Subjects were assigned to conditions according to a randomized block procedure, and all subjects received 12 individual sessions focusing on psychoeducational and interpersonal tasks and situations. The cognitive-behavioral condition received self-instruction training via coping modeling and behavior contingencies, while the behavioral treatment condition involved only task modeling and contingencies. Dependent measures included the SCRS and Conners hyperactivity rating scales, the MFF, the PH (Piers & Harris, 1969), the Wide Range Achievement Test (WRAT; Jastak, 1946) and behavioral observations of off-task behavior in the classroom. The cognitive-behavioral group showed significant improvement and maintenance of improvement on the SCRS, while the behavioral and control groups did not. On the teacher ratings of hyperactivity, both the cognitive-behavioral and behavioral groups showed significant change at posttest and maintenance of change at follow-up. The two treatment groups also produced significant improvement and maintenance on the latency measure of the MFF, while all three groups displayed significant improvement and maintenance on the error score of MFF. The cognitive-behavioral group produced significant changes on the reading, math, and spelling subtests of the WRAT, while the behavioral group also achieved significant change on the spelling and math subtests. Only the subjects in the cognitive-behavioral group showed improvement on the self-concept measure.

The classroom observations yielded a high degree of variability, but the cognitive-behavioral group displayed relative improvement in the categories of off-task verbal and physical behaviors. In terms of normative comparisons, subjects within the cognitive-behavioral group achieved self-control ratings within one standard deviation above the mean of a nonreferred group when assessed at posttest. Parent ratings of behavior in the home environment did not reveal significant treatment effects. Thus treatment generalization to the classroom did occur, as indicated by the teacher ratings and classroom observations, but generalization to the home did not. At one year follow-up, significant group differences did not persist on any of the treatment outcome measures.

These studies suggest that when self-instructional training with disruptive/impulsive children is conducted with social as well as cognitive problem-solving tasks *and* when the training is accompanied by behavioral contingencies, it is possible to achieve some change on both cognitive and social/behavioral measures. These changes appear to be detectable by both teachers and behavioral observers, although, as discussed previously, the optimizing of treatment generalization remains an issue.

In an effort to understand observed variations in outcome, Braswell (1984) examined the effects of the demographic variable of ethnicity while simultaneously assessing other psychological attributes of the child. Twenty-seven teacher-referred, non-self-controlled children from grades 2 through 5 were assigned to either the cognitive-behavioral or attention-control condition via a randomized blocks procedure. The sample (21 boys and 6 girls) included 16 black children, 10 white children, and 1 Asian-American child. Prior to the intervention, half of the children from each condition participated in a pretherapy preparation group in which the nature of the therapist–child relationship was explained and the children were allowed to state whether they wanted to participate. Children in both conditions received twelve 45- to 55-minute individual sessions and were exposed to the same psychoeducational tasks, games, and role-play exercises. Children in the treatment conditions received training in verbal self-instructions via direct instruction and coping modeling. Response-cost contingencies, as well as opportunities for earning bonus chips, operated throughout each session. The attention control group received neither the verbal self-instructions nor the behavioral contingencies, but were given prizes for "cooperation" that were comparable to those being earned by the treatment children.

Dependent measures included teacher ratings of self-control and hyperactivity, task performance assessment of planning ability and impulsivity, self-report questionnaires measuring locus of control and perceived competence, therapists' ratings of improvement, and observations of classroom behavior. These measures were administered at pretest, posttest, and 10-week follow-up. At posttest only the children also completed ratings of the therapeutic relationship and an attributions of change questionnaire. Therapists also completed brief ratings after each therapy session.

The results indicated the intervention did not produce the same relative magnitude of effects as observed in previous outcome studies. Teachers rated children from both groups as improved at posttest but only white subjects were rated as improved at follow-up. All subjects also displayed change on a measure on impulsivity. Significant changes in planning ability, locus of control, or perceived competence were not observed. The behavioral observations suggested some slight treatment versus control group differences, but the only statistically significant differences were those between the referred and nonreferred classroom controls, with the referred children displaying more behavior that involved frequent seat leaving and verbally bothering others. Intercorrelation of dependent variables suggested that the children who displayed improvement on the teacher ratings tended to have higher verbal IQs, more internal loci of control, and provided effort-oriented attributions for their own change. Thus, subjects like those in previous outcome studies (e.g., white, middle class, with at least average verbal IQs) tended to show positive change, while the amount of change decreased to the extent the subject differed from this prototype. The fact that all therapists were white may also be of significance, since blacks were therefore required to learn from models unlike themselves.

Ideal Clients and Contraindications

Much more research is needed before we can clearly understand the impact of various subject variables. However, the studies just reviewed raise a number of hypotheses about what types of children are best suited for this intervention. The data suggests greatest success when working with an elementary-school-aged majority culture child. Children of a range of IQ levels have obtained positive results; however, Braswell (1984) did observe that verbal IQ was positively associated with outcome in an ethnically and economically diverse sample. It may be the case that when the child is from a more deprived background, verbal IQ plays a stronger role, for this association between verbal IQ and outcome was not observed in previous studies. Being more internal in one's locus of control was also associated with positive outcome (Braswell, 1984). While the majority of the treated subjects have been male, the females that did participate showed comparable rates of improvement (see also Kendall & Urbain, 1981). The methods described in this chapter may be effective with a broad range of children; however, to the extent that the client differs from the subjects of the outcome studies the therapist must be particularly careful to tailor the methods appropriately.

While cognitive-behavioral methods can be utilized with many types of presenting problems, we believe that the methods outlined in this chapter should not be used for certain disorders. The treatment package was specifically developed to address the deficits of externalizing children, particularly their lack of self-guiding internal dialogue. Other types of children, such as those displaying overanxious or obsessive disorders, may already be engaging in excessive self-talk. These children might need assistance in changing and *decreasing* their self-statements. They would *not* benefit from learning more statements to insert between thought and action. Theoretically, these children could benefit more from cognitive-behavioral procedures modeled after Beck's cognitive therapy (Beck, Rush, Shaw, & Emery, 1979); Meichenbaum's stress innoculation training (Meichenbaum, 1975; see, e.g., Kendall, Howard, & Epps, in press, regarding programs for anxiety problems in general), or other programs that emphasize modeling, coaching, and modifying expectations (Kendall & Morison, 1984).

Future Developments

While this intervention has benefited from a relative wealth of research, the continued refinement of this approach depends upon further study in a number of areas.

More research is needed on the role of pre-existing cognitive sets or structures in affecting response to cognitive-behavioral interventions. While a great deal of work has focused on the relationship between locus of control and level of achievement in children, further exploration of when and how it is possible (and desirable) to alter the child's expectational/attributional style is needed. Future studies addressing the response of locus of control to therapeutic intervention would profit from including both generalized and more specific measures of locus of control. Assessment of the child's cognitive schemas and the extent to which change in schemas is associated with positive behavioral gains is the present mandate. A more complete understanding of the potential for change on these psychological dimensions would be valuable for therapists as well as educational personnel.

Concerning the form of the intervention, it would be advantageous to design studies that include more sessions, perhaps with the later sessions occurring at increasingly greater intervals. This change would lessen the dissimilarity between interventions conducted in the context of research projects versus those conducted in actual clinical settings. In addition to the time and resources these lengthier studies would require, researchers working in school environments would also need to develop an ongoing relationship with a school or school system and become better integrated into the curriculum and services of the school. The work of Sarason and Sarason (1981) represents an excellent example of an intervention project that achieved integration within the school environment; the effects of this intervention appeared to be maintained, at least within the context of the school setting.

The results considered in the previous section suggest that more research is needed on the role of various subject variables. For example, ethnicity, along with verbal IQ and locus of control, seem to exert some effect on outcome, at least as assessed by teacher ratings. Previous research with ethnically homogeneous samples indicated that change was not moderated by socioeconomic status. There may, however, be some type of interaction between the variables of socioeconomic status and ethnicity that is ultimately responsible for the type of results observed in this study. To be economically deprived *and* not of the majority culture may result in disadvantages or create barriers that are significantly greater than either factor alone. In order to explore this, future efforts will need to gather detailed family economic information in conjunction with other assessment methods. Concern with the additive effects of ethnicity and socioeconomic status received significant attention in the late 1960s and 1970s. Unfortunately, as often seem the case within psychology, research interests (and funding priorities) shift before key questions in an area have been sufficiently addressed.

While the efficacy of the cognitive-behavioral treatment approach described in this chapter has been relatively well-documented in comparison to other therapeutic efforts, the evidence for powerful, consistent generalization of treatment effects across different types of subjects is a goal that remains to be achieved.

REFERENCES

Achenbach, T. M. (1966). The classifications of children's psychiatric symptoms: A factor analytic study. *Psychological Monographs, 80,* (Whole No. 0.615).

Achenbach, T. M. (1978). The Child Behavior Profile: I. Boys aged 6–11. *Journal of Consulting and Clinical Psychology, 46,* 478–488.

Achenbach, T. M., & Edelbrock, C. S. (1978). The classification of child psychopathology: A review and analysis of empirical efforts. *Psychological Bulletin, 85*, 1275–1301.

Bandura, A. (1977). Self-efficacy: Toward a unifying theory of behavioral change. *Psychological Review, 84*, 191–215.

Beck, A. T., Rush, A. J., Shaw, B., & Emery, G. (1979). *Ccognitive therapy of depression*. New York: Guilford.

Braswell, L. (1984). *Cognitive-behavioral therapy with an inner city sample of non-self-controlled children*. Unpublished doctoral dissertation, University of Minnesota.

Braswell, L., Kendall, P. C., Braith, J., Carey, M., & Vye, C. (1985). "Involvement" in cognitive-behavioral therapy with children: Process and its relationship to outcome. *Cognitive Therapy and Research, 9*, 611–630.

Braswell, L., Kendall, P. C., & Urbain, E. S. (1982). A multistudy analysis of the role of socioeconomic status (SES) in cognitive-behavioral treatments with children. *Journal of Abnormal Child Psychology, 10*, 443–449.

Braswell, L., Koehler, C., & Kendall, P. C. (1985). Attributions and outcomes in child psychotherapy. *Journal of Social and Clinical Psychology, 3*, 458–465.

Braswell, L., Shapiro, E., & Kendall, P. C. (1983). *Verbal self-instructional training: A parent's guide*. Unpublished manuscript, University of Minnesota.

Camp, B. W., Blom, G. E., Herbert, F., & van Doornick, W. J. (1977). "Thinking Aloud": A program for developing self-control in young aggressive boys. *Journal of Abnormal Child Psychology, 5*, 157–168.

Chandler, M. (1973). Egocentrism and antisocial behavior: The assessment and training of social perspective-taking skills. *Developmental Psychology, 9*, 326–332.

Conners, C. K. (1969). A teacher rating scale for use in drug studies with children. *American Journal of Psychiatry, 126*, 884–888.

Copeland, A. P. (1983). Children's talking to themselves: Its developmental significance, function, and therapeutic promise. In P. C. Kendall (Ed.), *Advances in cognitive-behavioral research and therapy* (Vol. 2). New York: Academic Press.

Dodge, K. A., & Frame, C. L. (1982). Social cognitive biases and deficits in aggressive boys. *Child Development, 53*, 620–635.

Dodge, K. A., Murphy, R. R., and Buchsbaum, K. (1984). The assessment of intention-cue detection skills in children: Implications for developmental psychopathology. *Child Development, 55*, 163–713.

Dunn, L. M. (1965). *Expanded manual for Peabody Picture Vocabulary Test*. Minneapolis, MN: American Guidance Services.

D'Zurilla, T. J., & Goldfried, M. R. (1971). Problem solving and behavior modification. *Journal of Abnormal Psychology, 78*, 107–126.

Feldhusen, J., & Houtz, J. (1975). Problem solving and the concrete–abstract dimension. *Gifted Child Quarterly, 19*, 122–129.

Gottman, J., Gonso, J., & Shuler, P. (1976). Teaching social skills to isolated children. *Journal of Abnormal Child Psychology, 4*, 179–197.

Graziano, A. M., & Mooney, K. C. (1980). Family self-control instruction for children's nighttime fear reduction. *Journal of Consulting and Clinical Psychology, 48*, 206–213.

Gurucharri, C., Phelps, E., & Selman, R. (1984). Development of interpersonal understanding: A longitudinal and comparative study of normal and disturbed youths. *Journal of Consulting and Clinical Psychology, 52*, 26–36.

Hains, A. A., & Ryan, E. B. (1983). The development of social cognitive processes among juvenile delinquents and nondelinquent peers. *Child Development, 54*, 1536–1544.

Harter, S. (1982). The Perceived Competence Scale for Children. *Child Development, 53*, 87–97.

Hinshaw, S. P., Henker, B., & Whalen, C. K. (1984). Self-control in hyperactive boys in anger-inducing situations: Effects of cognitive-behavioral training, and methylphenidate. *Journal of Abnormal Child Psychology, 12*, 55–77.

Hudson, L. E., Forman, E. A., & Brion-Meisels, S. (1982). Role taking as a predictor of prosocial behavior in cross-age tutors. *Child Development, 53*, 1320–1329.

Ingram, R. E., & Kendall, P. C. (1986). Cognitive clinical psychology: Implications of an information processing perspective. In R. E. Ingram (Ed.), *Information processing approaches to clinical psychology.* New York: Academic Press.

Jastak, J. (1946). *Wide Range Achievement Test.* Wilmington: C. L. Story Company.

Kagan, J. (1966). Reflection impulsivity: The generality and dynamics of conceptual tempo. *Journal of Abnormal Psychology, 71,* 17–24.

Kanfer, F., Karoly, P., & Newman, A. (1975). Reduction of children's fear of the dark by competence-related and situational threat-related verbal cues. *Journal of Consulting and Clinical Psychology, 43,* 251–258.

Kendall, P. C. (1981). One-year follow-up of concrete versus conceptual cognitive–behavioral self control training. *Journal of Consulting and Clinical Psychology, 49,* 740–749.

Kendall, P. C. (1982). Individual versus group cognitive–behavioral self-control training: One-year follow-up. *Behavior Therapy, 13,* 241–247.

Kendall, P. C. (1985). Toward a cognitive-behavioral model of childhood psychopathology and a critique of related interventions. *Journal of Abnormal Child Psychology, 13,* 357–372.

Kendall, P. C., & Bemis, K. M. (1983). Thought and action in psychotherapy: The cognitive-behavioral approaches. In M. Hersen, A. E. Kazdin, & A. S. Bellack (Eds.), *The clinical psychology handbook.* New York: Pergamon.

Kendall, P. C., & Braswell, L. (1982). Cognitive-behavioral self-control therapy for children: A components analysis. *Journal of Consulting and Clinical Psychology, 50,* 672–689.

Kendall, P. C., & Braswell, L. (1985). *Cognitive-behavioral therapy for impulsive children.* New York: Guilford.

Kendall, P. C., & Finch, A. J., Jr. (1976). A cognitive-behavioral treatment for impulsivity: A case study. *Journal of Consulting and Clinical Psychology, 44,* 852–857.

Kendall, P. C., & Finch, A. J., Jr. (1978). A cognitive-behavioral treatment for impulsivity: A group comparison study. *Journal of Consulting and Clinical Psychology, 46,* 110–118.

Kendall, P. C., Howard, B. L., & Epps, J. (in press). The anxious child: Cognitive behavioral treatment strategies. *Behavior Modification.*

Kendall, P. C., & Morison, P. (1984). Integrating cognitive and behavioral procedures for the treatment of socially isolated children. In A. W. Meyers & W. E. Craighead (Eds.), *Cognitive behavior therapy with children.* New York: Plenum.

Kendall, P. C., Padawer, W., Zupan, B., & Braswell, L. (1985). Developing self-control in children: The manual. In P. C. Kendall & L. Braswell, *Cognitive-behavioral therapy for impulsive children.* New York: Guilford.

Kendall, P. C., Pellegrini, D., & Urbain, E. S. (1981). Approaches to assessment for cognitive-behavioral interventions with children. In P. C. Kendall & S. D. Hollon (Eds.), *Assessment strategies for cognitive-behavioral intervention.* New York: Academic Press.

Kendall, P. C., & Urbain, E. S. (1981). Cognitive-behavioral intervention with a hyperactive girl: Evaluation via behavioral observations and cognitive performance. *Behavioral Assessment, 3,* 345–357.

Kendall, P. C., & Wilcox, L. E. (1979). Self-control in children: Development of a rating scale. *Journal of Consulting and Clinical Psychology, 47,* 1020–1029.

Kendall, P. C., & Wilcox, L. E. (1980). A cognitive–behavioral treatment for impulsivity: Concrete versus conceptual training in non-self-controlled problem children. *Journal of Consulting and Clinical Psychology, 48,* 80–91.

Kendall, P. C., & Zupan, B. A. (1981). Individual versus group application of cognitive-behavioral strategies for developing self-control in children. *Behavior Therapy, 12,* 344–359.

Kettlewell, P. W., & Kausch, D. F. (1983). The generalization of a cognitive-behavioral treatment program for aggressive children. *Journal of Abnormal Child Psychology, 11,* 101–114.

Luria, A. (1959). The directive function of speech in development and dissolution. *Word, 15,* 341–352.

Luria, A. (1961). *The role of speech in the regulation of normal and abnormal behaviors.* New York: Liveright.

Mahoney, M. J. (1977). Reflections on the cognitive-learning trend in psychotherapy. *American Psychologist, 32,* 5–13.

Meichenbaum, D. H. (1975). A self-instructional approach to stress management: A proposal for stress-innoculation training. In C. Spielberger & I. Sarason (Eds.), *Stress and anxiety* (Vol. 2). New York: Wiley.

Meichenbaum, D. H., & Goodman, J. (1971). Training impulsive children to talk to themselves: A means of developing self-control. *Journal of Abnormal Psychology, 77,* 115–126.

Mischel, W. (1974). Processes in delay of gratification. In L. Berkowitz (Ed.), *Advances in experimental social psychology* (Vol. 7). New York: Academic Press.

Mischel, W., & Patterson, C. J. (1976). Substantive and structural elements of effective plans for self-control. *Journal of Personality and Social Psychology, 34,* 942–950.

Monohan, J., & O'Leary, K. D. (1971). Effects of self-instruction on rule-breaking behavior. *Psychological Reports, 29,* 1059–1066.

Mussen, P. H. (1963). *The psychological development of the child.* Englewood Cliffs, NJ: Prentice-Hall.

O'Leary, K. D. (1968). The effects of self-instruction on immoral behavior. *Journal of Experimental Child Psychology, 6,* 297–301.

Patterson, C. J., & Mischel, W. (1975). Plans to resist distraction. *Development Psychology, 11,* 369–378.

Patterson, C. J., & Mischel, W. (1976). Effects of temptation-inhibiting and task facilitating plans on self-control. *Journal of Personality and Social Psychology, 33,* 209–217.

Piers, E. V., & Harris, D. B. (1969). *The Piers–Harris Children's Self-Concept Scale.* Nashville: Counselor Recordings and Tests.

Porteus, S. D. (1955). *The maze test: Recent advances.* Palo Alto, CA: Pacific Books.

Richard, B. A., & Dodge, K. A. (1982). Social maladjustment and problem-solving in school-aged children. *Journal of Consulting and Clinical Psychology, 50,* 226–233.

Sarason, I. G., & Sarason, B. R. (1981). Teaching cognitive and social skills to high school students. *Journal of Consulting and Clinical Psychology, 49,* 908–918.

Schleser, R., Cohen, R., Meyers, A. W., & Rodick (1984). The effects of cognitive level and training procedures on the generalization of the self-instructions. *Cognitive Therapy and Research, 8,* 187–200.

Schleser, R., Meyers, A., & Cohen, R. (1981). Generalization of self-instructions. Effects of general versus specific content, active rehearsal, and cognitive level. *Child Development, 52,* 335–340.

Selman, R. L. (1980). *The growth of interpersonal understanding: Developmental and clinical analysis.* New York: Academic Press.

Shure, M. B., & Spivack, G. (1972). Means–end thinking, adjustment, and social class among elementary school-aged children. *Journal of Consulting and Clinical Psychology, 38,* 348–353.

Shure, M. B., & Spivack, G. (1978). *Problem-solving techniques in child rearing.* San Francisco: Jossey-Bass.

Spivack, G., & Shure, M. B. (1974). *Social adjustment of young children: A cognitive approach to solving real-life problems.* San Francisco: Jossey-Bass.

Urbain, E. S., & Kendall, P. C. (1980). Review of social-cognitive problem-solving interventions with children. *Psychological Bulletin, 88,* 109–143.

Vygotsky, L. (1962). *Thought and language.* New York: Wiley.

CHAPTER 6

Moving beyond Cognitive-Behavior Therapy: Integrating Gestalt Therapy to Facilitate Personal and Interpersonal Awareness

Iris Goldstein Fodor
New York University

INTRODUCTION

This chapter, drawing on my clinical experience in working on relationship issues and assertiveness training with individual clients in outpatient therapy, will focus on interpersonal issues that are typically neglected in discussions of cognitive-behavior therapy (CBT). Specifically, I will discuss some of the limitations of the standard CBT model for dealing with problems in relating to significant others.

Cognitive-behavior therapists for the most part have not paid sufficient attention to interpersonal variables. So much of the emphasis in CBT has been on the internal ideational system, that one often assumes that clients' major relationships consist entirely of the self-statements they are generating within their own heads (Ellis & Harper, 1975; Meichenbaum, 1977). Yet, relationship variables are quite central to both the process of being in therapy (which is after all a dyadic interaction) and to the most common issue that most clients are struggling with: getting along better with significant others. Furthermore, so many of the internal dialogues (or irrational beliefs) concern messages from significant others, appraisals of effects or consequences on behaviors of significant others, evaluations of significant others, and plans to court, or deal with significant others, that it is essential to study dyadic interactions within the context of CBT (Fodor, 1980, 1983). In approaching interactional issues, I will argue for a focus on *process* rather than on *symptoms*; that is, the study of recurrent patterns of behavior and how these patterns are characteristically and repeatedly reflected in the client's interpersonal interactions (Arnkoff, 1980; Guidano & Liotti, 1983). I will also argue for the therapist's becoming aware of how these patterns are revealed in therapist–client interactions and for using the therapist–client encounters as part of the process of therapy.

The first part of the chapter will describe my client population, the concerns that lead these individuals to seek out a cognitive-behavior therapist, and their expectations regarding therapy. In the second part, the strengths and limitations of cognitive-behavior therapy in the treatment of relationship issues will be discussed.

Behavior therapists typically begin with the client's presenting problems and develop therapeutic strategies to alleviate these symptoms. I will present a case for a widening of the assessment period by utilization of Gestalt techniques. Therapy will be viewed as an ongoing assessment process where therapist and client are engaging in cooperative exploration of characteristic patterns of behavior as revealed in therapist–client interactions. The third part of the chapter will present a model for the treatment of relationships within the context of individual therapy utilizing the combined Gestalt–CBT assessment strategies.

FRAMEWORK FOR UNDERSTANDING CLIENTS' EXPECTATIONS AND GOALS REGARDING THERAPY

Who Are the Clients?

Before proceeding with a theoretical overview of my model of therapy, I will delineate the nature of my client population: who I see, why these particular clients come to me, and what they hope to accomplish in therapy.

This chapter will draw on my private practice as a therapist in Greenwich Village, New York—a heterogeneous, middle-class community that has an overrepresentation of alternative life styles and single clients, and an underrepresentation of more conventionally married couples and families. Most of my clients are in their mid-20s to mid-40s. Diagnostically, most of these clients are either neurotics or have personality disorders. Some present the symptoms typically seen by behavior therapists such as phobias, work blocks, eating disorders, and depression. The remainder complain of stress or other less clearly defined difficulties.

Individual Client Problems

My clients represent some of the heterogeneity of New York. At one end of the range are young small-town adults who have come to the city to make it (e.g., aspiring actors working as waiters, writers working as typists, and political activists whose lives revolve around meetings and demonstrations). At the other end of the range are upper east siders whose lifestyles appear affluent and glamorous, but who come to therapy complaining of feeling empty. They are high achievers (e.g., the "type A businessman" and the "new entrepreneurial woman"), who feel they work too hard and receive too little nurturance and pleasure in their lives, as well as a large number of young, single professionals having difficulty coping with adult life in a stressful urban environment. About half of my clients are single and one fourth is lesbian or gay. Whatever their sexual orientation or presenting problem, they all seem to be attempting to cope with the problem of finding or dealing with a significant other.

Many of my clients have been in psychoanalytic therapy and have sought out a therapist with a behavioral orientation because of dissatisfaction with the former. They view the blank screen technique of psychoanalysis as negative and express a wish for more therapist contact and feedback. They also complain of a lack of structure and goals in psychoanalytically oriented therapy and, most important, a lack of progress. Many of my clients also come because they feel they can talk more honestly with a woman, or seek me out because of my feminist orientation after one or more negative experiences with male therapists. Some clients come because they think it will cost less to be in behavior therapy or are afraid to get too involved in "deep therapy."

I also see a number of therapists as clients (mostly behavior therapists) who seek a therapist with a behavioral perspective, but one who "works in-depth." These clients are often the ones most willing to experiment, and therapy with them is often collaborative and exciting.

My clients generally come for therapy when their usual life patterns break down, when ways of behaving that were learned in their family of origin don't work for them any more, or when they are thrown into a situation where the old supports or ways are no longer functional. Many of them are not prepared by familial and childhood learning to cope realistically with adult life. They assumed that it would all work out when they grew up, finished school, had their own apartments, or married. What they discover is that adult life is often overwhelming: There are too many decisions, too much work, and not enough money. What bothers them most is the emotional pain that comes from dealing with problematic relationships; they complain that no one ever told them it would be *"this* hard." For most of my clients, the area in which they seem least prepared to cope is that of their relationships. They come with questions such as these: "How do I make the lousy one I'm in better?" "Is this the best there is?" "Should I or shouldn't I leave this only partially satisfactory relationship; *is* there really anyone else out there for me?" My clients are so obsessed with these issues that whatever their presenting problem, we end up trying to work on their relationships. The other major area for my clients is work—"making it professionally" or at least surviving the New York rat race. Because life in this city is so stressful, and the single scene so off-putting, there is often great urgency about having a significant other with whom to share prime time.

Values and Societal Structures

Therapists and clients too often have highly internalized the philosophy of American individualism that says, "What we make of ourselves is up to us." They view the person as a sort of commodity, to be marketed in the best way, so that she or he can find the best job, or best mate, and be a "winner" rather than a "loser." Following this view, many of my clients view life as a competitive race against age peers, with the prize at the end being the perfect life. They use phrases, such as "Time is running out," and "At this age, all my other friends have married, [had children, have gotten doctorates, have bought a co-op, etc.]." They despair because they are "losers"—because they are 30 years old and without a mate, 40 and without a child, 50 and divorced with no money. In relationships, the concern with age is particularly apparent: "With my looks, money, and achievements, is this the best person I can get at this age?"

THE FUNCTION OF THERAPY

Perhaps because American culture places so great a value on individualism, in many ways behavior therapy, behavior therapists, and the self-help/self-management movement of the past decade have played into this therapy goal of the self as commodity. The message that we therapists often give is that it's all up to you the client what you make of your life. If you enter our workshops, buy our books and work with us, you will become more assertive, or thinner and more attractive, and thereby more successful: You will become a better commodity, have better relationships, and get ahead in life (Fodor, 1983; Fodor & Thal, 1984). As therapists we would do well to look into how much we are buying into the self-as-commodity aspect of therapy and using our cognitive–behavioral techniques to enable our clients to live the best of all possible lives. It is important to consider questioning these societal values of maximal self-development, work achievement, and material rewards as the only routes to happiness.

THE THEORY OF THERAPY: WHAT IS MY BIAS?

My theoretical perspective is that of a cognitive-behavior therapist operating within a social learning theory model. I view the therapist as a teacher/trainer, whose job it is to help clients understand themselves and what will make them happy, as well as, once these goals are articulated, to help clients systematically work on changing patterns of behavior that lead to poor choices and unhappiness (Mahoney, 1974). When I began work in CBT in the early 1970s, I believed that changing cognitions would lead to behavior change—that by identifying maladaptive self-statements and belief systems, and then substituting alternative belief systems (with some anxiety coping or other affect-management strategies thrown in) the client would change (Wolfe & Fodor, 1975; Fodor & Wolfe, 1977). My present view is that the above is too simplistic a view to encompass the complexity of people's problems and that people are remarkably resistant to substituting such therapist-generated rational adaptive thinking for their persistent irrational and maladaptive beliefs. Furthermore, after watching the emotional upheavals in many of my clients, I am convinced that affects cannot always be controlled by cognitions, that clients have affective patterns which influence behavior. Such affective patterns need to be explored more fully as routes into deep structures that cannot be so readily accessed or so readily controlled by surface conscious cognitions.

I now believe there are more general organizations of beliefs (both rational and irrational) that reflect more central processes than the above formulation would suggest. We need to look at more than strings of irrational beliefs: We need to examine cognitive structures that influence behavior (Beck & Emery, 1985; Turks & Speers, 1983). "For change to be maintained and generalized the deep structure must be altered" (Arnkoff, 1980, p. 350). Typically, when people come into therapy it is because their old system is not working. Traditional CBT often attempts to shore up the system by adding new coping strategies so that the client learns to manage new situations. When this works, it is the best work that behavior therapists do. However, for many clients the system may continue to break down, as we work piecemeal on anxiety management, assertiveness training, couples communication, self-control, and so on. As we see the same problems occurring and recurring in the same clients over a period of time, we would do well to reconsider our basic assumptions. By maintaining a focus only on symptoms rather than on patterns and process as well, we are failing to enable our clients to understand some of the redundancies that contribute to their persistent problems (Mahoney, 1980; Arnkoff & Glass, 1982). Furthermore, in the very act of carrying out our specific procedures, many of the problematic patterns experienced by clients in their lives are repeated in their interactions with the therapist. Behavior therapists have generally chosen not to focus on the dyadic interaction between therapist and client that occurs during therapy. I believe it is time for us to use these therapeutic interactions as important sources of data for both assessment and treatment.

Consider the following case seen over a 15-year span: In 1970, at age 25, the client sought behavior therapy for public speaking anxiety. She was a young administrative assistant, a perfectionist, and highly stressed. We did a standard behavioral treatment for speech anxiety, which enabled the client to conduct public demonstrations of her company's products and present her ideas at staff conferences. In 1970, I saw her for 12 sessions, using desensitization, relaxation, and graduated practice. A text book case, the client was now able to speak before her colleagues and was satisfied with the outcome of her therapy; and, by most criteria, she would be considered a definite treatment success.

Five years later, the client returned with a serious marital problem. Her husband was drinking heavily and refused to go for help. She had decided to leave him, but she was very anxious about supporting herself and living alone. She worried about breaking the news of the divorce to her Catholic parents. We worked on anxiety management, and did assertiveness training along with some feminist work on coping with being alone. (In the mid-1970s I was an active feminist therapist and assertiveness trainer [Wolfe & Fodor, 1975].) Therapy lasted 12 sessions. I helped the client restructure her beliefs that a woman needs a man to depend on in order to be happy, that a woman cannot live alone and take care of herself, and so on, countering them with statements such as, "I can learn to take care of myself" and "I can be happy on my own." The client was encouraged to put a feminist poster over her bed which said "A woman without a man is like a fish without a bicycle", and to behave more independently (e.g., go to restaurants alone). The client used therapy well. In 16 sessions over a 4-month period, her anxiety leveled off, she ended her marriage, and looked forward to living alone and becoming more independent. She valued her time alone, but still had few friends. The therapist urged her to go into a woman's group, but she declined, stating that she was a very private person and didn't feel comfortable talking about her problems with strangers.

At age 35, in 1980, the client called again, this time with a career crisis. She wanted to return to graduate school for an MBA. She was worried that she might not be able to handle the stress of the high status school she wished to attend. She was worried about finances, and about her ability to juggle school, work, and social life. By the 1980s, cognitive-behavioral therapists had developed techniques of stress management and training in coping skills. Again, the client responded well to the therapy and began her MBA program. At age 40, in 1985, she called me in a panic. She was exhausted from working full-time and trying to finish her MBA at night. She was being considered for a high-level management position, but she panicked about getting through the job interviews. (The anxiety appeared similar to the public speaking anxiety of 15 years earlier.) The man with whom she had been living over the past 3 years had moved out, just as she was leaning on him for the first time.

In many respects, this woman could be considered a behavior therapy success: She came for help every 5 years, required only 3 or 4 months of therapy, and moved on with her life. Yet, the case can illustrate the failure of piecemeal behavior therapy to access or tap into a more central system or structure that underlies the recurrent behavior patterns (Arnkoff & Glass, 1982; Beck & Emery, 1985; Guidano & Liotti, 1983). Behavior therapy only helped her cope with each crisis and achieve more control until the next situation overwhelmed her, but did not address her structural patterns. Furthermore, many of these structural patterns are out of the client's awareness (and thus are not so easily controlled by cognitions), and may result in behaviors that operate at cross purposes. In appraising the 15-year pattern of this case, the following is apparent: This woman asked for help only in a crisis. At these times, she felt out of control about the situation with which she was trying to deal and about her own anxiety. She picked unreliable, unsupportive men for her significant relationships. She viewed herself as independent and competent, and as striving to become more independent and more competent. As she got older, she picked bigger challenges as tests of her competency. When anxiety would break through, she would feel as though the entire system were breaking down and she would panic. Furthermore, in a city where psychoanalysts are everywhere, she sought out a behavior therapist and short-term therapy. She appeared reluctant to be dependent on a therapist, except in a state of panic.

In designing a treatment to alter these patterns, one needs to consider the following: (1) Why is the symptom so aversive: Why does being helpless, being alone, or seeming incompetent cause such panic? (2) How does the client use therapy? Does a cognitive-behavioral therapist with a feminist orientation ally him- or herself too early with the strong independent part and not explore the underside of the conflict, the helplessness and dependency? (3) What relation does the achievement drive (work) have to shoring up competency? Why is the client less happy as she gets more successful? What would make this client really happy? The issue that was not addressed until age 40 was her pattern of handling her life: seeing life as a challenging test of her ability to cope, trying to handle the crisis alone and then panicking when she can't cope, asking for short-term help and then going out to successfully meet the challenges until the next crisis. One also needs to explore the key features of the competing systems and the conflicts they generate: Can I be strong if I ask for help? Can I be independent if I'm with a strong man? Why is competency more important than nurturance as a goal?

For this client, all of the patterns were there with the first presenting symptom: The speech anxiety signalled a need for self-sufficiency competing with a fear of being out of control and looking incompetent to the world. The initial behavior therapy enabled her to shore up the independent and competent part of herself and avoid examining the more out-of-control, helpless side. Furthermore, in the very way the client interacted with me and made use of the therapy, her patterns were also revealed. She was very compliant and deferent, the good student. She didn't like to reveal too much and was very troubled about showing the extent of her helplessness, yet she depended on a therapist to "fix her" quickly. She also too readily accepted my values and those of behavior therapy—independence and self control—and never stopped to ask whether or not these goals or her therapy were really putting her on path of self-fulfillment or happiness.

I believe that the long-term issues raised by an examination of this client's therapy present a strong case for moving beyond traditional cognitive-behavior therapy, which focuses largely on the client's presenting problems and on a reappraisal of the belief systems that are assumed to underlie these problems. It is seen as desirable to use the therapy itself as a mechanism for a wider study of the patterns that contribute to recurring problems. Only after such patterns are discovered can the therapist begin to help the client make reasoned choices about what is realistic to change or not change and to aid in setting reasonable life goals.

The second section of this chapter addresses the issues inherent in the assessment of recurring patterns, focusing on therapist–client interactions as a vehicle for the study of such patterns. The third section presents a model for enabling clients to understand and deal with decision making in relationships. In particular, the author demonstrates how learning within an individual therapy session can be generalized to enhance a client's decision making and interpersonal interactions in outside relationships.

THERAPIST–CLIENT INTERACTION

Therapist–Client Interactions and CBT

The therapist–client model for CBT is for the therapist to be a teacher/ trainer/coach to a client/student. Much of the methodology of CBT involves the client taking an active part in the discovery process: self-monitoring, following through on homework assignments, and using therapy time to report on successes and failures. The three techniques most familiar to this author (self-control for weight problems, anxiety management for phobias and performance anxieties, and assertiveness training) all follow the model of therapist as teacher. Yet, there is little in the CBT literature about strategies for dealing with our neurotic clients who outmanueuver the best therapeutic efforts. Furthermore, many of their problematic patterns also occur during the session in the therapist–client encounters. What can the therapist do with an overweight client who reports eating three candy bars in the taxi after spending a substantial amount of money for a session in which she has worked up a plan to reduce caloric intake? Or consider the formerly agoraphobic client who, after a year of hard work in therapy, was now traveling on her own, but who (because she still felt anxious while driving) insisted that she had not been helped at all by the therapy and berated me for thinking she was significantly improved. When we have failures in such training we need to ask the following questions: What motivates a client to spend money on therapy and then binge immediately afterwards? Why do the therapist and the agoraphobic view progress so differently? What function does complaining serve? (Many clients begin a session with "You don't understand how hard my life is.") How often do we try to tell a client she or he is doing better instead of exploring the complaint that nothing has changed? In assertiveness training, the therapist uses role play to help the client develop more effective ways of responding with a significant other. A common failure is that when an emotionally laden situation occurs, the client freezes (Fodor & Epstein, 1983). Yet, we have opportunities in the therapeutic interactions to explore more fully these potentially upsetting situations, since clients exhibit a wide range of affects and behaviors in interacting with the therapist.

I believe that cognitive-behavior therapists need to pay more attention to the nature of therapist–client interactions, particularly in areas that are potentially confrontational, in order to enable clients to learn more in the therapy sessions about their interactive style and ways of handling powerful emotions with significant others.

CBT and Gestalt Therapy

While cognitive-behavior therapy does not present a model for analyzing therapist–client interactions, Gestalt therapy has seriously studied these dyadic issues and offers a theoretical and therapeutic model that has relevance for behavior therapy. Gestalt therapy is a learning-based therapy that focuses on present experience and enhancing awareness (Van De Riet, Korb, & Gorrell, 1980; Perls, Hefferline, & Goodman, 1951). What Gestalt therapy and behavior therapy have in common is the conception of the therapist as an educator. They both believe that the role of a therapist is to teach clients how to learn about themselves, although they approach the task in very different ways. Behavior therapists present techniques to clients as learning exercises that are assumed to foster change. Gestalt therapists set up experiments to help their clients to enhance their emotional experience. Gestalt therapists are not primarily interested in change for change's sake; rather, they believe that through increased awareness, responsiveness, and self-support, the client will change (Beisser, 1970; Harper, Bauer, & Kannarkat, 1976; Perls et al., 1951).

I am arguing in favor of cognitive-behavior therapists' making greater use of the Gestalt approach, both to enhance clients' awareness of their internal issues, and of the interactional process between therapist and client. In so doing, therapists may enable their clients to learn to be more effective in handling interpersonal interactions in general.

As Simkin and Yontef (1984) note, "Gestalt therapy focuses on process (what is happening) rather than content (what is being discussed). . . . Process refers to the observable development of behavior that occurs during the therapy hour . . . the focus on the interaction of the therapist and client. The emphasis is on what is, rather than on what was, might be, could be or should be" (p. 279).

In the case described earlier in which the client ate candy bars in the taxi following her therapy session, a behavior therapist might try to help the client improve her self-control techniques. A Gestalt therapist, on the other hand, might explore what it was like for the client to sit and work on a diet with her therapist. Such work might reveal that that the client as an overweight child was overly scrutinized by her mother during family meal times. She complied with the diet when watched, but stole money from her mother and binged on candy bars in private. The current therapist–client diet interactions tapped into the client's earlier resentful and rebellious structure. One doesn't need years of psychoanalysis to tap into this awareness. Instead, a combined CBT/Gestalt therapy would discover how prior dieting patterns influenced present dieting noncompliance by focusing on the client's awareness of the similarity of the present therapeutic situation to her childhood dieting struggles. After fully exploring these patterns, the therapeutic task would be to teach the client (using some variant of cognitive reframing) to separate her free choice to be on a diet as an adult, with the therapist as consultant, from the forced childhood structure where her mother was in charge of her dieting and she was the rebellious noncompliant child.

Gestalt Therapy: Basic Concepts

"Gestalt therapy . . . takes a phenomenological stance with regard to the therapeutic relationship. That is, there is a belief that the therapist can work best . . . by entering into the client's phenomenological world, experiencing along with the client the client's perspective . . . there is concern with the immediate, current experience of the client . . . it is of paramount importance for the therapist to stay with client's present experience and to facilitate his or her present awareness" (Van De Riet, Korb, & Gorrell, 1980, p. 90). Simkin and Yontef (1984) stress that "Gestalt therapy is an exploration rather than direct modification of behavior. The method involves contacting and focusing of awareness."

To illustrate the combination of CBT and Gestalt for the study of therapist–client interactions, three aspects of Gestalt practice will be highlighted: (1) teaching awareness, (2) exploring the dimension of contact (the therapist's use of feedback and sharing of her own awareness), and (3) blocks to awareness and contact.

In the last section of the chapter, I will present a cognitive-behavioral model combined with a Gestalt approach to facilitate decision making in interpersonal relationships.

Teaching Client Self-Awareness

"Awareness is a form of experiencing . . . it is the process of being in vigilant contact with the most important events in the individual/environmental field with full sensorimotor, emotional, cognitive and energic support . . . aware contact creates new meaningful wholes and this is in itself an integration. . . ." (Simkin & Yontef, 1984, p. 290). Laura Perls (1976) talks about an awareness continuum, where awareness emerges into a foreground, is experienced, changed, assimilated, and then falls back into the background as the next awareness emerges. Awareness fully involves the following modalities:

1. *Affects*. These are inner feelings, which involve the proprioceptive, kinesthetic experiences that occur within the boundary of the skin (e.g., tightening of throat, burning cheeks, or quivering lips).

2. *Sensory experiences*. These are awarenesses of the outside world, as it is experienced directly through the five senses (sight, hearing, touch, taste, and smell).

3. *Cognitions*. These are thoughts and fantasies (usually evaluations, memories of the past, or plans for the future). Gestalt therapists view awareness as always changing and evolving. Sensations and feelings happen in the present, while cognitions are viewed as reflections, memories, future projections, and plans. In Gestalt therapy, it is important for the client to learn all these distinctions, to know when one is experiencing a feeling and where it is located, as well as which thoughts, plans, or evaluations accompany it. Furthermore, since there is a tendency for individuals to hold back, interrupt, or direct the flow of experience, awareness training focuses on these processes as well (Perls, Hefferline, & Goodman, 1951). Gestalt awareness work begins by focusing on and amplifying body sensations, and turns to cognitions at the *end* of a piece of awareness work for reframing purposes. This is often done by having the client try out a sentence that seems to summarize his or her experience. (Harper, Bauer, & Kannarkat, 1976). Cognitive-behavior therapists, on the other hand, tend to use cognitions and cognitive control to handle or tone down powerful emotions (Ellis, 1975; Van De Riet, Korb, & Gorrell, 1980).

Instructions for Awareness Training

The following are exercises for enhancing awareness:

1. *General awareness exercise*. "(1) Maintain the sense that your awareness exists here and now. (2) Try to realize that you are living the expe-

rience: acting it, observing it, suffering it, resisting it . . ." (Perls, Heffer-line, & Goodman, 1951, p. 96).

2. *Zones of awareness.* "Take some time to pay attention to your aware-ness now. Just be an observer of your awareness and notice where it goes. Say to yourself, 'Now I am aware of ___' and finish this sentence with what you are aware of at the moment, and then notice whether this is something outside, something inside or a fantasy. . . . Where does your awareness go? Are you mostly aware of things outside your body, or sensations inside your skin? . . . Now direct your attention to whichever area you are least aware of, inside or outside, and become more aware of this . . ." (Stevens, 1973, p. 9).

3. *Focusing.* "Continue experimenting with your awareness, and realize that your awareness is like a searchlight. Whatever you focus your attention on is pretty clear, but other things and events tend to fade out of awareness. . . . Your awareness can shift from one thing to another quite rapidly, but you can be fully aware of whatever is in the focus of your awareness at the moment. . . . Take some time to become more aware of how you focus your awareness, and what comes into the focus of your awareness" (Stevens, 1973, p. 9).

4. *Generalizing.* "Notice when you begin generalizing, such as 'Now I am aware of the whole room . . .' if you notice that you are generalizing, return your attention to the focus of your awareness in the present moment, and see what you can actually contact clearly. . . ." (Stevens, 1973, p. 10).

Case Illustrations

Assessment of stressful work situation. The client, a young single lawyer, came to therapy for "bouts of crying that seem to come from nowhere." The following is from her second therapy session. She had rushed to therapy from work at 6:30 P.M. She dropped her briefcase on the floor, threw off her suit jacket, and collapsed on the couch.

CLIENT: (*in a rushed and somewhat breathless voice*) Sorry I'm late. I couldn't get a taxi and then traffic was impossible. There's so much work, I feel so intense, so many things on my mind.

After making contact, we began an awareness exercise, in which she was instructed to close her eyes and get in touch with the feelings and sensa-tions in her body.

CLIENT: I have so many things on my mind . . . all so intense, a lot of stuff there. Can't focus on anything else. . . .

THERAPIST: Continue paying attention to your body sensations. Notice the areas of tension. When you're ready, tell me what you're feeling.

CLIENT: I'm noticing how tense I am all over . . . God, I'm suddenly aware of being very fatigued. And I feel so hot . . . I didn't really know how hot I am. Now I feel an ache in my neck and my shoulders feel very tense, like I almost can't even move them.

At this point we could access directly the issue of how exhausted the client was from work pressures. CBT work may have focused directly on the cognitions and helped access some of the concerns about work. Gestalt therapy focuses on how exhausted the client was and how little she was aware of the tensions in her neck and shoulders during the work day. Through the use of these awareness exercises, the client was trained to pay more attention to what elements in her work setting contribute to her tension and fatigue. I could then use interventions to help her feel less drained at the end of the day. In the first month of therapy, the client was trained to self-monitor her fatigue and nonfatigue states at work by self-awareness exercises. We discovered that the overall work pressure was less problematic than her physical work environment. The client worked in an open room with many desks and phones. As she wrote her reports or briefs, anyone could come over to ask her a question or give her additional work or give another project priority status. She also felt pressured to answer the phone and deal with immediate requests. When the client came in early or went to work on Saturday, she didn't feel as tired. We explored the pattern of interruptions more fully via role play, for example.

THERAPIST: Could you handle this lease, it's due by noon today.

CLIENT: Okay.

THERAPIST: Ring. (*The client picks up the phone.*) Could you find the Levy file and bring it upstairs for the client?

THERAPIST: (*playing the secretary, walks over to her*) I've just typed this brief, could you go over and see if there are any changes before I photocopy it?

THERAPIST: What are you feeling?

CLIENT: My back is starting to ache . . . and I feel somewhat dizzy.

THERAPIST: Stay with the dizzy feeling.

CLIENT: Like I lose myself. I can't decide which direction to go. Feel like I have to do it all and I can't. It leaves me dizzy and shaky and I can't think straight.

THERAPIST: Let's work on ways of putting things on hold, on saying no to immediate demands and shielding yourself from interruptions. Let's work on your body first. What's happening as the demands are coming in?

As the client practiced saying no and studied her body posture, she discovered that she leaned her neck and shoulders forward with each request. As the requests continued, she reported feeling as though she were going in and out of her body. We explored nonverbally the body posture related to compliance and refusal.

THERAPIST: (*playing the secretary*) Could you go over this brief now before I xerox it?

(*The client leans toward the therapist.*)

THERAPIST: Are you aware of your body?

CLIENT: There I go again.

THERAPIST: Center yourself and say no.

CLIENT: (*sitting back in chair*) I'm in the middle of doing a project for one of the partners. I'll come by in 15 minutes.

THERAPIST: What was that like?

CLIENT: It seems easy to say no and mean it, when I don't lean forward.

Over the next few weeks, we fully explored the client's pattern of unassertiveness at work, her body posture, and saying no and its relation to her feeling so overwhelmed and fatigued.

Handling problems in relaxation training. The following case example illustrates the use of awareness exercises for an agoraphobic client who had been in behavior therapy previously. Many behavioral procedures had been presented to this client, but she still remained fearful and phobic. The client stressed that she suffered too much anxiety when trying to combat fears. However, she had also actively resisted learning and using relaxation techniques to handle anxiety. She seemed almost as fearful of relaxing as of confronting her fears. We set up an experiment to help her become aware of what happened when she tried to relax.

THERAPIST: Now try to settle into the couch and let me slowly give you relaxation instructions.

CLIENT: I don't want to do this.

THERAPIST: Stay with "I don't want to do this."

CLIENT: It's gonna be a disaster, like the last time.

THERAPIST: Let's see why you view relaxation as a disaster.

(*The therapist begins Jacobson procedure. The client begins the exercises but stops suddenly.*)

CLIENT: I can't do it.

THERAPIST: What are you feeling?

CLIENT: Scared.

THERAPIST: Dive into scared, describe it as fully as you can.

CLIENT: (*after a few minutes of focusing on 'scared'*) Like I'm falling apart. . . . It's worse than a panic attack, like total disintegration . . . like I'm going into death . . . like I'm already dead . . . in a black hole . . . and it's cold. (*Her voice quivers and she begins to shiver.*)

THERAPIST: (*putting a blanket on her*) Are you willing to tell me what's happening now?

At this point the client began to talk about how letting go of control, how relaxation felt like a total disintegration, like death. The terror she was experiencing was similar to the terror of her panic attacks. She had never fully felt this connection before and was now aware of why she had been avoiding both exposure and relaxation. As therapy progressed, the client, through awareness exercises, explored this death anxiety more fully. Treatment at this point had become a variant of flooding. As therapy continued, and the client increasingly exposed herself to feared situations *in vivo*. She wanted to have some relaxation procedures available to her; however, she still viewed relaxation as something foreign. Through the use of awareness exercises, she was helped to construct her own relaxation imagery.

THERAPIST: Close your eyes and imagine the most relaxing place you have ever been to and tell me about the experience as if it were happening now.

The client insisted she had never relaxed. After going through many different memories, with instructions to get more and more specific, the client produced the following scene:

CLIENT: I am lying on a beach. I'm lying face down on the hot sand. . . . The sun is shining down . . . on my back, there is a slight breeze from a palm tree overhead. I hear the waves break against the rocks and sea gulls are off in the distance.

THERAPIST: Can you feel it as if it is happening now?

CLIENT: If I stay with the picture, I can feel it.

THERAPIST: Stay with the image and describe it even more fully.

CLIENT: My whole body is sinking into the sand.

THERAPIST: Be more specific.

CLIENT: I am sinking further and further into the sand and I just let myself go. The warm soft sand envelopes me and I feel nurtured by the earth.

After months of therapy, focused awareness exercises had finally provided us with a specific relaxation image ("sinking into the warm sand and being nurtured by the earth") that could be utilized for the behavioral work on the client's phobias. Still another piece of work for us was to study her resistance to yielding control to a therapist.

Contact

The concept of contact is central to Gestalt therapy. There are three essential ingredients for Gestalt work with clients. First, the emphasis on therapy itself as a process involving contact between therapist and client. Second, the therapist uses the mechanism of contact to teach awareness. This is done by sharing and disclosing one's own sensations and feelings to the client. Third, the therapist uses the mechanism of contact to facilitate clients' development of their own awareness, their own supports, and responsibility for their own behavior and choices (Polster & Polster, 1973). Perls, Hefferline, and Goodman (1951) define contact as follows: "[F]undamentally, an organism lives in its environment by maintaining its differences and more importantly by assimilating the environment to its differences; and it is at [the] boundary that dangers are rejected, obstacles are overcome and the assimilable is selected and appropriated" (p. 270). Contact involves reaching out into the environment as well as reaching out to people. Contact occurs on a continuum. It's a process of moving in and out . . . or on a line. Contact is defined as the experience of the boundary between "me" and "not me" (Simkin & Yontef, 1984). The role of the therapist is to enable the clients to risk as much contact as they can tolerate and then withdraw, so they can learn to support themselves. That is, the client can learn to tolerate the affect that contact and withdrawal from contact generates.

The Therapist's Use of Contact

Gestalt therapy excludes the therapist teaching the patient directly. In other words, the therapist's main vehicle for enhancing client self-awareness is the sharing of her own observations and affective reactions (including stuckness), along with a willingness to create experiments in contact. Growth occurs from real contact between real people. Patients learn about their problems, but "from seeing how they and the therapist engage each other around the process" (Simkin & Yontef, 1984). Both this expanded form of self disclosure and experimentation in therapist/client relating go beyond what is typically done in CBT.

Case Illustration

A client entered therapy for help in making a decision about leaving her husband. She spent most of her sessions obsessing, going around and around the issue of whether or not to leave her husband. It was only toward the end of each session that the client typically became focused and made real contact with me, only to rush out and begin the cycle again the following week.

The beginning of the fifth session ran as follows:

CLIENT: (*speaking in a monotone, sitting stiffly on the couch, with her eyes toward the floor*) It was just another one of those weeks. We keep going back and forth. One day I'm all set to leave; the next day I work in the garden and I wonder how I could ever give up this wonderful house. But then on Saturday he spent all day in front of the TV watching the football game and I wonder, "What am I doing with such a man?"

THERAPIST: (*feeling bored and disconnected from client*) I am feeling that you're not talking to me right now, like you are talking to yourself. I am feeling disconnected from you when you talk that way.

CLIENT: Well, that's the way it feels.

THERAPIST: Look at me and try to tell me what's going on. I'm finding it hard to reach you. What are you feeling?

CLIENT: I'm feeling numb.

THERAPIST: Tell me how numb feels.

CLIENT: It's just numb, empty.

THERAPIST: Stay with numb and empty. Describe its shape, color . . . where it is in your body.

CLIENT: (*looking at therapist*) It's just black, empty, cold. (*Her hands start to shake.*)

THERAPIST: I see you shaking.

CLIENT: (*looking away again*) I'm so scared. (*She starts to wring her hands.*)

THERAPIST: I feel that you're running away again. What's happening to your hands?

CLIENT: (*looks at hands and makes teary eye contact with therapist*) They are shaking. I feel so scared!

THERAPIST: (*takes client's hands*) I know you're scared. It's hard to really focus on the fear. Let me stay close to you while you tell me about your fear.

At this point, the client shared with me her fear about separation. Feeling more in contact, I could now begin to work on the fears of being alone that kept the client trapped in this unsatisfactory relationship and contributed to her paralysis in making a decision. Through the contact work, I demonstrated to the client how she isolated herself with her obsessional thinking. I unmasked the fear by forcing a different kind of contact, so that the fear could now be worked with by a means of a variety of behavioral techniques, instead of being talked around. The client was shown how, by obsessing with me, she was postponing facing, both in the therapy session and after it, some of the fears she had about implementing her decision to leave her husband.

Use of Contact Work for Studying Patterns of Behavior

A young client complained that she never found any satisfactory sex–love relationships. She had been in and out of several lesbian relationships over 5 years, the longest lasting about 6 months. Typically, she would meet someone who appeared to her to be wonderful (warm, and loving); after the client had spent an evening or weekend with her, however, she would feel turned off and report that the person got under her skin. Often the other woman would hang on, hoping for a more positive response from the client, but the more the other person would try, the more the client would become oppositional, withdrawing further. When her lover was gone, the client would miss her and wonder why she felt so oppressed by what she now perceived as her lover's realistic demands. The client also complained of bouts of depression (feeling "sad, lonely, and empty") when there was no one around. At these times she would go on a search, meet a new woman, and begin the cycle all over again.

Therapeutic Interaction. After the third session, I noted the following pattern of therapist–client interaction. The client would come in with notes, ask for specific help, but often dismiss the therapist's opinion if she did not feel completely understood or listened to. At these times, if I insisted on presenting her point of view, the client would get angry and oppositional. I shared her impression of this process with the client, that is, that the client needed to have her environment exactly the way she wants it, and that when it was not, she would become resistant. I added that I found it difficult to present my point of view without the client becoming oppositional. The client was not sure she agreed with my account of her process. She agreed to participate in an experiment to explore this pattern more fully.

Sometimes, it is necessary to use experiential exercises to allow clients to discover their own patterns or to facilitate or heighten the awareness of their mode of interacting. This experiment involved tuning into music.

THERAPIST: I'm going to play a piece of music. I want you just to lie back and listen to it. Share with me what's happening as the music is playing.

CLIENT: Ok, but let me tell you, I'm not sure I'm going to like this.

THERAPIST: Let's see.

CLIENT: It's weird. What is it?

THERAPIST: Kitaro, "Silk Road." Just listen to it for a while.

CLIENT: It's too loud.

THERAPIST: I'll lower it. How is it now?

CLIENT: I don't like it . . . all those bells, it's weird.

THERAPIST: Just try to take it in and focus on what you do like.

CLIENT: I feel you are forcing me to listen to it. I don't want to listen to that any more. I don't like it.

THERAPIST: What did you dislike most about it?

CLIENT: The bells. They felt like they didn't belong to the music.

THERAPIST: What did you do when you heard the bells?

CLIENT: I shut myself off. I said, how can I trust you, if you can make me listen to such weird music?

THERAPIST: So, only if I played something *exactly* right—just the right loudness, tone, mood, no bells, could you feel trust?

CLIENT: Yes. It has to be just right. . . . Otherwise, I don't want to listen to it and I don't want to be with you!

At this point, both of us had accessed the client's need for perfect resonance, and the discomfort and alienation that resulted from a less-than-perfect fit. Only after many such experiments—studying the client's patterns of what she was willing to take in, felt oppressed by, or actively resisted—does the client begin to see what may be operating in her outside relationships. The experiments are set up not only to explore the need for a perfect fit, but also to teach ways of accommodating differences.

Use of Awareness and Contact to Enhance Client's Self-Support and Responsibility

According to Simkin & Yontef (1984), "Gestalt therapy balances frustration and support. The therapist explores rather than gratifies the patient's wishes . . . and this is frustrating for the patient" (p. 302). Gestalt therapy places on the client the major responsibility (in the form of responsive awareness) for developing her or his own supports. Moreover, the therapist steps back to allow the clients to struggle and test out some of the limits of self-support (Resnick, 1970).

Case Illustration

The "Take-Care-of-Me, Do-for-Me, My-Life-Is-So-Hard" Type of Client. Nancy was a successful 29-year-old children's book illustrator from a close Los Angeles family. She was now living alone in New York. She seemed chronically unhappy and dissatisfied with her life in the city. Each week she came into her therapy session with reports of minor and major crises, often whining about how much she suffered. Her weekly disasters include having her purse snatched, leaving her portfolio in a taxi, catching herpes from a one night stand, spraining her wrist before a major assignment is due, and falling in love several times where she is totally consumed with passion only to have the relationship end abruptly with her feeling hurt and rejected. She had been overly dependent on her widowed mother who was often available at a moment's notice to listen to her complaints or bail her out of her latest crisis, and now that she was alone in New York, she was seeking out a similar dependency with me. One week she was in a crisis about not being able to begin the assignment. She brought in her sketch pad.

THERAPIST: Let's see what happens if you just begin to draw.

CLIENT: I can't do it . . . nothing comes . . . it's just empty. I read the story and could identify with the girl caring for her retarded brother, but nothing comes.

THERAPIST: Why don't you try to see what happens?

CLIENT: It's too many choices. . . . I see maybe one big sketch with her looking at him in a distance excluded from other kids playing and then I see other possibilities, several smaller collages of images of them together. I can't decide.

THERAPIST: Why not begin someplace?

CLIENT: It's too hard. Whatever choice I make it will be suffering because then it will be decisions about how to tilt her face, what she's wearing, how many other kids to put in.

(*The client starts to cry.*)

THERAPIST: What's happening?

CLIENT: It's all so hard. My life is so hard. All I have is suffering. Ever since I moved to New York it's been so hard. Other people have it easy. They can just do things. Good things happen to them. Nothing good will ever happen to me.

THERAPIST: Do you really believe you were put on this earth to suffer?

CLIENT: Yes, I must have done something terrible in my last life, because all I get is suffering.

THERAPIST: We seem to spend a lot of time in therapy each week going over your sufferings. I can see sometimes when we sit here week after week how you feel overwhelmed. Many times I also feel overwhelmed by your problems. Sometimes it appears that you expect me to make it all better.

CLIENT: (*begins to sob even more*) You don't know how hard it is.

THERAPIST: Do you think you might be willing to try to see if you could work here at finding some other way to be in this world and not suffer? After all, if suffering is what you inherited as karma from your past life, maybe you were meant to overcome it.

CLIENT: (*still crying*) I feel so awful.

THERAPIST: Can you find another way to draw without suffering?

(*The client, stooping over the paper, stares at the paper*)

After a few minutes, she picked up the charcoal and began covering the page. The client made a huge sketch of a girl bending over. As she finished her body started to shake and she began crying again.

CLIENT: I can't handle the feelings. I get so anxious when I'm beginning something.

THERAPIST: Go on, tell me what happens as you begin to draw.

CLIENT: Well first there's nothing and I feel a rush to fill in the space, but once I look at it, I see all the decisions that have to be made and I know I can't do them all at once and I'm overwhelmed at what to do next. I can't do everything at once and that's when paralysis sets in and the pain begins.

THERAPIST: (*turning over a new page in the sketch pad*) Do it again. What you're describing is the rush of creative energy. I get it when I write. It's painful, but also exhilarating. Go ahead, allow the rush to happen. Let whatever comes out, come out.

CLIENT: (*draws again*) It's easier the second time, but now I have to look at the unfinished piece; all I see is what I have to do next and I can't do it all at once. I just give up.

THERAPIST: Try to figure out what to do next.

CLIENT: Like I'm being pulled all over the place. . . . Each piece . . . calls me to work on it . . . like I don't have enough hands.

THERAPIST: Let's see if you can now tell me what it's like, if you select any section, focus on what you need to do with that piece of the drawing, and shut out all other decisions. . . . Go on, I will just sit here while you do it. It's important that you learn how to break through this anxiety in your own way.

Additional work was indicated to explore the core beliefs that "I was put on this earth to suffer; I wasn't meant to have a good life." This is a common belief, and for this client, the patterns of behavior that reflected this belief needed to be systematically studied to enable the client to learn how to make better choices and be happier.

Helping Clients Explore "Unacceptable" or "Disowned" States or Competing Structures

Sometimes clients have the problem opposite to that of Nancy. They need to learn how to ask for help. They are too ashamed to appear incompetent or helpless and need to appear competent and self-sufficient. A client (similar to the client of the first case study) asked for help in preparing a talk. As I explored more fully the anxiety about public speaking, the client pulled back and it was clear she was ashamed to reveal her inadequacy to her therapist, whom she considered an authority in her own field. In this case, we didn't need to do an imaginal flooding for public speaking. Rather, we needed to help her explore her feelings of helplessness and incompetence in front of me without feeling shame. Further work was also needed in asking for help. We role played her giving her talk before the therapist.

(*The client begins to speak, but her voice shakes and she stops.*)

THERAPIST: What's happening?

CLIENT: I'm afraid I might fall apart.

THERAPIST: So, fall apart.

CLIENT: It would be awful.

THERAPIST: Tell me what's happening now.

CLIENT: My hands are shaking. I can't find the place in the talk. The words won't come out. You'll see how incompetent and unprepared I am and wonder what I am doing in graduate school.

THERAPIST: It's okay to feel incompetent sometimes.

CLIENT: (*beginning to cry*) You don't understand. . . . I'll just be a blob melt into a puddle.

THERAPIST: So, melt into a puddle.

CLIENT: (*bending over, hands over face*) I feel so helpless. I wish you'd go away . . . leave me alone, so I could sink down in a hole in the floor and just disappear. I feel so weak and helpless (*begins to cry*). I'm so ashamed. I feel like a cry baby now . . . in front of you.

THERAPIST: I know what it's like to feel like a cry baby. It's okay (*holding her while she sobs*). I know what it's like to be a cry baby too, we all get like this sometimes. When you feel ready, would you let me help you deal with that talk? You don't have to do everything yourself. You should see me when I have to write a paper. I ask all my friends for help.

CLIENT: You!

THERAPIST: How do you think I manage to write?

CLIENT: I see you as so independent, like you wouldn't have to ask anyone for help.

THERAPIST: I'm a lot like you. I like to feel like I can do it all myself, but I've learned how to ask others to help me. It has made my life much easier. So, let's work now on your asking for help. Let's explore what it's like to ask for help, and then receive it.

STRATEGIES FOR DEALING WITH
INTERPERSONAL RELATIONSHIPS

In New York City, with its large population and alternative lifestyles, serial relationships are very common. People often come for therapy for decision making about their relationships with others.

In particular, clients seek help in evaluating their interpersonal situations in the following areas:

- Am I getting what I want?
- Is this good enough?
- Can she/he change?
- How can I be sure I am doing the right thing (by staying or leaving)?
- How do I deal with all the conflicting feelings?
- How do I handle all the roller coaster effects I'm experiencing since the breakup?
- Is there anyone else out there for me?
- Do I dare be alone?
- How do I find someone else?

Ideally, the best solution for relationship work is for the person seeking help to work with the partner. Most often, the partner is not available for couple work, so the best one can do is to evaluate the situation from the client's perspective. The following is a model for dealing with relationship issues in individual therapy using the integrated Gestalt/CBT approach. This model is an expanded version of the "Progress Toward Assertiveness" steps outlining individual treatment of assertiveness problems (Fodor, 1980). The therapist helps clients to assess their situations and to make decisions by thinking through such questions as the following:

1. What do I want in my relationship? (What are the areas of dissatisfaction? Am I clear about what I am seeking from my partner?)

2. How do I communicate? (Do I have the skills to verbalize clearly, to ask for what I want?)

3. Can I assess whether my partner hears, is capable of responding to what I ask, understands the situation as I do, and is able to change?

4. As we work for change, am I aware of triggers and recurrent patterns that lead to problematic situations? How much am I contributing and how much is my partner contributing? Can we talk about this?

5. Which wants of my mine are primary and which are secondary? What am I getting from this relationship that does meet my needs? Am I expecting too much from this relationship? Am I focusing too much on what is not there and losing sight of what is there?

6. What are some of universal male–female issues with which we are dealing? Which aspects of problematic sex-role behaviors appear typical and/or incapable of changing much, and which behaviors are unique to us?

7. In gay and lesbian relationships what special issues do female–female and male–male coupling present? How are our issues typical or atypical?

8. What am I bringing to this relationship from my childhood patterns of relating?

9. In what ways is my partner expecting me to change? How does he/she handle not getting what is wanted? How do I handle my partner's unwillingness to change, and how does that contribute to our problems (e.g., do I withdraw, pout, have tantrums when I don't get my way?)?

10. If I decide I'm not getting enough of my primary wants met in this relationship or my partner is not capable enough of changing or not dealing with relationship issues in a constructive way, am I willing to risk separating?

11. How do I deal with the strong affects around separation and the conflict about making the right decision?

12. Can I say goodbye? What do I still want from this person?

13. Am I able to be alone?

14. How do I go about searching for another relationship?

15. When I meet someone new, how do I assess whether or not my potential partner is capable of meeting my wants? Am I repeating old patterns and expectations in the new relationship?

The case illustrations presented next will highlight the integration of Gestalt techniques with cognitive-behavior therapy around decision making and assertiveness issues in relationships. Not all 15 points will be covered in the case examples, though issues discussed in the previous section will be illustrated.

Decision-Making in Relationships

Case Illustration: Ann

Six months after she moved into a male friend's apartment, Ann returned for a consultation with me about how to deal with the weekend visits of the friend's 13-year-old daughter, Susan. Ann is 37 years old. She had come to me 2 years previously, following her divorce from a dominating husband, and together we had worked on weight, self-esteem, and assertiveness.

What do I need and what do I want?

CLIENT: Everything seems to be going fine. Jim and I get along well; I never thought I would have a relationship this good. Still, when Susan is around, I find myself getting irritable. I pick on little things she does and after she leaves, Jim and I bicker. I also feel turned off sexually after her visits.

THERAPIST: Think about her last visit. I want you to get in touch with everything you feel and think. When you are ready, I want you to talk aloud as if you were still in that moment of time.

CLIENT: I sleep late on Saturday morning and I come into the kitchen and Susan and Jim are having breakfast together. He is making her cereal and seems warmer and happier than I usually see him. I feel a tightening in my chest.

THERAPIST: Tell me more about that.

CLIENT: It's like an ache . . . right in the pit between my breasts.

THERAPIST: Stay with that feeling.

CLIENT: (*begins to cry*) I see Jim smiling at Susan in a way I don't usually see him. . . .

THERAPIST: Go on, what is happening?

CLIENT: (*begins to rock back and forth*)

THERAPIST: Don't talk. Just continue moving like that.

CLIENT: (*rocks back and forth more pronouncedly and then begins to cry*)

THERAPIST: What's happening?

CLIENT: (*sobbing now*) Like I want to, like I want to have a baby of my own . . . like I'd like for Jim and me to have a child together . . . I want a baby of my own, to love, my own baby.

How do I communicate what I want?

(*somewhat later in the session*)

THERAPIST: What would it be like to discuss the desire for a child with Jim?

CLIENT: What's the point? Jim doesn't want any more children. It's useless to go on. (*Ann stops talking and her body becomes rigid.*)

THERAPIST: Your body looks tense. Why are you stopping? What's happening with your hands?

CLIENT: (*looks at her hands, which are clenched in tight fists*) I feel tight, tense, angry. I want to let him know how much I want a baby.

THERAPIST: Why don't we practice telling him what you want.

Ann began to role play letting Jim know she wanted a child. She had started angrily, but gradually her voice began to be softer, more accommodating.

CLIENT: Jim, things are going so well between us that I have been thinking about how nice it would be if we could have our own baby. (*She tenses and stops herself again.*)

THERAPIST: What's happening?

CLIENT: I know Jim wouldn't hear of it. He thinks having Susan ruined his marriage. No, I could never bring it up.

THERAPIST: Try on this sentence. What he wants is more important than what I want.

CLIENT: What he wants is more important than what I want. It sure fits.

THERAPIST: Say it again.

CLIENT: (*begins to cry*) It's always that way. . . . My needs don't count. I can't put out what I want.

THERAPIST: Are you willing to give yourself the right to have a want different from Jim's?

CLIENT: I feel I'm back again at the beginning of therapy. I guess I have to risk it.

THERAPIST: Try this one on. It's okay for me to want something even if Jim doesn't like it.

CLIENT: (*in a shaking voice*) It's okay for me to want something even if Jim doesn't like it.

THERAPIST: Keep saying it louder and stronger until you mean it.

CLIENT: (*in a stronger voice*) It's okay for me to want something even if Jim doesn't like it. (*in an even louder voice*) It's okay for me to want something even if Jim doesn't like it.

THERAPIST: How does it feel now?

CLIENT: (*her voice resonates strength*) Like that first sentence is the story of my life, and it's going to change, and now I'm going to change.

Can I assess whether my partner hears, is capable of responding to what I ask?

Ann was given a homework assignment of telling Jim she wanted a child. She returned the following week with detailed notes about her communicating her wish for a baby. Jim had heard her request, but she reported that he seemed flabbergasted that she should want a child. He was also adamant about not having one.

As we work for change, am I aware of triggers and recurrent patterns? What are patterns of interaction of client and partner contributing to my problem?

For the next few sessions, Ann reported that she and Jim were not getting along too well. She was feeling depressed and anxious; he seemed an-

noyed, irritable, and withdrawn. We examined Ann's pattern of responding to similiar situations in her marriage. When she had finally had the
courage to ask for what she wanted, if her husband didn't immediately
agree to her request, she had backed off and allowed him to get his way.
Together we role played other ways of backing up her request: (1) asking
Jim to set aside some time to talk about having a baby so she could really
hear and understand his objections; (2) clearly letting him know that she
very much wanted a child with him and how important it was to her; and
(3) asking that he come into a therapy session with her to talk about the
issue. On being approached, Jim agreed to several therapy sessions and
there was much discussion about having a child, but he was still resistant
to the idea.

Which wants of mine are primary and which are secondary? Am I focusing on what's not there and not appreciating what is there?

As Ann faced Jim's resistance to having a child, she needed to assess
whether being in a good relationship without a child were good enough. In
addition, since she never seemed to have a wish for a child before and Jim
had made his attitude toward having another child clear before she moved
in, she needed to determine whether this were just a situation where she
was focusing on what she didn't have in the relationship and was overlooking all the positives. To help Ann assess whether or not she would be
willing to stay in this relationship if she did not have a child, we used a
Gestalt dialogue technique. Gestalt dialogue enables the client to articulate and debate both sides of a conflict. This Gestalt dialogue method is
often referred to as the empty chair technique (Van De Riet, Korb, &
Gorrell, 1980).

THERAPIST: Stay with the side of you that wants the child, and put out
all the reasons for wanting a child and talk to that empty chair next to you.

CLIENT: [side that wants the child] I'm 37 years old, it's now or never.
Jim is a wonderful father to Susan. I know he would be wonderful to a
new child. It would be so nice to have a family. If I don't have a child now, I
will regret it for the rest of my life. I'm really ready to connect up with a
baby.

THERAPIST: Now switch chairs and be the part that is willing to give up
having a child.

CLIENT: [side that doesn't want a child] You nut! You are in the best
relationship you ever had. Jim is wonderful. When Susan is around, you
have no privacy, it's no fun sharing him. Imagine how interrupting a baby
will be. If you have a child, you'll probably have to scrap plans to go back to
school and get your PhD. You've been dreaming about that for a while and
you'll never find time to take those short story writing courses, let alone

write. You want to try writing with a screaming baby demanding attention? Besides, you never really liked babies very much, imagine all those diapers, the spitting up. You are crazy when you don't get enough sleep, are you really ready to be up all night with an infant?

THERAPIST: Switch sides and continue the dialogue. Argue for your child.

CLIENT: [side for the child] It won't cost that much to have a child. I could still find time to write. I think Jim and I could get closer if we shared a child. If he really loved me he would want me to have his child. If he really loved me he'd want me to be happy (*voice begins to shake*).

THERAPIST: What's happening?

CLIENT: (*seems dazed and tearful*) I guess I feel if he really loved me . . . he'd give me a child. (*She begins to cry.*)

THERAPIST: What are you feeling now?

CLIENT: (*sobbing*) Like he loves Susan more than he loves me. I want to be loved in that very special way.

Over the next month, Ann had two sessions a week. Gestalt work had unearthed the following issues: (1) she was not really sure that she felt loved; (2) she was now considering the possibility that the desire to have a child was based more on insecurity and jealousy of Susan than sincerely wanting her own child; (3) she was sure she would choose Jim and this relationship over a child. She asked for help in learning to be less insecure with Jim.

Changing Patterns in Relationships

We needed to examine the pattern of behaviors that contributed to Ann's insecurity. The baby issue seemed to have highlighted a more basic structural pattern in this relationship. Jim appeared to have the power to dispense love and make important decisions. Ann felt insecure and she gave Jim higher status and believes if he leaves, he is not replaceable. Hence, she was afraid to put forward what she wants, felt insecure about whether he loved her enough and was unwilling to risk confrontation. For the next several weeks we studied the insecurity pattern by having Ann self-monitor the times when she felt most secure and the times she felt least secure. She felt most secure when she and Jim had an intimate conversation, when he spent all day Sunday with her, and when they made love on Sunday morning and he was willing to stay close to her. She felt most insecure when he preferred not to make love on weekend mornings, jumped out of bed to do his chores after love making, or spent the bulk of his weekend time watching baseball games, playing with his computer, and being noncommunicative.

What are some of the universal male–female issues with which we are dealing? What aspects of problematic sex role behaviors appear typical and/or incapable of changing much, and which behaviors are unique to us?

The pattern of the woman wanting more closeness than her male partner is typical of many male–female relationships. Recent work on male and female personality development suggests women are more emeshed in their relationships, while men are more separate. Furthermore, each sex is reported to experience anxiety about closeness differently. Women become anxious about too much separatedness and men about too much connectedness (Chodorow, 1978; Gilligan, 1982). Ann was given the homework assignment to read Carol Gilligan's book *In a Different Voice* to understand more about her dilemma. She needed to assess how much her problem followed a pattern typical of male and female relationships and what parts of the pattern were under her control and thus changeable. Furthermore, if she chose to be in a primary relationship with a man, and Jim's pattern of withdrawal may not be atypical, she needed to learn how to cope with not getting as much closeness and intimacy as she would like without feeling unloved.

While some of Ann's insecurity stemmed from typical male–female interaction patterns, her individual reactions to Jim required further study. Ann needed to learn how she handled the closeness–separateness aspects of her relationships. In particular, she needed to explore more fully, how she equated closeness with being loved and separateness with being rejected. She also needed to discover which behaviors she exhibited moved Jim closer and which drove him away. For this work, we studied more fully therapist–client contact. I suggested to Ann that she pay attention to the aspects of the therapist–client interactions that seemed similar to the problematic interactions with Jim. During the session, together we explored when she felt more secure and valued and when she felt less secure and less valued. For example, she felt more secure if I immediately greeted her in the doorway, if she sat facing me, if I didn't answer the phone and seemed fully attentive. She felt less secure when I was late beginning a session, expressed affection while saying goodbye to the previous client, appeared distracted, made less eye contact or took a phone call during the session. Even though her therapist was a female, a similar pattern of reaction emerged. Ann discovered from these observations how sensitive she was to rejection cues when she perceived me as not being in full contact with her. At these times she became anxious and worried whether or not I liked her and found her interesting enough to continue keeping her as a client.

To work more fully on these patterns, the experiential mirroring exercises of Stevens (1971) were utilized. While mirroring, we worked nonverbally and maintained eye contact.

A mirror instantly reflects exactly what is in front of it. If your partner has his left foot forward, put your right foot forward in a mirror image of his posture . . . as you do this be aware of how you feel as you mirror him . . . now I want you to mirror each other's position and movements at the same time. Begin by taking the same position and move very slowly so that you are not sure whether you are mirroring him or he is mirroring you. Let it become a slow dance . . . a dialogue of movement and interaction between you for five minutes or so. (Stevens, 1971, p. 136)

In mirror work, we worked on mirroring together, letting one another lead, and on independent movements as well. Ann discovered what it felt like to be confluent (fully mirroring and being mirrored by me), separate (aware of differences and feeling isolated and anxious), and separate but in contact. From this work, Ann became aware of how anxious she got over differences when I was not fully mirroring her every move or vice versa. Furthermore, when I moved in a different manner from her movements, she often experienced the difference as rejection. From this work, Ann learned that she often perceives difference as rejection.

Following the mirror experiments, we continued to explore these issues in the course of their therapeutic interaction. I shared with her the pressure she felt to always be "on" for her, to have to be overly sensitive to her, and how I often felt drained after such encounters. Following this work, Ann was instructed to monitor her reaction to difference at home, her sensitivity to rejection cues and her behaviors when Jim withdrew. She was also encouraged to pinpoint which of her behaviors influenced Jim's withdrawal patterns. By studying these patterns, Ann began to understand that she required more confluence than Jim and was intolerant of difference. She also began to understand that Jim might love her, but prefer to be more separate. Ann was also encouraged to share her observations of the interactive process with Jim.

After six months of therapy, Ann reported that she felt more secure in the relationship, talked more openly to Jim, experienced him as more communicative. When he pulled away now, she felt less personally rejected. While she still would have liked more closeness than he seemed to want, she was also more accepting of his wish for time apart on the weekends. Furthermore, Ann no longer felt an urge to have a child. She was working hard on not trying to get everything from Jim; she was spending more time with her women friends, and she also reported that she and Susan had become much closer and enjoyed doing things together on weekends.

Case Illustration: Richard

Richard, a somewhat overweight and balding 40-year-old man, came to therapy in a crisis. He was extremely anxious, unhappy and unable to sleep. His wife of 8 years, Debra, an artistic director for an advertising agency, told him she would like a separation. He worked long hours, did well financially, lives in a Manhatten co-op, had a ski house and a boat, and was a partner in one of the city's leading corporate law firms. He found it hard to believe that Debra thought the marriage so bad. While he viewed Debra as demanding, continually angry and finding fault with him, he could not comprehend her wanting a separation. He acknowledged that he had mostly handled problems in the marriage by avoidance and asked for help in figuring out how he could get her to stay, stating that he loved her and would never find anyone else who was as beautiful and interesting.

What do I want?

In doing the early assessment awareness exercises, Richard was aware that he didn't really know what he wanted. He was still in a state of shock. All he knew was that he wanted his wife to stay, but he was not sure why. He also wasn't even sure that he was that happy with her. Studying his desires seemed somewhat alien to Richard. Richard was asked to recall his most recent bout of unhappiness as if it were happening now.

CLIENT: It's 8:00, I've come back from work and am looking forward to spending some relaxing time with Debra. I'm tired. Debra is on her way out to a community board meeting with her friend Lynn. She looks terrific, full of energy. The two women are talking animatedly and I feel jealous. Debra has many close friends, I don't have any. She tells me to put some chicken in the micro. Now, I'm glad she's going out. At least I'll get some peace. The apartment is quiet. I get edgy. Not sure what to do. I pick at the food. Turn on the tube, turn it off. Go into the freezer for some maple walnut Haagen Daz . . . pick up *New York* magazine and flip through it and begin to wonder when she's coming back. I realize it's gonna be hard to get used to her being gone.

THERAPIST: It's like when Debra is with her friends, you have nothing to do.

CLIENT: When I don't have a plan for the evening or something to work on, I get edgy.

THERAPIST: What are you feeling?

CLIENT: (*looking tearful*) Like I'm really lost without her.

How do I express what I want?

Richard reports that he handles the problems in the marriage by second guessing and placating Debra. He was always trying to figure out what will please her. He bought her gifts, got tickets for plays, concerts, and operas as surprises. Even though he worked long hours, they went out frequently during the week and went away most weekends. They took numerous trips to Europe and Mexico during the year. Typically, when they traveled or socialized they were with other couples or groups. Debra did seem more responsive and sexual to him during those vacation periods. As Richard talked about Debra, he did not seem to have a clear picture of what Debra wanted and why she was unhappy enough to leave him. Although he acknowledged that she must have had some problems of her own (since she had been in analysis 3 times a week for 3 years), he said that she never talked to him about her therapy.

The therapist and Richard role played a recent deadlocked conversation he had with Debra during a 5-hour drive to Vermont.

CLIENT: I sure hope there's snow at Stratton this weekend.

THERAPIST: [as Debra] Nnnhh. . . .

CLIENT: We probably should take the Sappersteins up next week, their kids will be away then.

THERAPIST: [as Debra]: Okay.

CLIENT: And did I tell you I got the tickets for the new Neil Simon play? You really liked "Biloxi Blues"; this should be even better.

THERAPIST: What's happening as you're telling this to me, and I'm not responding?

CLIENT: I'm not sure . . . I guess I feel tired, worn out, like I have no more strength for this.

THERAPIST: I'm aware of how hard you are working to get a response.

CLIENT: It seems like it's work, work, work with her, and even then I don't seem to give her what she wants. She just sits there. You know she's very smart, a real intellectual, yet we never talk about anything any more. Those long drives up to Vermont are deadly.

Can I assess whether or not my partner hears, is capable of responding to what I want?
Richard and Debra did not talk about their relationship and she appeared to be unaware or oblivious of his unhappiness. Richard was given the homework assignment of communicating to Debra his unhappiness about the current situation, his fatigue, and his wish to work on the marriage. He also asked her if she were willing to join him for couples therapy. They had their first intimate conversation in a while. She said that she was working on her own issues with her analyst, that she was sure that the marriage was unworkable, and that she wanted a divorce. When Richard pressed her for reasons, she says she finds him rather insensitive to her and shut off emotionally. He reported that she said that he didn't appear to listen to her or really take time to know her and what she really wanted and that he didn't express what he really wanted. She also said she was

tired of doing most of the emotional work in the relationship, and that now it was her time to grow.

What are triggers and recurrent patterns in this relationship? What does the client contribute to these problematic patterns?
Richard reported that he was stunned by his wife's characterization of him as out of touch with her and unexpressive. He said that he was known as a very aggressive lawyer with a lot of initiative. We decide to study this pattern of his interactions. Debra was spending more and more of her free time with her women friends and was talking about a trial separation over the summer, two months from now. Richard wanted to talk with her about a vacation together to work on the relationship. Richard recorded the following interactions.

(Debra is dressing.)
CLIENT: That's a nice outfit, I like the grey striped top, is it new?

DEBRA: I'm in a hurry, Lynn is picking me up at 9:00.

CLIENT: Oh, where are you going?

DEBRA: *(in an irritated voice)* You know, to the hearing about the homeless. Lynn is trying to raise money for getting more housing. I may do some posters for them.

CLIENT: Yeah, it's a terrible problem, those people living on the street.

THERAPIST: What's happening as you're talking?

CLIENT: I am shrinking more and more into myself, like I don't dare bring up what I want to talk about, like I am walking on eggs with her.

THERAPIST: I experienced you as very evasive in the role play. What were you really feeling?

CLIENT: I was angry. She's running off in a new outfit to worry about the homeless while our marriage is falling apart.

THERAPIST: So, why don't you say that?

CLIENT: What's the point? She'll only get angry.

Further work on studying these interactions revealed that Richard's view of his role in marriage was to be a pleaser, to work hard to give a wife what he thinks she wants, and never to put his own wants up front or to express angry directly. When he was aware of his anger, he would back off and become evasive. He said he worked hard to win her and he had always been afraid of losing her. While he was very assertive and showed initiative at work, he had not brought these skills into the marriage.

What patterns am I bringing from the past?
Richard's way of interacting with his wife appeared to be similar to the way he interacted with his parents. He was the first son (after three

daughters) in a working-class family. He was considered special. His father was much older than his mother and his mother was depressed. She expected high achievement from her only son. Very early on he got into the pattern of giving his parents, particularly his mother, what they seemed to want from him.

Which needs are primary and which secondary?

Since Debra appeared to be leaving, an important issue now for Richard was what to do. What would make him happy?

CLIENT: All my life I thought that if I worked hard, had a great-looking, smart wife, lived in a wonderful apartment, and took great vacations, I'd be happy. I guess I was wrong. I don't know what I want any more or what would make me happy. I guess I never really stopped to think about it.

THERAPIST: Could you think back to some time in the past when you were most happy?

CLIENT: About 2 years ago, I took the boat out for a sail to Martha's Vineyard with a neighbor. Debra and this guy's wife were away at some woman's retreat. It was just wonderful, just the two of us, the open water, staying in Menemsha harbor, just doing nothing for ten days. He was a real easy-going guy and I didn't even have to talk to him much. We just existed, soaked up the sun and watched the stars. It was wonderful.

THERAPIST: So doing nothing with an easy-going guy was wonderful.

CLIENT: Yeah . . . You know I once met a woman at a ski lodge in Switzerland when Debra wasn't with me. She had such a warm smile and I fell in love with her just looking at her across the table. She just seemed to accept me with her smile.

THERAPIST: Try this sentence on: 'I have to work hard for everything I get.'

CLIENT: I have to work hard for everything I get. Yep, that's it. That's the story of my life. No one could just like me for myself.

Saying goodbye.

About 2 months after Debra had left, Richard asked for help in accepting the loss. We use a Gestalt technique of "saying goodbye" (Tobin, 1971). This work usually takes two to four sessions over a 2–4 week period of time. The client is encouraged to write down in a note book all thoughts she or he has about the relationship, using the following categories: (1) positive aspects of the relationship; (2) negative aspects of the relationship; (3) unfinished business; (4) future contact.

Positive Aspects of the Relationship. Richard was to list all the positive aspects of his relationship with Debra: what he liked about her, what he liked about them together, what he would miss. He brought in a long list of Debra's positive traits; she was "beautiful, exciting, intelligent, a talented artist, the most interesting woman he would ever meet, they had so many interests in common, they loved to ski, go to the theatre, art galleries, travel, they spent over ten years together and had all these memories. Sex was wonderful, she had such a beautiful body" and so on. As Richard goes over this list, he is instructed to go into each of these positive aspects of Debra, experience the pain, and talk about what he is losing.

Negative Aspects of the Relationship. Richard next listed the negative aspects of the relationship. What he wouldn't miss, what he didn't like about Debra and their relationship. His list of negatives was much shorter than his list of positives. In the therapy session, he was encouraged to get in touch with some of his anger at Debra and his own unhappiness about her treatment of him.

CLIENT: She's always dissatisfied with me.

THERAPIST: Tell me more about that.

CLIENT: Like, whatever I do, it's not enough, or not right. Like I can never satisfy or please her.

THERAPIST: What are you feeling now?

CLIENT: Quite angry. Why did everything have to be on her terms? God, she put the whole blame on me. But I see that she did a lot of putting me down, expecting me to change, to do most of the work . . . like she was a goddamn princess!

Unfinished Business. Through Gestalt awareness work, Richard focused next on what he was holding on to, what he still wanted from Debra, which was the unfinished business of their relationship that was hampering closure.

THERAPIST: What are you still holding on to?

CLIENT: Like, I'll never be able to find anybody who is as beautiful and exciting. Like, I'm still expecting her to come back. . . . I'm really angry, that she won't see that this could work.

In our next session, we explored each of these dimensions more fully. Richard began to focus on how he would never find anyone else so exciting or interesting.

THERAPIST: Tell me more about never finding anyone so exciting and terrific.

CLIENT: Like, without Debra, I wouldn't do anything. Just be a lump. She's my pacer, without her, my life is grey.

THERAPIST: Do you think you are not exciting yourself?

CLIENT: Yes, I need to have that other person to feel alive, sparkle, to have contact.

THERAPIST: Let's try to work on your contacting your *own* sparkle. That's what you are still holding on to.

The saying good-bye exercises leads to further work on ways to enable Richard to feel more interesting, emotionally alive, to sparkle.

Future Contact. Richard was encouraged to brainstorm what sort of contact he might like to have with Debra in the future (no contact, a friendship, dinner once a year, etc.). Richard was too angry to want any contact with Debra at this time. Sometimes clients have strong urges to contact the person again or are troubled by recurrent bouts of regret or memories of all they have lost. At these times a visual image or a sentence is useful. The client is encouraged to get in touch with some very unpleasant aspect of the relationship, for example, with Richard, one might capture Debra's putdown voice tone, and then focus on that image or sound when bouts of regret surface.

Am I able to be alone?

Richard was encouraged to generate ideas as to how he could experience pleasure in his own company, do what *he* wants to do. This was done to help him break his old pattern of always having to be with someone else in order to experience enjoyment in life. Richard has rarely spent any time alone. He was given homework assignments to spend anywhere from an evening to a weekend alone and take detailed notes on the experience. We worked on ways of enabling him to learn how to be with himself, schedule a day to meet his own needs, and enhance his pleasure in his own company. Richard had spent so much time tuned into others and trying to please them that the alone time was very difficult. At first, it appears, some of the early homework assignments were carried out to please me. Richard hated to be alone at first, but worried more about my disapproval. Several sessions were spent dealing with the need to second guess me. After a few months, however, Richard discovered that he liked to focus on himself; that he liked quiet, and reading mysteries in bed. He began to listen to chamber music, to go alone to concerts that he really wanted to attend. He also began to take piano lessons, swim every day, and was thinking about signing up for an Outward-Bound vacation. He was intrigued with the possibility of surviving in the wilderness alone for a few days.

How do I go about searching for another relationship?

As Richard began to enjoy his life again, he began the search for a new relationship. The search itself provided additional opportunities for Richard to seek out different women and to change his pattern of relating to women. He reported having gone to a party and immediately scanning the room for the best-looking woman. He then went over to her; when she wasn't interested in him, he tried the second best-looking one. He next approached the most interesting woman, who had a crowd around her. When that didn't click, he left, feeling depressed and hopeless. We then role played approaching other types of women, with the focus on learning how to make good contact. Richard also practiced just being interesting enough being himself. He enjoyed the animated role play with his therapist who, he admitted, is someone he would never approach at a party. Over the next weeks, he reported talking at a party to a young psychologist who was warm and was as easy to talk to as his therapist. She had seemed to like him too. He had enjoyed himself so much that he had forgot to scan the room again to see if any interesting beauties had entered. He expressed worry about being turned on to someone who was not beautiful. Through clearly stating her values and encouraging exploration of ways of being in a relationship other than adoration of a beautiful woman, I was able to help Richard on his way to experimenting with those other ways, rather than continuing to pick out someone who had to be won over and with whom he had to work so hard to please. In work with clients like Richard, one should not overlook the modeling aspects of therapeutic contact. Via the use of modeling, one can enable clients to have the experience of talking honestly and relating to someone who accepts them. For some clients, this type of contact is atypical.

How do I assess whether my new partner is capable of meeting my needs?

Sometimes people in new relationships are even more demanding than they were in marriage. After the trauma of separation and a long search for someone whose qualities are presumably a better "fit" than the last partner, even bigger storms may arise in the second relationship than the first. Richard might, for example, become even more demanding, so that the second relationship might generate thoughts such as "I picked you because I didn't have to work so hard; you accepted me and now you're starting to become critical and demanding." Or he might begin to feel so hopeless about ever being happy or getting what he wants that he falls into his old pattern of being Mr. Accommodating and trying to buy his partner off. As a new relationship begins, even if the client has stopped therapy, I encourage them to return for consultation to ward off the possibility of old patterns surfacing.

SUMMARY AND EVALUATION

Theory of Therapy and Principles of Behavior Change

I believe that change occurs from self-knowledge, understanding patterns, and attempts to engage in behaviors that change characteristic patterns of behavior. The role of the therapist is as a tutor or guide who facilitates such self-understanding. Often, clients' cognitions and behaviors are guided by core belief systems, which they feel helpless to change. These belief systems are usually tied in to core self-esteem issues regarding competency that are vocalized via such phrases as "I am helpless," "I can't depend on myself," "I am a fuckup," "I can't do anything right," "I was put on this earth to suffer," and so on. The CBT–Gestalt model highlights interaction issues with a focus on process, rather than on symptoms; it is one way of assessing and changing these belief symptoms and hence changing maladaptive behavior. However, the client will not fully integrate these new beliefs into the self-structure unless they are based on experience. The integration of CBT utilizes key features of both Gestalt and behavior therapy. Gestalt therapy in the form of focused awareness and experiential experimentation emphasizes the study of recurrent patterns of behavior and how these patterns are characteristically and repeatedly reflected in the client's interpersonal interactions. These experiments provide the framework to restructure core belief systems. Behavior therapy, with its step-by-step assessment and behavioral goals, moves clients along to actively work on changing the patterns of behavior that keep them locked into their symptoms and unhappiness.

Goals of Therapy

Behavior therapists have typically begun therapy with a presenting problem, focusing on a symptom and then constructing an assessment to discover more about the symptom in order to devise a treatment plan. Therapy outcome is determined by the client's progress in shedding the presenting problematic behavior. The CBT model presented in this paper argues for a shift from symptoms to patterns. Thus, therapy is seen as an ongoing assessment process, used to discover key patterns, core structures, and the way in which these are manifested in the client's interactions with significant others. The focus of change is on patterns and the client's goals are mostly those of self-awareness. Goal setting is based on the client's more realistic perceptions of her or his core issues. Hence, therapy could be construed as an ongoing series of assessment experiments to enhance the client's awareness. Consequently, outcome research becomes problematic, since the presenting symptom may not be the sole locus of change.

Who Can and Who Cannot Benefit from This Approach

My failures with this method have been more from *not* using it than from using it. Clearly, clients have to be open to self-exploration. Many clients who might benefit from self-awareness training do not like the exercises or place a high premium on avoidance. One recent failure was a 55-year-old man who was depressed following the announcement in January that his much younger wife wished to separate at the end of the children's school year. This client appeared to want quick symptom relief. I used more standard cognitive behavioral techniques to help him deal with his grief. He resisted any attempts to study the situation more fully and stopped therapy as soon as he felt better. However, 6 months later, when he actually had to sell the family house and watch his wife leave with the furniture and his three children for California, he became suicidal. Six months before, he was unwilling to anticipate what that day of departure might be like. He had felt better and that was all he had wanted from therapy. Later on, when coping with trying to find a place to live, facing the reality of his single state and the loss of the children, he fell apart. His pattern of avoidance in dealing with problems probably also contributed to the breakup of the marriage.

Another failure was a "wallower." The client was so open to her feelings and allowed herself to carry on so, it was impossible to use these techniques effectively to get her to see that the wallowing itself was a major factor in her problematic relationships.

Applications of the Model to Other Populations

The preceding model of therapy was evolved from work on a middle class, outpatient neurotic population of mostly young adults. However, the time and care devoted to the gaining of self-knowledge and one-on-one therapy is a middle-class luxury. Its application to other types of clinical populations requires further study. The author is working on an expansion of this model to assess coping skills of single-parent mothers in New York and other low-income, multi-ethnic disadvantaged populations in crisis. Many of my students use this approach in their field work in settings that cater to a disadvantaged clientele.

Training

As a trainer of beginning therapists, I have been using the combined CBT–Gestalt approach in training first-year doctoral students in the School Psychology and Child/School Programs at New York University. For example, from the first day of their field placement, students are taught Gestalt awareness exercises before beginning the more formal behavioral–observational assignments. In addition, from the first interactions they have with clients (parents, children, adolescents, teachers), they are encouraged to pay attention to process variables, how they feel about the person, what the dominant theme of interaction is (rebellion, take care of me, etc.), and how these considerations may or may not relate to the presenting problem. Students are also encouraged to use focus awareness exercises as an aid in learning to write clear descriptions of children, teacher–child interactions, and classroom settings for psychological reports.

Research

Gestalt therapists for the most part have not been interested in research. As a group, they write little and do not do careful data-based evaluations and follow-ups of their clients. What little research evidence exists for diving more fully into emotional experience to enhance behavior change comes from the behavioral literature on flooding. Foa and Kozak (1986) report that obsessive–compulsives who fully experience the emotional impact of exposure to contaminants, have superior treatment outcomes compared to those clients who use some form of cognitive distraction techniques. More creativity in designing experiments to measure what happens as clients dive more fully into an experience is needed. Behavioral researchers, for the most part, have specialized in particular types of symptoms and therefore have not focused on problematic patterns of behavior that cut across symptoms. I am currently carrying out such research with two of my students. We are exploring more fully the symptomatic processes of bulimics and agoraphobics.

To a great extent, researchers have neglected to study process issues in psychotherapy. There appears to be a gap between the issues researchers address and what the therapist deals with in therapy. How does the interaction of therapist and client influence outcome? Emmelkamp and van der Hout (1983), in reviewing negative outcomes for agoraphobics, believe that therapist–client interactions may be an important factor in determining outcome. They report that the clients who felt most understood by the therapist reported the most improvement. The study of process in Gestalt therapy is just beginning. Rice and Greenberg (1984) have edited a book on patterns of change, which describes both theory and methodology for such work. For example, Greenberg (1984) presents his research on task analysis to isolate components crucial for successful resolution. He studied in detail the Gestalt dialogue (in which client both talks and listens to the two parts of the conflict) to highlight the process of resolution and integration. Greenberg reports positive outcomes from using the Gestalt dialogue for conflict resolution. He also cites the unpublished research of Clarke (1981) that provides support for the two-chair dialogue being more effective than rational problem solving for conflict resolution.

Research on the training of therapists has also been a neglected area for behavior therapists. It may be that Gestalt techniques are very useful as therapist training aids. Clearly, research on Gestalt process and cognitive-behavior therapy has barely begun.

REFERENCES

Arnkoff, D. B. (1980). Psychotherapy from the perspective of cognitive theory. In M. J. Mahoney (Ed.), *Psychotherapy process*. New York: Plenum.

Arnkoff, D. B., & Glass, C. R. (1982). Clinical cognitive constructs: Examination, evaluation elaboration. In P. C. Kendall (Ed.), *Advances in cognitive-behavioral research and therapy* (Vol. 1). New York: Academic Press.

Beck, A. T., & Emery, E. (1985). *Anxiety disorders and phobias: A cognitive perspective*. New York: Basic Books.

Beisser, A. R. (1970). The paradoxical theory of change. In J. Fagan & I. L. Shepard (Eds.), *Gestalt therapy now*. Palo Alto, CA: Science and Behavior Books.

Chodorow, N. (1982). *The reproduction of mothering*. Berkeley, CA: University of California Press.

Clarke, K. (1981). *The effects of the Gestalt Tao-Chain experiment and cognitive problem solving on decision making*. Unpublished doctoral dissertation: Loyola University.

Ellis, A., & Harper, R. A. (1975). *A new guide to rational living*. Englewood Cliffs, NJ: Prentice-Hall.

Emmelkamp, P., & van der Hout, A. (1983). Failures in treating agoraphobia. In E. B. Foa & P. M. G. Emmelkamp (Eds.), *Failures in behavior therapy*. New York: Wiley.

Foa, E. B., & Kozak, M. J. (1986). Emotional process of fear: Exposure to corrective information. *Psychological Bulletin, 99*, 20-33.

Fodor, I. G. (1980). The treatment of communication problems with assertiveness training. In A. Goldstein & E. Foa (Eds.), *Handbook of behavioral interventions*. New York: Wiley.

Fodor, I. G., & Epstein, R. C. (1983). Assertiveness training for women: Where are we failing? In E. Foa & P. Emmelkamp (Eds.), *Failures in behavior therapy*. New York: Wiley.

Fodor, I. G., & Thal, J. (1984) Weight disorders: Overweight and anorexia. In E. Blechman (Ed.), *Behavior modification with women*. New York: Guilford.

Fodor, I. G., & Wolfe, J. L. (1977). Assertiveness training for mothers and daughters. In R. Alberti (Ed.), *Assertiveness, innovations, applications, issues*. San Luis Obisbo, CA: Impact.

Gilligan, C. (1982). *In a different voice: Psychological theory and women's development*. Cambridge, MA: Harvard University Press.

Greenberg, L. S. (1984). Task analysis of intrapersonal conflict resolution. In L. R. Rice & L. S. Greenberg (Eds.), *Patterns of change*. New York: Guilford.

Guidano, V. F., & Liotti, G. (1983). *Cognitive processes and emotional disorders*. New York: Guilford.

Harper, R., Bauer, R., & Kannarkat, J. (1976). Learning theory and Gestalt therapy. *American Journal of Psychotherapy, 30* 1, 55-72.

Mahoney, M. J. (1974). *Cognition and behavior modification*. Cambridge, MA: Ballinger.

Mahoney, M. J. (1980). Psychotherapy and the structure of personal revolutions. In M. J. Mahoney (Ed.), *Psychotherapy process: Current issues and future directions*. New York: Plenum.

Meichenbaum, D. (1977). *Cognitive-behavior modification: An integrative approach*. New York: Plenum.

Perls, F. S., Hefferline, R. F., & Goodman, P. (1951). *Gestalt therapy*. New York: Julian Press.

Polster, E., & Polster, M. (1973). *Gestaltt therapy integrated*. New York: Brunner/Mazel.

Rice, L. N., & Greenberg, L. S. (Eds.). (1984). *Patterns of change*. New York: Guilford.

Resnick, R. (1970). Chicken soup is poison. *Voices, 6*, 75-78.

Simkin, J. S., & Yontef, G. M. (1984). Gestalt therapy. In R. J. Corsini (Ed.), *Current psychotherapies*. (3rd ed.). Itasca, IL: Peacock.

Stevens, J. O. (1971). *Awareness: Exploring, experimenting, experiencing*. New York: Bantam.

Tobin, S. A. (1971). Saying goodbye. *Psychotherapy: Theory, Research, Practice, 8*(2), 150–155.

Turk, D. C., & Speers, M. A. (1983). Cognitive schemata and cognitive process in cognitive-behavioral interventions: Going beyond the information giving. In P. C. Kendall (Ed.), *Advances in cognitive-behavioral research and therapy* (Vol. 2). New York: Academic Press.

Van De Riet, V., Korb, M., & Gorrell, J. (1980). *Gestalt therapy: An introduction*. New York: Pergamon.

Wolfe, J. L., & Fodor, I. G. (1975). A cognitive/behavioral approach to modifying assertive behavior in women. *The Counseling Psychologist, 5, 4*, 45–52.

Yontef, G. (1976). Gestalt therapy: Clinical phenomenology. In V. Binder, A. Binder, & R. Rimland (Eds.), *Modern therapies*. Englewood Cliffs, NJ: Prentice-Hall.

CHAPTER 7

Marital Therapy: A Cognitive-Behavioral-Affective Approach

Gayla Margolin
University of Southern California

Had I been asked to write this chapter 10 years ago, rather than now, the task would have been much easier. In thinking back to the workshops that I gave and the writing that I did at that earlier stage of my clinical career, I realize that I was more certain then about how to conduct therapy than I am now. At times, I miss the clarity of my earlier model, particularly when faced with the task of communicating my model to others. I also miss the excitement of being a proponent of what then was a relatively new approach, and following in the footsteps of leaders such as Patterson, Weiss, Stuart, and Liberman (Liberman, 1970; Patterson & Hops, 1972; Patterson & Reid, 1970; Stuart, 1976; Weiss, 1978; Weiss, Hops, & Patterson, 1973). The changes that have occurred are due, in part, to seeing limitations in my earlier model. I think it comes as well from a maturing process in myself—in being able to understand more levels of clients' experience and pain and to appreciate better the obstacles impeding change. In writing this chapter, I know that my clinical work continues to undergo considerable change, influenced by each new client and by formal and informal input from colleagues. For myself, writing this chapter will serve as a marker to look back upon several years hence.

Since the time Neil Jacobson and I co-authored our book on marital therapy (Jacobson & Margolin, 1979), I have focused primarily on the treatment of specific problems, for example, jealousy (Margolin, 1981, 1985) or abusive conflict (Margolin, in press-a). Although it is relatively easy to get caught up in the exigencies of developing a course of action for a specific type of case, my goal in this chapter is to think in generalities across cases. My focus will be restricted to marital cases, however, since that is the primary form of therapy that I conduct.

THEORETICAL UNDERPINNINGS

The theoretical model underlying my work would best be described as a combination of social learning and systems theories. Each of these models offers a great deal toward the understanding of marital dysfunction, and translates into a variety of intervention strategies. In saying that social learning theory is a major influence in my work, I am not saying that I necessarily apply specific principles, such as reinforcement or modeling, in bringing about behavior change. Furthermore, while hoping not to offend some of my closest colleagues, I cannot say that my clinical activities are greatly affected by treatment outcome studies in behavioral marital therapy. As recently illustrated (Jacobson, Follette, Revenstorf, Baucom, Hahlweg, & Margolin, 1984), the data from these studies are not completely convincing. Moreover, I do not subscribe to a basic premise of these studies, that a systematic and uniform treatment is likely to work with most, or indeed, with even the majority of clients.

What I have found most useful is the experimental method of inquiry that characterizes the social learning approach. From this perspective, I have come to consider each case as a mini-experiment. By continuously collecting data about the couple, I can construct theories about what is contributing to their marital distress. By carefully monitoring the effects of my interventions, I allow for a self-corrective process in our change endeavors.

The social learning perspective also points me to certain dimensions as possible determinants of marital problems. Operant theory, of course, directs us to look at environmental consequences as determinants of behavior. The emphasis in social learning theory, however, is on social influences as the important environmental determinants in the development of behavior. Social learning theory, in addition, looks at the reciprocal influences between the individual and his or her social environment. As Bandura (1977), has indicated, persons and environmental factors determine each other. He states, "It is largely through their actions that people produce the environment conditions that affect their behavior in a reciprocal fashion. The experiences generated by behavior also partly determine what a person becomes and can do which, in turn, affects subsequent behavior" (p. 9). These concepts direct us to examine how spouses' reactions to one another continually shape each other's behaviors and mold dysfunctional behaviors (Jacobson & Margolin, 1979).

The concepts also suggest that the characteristics that spouses bring to the relationship are highly influenced by what has been learned in important relationships from earlier stages in life. People learn certain behavioral patterns in earlier relationships. They also acquire expectations and cognitive sets that serve as filters for processing information in the ongoing relationship. This aspect of the theory forms a bridge with psychodynamic theories. That is, certain preconceived expectations from early relationships then can lead to the evocation of confirming stimuli from the current relationship.

Social exchange theory (e.g., Jacobson, 1981; Jacobson & Moore, 1981; Rappaport & Harrell, 1972) offers the perspective that ongoing behavioral exchanges influence long-range subjective outcomes of relationships. This perspective elevates the day-to-day minutia of relationships to an important level. It also speaks to the importance of directly observing social exchanges and their effects on overall marital satisfaction.

What systems theory contributes to my conceptualization of marital dysfunction is a shift to a larger context or field of attention. Rather than focus on the individual, or on two separate individuals, my attention is directed to a system that encompasses and is created by those individuals. From this perspective, I have gained a better appreciation of the interdependence between the behavior of marital partners and between the marital system and larger systems. As Hoffman (1981, p. 348) says, "The family has to fit with its environment, just as the individual has to fit within the family, or the separate organs have to fit together in a system that is the biological self. And all have to fit together in the ecology of the whole." These ideas of one system being related to another system have led me to include more pieces in the puzzle of factors influencing and being influenced by the marital dysfunction. Questions of how the marital system fits within the family system and within the larger societal system are, of course, pertinent to this viewpoint. The importance of boundaries in keeping the marital system semiprivate and yet semipermeable to the children is one such consideration.

In addition, general systems theory, with its emphasis on redundancies in interaction, has helped me to develop "circular" rather than "linear" explanations for problems. No one element in a family system takes precedence over or controls another element. In fact, the whole notion of causation is suspended and replaced instead with an interest in how behaviors fit together in the family system.

The interpretation of symptoms is quite different in a systems perspective than it is in a social learning perspective. Although the social learning perspective tends to view symptoms as dysfunctional behaviors that must be changed, systems theory tends to view symptoms as signs that change is forthcoming. Systems theorists, particularly strategic therapists, such as Watzlawick, Weakland, and Fisch (1974), suggest that misguided attempts to solve a problem actually maintain or even intensify the problem. Watzlawick et al. capture this concept in their powerful image of

> two sailors hanging out of either side of a sailboat in order to steady it: the more the one leans overboard, the more the other has to hang out to

compensate for the instability created by the other's attempts at stabiliz-
ing the boat, while the boat itself would be quite steady if not for their
acrobatic efforts at steadying it. It is not difficult to see that in order to
change this absurd situation, at least one of them has to do something
seeming quite unreasonable, namely to "steady" less and not more, since
this will immediately force the other to also do less of the same (unless he
wants to finish up in the water), and they may eventually find themselves
comfortably back inside a steady boat (p. 36).

An important point of convergence between the social learning and
systems perspectives is the emphasis on understanding recurring patterns. The social learning perspective offers a structure for microanalysis
of interactional sequences. The systems perspective requires a more molar
analysis. From each of these analyses comes one or more hypotheses
about what maintains, though not necessarily what created, the dysfunctional pattern. Behavioral hypotheses often have to do with the behavioral
deficits or excesses observed in the interaction, as well as the ways that
partners mutually shape each other's behavior through reinforcement,
punishment and extinction. Systems hypotheses attempt to make sense of
and ascribe a positive connotation to each partner's or family member's
role with respect to the reoccuring pattern.

Blending the two perspectives offers a rich array of treatment options. From a social learning perspective, the hypothesis generally translates into a specific plan for change, that is, generating and training new
behavioral options. From a systems point of view, the hypothesis itself is
seen as more central. The hypothesis may be offered to the family as an
explanation of the distressing behavior with the expectation that the
explanation alone will stir the couple to new actions. Or, the hypothesis
might be offered in the form of a prescription for action that will break the
couple's pattern. The prescription may not attempt to change the behaviors per se but may positively reframe them or change the context or the
sequence in which they occur. In both perspectives, the hypothesis is
generated as a starting point for an investigation, with the reaction to the
hypothesis and its concomitant intervention taken as evidence of its work-
ableness. The reaction then is used to revise the hypothesis, to generate
new hypotheses, or to expand an intervention strategy that is working
well.

OVERVIEW OF THERAPEUTIC CHANGE

Underlying Assumptions

My intervention approach is grounded in several assumptions that I hold
about marital functioning. First, there are many different forms of
marital distress, with some of long standing and others more immediate,
some stemming from varied sources and others from one particular criti-

cal incident. Second, there are also many different forms of marital adjustment. Couples vary in their desired levels of intimacy and closeness, and in the amount of conflict that is acceptable to them. Couples also vary in what they view as the primary goal, purpose, or function of their union. Third, couples are differentially responsive to different aspects of a marital treatment, that is, some respond to affective interventions while some respond to cognitive or behavioral interventions. It also is likely that, within a given couple, the two spouses may differ on any of these dimensions. These differences may even be one of the primary factors underlying their tension.

In light of this view of couples, I try to make flexibility a key component in my intervention strategy. I do not presume to understand what is troubling a couple until I have completed a thorough evaluation and assessment. I try to avoid preconceived ideas of what a relationship should be like when our work is completed. Although I approach each new case equipped with knowledge about what often works with certain types of problems, I cannot assume that that is the best place to start with this particular couple. Instead, my overall intervention strategy takes shape based on the particular reactions of a given couple to each small step along the way.

Assessment

A thorough assessment requires taking account of and linking individual, interpersonal, and environmental processes as they affect marital functioning (Margolin, 1983a). What does each individual bring to the relationship that affects the problematic sequences in the relationship? How do recurring relationship phenomena and patterns affect the individuals involved as well as other systems? How do systems outside the marriage affect the relationship or, vice versa, how are they affected by the marriage?

The individual level alone is quite complex, with the relevant factors included being cognitive, affective, and behavior dimensions. One type of cognitive variable is the "cognitive sets" about relationships that individuals have developed through past learning experiences, either in their families of origin or in other intimate relationships as adults. Information regarding spouses' attitudes, beliefs, and expectations for intimate relationships are pertinent here. I find that these types of cognitions are readily forthcoming during the course of an interview regarding a couple's impressions of the relationship and of marriage in general. A second important cognitive variable concerns spouses' ongoing processing of relationship information. This comes from stop-action procedures whereby I inquire into how each spouse interpreted and reacted to what the other was saying or doing. Here I often use my own perceptions as a point of comparison against what the spouse was saying. If I see the spouse's behavior as an attempt to be helpful, while the mate interpreted it as demeaning, this may be indicative of a cognitive distortion, disabling the mate from accurately (or at least benignly) perceiving the partner's behavior. There must be repeating evidence of this pattern, however, before it can be labelled a systematic cognitive distortion. Furthermore, I must rule out some type of private meaning to what the spouse was saying that, indeed, does render it demeaning.

Affective dimensions to consider include affective involvement and affective expression. Affective involvement is, in many ways, the crux of whether the relationship will, or should continue. Affective involvement can be viewed as spouses' investment of themselves in the relationship: Is that investment high enough to maintain their desire to stay in the relationship and, moreover, to work on improving that relationship? In addition, is that investment high enough to sustain one another's interest in staying in the relationship? Sometimes, with some careful and sensitive questioning, it can be determined from the outset that the affective involvement is too low to warrant trying to improve the marriage. In other cases, this information is not available until the intervention has begun. The spouses' enthusiasm for and receptivity to the changes that accrue in therapy often are a good indicator of emotional investment.

Affective expression, or the way spouses convey the emotions that they feel, is also an important dimension. As stated elsewhere (Margolin & Weinstein, 1983), deficits in emotional expression have several different origins, including (1) labeling difficulties, or difficulties putting their feeling into words; (2) negative attitudes toward feeling expression (e.g., "It's a sign of weakness"); (3) discomfort due to inexperience (e.g., "I come from a undemonstrative family"); (4) beliefs that feeling expression is unnecessary (e.g., "Why should I have to spell it out? After being together this long, she should know what I'm feeling"); (5) a withholding attitude toward the partner (e.g., "I won't give him the satisfaction of knowing how I feel"); or (6) fear of being rejected or punished by the partner. Difficulties with affective expression or affective reception are common sources of miscommunication between spouses. The "stop-action" procedures used for identifying dysfunctional cognitions are also helpful in ferreting out these types of affective problems. Having the spouse articulate what emotion she or he was experiencing when the miscommunication occurred, and having the other partner label what she or he thought the partner was feeling points out discrepancies in this arena.

Behavioral competencies are, of course, another aspect to assess in the individual. There are a number of behavioral deficits, most notably in the area of communication, that affect marital adjustment. Being able to communicate sources of discontent and to evaluate possible solutions to problems both help to avoid an ever increasing build-up of marital tensions. The way I assess these particular skills is to ask the couple to discuss a problem issue. Often I have them do that at home, using a tape recorder so that I then can listen to the discussion. Or, if videotape equipment is available, they have the discussion in my office, without my being present in the room. In either event, I first review the tape carefully by myself, and then, in our next conjoint session, the three of us listen together and share impressions. We sort out what led to conflict escalation, to premature termination of the discussion, to feelings of frustration, anger and hurt, and to whatever processes appear problematic.

In addition to communication skills, being a good companion involves certain skills, e.g., being sensitive to one another's mood, being creative with leisure time. Being a good sexual partner similarly involves sensitivity and creativity, and is enhanced by information about sex, and by communication skills in giving and receiving feedback. There are also skills involved in managing a shared household (i.e., financial management, household organization) that typically are not crucial at the beginning of a relationship, but can affect relationship satisfaction later on.

Finally, before leaving the individual sphere, there are physiological components which serve as important determinants in a relationship. General energy or activity level, such as whether someone is an early riser or a night owl, affects how that person acts in an intimate relationship. It is not those characteristics per se that affect marital satisfaction, nor even differences between the spouses in those characteristics. What matters is how spouses interpret the differences. Negative interpretations of low energy level, for example, "Again she [he] won't go out with me! I guess that shows she [he] just doesn't care enough about me to do what I want for a change" lead to feelings of rejection and anger.

Moving into the relationship domain, I find it important to obtain a developmental perspective of the relationship and also a detailed analysis of what currently transpires on a day-to-day basis. The developmental intake interview, described by Jacobson and Margolin (1979) focuses on how the relationship began. This is important from an informational perspective, as well as for the affect that is elicited as the couple describes their initial meetings, early dates, and the decision to marry. After understanding the early stages of the relationship, I also want to know about other turning points in the marriage, with a particular focus on high points and low points. Even severely distressed relationships often include periods of content, if not bliss, just as satisfying relationships have weathered periods of discontent.

Couples generally are surprised by the amount of detail that I elicit and the interest that I place on what they regard as the mundane aspects of their day-to-day interaction, such as what happens in a typical evening from the moment that they reconvene after their separate days to when they go to sleep, how they usually spend their weekends or other free time, and how they split up the responsibilities of managing a home, or children. Without exception, my supervisees receive repeated recommendations to go back and get more information about the couple's daily interaction. I have them listen to what the couple is saying and try to imagine the senario. The gaps that remain after piecing the images together indicate what needs further exploration.

For some couples, the tenor of their daily interaction serves as a buffer against some relatively isolated but severe sources of tension. For example, some couples are quite satisfied with each other as companions, as co-parents, and as housemates, but have difficulty with deeper levels of intimacy. For others, the nature of their daily interaction provides a constant source of irritation, perhaps due to the partner's messiness in the house, unkempt appearance, uncommunicativeness, or constant preoccupation with work. However, when they can get beyond these daily annoyances, the spouses may sustain a strong attraction to one another.

As spouses report on what goes on in their daily interaction, they often speak in generalities and focus on the negative dimensions. I find it helpful in getting a more accurate and prospective picture to have them keep records on some relevant dimension of their lives together (Margolin, in press-b). One strategy is simply to have them keep records of what types of activities they do with or for one another through an instrument such as the Spouse Observation Checklist (Weiss & Perry, 1979). Analyzing the relationship between specific activities and daily satisfaction ratings directs attention to what types of relationship activities need to occur more or less frequently to improve overall satisfaction. Another more open-ended strategy is to have the couple rate (at least 3 times a day) some relevant affective dimension (e.g., feelings of closeness, openness, frustration, etc.), and then to speculate about what events in the relationship have contributed to those feelings. Thus, a wife who was concerned about her feelings of distance from her husband was instructed to rate herself on a closeness–distance dimension three times a day, and then to examine why she might be feeling that way. The husband had a parallel task that reflected his concerns with the relationship. These data are very useful in portraying the waxing and waning of emotional dimensions defined as important by the spouses, and in generating hypotheses on how to change those feelings.

External variables, the third general dimension of relationship influences, are elicited through interviewing and getting to know the spouses as individuals. During the course of the developmental interview, for example, external stresses on the couple are likely to surface. The pressures of being new parents or parents of adolescents, or of caring for aging relatives, are all relevant. In addition, there are the stresses that each spouse faces in his or her individual life, such as discontent with employment or lack of employment, coping with one's own health problems, and facing one's own aging. While I find it very important to learn about each spouse as an individual, I try to do this as efficiently as possible without taking too much time from relationship issues. Typically I gather this information in the conjoint session although occasionally I rely upon individual interviews.

Overall, the assessment that I conduct is a balance between obtaining information, establishing a relationship with the couple, and helping both partners become comfortable with the therapy process. For assistance in gathering information, I rely on several questionnaires that can be completed at home. Typically, I use the Dyadic Adjustment Scale (Spanier, 1976) for an assessment of overall satisfaction relative to other couples, the Areas of Change Questionnaire (Weiss & Perry, 1979) for an assessment of specific problem areas as well as spouses' perceptual accuracy in identifying those problems, and the Conflict Inventory (Margolin, Fernandez, Gorin, & Ortiz, 1982) for a picture of conflict strategies.

My overall impressions, however, are largely formulated on the basis of direct observation. What always has appealed to me about couples' therapy is that, with both spouses present in the therapy room, I have the opportunity to directly see many of the problems acted out rather than have to rely on patients' reports of problems that occur outside the therapy situation. In addition to those informal observations, I almost always get structured samples of the couples' communication, as described above.

Structure of Therapy

Although the organization of my therapy is relatively loose, there are some distinct stages at the beginning and end of therapy. The first session is used to determine whether or not marital therapy is appropriate and to decide whether or not to embark on 3- to 4-week assessment. The assessment is used to decide whether to enter therapy. The structure of the therapy itself is rather freewheeling but toward the end there is a consistent fading-out period.

The first stage, for determining whether or not marital therapy is appropriate, is distinct from the larger assessment by virtue of the way it is set up during the telephone intake. To ease one or both spouses' ambivalence about entering therapy, I always suggest that they have one meeting with me to decide whether or not we should proceed further. Toward the end of that meeting, I indicate that, should they want to continue, we would do a more formal assessment. Having that choice point, followed by at least one other choice point, means that, over time, each spouse makes an independent overt commitment to therapy.

The main purpose of the first session is to determine whether marital therapy is a appropriate form of therapy. During the course of the first session, I have the couple address the question of what they want from therapy. As long as both spouses are interested either in improving the relationship or in determining the future course of the relationship, then marital therapy is an appropriate treatment. Marital therapy is not appropriate, however, if one partner has already made the decision to leave the marriage or if one partner wants to maintain the relationship but in its current form. In these instances, individual therapy may be the best choice, particularly for the person who wanted marital improvement. Marital therapy also may not be appropriate if one or both partners suffers from drug or alcohol dependency, or a severe emotional disturbance. Depending upon how the marriage affects or is affected by the individual problem, I will either do marital therapy concurrent to an appropriate individual therapy or suggest deferring the marital therapy until the other problem has been treated.

It should be noted that while an initial decision about whether marital therapy is appropriate may be reached in the first session, this may not be the ultimate decision. Often this is a very complicated decision, with one spouse feeling unsure about whether to commit to therapy or to the relationship at all. In such cases, I postpone the decision regarding the appropriateness of marital therapy at least until our initial assessment has been completed. That gives spouses more time to think about what they want with therapy and to experience what therapy is like.

Presuming the presenting problems and goals are compatible with a relationship-oriented therapy, I will suggest to the couple that we proceed with the 3- to 4-week evaluation period. In other words, at the end of the first session, I do not ask for a commitment to therapy but ask only that the two partners engage in a full assessment, thereby giving both them and me time to make a more informed decision. Although the assessment is not designed to bring about major improvement, it tends to have some very important effects. It is a time for the spouses to experience what it is like to discuss with an outsider issues that they may never have divulged to anyone, even the partner. It also is a time for the two partners to focus intensively on one another and on the marriage; that, in itself, can be a powerful emotional experience. While it is not my intention to solve the major relationship problems during the assessment phase, it is my intention to help the spouses begin to develop more good will toward one another. This occurs by creating an atmosphere in which the spouses talk thoughtfully and nondefensively about the marriage, by slowing things down so that they actually hear what the other is saying, and by reframing some of their interpretations of problems.

At the end of the 3- to 4-week assessment period, I summarize for the couple what I have learned that bears directly on my ideas for an intervention. In some cases, I sort out which among the spouses' goals can be dealt with in therapy and, as much as possible, inform them of how we will deal with each goal. In other cases, I bring attention to problems I have observed that the couple has not mentioned, such as a structural problem in terms of their schedules or an imbalance in power, and see if they are interested in overhauling these aspects of the marriage. The couple's reaction will determine whether or not these become intervention targets.

The intervention, which is described in detail below, can be thought of as incorporating two predominant stages, sometimes in tandem and sometimes sequentially. One stage is building up good will, while the other is the tackling of serious problems. The building up of good will is designed to heighten spouses' feelings of support and caring for one another. The good will serves as a cushion for the hard work and difficult decisions that the spouses face when they then confront their major problems, whether they are conflicts of values, life style, or shared resources.

If we are successful at improving the overall tenor of the marriage as well as resolving some of the major battles, we then enter a maintenance stage. Ostensibly, this stage is directed to picking up on less significant problems that have been pushed into the background or on problems that arise on an ad hoc basis. In reality, the importance of this stage is that the major changes already in effect have a chance to solidify, and that the spouses themselves assume more responsibility for healing their marriage.

The maintenance stage gently flows into the final stage, that is, the fading out of therapy. I find that the more successful therapy has been, the more reluctant clients are to give it up. One hour a week becomes a small investment for maintaining a more satisfying relationship. Because of these feelings of wanting to 'hold on' and because relationship problems tend to ebb and flow over time, I find it very useful to end by lessening the frequency of the therapy sessions, for example, every other week and then every month. In the final phase, I frequently recommend that we touch base and assess how things are going after 6 months have elapsed. This gives the couple a target date to reevaluate the relationship themselves and possibly take action to avoid backsliding. It also normalizes the process and reduces concerns of the perceived failure involved in recontacting me to consult further about their marriage.

The Structure of Sessions

The continuity of my therapy comes from the homework assignments that the couple is asked to complete between sessions. It is extremely rare that the couple leaves my office without some task to do or to practice, or at least something to think about before we meet again. I do this so that couples are actively working on their relationship on their own and in their natural environment. It is my view that structured homework assignments are essential if the gains made in the therapy session are to generalize, be encorporated in daily routines, and take on personalized meaning.

The strong emphasis on work between sessions has an important impact for the structure of our meetings together. The first order of business always is to review what has gone on during the week relevant to the specific assignment that I made or that the couple gave themselves. Issues about how the homework was done, what the outcome was, or why it was not done all are given ample attention. Then other pertinent details of the week also are examined, such as, particular high or low points or unusual stresses in the spouses' lives. Issues that arise from this discussion may require our attention for the full therapy hour. More typically, however, following such a discussion we can then turn to the "new business" of therapy, which may be devising the next step in our efforts to improve the quality of their interaction, or the next phase of communication training, or the next topic to which we will apply problem-solving techniques. Whatever the topic, my goal is to take this new business and transform it into something that the couple can go away with and work on before our next meeting. Before ending the session, we review exactly what the next step is that the spouses will do on their own, so that the homework itself does not become an additional source of conflict for the couple.

Active Ingredients

In thinking about active ingredients, I tend to believe that there are two different types—ones that evolve from the situation of being in therapy, and ones that evolve specifically from my suggestions or from the agenda that I structure. Simply to be in a room together, focusing on their relationship, with no distractions, and with an interested, encouraging third party is quite a powerful experience for most spouses. The habit of letting issues slide as each partner gets caught up in the exigencies of daily life is directly challenged just by scheduling this time together. This impact is further reinforced when the assignments between sessions require each spouse at least to think about some aspect of their marriage or, more typically, to interact with one another in a specific fashion. In essence, being in therapy and complying even minimally requires making the relationship more of a priority in relation to other demands.

The active ingredients for which I am willing to take more direct credit fall into the general category of making it possible for spouses to take risks with one another. The risk may be as small as allowing oneself to listen to what the partner really is saying or to try to explain something in a different fashion. The risk may be as large as attempting to be intimate after years of distance, making a major change in one's personal life (e.g., taking a new job, giving up an affair), or restructuring patterns of daily interaction. To facilitate this risk taking, I need to help the couple reach the level at which they expose their vulnerability but also become strong enough to attempt change, either in attitudes, actions, or feelings. My input is most direct when it comes to structuring the change such that it is reasonable in scope and has a chance of succeeding.

SPECIFIC TECHNIQUES

What I do in therapy can be most generally described as altering transactional patterns. The patterns may be molar or molecular in scope, that is, my focus may be on altering a pattern of conflict escalation that develops in less than one minute or on altering a pattern of withdrawal that evolves over a several month period. Within each individual, the patterns reflect an interplay between covert and overt processes. Between individuals, the overt events exhibited by one person affect both the overt and covert reactions in the other. Complicating this never-ending circular feedback loop are the metaperceptions that each spouse has about the other's overt behavior. Each spouse not only observes what the other does but has his or her unique interpretation of that action, as well as his or her unique perceptions of how the other person interprets the same action.

To change these continuous interactional cycles requires choosing a target of intervention. The ultimate goal generally resides in the affective domain. That is, therapy is deemed successful if spouses feel more comfortable with, more satisfied with, or happier about the relationship. Occasionally interventions are directed immediately at affective processes, but more typically the interventions are directed toward behavior-affective links, cognitive-affective links, or behavior-cognitive-affective links.

Choosing the target point for changing these cycles is, in my view, one of the more important decisions that we face. As seen in certain examples below, there are some instances in which cognitions and behaviors can be changed simultaneously. At other times, however, this would be overwhelming and it is best to focus change on one domain and then to help that change generalize to other domains. Factors to consider in choosing the entry point for a given transaction include the following: What seems most dysfunctional in the given interactional sequence—the behavior or the cognition? What seems most malleable? Are the spouses more receptive to dealing in the cognitive or behavioral domain? Will it be most beneficial to work within the domain that is most comfortable and familiar to the couple or to work within an alternate domain? How can the dysfunctional pattern by interrupted or changed most dramatically while still substituting a new pattern that is acceptable and desirable to the clients?

Cognitive Interventions

Sharper Focus

I cannot imagine a course of therapy that does not lead to some cognitive change, whether such is a direct or an indirect target. Within the initial session (and probably within the first 15 minutes) therapy requires the clients to take a closer and deeper look at their relationship. It is the therapist's supportive, yet questioning, stance that enables the spouses to get beyond the superficial layers of their impressions and dissatisfactions.

One process that I find helpful for bringing the relationship into sharper focus is described in detail by Wile (1981). According to Wile, a major component of couples' therapy is helping each spouse clarify his or her position. Clarifying positions does not mean talking about the problem in the repetitive, circular fashion that repeatedly goes on at home but rather helping each spouse develop a full and complete statement of his or her position without being interrupted or having that position disqualified. The therapist's task in accomplishing this is to make each spouse feel that his or her position is understood and appreciated. Probing questions and paraphrasing allow follow-up on each point until underlying impressions and feelings are expressed.

This particular intervention is based on the premise that what is spoken is generally far less threatening than what remains unspoken. The person who is opening up learns that fully expressing his or her position is not catastrophic, even if that viewpoint includes doubts about the relationship. For the other spouse, this might be a rare instance in which the opportunity for avoidance or rebuttal is blocked. In the process of really listening to the partner and listening to a deeper meaning of the partner's message, this spouse may come to better appreciate the other's experience in the relationship.

In one particularly difficult case, the couple was stalemated about whether or not to enter into a course of therapy which would improve the relationship. The husband was certain of his desire to improve the marriage but the wife did not know if she was prepared for that type of emotional investment. In fully exploring her feelings, the wife finally was able to articulate her questions about whether or not she loved her husband, which the husband had suspected was a problem for some time. However, the wife also was able to clarify that her lack of loving feelings was not because the husband was a horrible person but because her life with him was quite different from her expectations of marriage. The husband still was tremendously disappointed by his wife's statement but, contrary to the wife's fear, was not surprised and actually was somewhat relieved to learn the basis of his wife's disaffection.

Attributional and Efficacy Focus

As part of bringing the relationship in general into sharper focus, the issue often arises as to who is in control of and responsible for the relationship problems. Recent evidence supports what has long been suspected: Distressed spouses tend to attribute the partner's negative behaviors to dispositional, voluntary, and intentional factors, while attributing positive behaviors to involuntary, unintentional, or situational factors. This is the opposite pattern of satisfied spouses who give their partner credit for their positive behaviors by invoking dispositional, stable, global, intentional, and voluntary explanations while writing off the partner's negative behaviors as situationally based, involuntary, and unintentional (Baucom, Bell, & Duhe, 1982; Fincham & O'Leary, 1983; Holtzworth-Monroe & Jacobson, 1985; Jacobson, McDonald, Follette, & Berley, 1985).

One goal of therapy thus involves spouses shifting this attributional pattern in such a way that each gives his or her spouse credit for positive behaviors and does not assume the worst motives on the part of his or her spouse for negative behaviors. A number of factors figure into this shift. First, it is important for spouses to compare notes on what constitutes positive and negative behaviors. Often what the recipient perceives as a negative behavior is, in the actor's mind, intended as neutral or even positive. To accurately label that actor's behavior would be to call it unknowing or inconsiderate rather than purposely or intentionally negative. One wife, for example, was disparagingly recounting all the times in their 28 years together when the husband had failed to remember her birthday or their anniversary with even a card. The husband quietly took this all in and then started itemizing all the life insurance policies he had purchased so that she would be cared for after he was gone. He could not reconcile her criticisms of 'uncaring' and 'inconsiderate' in light of his careful planning for her future. Ignoring the thousands of dollars devoted to future planning, she simply wanted a one dollar token of his attention now. Pointing out the mismatch in these spouses' currencies of positive attention provided a less blaming way for them to discuss their disappointments.

Another step is dependent upon careful exploration into the meaning of each spouse's behavior. Often, when spouses fully understand the significance of a given response by the partner, out-of-proportion reactions become more predictable and seemingly malevolent responses become explainable, even if still undesirable. The husband who seems irrationally enraged when his wife overspends their budget by a few dollars may be viewed by the wife as a skinflint and as having purposely constructed a budget that is unworkable. His reaction becomes more understandable, however, if the wife listens to how badly he feels about his low salary and how miserable he is each hour that he spends on the job. To him, even an overexpenditure of a few dollars condemns him to more time on the job he detests.

In focusing on attributions, one also must consider who is to blame for the problems: oneself or one's partner. Blaming one's partner and ignoring one's own role in a problem is commonly observed in couples seeking treatment. To undo this pattern, it is helpful to introduce the concept of reciprocal cycles, in which there is no beginning or cause, but just a series of reactions and counterreactions. Any behavior that escalates or even does not stop a downward cycle between spouses is seen as contributing to the problem. Spouses need to be able to take a hard look at their own behavior in a nondefensive fashion to appreciate the impact of what they do. Letting spouses review their audiotapes and videotapes can offer the objective mirror that assists in this process. At times, I have found it very useful to review such videotapes separately with each partner so that they can study themselves carefully without being accountable to or fearing criticism from the partner. When observing themselves, spouses are asked to address the question "How well do you carry out your own goals during this discussion?" By identifying the places that they got sidetracked from their objectives, they begin to take responsibility for their role in the interactional process.

Couples therapy requires the therapist to play an active role in distributing blame for the relationship problems. As Broderick (1983) describes, spouses often "are skilled at making their own sins seem small, reactive, and misperceived, while their partners' are manifestations of incredible and well-nigh unforgivable insensitivity, selfishness, and even cruelty" (p. 26). The therapist's task is to help spouses shift their positions of victim versus villain roles to perceptions of how both have contributed to the cycle of miscommunication and distancing. In one couple, for example, the wife was ferocious in her attack whenever her husband said something that displeased her. At such moments, the husband seemed to shrink from her but also assumed a somewhat smug posture, as if to say, "Look how crazy she is!" My initial reaction was, in fact, that this woman's reaction, if indeed not crazy, was greatly out of proportion. By observing more cyclically, however, I came to appreciate how confusing the husband's message was. On the one hand, he said he wanted her to be completely open with her feelings. On the other hand, he gave nonverbal messages of being unable to cope with her emotional reactions and unwilling to reciprocate by expressing his feelings. Once her emotional spiral began, his lack of responsiveness contributed to her escalation.

As Broderick (1983) explains, even when one spouse has unjustly wronged the other (e.g., by violating the other's trust), and even when there can be no balance of responsibility, there may be a balance of pain. That is, even the violating partner, who has acted in a cruel and unthinking fashion, may be experiencing tremendous remorse for what has transpired. I have repeatedly found that no matter how upset and frustrated spouses are with one another, they rarely want to cause each other pain. Acknowledging the pain that each spouse experiences helps avoid the trap of being evaluative and contributes to each spouse feeling understood. It also helps spouses get beyond their own feelings and hear about one another's despair.

Finally, reattributions also can take into account factors external to the partner. In looking at the broader picture of spouses' lives, one sometimes finds that relationships have slowly eroded due to situations and problems that have taken priority over the relationship, and over which the spouse has little control. A couple who came to therapy after only 2 years of marriage had, for the past 15 months, been dealing with the imminent death of the husband's father. The father's illness drained the husband of his free time, energy, and spirit. The wife, who herself had lost her mother only 5 years previously, could rationally understand the pressures that her husband was experiencing. She had, however, entered this marriage hoping to diminish the feelings of the loss she still experienced. With this situation looming so large over the brief span of their relationship and with the relationship not offering enough nurturance to compensate for other losses, both partners were starting to question the viability of the marriage.

Deaths, the loss of one's job, and other life crises are dramatic examples that can push the relationship into the background. There are, in addition, other more 'normal' and even positive events that can have a similar, albeit lesser, impact. With the birth of children, or with demanding career advances, there is a tendency to "put the relationship on hold." Or, there may be developmental disjunctures between the two partners, such that one grows intellectually or emotionally in a way that separates him or her from the partner. With any of these situations, there is the potential for one or both spouses to lose sight of why they are not getting along and to blame it on the partner's bad intentions. Reattributing the blame to the external factors and helping spouses to label their dissatisfactions can help them feel that they are on the same, rather than opposite, sides of the struggle.

Although the goal of reattributional procedures, as described thus far, has been to alter attributions, (e.g., from partner to self, from negative to positive, from internal to external), sometimes the objective is strictly to halt runaway attributions. A stop-action assessment may reveal a process whereby a brief action or statement by one partner elicits a global negative attribution in the other (e.g., 'There she goes again with one of her rampages, if she keeps this up, I'll just . . ."). In essence, there are certain red flags that result in one person tuning out and going into a dead-end cognitive spiral about how miserable she or he is. It is important for the sender to be made aware of the behavior that elicits these spirals. It also is important for the receiver to interrupt this cognitive process. If the receiver can come to recognize the futility of a process that only contributes to his or her own discomfort, then that person can be taught how to interrupt the process. With this intervention, there is no attempt to replace the pathogenic attributes with benign attributes but simply to have the receiver use the negative attributes as a cue to refocus his or her attention on the interaction and to interrupt the process by giving feedback on his or her reaction and to allow for the possibility that the spouse had intended to send a different message from what was received.

Efficacy and Outcome Expectations

In coming to see how the relationship is a two-sided process and coming to recognize one's own contribution, the spouses may also gain a sense of greater control, depending upon both efficacy and outcome expectations. According to Bandura (1977), outcome expectancies reflect a person's estimate that a given behavior will lead to a certain outcome. Efficacy expectations reflect the conviction that she or he can successfully execute the behavior required to produce the outcome. As spouses become careful observers of the action–reaction units in their relationship, they generally are surprised how much impact their behavior has, even in a negative way. Often that sense of impact helps them formulate new possibilities for their interaction, (e.g., "If only I can remember to stay calm, then . . ."). Although they may not already have the outcome expectation, that is, they may not know what will happen if they do execute the new behavior, the important ingredient is the willingness to try to a new behavior. Thus, engendering positive outcome expectations (e.g., "I know that I can affect what occurs between us"), is important.

Positive Focus

Decreasing negative tracking is another important cognitive shift. This selective attention to negative events characterizes distressed spouses, and it is necessary to counteract it by increasing positive tracking. One way to foster this is to focus on positive events in the therapy session. The distressed couple typically comes to therapy primed to review in great detail all that has gone wrong during the previous week. That material, while certainly important to discuss, can be balanced by paying attention to what has gone well, which the couple may not even think to mention.

To elicit this material, I often use the Spouse Observation Checklist (Weiss & Perry, 1979) to contrast the most satisfying and the least satisfying day of the week. Spouses are asked to generate hypotheses about what might have contributed to one day being more satisfying than another and then, more generally, to consider what contributes to their relationship satisfaction on a day-to-day basis. This procedure helps spouses shift from an attacking mode to a suggestion mode and from global ideas for change to ideas that can be accomplished within the framework of their day-to-day lives.

One couple, for instance, was convinced that the only way that they could continue to coexist was to arrange their lives so that they rarely saw each other. These spouses could truly be described as ships passing in the night, with the wife returning from her day shift 1 hour after the husband left for his night shift. Although they sometimes bumped into each other in bed, days might pass without an opportunity for conversation. Having charted daily satisfaction and what was going on in their lives for about 6 weeks, this couple was confronted with data that contradicted their assumption about the importance of maintaining distance. On the few occasions when they both were off work, their charting unexpectedly indicated that their time spent together was quite satisfying. The records kept by these spouses not only helped them generate ideas about what made those days go better than anticipated, but also raised their hopes about what to anticipate in being together.

A positive focus can also be elicited by positive reframing procedures. The goal here is to take negative labels and look for the positive dimension within them. Within someone's dependency may be a component of loyalty and devotion. Behind someone's frustratingly quick temper, there generally is a great deal of caring rather than merely disinterest. The purpose of such reframing is not to minimize or trivialize each spouse's complaints. That would quickly become frustrating and discourage spouses from expressing what they experience in the relationship. Rather, the intent is to use language to reduce some of the immobilizing hopelessness of negative labels. The complainer may begin to see how the same characteristic, expressed in another fashion, would be less objectionable. The person's whose behavior is being criticized will be less likely to respond defensively.

Acceptance

Another very important cognitive change can take place in marital therapy by spouses gaining awareness and acceptance of their differences. The differences may occur at a relatively superficial level (e.g., "He likes this while I like that" or "His way of doing something is X while my way is Y"), or they may surround important underlying values and beliefs regarding life, love, and people in general. In either case, the differences can be agonizing. In one couple that I saw, the wife was mortified when her husband, who was somewhat overweight, went out in public in what she perceived as "sloppy clothes." From the husband's perspective, weekends were the only time when he did not have to dress in a shirt and tie and he wanted to enjoy that freedom. This issue conveyed all sorts of meanings including the wife not feeling important enough to warrant the husband attempting to look nice for *her*, her guilt feelings at being attracted to men who paid better care to their appearance, the husband's frustration with his weight problem, as well as his feeling unaccepted by his wife. Although compromise (i.e., the husband dressing to please the wife *some* of the time) was one way to address this problem, this did not resolve the underlying issues. It was important for the wife to examine her sense of responsibility for how the husband looked, her inability to control how he looked, and her lack of acceptance of him through the inevitable fat periods. On the husband's part, it was important for him to examine what he might be communicating through his clothes, to accept the fact that he could not change the wife's views about how people ought to appear in public, and to accept the consequences of his wife being less attracted to him if he dressed in his favored way. The spouses thus were helped to examine their own assumptions, motivations, and behavior, and to accept their differences on this topic. While there was no magical answer that would relieve the tension between them, it was helpful to explore this controversy in its entirety and then to examine its importance in the context of the relationship as a whole.

There are other topics on which value differences loom monumental. A particular painful example is the couple in which one partner wishes to have a child and the other is equally determined not to become a parent. One wife, frustrated by her husband's reluctance to become a parent, simply took charge, stopped using birth control and became pregnant. Having his right to contribute to this decision violated, he then was left with the choice of whether or not to stay in the marriage. Alternatively, another husband who wanted children but could not reconcile his wife to his way of thinking, was forced to choose between accepting a childless marriage or terminating the marriage.

As we can see from these examples, issues of acceptance may eventually lead to the question of whether the marriage will continue. Each spouse must confront the question "Do I want to remain with my partner even if that means accepting this difference and accepting the fact that I am not going to change my partner's position on this topic?" When talking about acceptance as an intervention strategy, the goal is not merely reaching a grudging truce, but rather an easing or "letting go" of the issue. If spouses actually come to understand and accept their differences, the pressure on each to continue fighting and convincing the other will cease. Hopefulness for agreement on the issue also will cease. Although the issue may always be a point of sensitivity, the acute pain and frustration will ease. Spouses can learn to respect and be sensitive to each other's feelings, and even to touch base with each other on how each is coping with the issue. The wife of the husband who wanted a baby may inquire into his feelings, for example, when they learn that close friends are expecting a child. Nonetheless, the acceptance itself is the outcome; there is no further attempt to solve the conflict or make it disappear. I imagine that most couples who have been together for some time have reached a number of such acceptances, either major or minor.

Reawakening

What I am calling "reawakening" for lack of a better term is a process whereby the therapist tunes in to the aspects of each spouse that represent what that individual believes or fantasizes she or he can be, or indeed has been. In other words, the therapist exhibits faith in each spouse's capability to be a creative, spontaneous, and romantic partner. The goal is for spouses to indulge in fantasies of themselves that reveal these characteristics, the next step being to display them. However, the reason for displaying them is not to please the partner but for oneself, to be the person that one really wants to be in a marriage. Most spouses are, in fact, somewhat disgusted and bored with themselves in the marriage, but are waiting for the right circumstances to allow themselves to exhibit the marvelous characteristics that they possess. The goal here is to dust off that lovable side and to try it out, even if one does so strictly to prove something to oneself.

Given the riskiness of this intervention, timing is essential. This is not to be tried when spouses are feeling angry and resentful. It has proven useful, however, when spouses are stagnating in an intellectual self-analysis of their relationship or are feeling lukewarm to each other but warily waiting for the other to make the next move. The cognitive goal is for spouses to remove the rational, careful glasses through which they normally see the world and that are normally quite functional, and to allow their more creative, feeling selves to shine through. The actual behavioral changes that they might exhibit are, of course, of their own choosing.

Behavioral Strategies

Cognitive strategies were presented before behavioral strategies because cognitive change is often necessary to set the stage for behavioral change. The majority of the behaviors that we ask spouses to engage in are not all that unfamiliar or complicated. The difficult part involves helping spouses to overcome their ambivalence about reinvesting and committing themselves to the relationship, getting them to entertain the idea that by doing something the relationship might improve, and encouraging them to try the very behaviors that they may have been avoiding. With some spouses, it simply takes the direct instruction from the therapist, as the expert, for them to engage in prescribed behaviors without losing face. With other spouses, the solutions must be self-generated to be acceptable. As a general rule, for spouses to engage in new behaviors requires them to challenge currently held assumptions regarding their behavior in the relationship.

The behavioral strategies described below all involve building up new behavioral patterns of interaction. Some focus on molecular interactions while others focus on molar interactions. The goal in both cases is to substitute new patterns for old by changing something in each partner's actions. As can be discerned from this description, the goal is not simply that of resolving sources of conflict or eliminating sources of annoyance. These outcomes are important but not as important as changing the couple's process of interaction so that they themselves can cope with the downward spirals that they are bound to encounter in the future.

Changing Molecular Patterns

Communication training approaches (e.g., Birchler, 1979; Guerney, 1977; Rappaport, 1976) and problem-solving approaches (e.g., Jacobson, 1977a, 1977b; Jacobson & Margolin, 1979) are directed toward improving the moment-to-moment interaction patterns between spouses. Communication training refers to accurate and empathetic listening skills, the expression and reception of feelings, and conflict resolution. Problem-solving training, which sometimes is subsumed under the general category of communication training, teaches couples how to communicate in order to facilitate the resolution of conflict. When I began doing marital therapy in the early 1970s, I did communication training and problem solving with all of my clients—in fact, this comprised a good portion of our work together. I would estimate that now I do some type of communication training with about 80% and problem-solving training with about 50% of the couples that I see.

My decision to do communication training stems from an assessment that a couple's manner of talking to one another, particularly about conflictual or emotion-laden issues, confuses rather than clarifies issues and creates negative feelings between them. The direction that I take in the communication training varies depending upon whether the couple's general style is one of withdrawal from discussions or one of escalating patterns of verbal aggression. The other distinction that I draw is between communications in general versus communications around conflictual topics. Sometimes spouses need assistance in sharing any information, even information as commonplace as how their days went. Other times, the problems are specific to issues over which they disagree.

For couples whose communication is riddled with rapid, angry cross-fire, the most important order of business is interrupting these exchanges in order to slow down the communications so that messages are thoughtfully sent and accurately received. If spouses can learn to recognize angry reactions in themselves early enough, they can then use those reactions as discriminative stimuli to interrupt rather than to reciprocate the negative behavior. Spouses are first taught to be more sensitive to their own ways of registering anger, whether it is through a physiological reaction (e.g., rush of blood, clenched jaw), or through a specific cognitive reaction (e.g., "I've heard this all before . . ."). Then spouses are taught to monitor these reactions in themselves, and to a lesser degree in one another, and to use them as cues to disrupt the discussion.

Initially the disruption may be something as simple as having the spouse who is getting angry motion T for "Time out." At this point, I can intervene and inquire into what that spouse is experiencing, and what triggered that reaction. I am interested in whether the listener has, in fact, accurately perceived the message. To figure this out requires that the listener paraphrase what she or he has heard and the speaker indicate whether the paraphrase is accurate. If it is inaccurate, the speaker is to restate and rephrase the intended message, making it as clear as possible. This process goes back and forth until the message can be stated and perceived without eliciting a "red flag" reaction. Over time, I play a less active role in intervening and checking out both sides of the message and the spouses do this on their own. Spouses must find a way to interrupt the process that is comfortable for them. It is important to convince them that they have permission to stop the discussion and to demonstrate that stopping it can be a constructive action rather than another cause for reproach.

The overriding goal is not to squelch angry exchanges but to make sure that spouses are accurately sending and receiving messages. Some of those messages will genuinely evoke anger. Some messages will evoke other emotions, such as hurt. Careful discrimination between emotions is important for both the sender and the recipient.

Accurate sending and receiving of messages is also the goal for withdrawn partners and, in some ways, the process for attaining this goal is quite similar. What differentiates these two patterns is that there is not a need for disrupting the interaction. Instead, the withdrawing partner needs to be encouraged to express his or her position. Sometimes the reluctance is due to feeling inadequate in verbal expression, particularly if the other partner is more articulate. Other times the reluctance is due to feeling that verbal expression is unnecessary, or that the partner should know what she or he is feeling, and why she or he is feeling that way. It must be demonstrated to the withdrawn partner that his or her opinion really is important and that no one will know what that position is unless it is explicitly stated. Initially, I find that I need to be quite active with withdrawn partners in paraphrasing and drawing them out. Finding a topic that is truly of interest to the withdrawn spouse, be it his or her work, family, friends, or hobbies, may be the key to increasing that person's sharing of his or her opinions.

Once communication is started, the steps for training withdrawn couples in communication skills are quite similar to those for training overtly angry couples. As speakers, the spouses need to practice emitting clear content messages and identifying the accompanying affect. As listeners, the spouses need to practice basic listening skills to communicate interest, to indicate when a message is unclear, and to bring a drifting topic back into focus.

When an attacking spouse is paired with a withdrawing spouse, it is readily apparent how this pattern feeds on itself. The attack leads to more withdrawal, which leads to more attack and so on. Here, spouses need to become aware of how their behavior contributes to the reaction they find so offensive in the other. Each spouse needs to become a careful observer of this pattern and to identify it quickly. The therapist can help to undermine the pattern by attempting to balance the spouses' talk time in the session and by not allowing one spouse to speak for the other.

As noted previously, the other decision is whether to focus on problem-oriented or non-problem-oriented discussions. For spouses who are experiencing distance from each other, it is important to begin by establishing a base for contact. With these couples, it is useful to practice the expressive and listening skills around every day topics, (e.g., sharing the most important thing that happened that day). Sometimes sharing a meaningful event such as an emotion-evoking movie, helps provoke discussion. For these couples, the structuring of such discussions proves to be an important component; the actual scheduling of such discussions (e.g., a brief cocktail hour before dinner or after the kids are in bed), overcomes the inertia that has stymied such couples.

There are a number of additional skills to add when helping a couple deal with conflictual topics. The guidelines that I follow are the ones outlined by Jacobson and Margolin (1979), which involve several distinct phases. An issue that is currently unresolved and that creates ongoing tension is chosen as the topic. Spouses then work to develop a problem statement that identifies what the problem is in a nonblaming, specific fashion. A problem such as "Betty thinks that Bill is rude to her mother" might be restated as "Betty feels uncomfortable about the way Bill and her mother talk to each other." The objectives in developing a problem statement involve using specific behaviors rather than derogatory labels or overgeneralizations to describe what is bothersome, making connections between those specific behaviors and the feelings that arise in response to them, and being brief by maintaining a current or future focus.

After developing a problem statement that both spouses are willing to work on, they then enter a brainstorming phase in which each spouse offers as many solutions as possible, either serious or humorous, and without any evaluation of each suggestion. For example, possible brain-storming solutions to Betty's and Bill's problem might include: Betty visits her mother without Bill or, vice versa, Bill visits his mother-in-law without Betty; Betty asks her mother whether or not she is upset by Bill; Bill makes special efforts to say something nice to his mother-in-law; Betty signals Bill when she is feeling uncomfortable due to something he has said; Bill and Betty's mother enter therapy together. I usually strive for 15–20 brainstorm ideas. From this list of solutions, spouses indicate which solutions they would be willing to consider further, thereby eliminating all suggestions that are totally unacceptable to either spouse. Even the most argumentative couples find some degree of overlap in the suggestions that remain on the list. From here, they rank their preferences and discuss their reasons for their preferred orders.

The final stage is agreeing upon some course of action that both are willing to endorse for at least one week. When making these final deci-sions, spouses need to do the following: consider solutions that involve change by both partners; accept, as a beginning, a change less than the ideal solution; discuss the advantages and disadvantages of each sugges-tion before reaching agreement; and prepare a final change agreement that is spelled out in clear, descriptive, behavioral terms, that is recorded in writing, and that includes cues reminding each partner of changes she or he has agreed to make.

Generally I give spouses a copy of the problem-solving manual (Jacob-son & Margolin, 1979) prior to our attempting this process. Since this manual contains many "do" and "don't" examples for each guideline, spouses readily identify shortcomings in their current problem-solving strategies. One of my goals in introducing this problem-solving process is to clearly distinguish it from previous unsuccessful attempts to discuss conflict topics. Toward this end, we establish certain conditions surround-ing the problem-solving process. Rather than slide into problem solving, we specifically delineate problem solving as an agenda for the therapy session or for a discussion at home. We also clearly identify the topic of the problem-solving session, and then also specify what topics we should watch out for as potentially sidetracking issues. One spouse is designated to take notes from the discussion. The agreed-upon problem definition is put in writing, as well as each of the brainstorm suggestions. Putting the final change agreement in writing emphasizes the importance of the negotiated agreement. It also circumvents any memory problems as to the specifics of the agreement while serving as a concrete reminder to carry out the agreement. Finally, a meeting between the spouses is scheduled approximately one week later, at which time the couple will review how the contract has gone and decide whether to continue the contract as it currently stands or to change it. Thus, all agreements are entered into on a trial basis.

I find there to be three major benefits to teaching couples problem-solving procedures. First, it offers them a structure that serves as an alternative to what they have been doing when confronted with a disagreement or major problem. Second, the brainstorming component unleashes spouses' creativity such that they can generate points of convergence in their positions rather than being stuck in extreme, nonoverlapping stances. Third, spouses discover that problems can, in fact, sometimes be resolved. This relieves some of the overriding tension currently in the relationship and also makes problems that arise in the future less threatening.

There are, however, two common pitfalls in problem solving against which to guard. Unless carefully monitored, problem solving can be used to generate premature conciliations, which are not satisfactory to one or both partners but are agreed upon just to establish closure. Generally this occurs when a spouse is "fight-phobic" and will agree to anything to end the discussion, or when a spouse does not feel entitled to his or her position and will overtly agree but covertly sabotage. When contracts are not carried out which, in my experience, is quite rare, it is good to check into these possibilities.

Second, it is important that problem solving not become the *modus operandi* for all conflictual discussions such that there is no place for simply venting feelings. Before entering a problem-solving discussion, spouses need to check out whether a *change* agreement really is the desired outcome. Sometimes one spouse may not be ready for the structured rational approach of problem solving and may want a format simply for expressing what she or he is experiencing. If the other spouse pursues problem solving, even with the best of intentions, this discussion is bound to fail and even result in increased tensions.

Changing Molar Patterns

I have described regarding molecular patterns how, although I provide the couple with a new problem-solving process, they generate solutions to their problems. In working on larger patterns, however, I find that I assume a lot more responsibility for formulating the actual solutions. The overall change pattern usually involves a cognitive shift that sets the stage for a behavioral intervention. Hopefully, the behavioral change leads to another cognitive–affective change reflecting an improvement in feelings and impressions of the partner.

The "stage setting" cognitive interventions are of two types. The first is a refocusing or relabelling of the problem so that it is no longer an accusation of one partner but instead reflects the underlying feelings of that partner. Thus, one person's jealousy may be relabelled as fear of rejection. Another spouse's nagging may be a sign of being overwhelmed or feeling unappreciated. The problem is made into a dyadic process by examining the second spouse's internal feelings (e.g., frustration and helplessness at being unable to gain the other's trust, hopelessness that whatever she or he does is inadequate).

The second stage, which is necessary when the intervention is particularly anxiety arousing, involves asking the couple to engage in a therapy procedure that requires their unquestionable willingness. In this procedure, which is described by Tiesmann (1979), I indicate that I have an intervention that is likely to have powerful effects but that is going to be challenging and demanding. The procedure is likely to conflict with some of their assumptions about themselves and one another. While describing the intervention as difficult, I indicate that it is accomplishable if they truly want to succeed. I then ask the couple to weigh the risks of a demanding and experimental therapy against learning to live with their situation as it is. They are told to think about this decision and then to return with their response the following week.

Why is such a build-up necessary? First, asking spouses to change a major pattern that has been the source of considerable emotional upheaval requires taking a risk on their parts. I want them to know that I understand and appreciate the riskiness. Often I actually exaggerate the riskiness to pique their interest and arouse some anxiety so that when I actually describe the intervention they relax a bit and think, "Well, it's not that bad; I can do this." Second, I realize that the actions I am about to prescribe may be the very behaviors that they have been avoiding. To an outsider the actions may not seem particularly difficult and may, in fact, seem rather normal and pleasureable, (e.g., going out on a date together). For certain couples, however, that event may reflect a momentous change. Thirdly, I am going to present a whole package for change and want to avoid nitpicking over details. By building up the commitment phase of the intervention, I circumvent many of the overt and covert problems of compliance with all or part of the intervention. Spouses are instructed to take an entire week to make their decision, which then is taken very seriously by them and by me.

The behavioral part of the intervention is directed to introducing new patterns of interaction that undermine the negative interaction cycles that currently are functioning. The interventions are not as much of a "block-ing" variety, as seen in the molecular interventions, but more of an attempt to anticipate and circumvent the escalation of negative patterns by introducing an alternative course of action.

For some couples, for example, disappointments experienced within the first few minutes of rejoining at the end of the day can set off a whole evening of uninvolvement and resentment. One way to change this pattern of disappointment and alienation is to change the interactional sequence that occurs as soon as the spouses greet each other. It is important to know exactly what each really would like to happen as soon as they reunite after their separate days. From this, it becomes obvious whether the desired patterns simply have not been made explicit or whether they are in conflict, (e.g., husband wants a period of quiet and solitude while wife wants some attention and interest). The goal is to structure the couple's reuniting so that each spouse actually gets his or her needs met. Normalizing each spouse's preferences and letting each spouse state his or her position in its entirety sometimes reveals that the differences are not as extreme as anticipated. That is, the husband is perfectly willing to sit down and talk if he can have one hour to himself. Knowing that the time for closeness will come, the wife may be content to allow the husband his time alone. Or, the wife simply may need for the husband to look up from his newspaper and greet her rather than ignore her when she walks in the door.

In examining and changing these patterns, expectations must be translated into concrete steps and very often those concrete steps must be role played. As with any new behavior, the therapist must be certain that the spouses have the skills for carrying out the new sequence, that is, that they know what an interested and concerned greeting entails, and also are committed to try this new pattern. I have found it useful to predict how forced and awkward the new interaction may feel at the time that I ask for an unequivocal commitment to try the new sequence during the upcoming week.

Appreciation is another problem that I often work on through changing daily interaction sequences. Here my goal is to change reaction/feedback loops, first by having spouses become better observers of one another's behavior and then by giving feedback to each other. When spouses complain of feeling unappreciated, the problem may stem from the partner not noticing the other's behavior or noticing but not commenting upon the behavior, or from the comments not being received. To change this, I make all of these steps more overt through a procedure that I call "appreciation notes." Both spouses are instructed to start to pay close attention to each other's actions so that they can identify one thing each day that they have appreciated. They then are to communicate this appreciation to one another through a brief written note. Sometimes the assignment is carried out with a serious, practical flavor, (e.g., a note left next to the spouse's toothbrush reading "Dear Sam: Thank you for sitting down with Jimmy and helping him with his homework") while other times it takes a more creative approach, (e.g., one woman wrote her note on her thigh and showed it to her husband while they were dining out).

In general, this assignment serves an informational and affective function. The spouses become attuned to what they do like in one another as well as what the other appreciates in their own actions. It also eases tensions by refocusing attention on something that is going well in the relationship. Having the communication in writing involves a bit more work for the spouses but, for some, is easier than addressing the spouse directly. The other advantage of the written record is that there is concrete evidence whether or not the communication has occurred and whether or not it was a whole-hearted appreciation or a disguised complaint.

Other patterns can be introduced by establishing new daily, weekly, or monthly rituals. As described earlier, mutual withdrawal is one common pattern found in spouses who are disappointed with each other or who have too many competing priorities in their lives. Such couples have given up the very activities through which they initially established their relationship, that is, time spent by the two of them in mutually enjoyable activities. For such couples, introducing a weekly 'date' into their lives can be a major change. I have found this to be particularly true of couples with young children who, by not planning ahead for babysitting, find that they never go out. One couple, who had 6- and 4-year-old boys and had not gone out alone as a couple for 6 years, began to reserve Saturday nights just for each other. They took turns planning the dates and renewed a sense of intimacy in their relationship that had been lost for too long.

While it seems somewhat strange to spend a whole hour in therapy helping a couple plan a date, this intervention can have a powerful impact. With some couples, it takes considerable energy and input on the part of the therapist to get this date off the ground. In addition to helping the couple overcome their inertia, the therapist has to help them think through what types of dates are likely to free them from usual negative interaction cycles. Sometimes spouses get beyond their typical patterns if they do something that is really out of character, (e.g., an intellectual couple goes bowling, an activity which they never have done together and for which they have no emotional investment at being "the best"). Sometimes it also works to resurrect an old activity that they used to enjoy very much but have not done for a long time, such as going dancing or watching a favorite old movie. It is also recommended that the therapist help the couple identify all obstacles that may interfere with the date, and ways to circumvent those obstacles. When successful, this intervention demonstrates to the couple that, despite their serious problems, they can still enjoy each other's company.

The goal of circumventing problems before they escalate also can be addressed by building in a format for regular discussion of topics that the couple would typically avoid. One couple, presented in detail in Margolin (1985), sought therapy for a crisis surrounding the husband's affairs. In fact, there had been a series of such crises over the past 12 years. The crises erupted when, after weeks of suspicion, the wife would finally confront her husband about whether he was involved with another woman. The husband, in an effort to protect his wife, would adamantly deny the affair. Eventually, however, she would wear him down and he would admit to having an affair. This, then, would result in a big blow-up, followed by the husband temporarily ending the affair and, for a period of time, the marriage going more smoothly.

The problem was reframed as one of trust. The husband complained bitterly that he never felt trusted even though most of the time he was being faithful. The wife, of course, felt untrusting, having been correct several times in her suspicions, despite his repeated promises not to have affairs. The solution for this couple was for them to discuss trust on a regular basis. The husband was asked to suspend his assumption that protection, through lying, was a good strategy—obviously it was not working. The wife was asked to stop her attempts to hold back her suspicions and, instead, to try confronting the husband immediately. These changes simply restructured the old cycle by bringing the crises out into the open quickly rather than allowing suspicions and denials to fester.

To put these changes into action, the couple was instructed to have weekly "trust meetings," in which each one told the other whether they felt trust and, in return, whether they were to be trusted. Thus, most every week, this couple engaged in an affirmation of trust. The few times when suspicions did arise, they were dealt with immediately, thereby circumventing the painful sequence of accusations, denials, and lack of trust. Eventually, as trust became less of an issue, this couple expanded their meetings to discuss other important issues and to maintain a consistent time for contact in the midst of their busy week.

For patterns surrounding trust, I have often found it useful to disrupt the couples' typical pattern by actually exaggerating some aspect of that pattern. In two other cases, one involving a wife who was a cocktail waitress and another wife who was a realtor, the husbands were suspicious and jealous. For the husband of the realtor, suspicions were fueled by bits of paper with phone numbers that he would find lying around the house. His demands to know whose numbers these were irritated the wife. The strategy here was to get the husband more, as opposed to less, involved in the wife's phoning by having him actually organize the phone messages for her. This idea intrigued her since it would be of assistance in her work and pleased the husband since he would have all of his answers. Predictably, he grew tired of this activity within two weeks and also stopped bothering her with questions about the phone numbers.

Similarly, the husband of the cocktail waitress was worried about how much contact his wife had with men on her job, and whether she could handle their advances. He would grill her when she was late and never quite be satisfied with her answers. Here, too, the strategy was to shower the husband with information. The wife agreed to keep notes about how men made advances and how she responded and then to "show off" her clever responses to her husband the following day. She also agreed to hide little notes to him around the house, so that he could search for them and experience some sense of involvement, even in her absence. The husband found he really was not all that interested in hearing the details of how men made advances but did really enjoy the notes.

Other escalation patterns, in addition to those surrounding trust, can be circumvented by regularly scheduled touch points. One of the most common solutions devised by couples in response to quarrels over finances is to divide up the resources and responsibilities. That is, they often decide to keep separate accounts for their money and to be in charge of separate financial responsibilities to obviate having to discuss finances and thereby avoid arguments. Although this may work in the short-run, problems generally arise over time. Moreover, with this arrangement there is no structure for dealing with the problems. My strategy with these sorts of problems is first to introduce some doubt about the assumption that arguments will be avoided by avoiding discussions altogether. I then help the couple to develop a structure for discussion at frequent enough intervals that they can anticipate and discuss a potential problem. Thus, weekly meetings to discuss what has been spent, what are upcoming expenses, what are some luxury expenses that each would like, and so on, can short-circuit the frustrations that develop when the situation goes undiscussed for long periods of time.

In general, changing a long-standing, repeating pattern requires fully understanding the interlinking parts of that pattern, that is, how an action by one leads to an action by the other and what each spouse was thinking and feeling about each action. In putting the pieces together for the couple, I try to point out instances in which they may have been motivated by good intentions, but show how the overall outcome is detrimental. I then challenge them to try something new. Very often what they are trying is not all that new but the situation or timing has been changed. In the example regarding the husband's affairs and trust, for instance, I built an acceptable and regularly occurring structure wherein the confrontations regarding trust could occur. Very often, I find myself structuring an opportunity for the spouses to engage in the actions that they fear, but are nonetheless doing in a subtle and ineffectual manner.

Nonbehavioral and Noncognitive Strategies

As the above interventions illustrate, the systems approach is the theoretical school from which I borrow most heavily from to carry out what are basically cognitive and behavioral interventions. The use of reframing, and paradoxical instructions that prescribe the problematic behavior but within a different context are basic tools of systems and more specifically strategic therapists (e.g., Watzlawick *et al.*, 1974). Couples' well-meaning but inept solutions to their problems, which maintain rather than solve the problem, are another important target of this approach. The compatible fit between behavioral and strategic interventions also has been noted by others (e.g., Birchler & Spinks, 1980; Coyne & Biglan, 1984; Weiss, 1980).

To lesser degrees, Gestalt and humanistic therapies play some role in the therapy that I do. The notion of awareness, which is central to Gestalt therapy, is something that I tend to pursue in helping spouses to tune into their personal experience as they interact. In the role playing that involves the two spouses that I have described, I sometimes alter this procedure and have one spouse play both roles. In either format, my objective is to help spouses gain a full understanding, for themselves and for one another, of what is being sensed, felt and thought. Attention to spouses' nonverbal behavior and discrepancies between verbal and nonverbal behavior certainly are essential in this process. From the humanistic school, I have borrowed the concepts of personal responsibility and choice. Most typically, I find myself using these concepts when there is a lot of blaming and when spouses are trapped in indecision about whether or not to continue the marriage. Despite all the complexities that bind two spouses together, spouses always have a choice about whether or not to continue in an unhappy marriage. Spouses also choose to be the person they are in the marriage. If they do not like who they are in that marriage, they have a choice about whether or not to change.

Finally, from a variety of schools, but particularly from object relations theory, comes the idea that satisfactions and dissatisfactions in the marriage are a function of the expectations that spouses bring to the relationship. A spouse's reactions to the marriage are determined not only by how the partner behaves toward him or her, but how the behavior is perceived and integrated. In some cases the distorted perceptions are related to what the spouse has experienced in other relationships, particularly in his or her family of origin. While I do not assume that to be the explanation in all instances, I do find that information about family history is important. When a spouse is overgeneralizing from his or her experience with a historical family figure and making inaccurate assumptions about the partner, I find Segraves's (1982) discrimination training to be useful. That is, I point out the discrepancies between how one spouse describes the other's behavior versus the actual behavior of the second spouse, and may go on to examine how the misperceptions have been carried over from a previous relationship. The explanation for the misperception can make it easier to give up that perception and to move on to more constructive perceptions and behavior patterns.

ROLE OF THE THERAPIST

I find that the following four therapist characteristics play a key role in carrying out the therapy just described: expertness, teaching capacity, an ability to engage the couple, and basic caring. Each of these four dimensions must be sensitively regulated in order to comply with the needs of the clients at any particular moment. The effectiveness of even the most well conceived interventions can be undermined by a delivery that conveys too much or too little of these characteristics.

Expertness

For spouses to take risks in therapy, they need to believe that I know what I am doing and that I have their best interests in mind. I prefer that couples do not enter therapy having immediate confidence in me, but rather that their confidence builds as they see that I am not going to be overwhelmed by the extent of their problems or the enormity of their feelings, and they discover that our actions in therapy are to their benefit.

Expertness, in my view, involves assuming responsibility for the overall structure and flow of therapy. I set up and implement agendas so that the goals of therapy are met. This means keeping track of an overriding structure that goes across sessions as well as the agenda and structure within each session. Equally important, however, is being flexible and knowing when to dispense with agendas. Sometimes I remind the couple what our agenda is for the session and then get their opinions as to whether another issue is more important and we should put aside the scheduled agenda. Thus, I lay the goundwork for the direction of therapy and then consult with the couple and elicit their feedback.

This role also includes recognizing when therapy is stagnating, initiating discussion about why that may be the case, and taking some responsibility for that process. When things are not going well, I tend to share my concerns and frustrations, as well as admitting when I think that I have been heading in a futile direction. For example, following a nonproductive session, I usually begin the next session by commenting on my reactions to what occurred the previous week, saying, "I've been giving last week's session a lot of thought. I think we really got bogged down when we focused all our attention on that argument that you had on the way over here and lost sight of what happened during the rest of the week." The spouses generally have had strong reactions themselves to nonproductive sessions and are happy for an opportunity to share them.

Expertness does not mean having all the answers, despite the fact that there are some couples who would like that. Even those couples, however, generally understand that there is no one answer with respect to questions of intimacy. Moreover, no matter how much I might actually have answers or ideas, it is the spouses who must put those answers into action. The hard work of therapy definitely falls on the clients' shoulders.

Although I am the expert on marital therapy, the couple is the expert on their own relationship. I need for them to teach me about the way that they think and feel in the marriage. My job is to take what they say, use my perspective to integrate the information, and then give the information back to them within a somewhat different context. In other words, what I know about the relationship is basically what they tell me and show me. However, by turning the information around a bit, I offer them a new perspective, hopefully enabling them to take the steps to improve the marriage.

Teaching

As emphasized already, much of what goes on in marital therapy involves teaching the couple new styles of interaction. Thus, to be a good marital therapist requires being a good teacher. As Jacobson (1983b) suggests, one aspect of being a good teacher is knowing at what level to pitch the information. It is easy to err by overestimating the capacity of clients to enact certain skills and process certain information. Even bright, competent individuals who are socially skilled with persons other than their partner may not be ready to carry out the same interpersonal skills with the partner. Despite the fact that the desired behaviors are indeed being exhibited under certain situations, the skills still need to be carefully practiced with the spouse. I have seen many beginning therapists be apologetic for requiring the clients to practice such "easy" skills as paraphrasing, thereby setting up the clients for embarrassment when they have difficulty with this. It also is possible to err on the other side, however, by trying to teach something that the spouse already knows but failing to attend to why the spouse is not performing the behavior. A similar risk is that of being overly simplistic in an attempt to be specific and clear. When presenting a new approach, I generally ask spouses whether or not they have already tried something similar. I then focus on the differences between what they have already tried and what I am suggesting.

A major component of being a good teacher is creating an atmosphere conducive to trying out new behaviors, both in the session and at home. This requires, for example, making the session a safe place, in which clumsy and awkward attempts at new behaviors will not be punished by the partner. Fostering this atmosphere may involve setting up a few key rules, such as "no name-calling in the session." Then both the therapist and clients are responsible for maintaining this rule by interrupting the process whenever it has been violated. Another component toward the desired atmosphere is making it clear that, when feeling uncomfortable, anyone can stop the action of the session to examine what is going on. Still another consideration is how to give feedback while guarding against being judgmental. To draw attention to the fact that the husband's rebuttal led to the wife's blame that resulted in both feeling frustrated links an interaction pattern to an outcome. That type of feedback is more constructive than simply saying that their interaction is not working.

Jacobson (1977a, 1977b, 1981; Jacobson, Berley, Newport, Elwood, & Phelps, 1985) has offered some of the most useful and specific information about applying principles of learning to the business of helping couples. Focusing on communication training, he divides the procedure into three components: instructions, feedback, and behavioral rehearsal. Instructions refer to the way that information is imparted about what is necessary for effective communication. To help couples understand the general principles underlying a new skill as well as clearly envision how that new skill will be enacted, I generally supplement verbal instructions with written materials, such as the aforementioned problem-solving manual by Jacobson and Margolin (1979). I may illustrate the new skill through role-play demonstrations, in which I take the place of one of the spouses. In addition, occasionally couples have asked to take home audiotapes of our sessions so that they can listen to the material more than one time, which is a suggestion that I have supported.

Once the skills are presented, the spouses repeatedly practice the new behaviors until achieving competency. As with most behavioral rehearsal, the couple works up to skills of greater complexity and problems of greater proportion, after first achieving competency in simpler tasks. Thus, in working on listening skills, I may first have the spouses practice the reflection of feelings with me and then with each other, on nonproblematic topics, and then on problematic topics. Through this process, I work to refine the spouses' behaviors by giving frequent and detailed feedback describing ways that their behaviors approached and did not approach the desired response.

I also have them practice at home whatever we have been working on in the session. Thus, if we are working on listening skills, the homework assignment might be for them to sit down with a tape recorder twice during the upcoming week. During that time, they are to take turns in the listener and speaker roles. The speaker is to be prepared to speak briefly about a topic of interest to him or her while the listener is to practice reflecting and paraphrasing skills. During problem-solving training, we might begin to define a problem in the session and then I will ask the couple to further refine the definition or to do brainstorming on their own.

Getting the Couple's Attention

None of what I do matters if I cannot captivate the couple and draw them into the therapeutic process. If I am worried about spouses I let them know that, which usually strikes a responsive chord since they are worried about themselves. For spouses who are too cavalier about their problems to get down to the work of therapy, I usually confess to being more worried than they are, which also gets a response. Yet, for couples who are bogged down in their hopelessness, I generally share my perceptions of greater optimism, which are a relief for the couple to hear. Similarly, when someone becomes overly self-critical, I point out that she or he is being too hard on himself or herself.

When couples come in for marital therapy, just as with any other type of therapy, they are ambivalent about actually wanting help. While they may want the problems to disappear magically, they may not want to go through the effort required for them to make the relationship better. Engaging them in this process usually is a function of making the sessions emotionally involving and rewarding. I find therapy works best when it elicits a combination of positive and negative emotions. Strictly negative emotions become too painful for most clients to tolerate. Strictly positive emotions generally mean that therapy is not necessary or is focused on superficial tasks.

Once we are seriously involved in therapy, there still is a need to get the attention of clients. Sometimes this means livening the sessions up, particularly if we are into the rather serious and sometimes tedious business of communication training. Other times this means helping spouses experience some deep and long-time denied emotion.

Certainly humor and playfulness have an important role in marital therapy. Certain agendas, such as planning a date, lend themselves to a light-hearted atmosphere. When debriefing a good week, it is nice also to join the couple in an optimistic spirit. When spouses come for a therapy session in a playful mood, it would be a missed opportunity not to capitalize on that. On occasion, I also have found humor to effectively disrupt an extremely tense and nonproductive interaction, but only if the spouses show the capacity to laugh at themselves.

Getting attention also applies to disrupting the repetitive, nonproductive patterns that the spouses experience *ad nauseum* at home. In many instances, simply commenting on the process will suffice. However, for the die-hard couple who slips right back into the argument I rely on nonverbal actions. Standing up, walking between the two spouses, suggesting a 3-minute break, and actually leaving the room are all ways to get the attention of spouses and show them that I think therapy can offer more than a context for fighting.

Self-disclosure is another powerful vehicle for getting the couple's attention. In my view, self-disclosure does not just serve a rapport-building function but also serves to normalize certain problems. Couples who maintain a high degree of privacy about their married lives find themselves extremely isolated in their problems and have no idea how typical their situation may be of others. I, too, tend to be quite private and thus, use self-disclosure sparingly. However, I have found that couples are tremendously relieved to learn that I have experienced something similar, and I try to keep this in mind when the opportunity presents itself. My having experienced similar situations and feelings rather than my particular solution to the problem is the dimension that I stress.

Self-disclosure also includes sharing feelings I experience during the session. I have come to rely increasingly on my own affective reactions in the session and to use them to determine what is happening. If I am feeling frustrated, that is usually a good indicator that the session has reached an unproductive impasse and it is time for a process intervention. I have learned that if I label my feelings rather than make an intellectual comment, my message gets across more powerfully.

Generally I have found therapy to be a self-regulating process with respect to the dimension of getting attention. A number of sessions may pass in which we are consistently engaged in some aspect of therapy, such as problem solving. At one point where this bogs down, there usually is a crisis which initially may distract us from our overall objectives but, in the long run, may help us to rethink those objectives and restore our energy for the next stage.

Caring

I believe that for marital therapy to be effective, the couple must know that, first of all, I care about them as individuals, and, secondly, I care about their marriage. It is no great news that this is a bit more complicated in marital therapy than in individual therapy, since I have to balance my caring. I have done this by getting to know both spouses as individuals and trying to put myself in each of their positions. I usually tell the couple that, in order to work on couple issues, I will be trying hard to see the situation from each of their perspectives. At the same time, I invite them to tell me if they feel that I have become partial to one or the other. An overall balancing in my alliance and caring does not mean that balance can be obtained at every moment or within every session. When there is a reason for me to be temporarily imbalanced, I warn the couple of this so that it is overt and, hopefully, not the cause of resentment.

One of the ways that I show caring is to question the appropriateness of therapy at certain times. If, for example, I know that one of the spouses has a lot going on in his or her life in addition to the marital problems, I may express concern for that person becoming overloaded by taking on the demands of therapy as well. Or if one spouse is obviously committed and the other is considerably less committed, my concern for the committed one takes the form of advising against any course of action that may increase his or her commitment and thereby intensify his or her disappointment. On the other hand, for couples who are hesitant about therapy and who have a lot to lose by not entering therapy, I will attempt to be quite persuasive in my recommendations for trying out therapy.

In general, being caring means being supportive and gentle and being tuned into spouses' emotional turmoil during this trying period. When something occurs in therapy that elicits a strong affective reaction, it is important for me to focus attention on it. To not do this would be two opportunities lost—one for furthering the relationship between me and that spouse and one for modeling the emotionally nurturant activities that hopefully will be taken over by the other spouse.

COMMON CLINICAL ISSUES

Resistance and Noncompliance

Resistance and noncompliance are to be expected in marital therapy just as they are in most individual therapies. The difference, however, is that in marital therapy the couple can collude in their resistance such that the system remains resistant but the roles of the spouses keep reversing. Almost always, at the beginning of therapy, one spouse is more enthusiastic than the other about entering into therapy. Usually during the evaluation phase I attempt to balance that enthusiasm by building interest and commitment in the hesitant spouse, that is, showing that person how therapy might promote his or her interests, which might also have the effect of tempering the enthusiasm of the other partner. I also attempt to normalize feelings of uncertainty and caution by encouraging spouses to give considerable thought to whether or not they want to enter therapy at this time.

I view as more serious resistance when, just as the reluctant spouse becomes more involved, the enthusiastic spouse draws back, precipitates a crisis, or somehow keeps us from moving forward, and when this role reverse occurs more than once. This process of shifting enthusiasm usually characterizes a larger relationship pattern of wavering relationship commitment. That is, as one spouse decides to put his or her all into the relationship, the other suddenly has a lot of questions. A system such as this tends to be quite stable but also quite stuck.

One interpretation of couples with shifting levels of commitment is that the pattern is necessary to maintain what for them is a maximal level of intimacy. While distance certainly is the outcome of such a pattern, I believe that there is a more benign interpretation. I think that, in general, these people already are feeling disappointed, and frustrated. As much as they want to believe that the relationship can offer more, they are protecting themselves from further hurt. Thus, I tend to believe that many partners do have the capacity to achieve greater intimacy but must be nurtured to the point of taking that risk. The nurturing involves some of the previously described procedures by Wile (1981). Namely, the goal is to help spouses fully develop their perspectives of what they want from a marriage and to help the partner listen to those perspectives without necessarily believing that it is his or her responsibility to meet the other's desires. Only when spouses stop holding back their feelings in efforts to protect themselves and one another can they move forward.

The resistance also may take the form of one spouse continuing to be reluctant. In that case, I react by respecting that person's position and not moving ahead with marital therapy. I spend time exploring what that resistance represents; perhaps the person is too busy starting up a new business to get involved in therapy but might be willing at a later date, or the person really wants to terminate the relationship and wants to use therapy as a way to prove that the relationship is hopeless, or the person has concerns about his or her emotional state and finds the patient role too threatening. While I may direct a lot of my attention to the reluctant spouse, my concern is equally if not more for the other spouse. I consider it a real disservice to that person to increase his or her hopes and enthusiasm if therapy is likely to fail. Thus, I encourage discussion about the reluctance and label overt, as opposed to covert, signs of reluctance as showing concern and consideration for the partner.

With each marital therapy case, I ask for an overt statement of commitment at the transition between our initial evaluation and therapy. The commitment is to try therapy, usually for a three to four month period, with there being a strong likelihood that we will make an additional commitment at that later date. The time-limited commitment to therapy symbolizes a time-limited commitment to the relationship as well. For some couples this eases the immediate burden of making a more long term commitment to the relationship. The commitment to therapy is, in reality, strictly symbolic. It serves to increase the couple's investment in the therapeutic process while emphasizing the importance of this process.

With each marital therapy case, I also take specific steps to prevent noncompliance. Before making any assignment, I have the couple generate all the reasons why they may not be able to complete the assignment. We then discuss how to circumvent those reasons. I also try to have the couple as involved as possible in deciding upon the exact format of the assignment. While I set up the objectives and specify a general structure, the spouses fill in the details so that it fits their needs and fits into the structure of their lives. In planning assignments, I often go more slowly or take smaller steps than the couple would assign themselves. If they go ahead and actually do more, that, of course, is fine with me, although I may chide them about moving too quickly.

With some couples, of course, it becomes obvious that one or both spouses are really not prepared to become involved in therapy, despite their stated commitment. Although they are not ready to recognize the extent of their ambivalence about the marriage, even to themselves, the reluctance is exhibited in the form of noncompliance. When encountering a noncompliant couple, I first check into whether there is something about the nature of the task itself that made it more difficult than we anticipated. If this is the case, we then restructure the task or devise a new task that is still toward the same objective. We also discuss and decide whether the objective itself was ill conceived. However, when there are repeated signs of noncompliance, I take it as an indication that we must re-examine our initial commitment to therapy.

Crises

Although most couples enter marital therapy for problems of long duration, as opposed to a crisis, there are some exceptions. Sometimes couples seek therapy when one spouse has threatened to leave the marriage. This threat might be due to long time frustrations or may be on the heels of a recent and major upheaval (e.g., learning of the spouse's affair, or having a particularly violent argument). With any couple, it is helpful to learn what motivated them to seek therapy at the particular time that they did. Whatever motivated them to take that first step perhaps also can be used to motivate them to work in therapy.

From the couple's perspective, a crisis is something that they want to be quickly resolved such that their pain is lessened. Typically, however, there are no quick resolutions to such problems unless the spouses choose to turn off their feelings and return to "life as normal." I have encountered some couples who quickly resolve their crises in that fashion and thereby alleviate their need for therapy. Although such couples clearly could benefit from a more major overhauling of their relationship, they reject that prospect as too threatening. I am generally disappointed when a couple makes that choice, but figure that the relationship has stabilized for now and, if the problem reoccurs, they can re-evaluate whether they want therapy.

When one person threatens to leave, the decision involves whether to enter a decision-making process of whether or not to end the marriage, or whether to postpone that decision and try to make the relationship better, and then reevaluate the decision. Perhaps the decision to leave is already a *fait accompli*, in which case efforts toward relationship improvement are of no value. Alternatively, the threat to leave might simply be a signal that one spouse is ready for change.

One of my concerns when discussing the possibility of ending a relationship is to balance the power vis-à-vis that decision. Generally one person is threatening and the other is awaiting the decision. In reality, however, each person has that choice and each person has his or her breaking point. Thus, I ask the person who has not been threatening to leave under what conditions she or he would make that choice. Even the most committed spouse can generate several conditions that would be intolerable. Recognition of both persons' decision-making power tends to deintensify the impact of the original threat. It also poses some alternative goals should we decide to work on relationship improvement.

Although I am not an advocate of keeping marriages together, I do believe that such decisions need not be made in a hurry. That is, couples who have been miserable for a number of years may want to consider giving themselves several more months in which to work on the relationship before making that decision. Couples who are relieved at this prospect generally are good candidates for therapy. Couples who react to this suggestion with the thought "It's already been so long," probably have already made their decision.

Although I believe that the decision about whether to stay together or separate should come from the couple, it is hard to remain neutral about this decision. I see my job as helping the couple to explore this decision in a thoughtful manner. I also find myself frequently pointing out that this is not likely to be a mutual decision. For a separation to occur, it takes just one person to decide that is the best choice for him or her.

The one occasion when I do take a more active role in such decision making is when one spouse would be at physical risk if the relationship were to continue. With battering couples, I interview the two spouses independently to evaluate the risk and to determine their feelings about staying in the marriage. If both spouses show a preference for trying to work on the marriage, I will try a no-violence contract, complete with contingencies and plans for one or both partners to leave the situation (e.g., Margolin, in press a). The breaking of such contracts is reason for me to strongly urge a separation.

Although I have focused on crises that precipitate therapy, crises also may arise in the midst of therapy. My reaction to these crises is much the same although, by knowing the couple for some time, I am better able to determine what the crisis means. In some cases, these crises are a way for one spouse to register his or her desperation more forcefully. In one couple, for example, the husband suddenly made a threat to move out of the house when he felt that the wife was not fully involved in therapy.

Based on the hunch that the husband really did not want to leave, I called for an emergency session to discuss the husband's threat. That session gave the husband an opportunity to express his frustration with his wife. He really was not interested in leaving the marriage but was demanding a decision from the wife either to get involved in therapy or to disengage altogether.

Crises in the midst of therapy can often be used to reenergize a dragging system and refocus attention on a more serious problem. Other times, however, they are indicators that marital therapy may be a mistake. Thus, I find myself reacting on two levels: responding to the emotional needs of each spouse at that time, and sorting out what this means for therapy and for the relationship more generally.

Termination and Maintenance

As stated previously, I try to arrange for periodic renegotiations of the therapy contract so that the couple and I are in touch about where the therapy is going. Whenever we reach one of these points, I raise the following questions: Are we making the type of progress that would indicate that continued therapy is advisable? Have we gone as far as we can go? Have we reached a plateau such that a rest from therapy is in order?

In general, I gradually wean couples out of therapy. The sign that it is time to start this process is when our sessions, although enjoyable, are less productive and take on a flavor of "checking in." As we move to a schedule of alternate weeks and then once a month, I always let couples know that they can contact me sooner if they wish. Eventually we move to an on-call basis.

There are specific suggestions that I make in efforts to facilitate maintenance. First, since much of my work is skill-training and not just solving individual problems, it is anticipated that these skills will be useful when future problems arise. I find it useful to review the various skills we have worked on and to identify a few specific ones that they have found useful and are comfortable with. I often ask them to speculate on what they believe to be the underlying change process that has occurred. I attempt to demystify that process and attribute responsibility to the spouses for the benefits they derived. My overall goal here is to bring to the forefront two or three strategies to which they can turn on their own.

Second, I always predict relapse, both in the course of therapy and when preparing for termination. Since all couples encounter problems, I want them to be prepared to cope with problems as opposed to panicking and thinking that therapy has been of no avail. In our planning, I ask them to generate ideas about how they would recognize that the relationship was heading in a downward trend, focusing particularly on the early signs. From there, we talk about how to head off such a trend. I also ask them to imagine the worst situation (e.g., a flareup of their most sensitive issue), and then have them imagine how to move beyond it.

Third, I attempt to build in a structure whereby they can keep in close contact with each other about how the relationship is doing. One suggestion that I make, for example, is that they reserve the hour that they had been in therapy to spend with each other discussing how the relationship is going. I urge couples to develop that habit during the time that we meet biweekly.

Ethical Issues

As I and others (Margolin, 1982, 1986; O'Shea & Jessee, 1982) have discussed at length, the sheer practicalities of seeing two as opposed to one client as well as the theoretical implications of an interpersonal as opposed to individual model complicate and create new kinds of ethical and value dilemmas. Although there are a variety of issues to consider, the ones that I encounter most frequently include the following questions: "Whose agent am I?" "Am I being overly eager to maintain the relationship system?" "How do I handle confidentiality?"

The question regarding whose agent I am reflects the difficulty in balancing my responsibility to each spouse. By virtue of the fact that the spouses are in conflict about a variety of issues, it is difficult to guard and promote the welfare of each client at all stages of therapy. My solution to this dilemma is to attempt to balance my support for the two clients over the long run. Furthermore, I attempt to insure that improvement in one spouse does not occur at the long-range expense of the other. I have come to accept, however, that an intervention that benefits one spouse may cause some temporary distress and discomfort in the other. My overall strategy for coping with this issue is to confront it outright with the couple so that they know that my goal is to balance the benefits of therapy and that they can help me monitor the effects of the interventions.

Another dimension of the balancing that goes on in marital therapy concerns my role as an advocate of the relationship system versus as an advocate of either or both individuals. As noted above with respect to wife battering, there are times in which I automatically abdicate my role as relationship advocate and immediately turn my attention toward the protection of one individual. For the most part, however, I rely on the three-way decision that evolves out of our initial evaluation as to whether we pursue improvement of the relationship or focus on deciding whether to continue the relationship. Toward the goal of relationship improvement, I find that, by becoming a relationship advocate, I am able to see beyond the futility that spouses themselves experience and help to unstick a stuck system. However, I still try to remain watchful of signs that pursuing this course is detrimental to one of the individuals. In deciding whether or not to continue the relationship, the focus is much more on the welfare of the individuals. I am helping each individual to consider how his or her personal well-being is affected by remaining in the marriage.

Another direction in which I have been moving that of extending my advocacy beyond the two-person marital system. Seeing how affected children are by the actions of their parents, I find myself inquiring into the impact of the marital problems on the children. Parents generally have thought about and are concerned about the impact of their marital problems on the children. A side benefit of this discussion is that it often helps promote an atmosphere of good faith as the partners hear each other's commitment to good parenting. When the discussion gets more specific, however, it is often revealed that the couple is in conflict over a number of issues regarding childrearing. Understanding how the children might get 'caught' in a conflictual marriage is important. When I believe that the children are at risk for problems themselves, I either renegotiate my contract with the couple and switch for a period of time to family therapy or else I make an outside referral for an evaluation and treatment that focuses on the children.

Confidentiality poses another major issue with which to contend. To what extent do I maintain the individual confidences of my two clients? For many years, I solved this dilemma by simply never seeing spouses alone and thereby never having access to individual confidences. I came to realize, however, that a set policy such as this was unnecessary. I was losing out on some important information as well as relationship-building benefits that could be derived from individual sessions. At this time, I would estimate that I have at least one individual session with about half of the couples whom I treat. When the same information that would come out in an individual session also can be obtained in a conjoint session, my preference is for conjoint sessions so that the other spouse also has the benefit of hearing the information. My most common reason for scheduling individual sessions is that I feel that I simply have not established a firm relationship with one of the spouses and thus that I cannot understand his or her perspective. I may also use individual sessions when therapy is really stuck and I feel that I am missing some important key to what is going on. Sometimes the initiative for individual sessions comes at the request of one of the spouses.

When I do schedule individual sessions, I always balance my time with both spouses. That is, either I schedule separate hours with each or I split the hour, but I never see one without seeing the other. Secondly, I let spouses know that, in order to continue our primary thrust of working as a threesome, I cannot maintain individual confidences. Anything that they tell me may be brought into the larger three-person session. That does not mean, however, that everything necessarily will be brought in. Before scheduling such sessions, I make sure that both spouses are comfortable with this plan, which they usually are. The benefit to the spouses is that they sometimes can sort out their own positions better without the other spouse present. When spouses do reveal sensitive material under these conditions, they typically are searching for ways to bring up that information with the spouse. I then can work with that individual on how to introduce the material in our conjoint session. Because of the no-secrets nature of our agreement, I may of course be depriving myself of some important information that one spouse is determined that the other should not know. I am willing to take that risk, however, to avoid finding myself in the situation in which I obtain information that I cannot use openly and thereby enter into a special, protective collaboration with one spouse.

Sex Role Issues

I have come to the conclusion that attitudes regarding sex roles pervade most every dimension of a spouses' lives together. Likewise, the couple's sex-role attitudes, in combination with the therapist's attitudes, play a role in every aspect of the intervention. I go back and forth between the viewing of the effects of sex role as background noise to viewing them as the underlying core of many relationship problems and the most important target of the intervention. Clearly, the sexist society in which most of us were raised has left a negative mark on intimate relationships, including, for example, differential roles and an imbalance of power. Couples now struggle with the dissatisfactions arising from those issues as well as from the bewilderment of redefining their relationship in a time of rapidly expanding sex-role options.

For me, the issue is whether to tamper with a couple's sex-role values, thereby overhauling the relationship in a more profound way than they requested, or whether to accept those values and work within them. I find myself debating this issue regarding almost every couple with whom I work and varying considerably from case to case in my decision. As I evaluate couples, I generally elicit information about sex-role expectations. I also consider how discrepancies between their goals in comparison to their current patterns reveal underlying dissatisfactions with sex roles. Interventions can then be construed at two different levels—one that creates more satisfaction and harmony within the current structure of sex roles or one that alters those fundamental structures. For instance, dissatisfaction with the household (husband thinks it is too messy; wife thinks husband should do more housework) can be resolved by having the husband help out more or by questioning the underlying assumption that the household is the wife's domain (Gurman & Klein, 1983).

In deciding how to proceed, I evaluate the extent to which confusion and conflict over sex-role issues are unifying themes in the couples' complaints, even if they do not label them as such. This assessment does not commit me to intervening in this area but provides me with information to decide whether an intervention around sex-role issues is warranted. The more pervasive sex-role issues are, the more likely I am to recommend that we deal with those issues per se as opposed to dealing with a string of individual complaints that reflect the issues. In any event, I try to be open with couples in terms of discussing the two levels of intervention and eliciting their reactions. When spouses agree on the level of intervention, whether it is the more or the less traditional, I go with their preference. A disagreement regarding level of intervention, however, indicates that sex-role conflict, indeed, may be important. I also try to be open with the couple about what my preference would be, not so that they will adopt that preference but so that they can help monitor the effects of my influence and not feel subtly coerced. The recent attention to sex-role issues by several authors (Gurman & Klein, 1980; 1983; Hare-Mustin, 1978; 1983; Jacobson, 1983a) has led me to reevaluate specific procedures, such as the male bias in problem solving (Margolin, Talovic, Fernandez, & Onorato, 1983), and probably will continue to be a major force in shaping my therapy over the next few years.

Cultural Values

Cultural values, similar to sex-role values, influence what is perceived as being functional versus dysfunctional behaviors and interactions in relationships. In working with a post-Korean-war marriage between an Asian woman and a black man, for example, it was clear that the ethnic differences between the two of them, as well as between them and me, added layers of complexity to our work together. The wife's deference to the husband was certainly common to her culture but, from a systems perspective, was problematic. She was quite passive in expressing her dissatisfactions, which the husband chose to interpret as acceptance of his behavior. The question I faced was whether encouraging her to be more assertive in her complaints, which reflected my cultural bias, would increase or decrease her discomfort.

Once again, I rely on a careful assessment to understand how spouses' beliefs, expectations, and traditions are shaped by their cultural background. Based on Falicov's (1983) recommendation, I try to avoid labelling an attribute as dysfunctional when it is normative in the person's culture as well as erring in the opposite fashion and failing to recognize dysfunctional processes due to my own cultural stereotyping. I often find it useful simply to admit to my own ignorance and confusion in this area.

When the spouses share a cultural background but it is different from my own, I often consult them about how our therapeutic plans mesh with their values and modify the plans accordingly. When the couple and I share a cultural background, I might make use of our similarities to establish rapport, but will try to guard against going too far in assuming a similarity of values. When the spouses themselves are from different cultures, I inquire as to how they are accommodating that difference. Effective coping with those differences gives couples a source of strength that sometimes can be generalized to other areas of the relationship. Ineffective coping, however, can be a tremendous source of tension that effects most every aspect of their lives.

It is my impression, however, that the differences among couples are not as much a function of being from a particular ethnic background as from the diversity among individuals in general. A cultural perspective is only one component of the complex decision making that goes into matching interventions and couples.

EVALUATION OF THERAPY APPROACH

The approach to therapy described here is an amalgam of the theories and procedures of several different models and is very much attuned to the needs of the individual couple. Thus far I have done no formal evaluation of this approach nor is there any therapy outcome study in the literature that represents this approach. Certain components of the approach that represent behavioral marital techniques have been evaluated by others (e.g., Baucom, 1982; Hahlweg, Revensdorf, & Schindler, 1982; Jacobson, 1978; 1984; Turkewitz & O'Leary, 1981). However, it is hard to draw generalizations from studies that evaluate a standardized treatment to the more individualized approach that I have described. While the scientist in me demands a formal evaluation of efficacy, the practitioner in me is bewildered as to how to adequately assess the approach at this time.

What I believe still needs to be developed before such an evaluation can take place is a clear blueprint identifying under what conditions what interventions should be offered. When I can better describe this approach in if-then statements, I think its efficacy could be researched: For instance, if the couple has such and such problems and if they have tried X, Y, and Z solutions thus far, then I might prescribe a cognitive intervention that includes A, B, and C components followed by a behavioral intervention that includes D, E, and F components. In principal, I would like to move in that direction of order and specificity. Nonetheless, in reality, I find myself moving toward a model that keeps adding dimensions to the "if" clause and increasing the number of alternatives in the "then" clause.

Thus, at this point, I find myself relying upon the feedback of individual couples as to the overall success of our work together. In defining success, my criterion is that the spouses feel they have benefitted from therapy, regardless of whether the relationship improves or ends in separation. Alternatively, failure is defined as continuing in the same degree of "stuckness' and feeling equally or more uncomfortable with that stuckness. Success is not an all or none prospect. Rather, I see therapeutic effectiveness as a series of stages of relationship growth. Some spouses are content with experiencing a few of these stages while others want to explore many.

Sometimes I do not know the long-range effects of therapy until well after our work together has discontinued. One couple, for example, with whom I met over a 2-year time frame and then had periodic follow-up meetings, decided to divorce approximately 4 years later. The goal of our work together had been defined as relationship improvement, which, upon ending therapy, we had achieved with limited success. The couple reported being satisfied with therapy, even after their divorce. Given their intense involvement in therapy, they felt satisfied that they gave the relationship their best efforts. Whether or not the therapy actually helped them arrive at the decision to divorce, which appears to be a good decision on both sides, remains unknown. Is that a success or failure? Another couple, who had lived together for approximately 10 years, entered therapy to improve their relationship and also to decide whether or not to marry. They made some gains in terms of communication and overall satisfaction but left therapy still undecided about whether their relationship was good enough to warrant committing themselves to marriage. One year later, however, they married and 1 year after that they still were pleased with their decision. Is that a therapy success?

Because of the flexibility of this approach, I can think of no specific relationship problems that are not amenable to this approach. However, I have recognized two patterns that emerge during the course of therapy with which I have not been very successful. The first has to do with therapy becoming part of an overall pattern of severe coercion on the part of one spouse. Mild coercion by one spouse to get the other into therapy is characteristic of many couples' initial decision to seek therapy. Nonetheless, most of the time, I can get beyond that coercion such that both spouses feel they have made an independent choice. When that does not happen, however, and one spouse continues to feel coerced, therapy generally does not get off the ground. In one couple, for example, the wife initiated therapy; the husband was a greatly overworked young teacher who was feeling multiple stresses from all sides. One of their major issues was whether to practice birth control. The wife claimed that this violated her newly found religious beliefs, as well as that she was emotionally ready for a child. The husband, however, was terrified at such a prospect.

Just as we were getting started in therapy, the wife got pregnant. The husband, still viewing therapy as the wife's idea, and feeling completely overwhelmed at that point, chose to discontinue therapy. Leaving therapy was one means of escape from a relationship that he was experiencing as beyond his control.

The other pattern that I find to be difficult is when a highly intellectual and obsessional couple becomes stuck in the decision of whether to try to improve the relationship or whether to separate. Such couples can go through several cycles of trying to improve the marriage, interrupted by severe doubts about whether they should be together and wondering whether they can find a better relationship. Thus, they never really give relationship improvement an adequate trial and, at the same time, they fail to make any decision about the direction of their marriage because they are terrified of making a mistake. These couples systematically avoid anything that will push them in either direction, (i.e., anything warm and exciting and anything that increases the level of tension). When I first start feeling stuck with such couples, I usually try to help them to be more action-oriented and emotive with one another, (e.g., considering the worst scenario if they separate, setting up situations in which they might act on impulse). If we remain trapped in this obsessive cycle after a number of such attempts, I generally suggest a break from therapy and sometimes make individual referrals. Sometimes the passage of time helps these couples to become clearer as to what they want; in other cases they continue in highly compromised and dissatisfied relationships.

On the other side of the coin, although I know which types of presenting problems are easier to treat, I am not sure that I can typify what couples ultimately benefit the most from this therapy. Certainly therapy is easier if spouses actually suffer from a skills deficit, as opposed to a reluctance to perform desired behaviors with the partner. Teaching the new skills quickly opens new relationship possibilities for such couples. It also always is helpful if spouses have maintained strong feelings for each other, despite what may be extremely destructive patterns. In such cases, their underlying feelings will supply the motivation to develop new patterns. This is in contrast to the couples who are distant, withdrawn, and depressed, with whom it is an ordeal to conjure up the emotional and physical energy just to enter into the therapy process. A parallel distinction is the difference between blocking angry interactions versus eliciting caring, loving interactions. For me, the former is much easier than the latter.

In most instances, couples present with a mixture of positive and negative feelings, and in some need of new skills, but without that being the major problem. I think that the overall characteristic most important to making therapeutic gains is the spouses' willingness to maintain and act upon the shred of hope that they can make the relationship better.

FUTURE DIRECTIONS

My thoughts about future directions split into the two categories of short-range versus long-range objectives. In terms of the short-range objectives, I think that the most important concern for this therapy as well as for other marital therapies is developing a diagnostic scheme. Currently, our literature is limited to the differentiation between distressed and nondistressed couples. I am not recommending a diagnostic system simply for the purposes of labelling couples but rather to help us conceptualize different types of marital problems and to associate those types with different types of treatment. What I personally have been exploring is differential treatment based upon whether a couple is openly conflictual or emotionally withdrawn. I plan to clarify further the diagnostic picture of these two types and to explore further differential treatments. This is only a beginning step, however. This differentiation may not be the most important one and certainly is not the only one. Given the diversity among marital complaints, greater delineation of problem types and treatments is needed.

Due to my current research interests in marital violence, I have been focusing on understanding and treating couples who experience this one extreme form of conflict. Further understanding is needed as to why some spouses cross over this important threshold and resort to physical aggression while other spouses, though equally angry and disappointed, do not. Although I believe that individual treatment and legal action is the most important intervention in many cases (Margolin, Sibner, & Gleberman, in press), further development of conjoint treatments, such as those described above, will play an important role in light of the many aggressive couples who elect to remain together.

On the other side, I also think that more attention needs to be paid to treatment of the withdrawn, devitalized but stable couple. The pain experienced by these spouses is more subtle than that in the overtly hostile couples. Furthermore, the withdrawal often is a maneuver to dull the experience of that pain. While I have suggested an overall strategy of increasing these couples' affective experience, there are a number of questions to be addressed. How do we balance the escalation of positive and negative emotional experiences? What are the effects of this emotional escalation?

Overall, there is much to be learned about enhancing affective experience in marital therapy. The chapter, like most of the marital literature, has focused considerably more on cognitive and behavioral, as opposed to affective, dimensions of relationships. I think that this reflects therapists' greater confidence in how to promote cognitive and behavioral change and their uncertainties about affective change. Yet, if we were to poll the couples on their priorities, I imagine that affective change would be rated as least as high, if not higher, than either of the other two dimensions. As an immediate goal for therapy, I think that emotional expressive procedures need more exploration and elaboration, perhaps along the lines recently suggested by Greenberg and Johnson (1986).

In addition to a fuller experience and expression of feeling emotions, there are more stable emotions that ideally accompany marital relationships. Jacobson (1983c) and I (Margolin, 1983b) have debated the role of intimacy, passion, and love in marital therapy. The procedures described above are designed to promote closeness and intimacy. While I would like to believe that at least some of the procedures are related to enhanced feelings of love, I really cannot claim that. Jacobson (1983c) suggests that we are on most secure ground in believing that treatment procedures help to promote the right conditions for love. An important future direction is to figure out whether this therapy gets beyond promoting more compatible, companionate relationships (not a trivial goal in itself) and actually fosters the special type of intimacy that spouses hope for in a marriage.

My long-range goals are directed to the prevention of marital distress. Overall, I think that there is a considerable need for educating young people as to what is involved in maintaining an intimate relationship. Despite the fact that the vast majority of people marry in their life times, it is estimated that approximately 58% of all children will be spending at least some of their childhood in single-parent homes (Brazelton, 1985). This figure overlaps with but does not fully account for the number of children who grow up witnessing unhappy marriages. Without readily accessible parental models, and with the extremely unrealistic models available through television and movies, many individuals enter intimate relationships with misguided expectations. Couples that I see in therapy repeatedly surprise me by how little they know about what goes on in other people's relationships. The lack of exposure that they might have experienced as children and adolescents often is further exacerbated by their current isolation as adults from other couples.

My recommendation is that there be more educational experiences regarding marital relationships. This education could be directed toward normalizing the common stresses that couples experience as well as demonstrating some coping strategies. Currently such an educational blitz in going on with respect to wife battering through television shows, newspaper and magazine articles, public lectures at community agencies and religious centers, and special classroom discussions in the high schools. I think that there is an important need for similar educational activities for marital problems more generally.

SUMMARY

In sum, what I have attempted to portray in this chapter is my personal integration and elaboration of treatment models that are best attributed to others. I have tried to indicate those models that I have drawn upon most heavily but I probably am not even aware of all the influences that have shaped my therapy. How my therapy evolves in the future, will probably reflect how the field in general evolves, and in particular what I learn from a handful of colleagues with whom I maintain close contact. In return, I hope that my perspective will offer something new to them. More importantly, however, I am sure that my clients will continue to serve as a major source of inspiration. Knowing how much I learn from clients, I like to believe that those relationships also are reciprocal and that they, in return, learn as much from me.

REFERENCES

Bandura, A. (1977). *Social learning theory*. New York: General Learning Press.

Baucom, D. H. (1982). A comparison of behavioral contracting and problem-solving/communication training in behavioral marital therapy. *Behavior Therapy, 13*, 162–174.

Baucom, D. H., Bell, W. G., & Duhe, A. G. (1982, November). *The measurement of couples' attributions for positive and negative dyadic interactions*. Paper presented at the 16th Annual Convention of the Association for the Advancement of Behavior Therapy, Los Angeles.

Birchler, G. R. (1979). Communication skills in married couples. In A. S. Bellack & M. Hersen (Eds.), *Research and practice in social skills training*. New York: Plenum.

Birchler, G. R., & Spinks, S. H. (1980). Behavioral-systems marital and family therapy: Integration and clinical application. *American Journal of Family Therapy, 8*, 6–28.

Brazelton, T. B. (1985). *Working and caring*. Reading, MA: Addison-Wesley.

Broderick, C. B. (1983). *The therapeutic triangle*. Beverly Hills, CA: Sage.

Coyne, J. C., & Biglan, A. (1984). Paradoxical techniques in strategic family therapy: A behavioral analysis. *Journal of Behavior Therapy and Experimental Psychiatry, 15*, 221–227.

Falicov, C. J. (1983). Introduction. In J. C. Hansen & C. J. Falicov (Eds.), *Cultural perspectives in family therapy*. Rockville, MD: Aspen.

Fincham, F., & O'Leary, K. D. (1983). Causal inferences for spouse behavior in maritally distressed and nondistressed couples. *Journal of Social and Clinical Psychology, 1*, 42–57.

Greenberg, L. S., & Johnson, S. M. (1986). Affect in marital therapy. *Journal of Marital and Family Therapy, 12*(1), 1–10.

Guerney, B. G. (1977). *Relationship enhancement*. San Francisco: Jossey-Bass.

Gurman, A. S., & Klein, M. H. (1980). The treatment of women in marital and family conflict: Recommendations for outcome evaluation. In A. Brodsky & R. T. Mustin (Eds.), *Women and psychotherapy*. New York: Guilford.

Gurman, A. S., & Klein, M. H. (1983). Women and behavioral marriage and family therapy: An unconscious male bias? In E. A. Blechman (Ed.), *Behavior modification with women*. New York: Guilford.

Hahlweg, K., Revensdorf, D., & Schindler, L. (1982). Treatment of marital distress: Comparing formats and modalities. *Advances in Behavior Research and Therapy, 4*, 57–74.

Hare-Mustin, R. T. (1978). A feminist approach to family therapy. *Family Process, 17*, 181–194.

Hare-Mustin, R. T. (1983). Psychology: A feminist perspective on family therapy. In B. Haber (Ed.), *The women's annual: 1982–83*. Boston: G. K. Hall.

Hoffman, L. (1981). *Foundations of family therapy*. New York: Basic Books.

Holtzworth-Munroe, A., & Jacobson, N. S. (1985). Causal attributions of married couples: When do they search for causes? What do they conclude when they do? *Journal of Personality and Social Psychology, 48*, 1398–1412.

Jacobson, N. S. (1977a). Training couples to solve their marital problems: A behavioral approach to relationship discord. Part I: Problem-solving skills. *International Journal of Family Counseling, 5*(1), 22–31.

Jacobson, N. S. (1977b). Training couples to solve their marital problems: A behavioral approach to relationship discord. Part II: Intervention strategies. *International Journal of Family Counseling, 5*(2), 20–28.

Jacobson, N. S. (1978). Specific and nonspecific factors in the effectiveness of a behavioral approach to the treatment of marital discord. *Journal of Consulting and Clinical Psychology, 46*, 442–452.

Jacobson, N. S. (1981). Behavioral marital therapy. In A. S. Gurman & D. P. Kniskern (Eds.), *Handbook of family therapy* New York: Brunner/Mazel.

Jacobson, N. S. (1983a). Beyond empiricism: The politics of marital therapy. *American Journal of Family Therapy, 11*, 11–24.

Jacobson, N. S. (1983b). Clinical innovations in behavioral marital therapy. In K. Craig & D. McMahon (Eds.), *Advances in clinical behavior therapy.* New York: Brunner/Mazel.

Jacobson, N. S. (1983c). Expanding the range and applicability of behavioral marital therapy. *the Behavior Therapist, 6*, 189–191.

Jacobson, N. S. (1984). A component analysis of behavior marital therapy: The relative effectiveness of behavior exchange and communication problem solving. *Journal of Consulting and Clinical Psychology, 52*, 295–305.

Jacobson, N. S., Berley, R., Newport, K., Elwood, R., & Phelps, C. (1985). Failure in behavioral marital therapy. In S. Coleman (Ed.), *Failures in family therapy.* New York: Guilford.

Jacobson, N. S., Follette, W. C., Revenstorf, D., Baucom, D. H., Hahlweg, K., & Margolin, G. (1984). Variability in outcome and clinical significance of behavioral marital therapy: A reanalysis of outcome data. *Journal of Consulting and Clinical Psychology, 52*, 497–504.

Jacobson, N. S., & Margolin, G. (1979). *Marital therapy: Strategies based on social learning and behavior exchange principles.* New York: Brunner/Mazel.

Jacobson, N. S., McDonald, D. W., Follette, W. C., & Berley, R. A. (1985). Attributional process in distressed and nondistressed married couples. *Cognitive Therapy and Research, 9*, 35–50.

Jacobson, N. S., & Moore, D. (1981). Behavior exchange theory of marriage: Reconnaisance and reconsideration. In J. P. Vincent (Ed.), *Advances in family intervention, assessment and theory: A research annual* (II). Greenwich, CT: JAI Press.

Liberman, R. P. (1970). Behavioral approaches to family and couple therapy. *American Journal of Orthopsychiatry, 40*, 106–118.

Margolin, G. (1981). A behavioral–systems approach to the treatment of marital jealousy. *Clinical Psychology Review, 1*, 469–487.

Margolin, G. (1982). Ethical and legal considerations in marital and family therapy. *American Psychologist, 37*, 788–801.

Margolin, G. (1983a). An interactional model for the assessment of marital relationships. *Behavioral Assessment, 5*, 103–127.

Margolin, G. (1983b). Behavioral marital therapy: Is there a place for passion, play, and other non-negotiable dimensions? *the Behavior Therapist, 6*, 65–68.

Margolin, G. (1985). Building marital trust and treating sexual problems. In A. S. Gurman (Ed.), *Casebook of marital therapy.* New York: Guilford.

Margolin, G. (1986). Ethical issues in marital therapy. In N. S. Jacobson & A. S. Gurman (Eds.), *Clinical handbook of marital therapy.* New York: Guilford.

Margolin, G. (in press-a). Marital conflict is not marital conflict is not marital conflict. In R. de V. Peters & R. McMahon (Eds.) *Marriage and families: Behavioral treatments and processes.* Champaign, IL: Sage.

Margolin, G. (in press-b). Participant observation procedures in marital and family assessment. In T. Jacob (Ed.), *Family interaction and psychology.* New York: Plenum.

Margolin, G., Fernandez, V., Gorin, L., & Ortiz, S. (1982, November). *The Conflict Inventory: A measurement of how couples handle marital tension.* Paper presented at the 16th Annual Meeting of the Association for the Advancement of Behavior Therapy, Los Angeles.

Margolin, G., Sibner, L. G., & Gleberman, L. (in press). Wife battering. In V. B. Van Hasselt, R. L. Morrison, A. S. Bellack, & M. Hersen (Eds.), *Handbook of family violence.* New York: Plenum.

Margolin, G., Talovic, C., Fernandez, V., & Onorato, R. (1983). Sex role considerations and behavioral marital therapy: Equal does not mean identical. *Journal of Marital and Family Therapy, 9*, 131–146.

Margolin, G., & Weinstein, C. D. (1983). The role of affect in behavioral marital therapy. In M. L. Aronson & L. R. Wolberg (Eds.), *Group and family therapy 1982: An overview.* New York: Brunner/Mazel.

O'Shea, M., & Jessee, E. (1982). Ethical, value, and professional conflicts in systems therapy. In J. C. Hansen & L. L'Abate (Eds.), *Values, ethics, legalities and the family therapist* (pp. 1–22). Rockville, MD: Aspen.

Patterson, G. R., & Hops, H. (1972). Coercion, a game for two: Intervention techniques for marital conflict. In R. E. Ulrich & P. Mountjoy (Eds.), *The experimental analysis of social behavior.* New York: Appleton-Century-Crofts.

Patterson, G. R., & Reid, J. B. (1970). Reciprocity and coercion: Two facets of social systems. In C. Neuringer & J. L. Michael (Eds.), *Behavior modification in clinical psychology.* New York: Appleton-Century-Crofts.

Rappaport, A. F. (1976). Conjugal relationship enhancement program. In D. H. L. Olson (Ed.), *Treating relationships.* Lake Mills, IA: Graphic.

Rappaport, A. F., & Harell, J. (1972). A behavioral exchange model for marital counseling. *Family Coordinator, 22*, 203–212.

Segraves, R. T. (1982). *Marital therapy: A combined psychodynamic–behavioral approach.* New York: Plenum.

Spanier, G. B. (1976). Measuring dyadic adjustment: New scales for assessing the quality of marriage and similar dyads. *Journal of Marriage and the Family, 35*, 15–28.

Stuart, R. B. (1976). An operant interpersonal program for couples. In D. H. L. Olson (Ed.), *Treating relationships.* Lake Mills, IA: Graphic.

Teismann, M. W. (1979). Jealousy: Systematic problem-solving therapy with couples. *Family Process, 18*, 151–160.

Turkewitz, H., & O'Leary, K. D. (1981). A comparative outcome study of behavioral marital therapy and communication therapy. *Journal of Marital and Family Therapy, 7*, 159–169.

Watzlawick, P., Weakland, J., & Fisch, R. (1974). *Change: Principles of problem formation and problem resolution.* New York: Norton.

Weiss, R. L. (1978). The conceptualization of marriage from a behavioral perspective. In T. J. Paolino & B. S. McCrady (Eds.), *Marriage and marital therapy: Psychoanalytic behavioral and Systems theory perspectives.* New York: Brunner/Mazel.

Weiss, R. L. (1980). Strategic behavioral marital therapy: Toward a model for assessment and intervention. In J. P. Vincent (Ed.), *Advances in family intervention, assessment, and theory: An annual compilation of research* (Vol. 1). Greenwich, CT: JAI Press.

Weiss, R. L., Hops, H., & Patterson, G. R. (1973). A framework for conceptualizing marital conflict, a technology for altering it, some data for evaluating it. In L. A. Hamerlynck, L. C. Handy, & E. J. Mash (Eds.), *Behavior change: Methodology, concepts, and practice.* Champaign, IL: Research Press.

Weiss, R. L., & Perry, B. A. (1979). *Assessment and treatment of marital dysfunction.* Eugene, OR: University of Oregon & Oregon Marital Studies Program.

Wile, D. B. (1981). *Couples therapy: A nontraditional approach.* New York: Wiley.

CHAPTER 8

The Multimodal Approach with Adult Outpatients

Arnold A. Lazarus
Rutgers—The State University of New Jersey
Private Practice, Princeton, New Jersey

THEORETICAL MODEL OF BEHAVIOR DISORDERS

In a broad sense, we are products of the interplay among our genetic endowment, our physical environment, and our social learning history. Adolf Meyer (1915) was among the first to emphasize the need to assess and treat biological, psychological, and sociological factors, instead of resorting to mind–body dichotomies. We all recognize that conflicts, traumata, and other adverse environmental factors play a role in psychological disturbance (behavior disorders), but this is far too global. What specific constructs, theories, principles, terms, and concepts are needed to account for the vagaries of human conduct? The multimodal orientation is predicated on the following assumptions:

1. Human disquietude is multileveled and multilayered—few, if any, problems have a single cause or a unitary "cure."

2. We are beings who move, feel, sense, imagine, think, and relate to one another. At base we are biochemical/neurophysiological entities. Our personalities are the products of our ongoing *behaviors, affective processes, sensations, images, cognitions, interpersonal* relationships, and biological functions (wherein psychotropic *drugs* are most commonly used to remedy dysfunctions). The first letters of each of these modalities form the acronym BASIC ID (or the preferred acronym BASIC I.D.). It is crucial to realize that "D." stands not only for drugs, medication, or pharmacological intervention, but also includes nutrition, hygiene, exercise, and all basic physiological and pathological inputs.

3. Psychological disturbances are a product of one or more of the following: (a) conflicting or ambivalent feelings or reactions; (b) misinformation; (c) missing information (includes skill deficits, ignorance, and naiveté); (d) maladaptive habits (includes conditioned emotional reactions); (e) interpersonal inquietude (e.g., undue dependency, misplaced affection, excessive antipathy); (f) issues pertaining to low self-esteem; (g) biological dysfunctions.

4. At the physiological level, the concept of *thresholds* is most compelling. People have different frustration-tolerance thresholds, different stress-tolerance thresholds, different pain-tolerance thresholds—all of which are largely innate. While hypnosis and other psychological methods can modify certain thresholds, the genetic diathesis will usually prevail in the final analysis.

5. The main learning factors responsible for behavior disorders are conditioned associations (respondent and operant responses); modeling, identification, and other vicarious processes; and idiosyncratic perceptions (addressing the fact that people do not respond to some *real* environment, but rather to their *perceived* environment, thus factoring in the personalistic use of language, semantics, expectancies, encoding and selective attention).

6. Since much of our learning is neither conscious nor deliberate (Shevrin & Dickman, 1980), it is necessary to include *nonconscious processes* (not to be confused with "the unconscious" that has become a reified entity). We are merely noting that (1) people have different levels and degrees of self-awareness, and (2) that unrecognized (subliminal) stimuli can nevertheless influence one's conscious thoughts, feelings, and behaviors.

7. People defend against or avoid pain, discomfort, or negative emotions such as anxiety, depression, guilt, and shame. The term *defensive reactions* avoids the surplus meanings that psychodynamic theory attaches to "defense mechanisms." It is not necessary to fall into the quagmire of Freudian constructs when acknowledging that a truly comprehensive understanding of human personality needs to address the fact that people are capable of denying, disowning, displacing, and projecting various thoughts, feelings, wishes, and impulses.

8. As we examine dyadic and more complex interactions, another explanatory construct is required. People do not only communicate, they also *metacommunicate* (i.e., communicate about their communications). Communication tends to break down when one is incapable of stepping back, as it were, and examining the content and process of ongoing relationships.

The foregoing are the main theoretical tenets that underlie multimodal assessment and therapy. For more detailed accounts see Lazarus (1981, 1984a, 1985).

THEORY OF THERAPEUTIC CHANGE

Rationale for Treatment Approach

Given the preceding theoretical model of behavior disorders, it follows that multimodal practitioners have a pluralistic conception of etiology and treatment. A fundamental premise is that clients are usually troubled by a multitude of specific problems that should be dealt with by a similar multitude of specific treatments. It is assumed that durable results are in direct proportion to the number of different modalities deliberately addressed, that lasting change is at the very least a function of combined *techniques, strategies,* and *modalities*. Basically, the more a client learns in therapy, the less likely he or she is to relapse afterward. This vitiates the search for a panacea, or a single overriding therapeutic modality. In essence, the multimodal position is that comprehensive treatment at the very least calls for the correction of deviant behaviors, unpleasant feelings, negative sensations, intrusive images, irrational beliefs, stressful relationships, and possible biochemical imbalance. Of course, not every case requires attention to each modality, but this conclusion can be reached only after a thorough assessment of each area has been conducted (i.e., comprehensive problem identification). To the extent that interactive problems in behavior, affect, sensation, imagery, cognition, interpersonal relationships, and biological functioning are systematically explored, the diagnostic process is likely to be thorough. And to the extent that therapeutic intervention remedies whatever deficits and maladaptive patterns emerge, treatment outcomes are likely to be positive and long-lasting.

The "idiosyncratic perceptions" alluded to in the preceding section call for the adoption of various treatment styles, and place heavy emphasis on flexibility and specificity. Multimodal therapy calls for a precise tailoring of the therapeutic climate to fit each client's personal needs and expectancies. The term *bespoke therapy* has been used to describe the multimodal orientation (Zilbergeld, 1982) and aptly conveys the custom-made emphasis. The form, cadence, and style of therapy are fitted, whenever possible, to each client's perceived requirements. The basic question is "Who or what is best for this particular individual, couple, family, or group?" With some clients, it is counterproductive to offer more than a sympathetic ear; with others, unless therapy is highly structured, active, and directive, significant progress will not ensue (cf., Davison, 1980). By endeavoring to determine what works, for whom, and under which conditions, multimodal assessments try to spell out when to treat family systems rather than individuals, and vice versa. Even effective therapists will make mistakes relative to gauging the foregoing complexities, but capable therapists, on observing these errors, will usually make adjustments to change the course of therapy.

Overall Strategy for Bringing About Behavior Change

Assessment Procedures

In multimodal therapy, the initial interview and the use of the Multimodal Life History Questionnaire (Lazarus, 1981)[1] are the mainstay of assessment and problem identification. The initial interview is used to arrive at 12 determinations:

1. Were there signs of "psychosis" (e.g., delusions, thought disorders, bizarre or inappropriate behaviors, incongruity of affect)?
2. Were there signs of organicity, organic pathology, or any disturbed motor activity (e.g., rigid posture, tics, mannerisms)?
3. Was there evidence of depression, or suicidal or homicidal tendencies?
4. What were the presenting complaints and their main precipitating events?
5. What appeared to be some important antecedent factors?
6. Who or what seemed to be maintaining the client's overt and covert problems?
7. What did the client wish to derive from therapy?
8. Were there clear indications or contraindications for the adoption of a particular therapeutic style? (Did a basic directive or nondirective initial stance seem preferable?)
9. Were there any indications as to whether it would be in the client's best interests to be seen individually, as part of a dyad, triad, family unit, and/or in a group?
10. Could a mutually satisfying relationship ensue, or should the client be referred elsewhere?
11. Why was the client seeking therapy at this time—why not last week, last month, or last year?
12. What were some of the client's positive attributes and strengths?

In multimodal assessment, there is no slavish attention to order. When intervening in a crisis situation, the clinician may offer no more than immediate support, reassurance, and perhaps guidance. A primary purpose of the initial interview is to determine how to fit the treatment to the client (and not vice versa). Whenever there is any suspicion of organicity, a typical mental status examination is performed. When neurological impairment is suggested, a thorough testing of the client's attention, comprehension, grasp, reasoning, judgment and other neuropsychological factors is called for. The client's interests are best protected when the therapist has a network of competent physicians (e.g., psychiatrists, neurologists, internists, endocrinologists) for consultation.

Information derived from the initial interview and the 12-page Multimodal Life History Questionnaire usually provide the therapist with information sufficient to design a comprehensive treatment program. The questionnaire, in addition to obtaining routine background information, contains a "Modality Analysis of Current Problems" via behavior, affect, sensation, imagery, cognition, interpersonal relationships, and biological

1. The Multimodal Life History Questionnaire is published by Research Press, Box 3177, Dept. G., Champaign, Illinois, 61821.

factors. In tandem with observations obtained during the initial interview, after the client completes the Multimodal Life History Questionnaire, the therapist constructs a BASIC I.D. Chart or Modality Profile—a distinctive feature of multimodal therapy. The Modality Profile establishes a clear nexus between assessment and therapy. It seldom takes longer than 15 to 20 minutes for the construction of a comprehensive Modality Profile. Each item on the Profile is viewed as a specific problem that calls for direct therapeutic attention. These problem checklists serve as "working hypotheses" that may be modified or revised as additional factors come to light.

Clients are frequently asked to draw up their own Modality Profiles; it is sometimes particularly valuable for therapist and client to perform this exercise independently and then compare notes. Clients are provided with a brief explanation of each term in the BASIC I.D. A typewritten instruction sheet with the following information usually suffices:

Behavior. This refers mainly to overt behaviors: acts, habits, gestures, responses, and reactions that are observable and measurable. Make a list of those acts, habits, and so on that you want to increase and those that you would like to decrease. What would you like to start doing? What would you like to stop doing?

Affect. This refers to emotions, moods, and strong feelings. What emotions do you experience most often? Write down your unwanted emotions (e.g., anxiety, guilt, anger, depression, etc.). Note under "behavior" what you tend to *do* when you feel a certain way.

Sensation. Touching, tasting, smelling, seeing, and hearing are our five basic senses. Make a list of any negative sensations (e.g., tension, dizziness, pain, blushing, sweating, butterflies in stomach, etc.) that apply to you. If any of these sensations cause you to act or feel in certain ways, make sure you note them under "behavior" or "affect."

Imagery. Write down any bothersome recurring dreams and vivid memories. Include any negative features of the way you see yourself, of your "self-image." Make a list of any "mental pictures," past, present, or future, that may be troubling you. If any "auditory images"—tunes or sounds that you keep hearing—constitute a problem, jot them down. If your images arouse any significant actions, feelings, or sensations, make sure these items are added to "behavior," "affect," and "sensation."

Cognition. What types of attitudes, values, opinions, and ideas get in the way of your happiness? Make a list of negative things you often say to yourself (e.g., "I am a failure," "I am stupid," "Others dislike me," or "I'm no good"). Write down some of your most irrational ideas. Be sure to note down how these ideas and thoughts influence your behaviors, feelings, sensations, and images.

Interpersonal Relationships. Write down any bothersome interactions with other people (relatives, friends, lovers, employers, acquaintances, etc.). Any concerns you have about the way other people treat you should appear here. Check through the items under "behavior," "affect," "sensation," "imagery," and "cognition," and try to determine how they influence and are influenced by your interpersonal relationships. [Note that there is some overlap between the modalities; don't hesitate to list the same problem more than once, (e.g., under "behavior" and "interpersonal relationships")].

Drugs/Biology. Make a list of all drugs you are taking, whether prescribed by a doctor or not. Include any health problems, medical concerns, and illnesses that you have or have had.

Table 8-1 presents a Modality Profile that a client drew up on her own after reading the foregoing instructions.

In addition to Modality Profiles (i.e., specific problems and proposed treatments across a client's BASIC I.D.) the use of Structural Profiles (Table 8-2) often yields important information, especially in couples therapy. The following instructions are sufficient for drawing up these Structural Profiles: "Here are seven rating scales that pertain to various tendencies that people have. Using a scale of 0 to 6 (0 means that it does not describe you, or you rarely rely on it; 6 means that the description

TABLE 8-1. Modality Profile

Behavior	Procrastination. Disorganized/sloppy.
Affect	Self-blame, guilt, jealousy, fear. I'm especially afraid of criticism and rejection.
Sensation	Tension, especially in my jaws. Low back pain. Fatigued a lot of the time.
Imagery	Lonely images. I picture myself failing at many things. I often picture myself appearing foolish.
Cognition	Trouble making decisions. I'm often thinking about negative things. I don't feel entitled to happiness. I think of myself as less competent than most others.
Interpersonal relationships	Basically suspicious and nontrusting. I don't speak up when I am hurt or angry. I feel that I am too dependent on my parents. I don't have any good, close friends.
Drugs/biology	Insufficient exercise. Smoke ±2 packs of cigarettes a day. Use Valium from time to time.

TABLE 8-2. Structural Profile

1. *Behavior:* How active are you? How much of a "doer" are you? Do you like to keep busy?
   Rating: 6 5 4 3 2 1 0

2. *Affect:* How emotional are you? How deeply do you feel things? Are you inclined to impassioned, or soul-stirring inner reactions?
   Rating: 6 5 4 3 2 1 0

3. *Sensation:* How much do you focus on the pleasures and pains derived from your senses? How "tuned in" are you to your bodily sensations—to sex, food, music, art?
   Rating: 6 5 4 3 2 1 0

4. *Imagery:* Do you have a vivid imagination? Do you engage in fantasy and daydreaming? Do you "think in pictures?"
   Rating: 6 5 4 3 2 1 0

5. *Cognition:* How much of a "thinker" are you? Do you like to analyze things, make plans, reason things through?
   Rating: 6 5 4 3 2 1 0

6. *Interpersonal relationships:* How much of a "social being" are you? How important are other people to you? Do you gravitate to people? Do you desire intimacy with others?
   Rating: 6 5 4 3 2 1 0

7. *Drugs/Biology:* Are you healthy and health conscious? Do you take good care of your body and physical health? Do you avoid overeating, ingestion of unnecessary drugs, excessive amounts of alcohol, and exposure to other substances that may be harmful?
   Rating: 6 5 4 3 2 1 0

characterizes you, or you rely on it greatly) please rate yourself in the following areas." (See Table 8-2.) These subjective ratings are easily depicted on a graph. Despite their arbitrary nature, these ratings often enable one to derive useful clinical information. Important insights are gained when the therapist explores the meaning and relevance of each rating. In couples therapy, when husband and wife each fill out a Structural Profile, various differences and areas of potential incompatibility are readily discerned. With couples, it is also useful to have them rate how they think their spouse would depict them. This metacommunication usually provides additional inputs that can be put to good effect. Furthermore, it is also useful to determine the way a person rates himself or herself and to compare this with the way he or she rates his or her spouse. (At present, a standardized instrument is being designed to obtain Structural Profiles.)

When necessary, the multimodal therapist may call for standardized tests and additional diagnostic and assessment procedures (in the same technically eclectic spirit as a therapeutic method may be employed) but the mainstay of multimodal assessment centers on Modality Profiles and Structural Profiles.

Typical Stages of Treatment

The emphasis on flexibility and idiosyncratic necessity produces a high degree of heterogeneity on the part of the multimodal therapist. There are some clients who first require weeks or months of "trust building" before any techniques or assessment procedures can be broached. Others are too depressed or too anxious to cope with the rigors of filling in a 12-page Multimodal Life History Questionnaire. Some clients require immediate advice, guidance, and behavior rehearsal to deal with a current and pressing problem. Bearing in mind that there are exceptions to every rule and procedure (aside from two absolutes—sexual contact with clients is taboo, and clients should never be deprived of their dignity) most people nevertheless follow a similar therapeutic path.

Typically, initial interviews focus on the establishment of rapport, on assessing and evaluating presenting complaints, and on arriving at the best course of treatment. By dwelling on who or what is best for the client, the first question centers on whether or not alliance building and the development of a mutually satisfying relationship are likely, or whether referral to a different therapist or resource would be of greater benefit to the client. Sometimes, a definite mismatch is evident between client and therapist (e.g., in terms of the client's expectations, or clash-points vis-à-vis their respective "personalities"), and rather than "work through" these differences, my associates and I prefer to effect referral to a more compatible resource. Earnest attempts to match the client to the type of therapist and therapy that he or she seems most likely to profit from, makes *referral* an important procedure.

On what basis are referrals determined? It has been argued that there are three kinds of clients: good clients, who get better no matter who the therapist is; bad clients, who are untreatable regardless of how good the therapist is; and those clients who respond only to certain therapies and specific therapists. Clearly, the need for referral would apply to the second and third categories. There are often clear-cut indications for effecting a judicious referral. Sometimes, it seems obvious that a client will relate better to a therapist who is younger, older, of the opposite sex, whose background and race are more in keeping with the client's, who speaks Spanish (or another language that would facilitate rapport), or someone with specific expertise in a given area or with a particular population (e.g., children, adolescents, or geriatric clients).

Recently, while seeing a 19-year-old man who was experiencing difficulties at home and at college, I felt myself "rowing upstream" for three sessions. In essence, we did not seem to be getting anywhere. Consequently, I referred him to an associate who was much closer to him in age, on the hunch that he might be able to achieve a better alliance. I was correct. In the initial session, the client addressed issues he had withheld from me—the fact that he smoked marijuana daily, and a basic fear that he might be homosexual. When my colleague inquired why he had not shared this information with me, the client said, "Dr. Lazarus reminds me too much of my father, and I was unable to open up to him, just as I am unable to discuss things with either my mother or father."

Given the absence of untoward features that would undermine the development of a therapeutic alliance, relationship building becomes an integral part of the problem-identification sequence. In other words, while eliciting information from the client, while searching for antecedent factors, ongoing problems, and maintaining variables, and while ferreting out those subtle and elusive clues that point to appropriate technique selection (to be discussed in greater detail elsewhere in this chapter), one reflects empathy when appropriate, provides evidence of genuine caring, understanding, acceptance, and similar basic facilitative conditions. For a small minority of clients, "relationship therapy" is both necessary and sufficient; for the majority, the context of client–therapist rapport is the soil that enables the techniques to take root (Lazarus & Fay, 1984).

Armed with data from Modality Profiles, Structural Profiles, and other sources, the sessions become task oriented as emphasis is placed on mitigating the specific problems across the client's BASIC I.D. The therapist endeavors to pinpoint the types of interventions that are most likely to be of specific help in each instance. Whether or not the practitioner who carried out the multimodal assessment will perform the necessary treatments depends on his or her technical armamentarium. For example, a client may be referred to a biofeedback expert for help with sensory problems, while the primary therapist continues to work with the client in other areas.

While many psychotherapeutic systems refer to a beginning phase, a middle phase and a sequence devoted to terminating therapy, in most instances, multimodal therapy does not follow this typical format. After establishing the working alliance and developing the problem check-lists, therapy continues until most of the major items on the Modality Profile no longer constitute a problem, at which point the treatment comes to a logical and operational end. Much more frequently, clients elect to terminate therapy long before each and every entry on their problem profile has been addressed and successfully resolved. In most cases, when the more disturbing or debilitating features have been overcome, the client will decide to "go it alone." He or she usually feels capable of living with the remaining problems, or has acquired sufficient coping skills from the therapy to apply them in a self-help capacity and thereby further attenuate residual difficulties. It is not my practice to discourage clients from discontinuing therapy unless I have good reason to suspect that serious consequences may result. It might also be mentioned that some clients elect to undergo several different courses of therapy, preferring to deal with different problems at different times (and perhaps with different therapists). In several instances, booster or check-up sessions are necessary at 3-month or less frequent intervals, and this may be required for several years. I have clients with whom ongoing therapy has long since terminated, who consult me from time to time for situational crises, or who request "annual check-ups." There have been some clients, who, despite the goal-directed and task-oriented nature of the approach have nonetheless developed undue dependency and with whom treatment termination became a problem unto itself. These cases are very much the exception rather than the rule.

The fact that many clients are inclined to leave before all problems throughout the BASIC I.D. have been dealt with may suggest that our treatment plans are too elaborate, and that the goals we set for our clients are loftier than their goals for themselves. It should be understood that the Modality Profile (BASIC I.D. Chart) endeavors to list a wide range of problems, and that the goal of therapy is very rarely to eliminate each and every item. To aim for a completely problem-free *modus vivendi* is at best unrealistic. (Perhaps this is what is meant by "self-actualization.") Rather, the aim of multimodal therapy is to deal with as many specific problem areas as seem feasible, cost-effective, and worthy of attention. Thus, a client who has overcome debilitating anxiety, whose interpersonal dealings are no longer sources of emotional anguish, and who has triumphed over previously incapacitating guilt reactions might say, "I know that I am still a little too concerned about public opinion, and I do still tend to fuss over my kids more than I should, and I have one or two other hang-ups, but nobody's perfect, and I can live with myself just the way I am."

Thus, it should be clearly understood that the Modality Profile provides the total "blueprint" of the major and minor problem areas, and that the specific treatment goals are then selected from the total list. In some instances, the goal might be to focus on one or two of the main problematic modalities; in other cases, we would shoot for all seven (without necessarily aiming to *eliminate all*) problem items. It is most important for the therapist to avoid suggesting treatment goals that clients are unlikely to attain.

Structure of Treatment Sessions

Typically, treatment sessions begin by asking the client for an update. "What has happened this week?" If specific homework assignments had been suggested, the session would probably open by addressing these issues. "Did you have that conversation with your brother-in-law, and did you count calories and note them down?" I take notes during sessions, usually jotting down reminders to review certain issues, check-up on assignments, and raise particular matters that may clarify hitherto obscure points. Sometimes clients have pressing problems or other immediate agenda items that supersede the ongoing treatment plan. Reticent clients may have to be prodded to bring additional matters to light. "Before we continue with the relaxation and imagery exercises, is there something you'd like to talk about?"

A caveat at this juncture seems timely. Many years ago, one of my supervisors erroneously stated that whatever a client elects to discuss is important. Nonsense! Some clients may dwell on trivial events as a smokescreen, blotting out and avoiding the real issues. They may ramble or babble on tediously about irrelevant matters. There are gentle and effective ways of cutting into the flow. "You have told me a good deal about Paul and Amy's marriage, but I'd much rather hear about your own relationship, particularly how you feel about Ron's new job." With some clients, considerable vigilance is required to ensure that the therapy remains on target. In this regard, a technique called "bridging" has proved most effective.

Bridging refers to a procedure in which the therapist deliberately tunes into the client's preferred modality before branching off into other dimensions that seem likely to be more productive. Thus, if the therapist is eager to hear about the client's feelings, emotional reactions to a given incident, but is receiving no more than intellectual barriers from the client, the bridging maneuvers might proceed as follows:

THERAPIST: How did you feel when Sol just walked out and drove away?

CLIENT: Well Sol probably inherited his irascible nature from his mother. I could speak for hours about his family background.

THERAPIST: [trying to remain problem focused] Did his behavior upset you, the way he just got up and left?

CLIENT: His brother behaves the same way. They learned it from their mother. The old man, their father, was a sweet guy . . .

Comment. At this juncture, many therapists might be inclined to interrupt the client by pointing out that she is not answering the question, by challenging her intellectualizations, or perhaps by interpreting her "resistance." In many instances, these onslaughts are counterproductive. Clients often feel hurt, misunderstood, criticized, or attacked when therapists countermand their flow of ideas. In this example, we have a therapist who wishes to enter the client's affective domain, while the client is insistent upon remaining in the cognitive modality. Gaining access to the affective modality via the bridging tactic would require the therapist to go along with the client's cognitive content (usually for no more than 2 to 5 minutes) and then switch to a less threatening modality (e.g., the sensory area) before finally readdressing the affective reactions. Thus, the interchange might continue as follows:

THERAPIST: [continuing to join the client's cognitive output] So Sol in some ways is a carbon copy of his mother.

CLIENT: He has a few more redeeming features or I would never have married him, but it is interesting how Sol and his brother took after the mother, whereas their sister is just like her father—the Freudians would have a field day analyzing the family identifications. Mildred, that's the sister, chose to marry a man who is a lot like Sol in some ways. . . . [The discussion remains focused on Sol's family dynamics for the next several minutes.)

THERAPIST: [bridging] By the way, while we've been talking about Sol and his family, have you noticed any particular *sensations* anywhere in your body?

CLIENT: Sensations? (*pause*) I don't know what you mean exactly, but I would say that my chest, well really it's more my throat and jaws feel tensed up.

THERAPIST: Let's just pay attention to those tense sensations in your throat and jaws. Would you mind closing your eyes and studying those sensations for a few moments?

CLIENT: (*complies; sits with eyes closed for about 45 seconds*) I notice that my breathing is very shallow.

THERAPIST: Is the tension and the shallow breathing in any way connected to feelings and emotions?

CLIENT: (*opens her eyes*) I don't know what you mean. (*pause*) Damn! I think I'm going to cry! He can be such a bastard! (*tearfully*) Let me tell you something. I don't deserve to be mistreated by him. (*cries*)

THERAPIST: So I guess you feel both sad and angry.

CLIENT: (*sobbing*) And I feel abandoned. (*continues crying*) Oh well, I guess there's no point in sniveling about it.

THERAPIST: Well, have you expressed these feelings to Sol, or have you continued to pretend that it doesn't bother you?

CLIENT: (*drying her tears*) I think you and I ought to rehearse a little speech, like we did that time with Margery [her employer].

Comment. It should be reemphasized that a therapist's failure to tune into the client's presenting modality can lead to feelings of alienation—the client may feel misunderstood, or may conclude that the therapist does not speak his or her language. Thus, multimodal therapists *start where the client is* and then bridge into more productive areas of discourse. Usually, I would have stayed with the affective reactions until I felt fairly convinced that the client had fully accepted her feelings, but since she obviously wanted to move towards an action-oriented solution that seemed quite relevant and appropriate, we launched into assertiveness training.

Second-Order BASIC I.D. Assessments

The initial BASIC I.D. Chart (Modality Profile) translates vague, general, or diffuse problems (e.g., depression, anxiety, unhappiness) into specific, discrete, and interactive difficulties. Thereafter, while avoiding push-button panaceas, the initial selection of techniques is usually straightforward. Relaxation training is applied when undue physical tension is evident; dysfunctional beliefs will call for the correction of misconceptions; timid and unassertive behaviors suggest the application of assertiveness training. Nevertheless, treatment impasses arise—for example, when a client's unassertive reactions are not being changed despite the diligent application of role playing, behavior rehearsal, modeling, and other assertiveness training. When this occurs, a more detailed inquiry into associated behaviors, affective responses, sensory reactions, images, cognitions, interpersonal factors, and possible biological considerations, may shed light on the situation. This recursive application of the BASIC I.D. to itself adds depth and detail to the macroscopic overview afforded by the initial Modality Profile. Thus, a client who was not responding to assertiveness training, when asked to examine, in detail, the repercussions of assertive responses across the BASIC I.D., revealed a significant "cognition" that seemed to account for his "resistance." In essence, it seemed that he did not feel *entitled* to certain rights and privileges. Consequently, "cognitive restructuring" was required before role playing and other behavioral measures proved effective.

Hypothesized Active Ingredients of Treatment Approach

In most forms of effective therapy, clients receive a desideratum not usually available in many situations, that is, an active listener who is essentially nonjudgmental, accepting, tolerant, patient, considerate, honest, and nonpejorative. For some, the mere exposure to a respected professional who displays genuine caring and sustained good-will is sufficient to induce what Franz Alexander (1932) called "a corrective emotional experience." Indeed, for a number of clients, therapy seems to be a constructive reparenting experience.

The main hypothesized ingredients of change, from a multimodal perspective, may be listed as follows:

- Behavior: Positive reinforcement. Negative reinforcement. Punishment. Counterconditioning. Extinction.

- Affect: Admitting and accepting feelings. Abreaction.
- Sensation: Tension release. Sensory pleasuring.
- Imagery: Coping images. Changes in self-image.
- Cognition: Greater awareness. Cognitive restructuring.
- Interpersonal relationships: Nonjudgmental acceptance. Modeling. Dispersing unhealthy collusions.
- Drugs/biology: Better nutrition and exercise. Substance abuse cessation. Psychotropic medication when indicated.

SPECIFIC TECHNIQUES

Behavioral Strategies

Multimodal therapists are technically eclectic (as opposed to theoretically eclectic) and endeavor to select methods from diverse disciplines without necessarily subscribing to the theoretical doctrines that gave rise to them. The evidence (e.g., Rachman & Wilson, 1980) points to the efficacy of behavioral and cognitive-behavioral procedures over most (but not all) other interventions. Consequently, the majority of techniques employed by multimodal therapists are the standard fare of routine behavior therapy, and certainly fall comfortably within the realm of cognitive-behavior therapy. (The role of nonbehavioral and noncognitive strategies will be discussed in a later section of this chapter.)

The differences between technical eclecticism and theoretical eclecticism need to be underscored. Basically, the theoretical eclectic (also known as "synthetic eclecticism") attempts to integrate diverse theories, whereas the technical eclectic uses a variety of techniques within a carefully selected and delimited blend of compatible theories. The main problem with theoretical eclecticism is that it ends up with a haphazard mixture of incompatible notions. Technical eclecticism (or "systematic eclecticism") uses a variety of techniques within a theoretical structure that is open to verification or disproof. Many theoretical systems rest on entirely different and incompatible epistemological foundations. Attempts to integrate these systems are as futile as trying to mix oil and water. Technical eclecticism sidesteps the syncretistic muddles that arise when attempting to blend divergent models into a super-organizing theory. As the introduction to the present chapter implies, the multimodal framework rests on *social learning theory, general systems theory,* and *group and communications theory.* These theoretical systems blend harmoniously into a congruent framework.

As Wilson (1980) underscored, "the most potent methods of therapeutic change appear to be those that are performance based" (p. 291). The essence of effective therapy seems to be the capacity to persuade our clients to do different things, and to do things differently. There are two major components that enter into the successful application of behavioral techniques: (1) The therapist should be well versed in the specifics of the various procedures so that he or she displays an aura of genuine knowledge, confidence, and competence; and (2) An effective practitioner should know how to instigate clients to adhere to treatment prescriptions. The first condition is relatively simple. Many paraprofessionals have been adequately trained to conduct *in vivo* desensitization, to administer token economies, to employ stimulus control, modeling, nonreinforcement, and to assist clients who are recording and self-monitoring various behaviors. Technique proficiency *per se* is not at all difficult to achieve. There is, however, another level that involves knowing when and when not to use a particular procedure, how to introduce it and, if necessary, "sell it" to the client, and whether to make modifications that will jibe with a client's idiosyncratic perceptions. These skills demand special knowledge and training. And as for achieving cooperation and compliance from one's clients, this is no less a problem in the practice of medicine than it is in psychotherapy, and entire books have addressed this crucial topic (e.g., DiMatteo & DiNocola, 1982; Shelton & Levy, 1981).

To illustrate some of the foregoing points, the case of Mrs. Graham, a 32-year-old dental assistant who complained of depression and general anxiety since her divorce, seven months earlier, should underscore some important elements. She had consulted a psychiatrist, but discontinued therapy with him when he had recommended an antidepressant. "I don't believe in drugs!" she declared. The second therapist she consulted was fired when he attempted to introduce imagery techniques. "I don't believe in mind games," Mrs. Graham stated. Next, she saw a therapist whose psychoanalytic penchant was a turn-off. "I don't believe in rehashing my childhood!" she said. What did Mrs. Graham believe in? It was simple to ascertain that she was a firm believer in astrology, the occult, and especially in the impact of "magnetic field forces" *vis-à-vis* sickness and health.

My assessment revealed that Mrs. Graham was extremely tense and suffered from various muscular aches and pains that seemed to be a direct consequence of her inability to relax. Even more importantly, she satisfied most of the diagnostic criteria of a major depressive episode as listed in DSM-III: Her appetite was poor and she had lost weight; her sleep was light and fitful; she had lost interest in many formerly enjoyable activities; she complained of chronic fatigue; she blamed herself for the breakup of her marriage and was filled with self-reproach; she complained of a diminished ability to concentrate. Moreover, there was a family history of depression, her mother and two paternal aunts having received courses of electroconvulsive therapy.

There were other problem areas, but in order to achieve significant inroads, it seemed necessary to overcome her debilitating depression and chronic tension as rapidly as possible. Significantly, before consulting me, she had purchased a popular book on the cognitive treatment of depression. "I soon realized that that stuff would not work for me," she said. I concurred with the psychiatrist who had recommended anti-depressant medication. It was also my opinion that Mrs. Graham would derive benefit from training in deep muscle relaxation. Given her negativism, the clinical challenge was how to gain her cooperation and compliance. The obvious answer was to provide a context that made sense in terms of her expectancies and addressed her phenomenological perspective.

THERAPIST: Are you familiar with the concept of homeostasis?

CLIENT: It's sort of like equilibrium isn't it?

THERAPIST: Right. Our bodies, our physiological processes endeavor to keep things balanced, stable, somewhat constant. But various factors can disrupt this process and throw us off balance.

CLIENT: Like what?

THERAPIST: Well, let's talk about electromagnetism. Physicists have been studying the magnetic properties of electrical currents for many years. As you know, our central nervous system generates and works through electrical impulses. Our brains are partly made up of neurotransmitters and receptor sites. Now if something goes wrong with the way these electromagnetic impulses travel to and from certain parts of the brain, psychophysiological disorders result. We end up feeling depressed, anxious, tense, and fatigued. Are you following me?

CLIENT: More or less. It seems to make a great deal of sense to me.

THERAPIST: Have you ever heard of Mesmer?

CLIENT: Can't say that I have.

THERAPIST: Well he was one of our psychiatric forefathers who practiced what he called "animal magnetism" in the late eighteenth century. Anyhow, if he were alive today, he might say that the break up of your marriage plus various other stressors have thrown your magnetic field forces off center, and that we have to remedy this situation before you can start feeling better.

CLIENT: Well, I must say that you're the first therapist who has talked sense to me.

THERAPIST: Thank you. But you haven't asked me how we go about changing your magnetic field forces.

CLIENT: Well you're the doctor.

THERAPIST: Ah, but I don't think you will like or agree to one of my remedies.

CLIENT: What's that?

THERAPIST: Let's first talk about biofeedback. Do you know what that is?

CLIENT: Like EEG machines?

THERAPIST: Yes, and there are EMG machines—that's short for electro-myogram—and many other devices that can measure your magnetic field forces. But even without these machines, if you are willing to practice certain relaxation exercises, and if you work to acquire the skill of relaxing, letting go of tense muscles several times a day, it will modify your electromagnetic impulses and begin to get back to a state of neuromuscular and central and autonomic nervous system equilibrium, and this could make a big difference.

CLIENT: So why would I disagree with that?

THERAPIST: There's another component. The two go hand in hand. In the same way that you require positive and negative terminals for electricity to be conducted, I don't think that one strategy alone will work. While you are altering the electromagnetic impulses in your neuromuscular areas through specialized relaxation training, it is also necessary to deal directly with the neurotransmitters and receptor sites in your brain. As I said, either method alone will not do the trick—we need the synergestic properties of both.

CLIENT: Are you suggesting that I need brain surgery?

THERAPIST: (*laughing*) Brain surgery? No, no. There are certain medications that directly alter the receptor sites in the brain. But you told me that you refuse to take medication.

CLIENT: That's what they give to schizophrenics. Are you saying that you think I'm schizophrenic?

THERAPIST: Many schizophrenics are treated with medicines called "phenothiazines." I am talking about something entirely different. I believe that a first rate psychopharmacologist, that is a psychiatrist who specializes in the use of psychotropic or neuroleptic medication, will prescribe either a monoamine oxidase inhibitor, or a tricyclic, but since you refuse to go this route, frankly I feel like an electrical engineer with one wire instead of two, and with half a magnet.

CLIENT: When I said that I was anti-drugs, I was referring to tranquilizers and those sorts of things that make you into a zombie.

Comment. Is there anything unprofessional or unethical about bending the truth to achieve compliance and obtain a salubrious result? I think not. The package in which the technique is wrapped will often determine if it remains unopened, is opened and discarded, or put to good use. For example, it has been established that the effective treatment of obsessive-compulsive disorders requires such techniques as response prevention and flooding (e.g., Steketee, Foa, & Grayson, 1982). However, as already stated, technique selection is one facet; how techniques are introduced, the manner in which they are delivered, and the way they are implemented will make the difference between compliance and noncompliance.

In behavior therapy, one of the most central aspects, regardless of the problem being treated, is the use of homework assignments. Certainly, the way I practice therapy renders most of the behavioral strategies applied in my office preludes to excursions, confrontations, and other activities that will take place in the client's day-to-day milieu. Thus, the first article on "behavior rehearsal" (Lazarus, 1966) suggested that when clients role play and rehearse appropriate, albeit difficult, interpersonal encounters, they are far more likely to put these skills to good effect *in vivo* than when they are merely given advice, or when they receive a nondirective reflection of their fundamental feelings. As already stated, it is the extent to which clients engage in new or different activities between therapy sessions that usually constitutes the difference between success and failure. Certainly, the evidence from many outcome studies (see Wilson, Franks, Brownell, & Kendall, 1984) suggest that without specific homework assignments (*in vivo* activities), it is unlikely that phobic disorders, social skills problems, obsessive–compulsive behaviors, or sexual dysfunctions could be significantly changed.

Giving homework assignments with which clients are likely to comply calls for attention to specific details (Shelton & Ackerman, 1974; Shelton & Levy, 1984) among which the more obvious are:

1. Be explicit and extremely clear about the precise actions you wish the client to carry out.
2. Specify the exact frequency, time, duration of each assignment.
3. Ascertain that the client regards the assignment as pertinent and relevant.
4. Determine that the client does not view the assignment as too time-consuming in terms of its "cost effectiveness."
5. Ensure that what is being asked of the client is not too threatening. (First provide direct skill training when necessary.)
6. Commence with assignments that are easy to carry out.
7. When giving homework assignments, present them as requests, or as suggestions, rather than as orders or instructions.

The following clinical excerpt illustrates some of these points:

THERAPIST: Do you think it makes sense for you to talk to your husband about that incident with his secretary?

CLIENT: I know there was nothing serious going on between them, but even though I know this, and even though she no longer works there, I feel I want to let him know exactly how I was feeling at the time.

THERAPIST: I agree with you. I think that if you just let it slide and said nothing more about it, history will repeat itself simply because your husband won't be aware of a basic groundrule in your marriage.

CLIENT: I should have brought it up two weeks ago, but I've kept putting it off. I guess I'm waiting for the right time or something.

THERAPIST: Actually, after you and I rehearsed what you would say I thought you would go straight home and discuss it then and there.

CLIENT: That would have made sense. I don't know why I keep putting it off.

THERAPIST: Well, something is making it difficult for you. What's the worst thing that could happen?

CLIENT: I don't know. (*pause*) I guess I don't want to seem picky.

THERAPIST: Do you think your opinion on the matter is picayune? It seems to me that you have a valid point, that you are entitled to your feelings, and that you have every right to express them.

CLIENT: No, I agree.

THERAPIST: Well does it make sense if, right after dinner tonight, you tell him that you want to discuss an important issue with him?

CLIENT: Yes. Basically, my point is that there are other ways of building up employee morale than by going out for private lunches, and leaving the office to drive someone's else's kids home from school is above and beyond the call of duty.

THERAPIST: Tell me truthfully, is your main objection that this could have turned into a romantic interlude? What I am asking is whether the fact that he was doing this for a woman is the main objection.

CLIENT: Not really. My point is that Bill tries so hard to be Mr. Nice Guy that he may end up a dead-end street. Like the time he left the conference to drive Martin, that kid who had just joined the firm, to the train station. . . .

THERAPIST: Fine. So let's make sure that you don't merely talk about the secretary but that you also bring up other matters that concern you about his going too far to please other people. Let's role play it again. Okay? Let me play the part of your husband. We have finished our dinner and you tell me that you have something important to discuss with me. [Role playing and behavior rehearsal continue for about 10 minutes.]

CLIENT: Well, Professor Higgins, I think I've got it.

THERAPIST: Good! So when will you *do* it? No more procrastination.

CLIENT: Tomorrow evening, for sure. I don't want to get into it tonight because we're having dinner with some friends, and I'd rather not bring it up before going to bed in case it turns into a lengthy discussion.

THERAPIST: Are you afraid that it will lead to an argument?

CLIENT: No, but I want to be sure that Bill really sees my point and doesn't humor me, or pretend to agree just to get me off his case.

THERAPIST: Fair enough. Let's see. Today is Tuesday. (*opens appointment book*) Can you give me a call on Thursday between one and two just to let me know how it went?

CLIENT: Sure.

THERAPIST: I have the feeling that you will discuss those issues with Bill because I am pushing you, prodding you, and that you will do it mainly to get me off your back. I want you to do it for *you* not for me.

CLIENT: No, no. It's for me all right. As you know, I procrastinate and I need a little shove from time to time.

Comment. Most therapists seem to agree that the role of new experiences provided to the client are crucial for facilitating change. Davison (1980) stated: "In my own clinical work, I view the therapy situation as one in which the client can try out new ways of thinking, feeling, and behaving, both within the therapy relationship (that is, to myself) and outside the consulting room . . . As for *how* such experiences are created, I sometimes become more heavy-handed under certain circumstances" (p. 273). Behavior change requires *work*—both from client and therapist.

The Role of Cognitive Therapy

In late 1969 and early 1970 a detailed and systematic follow-up inquiry of 112 cases, randomly selected, led me to question the durability of "pure" behavior therapy. The findings revealed that 36% had relapsed anywhere from 1 week to 6 years after therapy. On the other hand, certain clients had maintained their therapeutic improvements despite the intrusion of inimical circumstances. Referral to the case notes of these individuals revealed that their improvements were often contingent upon the apparent adoption of a different outlook and philosophy of life and increased self-esteem—in addition to an increased range of behavioral skills. *Thus, the synergy of behavioral and cognitive methods became evident.* These findings were published in my book *Behavior Therapy and Beyond* (Lazarus, 1971), which advocated a "broad-spectrum" approach and was one of the first texts on "cognitive-behavior therapy."

Clinicians who limit themselves to conditioning procedures and who eschew cognitive processes, will soon find that people are capable of overriding the best-laid plans of contiguity, reinforcements, and modeling by their own thinking. The cognitive domain addresses the subjective use of language, semantics, expectancies, problem-solving competencies, goals, and the selectivity of perception, as well as the specific impact of beliefs, values, and attitudes on overt behavior. Some of the main cognitive errors include overgeneralization, dichotomous reasoning, perfectionism, categorical imperatives, nonsequitors, misplaced attributions, "catastrophizing," jumping to conclusions, and excessive approval seeking. To the extent that our clients engage in one or more of these dysfunctional cognitions, they will be prone to a variety of behavioral problems and affective disturbances.

Many years ago, Ellis (1962) stressed that a human being, unlike an animal, "can be rewarded or punished by his *own* thinking, even when this thinking is largely divorced from outside reinforcements and penalties" (p. 16). Beck (1976) in his classic test on cognitive therapy underscored that "the specific content of the interpretation of an event leads to a specific emotional response" (p. 51). He then emphasized that "we can generalize that, depending on the kind of interpretation a person makes, he will feel glad, sad, scared, or angry—or he may have no particular reaction at all" (pp. 51-52).

The following dialogue illustrates typical cognitive interventions:

CLIENT: When people first meet me they think I'm sweet, charming, lovable, and kind, but when they get to know me better, they discover that I'm a nasty bit of work.

THERAPIST: What does your nastiness consist of?

CLIENT: I can be spiteful. I get envious and jealous when other people do better than I do. I have a sharp tongue and can use it like a knife to cut other people down. I can act considerate and concerned, and good-hearted, but the real me is the opposite—nasty, selfish—that's what I really am.

THERAPIST: Instead of believing that there is one *real you*, and that this true and basic you is a negative, nasty, spiteful, or even hateful person, I'd like you to consider that you have different facets to your personality, that each aspect is just as real as any other. Thus, the kind, warm, loving, giving, accepting part is no more or less real than the nasty part. So I am saying that in certain situations, and at various times, the positive components are brought out, and at other times, in different settings, under other circumstances, the negative aspects come to the fore. But each is equally "real." What do you think about that?

CLIENT: Well, I'm pretty sure I know where and how I learned to dislike myself. I had two, not just one, overly critical parents. "You're bad!" "You're nasty!" "You're a wicked child!" That's what I grew up with.

THERAPIST: Okay, so now it's time for you to unlearn that faulty labeling and reframe your own thinking. If your parents understood logical and rational thinking, they would never have called you bad. They would have pointed to a specific thing that you did and they would have called that behavior "bad." Do you understand that fundamental distinction?

CLIENT: Yes, but instinctively I look at things more . . . what's the word? . . . globally. Here's a perfect example. I caught my girlfriend out on a lie, and as far as I'm concerned, that makes her a liar, and I want nothing to do with liars. Don't you agree that if she has told a lie once, it follows that she can and will lie again and again?

THERAPIST: Here are two quick reactions. First, it would depend on the magnitude of the lie and the motive behind it. And secondly, if your girlfriend tells lies 10% of the time, that makes her 90% honest.

CLIENT: Isn't that like being a little bit pregnant?

THERAPIST: All or none? Not at all. Tell me, if someone is selfish 20% of the time, and distinctly unselfish the other 80% is this person selfish or unselfish?

CLIENT: (*pause*) I see what you're getting at.

THERAPIST: You do? Tell me.

CLIENT: Well I sort of get this idea of a balance scale, and you weigh everything to see which is greater or more frequent.

THERAPIST: My analogy of your style of thinking is that you reach into a basket of apples, pull out a rotten one, and conclude that the entire basket is made up of rotten apples instead of looking further. So your definition of a liar is anyone who ever told a single lie. If someone acts stupidly on a given occasion you would conclude that the person is totally stupid.

CLIENT: But that's the way I was raised . . . .

THERAPIST: I'm not blaming you for being the way you are. Whether or not the reason you think as you do is 100% due to your critical parents is beside the point. Let's get you to change your way of thinking here and now and forever more. Try this sentence on for size. Will you close your eyes and repeat this five or six times? "The nice part of me is just as real as the nasty part." Will you say that aloud and then think it silently?

CLIENT: (*complies, and after a pause says*) I'm going to have to work to let that sink in.

THERAPIST: True. It will take some effort from you. I'm going to give you a book that I wrote with a good friend and colleague [Lazarus & Fay, 1977], which lists some of the common mistakes that many people make in the way they think and act. I'd like you to read it carefully and tell me which of the mistakes you identify with. Will you do that?

CLIENT: Sure.

THERAPIST: If a picture is worth a thousand words, certain books can be worth, not a thousand sessions, but give or take a dozen.

Comment. In multimodal therapy, cognitive restructuring is seldom a necessary and sufficient intervention, but modifying dysfunctional beliefs is often essential if constructive change is to ensue. To be pedantic, I use "bibliotherapy" fairly extensively with clients who enjoy reading, and it certainly has expedited the treatment process with innumerable individuals. Readers who are familiar with Albert Ellis's treatment procedures will note from the foregoing excerpt that while I concur completely with his reasoning, my therapeutic style is rather different. As an aside, I have seen many of Ellis's trainees trying to emulate his style—right down to his Bronx/New York accent—instead of learning from this giant and remaining themselves. My style also differs from Beck's Socratic method of asking questions, although clients who are averse to didactic instruction would be treated in the Beckian manner. In general, I find a directive stance more rapid and effective; it exemplifies the psychoeducational thrust of multimodal therapy. I find no difficulty in integrating cognitive and behavioral strategies. If, for instance, while teaching a client to dispute his or her own dysfunctional beliefs a significant degree of anxiety seems to occur, it is simple and natural to shift to a relaxation or desensitization sequence. If, while examining irrational ideas, we come upon response deficits, the use of behavior rehearsal is readily introduced. In short, it is my experience that cognitive and behavioral methods are positively synergistic.

The Role of Nonbehavioral and Noncognitive Strategies

The most obvious caveat concerns the use of any psychological technique by itself in the face of major biological disturbances that are amenable to somatic interventions. People who are grossly psychotic—delusional, extremely confused, markedly withdrawn and behaviorally inappropriate, homicidal, or suicidal—usually require drug therapy to become amenable to psychological interventions. From a multimodal standpoint, as Fay (1976) underscored, "It is clear that the taking of drugs is affected by the six other modalities and in turn produces results which affect the other modalities" (p. 66). A client with a clear-cut bipolar depressive disorder in the manic phase of the illness is referred to a psychiatrist who most likely prescribes lithium. When the medication has taken effect, one or more of the following interventions are administered: behavioral, sensory, imagery, cognitive, interpersonal.[2] The "D." modality also involves the encouragement of health habits—good nutrition, exercise, and recreation.

---

2. Unlike other modalities—behavior, sensation, imagery, cognition, interpersonal relationships, biological considerations—affect cannot be treated directly. Affect is a product of the reciprocal interaction of the other six modalities, and can be worked with only indirectly. "I arouse emotion directly by getting people to scream while pounding foam rubber cushions," one therapist informed me. "No," I replied, "you are arousing emotions via behaviors (screaming and pounding are not emotions) and by generating sensations and images." Affect is derived from and can only be reached through behavior, sensation, imagery, cognition, interpersonal relationships, and biological processes. This conception is the core of the multimodal position. Regardless of the affective disorder under scrutiny, it holds that thoroughness in assessment requires an inquiry into the other six modalities: B-S-I-C-I-D.

Outside of the biological modality, is any intervention nonbehavioral or noncognitive? Surely nearly all forms of psychotherapy try to teach people to think, feel, and act differently. Nevertheless, I employ techniques that are regarded as outside the purview of cognitive-behavior therapy by certain authorities (e.g., Kazdin & Wilson, 1978; Wilson, 1982; Wolpe, 1984) and have been criticized for polluting the system by so doing. Thus, I shall describe some of these "non-cognitive-behavioral" techniques and attempt to justify their value.

Time Projection (Forward and Backward)

Clients with fairly vivid imaginations can readily picture themselves going forward or backward in time. By going several months into the future and picturing themselves adding more and more rewarding events to their daily lives, some depressed individuals experience a diminution in negative affect (Lazarus, 1968). "Time tripping" into the past can help clients relive, modify, and work through various events. Here is an example:

CLIENT: I was a kid when all this garbage was shoved into my head. What the hell does a 5-year-old know? How could I stand up to my parents and tell them that they're talking crap? So these tapes are still there, and often play on "automatic." Today, as a 24-year-old I realize the truth, but back then I had no measuring stick to show me that it was all clap-trap that they were handing me, and somehow there must be a part of me that still believes it.

THERAPIST: Would you mind trying out a little fantasy excursion? Sit back and relax, let yourself ease comfortably into the chair. (*pause*) Now please close your eyes, and imagine that we have a Time Machine that can transport you into the past, and then bring you right back into the present. I'd like you to pay a visit to yourself in the past. You can visit little Michael aged 10, 9, 8 or whatever. At what age would you like to visit yourself in the past?

CLIENT: Say around 5 or 6.

THERAPIST: Okay. You step into the Time Machine, and instantly you go back and visit yourself at age 5. The 5-year-old Michael looks up and sees a man walking towards him. Of course, he doesn't realize that this is himself, grown up, 24 years of age, coming back out of the future. But he senses something special about that man, he feels a deep affinity for him, and so he will listen to him. Can you get into that picture?

CLIENT: (*pause*) Yes. The 5-year-old me is playing in the yard and the 24-year-old me comes up to him, puts a hand on his shoulder, and says, "Michael, I want to talk to you."

THERAPIST: Excellent! Now talk to him. What do you want to tell him?

CLIENT: Michael, your mom and dad have told you a lot of things about sin, and the devil, and hell, and all that sort of thing. That's all nonsense, Michael, just nonsense! Don't believe it. Just pretend to go along with it because if you tell them it is nonsense, they will punish you. But listen to me, Mike. You're a good kid. (*pause*)

THERAPIST: Can you explain to 5-year-old Mike that it's all right if he doesn't do brilliantly at school? [The session continues in this vein for another about 5 minutes.]

CLIENT: (*very emotional at this juncture*) Mike, remember what I'm telling you. It's the truth.

THERAPIST: I guess it's time to come back to the present now. Do you have any final words of wisdom for little Michael?

CLIENT: Just remember that Mom and Dad are wrong. They mean well, but they talk a lot of crap about religion.

Comment. Imagery procedures that metaphorically tap "right brain" material are often effective in achieving what pure "left brain" cognitive disputation and rational reasoning are unable to do. Elsewhere (Lazarus, 1985) I described the case of a man who went back in time and enacted several imaginary dialogues with his father and grandfather (to whom he attributed his current lack of self-confidence). In these dialogues, he persuaded his father and grandfather (and thus convinced himself) that their standards of manliness were irrational and obsolete. In my view, these and several other imagery techniques (Lazarus, 1984b) can readily be seen as being within the compass of cognitive-behavior therapy, but since they did not emanate from laboratory studies, and since their value is purely clinical and anecdotal (as opposed to experimental and confirmed via controlled studies) many behavioral practitioners tend to "boycott" them.

The Deserted Island Fantasy Technique

Here is another "non-cognitive-behavioral" technique that I have found extremely useful and that I have been taken severely to task for employing (since it too lacks an empirical data base vis-á-vis its controlled clinical effectiveness). Many years ago, a particularly frustrating client led me to remark that I'd need to observe her 24 hours a day to get beyond her enigmatic facade. She retorted, "Well, let's go and spend a few months on a desert island." Ignoring the possible seductive undertones, I asked her what I would learn about her on the island. She painted a verbal picture that proved highly informative. Her fantasies about our island sojourn enabled me to infer a great deal about her. Despite the subjective nature of this interaction, I had indeed emerged with considerable knowledge about her significant thoughts, feelings, and actions. Subsequently, I found that this fantasy journey yielded important clinical information with many clients. Initially (Lazarus, 1971) I used to refer to it as a *desert* island, but the term *deserted* seemed more accurate (i.e., it was not a barren wilderness, being lush and green but uninhabited). Secondly, there are advantages to conjuring up a person other than the therapist on the island. An entire chapter replete with an actual therapy transcript has spelled out this technique in considerable detail (Lazarus, 1981).

Basically, the client is enjoined to enter into a fantasy experiment wherein a magician tells him or her, "When I wave my magic wand you will instantly appear on a deserted island and you will remain there for 6 months." The client is informed that while he or she is on the island, the rest of the world will remain in suspended animation: Time will stand still. Being a magic island, there are no dangers and there is an adequate supply of food and provisions. "Now, before waving his magic wand, the magician gives you a choice: He allows you to choose company or solitude. Would you prefer spending 6 months alone, or would you rather find a pleasant person of the opposite sex [or, when dealing with homosexuals, a person of the same sex] waiting for you on the island?" Thereafter, the client is encouraged to "run with the fantasy," with less imaginative clients being given prompts to help them along: "How will you occupy your time?" "What will happen?" "Do you think you'll be bored?" One gets a clear picture from this procedure of the client's capacity for developing and maintaining close, genuine relationships. With this technique, one can readily detect how much manipulation, deception, asocial, antisocial, and other maladaptive patterns are likely to be present.

There are several other techniques drawn from various nonbehavioral disciplines that I use fairly extensively—but within a cognitive-behavioral framework. For example, the well-known "empty chair technique" drawn from psychodrama and Gestalt therapy is particularly useful in many cases for instigating assertive behavior. Another nonbehavioral technique is Rogerian reflection. Frequently, it is judicious merely to make clear by mirroring for the client the affective impact of his or her meandering. This seems to be especially helpful when clients express conflicts and other ambivalent feelings. In these instances, by holding up a "psychic mirror," the therapist is often more facilitative than when offering direct advice. Unlike Rogerians, we seldom find empathic reflection, genuineness, unconditional positive regard, and so on, both necessary and sufficient for effecting behavioral change. Rather, when the client has been helped to clarify certain areas of confusion and uncertainty via nonintrusive acceptance and reflection, it is time to take action. At this juncture, we revert to behavioral rehearsals, assignments, and other objective coping strategies. But the point is that while adopting a Rogerian stance, we are into a "nonbehavioral" realm.

Let me stress again, that while drawing on Rogers, or Perls, or Freud, or any other personage or system for particular techniques, we do not necessarily subscribe to the theories that are embraced by any of the specific school adherents. We may have a client reclining on a couch, free associating, for reasons that are entirely different from those that Freud and his followers espouse. I consider it a serious error for a therapist to bypass or ignore techniques that do not emanate from or readily fit into his or her theoretical predilections. As McFall (1985) has underscored: "Most psychologists probably would agree that no single existing theory, perspective, or approach in psychology is capable of explaining everything observed in human behavior" (p. 28). As London (1964) emphasized: "However interesting, plausible, and appealing a theory may be, it is techniques, not theories, that are actually used on people. The study of the effects of psychotherapy, therefore, is always the study of the effectiveness of techniques" (p. 33).

ROLE OF THE THERAPIST

Clinical Skills and Other Crucial Therapist Attributes

Obviously, from what I have said in the preceding section, in my book, a good therapist will have at his or her disposal an arsenal of many different techniques. But there is more. Knowing how to administer various techniques must go hand in hand with knowing *when* to select a given procedure. One must also know how to introduce it into the therapy so that the client understands the rationale and is most likely to cooperate. Also, a good therapist is, at the very least, an intelligent consumer of research in the field. For example, therapists who treat phobias with Rogerian reflection, or with psychodynamic insights, or with cognitive disputation, are unlikely to make significant clinical headway, because, as the research evidence has shown, some form of *exposure*—imaginal and/or *in vivo*—is called for. In the successful treatment of obsessive–compulsive disorders response prevention and flooding techniques are a *sine qua non* (Steketee, Foa, & Grayson, 1982). Several specific behavioral techniques are the treatments of choice for the management of sexual problems such as impotence, orgasmic dysfunction, premature ejaculation, and dyspareunia (Leiblum & Pervin, 1980). Marital dysfunction usually requires techniques aimed at teaching more positive and productive interpersonal behaviors (Jacobson & Margolin, 1979). A therapist who is not *au courant* with the pertinent literature on treatment effectiveness will often end up wasting his or her clients' time and money, will fail to help many who could have benefitted from someone more knowledgeable, and may even exacerbate matters in certain instances (Mays & Franks, 1985).

Technical proficiency should neither be minimized nor underestimated, yet it has often been said that the client–therapist relationship is paramount, and that techniques *per se* are of little consequence. There are some clients for whom, as Schofield (1964) emphasized, psychotherapy is essentially the purchase of friendship. In my experience, if measurable gains are to be achieved, client and therapist have to *work*, not merely *relate*. Those for whom a warm, empathic, genuine, and caring relationship are both necessary and sufficient to achieve significant gains, constitute a very small minority. Nevertheless, as already mentioned earlier in this chapter, without a client–therapist rapport, the best engineered techniques are unlikely to take effect. Thus the mechanisms of change cannot be divorced from the person administering the particular procedures. As surgeons are apt to point out, it is the person wielding the scalpel who can use it as an instrument of destruction or of healing. In psychotherapy it is virtually impossible to separate specific mechanisms and techniques from the person administering them.

Certain common characteristics have been very apparent to me among all highly successful therapists I have been privileged to know. The term "hostile" could not be applied to any one of them. On the contrary, their degree of patience, tolerance, and nonjudgmental acceptance was sometimes astonishing. This is not to say that they lacked assertiveness. However, when they took a firm stand with a client, it was done in a supportive, nonattacking manner. In thinking about these clinical virtuosos, their genuine respect for people stands out, as does their flexibility and fundamental responsibility. And each one of them is funloving, articulate, and unpretentious, with a delightful sense of humor. There is more. They practice what they preach; they are authentic and congruent, and they are unafraid of revealing their shortcomings. Interestingly, the majority of these spectacular therapists are unknown beyond the confines of the small towns or large cities in which they practice. They are not internationally revered giants who bask in the limelight of their colleagues' admiration. Indeed, they have been too busy practicing good therapy to find time for self-serving promotions of their wares. I have met many of them by chance—at clinical meetings, at workshops, and through the happenstance of being cotherapists or consultants for certain enmeshed couples and families.

Many people resolve their conflicts, solve their problems, and overcome their disturbances as a result of processes that lie outside their therapists' attributions. Extratherapeutic factors such as environmental changes, biological shifts, and various fortuitous effects (Lazarus, 1980) will produce salubrious outcomes, perhaps even in those instances where the therapist is a somewhat noxious human being. Thus, even the poorest practitioner is likely to develop a coterie of supporters. The truly gifted clinician is exemplified by a demonstrable capacity to be of help to a wide variety of clients, while remaining fully cognizant of his or her limitations, and constantly seeking for the active ingredients of psychological change—instead of taking credit for unintentional influences. Let us take a close look at the "bad guys."

Common Treatment Errors Leading to "Bad Therapy"

It is my impression that "bad therapy" is often carried out by well-intentioned but poorly trained practitioners who apply incorrect techniques or, perhaps, select the correct techniques but administer them incorrectly. While ignorance and incompetence on the therapist's behalf do not constitute desirable attributes, they are infinitely less pernicious than narcissism, hostility, seductiveness, and a need to exploit the client due to greed, insecurity, or downright sadism. Unfortunately, I have encountered more than a small number of therapists whose personalities are well-suited to tossing hand grenades into enemy bunkers, and who treat their patients like dangerous adversaries or antagonists. They use diagnostic labels like bayonets. "My doctor said that I have a borderline personality." "She said that I was an obsessive and passive–aggressive something or other." "Dr. K. said that I have schizophrenic tendencies." The foregoing are literal quotes from three clients who were members in the same therapy group led by "Dr. K."

Among my trainees, perhaps the most common error is that of trying too hard to effect change. The students are often eager to prove to their supervisors (and to themselves) what effective change agents they are, so that they tend to rush their clients to take action—very prematurely at times.

Another common error is that of pursuing a favorite line of inquiry, or employing a particular procedure despite no evidence of change. I find this especially true of those who are strongly devoted to cognitive therapy. They tend to continue to argue, cajole, dispute, challenge, explain, interpret, and reframe. Instead of switching to a different modality (e.g., imagery) they seem of the opinion that a change in cognition is the be-all and end-all.

In listening to one of my student's therapy tapes, I noted that he had launched into a lengthy self-disclosure regarding some of his own shortcomings and limitations. When asked to justify this procedure, he claimed that he was modeling anti-perfectionism and the virtues of fallibility. While selective self-disclosure is often an effective strategy, it was evident to me that the student's motive was more one of receiving, than of giving, therapy. I pointed this out and after a few moments of reflection he admitted that I was correct. It is most important for therapists to be aware of their own motives—otherwise the possibilities of making endless errors are rampant.

Wolf, Wolf, and Spielberg (1980) have addressed the most salient helpful and harmful responses that typify good and bad therapy. At the top of their list of destructive responses are examples of grossly judgmental and intolerant attitudes. Therapists who display disgust, disdain, impatience, blaming, disrespect, intolerance, and guilt-induction, are included in this category. Here are some typical responses:

- *Disdain:* "Yes, I know what you are all about alright. Unfortunately, your type is all too common."
- *Guilt:* "Why didn't you wake up and do something *before* your son got hooked on drugs?"
- *Blame:* "You made a mess of that situation and now you expect me to pick up the pieces."

Next, Wolf *et al.* refer to "blatant insensitivity and inaccuracies," wherein the therapist fails to appreciate the client's feelings, or is highly inappropriate in the timing of his or her remarks. They also mention the destructive impact of the clinician's anger and defensiveness, as well as the fostering of dependence. A classic example of the latter is the following statement: "You've come a long way during these past 18 months, but if you terminate therapy now, you'll be right back to square one before you know it." Less damaging, but nonetheless disruptive, are instances of poorly timed or irrelevant questions, confusing remarks, and false reassurance.

To end this section on a positive note, Wolf *et al.* (1980) point out that "very helpful responses" and "extremely helpful responses" share a number of common features. They include: concise and accurate phrasing, perceptiveness, sensitivity to relevant and highly charged emotional issues, the display of profound respect and significant understanding, and the appropriate use of humor. Their major facilitative conditions include empathy, respect, genuineness, warmth, concreteness, self-disclosure, and immediacy. Whether or not these facilitative core qualities can be taught or "techniqued" is an open question. Personally, it is my belief that these are attributes that students bring with them into their training programs. Those who do not possess them to start with will inevitably end up without them—regardless of their academic credentials, or the excellence of the clinical training programs to which they are exposed.

COMMON CLINICAL ISSUES

Preventing Resistance and Noncompliance

Throughout this chapter, several allusions have been made regarding the attainment of the client's active cooperation. There is an additional strategy that has not been mentioned: *tracking the "firing orders" of the specific modalities.* This refers to the fact that different people tend to generate negative affect through individualistic perceptions of the BASIC I.D. Thus, some clients dwell first on aversive images (I) (pictures of dire events and a variety of horrors), followed by unpleasant sensations (S) (tremors, sweating, palpitations, and shortness of breath), to which they attach negative cognitions (C) (ideas about their impending death), leading to maladaptive behavior (B) (withdrawal, avoidance, and isolation). This ISCB firing order (Imagery–Sensory–Cognitive–Behavioral) will tend to require a different treatment strategy from that employed with say a CISB reactor (Cognitive–Imagery–Sensory–Behavior), or with someone with yet a different sequence. For example, our clinical findings suggest that it is usually better to select techniques that adhere to the client's chain reaction. When someone reports that he or she starts with the *sensory modality*, it is usually advisable initially to introduce biofeedback, relaxation, and so on. "My anxieties usually begin to develop when I tune into the fact that my body is feeling a little "off," such as a queasy feeling in my stomach, or a little tension in my neck. This sets off the chain. These feelings grow stronger as I attend to them, and then new ones develop, and pretty soon I start *thinking* that something dreadful is going to happen to me. These thoughts start up a whole series of *memories and pictures* of the time I came down with pneumonia—which went undiagnosed for 6 weeks." Here we have a Sensory–Cognitive–Imagery pattern. Thus, after teaching the client several sensory techniques (relaxation, specific biofeedback, breathing exercises, etc.), the cognitive modality is attended to (e.g., instructing the client in positive self-talk) followed next by imagery methods (e.g., the use of specific pictures wherein the client sees him- or herself being healthy, warding off disease, etc.).

On the other hand, if a client's anxiety is triggered first by cognitions ("I'm doing fine when suddenly I start thinking of all the things that could possibly go wrong"), followed by images ("Then I see myself, quite vividly, passing out and making a complete fool of myself"), leading to negative sensations ("My hands get clammy, my chest tightens up, and I get butterflies in my stomach"), the use of biofeedback/relaxation as a first line of attack would usually not be especially effective, since the sensory mode is the *third* sequence in the chain. My clinical observations suggest that when one selects techniques that follow the client's individual sequence, the therapeutic impact is augmented. And in my experience, most clients have little difficulty tracking their respective "firing orders" when asked to do so. Some clients demand a rationale for technique selection, and by explaining that their own patterns of response will be matched to the specific ordering of techniques, many thereby prove less resistant.

Some Additional Tactics for Overcoming Resistance

At times, a client's resistance or noncompliance may be a function of his or her view that the therapist's investment and involvement with and interest in resolving his or her problems is insufficient (i.e., below his or her expectations). Under these circumstances, some remedies proposed by Fay and Lazarus (1982) include:

- An unsolicited telephone call by the therapist to follow up on something that was discussed in the session.
- Shifting the locus of therapy to outside the office, such as outdoor walking sessions, a session in the park, or, under certain circumstances, a home visit by the therapist.
- Sharing a mutual avid interest such as playing tennis or chamber music together.

We must not continue making the same mistakes with clients who are not responding, repeat the mistakes other therapists have made, or in general fit the client in a procrustean fashion into a unimodal framework.

Many therapists believe that contact with the client outside the normal confines of a therapist's office creates "boundary" problems. The personalistic emphasis of the multimodal tradition would oppose any such blanket taboo. There are indeed clients with whom all dealings should always be strictly "professional" and who would take unkindly to extramural contact. In my experience, these people are in the minority, and have usually comprised the more seriously disturbed individuals who have consulted me.

The most uncooperative clients are generally those individuals who are not seeking therapy voluntarily, but who have been coerced into coming. People referred by the courts, and children reluctantly dragged in by their desperate parents fall into this category. In these instances, practicing paradoxical techniques, or simply doing something that is out of character, thereby violating the client's expectations, can initiate a major change. Thus, the following dialogue ensued with a hostile 16-year-old boy who had been cutting class, fighting with his two siblings, and allegedly using marijuana to excess:

THERAPIST: I decided to ask your parents to remain in the waiting room so that you and I could talk privately. I gather that you've been having a pretty rough time of it at home and at school. If you'd like to fill me in, share with me what's been going on with you, I might be able to help.

CLIENT: I don't need any help.

THERAPIST: Well, it seems to me that a lot of people are on your back. Is that true?

CLIENT: No.

THERAPIST: How's school?

CLIENT: School's school.

THERAPIST: They said you were cutting classes.

CLIENT: That's their problem, not mine.

THERAPIST: Nothing and nobody is bugging you?

CLIENT: Right.

THERAPIST: So your parents brought you to me under false pretenses. I see people who are unhappy in some way, shape, or form, and together we figure out ways and means of overcoming their problems. With you, I'm going to earn my fee the easy way—without working. If I simply discharge you and tell your parents that you have no troubles or problems, they will take you to another shrink. So here's what I'm going to do. I have a lot of work and reading to catch up on. You just sit here until the hour is up while I do my reading. Then I charge your parents for my time anyway. This way, we both come out ahead. I get to do my reading, and you are not pestered by a therapist trying to help you. (*selects a book and starts to read*)

CLIENT: (*after 2 to 3 minutes*) How much do they pay you?

THERAPIST: Who?

CLIENT: Like my parents.

THERAPIST: At least $80 an hour. Isn't that nice? I'm getting paid by your parents to catch up on my reading. I wish all my clients were like you.

CLIENT: Do you ever *really* help anyone?

THERAPIST: Unfortunately I don't get paid by other people simply to sit here and read my books—I have to work hard and really help them.

CLIENT: Yeah, but all this garbage of going back into my childhood and examining my dreams, I don't see how that can help.

THERAPIST: I don't work that way. I prefer to stick to the here-and-now and to get into real problem solving. I believe simply that two heads are better than one, and that when my clients and I look at problems from different angles, we usually come up with solutions.

CLIENT: Yeah, but you don't know my parents.

THERAPIST: True, but if you fill me in, maybe I can come up with something useful.

CLIENT: What if I said my mother's a real ball-buster.

THERAPIST: I'd believe you and I'd try to help you figure out a way of coping with her.

CLIENT: Well she's always on my case.

THERAPIST: Does she treat you differently from the way she treats your sister and brother?

CLIENT: You're damn right she does. She's always played favorites. My sister can do nothing wrong. . . .

Comment. We were soon off and running, and within 15 minutes had established a working liaison. After a few additional individual sessions with the young man, it became evident to me that family therapy was indicated. I had no trouble shifting from an individual therapy format to a family systems arrangement, although working with the five of them made me feel that I was indeed earning my fee the hard way!

Typically, when a treatment impasse is reached, one or more of the following factors seems to be operative:

1. An absence of rapport, or inappropriate matching. (In these instances, referral to a more appropriate resource is usually the best solution.)
2. Inaccurate assessment (especially the therapist's failure to identify relevant antecedents and/or maintaining factors).
3. An exclusive focus on intraindividual factors, thereby leaving ample room for saboteurs in the client's social network to undermine the therapy.
4. Therapist errors and blunders (especially the use of inappropriate techniques).
5. The faulty or incorrect use of appropriate techniques—usually a function of inadequate training.
6. Extreme degrees of "psychopathology" in the client.
7. The client's unwillingness to expend the necessary effort to effect meaningful change.

Note that most of the variance, in my view, rests with the therapist, and pertains to his or her skills, or the lack thereof. Only the last two items reflect possible excesses and deficits within the client. (For comprehensive coverage of these and other aspects of "resistance," see Lazarus and Fay, 1982.)

Fostering Generalization and Maintenance of Therapeutic Gains

As already stated in several places throughout this chapter, to facilitate *in vivo* transfer from the client–therapist relationship to significant others and to ensure generalization from the treatment setting to work, home, and social environments, one of the major tactics has been the systematic use of *homework assignments*. Furthermore, generalization may be enhanced by involving important members of the client's social network. Involvement of the social network permits the therapist to mitigate negative attitudes within the family toward change in the client. Moreover, by bringing family members into the office, one is better able to control noncontingent reinforcement in the client's natural environment. Collaboration by therapist, identified patient, and social network facilitates many aspects of behavioral retraining, emotional growth, and value transformation.

While it is not routinely feasible for therapists to go into the client's natural environment, extramural excursions are sometimes necessary for generalization to occur. At times, a paraprofessional or auxilliary therapist works with the client at home or in work or recreational settings under the therapist's direction. Participant modeling and reinforced practice *in vivo* may be particularly helpful in this situation.

It is often valuable for the therapist to maintain telephone contact with the client in the interval between sessions. For example, a client may practice social skills in an individual or group therapy setting, but frequently will not take emotional risks in life unless prompted, exhorted, monitored, reinforced, and encouraged by daily telephone calls.

One of the most useful tactics for generalizing control of punitive responses in couples is the use of a tape recorder at home, on vacations, in the car, or even when talking on the telephone. Couples and families quickly learn to refrain from aggressive exchanges in the therapist's office but revert to destructive habits in other settings. The use of a tape recorder heightens self-awareness and tends to inhibit destructive communication in natural settings. Clients may bring in the tapes for review during the sessions to further facilitate the learning of prosocial and effective communication styles, and the unlearning of dysfunctional ones.

Two of the most effective techniques that provide an important prelude to the transfer of therapeutic gains are *behavior rehearsal* and *coping imagery*. Behavior rehearsal, using audiocassettes or even videotapes as ancillary aids, employs role playing to ensure that the client develops appropriate interpersonal skills. Coping imagery consists of evoking systematic mental pictures in which the client sees him- or herself dealing with inimical situations, and yet managing to get through them. The rationale for recommending several brief coping imagery practice sessions per day is that most of us need to see ourselves performing adequately in our mind's eye *before* we can venture forth into the real-life situation with any sense of confidence.

In terms of *maintenance*, it is generally accepted that with addictions, frequent booster sessions and careful after-care tactics are required if relapse is to be avoided. In general, however, my follow-up inquiries have shown that a number of clients retain their recoveries until significant, but often predictable, circumstances take them by surprise. Relapse would often not have occurred had clients been prepared to cope with events that resided in their future. This can be achieved through rehearsal via projected imagery. By taking stock of challenges that are most likely to occur and by encouraging the client to visualize him- or herself coping with these events, one can enhance the client's capacity to deal with them effectively. These "emotional fire drills" tend to ward off the hazards of "future shock."

In essence, comprehensive therapy probably offers the best prevention against relapse, thus maximizing the likelihood of long-term maintenance. When treatment outcomes and therapeutic gains were shortlived, follow-ups (Lazarus, 1981) revealed not that therapy was too shallow, but that an insufficient number of areas had been covered (i.e., therapy was too narrow).

Other Populations

While I have confined my comments throughout this chapter to the multimodal treatment of adult outpatients (since that is the population I deal with in most instances) it should not be thought that the approach has no value with different populations in various settings. Brunell and Young (1982) have edited a compelling volume detailing the application of multimodal assessment and therapy to psychiatric inpatients. Keat (1979) described multimodal therapy with children. Pearl and Guarnaccia (1976) discussed multimodal therapy and mental retardation. Slowinski (1985) described the use of multimodal methods with two recalcitrant "ghetto clients." Ridley (1984) commented on the specific virtues of the multimodal approach for the nondisclosing black client. Edwards and Kleine (1986) have addressed multimodal consultation with gifted adolescents. There is scarcely a clinical entity for which multimodal assessment and therapy cannot be proposed and implemented. The BASIC I.D. paradigm has even been applied to community disasters (Sank, 1979).

Multimodal therapists are drawn from the full range of "health service providers." Psychiatrists, psychologists, social workers, pastoral counselors, and other mental health workers have members who are well versed in and employ multimodal methods. This is consonant with the trend in current psychotherapy toward multifaceted, multidimensional, and multidisciplinary interventions. Multiform and multifactorial assessment and treatment procedures have become widespread. Nevertheless, it needs to be underscored that while all multimodal therapists are (technically) eclectic, all eclectic therapists are not multimodal practitioners.

OVERALL EFFECTIVENESS

At present there are Multimodal Therapy Institutes in New York, Illinois, Ohio, Pennsylvania, and Virginia. Data obtained from several colleagues at the different institutes plus the findings from my own outcome and follow-up studies have been reliable and reasonably impressive. Multimodal therapy is an approach that endeavors to incorporate state-of-the-art research findings into its framework. It is not intended as yet another "system" to be added to the hundreds already in existence. The multimodal practitioner tends to scan the field for better assessment and treatment methods and tries to be at the cutting edge of clinical effectiveness.

A 3-year follow-up of 20 "complex cases" who had completed a course of multimodal therapy (e.g., people suffering from extreme agoraphobia, pervasive anxiety and panic, obsessive–compulsive rituals, or enmeshed family or marital problems) showed that 14 maintained their gains or had made additional progress without further therapy. Moreover, a recent survey of 100 clients who had failed with at least three previous therapists (thereby ruling out the "placebo reactors" and those mildly disturbed individuals who require little more than a good listener and a touch of empathy) revealed that 61 had achieved measurable and unequivocal benefits. For example, there were quantifiable *decreases* in compulsive behaviors, depressive reactions, marital and family disputes, panic attacks, sexual inadequacy, and avoidance behaviors. There were corresponding *increases* in assertive responses, work-related achievements, and prosocial behaviors. Significantly, many of these clients were regarded by their previous therapists as "intractable." In terms of overall statistics, during the past seven or eight years, more than 75% of the people who have consulted me have achieved their major treatment goals. Data from other multimodal practitioners are in keeping with my own findings. Failures are minimized by a strong willingness to use teamwork, cross-referrals, and by explicitly seeking second and third opinions when doubts arise.

The populations with whom we have been least effective include drug addicts and substance abusers in general, character disorders, grossly inadequate personality disorders, a certain number of bipolar depressives (despite the use of lithium in addition to a thorough attempt to traverse the BASIC I.D.), and a number of people with florid psychoses. At times, we have failed because someone in the client's social network managed to sabotage what we were attempting to achieve (Kwee, 1984). There are some clients who appeared to be receiving too many secondary gains for them to relinquish their maladaptive behaviors. (See Lazarus, 1986, for additional details on applications and research.)

In terms of future directions, perhaps the first point of emphasis should be on controlled experimentation. Attempts to receive the necessary funding to test certain propositions have been unsuccessful. Consequently the virtues of employing Modality Profiles, Structural Profiles, Second-Order BASIC I.D. assessments, and the use of tracking modality "firing orders" are all based on uncontrolled clinical observations. It should be remembered that the multimodal orientation is an open approach, not a closed system. Consequently, its practitioners maintain a vigilant lookout for state-of-the-art assessment and treatment strategies that are readily incorporated into the technically eclectic framework. Thus, depending on what the field at large generates over the next decade, the entire spectrum of multimodal methods may, or may not, undergo extensive changes.

CONCLUDING COMMENT

The editor of this volume has asked me to address a specific issue. He said:

> With your approach more than most of the others discussed in this book, I have a problem distinguishing between the therapy technology and the therapist who is providing the technology. I have always wondered when

reading your work, what proportion of the variance in your effects result from your modalities and strategies per se, and what proportion results from your own unique clinical skills. Furthermore, it is not just Neil Jacobson who has wondered about this. Do you frequently experience frustration with students who may apply the multimodal approach effectively, but get inferior results because they lack your natural clinical skills?

I have been accused, quite justly at times, of being an elitist. This is because I refuse to work closely with students who do not possess "natural clinical skills." For me, it is a given that any aspirant multimodal clinician is basically warm, empathic, perceptive, insightful, caring, and has a history of having been the confidant and counselor of friends and associates long before entering any professional training program. Given these fundamental attributes, we then teach our students to think more critically, to reason more logically, to become more astute observers (i.e., to be hyper-alert to inconsistencies and anomalies), and to develop courage and boldness in doing what has to be done to best serve one's clients. Thus, I am seldom frustrated by my students' clinical performance. At times, they are inept, but so is virtually any therapist, no matter how skilled and how well-trained. Clearly, while practice does not make most things perfect, it usually does enable one to make fewer and fewer blunders. After having practiced therapy for more than a quarter of a century, I have acquired a "data bank" that not only renders me a lot more effective than I was 10 to 15 years ago, but also signals when best to quit trying to achieve the impossible. Knowing one's personal limitations as well as the upper limits of existing psychotherapeutic knowledge, saves time and money, and reduces frustration.

A most important point about the multimodal orientation is that it tries to articulate specific procedures that expedite assessment and therapy. In retrospect, the multimodal tradition had its inception in 1963 when, as a visiting assistant professor in the Department of Psychology at Stanford University, I was teaching "behavior therapy" to graduate students. I made liberal use of one-way mirrors: Students would observe me treating numerous clients, and we would subsequently discuss the rationale behind the choice of specific techniques. Frequently, a student would inquire why I had selected one procedure rather than another; how I had deduced certain factors or inferred others. Sometimes, there were reasonably clear-cut and objective reasons, but just as often, I would say that my previous "clinical experience" or my "intuition" had led me to pursue (or avoid) a specific issue, or had pointed the way to an effective intervention. They were not impressed. Indeed, they had every right to feel that the didactic virtues of such answers left much to be desired. It is incumbent on a teacher to be able to specify, to articulate, and to pinpoint the verbal and nonverbal cues that elicit certain hunches and lead to the selection of particular methods and interventions. Thus, instead of providing glib answers, I really started thinking, "soul-searching," to discover the precise mechanisms that guided my clinical inventiveness.

For example, it is rarely for capricious reasons that a seasoned veteran says to a client, "Can you form a *mental image* of that event?" whereas to someone else under seemingly identical circumstances, he or she asks, "Can you notice a *sensation* somewhere in your body?" Nevertheless, when asked to explain the precise reasoning behind the particular point of emphasis, the expert may be hard-pressed to do so and might contend that "clinical experience," "know how," and "intuition" had all played a part. Closer introspection will probably reveal that the therapist was at least subliminally aware that the first client was especially prone to vivid imagery as a potent agent of change, whereas the second one was much more of a "sensory reactor." Alternatively, the first client may have been *avoiding* any imagery referents, and thus it was likely that an inquiry into this modality might "strike oil" (and likewise for the second client who might have been playing down his or her sensory reactions). My novice students who have learned the tenets of multimodal therapy and are trained to think in BASIC I.D. terms, are told to pay attention to clients' favored modalities and to those they eschew or gloss over, and to zero in on those dimensions when therapy falters. In this way, these novices end up acting like experts.

Many of the multimodal assessment techniques have been formulated to provide beginners with a map, a set of directives, and a template with which to design effective interventions. All good, intuitive, experienced therapists use some form of "bridging" and "tracking" procedures, but it is my contention that there is much to be gained by writing this into the treatment manuals as explicitly as possible. I have been told by some experts that this has sharpened many of their already well-honed procedures, and beginners have told me that they have gained a sense of direction and confidence from having these tactics spelled out for them. It is towards the foregoing ends that multimodal assessment procedures have been designed.

ACKNOWLEDGMENT

My special thanks to Allen Fay, MD, for his cogent criticisms.

REFERENCES

Alexander, F. (1932). *The medical value of psychoanalysis.* New York: Norton.

Beck, A. T. (1976). *Cognitive therapy and the emotional disorders.* New York: International Universities Press.

Brunell, L. F., & Young, W. T. (Eds.). (1982). *A multimodal handbook for a mental hospital: Designing specific treatments for specific problems.* New York: Springer.

Davison, G. C. (1980). Some views on effective principles of psychotherapy. *Cognitive Therapy and Research, 4,* 273.

DiMatteo, M. R., & DiNicola, D. D. (1982). *Achieving patient compliance: The psychology of the medical practitioner's role.* New York: Pergamon.

Edwards, S. S., & Kleine, P. A. (1986). Multimodal consultation: A model for working with gifted adolescents. *Journal of Counseling and Development, 64,* 598–601.

Ellis, A. (1962). *Reason and emotion in psychotherapy.* New York: Lyle Stuart.

Fay, A. (1976). The drug modality. In A. A. Lazarus (Ed.), *Multimodal behavior therapy.* New York: Springer.

Fay, A., & Lazarus, A. A. (1982). Psychoanalytic resistance and behavioral nonresponsiveness: A dialectical impasse. In P. L. Watchel (Ed.), *Resistance: Psychodynamic and behavioral approaches.* New York: Plenum.

Jacobson, N. S., & Margolin, G. (1979). *Marital therapy: Strategies based on social learning and behavior exchange principles.* New York: Brunner/Mazel.

Kazdin, A. E., & Wilson, G. T. (1978). *Evaluation of behavior therapy: Issues, evidence, and research strategies.* Cambridge, MA: Ballinger.

Keat, D. B. (1979). *Multimodal therapy with children.* New York; Pergamon.

Kwee, M. G. T. (1984). *Klinische multimodale gedragstherapie* Lisse, Holland: Swets & Zeitlinger.

Lazarus, A. A. (1966). Behavior rehearsal vs. non-directive therapy vs. advice in effecting behavior change. *Behaviour Research and Therapy, 4,* 209–212.

Lazarus, A. A. (1968). Learning theory and the treatment of depression. *Behaviour Research and Therapy, 6,* 83–89.

Lazarus, A. A. (1971). *Behavior therapy and beyond.* New York: McGraw-Hill.

Lazarus, A. A. (1980). Toward delineating some causes of change in psychotherapy. *Professional Psychology, 11,* 863–870.

Lazarus, A. A. (1981). *The practice of multimodal therapy.* New York: McGraw-Hill.

Lazarus, A. A. (1984a). Multimodal therapy. In R. J. Corsini (Ed.). *Current psychotherapies* (3rd ed.). Itasca, IL: F. E. Peacock.

Lazarus, A. A. (1984b). *In the mind's eye: The power of imagery for personal enrichment.* New York: Guilford.

Lazarus, A. A. (1985). A brief overview of multimodal therapy. In A. A. Lazarus (Ed.), *Casebook of multimodal therapy.* New York: Guilford.

Lazarus, A. A. (1986). Multimodal psychotherapy: Overview and update. *International Journal of Eclectic Psychotherapy, 5,* 95–103.

Lazarus, A. A., & Fay, A. (1982). Resistance or rationalization? A cognitive–behavioral perspective. In P. L. Watchel (Ed.), *Resistance: Psychodynamic and behavioral approaches.* New York: Plenum.

Lazarus, A. A., & Fay, A. (1984). Behavior therapy. In T. B. Karasu (Ed.), *The psychiatric therapies.* Washington, DC: American Psychiatric Association.

Leiblum, S. R., & Pervin, L. A. (Eds.). (1980). *Principles and practice of sex therapy.* New York: Guilford.

London, P. (1964). *The modes and morals of psychotherapy.* New York: Holt, Rinehart & Winston.

Mays, D. T., & Franks, C. M. (Eds.). (1985). *Negative outcome in psychotherapy and what to do about it.* New York: Springer.

McFall, R. M. (1985). Nonbehavioral training for behavioral clinicians. *The Behavior Therapist, 8,* 27–30.

Meyer, A. (1915). Objective psychology or psychobiology with subordination of the medically useless contrast of mental and physical. *Journal of the American Medical Association, 65,* 860–862.

Pearl, C., & Guarnaccia, V. (1976). Multimodal therapy and mental retardation. In A. A. Lazarus (Ed.), *Multimodal behavior therapy*. New York: Springer.

Rachman, S. J., & Wilson, G. T. (1980). *The effects of psychological therapy* (2nd ed.). New York: Pergamon.

Ridley, C. R. (1984). Clinical treatment of the nondisclosing black client. A therapeutic paradox. *American Psychologist, 39,* 1234–1244.

Sank, L. I. (1979). Community disasters: Primary prevention and treatment in a health maintenance organization. *American Psychologist, 34,* 334–338.

Schofield, W. (1964). *Psychotherapy: The purchase of friendship*. Englewood Cliffs, NJ: Prentice-Hall.

Shelton, J. L., & Ackerman, J. M. (1974). *Homework in counseling and psychotherapy*. Springfield, IL: Charles C. Thomas.

Shelton, J. L., & Levy, R. L. (1981). *Behavioral assignments and treatment compliance: A handbook of clinical strategies*. Champaign, IL: Research Press.

Shevrin, H., & Dickman, S. (1980). The psychological unconscious: A necessary assumption for all psychological theory? *American Psychologist, 35,* 421–434.

Slowinski, J. W. (1985). Three multimodal case studies: Two recalcitrant '"Ghetto Clients" and a case of post-traumatic stress. In A. A. Lazarus (Ed.), *Casebook of multimodal therapy*. New York: Guilford.

Steketee, G., Foa, E. B., & Grayson, J. B. (1982). Recent advances in the behavioral treatment of obsessive-compulsives. *Archives of General Psychiatry, 39,* 1365–1371.

Wilson, G. T. (1980). Toward specifying the "nonspecific" factors in behavior therapy: A social-learning analysis. In M. J. Mahoney (Ed.), *Psychotherapy process: Current issues and future directions*. New York: Plenum.

Wilson, G. T. (1982). Clinical issues and strategies in the practice of behavior therapy. In C. M. Franks, G. T. Wilson, P. C. Kendall, & K. D. Brownell, *Annual review of behavior therapy: Theory and practice* (Vol. 8). New York: Guilford.

Wilson, G. T., Franks, C. M., Brownell, K. D., & Kendall, P. C. (1984). *Annual review of behavior therapy: Theory and practice* (Vol. 9). New York: Guilford.

Wolf, S., Wolf, C. M., & Spielberg, G. (1980). *The Wolf counseling skills evaluation handbook*. Omaha, NE: National Publication.

Wolpe, J. (1984). Behavior therapy according to Lazarus. *American Psychologist, 39,* 1326–1327.

Zilbergeld, B. (1982). Bespoke therapy. *Psychology Today, 16,* 85–86.

CHAPTER 9

A Contextual Approach to Therapeutic Change

Steven C. Hayes
University of Nevada, Reno

The behavior therapy movement was never primarily a movement to bring behaviorism into applied psychology. If there was ever any doubt about this, the trends over the last 10 years within behavior therapy should have resolved the doubts. We have seen the ascendance of cognitive analyses, self-based analyses, and mere empiricism as substitutes for a truly behavioral analysis of clinical problems.

Perhaps there is nothing wrong with this. Cognitive analyses, for example, have a long tradition within both psychology and the culture at large. Presumably they haven't survived without having some value. What seems unfortunate, however, is that behavior therapists often have little facility with behaviorism and with behavior theory. Because of this, the possible contribution of a very different perspective on human behavior has been greatly attenuated.

My purpose in this chapter is to show one way in which what I take to be the essence of radical behaviorism might be applied to adult clinical problems. I am not claiming that this is the only way to apply this perspective to adult problems—it is just one way that I hope is of some value. Before describing the therapy approach itself, I shall need to discuss briefly the basic philosophical moves I take to be at the heart of radical behaviorism. Many psychologists easily become frustrated with philosophy and hope to escape having to take philosophical stands by retreating into empiricism (e.g., Adams, 1984). There is no way, however, to understand the present approach to therapy without also understanding the assumptions it stands on and to distinguish these assumptions from those within the mainstream culture. The reader will quickly note that I have no interest in promoting the caricature of radical behaviorism presented so often in our behavioral journals and texts. I shall then need to explore the fringes of behavior theory to gleen principles and analyses that might apply to humans with verbal abilities. Most well-known behavioral principles were developed with nonverbal organisms. There are good reasons to believe that verbal organisms are very different creatures. This is one reason why many behavior therapists have "gone cognitive." In my opinion, this is the right problem but the wrong solution.

RADICAL BEHAVIORISM

The core of radical behaviorism can be summarized in four words: contextualism, monism, functionalism, and antimentalism. This is obviously not the place to engage in an extended discussion of radical behaviorism, but fortunately for our present purposes we can focus on just a few aspects of the nature of behavior and causality within behavior analysis, and then apply this to the possible role thoughts might play in human action.

What Can Science Study?

It is common in our everyday language to distinguish thoughts, feelings, intentions, and so on from behavior. The entire cognitive-behavioral movement was originally based on this distinction. If behavior therapy treats behavior, so the thinking went, then we need some way to treat thoughts as well. Even the title of this book is based on such a distinction between behavior and cognition.

To understand the historical context of this distinction in psychology, it is useful to distinguish four perspectives: Watsonian metaphysical behaviorism, Watsonian methodological behaviorism, contemporary methodological behaviorism, and radical behaviorism. As Skinner has pointed out (Skinner, 1969), Watson created several long-term problems for behaviorism by the philosophical perspectives he embraced. Useful as they were at the time, it has long since been time to move on. Most psychologists have done so, but unfortunately they have often embraced even more deficient philosophical perspectives. Meanwhile, the word "behaviorism" has retained much of the flavor of these earlier positions.

Watson, reacting to the foundering of introspectionism, was taken to have said two things: (1) nonpublicly observable events do not exist, and (2) all science can study is publicly observable events anyway. The first position can be called Watsonian metaphysical behaviorism. Actually, a sympathetic and careful reading of Watson does not have him taking such a position, but he was widely understood to have advanced it. It is obviously a position that most people will reject since the reality of our own thoughts can hardly be denied. The second position formed the foundation of methodological behaviorism, a position that profoundly influenced American psychology during this century. Basically, this position says that there is a distinction to be made between thoughts, feelings, and other private events on the one hand, and behavior and other publicly observable events on the other. According to this position, only publicly observable events can be considered in science because of the requirements of scientific methodology. Other types of events may exist, but they are scientifically illegitimate, or at least unanalyzable. Originally, this position was used to exclude from scientific consideration the "mental" events being sought by the introspectionists. Over time, however, it had a second and more damaging effect. Since methodological behaviorism does not state that nonscientifically analyzable events do not exist—only that they are unanalyzable—it was possible for psychologists to act as if there were two ontological categories in the world. In other words, methodological behaviorism is implicitly dualistic (Moore, 1981; Skinner, 1969). Contemporary methodological behaviorism (e.g., Mahoney, 1974) has stepped in to take advantage of this obvious gap. In contemporary methodological behaviorism, the definition of what is scientifically analyzable is once again accepted to be publicly observable events, but we are said to be able to use the scientifically analyzable world to make inferences about the scientifically unanalyzable world. Thus, for example, we may not be able to see thoughts directly, but we can see the influence of thoughts on other types of human behavior such as reports on an inventory. The same argument can be applied to events that are completely inferential and *in principle* can never be observed directly by anyone, not even the person "doing it," such as levels of processing, or deep mental structures. Over time, the influence of contemporary methodological behaviorism has led to more and more inferential models, since we must seemingly allow a great deal of inference simply to address questions of fundamental human significance.

Literal dualism is not often embraced by scientists, because of its obvious scientific deficiencies. If spirit is "nonmatter," then it cannot be the qualities of matter such as a beginning or end, mass, acceleration, size, or indeed any discernable properties. How "it" could even be known is problematic under these conditions (Hayes, 1984; Hayes & Brownstein, 1986b). Adherents of methodological behaviorism, which unfortunately include most behavior therapists, thus often deny literal dualism while maintaining that scientific methodology forces a kind of dualism on us all. The problem with this type of dualism for science is that it handcuffs scientific analysis by putting some of the most interesting phenomena out of its direct range.

Radical behaviorism is most often confused with Watson's positions. Contemporary behavior therapy texts still act as if Skinner somehow felt that thoughts, feelings, and the like are illegitimate objects of scientific study. The problem exists because Skinner's position is a fairly sophisticated one that fundamentally changes the way we address this issue. Skinner's point is basically this: Behavior is the observable activity of organisms. Note that the word "publicly" does not appear in this definition. In radical behaviorism, an event that even one person can observe is open to a scientific analysis (Skinner, 1945). How this is possible will be discussed shortly, but the implication is that thoughts are not substantially different by virtue of their private nature. They may have special properties because they are verbal, but they are still behavior.

In summary, Watsonian metaphysical behaviorism is monistic, but excludes the private world from consideration on its own terms. Methodological behaviorism (in both its varieties) is implicitly dualistic. Radical behaviorism is monistic, but includes the world of private experience. Note that in a radical behavioral perspective the distinction between mental and physical is a false one. The distinction between private and public is a real distinction, but it has nothing to do with the mental-physical dicotomy, and is not at all the same as the distinction between subjective and objective. It is quite possible, for example, to do objective analyses of private experience, or subjective (and therefore scientifically invalid) analyses of publicly observable events.

Causality and the Analysis of Behavior

If radical behaviorists view thoughts as behavior, why do they often object to the kinds of analyses so popular in the cognitive–behavioral literature? The problem is not with the phenomenon being studied, but with (1) the implicit dualism inherent in most accounts, and (2) the type of analysis conducted (Hayes & Brownstein, 1986a, 1986b).

Radical behaviorism embraces contextualism, pragmatism, and functionalism. Among other things, this means that behavior can only be understood in context. Literally, behavior can make no sense—even its units of analysis will be unknown—unless the context in which the behavior is occurring is understood. Context is just another word for contingencies of reinforcement, survival, and cultural evolution. Contingencies simply describe the functional relationship of behavior to the events in space and time that precede and follow the behavior, in the lifetime of the individual (reinforcement), in the lifetime of the species (survival), or in the lifetime of a cultural group (cultural evolution). Thus, a behavioral analysis will always come down to the task of contingency analysis. This is the reason that public agreement is not a requirement of scientifically valid observations within a radical behavioral analysis. Even the behavior of scientists is subjected to a contingency analysis. A valid scientific observation occurs when the contingencies controlling the observation establish control by the stimulus environment described in the observation (Skinner, 1945). Events can be publicly agreed upon but still invalid, as when a group of teenagers all mistakenly agree that a glimpsed stranger is actually a well-known rock star. Conversely, events can be private but valid, as when a stranded seaman makes careful daily note of the depletion of the available water supply. In short, observations are scientifically valid to the degree that they are based on *tacts* (Skinner, 1957): verbal behavior under the control of the presence or absence of specific stimuli rather than audience control, states of deprivation, or other such factors (Hayes & Brownstein, 1986a). The teenagers above "see" the rock star because they are motivated to do so and because their peers also "see" the same thing. The sailor's observation is controlled by the water itself, even though it might be more reinforcing to "see" the water supply remain.

In accordance with what has been said so far, a question like "What role do thoughts play in controlling human behavior?" would be changed to "What types of contingencies would lead one behavior to occur and to influence another behavior?" Some authors (e.g., Killeen, 1985) have criticized the usefulness of calling private actions "behaviors," but their are strong reasons to do so. First, it emphasizes that it is the job of psychology to explain these events. If we seek to understand the behavior of an individual, considering thoughts to be behavior requires that we also understand thoughts. Second, it prevents incomplete explanations that are useless for prediction *and* control (see Hayes & Brownstein, 1986a for an extended discussion of this topic). We intuitively recognize that an explanation of one behavior by another is incomplete. For example, if we claimed that a person played racquetball well because she played squash well, we would immediately wonder why she played squash well and why the two are related. We can use the relationship to predict who will be good at racquetball, but it cannot in itself tell us how to produce excellent racquetball playing. Suppose, however, we seemed to change the realms of the two related events. Suppose we claimed that the person played good racquetball because she was confident, enthusiastic, and had high self-esteem. Notice that this explanation does not seem as obviously incomplete as the first. It looks as though the explanatory events are of a different kind than the explained event, and thus are possibly complete. By using the term "behavior" for all organismic activity, this self-deception is made less likely. The operating characteristics of behavior–behavior relationships as scientific explanations are the same whether the relationship is between two overt actions, or between a thought and an overt action. Note that in this last example one could predict based directly on the relationship between thoughts and overt behaviors, but could not use it directly to control the event in question.

There is a final reason to consider private actions to be behaviors. Once we get used to thinking of cognitive control as a matter of behavior-behavior relationships we can begin to think of behavior–behavior relationships in contingency analysis terms. To do this requires that we understand the contingencies giving rise to each behavior *and*—this is the crux of the matter—the relationship between them. Thus we must ask, "What are the contingencies that support the relationship between thoughts and other forms of human action?" In this view the thoughts do not necessarily produce any effect on other behaviors. It is only because of the context (the contingencies) that one form of behavior relates to another. All of what I have said so far has been said simply to justify the behavioral sensibility of this one point. As I shall attempt to show, it can make an enormous difference in the way we approach therapy.

BEHAVIORAL PRINCIPLES RELEVANT TO COGNITIVE CONTROL

It is not an adequate behavioral analysis of thoughts simply to speak broadly about thoughts being behavior. Why, other than the issue of privacy, are thoughts, feelings, attitudes, intentions, purposes, plans, and so on given so much attention? One major possibility is that these behaviors are all to some degree verbal. By examining each of the words above one can see that, with the possible exception of feelings (and it ends up not being an exception), each of these terms adds little unless we think of them occuring in a verbal organism. Suppose, for example, a person says "I have a plan." When asked to explain the plan, he says, "I cannot because I have no idea what the plan is." This would seem very strange. When verbal humans have plans, intentions, or thoughts, and so on we expect them to have these behaviors in a verbally sensible form. Consider, then, the possibility that cognitive control is really a matter of verbal control.

Why would verbal control be at all different from any other type of control? According to Skinner, all behavior is ultimately contingency shaped, but an important subset of behavior is said to be rule governed (1966, 1969). A rule for Skinner, is a contingency-specifying stimulus. I believe we should define a rule as a verbal contingency-specifying stimulus. What I mean by "verbal" will be discussed shortly. Skinner (1969, p. 146) provides an interesting example of rule-governed behavior. An outfielder moves to catch a fly ball. Following its trajectory, he moves under it and grasps it with his glove. The outfielder has done this hundreds or thousands of times. His behavior is presumably largely contingency shaped—that is, moving to the ball is controlled by the position and trajectory of the ball and the outfielder's history of catching balls under similar situations. A dog can easily acquire the same behavior in much the same way (e.g., in catching a Frisbee). Now consider the behavior of a ship captain who is moving her ship to catch a falling satellite. The trajectory of the falling object is analyzed in detail. Mathematical models that take into account a host of factors such as wind speed and drag coefficients are consulted. The place of impact is predicted based on these verbal rules, and then approached. If the rules are adequate and if they are followed carefully and correctly, the satellite will be caught—not because of the ship captain's past success at reacting to the trajectory of satellites, but because of her past success in following rules and the adequacy of the rule itself.

At first it may seem as though rules, since they are stimuli, must operate through the processes of stimulus control identified in the animal laboratory. Skinner has been quite insistent that verbal control over the listener is not itself verbal because it is simply a matter of discriminative control (1957). There is nothing in behavior theory, however, that requires such a solution. Plausible as it seemed 30 years ago, more recent evidence suggests that verbal control has properties that are difficult to extrapolate from discriminative control as seen in the infrahuman laboratory. There is a growing body of evidence that indicates that different processes occur in human stimulus control. The sense that nonbehaviorists have long had that the behavioral processes that influence humans are different from those that influence infrahumans may turn out to be largely correct, at least as far as the degree of influence is concerned. Paradoxically, behavior theory may be well-positioned to study the exact differences between human and infrahuman performance precisely because it has taken an inductive approach to human behavior, emphasizing its continuity with infrahuman behavior.

The Effect of Rules

Human operant behavior often differs significantly from the behavior of other species. In many situations, humans tend to be relatively insensitive to changing contingencies when animals would surely be quite sensitive (Ader & Tatum, 1961; Harzem, Lowe, & Bagshaw, 1978; Hayes, Brownstein, Zettle, Rosenfarb, & Korn, 1986a; Matthews, Shimoff, Catania, & Sagvolden, 1977; Shimoff, Catania, & Matthews, 1981). Humans show patterns of responding that differ markedly from those shown by infrahumans, even on the simplest schedules of reinforcement (Leander, Lippman, & Meyer, 1968; Lowe, Harzem, & Hughes, 1978; Weiner, 1964, 1969). There are many similar differences, all of which underline the fact that human and infrahuman responding may at times be controlled by different variables (Hayes, in press). In the past few years, it has become more and more plausible that some of these differences can be explained as being due to the effects of rules on human action (Baron & Galizio, 1983; Lowe, 1983).

Evidence for this view comes from several findings. First, humans behave just as infrahumans do on simple schedules of reinforcement before they acquire extensive language skills (Lowe, Beasty, & Bentall, 1983). There is considerable evidence that verbal humans are extraordinarily sensitive to instructional control (see Baron & Galizio, 1983 for a recent review). In general, human performance is more like that of other animals when the task is indirect or complex, and when steps are taken to make less likely the direct use of verbal abilities in accomplishing the task (e.g., Lowe et al., 1978; Lowe, Harzem, & Bagshaw, 1978). Compared to shaped responding, instructed performances are far less sensitive to changing contingencies, even in verbal adults (Matthews *et al.*, 1977; Shimoff *et al.*, 1981). With proper instructions, verbal humans can be made to respond in ways that appear to mimic the behavior of infrahumans (Baron & Galizio, 1983), but other research has shown that unlike infrahuman responding, these performances will also be fairly rigid when the contingencies subsequently change (Hayes, Brownstein, Haas, & Greenway, 1986b; Shimoff, Matthews, & Catania, 1986).

What is it about rules that might lead to such profound and generalized effects on the ways in which the environment has an impact upon behavior? In some sense, this is the central question of the cognitive movement within behavioral psychology. More generally, it is the central question we need to answer to understand adult clinical phenomena.

One possible explanation is that rules can generate patterns of responding that preclude effective contact with the contingencies (Galizio, 1979). This requires no special analysis of rule-governed behavior per se. It is well known that it is the actual contingencies we contact, not the programmed contingencies, that influence behavior (e.g., Anger, 1956; Herrnstein, 1970). Thus, if we are led by a rule to behave in ways that keep us from contacting the environment in effective ways, it would not be surprising to see long-term and generalized effects from rules. Several studies, however, have shown that instructions have generalized and detrimental effects on behavior *even when the contingencies are contacted* (e.g., Hayes *et al.*, 1986a). It is also known that rules can easily engage social contingencies that might then profoundly influence behavior—a notion to which I shall return later in the chapter.

An interesting alternative and more exotic possibility has arisen over the last decade. Recent research has shown that humans can readily develop a special type of stimulus control. Consider a situation in which a human is taught that some arbitrary stimulus goes with several others. For example, suppose that we show a young child a picture of several imaginary animals. We tell the child to pick out the "wheezu," and say "correct" only when she points to an animal with eight legs. Now we ask the child to pick out the name wheezu from a list of names and say "correct" only when the written work *wheezu* is selected. In other words, we teach the child that *A* goes with *B*, and *A* goes with *C*, where *A* refers to the spoken name, *B* to the picture, and *C* to the written name. Animals can learn discriminations of this sort quite well. However, if we now ask the child to select the picture that goes with the written word *wheezu* (i.e., to match *B* and *C*) she will do this quite readily (Sidman & Tailby, 1983), even though the choice of *B* in the presence of *C* has never been explicitly reinforced. Similarly, the child will readily match the picture of a wheezu to itself (i.e., will pick *B* given *B*), and will probably be able to say "wheezu" in response to the picture or the word (i.e., will select *A* given either *B* or *C*). This phenomenon is called "stimulus equivalence" and seems to represent a fundamentally different kind of stimulus control. So far as we know, humans are the only animals who show this ability readily. Even primates have not been found to make these kinds of untrained associations (Sidman, Rouzin, Lazar, Cunningham, Tailby, and Carrigan, 1983).

It is possible to interpret stimulus equivalence as a special case of a more general phenomenon (Hayes, 1986; Hayes & Brownstein, 1985). When a human learns that A "is the same as" B, this will always mean that B is the same as A. Over many examples humans may learn to respond to stimuli based on a history with a particular arbitrary relationship between stimuli, or what we have termed a "relational frame." For example, if the relationship is synonymic, when a person matchs B to A, the frame implies that matching A to B will also be reinforced. The combination of two such synonymic frames form the special case called "stimulus equivalence", but in principle many other kinds of relationships can be trained (e.g., opposites). In short, humans can learn that arbitrary stimuli symbolize other stimuli because they can respond to indications of a relationship per se without a need for a direct history in a particular instance (Hayes, 1986; Hayes & Brownstein, 1985).

Let us return to my statement that rule-governed behavior involves control by stimuli that are effective because of their verbal nature. We can now define a verbal stimulus as a stimulus that has its eliciting, establishing, reinforcing, or discriminative properties because of its participation in relational frames (Hayes & Brownstein, 1985). Verbal behavior can be defined as behavior that provides verbal stimuli and has been established and maintained because it does so. If this perspective is worthwhile, there should be a clear relationship between an ability to speak and an ability to respond to stimuli based on arbitrary relationships. There are data suggestive of this. It has recently been shown that children without productive speech or signing do not form equivalence classes (Devany, Hayes, & Nelson, 1986). If the present analysis has validity, we should also be able to show that humans can respond to stimuli based on their participation in relational classes and not just on direct training. Such effects seem to be common in verbal control. For example, suppose a young girl has an equivalence class established among the written word *cat*, the spoken word *cat*, and cats themselves. Suppose further that this child loves to play with cats and that if she sees a cat, she will approach it and play with it. Having this history, if the child sees someone looking behind a door while saying, "Oh, a cat," she may go behind the door *without ever having responded to such a rule in the past and thus without previously securing reinforcement for responding to this stimulus*. Similarly, if the word *good* is a conditioned reinforcer for the child and she is now told that in Spanish the word for *good* is *bueno* and that in French the word for *bueno* is *bon*, it seems quite likely that she will now respond to *bon* as a conditioned reinforcer *without ever having* bon *paired with reinforcement*. This automatic transfer of control within relational classes has recently been experimentally demonstrated both for discriminative and conditioned reinforcing effects (Hayes, Brownstein, Devany, Kohlenberg, & Shelby, 1985).

Based on this analysis, verbal control is truly a special form of stimulus control. Verbal stimuli are essentially effective because of their arbitrary relation to other stimuli—in short, because of their symbolic nature. When verbal stimuli are effective because they specify contingencies, they are called rules. Verbal stimuli can have other effects as well, such as when they function as reinforcers, but because of the importance of rules, I shall limit my discussion of verbal control to rule governed behavior for the rest of the chapter.

To summarize, I take the question of cognitive control in humans to be reduceable to the following question: What are the contingencies that might produce verbal rules and might cause them to influence other forms of human action? This is a very different kind of question than the kind of question asked by cognitive-behaviorists who treat cognition as other-than-behavior, or who analyze cognitive control in terms of the influence of one behavior over another, without adequately examining the contingencies that gave rise to and maintain that relationship. Essentially, the traditional cognitive position is much more like a stimulus–response position, because overt responding is automatically and directly produced by thoughts.

To give a hint of where this will lead, note that in my analysis a modification of the control exerted by rules may involve alteration of the contingencies surrounding verbal control, *without having first to change the rules themselves.* Furthermore, it might involve alternation of the nature of the relational classes in which the rule participates, again *without actually changing the form of the rule itself.* While a skeptical reader might claim that the special nature of verbal control to which I am pointing is exactly what the cognitive theorists have held all along, the occurrence of this analysis in a behavioral context gives rise to fundamentally different conclusions and techniques.

I shall need to discuss several other aspects of rules in order to make my approach to therapy comprehensible, but these I shall discuss in the context of the therapy approach itself. It is to the approach that I now turn.

A CONTEXTUAL APPROACH TO THERAPEUTIC CHANGE

In order to make this discussion more focused, I will limit what I have to say to the following situational framework: A client enters therapy complaining of certain problems. As the problems are examined, it is clear that the client believes that his problems are certain private behaviors: thoughts, feelings, attitudes, beliefs, memories, and the like. For example, he might say that he is depressed, anxious, bored, or angry. Similarly, he might say that he believes the wrong things or fails to believe the right ones—he might, for instance, believe that he is no good, or fail to trust others. Usually, if the clinician probes, she will find that the client feels that these things are bad because of other effects they seem to have. The anxious person may believe that the anxiety is causing avoidance, the depressed person that the depression is causing social withdrawal or a lack of activity. The obsessive-compulsive may feel that the obsessions are leading to senseless rituals or to an inability to concentrate on other things. The jealous spouse may feel that the jealousy is leading to arguments. It is only clients of this type that I plan to discuss in this chapter, but this is not a major restriction because any clinician will quickly see that the great majority of adult voluntary outpatient clients fit within this definition.

The System

When clients arrive in therapy they bring a great deal of excess baggage with them. They not only have problems, they have been struggling with their problems, they believe their problems are caused by this or that, they believe that what they need to do to solve their problems is one thing or another, or they believe that their problems are unsolvable. These actions and beliefs originated within a social–verbal community that undoubtedly helped give rise to them. In talking to clients, I like to call this entire context "the system in which your problems are being held." Recall that according to a behavioral perspective, behaviors are to be analyzed in context. The "system" points to an important aspect of the context in which clients problems occur: the "logical" contexts of the social-verbal community.

This system can be fairly well expressed as a logical syllogism. I don't mean to say that clients actually recognize the logic of it—it is more implicit than explicit—but simply that the syllogism expresses the essence of it fairly well. Indeed, I use this syllogism in therapy, though not at the beginning. I am placing it at the beginning in order to set an intellectual context for the chapter.

The first aspect of the syllogism is that *all behavior is caused*. Despite the fact that most clients are not determinists (or so they would claim), their very presence in therapy suggests that at least to some degree they believe that their behavior is controlled. Otherwise, why would they pay someone $50 or $100 an hour in order to try to bring about change? Behaviorists would tend to have little problem with this aspect of the system.

The second proposition in this syllogism is that *reasons are causes*. By reasons I mean simply the verbal explanations and justifications that people give for their actions, beliefs, feelings, and so on. Typically, these reasons are given in response to questions that, if one takes them literally, ask about causes, so that it seems sensible to view the answers as attempts at descriptions of causal relations. Thus, for example, a person may ask someone else, "Why did you have an argument with your husband?" The answer may be, "He made me mad" or "I didn't like the way he has been treating me." An agoraphogic, when asked, "Why did you avoid the mall?" might say, "Because I was so anxious." A depressive, when asked, "Why are you restricting your activities so much?" might answer, "Because I don't feel like doing anything anymore."

There are major problems, however, in viewing reasons as causes (Skinner, 1974). It seems extraordinarily unlikely that people would have access to much of the material that is needed to understand their own behavior. As I tell my clients, if this were not true, we could all be given PhDs in psychology. Behavioral scientists have just begun to understand the simplest behavior of the simplest organisms in the simplest environments. Entire academic lifetimes have been spent on understanding why a flatworm turns left in a T-maze. Humans are enormously complex organisms with enormously complex histories. We know very little about such key topics in human behavior as verbal behavior. The idea that the kind of verbal explanations we give about why we do things has very much at all to do with why we really do things is simply absurd. Even if a reason is true, it is such a small part of the picture as to be functionally false. So, for example, if a person says that a fight with a spouse occurred because "He made me mad," it may be literally true—a reaction called anger may indeed have been present—but it is functionally false because we don't know (1) why the anger occurred, (2) what else other than anger contributed to the fighting, and (3) how anger has come to control fighting of this sort. Presumably a comprehensive answer might analyze the phylogenetic and ontogenetic contingencies that gave rise to all these considerations. We might need to know, for example, about the person's history with regard to anger, fighting, social control, and so on. Unfortunately, most people can hardly remember what they have had for breakfast yesterday, much less what events in the remote past constitute their learning history with regard to a given situation. The difficulty is more than just access to the events. Even if we did know *all* of the events in a person's life, we still would not know how to organize them into meaningful functional units. For all these reasons, it seems impossible that reasons could have very much to do with causes.

This is not to say that reasons are not very interesting behavioral phenomena in their own right. Reasons undoubtedly have some important role. We spend a great deal of time teaching children to give reasons. A very young child, for example, will often answer, "Just because" in response to a request for a reason, but this would not be permitted in an older child. One must have a reason to give, in part because reasons are the way the verbal community can establish whether or not a person can justify his or her own behavior consistently and in terms of socially established rules of conduct. Thus, for example, if a young child is asked, "Why did you hit your sister?" and answers, "Because she made me mad," we may explain to the child what to do when he gets mad. We are not asking the child to engage in scientific speculations about what caused the behavior. This is easy to see when we examine answers that may be more scientifically correct, but that lose contact with social norms. Suppose this same child is asked the same question and responds, "Because she did things that I experienced as aversive. Aversive stimulation is an establishing operation that leads to a heightened state of reinforceability with regard to the sensory stimulation provided by forcefully striking my knuckles against her face. Furthermore, I have had extensive experience with regard to the immediate social consequences of aggression that has reinforced my hitting." It seems likely that such an answer—even though it may be more nearly a description of causality in the situation—would secure less support from the verbal community than would the obviously inadequate former answer. All of this would not be such a problem were it not for the fact that people eventually begin to take their own reasons quite seriously and truly treat them as if they were causes. For the verbal community this is desirable because it means that behavior that cannot be justified in terms of social norms is made less likely—it is not "reasonable" to do it.

Clinically, it seems as though most clients explain their behavior in part based on thoughts, feelings, attitudes, memories, beliefs, bodily sensations, and so on. Even when clients are seemingly not trying to explain behavior per se, they evaluate their life in terms of these same things. For example, a person's life is said to be not going well if he or she is "depressed" or "anxious." This is a kind of reason giving at a higher level. To shorten the list, let the words *thoughts and feelings* stand for all the private behaviors and private stimuli that are commonly pointed to as the reason for human action or the basis for the evaluation of human success or failure. The third statement of the syllogism is that *thoughts and feelings are good reasons*.

Clinical experience suggests the ubiquity of this part of the system. Clients often come into therapy complaining, for example, of "anxiety" or "depression." Typically, there are real-life problems these private behaviors are being used to explain. Such people may be withdrawing from those around them, failing in relationships, avoiding certain necessary situations, and so on. In the rarer case when a person is behaving fairly effectively at an overt level and is complaining of depression or anxiety, the person is usually not responding just to the feeling or thought but to its meaning according to the verbal community. The presence of anxiety, for example, "means" that one's life is not going well. Our field has so bought this general context that we even label disorders and treatments in these terms. If someone is said to have an "anxiety disorder," we are obviously implying that the anxiety itself is the problem. In my view, however, it is the very system that makes this seem sensible that is the problem.

What evidence is there that people tend to use private events to explain behavior, and that these explanations are seen to be "good" reasons? A few years ago, Elga Wulfert, Suzanne Brannon, and I collected some data on this question. We constructed a set of several common clinical situations in which a client engaged in clinically undesirable behavior. We then asked a number of undergraduates to read the description and write down several reasons that the client might be likely to give if asked why the behavior occurred. For example, if an alcoholic client got drunk, what reason might he give for his behavior? About 80% of the reasons people listed for a wide variety of situations referred only to private events, and not at all to external events of which the behavior might be a function. When we asked people to write down reasons they themselves might give if they were in such a situation, the answers were similar. Even the few reasons that pointed to external events also typically included private events (e.g., "He made me mad when he did X"). We then asked these same respondents to rate the validity of each reason on a scale of 1 (low validity) to 7 (high validity). The average ratings were quite high (about 5.8) and did not differ between purely private behavioral reasons and those that involved the external environment. In short, people told us that thoughts and feelings are the most common reasons given by themselves or others for clinically undesirable behavior and that these reasons were quite valid. Please note that self-reports in this situation are in fact the behavior of interest. It shows that the social–verbal community (that establishes the system I am discussing) will support reasons of this kind.

The fourth statement in the syllogism flows quite naturally from the first three: *Thoughts and feelings are causes.* I have already discussed how this is not a radical behavioral perspective. In such a perspective, only contingencies are causes. This is not as arbitrary as it might sound. Obviously, behavior influences the environment, which in turn influences future behavior. In the case of behavior–behavior relationships, obviously the first behavior has stimulus properties that can assist in the control of the second. We can notice our own thoughts, for example, just as we might listen to instructions given by others. However, there is good reason to take the sequence back to the environmental level before calling an event a cause. In the pragmatic view of science encompassed by radical behaviorism, the purpose of contingency analysis is to allow us to predict, control, and thus to understand phenomena. If behavior is allowed to be viewed as a cause of behavior, this can lead directly to prediction but not to control. We cannot manipulate behavior directly—we can only manipulate environmental events (see Hayes & Brownstein, 1986a, 1986b for more extended discussions of this issue). Thus, behaviors—and their private stimulus products—can participate in overall causal relationships but should not themselves be seen as causes of other behaviors of the same individual. In any case, I just want to note here that the lay perspective we are analyzing differs dramatically from a radical behavioral account, though not from a cognitive-behavioral account.

The fifth statement is a logical requirement: *To control the outcome we must control the causes.* For the word *cause* to mean what it says, this is a truism.

With these five statements the trap is sprung, because it must then logically follow that *to control the outcome we must control the thoughts and feelings.* At first it may not be obvious why this is a trap. Indeed, the field of psychotherapy (especially behavior therapy) has often *defined* its procedures in terms of controlling thoughts and feelings. Thus, for example, we speak easily of "anxiety management" procedures, or of "cognitive restructuring." Psychology has almost completely bought into the cultural mainstream that dictates the need to control private events in order to live a successful life. There are good reasons to believe, however, that the attempt to control thoughts and feelings is often counterproductive—particularly with persons who have clinical disorders.

To some degree the last sentence is the central theme of the entire chapter; I can thus only give a partial defence of this assertion presently. Consider the fact that deliberate attempts to do anything are, in fact, instances of rule-governed behavior. When we add qualifiers to human action such as "deliberate, purposeful, conscious, intentional," and so on we are doing so because we recognize that the behavior is not just contingency shaped. Infrahumans, for example, are not said to be "deliberately" doing anything—they just do or do not based on the current situation and their prior history. Thus, deliberate attempts to control thoughts and feelings boil down to attempts to control thoughts and feelings by following a rule (e.g., "Don't feel X"). In most clinical situations the feeling or thought we are attempting to control is seen to be problematic and thus the goal is to get rid of it or diminish it in some way.

Consider what is likely to happen, however, if we use a rule to, for example, get rid of a thought. In order to do so, we must specify the thought to be eliminated. The thought, however, must be in a relational class with the rule in order to be specified. That is, the words contained in the rule must to some degree be equivalent to the form of the thought itself. Under these conditions, the rule will itself actually help create the very private event the person is trying to avoid. Obsessive–compulsives often attempt to follow rules such as "You must not think about hurting other people." A rule of this sort is itself likely to create thoughts about hurting others because it contains events that are in an equivalence class with the thought. Thus, the more one tries to follow it, the worse it will get. I shall discuss this concept and the theoretical basis of it further when I describe my approach to therapy.

For now, it is only necessary to recognize that I am claiming that there is a problem; According to the system we have in place by virtue of our participation in this verbal community, a client's goal is likely to be the elimination of thoughts and feelings by following a rule. This may be fundamentally faulty because, despite appearances to the contrary, we need not change thoughts and feelings to either change other behaviors or live a successful life, thus, thoughts and feelings are not really the problem anyway. Moreover, trying to eliminate thoughts and feelings deliberately is often ineffective. If this be so, the social-verbal system we have been describing creates a trap that can frustrate attempts to change a person's actual life situation. Seeing thoughts and feelings as the "problems" is itself part of the problem. Furthermore, the solutions generally proposed for this "problem" are also part of the problem.

Comprehensive Distancing

Over the last 7 years I have developed a particular approach to therapy based on an attempt to undermine the system I have just described. It is not so much a set of techniques as it is a context in which various techniques might be placed. Every client I see who fits the description that I gave at the beginning of this section is likely to be treated within this context. The approach is called comprehensive distancing. Typically, the first several sessions after the initial assessment will be taken up establishing this working context. After that, I do many of the things other therapists may do, but always from within this continuing context. I believe the approach transcends the distinctions between cognitive therapy and behavior therapy in that it is a behaviorally rationalized approach that can incorporate both sets of techniques. Comprehensive distancing has several goals that can be arranged more or less according to their normal sequence in therapy.

Goal 1: Establish a State of Creative Hopelessness

When people come into therapy they will readily describe aspects of their life that they feel need to be changed. Problems are identified and solutions are proposed based on our history with a verbal community that teaches us to evaluate our life and to modify events accordingly. This is the "social-verbal context" of our problems. By context I simply mean contingencies and sets of contingencies; the contingencies are social-verbal in the sense that they are established and maintained by a community of verbal organisms. In a contextual approach to therapeutic change, it is not necessarily the "problems" themselves that are problematic, but the social–verbal context in which they occur.

There are three major and related contexts (i.e., sets of contingencies) that are established by the social–verbal community. First, there is the context of literality. Words have meanings and events are conceptually categorized based on the way the verbal community constantly refreshes the relationship between various stimuli. For example, the word *anxiety* is used over and over again in everyday talk and each time it is used another bit of learning occurs. Anxiety means that, this is called anxiety, anxiety is bad, and so on. It is like the earlier example of the matching to sample involving the child and the wheezu, except that the trials never end. This is what I mean by the "context of literality." It is so ubiquitous that it is hard even to see it as a context—it is like a fish trying to see water as water. Indeed, as you read this chapter you are swimming in the very sea I am pointing toward. You do not see these words as squiggles on a piece of paper; you see (or more often almost "hear") the "words themselves." In exactly the same way, when a person has a thought it immediately "means something," whether or not this meaning contributes to successful living. The person may seemingly have to respond to the meaning of the thought *given this context*. A particular behavior–behavior relationship is established.

Second, there is the context of reason giving. I have already explained this context in some detail. According to the social–verbal community, certain events explain other events. This context can then contribute to control by the presence or absence of these same events. For example, a depressed person may explain in all sincerity that it is impossible to perform some action because of a lack of energy. In fact, the person will most often receive some degree of support for the sense of the explanation itself. Thus, a feeling called "a lack of energy" may truly come to control behavior *given this context*. A particular behavior–behavior relationship is established. The context of reason giving is so powerful and pervasive that the reader may think that it is odd to claim that a person could perform an action without some energy. I am suggesting that, given other contexts, people can in fact behave energetically *and* feel that they have no energy whatsoever. That this seems unlikely is itself the evidence I would point to of a context of reason giving in the social–verbal community that influences us all. Given such a context, if one were to feel that one has no energy whatsoever, it would seem "reasonable" to refrain from doing anything energetic.

The final context is that of control. Basing our logic on literality and reason giving, we come to believe that certain things must change before others may change. That is, we must control *A* in order for *B* to happen. A person must get rid of depression in order to be happy. A person must get rid of anxiety in order to do frightening things. Thus, the presence of *A* must seemingly lead to efforts to get rid of *A*, *given this context*. Another type of behavior–behavior relationship is established.

I believe that each of these contexts can produce pathological results at times. Since each is a set of contingencies established and maintained by the mainstream verbal community, the first goal of therapy must be to create a new verbal community, which operates within a different context—that is, within a different set of contingencies. This is very difficult because the client brings a behavioral history in the door. Thus, when a therapist says something to a client, it is heard within the very contexts that need to be changed.

For these reasons, my first goal in therapy is to challenge these contexts themselves. The only way I know to do this is to behave in ways that do not fit within these contexts. The contexts of literality, reason giving, and control are so fundamental that it is impossible to alter them by behaving "reasonably." Many of traditional "hard-nosed" behavioral interventions, for example, try to ignore these contexts without challenging them directly. In the long run, this strategy seems doomed to failure if the contexts themselves are part of the problem, because it leaves those contexts ignored but intact. The only way to alter them is to do things that do not fit within them.

The section that follows is a rough approximation of what might be said in the first therapy session after the initial assessment phase. Throughout much of the rest of the chapter, I will intersperse the session descriptions with textual asides to the reader. I shall assume the client has an "anxiety disorder" such as agoraphobia, since this disorder represents fairly well some of the major dynamics of the system in which clients function. Although most of the case descriptions will be hypothetical (in the interest of efficiency and clarity), virtually every sentence within these descriptions are sentences I have actually said, or a client has actually said. They are not just "made up."

THERAPIST: I want to begin to lay some groundwork today for us to work on your problems. You see, you've come in here wanting a solution to these problems, but I'm worried lest we first do things that will just dig you in deeper. It may be hard to see that part of the problem is what you have been calling "the solution." You have an idea of what you want and need in order to be able to handle these problems—but you had these ideas before you came in. You've tried this and you've tried that. Don't you sometimes wonder why none of these things have really worked? Sure, sometimes they have seemed to work, but ultimately they didn't—otherwise you wouldn't be in here. Well, what if the problem is actually in part the very solutions you have been attempting? It is as if a person who came in to a doctor with a headache had been trying to cure the headache by hitting himself on the head. The first job the doctor would have would be to stop the hitting. Well, we are in a situation exactly like that. So I can't just run in and try to help. First I have to stop what has been getting things stuck. To do that you will have to allow me to take a fair amount of control over the next several sessions. I want you to know, however, that this is not the way therapy will be permanently. You may think at times over the next several sessions that I am just confusing you or maybe even not listening to you. That's part of what needs to happen to break down the system that has been keeping you stuck.

My purpose in these opening remarks has been to do two things: to put on the table that I shall not do what the client expects me to do and that I want the client's permission to take temporarily the control I need to get the job done. I want to have the client going into therapy with fair warning.

THERAPIST: If we strip away all of the details, you are saying that what you need to be able to move ahead in your life is to rid yourself of an undesirable emotion: anxiety. If you could just eliminate, reduce, manage, or otherwise control your anxiety, *then* you could move ahead. In other words, it is the anxiety that is the problem: As long as it is here, at least as long as it is so intense, your life will never work.

CLIENT: That's right. No one could live with the anxiety I have.

THERAPIST: Okay. And what I want you to notice is that a great deal of behavior has emerged from this perspective. You've really tried hard to accomplish this goal. You've done everything you know how to do.

CLIENT: Yes, but nothing has really worked. Some things work a little—I don't know what I'd do without tranquilizers, for example. Still, I haven't really licked it yet.

THERAPIST: And you're here for me to help do that, but what I want you to know right from the beginning is that I can't and I won't. You think that there is a way out; that you just don't have the right technique. So I'm supposed to give you the right one. *I don't have it to give.* It doesn't exist. There is no way out. Within the system in which you're functioning you are trapped. Look, don't you deep down have the feeling that you're hopeless? Haven't you thought that? And that's scared you, hasn't it? Well, I'm sorry to have to be the one to tell you, but your fears are correct. Held in the way you are holding it, the situation is hopeless. No joke. No fooling. I mean it. There is no way out.

CLIENT: Well, then why am I coming to see you? Why am I paying you money to help me? What can you do for me?

THERAPIST: I don't know. I'm certainly not going to help you get rid of your anxiety, to get rid of your worries, to get all your thoughts lined up in a row. You've played that game for years *and it hasn't worked*. You know that. Well, I'm here to say that it never will.

CLIENT: You mean I'm just hopeless. I should give up.

THERAPIST: In a sense, yes. Actually, you are not hopeless. But the system within which you are functioning has no hope of working. It will never make your life work.

CLIENT: So what is the other system? You seem to be implying that there is another way.

THERAPIST: Well, first, there is *not* another way to get accomplished what you want accomplished. There is a way to have your life get unstuck, but right now I can't tell you what that is because you wouldn't hear me. You'd hear the words, and then promptly put them back into the same old system that is the real problem in the first place. That system is everywhere. It's in the room right now. If fact, I can say with complete confidence that what you think I'm trying to say is not what I'm saying at all. If you think you understand me right not I want you to know that what you think I'm saying is not what I'm saying.

The use of paradox in this way, if done in moderation, is one of the fastest ways to loosen up the verbal system with which the client comes into therapy. It puts clients in an untenable situation—if they understand it, they don't. This is a direct attack on the context of literality. As clients notice their opinions about what the therapist is saying, they also cannot take them literally because whatever they think is being said isn't. This allows the therapist to say things to clients that wouldn't have an impact if the sentence first had to be understood to be useful.

THERAPIST: Let me give you a metaphor that might help you see what I'm saying. The situation you are in is something like this. Imagine a large field. You are blindfolded, given some tools, and told to run through the field. Unknown to you, though, there are holes in this field. They are widely spaced in most places but sooner or later you accidentally fall into one. Now, when you fall into the hole, you start trying to get out. You don't know exactly what to do, so you take the tool that seems most useful, and you try to get out. Unfortunately, the tool you were given is a shovel. So you dig. And you dig. But digging is an action that makes holes, not a way to get out of them. You might make the hole deeper, or larger, or there might be all kinds of passageways you can build, but you'll probably still be stuck in this hole. So you try other things. You might try to figure out exactly how you fell in the hole. You might think, "If I just hadn't turned left at the rise, I wouldn't be in here." And of course that is literally true, but it doesn't make any difference. Even if you knew every step you took, it wouldn't get you out of the hole. So we're not going to spend a lot of time trying to figure out the details of your past—many of these will come up for other reasons and we will deal with them, but not as a way to get you out of the hole you're in. Another thing you might do when you're in the hole is try to find a really great shovel. You think that maybe that's the problem; you need a gold-plated steam shovel. That's really why you're here. You think I have a gold-plated steam shovel. But I don't, and even if I did it wouldn't do any good because shovels don't get people out of holes. To get out of a hole you need a ladder, not a shovel.

CLIENT: So what is the ladder? How do I get out?

THERAPIST: See, the reason I can't answer that now is that it wouldn't do any good until you really let go of this determination to dig your way out. Right now if you were given a ladder you'd try to dig with it. So let me go back to it and say that we can't begin to go on until you really start to face up to the fact that there is no way out, given the way you are holding it. It doesn't matter how you do it, you can't dig your way out. Digging faster won't work. Putting more effort into it won't work. And there is no room to do what will work until you put down the shovel.

I usually stay on this topic for at least one full outpatient session. I use several other kinds of metaphors to get the point across. Metaphors are excellent ways of talking to clients because they allow the therapist to use language without having to use it literally, and thus without strengthening the very context creating the problem in the first place. Whatever clients throw out during this part of the treatment—frustration, determination, unthinking cooperation—is just more behavior that is at strength, and the only behavior really at strength by definition is behavior that hasn't worked in the past. Thus, I make note of what the client is doing and point out that *that* behavior is old stuff too, and also won't work. The goal is to establish a state of creative hopelessness. That is, I want all avenues of escape cut off so that behavior controlled by the contexts of literality, reason giving, and control can be weakened a little. This allows the client to begin to engage in some new behaviors that exist only outside of these contexts and that might actually work. It also tends to heighten greatly the client's motivation to change. In the language of rule-governed behavior, it serves as an *augmental*—that is, as a rule that works in part by changing the reinforcing effectiveness of certain consequences (Zettle & Hayes, 1982). In this case, finding a new way to approach the situation becomes of paramount importance. It is then that clients will really begin to search their assumptions in a way they haven't before.

Undoubtedly some readers see this approach as harsh or even dangerous. It could be if clients had the sense that the therapist were criticizing them or that the therapist were saying that they themselves were hopeless. The issue that must be present in the session, however, is that of a challenge to the system that confines them, not a challenge to them as a person. I approach this in a kind of firm, confrontational, but bemused approach. I'm not attacking them—I'm attacking the system. A slight twinkle in the eye helps make that clear. The way it actually works in therapy can be seen from the following interchange from a transcript of a workshop I gave for clinicians, which was also attended by one of my agoraphobic clients:

COMMENT FROM AUDIENCE: I'm surprised they come back for a second session.

SCH: I've never had a client drop out at this point. They're usually quite interested—they've never had anyone talk to them in this way before.

AUDIENCE: I'd hate for a client to go out and commit suicide when you say there is no way out.

CLIENT SITTING IN: But along with that rap comes a feeling of hope too. You go into therapy thinking you've done everything you can possibly do. You want the therapist to give you a trick and yet deep down you know that can't happen. If it could have, you'd already have done it. So you sort of feel relieved to hear that you have tried everything. And with this you also feel hope because you figure he must know something you don't. So it really wouldn't create a suicidal feeling. You can't wait to find out where he is going with this thing.

Often in the beginning of therapy I try to distinguish fault from responsibility, which helps alleviate the possibility of an unproductive reaction to a confrontation of the client's system. The man-in-the-hole metaphor can help make this point, as is described below.

THERAPIST: There is something I want you to notice about this. In the metaphor it is not the person's fault that he fell in the hole and it's not his fault that he can't get out. If it hadn't been this hole, it might have been another. Fault and blame are established when we add in social condemnation to try to motivate someone to change. You don't need that. You are already motivated to change. So it's not your fault. You are not to blame. You are, however, responsible in the sense of response-ability. You had an ability to respond differently in the situation than you did. You just didn't know that you did. You didn't have to spend years digging furiously, as you have. If that's not true, then nothing can be done now, so don't try to avoid responsibility—just know that the ability to respond is not the same as blame. We have no need of blame here. The consequences themselves are plenty aversive enough already without having to dump social condemnation on top of them. I want you to know that it is very clear to me that you would like your life to work. If you had known what to do you would have done it.

Theoretically, the purpose of all of this is to begin to establish a different set of contingencies than the contexts of literality, reason giving, and control. By using such statements as "What you want me to do I can't do" or "What you hear me saying isn't what I'm saying," I attack literality and reason giving. Raising the issue of responsibility is meant to tell the person that we are indeed talking about behavior: there are things to be done. The metaphor of digging is utilized to begin to attack the context of control to which I now turn.

Goal 2: The Problem is Control

The next issue that is typically covered is the nature of the system that has created the trap. As is apparent from the section above, I believe the nature of this is the inappropriate attempt to control private behaviors. This effort is based on the view that these behaviors are themselves causes of major life difficulties. Rather than expand on my theoretical rationale for this at this point, I shall go directly to a description of the approach taken with clients.

THERAPIST: The situation you are in is something like a person trying to deal with an inappropriately placed public address system. Have you ever been at a speech and heard a feedback screech? Well, what happens there is that the speaker is too close to the microphone, given the setting of the amplifier. When the speaker speaks into the microphone, the amplifier amplifies it and sends it out the speakers. If it gets picked up again by the microphone and if it is just a bit louder this time compared to the first time, then as fast as the speed of sound and electricity, the sound will be amplified, picked up, amplified, picked up, amplified, and so on. The result is a feedback screech. You're sort of in that situation. The sound is emotion. The feedback screech is being overwhelmed by or controlled by your emotion. But notice that we might easily feel in such a situation that the sound itself is the problem. So we might live our lives tiptoeing around trying not to make any noise. But noise is not the problem. It's the amplifier that's the problem. I don't want to help you live your life very quietly. I want to help you find the amplifier and turn it off. When you do this you'll still have noise (i.e., anxiety), and maybe it will be frequent and loud or maybe it won't. Either way it won't be overwhelming.

CLIENT: So what's the amplifier? How do I turn it off?

THERAPIST: In the real world, an amplifier is used to regulate and modulate the volume of a given sound. It's the same thing here. Your amplifier is the part of you that is spending its time regulating and modulating your emotions—or at least trying to do so. In a word: control.

In the huge proportion of human existence, conscious, purposeful control works beautifully. It is what has made humankind as a species what it is today. The rule is: "If you don't want something, figure out how to get rid of it, and get rid of it." That rule works wonderfully in the realm of the physical things in our life. If you don't like poverty, get a job. If you don't life the dirt on your floor, vacuum it up. This is not to be ridiculed or minimized. If you examine what the rest of living creation is doing, it's quite an advance. We are warm and dry because of our ability to think things out and then to follow such rules; that is, because of conscious control. It is a problem, though, that the same system that works so well for us as a species can be a disaster for us in the areas that determine the degree to which we are satisfied with our lives. When you apply the system of conscious control to the world of our private experience, the rule changes fundamentally. In this realm the rule is: "If you are not willing to have it, you've got it." In other words, attempts to control your thoughts and feelings so as to get rid of "bad" ones will ultimately doom you to being stuck with and controlled by these very same thoughts and feelings. That's what I meant by the person with the shovel: Digging is simply the attempt to control what you think you feel.

Imagine this. Suppose I had you wired up to a very fine polygraph. It is such a fine machine that there is simply no way you could possibly be anxious without my knowing it. Now imagine that I have given you a very simple task: to not get anxious. However, to help motivate you I pull out a gun. I tell you that to help you work on this task I will hold the gun to your head. As long as you don't get anxious, I won't shoot you, but if you get anxious you will be shot. Can you see what would happen?

CLIENT: I'd be shot for sure.

THERAPIST: Right. There is no way you can follow this rule. If it is critical not to be anxious, guess what you get? This is not a far-fetched situation. It is exactly the situation you are in right now. Instead of a polygraph you have something even better: your own nervous system. Instead of a gun, you have your self-esteem or your success in life apparently on the line. So guess what you get?

Haven't you noticed that about the most depressing thing to do is to try to stamp out your depression? Anger seems to make you mad, anxiety makes you anxious. It's a set-up. We are applying a rule that works perfectly well in one situation to a situation in which the same rule is a disaster. And it's not only so with feelings. Suppose you have a thought you cannot permit. So you try not to think it. That really works great, doesn't it? Try it now. Don't think of jelly donuts; don't think of race cars; don't think of your mother. Guess what you get?

CLIENT: I guess I see the problem. But what is the alternative? No one could be as anxious as I am and be calm about it.

THERAPIST: Well, one thing you should notice is that you really don't know what it would be like to feel anxiety when you weren't also trying to control it. It would be like a person who had gasoline all over the floor and was convinced that flame is a horrible thing. In the context of gasoline, it is. But maybe it isn't in another context. In other words, when anxiety isn't being held in the context of deliberate attempts to control it, anxiety may work very differently.

CLIENT: You mean if I'm willing to be anxious, it'll go away?

THERAPIST: I didn't say that. I said it might work differently. Whether anxiety is present or absent is another matter. If you are willing to be anxious, one of two things will happen: it will go away . . . or it won't go away.

CLIENT: Very funny.

THERAPIST: No, look. I wasn't trying to be funny. If you were willing to be anxious in order to get it to go away, than you *aren't* willing to be anxious and it won't go away. You can't fool yourself. This is not a trick. If you are willing to be anxious, then you are willing to be anxious. When you are holding things this way the only words to describe what it's like is "Either you will be anxious or you won't." In other words, the outcome isn't an issue anymore.

CLIENT: But I want to get rid of my anxiety.

THERAPIST: Indeed. And you are acting as if reality cared, so that if you hold out, sooner or later you'll get what you want. Guess what? Reality doesn't care. Your experience tells you that trying to get rid of anxiety doesn't work. So which will you believe? Your beliefs or your experience? If you notice that you want to be rid of anxiety, the question is, do you buy this literally? Are you going to follow this rule? If so, you'll be stuck. Of course, wanting to be rid of anxiety is also something that just pops up—you don't need to control this thought or feeling either. So I'm not asking you to stop wanting to be rid of anxiety. I'm suggesting that you not actually buy that thought literally. I'm suggesting that the name of the trap you are in is "control" and if you continue to try to get rid of your thoughts and feelings before you can get on with your life, you will continue to be stuck. I'm saying the way that it works is "If you're not willing to have it you've got it."

CLIENT: I'm confused.

THERAPIST: Good. If you understood this intellectually, it couldn't be it. Confusion is what happens when the system that has you stuck starts to break down. I'm not suggesting you try to figure this all out. If this has value, you will get the value independently of figuring it out.

As should be clear, this is all a deliberate attempt to attack the three problematic contexts. "If you're not willing to have it you've got it" is a beautiful saying because if one takes it literally, there is nothing that can be done with it. Trying to use it to get rid of anxiety immediately violates it. It can't be used reasonably and it can't assist in control. Thus, the client becomes confused. The normal social–verbal contexts do not fit. This part of therapy may take a full session or more. Multiple examples and metaphors are used. For example, with a man who has had problems with sexual dysfunction, I would relate what I am saying to trying to avoid being sexually turned-off. Most men have experienced the odd fact that trying to avoid losing an erection is almost sure to create this very situation. When the client begins to see that control is what he or she has been trying to make work, I begin to expand on this perspective and to point to the alternative.

THERAPIST: Think of two scales, each going from 1 to 10. Let's call one anxiety and one control. By "control" I mean deliberate, purposeful attempts to control your private experiences. You come in here with anxiety at a 10 and control at a 10. What you are asking me to do is to get the anxiety down to a 1. But that is what you have been trying to do right along. It hasn't worked. You know that. What you may not yet realize is that it never will. Anxiety can't get unstuck as long as the control scale is at a 10. What I want to do is get the control scale down to a 1; then the anxiety will go wherever it goes. It's free to move. When control is high and anxiety is high, anxiety is stuck because now the anxiety itself is something to be anxious about—so it feeds on itself.

If what I'm saying is true, it seems strange that we can stay stuck on it for so long—literally years. I can think of four reasons why this might happen. First, deliberate control works beautifully in so many other situations. You have learned if at first you don't succeed, try, try again. You know that usually conscious effort makes a difference. It may be hard to see that the rule doesn't work in this situation. Second, you've been told this is what you need to do. When you were very little you were already hearing things like "Don't be afraid", or "Don't cry—there's nothing to cry about." The message was that you could control your thoughts and emotions, and furthermore that you needed to do so to be able to be successful in life. It was important to be able to do so, or so you were told. Third, you looked around you and sure enough other people seemed to be able to pull this off quite well. Other people didn't seem to be as afraid, or insecure, or whatever. Of course, that was often just on the outside. Now these two things alone probably wouldn't do it—these wouldn't keep you stuck indefinitely. But the kicker is the last reason: It even seems to work for you. It seems to. For example, suppose you are bothered with a "bad thought." You try to get rid of it by distracting yourself. Sure enough, when you distract yourself it "goes away." So the immediate effect seems to confirm the rule. The problem is that it comes back, and often it comes back even stronger. So we do something else, and round and round it goes until ultimately we are in this monstrous struggle with our own thoughts.

For example, I'd be willing to bet that at some time—probably when you were pretty young, you first realized that deep down there might be something wrong with you. So what did you do? You tried to be good, or maybe you rebelled—same thing really. You put on a good act. You tried to get social approval. And a lot of this seemed to work. But do you notice that that basic insecurity is still there? Not only that, but now you also have to deal with having "fooled" people all these years. There's not only something wrong with you, you are also a fraud. The problem is this: If it is critical that thinking that you are no good has to be gotten rid of before you are good, this very attempt confirms the view that there is something wrong with you in the first place. If you buy the thought, then try to get rid of it now that you've bought it, it's too late because you already bought it. In other words, you would only be trying to get rid of the thought or feeling because you are already treating it as literally true, so what you get in the end is based on (and therefore must have the quality of) it being literally true. That's why control can't work.

Naturally, when I do this in therapy there is a great deal more interaction, but this captures the flavor of the discussion. Why might it be the case that trying to control thoughts and feelings can be a destructive effort? If one is using a rule to avoid certain private verbal stimuli (i.e., thoughts) this is quite dangerous for two reasons. First, as I've already discussed, the rule itself must specify these stimuli, and thus the avoidance cannot be completely successful. Second, as I said to the client above, even if it could, the avoidance itself establishes a controlling function for the avoided verbal stimuli. For example, if one avoids the thought "I am bad," it gives that thought a controlling function that is itself consistent with the class "bad." If a person has to change something in order to be good, it means that right now the person is not good. It makes the thought functionally bad, and therefore confirms the thought in the effort to avoid it. As I say to my clients, it is like playing a game where the rule is "First you lose, then you play." The only way "bad" thoughts or feelings can lose their power is if they stop controlling a great deal of behavior. Fighting against thoughts is as much behavior as is doing what they say. My whole purpose is to undermine the destructive behavior-behavior relationship. For this to occur, the person must have the first behavior and not the second.

Feelings present much the same dilemma. Anxiety, for example, is a natural response to a situation in which punishment is likely. The rule "It is critical not to be anxious" signals punishment for the occurrence of reaction to the probability of punishment. Normally that might not be a problem because the probability of considerable anxiety seems so low. An agoraphobic knows, however, that extreme anxiety is possible. That knowledge will never change. Thus the apparent probability of punishment is very high and the rule thus produces exactly what it warns against.

It is more difficult to account for why the actual contingencies don't take a stronger hold. If following rules of this sort is counterproductive, why don't we stop? To begin to understand this requires a brief expansion of the concept of rule-governed behavior. There seem to be at least three basic kinds of rules. The first is rule-governed behavior under the control of an apparent correspondence between the rule and the natural (i.e., nonarbitrary) contingencies (Zettle & Hayes, 1982). This kind of rule is called a *track*, and the behavior it controls is called *tracking* to denote following a path. For example, if I say to someone, "The way to get to Greensboro is to follow I-85," and if getting to Greensboro would be a reinforcing state of affairs, he or she may follow the rule as a track. In a sense, this kind of rule-governed behavior simply adds another discriminative stimulus (though a verbal one) to the environment.

A second kind of rule is termed *pliance* (from the word compliance). The rule itself is a *ply*. Pliance is rule-governed behavior under the control of apparent socially-mediated and arbitrary consequences for a correspondence between the rule and relevant behavior (Hayes et al., 1986a). What is different about pliance, as compared to tracking, is not the nature of the consequences (social consequences can certainly be natural in the sense of nonarbitrary) but that these consequences are for another unit of behavior. They are delivered not for the behavior itself, but because that behavior is also an instance of rule following. Thus, for example, if I tell my daughter, "PUT on your jacket right now," she may put on the jacket not because she will be warm but because I would deliver consequences differentially for following or not following my instructions.

The third unit is called *augmenting*, and I have already briefly described it. Essentially, an augmental is a rule that works because it is an establishing stimulus (Michael, 1982); that is, a stimulus that changes one's motivation for a particular consequence.

Each of these three units can be thought of as crossing with another dimension, namely the degree to which the rule is taken literally. Recall that rules are verbal stimuli and that verbal stimuli have their effects based in part on their participation in equivalence (or other relational) classes. These classes can be thought of as relatively tight, in which case each stimulus can essentially stand in for others in the same class in a given situation, or relatively loose, in which case the stimuli are related to each other, but are also functionally distinct in many situations. Verbal stimuli are purely arbitrary stimuli and thus there are a few impediments to fairly tight equivalence classes emerging. For example, suppose I said to a man crossing the street with me, "Look out, a truck!" Treating this as if he had actually seen a truck would probably be to his advantage.

We have extensive histories from the verbal community for maintaining a rough equivalence between words and events. We are encouraged to engage in formal analyses of situations and then to respond to these analyses. Thus, the verbal community is constantly tightening the equivalence between our talk and the world. We are told that our view is right or correct, or that a given way of talking is a good way to talk about events. We also have extensive histories of behaving consistently or inconsistently with our stated rules. When we think something, it is not always obvious that it is even a thought. In a sense, the class is so tight that it is hard to see that it is a class. For example, if I think, "This interpersonal relationship will crush me—I have to get out," I may act as if it were literally true. That is, I may act as if I am actually in a situation in which I will be crushed. I may even miss that it is just a thought that might or might not correspond with the real world.

The question of why we follow destructive rules can thus come down to this question: Under what conditions do rules produce an insensitivity to the natural contingencies? Literal tracks could produce insensitivity because the rule is followed in much the same way that the actual environmental events would be followed, and these events may entail real contingencies. If I really did need to avoid being crushed, (situation A), then getting out would be reinforced. If I think I need to do so, (situation B), and respond the same way, I may not be reinforced but the history with regard to the equivalence between A and B may delay this discrimination.

Pliance could also create mischief, especially if the ply is relatively literal. In this case, socially mediated contingencies are actually added to the situation for rule following, so it wouldn't be surprising to see an insensitivity to the natural contingencies. There is evidence that pliance does indeed produce an insensitivity to natural contingencies (Hayes *et al.*, 1986a).

Augmentals can also create notable insensitivity, if they are literal. For example, if one is told that everyone should be able to do something (e.g., control feelings), a failure to do it may be much more punishing than the natural contingencies themselves would have established.

Examination of the explanations I gave to the client for a failure to let go of the control rule will reveal that they imply several possible mechanisms in these terms. To begin with, deliberate control works in many other situations, which would tend to strengthen following of this rule in new situations. It is a tested and successful track. Secondly, as a matter of pliance, we are taught to try to follow the rule in social situations. We learn that we can and should control our private behaviors. Of course, most often we need only control the overt expression of these behaviors, but because the ply has a literal quality, we continue to apply the rule even when the expression of undesirable private behaviors is suppressed. Thirdly, it seems as though other people can follow the rule. To the extent that the rule is also a track, this would tend to lead to increased rule following, since it implies that the natural consequences are as stated in the rule. To the extent that the rule is a ply, this may strengthen rule following by setting a socially available standard against which performance can be evaluated (Hayes, Rosenfarb, Wulfert, Munt, Zettle, & Korn, 1985; Hayes & Wolf, 1984; Rosenfarb & Hayes, 1984; Zettle & Hayes, 1983). The verbal community can say things like "I know you can do better. Look at Johnny. He's not crying." To the extent that the rule functions as an augmental, the apparent success of others may make our own failure sufficiently aversive so that we do everything to avoid the awful possibility that we cannot control our private experience. Finally, the short-term effects of following the rule mimic the contingency stated in the rule, which would tend to reinforce tracking.

Based on this analysis, we can undo the damage by several methods:

1. Teach different rules that have more beneficial effects. This is essentially the move made by cognitive therapy. It is a reasonable strategy, but I am concerned that it buys into the social–verbal context I am talking about. If we have to change our thoughts to be fine, what does that say about us now?

2. Reduce destructive forms of pliance. If we can eliminate the possibility of social compliance with literal rules, the natural contingencies may be able to take more of a hold. This is part of what I have already been describing. Putting a client in an untenable or paradoxical situation with regard to therapist-given rules, for example, should make pliance weaken. There is no longer any way to do "the right thing."

3. Reduce the literality of rules. Paradox is an aid here, but there are additional techniques. Notice, for example, when I am talking about a client's thoughts, I say, "You are having the thought that. . . ." so as to accentuate the difference between the thought as a thought and its literal meaning.

Consistently avoiding the trap of literality, however, is difficult. If one logically points out the problem with literality, one is still supporting literality because your very logic is based on it. Rational argument, therefore, cannot easily accomplish this task to its fullest. Even paradox is based to some degree on the literal meaning of the words themselves. There is another way to undermine literality. How that can be done is a topic to which I shall now turn.

Goal 3: Distinguishing People from Their Behavior

This next section is one of the more complicated ones from a behavioral point of view. Parenthetically, it will also require an even greater tolerance of nontechnical language for me to be able to explain the issue adequately.

Let the word "seeing" represent all of the major things we do with regard to the world (feeling, moving, etc.). To nonverbal organisms there is just the world and seeing. Seeing is controlled entirely by the direct contingencies (of survival and reinforcement). Seeing is simply a response to these nonarbitrary contingencies (Hayes, 1984).

With the advent of verbal behavior this changes. According to the Skinnerian view, something else called self-knowledge or self-awareness is added. Skinner has described it this way: "There is a difference between behaving and reporting that one is behaving or reporting the causes of one's behavior. In arranging conditions under which a person describes the public or private world in which he lives, a community generates that very special form of behavior called knowing. Self-knowledge is of social origin (1974, p. 30). In other words, the verbal community establishes additional arbitrary contingencies for a behavior that it is hard to imagine could emerge any other way: not only seeing but what we might call "seeing seeing" or self-knowledge. Supposedly this happens through such questions as "What did you do yesterday?". There emerges a generalized tendency to respond discriminatively to one's own behavior in order to be able to give the verbal community access to our experiences. As Skinner says, "It is only when a person's private world becomes important to others that it is made important to him" (1974, p. 31).

But there seems to be more to it than that (Hayes, 1984). It is also critical to the verbal community that this behavior occur from a given and consistent perspective, locus, or point of view. That is, we (the verbal community) must not only know that one sees seeing, but that one sees seeing from the point of view of oneself. In this way, the verbal community creates a sense of self that has some very special properties.

The behavior of seeing seeing from a perspective might emerge in several ways. Children are taught deictic words (e.g., "here" and "there"), which do not refer to events but to the relationship between events and the child's point of view. Similarly, children are taught to distinguish their perspective from that of others. Young children, when asked what they ate, may report what their brother ate. If seated across from a doll and asked what the doll sees, they will report what they themselves see, not what the doll sees. Gradually, however, the verbal community teaches us to report from our own point of view. Finally, it is also possible that perspective emerges by process of elimination or by metaphorical extension. We are taught to respond generally to questions of the form "What did you X", where X is a wide variety of events such as eat, feel, do, watch, and so on. The events themselves constantly change. Only the locus of the observation does not. The invariant is that "you" is placed in sentences when reports are to be done from the point of view of you.

In a sense I am arguing that the verbal community creates a kind of "content-less" behavior called "seeing seeing from perspective," and gives it the name "you." I have argued elsewhere that this behavior is the basis of the matter/spirit distinction so prevalent in our culture (Hayes, 1984). We, of course, use the term "you" in other ways as well (e.g., "you as a physical organism"), but the sense of the word "you" that is of special relevance to comprehensive distancing is this former sense.

The behavior of, for example, observing thoughts from a perspective is quite different from the behavior of following self-rules. By helping the person distinguish between seeing seeing from a perspective and the things seen, it may make it more possible to generate a rule without also following that rule or taking it literally. This is a difficult distinction, and it takes quite a bit of work in therapy to get it solidly established. Parenthetically, in the next section of the chapter I shall be using the therapist monologue more to address the reader than to mimic a therapy session. In the interests of space I cannot afford to present the large amount of client–therapist interaction that actually takes place in these middle sessions.

THERAPIST: As it is right now, it is very difficult, if not impossible to stay out of the struggle to get rid of "undesirable" thoughts and feelings. You are too much controlled by your own thoughts about what you need to do. The way we normally operate, we confuse the content of our own conditioning with the behavior of seeing the results of that conditioning. Because of that, when we think a thought, it is as if that thought is also now what is real, not just as a thought but as what the thought says it is. When that happens, we are in what I call the "about" world. We get caught up in what the thoughts are about—not what they are. In other words, you aren't just noticing behavior called thinking, you are actually in the situation described by the thought. If you think you are bad, you *are* bad. Often you don't even notice that it is a thought. Right? So if you think a thought like "I can't stand this. I have to get out of here," it is not at all clear that what actually happened is that you experienced yourself thinking. You did *not* experience what the thought actually said. The form of the thought says one thing, but you actually only experienced that you thought that thought.

The "copy theory" overtones of the next example are due to its use clinically. The reader should not take it too literally.

THERAPIST: Here's a metaphor that may help. Imagine two people sitting in front of two identical computers. Given a particular set of programming, a given input will produce a given output. The programming of these computers are like what has happened to you in your life. Given a certain situation, a certain response is likely. Let's say that we type something in on the keyboard and the output on the screen is "Deep down, you are a bad person." In one case, let's imagine that the person sitting in front of the computer is well aware of the distinction between herself and the computer. When the readout appears on the screen, it may be interesting to this person, or maybe something to consider, or maybe something to show to others. It probably doesn't have to be changed, covered up, followed, not followed, disbelieved, and so on. The second person, however, is totally absorbed by the screen. Like a person at the movies, he has gotten so far into it he has forgotten that there is a distinction between him as an observer of the screen and what is on the screen. A readout like the one I just mentioned would be far more unacceptable to this guy. To him it would probably be something to be denied, forgotten, changed, and so on. In other words, when you identify with the content of your private experiences, you will almost automatically be controlled by them, at least to the extent of trying to get rid of them.

Here is another metaphor that will help make the point. Imagine a chessboard that goes out indefinitely in all directions. On this board are a lot of chess pieces, of all different colors. To keep it simple, let's just concentrate on the white pieces and the black pieces. Now in chess, the pieces are supposed to ally with their friends to beat up on their enemies. So the black pieces sort of hang out together and try to knock the white pieces off the board and vice versa.

These pieces represent the content of your life: your thoughts, feelings, memories, attitudes, behavioral predispositions, bodily sensations, and so on. And if you notice, they do indeed hang out together. For example, the "positive" ones might cluster together—you know, the ones that say things like "I'm going to make it," and so on. And the negative ones work together too. So you'll notice that "bad" thoughts are associated with "bad" memories, "bad" feelings, and so on.

Now the way we usually try to work it is that we nominate one of the teams as "our team." It is as if we get up on the back of the white queen, and ride off to do battle with the black pieces. There is a big problem with that, however. As soon as we do this, whole great portions of us are our own enemy. In addition, if it is true that "If you are not willing to have it, you've got it," then as you battle with the undesirable pieces and try to knock them off the board, they loom larger and larger and larger. And that's in fact what has happened, isn't it? Anxiety, for example, has become more and more and more the central focus of your life.

Within this metaphor, the sad thing is that when you act as if only part of your programming is acceptable, you must also go from who you are to who you are not. To be even more precise, you have to act as if you are no longer who you experience yourself to be. You have to forget that you are not the computer, in that last metaphor. Within this metaphor can you see who "you" are?

CLIENT: I don't know. I always thought I was the pieces. Who else can I be?

THERAPIST: Well, think about it.

CLIENT: The board?

THERAPIST: Yeah. Do you see? You are the board. You are the context in which all these things can even be seen. If there was a thought and no one to see it, it'd be as if it wasn't there at all. Now you notice that a board, while it is being a board, can only do one of two things. It can hold what is put on it or it can move everything, as when you pick up the board and move it in the middle of a game. Note also that it requires no effort to hold the pieces. If the board wanted to move the pieces around one at a time, however, it would have to go from the board level to the piece level. So if you get in the middle of the pieces in the name of moving the pieces you have to forget that you are actually the board. And once you are on the piece level you have to fight, because at that level other pieces seem to threaten your very survival. That's why you can't logically force yourself not to struggle with your emotions. It's a lost cause. What you can do is to distinguish yourself as you experience yourself to be from the events you experience. That is, you can get clear that you are actually on the board level anyway. From that level it is possible to watch the war between your own pieces without actually getting hooked by them—that is, without having to take them literally, or without having to change them before you can get control over your life. It is only by realizing that you don't have control over the pieces and that you don't need it, that you can have control over your life.

This previous metaphor may seem strange, especially for a radical behaviorist. It seems as though I am encouraging a kind of disembodied self: a distinction between the "real person" and behavior. But the verbal community, which established this kind of self to begin with, wasn't trying to establish a literal scientific truth. There are many advantages to helping people get in contact with themselves in this sense. Note that I spoke of "who you experience yourself to be." My argument is that a person can only experience this sense of "you" because of the verbal community. The "you" one experiences oneself to be is primarily "you as perspective," because that is what the verbal community has an interest in establishing as "you." The next section is an exercise drawn largely from a book by Assagioli (1971).

THERAPIST: Okay. I want to do a little exercise to help you get in touch with your actual experience of the events we have been talking about. Remember, I don't want you to believe what I've been saying here. It is not a matter of belief. I don't want just to add to the pieces you have already. What I want you to do is to check and see if in your actual experience the distinctions I've been making aren't evident. When you do that it won't be a matter of words—you'll have made contact with the events directly. It's like how you don't really have to believe in chairs. You know about them from your direct experience and that's more than enough. It's just like that.

I want you to start out by closing your eyes. Notice what your body is doing right now. . . . Notice if you are feeling any feelings or having any emotions. . . . See if you are thinking anything.

And now I want you to notice that when I asked these questions, you were there noticing the reactions. That is, see if it isn't true that behind the content there was a sense of you looking at the content. I'll call that the "observer you." Now from the point of view of the observer you, I want you to look at several areas.

Let's start with your bodily sensations. I want you to notice all the things your body is doing right now. Now think of all the changes your body has been through in your life. Once it was very small but now you are grown. Sometimes it is sick, and sometimes it is well. Sometimes your body is strong, and sometimes it is weak. And now I want you to notice that as your body has changed, that sense of you being you—that observer you—has stayed the same. Remember when you were, say, 10 or 11. Now let me ask you a question. Do you remember being you back then? Do you remember looking out at the world? Now let me ask you another question. Isn't the you that is here now the same you that was there then? Don't answer logically. I'm not asking about your beliefs. I'm asking, Is that experience of observing your life that is here now what was there then? Isn't it true that you have been you your whole life? Now if you have experienced your body rapidly changing and yet the you that you really call you has stayed the same, this must mean that while you have a body, you don't experience yourself to be your body. Please, don't believe this. I'm not giving you more dogma to believe or not believe. I'm simply asking you to acknowledge your experience. Think of these questions. If you lost a hand, wouldn't you still be you? If you had an operation, and an organ was removed, wouldn't you still be you? If you were paralyzed, wouldn't you still be you? In fact, as long as you are here to see your own experiences, you will be you, right? So just spend a few moments watching your body, then notice who is watching.

Okay, now let's go on to another area. Let's look at your emotions. Think of all the emotions you have experienced in your lifetime. Sometimes you are happy, sometimes sad. Sometimes you are angry, sometimes at peace. As you go through your day, one emotion gives way to another, and to another. But notice that you are still there seeing your emotions. So if your emotions are rapidly changing and yet the you that you call you—this observer you—stays the same, it must be that while you have emotions, you don't experience yourself as being your emotions.

Again, don't believe this. It's not a matter of belief. Just notice your emotions right now, and then notice who is noticing them. Spend a few moments just noticing that.

Now let's go to another area: your thoughts. This is a hard one because the very system that allows us to know that we know is the system we are observing when we are looking at our own private speech. Think of all the thoughts you think in a day. Notice how they are also constantly changing. In fact, even as I speak, your thoughts are changing, and changing, and changing again. No sooner do you have a thought about what you are experiencing than you are ready to move on to something else. Notice how your thoughts have changed over the years. When you were small, you used to think thoughts that you no longer think. And you had areas of ignorance that you now have changed. As you live your life this is continuing to happen and happen again. Now notice once more that while your thoughts are constantly changing that sense of being you has stayed the same. This must mean that while you have thoughts, you don't experience yourself as being your thoughts. So just go on noticing your thoughts for a while. Now notice who is noticing them.

This exercise can be expanded to include any behaviors the therapist wants to distinguish. I typically start with roles, for example, and will commonly include memories or other behaviors. I also spend much more time on each section than the abbreviated version here suggests.

In what sense is it possible that the socially created sense of "you" can be independent from all these behaviors? This is possible only because the behavior of seeing seeing from a perspective is itself content free. That is, it is a behavior that cannot itself be seen as a thing by the person behaving in this way (Hayes, 1984). No sooner does a person notice this behavior than the behavior has fundamentally changed. If conscious organisms were to see their own perspective, from what perspective could it be seen? Thus, the sense of self established by the verbal community can be looked from, but cannot be looked at—or at least, as soon as it is looked at, the behavior being examined is no longer occuring in the same place. The "observer exercise" above simply allows clients to get a fleeting glance at what people know very well anyway, that the sense of being "you" stays the same through life. It has to because all it is is the sense of viewing from perspective. If that were to change, one would no longer be that same "you."

There is something enormously calming about this exercise. I have had many clients who were very different after this one session. To give a sense of how I use this exercise, I shall relate how I conclude it.

THERAPIST: So now notice that as an experiential matter (in addition to whatever you believe), you know you are not your thoughts, your roles, your emotions, or your body. You are the context in which all of these things can be seen as things. Without you they would not exist. They are in your life but they are not who you are. So all these things you have been struggling with, all these things you have been trying to change, *aren't you anyway.* I want you to notice that you are big enough for all these things to be there. You don't have to change something in order to move ahead—in order to earn your right to be acceptable. You are acceptable just the way you are.

The point is that is it only when a distinction is made between this sense of self and the things in one's life that it is possible consistently to do anything else with these things other than struggle with them, follow them, try to get rid of them, and so on. We have lots of socially established rules about self-worth. People want to be acceptable to themselves and others. Unfortunately, because of verbal evaluation, at the level of content no one is truly acceptable. I sometimes ask my clients to name one thing in the physical universe that they can't find fault with. Usually they can't. Then I ask, "So why should you be an exception?"

If the "you" one takes oneself to be is this observer "you," these rules of self-worth are handled fairly easily. Since the observer "you" is in a sense "content free," there is no-thing about "you" to be unacceptable. Only things can be evaluated, and at the deepest level one cannot experience oneself in the sense of "you as perspective" to be a thing.

Goal 4: Letting Go of the Struggle

There are many ways clients can get pulled into a struggle with their thoughts and feelings. At this point in therapy, I typically point out several ways that we can be hooked by the literal sense of our thoughts and descriptions of experiences. I shall go through some of these briefly, but the reader should know that I am obviously skipping quite a bit in all of these sections. As is probably noticeable, a contextual approach differs in many basic ways not only from behavior therapy or cognitive therapy, but also from our mainstream culture. For these reasons, I cannot describe the approach fully even within the confines of a lengthy chapter.

One way people can get pulled back into a struggle is by confusing evaluation with the things evaluated. When we say, "That is a cup," and when the statement is controlled by the cup itself, the statement is a tact. The tact is a case when the equivalence between verbal stimuli and the world can afford to be very tight. If all tracks were based on tacts, literality would present no problem, because the rule would only be present when the events the word tacts are also present. Unfortunately, many other apparent descriptions are not actually tacts, but they can nevertheless be tracked (Zettle & Hayes, 1982). For example, a person might say, "That is a good cup." The word *good* is in all likelihood not a tact. There is no stimulus "good" present. Actually, we are probably reacting to such things as whether or not we like the cup. Rather than describing our reactions to the cup, however, we seem to be describing the cup itself: "That is a good cup."

There are two things that are destructive about this. First, we are then likely to track this rule literally, even though it is not literally true: It is not a tact. Second, we cannot allow tacts to change readily. If I say of a cup, "That is a race car," the verbal community cannot afford to reinforce that kind of talk. To do so would result in chaos. In other words, tact like terms must be very resistant to change. If "good" is allowed to be treated as a tact, it too cannot change. Thus, our evaluations must be held on to, defended, followed, made right, and so on. One can see the terrible irony of this when clients have been hooked by such thoughts as "I am bad." Pseudo-tacts cannot easily change, so once one thinks one is bad one must continue to be bad. If a person approaches this as an issue of being as one is *and* also having the thought that one is bad then no such artificial rigidity is created. The person may sometimes think "I'm bad" and sometimes not: As thoughts come and go, so do the terms "bad" and "good," since they have lost their literal status.

In the area of evaluation, I encourage clients to name evaluations as evaluations. For example, instead of saying, "My job is awful; I have to get out of there," clients would learn to say, "My evaluation of my job is that it is awful, and I'm having the thought that I have to get out of there." After several weeks this cumbersome usage can be reduced, but if at any time it seems as though clients are getting pulled back into a struggle, this convention can be reestablished for a short period of time. It can make a remarkable difference in the control exerted by client talk of this sort.

Evaluations can also present a problem when clients confuse a willingness to experience feelings (i.e., letting go of control) with the evaluation that the experience is desirable. A metaphor I use is that of an open house party to which everyone in the neighborhood is invited. Unfortunately, the bum who sleeps behind the supermarket shows up. It is still possible to *welcome* him without having to *like* the fact that he has shown up. If the host doesn't like it, that very dislike is just yet another bum at the door, or what one of my students called the "bum's chums." So evaluation is not the same as willingness. The client need not like his or her anxiety—the issue is the willingness to have it when he or she has it.

Another way clients encourage struggle is by the use of language that implies that struggle is necessary. The clearest example of this is the use of the world *but*. *But* is typically used to denote some sort of incompatibility between one event and another. The incompatibility, however, arises from social conventions about consistency and compatibility. For instance, if a client says, "I want to go into the mall, but I am afraid," it suggests that fear is incompatible with approach. This is nothing more than giving an emotional reason as a cause of behavior. Thus, *but* almost always supports the context of reason giving. In therapy I encourage clients to change every *but* to the word *and*. In almost every situation the word *and* fits better and is more truthful, in that it describes the client's experience more closely. In addition, because the context of control is based on the context of reason giving, undermining the context of reason giving greatly weakens unnecessary efforts to change private events before life changes are possible. A client saying, "I want to go into the mall, and I am afraid," is just describing two emotional events. Neither has to change before an action is taken. The next question for the client is, "Are you willing to go into the mall *and* feel afraid?"

Goal 5: Making a Commitment to Action

After the above work, the client is now more ready to take directive action to change the quality of his or her life. Since reasons are now just verbal behavior, not literal causes, the person can make promises and know that there will be no excuses for a failure to follow through.

It is at this point that traditional behavioral techniques become of more importance. They are always placed, however, into the context of a contextual approach to private experience. Sometimes this takes a bit of conceptual reorganization, since many of these techniques originally emerged within the context of control, and control is what limits the horizons of clients in the first place. I know of no behavioral technique that cannot be rationalized within a contextual approach, except for some forms of cognitive therapy.

For example, when I am working with agoraphobics, we generally start to do deliberate approach exercises at about this point (about six sessions into therapy). The exposure work, however, is not designed to reduce anxiety. Instead, exposure gives people an opportunity to practice experiencing anxiety without also struggling with anxiety. It is as well an opportunity to make and keep commitments. The question I always ask clients before they try exposure is, "Out of the place in which there is a distinction between you and the things you experience, are you willing to experience your thoughts and feelings without defense, denial, covering up, avoiding, trying to change, or any other kind of struggle—*and* do what really works for you in this situation by keeping your commitment?" If the answer is "no," we go back to the earlier part of therapy and find out what the hang-up is. If the answer is "yes," it is time to go to exposure. During exposure, I continually work with the client to recognize the distinction between them as a person and the private behaviors they are experiencing. I encourage the client to feel whatever is there to feel, including anxiety, and not to struggle with it. The commitment to experiencing one's own feelings must be fairly strong. I use the example of a child throwing a tantrum to get candy. If the child knows that the parent has a limit and will give in if it is reached—perhaps 5 minutes—guess how long the tantrum will last? In the same way, if a client is willing to be anxious, it is important not to let it be a half-measure. Like the child, a client's emotions will know the limits and likely exceed them. There is no bluffing oneself.

Imaginal exposure such as desensitization is now an opportunity to both feel anxiety and let go of the struggle with it. As I say to my clients, "Just keep your eyes open, your feet on the floor, and your hands off." By this I mean that the client should see the emotion or thought, but neither run from it nor struggle with it. A metaphor suggested originally by a client that I sometimes use is this: "Imagine you are in a tug-of-war with an enormous monster, who seems intent on pulling you into a pit. You struggle more and more, but the harder you struggle the stronger he becomes. Instead of struggling, you can do something even more effective: drop the rope. Unless you join the battle, the monster (e.g., anxiety) can have no control." I sometimes use deliberate "willingness exercises" to practice "dropping the rope." For example, I sometimes have the client sit about a foot from me and look me in the eyes for two minutes without talking or laughing. As I do this, I encourage the client to experience but not buy into any feelings, thoughts, and so on that, if taken literallly, would interfere with the exercise (including such "helpful" thoughts as "I'm going to do this right").

Some forms of cognitive therapy as it is usually taught can also be used to some degree. Rational–emotive therapy is very difficult to integrate within this perspective because it comes so close to saying that you shouldn't think certain thoughts. This seems likely to increase the pathological control of socially established rules, though those very rules are now those established in therapy itself (see Zettle & Hayes, 1980; 1982). RET seeks to change the thoughts. Comprehensive distancing seeks to change the context within which thoughts occur.

Beck's approach (e.g., Beck & Emery, 1985) is more compatible, at least in some of its elements. There is certainly much to be said for teaching clients to formulate rules in testable form, and to test the accuracy of rules. Essentially, this can be thought of as training in tracking (Zettle & Hayes, 1982). Beck also has his "distancing," though it is not as comprehensive as the present approach.

Comprehensive distancing shares many attributes with various experiential therapies. I frequently use Gestalt exercises, for example, because they lead quite naturally to some sense of distance between the content of experiences and the person engaging in the process of experiencing them. Essentially, Gestalt exercises are ways to do imaginal exposure to private events that clients are struggling with, avoiding, or trying to change. For example, I often have clients put their emotions out in front of them and describe them physically.

I occasionally use some psychoanalytic techniques as well. A form of free-association exercise I like is one that one of my clients invented. She called it the "soldiers in the parade" exercise. She imagined that her thoughts were soldiers marching by carrying signs with the thought on them. The game was to watch the parade as from a reviewing stand and to see how long she could go without stopping the parade. Invariably, clients discover that the parade will stop when one of the thoughts is taken literally. At that moment the client loses what Freud called the proper attitude of "quiet, unreflecting, self-observation." Rather than looking *at* the thought, the client is now looking *from* the thought, and the parade ends. This is an exercise that can easily be done at home.

Another association exercise that can be done in session begins by selecting a private event with which the client is struggling. With eyes closed, the client gets in close contact with it. The therapist then asks the client to name one bodily feeling that seems associated with the event. When a single specific symptom is named, the therapist encourages the client to see if it is possible to feel just that bodily symptom without defense, denial, or struggle—that is, without an attempt to control it. In this manner the therapist takes the client through several bodily sensations, then several emotions, several thoughts, several behavioral predispositions, and finally several memories. In each case the therapist helps the client actually experience the associated item fully. It can be a powerful exercise. There are many more metaphors and exercises that fit well within a contextual approach, but the explication of these will have to await another even more extended forum.

DIFFERENTIATING TECHNIQUE FROM THEORY

The present volume asks, "What is the relationship between behavior therapy and cognitive therapy?" From a radical behavioral point of view, all effective therapy is behavioral. By this I obviously don't mean that only techniques commonly called "behavioral" will work. I mean, if we intend to have a comprehensive account of human behavior, and if we call all the principles that explain behavior "behavioral principles," and if a therapy changed behavior, then it must have occurred because of behavioral principles. This does not mean that we currently know all the behavioral principles needed to account for human action. We don't. Our task is to discover them. Sometimes behaviorists act as if all behavior must be accounted for by known behavioral principles, but really this is not at all inherent in the position. It is an arrogant abberation of it.

In my opinion, behavior therapy is not a body of techniques. Rather, it is an approach to therapy that is organized, rationalized, and evaluated in terms of behavioral philosophy, concepts, and methodology. Thus, "psychodynamic," "Gestalt," or any other set of techniques can be part of behavior therapy when (but only when) this occurs. In fact, many so-called behavior therapy techniques are really not behavioristic in a radical behavioral sense of the term.

Within contemporary methodological behaviorism, only two sensible uses of the term "behavior therapy" seem possible. One could claim that all empirically established techniques are behavioral. Essentially, then, behavior therapy becomes empirical clinical psychology. Conversely, one could view techniques that obviously treat overt behavior as "behavioral." In this case, however, behavior therapy will forever be a mere subset of therapeutic approaches, and theoretical eclecticism will be confused inextricably with technical eclecticism.

THE ROLE OF THE THERAPIST

Within a contextual perspective, the therapist must be able to discern and react to sources of control over behavior that are nearly ubiquitous in our culture. The contexts of literality, reason giving, and control are the dominant contexts within which we all function. Since the goal of comprehensive distancing is to change these contexts, it means that we cannot rely on the form of the behavior, but must discern its function.

Behaviorists are particularly attuned to the form/function distinction, so it would seem that they would be fairly well prepared for this task. In general, this seems to be true, but not always. Successful work within this perspective seems to require the following:

1. *Sensitivity to destructive rule control.* Clients can learn to function within a contextual perspective, but it is not easy. Therapists need to be on the look out for such statements as "I'm finally learning to ignore this anxiety." Such an innocuous sounding statement is dangerous because usually it means that the person thinks that anxiety has to be ignored in order for its effects to weaken. This begins once again to set up a struggle to reduce or eliminate anxiety. Similarly, clients may say in a response to a question about how things are going, "I feel pretty good." This is a bit worrisome because it implies that the measure of success or failure should be feelings. It is but a short jump from "I want to feel good" to "I don't want to feel bad." There is nothing wrong with these wants per se, but if they are taken literally, the struggle will recommence. I often warn clients that if anxiety drops after the "control scale" drops (as it nearly always does), this is a tricky time. Seeing that the anxiety has dropped, clients often act as if they now know how to control their anxiety. They are grateful it has finally gone away. As soon as clients start to take this self-talk literally, the control scale is moving back up again. Then when anxiety raises its head once more, as it always eventually does, rather than just let

it assume a natural level appropriate to the moment, the struggle begins anew because of the attitude that says, "I thought I had it licked, but I didn't." Therapists must therefore be very sensitive to the early stages of this kind of struggle and to the multiple pathways that can give rise to it.

2. *A rapid and flexible (but nondominating) approach.* Therapists must also be able to act on their observations rapidly. The therapist must be capable of restating the basic issues in new ways that fit the situation at hand without simultaneously dominating the client. The therapist has to let the client discover some of these things, but the therapist also has to be flexible and creative in fostering this discovery. Good therapists are ready to fit their points into a form that is nondominating and often nonliteral, when the client requires it. The creative use of metaphor and allegory, for example, is extensive in this approach. This tends to allow clients to discover points without linear rationality. Much of this chapter may have seemed to indicate that one can just tell people a few stories and expect to create change. In reality, the interaction itself is critical. The didactic material simply sets up a rationale to do the truly important work: discriminating and reacting to the client's "system" moment to moment. In an average session in the early parts of therapy (but after the relatively didactic first five or six sessions), I may have to reorient a client by pointing out the implicit struggles they are setting up perhaps four or five times, and each time may take a few minutes to deal with. Thus, rapid assessment and a flexible approach is essential to success in this therapy.

3. *Placing techniques in proper context.* A difficult area in this approach is the necessity of fitting techniques and exercises into a general context that is not well-established within the culture. I find that novice therapists often slip into using techniques in the name of outcomes that don't fit within this approach. For example, they often will propose relaxation training as a way to help the client relax rather than as practice in letting go of the struggle with anxiety. Similarly, novice therapists will tell clients that being more assertive will make the client feel better, when in fact that is not the purpose (nor the necessary outcome) of this training within this context.

4. *Practicing what one preaches.* A final therapist characteristic is perhaps the most difficult. Because a contextual approach clashes with the mainstream cultural view, most therapists at first have a hard time practicing what they are preaching. In general, a therapist who intends to practice from this context must do so not as a technique or rap to be laid on others, but as a context for the behavior of the therapist and client alike. The problems above (sensitivity, flexible intervention, and the creative use of specific techniques) probably all flow from this point. We can be more sensitive to the traps others lay only when we see some of our own. Thus, therapists can point out the relevance of this context to specific events only if they have been examining such relevance frequently and in detail—

as will be the case if they are applying it to their own lives. Finally, therapists will use techniques consistently only when the general approach is thoroughly integrated into their own lives. A contextual approach is not a technique.

COMMON CLINICAL ERRORS

To some extent I have already dealt with this issue above, but there I was concentrating more on the mistakes made within this approach. If I examine the mistakes as seen from this approach, the list expands. By far the easiest error is to take content rather than context as the issue. That is, we may be tempted to take the client's report of what bothers him or her as an accurate assessment of what needs to be changed, when in fact this event is problematic only within a given context. This is especially sad when it sets up the client for a continuing problem and superficial improvement. For example, many of the so-called anxiety management procedures seem to lead to only limited improvement. I believe this is because they seek only to change the form of the behavior, not to alter the behavior in a full functional sense. Other approaches sometimes work but leave untouched the system that created the problem in the first place. For example, paradoxical instructions (Weeks & L'Abate, 1982) can short-circuit the attempt to control private experience, but leave in place the social–verbal support for this kind of control to emerge once again.

A second type of error can occur when therapists act as if the problems clients are facing indicate that they are somehow broken, or deficient, or that they need in some basic way to be shown how to behave. Most commonly this reveals itself in a tendency to give advice needlessly or to instruct people about the *form* their behavior should take. When we therapists take this parental role with clients, we sometimes incapacitate their ability to experience the contingencies directly and to find that they have the resources to learn and to grow. For all of the directive talk that some readers may have discerned in this chapter, note that very little of it tells the client what form of behavior to adopt. The confrontation is more like presenting a client with a dilemma than a prescription.

I am very suspicious of advice and instructions. Most often what we tell clients are things they have already heard. If the problem is a lack of proper instructions, why hasn't this been enough? Of course, there are some kinds of problems that are amenable to simple instructional interventions, but probably far fewer than we pretend. Furthermore, instructions seem to have a great likelihood of trapping clients even if they do work (Hayes et al., 1986b). For example, when we tell a person what to do to behave in a socially skillful manner, we may also be setting a ceiling on the excellence of the performance that person will show. They are too busy following the rule to learn from the direct contingencies themselves (Azrin & Hayes, 1984).

A final type of error that is crucial in this approach is inconsistency. A therapist can't expect to make a permanent or lasting change in the context of client behavior if the context established in therapy keeps changing. In a technique-oriented approach, in which various techniques stand more or less independently of each other, inconsistency is not a great problem. Comprehensive distancing is a bolder approach that seeks to alter fundamentally a basic mechanism of behavioral control. For this, greater consistency is required.

COMMON CLINICAL ISSUES

Resistance

In some sense, my entire approach is oriented toward handling the problem of resistance. The client is, in a way, resistant before even coming to therapy. Why hasn't the problematic behavior changed as negative consequences were contacted? This kind of resistance, as I've already stated, I believe usually comes from a problem in rule control.

In comprehensive distancing, resistance is prevented by distancing the client as a conscious organism from the content of what we experience. This is *not* done to diminish these experiences, or to make them less powerful, important, or felt. The purpose of distance is not to get the events away from the client, but to give him or her the room to experience them fully as they are without actually taking them for what they say they are literally. Thus, for example, sadness is sadness—nothing more or less—and something to be felt, not to be run from or controlled by. Much of resistance is actually a "control move," thus distancing may automatically reduce resistance.

By undermining reason giving and searches for needless explanations, the therapist is able to reduce the client's ability to invoke the social norms or standards that are used to justify and explain resistance. Even if a great reason is given for resistance, the question will still come back to "And does buying into that rule work for you?" Thus, an explanation can be great yet irrelevant, and not something to be followed. Resistance doesn't work. When we face up to that and see our attempts to explain our way out as just more behavior, the defense created by resistance crumbles.

I also prevent resistance by having clients make personal commitments to change. I explain that it is no skin off my nose if their problems continue. I will still think well of them as people, though I will feel sorry that they are so stuck. Thus, the commitment isn't to me—it is a simple recognition and acknowledgment of the way things are. When a client admits that X doesn't work and Y does work, the simple question is "Do you agree to do what works?" If so, it needs to be done. I make it clear that it doesn't help for clients to give me the reasons that they can't do what works. If clients do not agree, then so be it—but then they must be honest with themselves about why they are where they are. This kind of rule making and following is essentially a matter of tacting and tracking. When one takes away the verbal defenses, as this approach does, people are led quite naturally to this kind of rule control. A metaphor I sometimes use is that of a driver of a bus. The passengers are thoughts and feelings. They will tell the driver (the person having those thoughts and feelings) which way to turn, and threaten that if the driver doesn't obey them they will come forward and make the driver look at them. Trying to throw them off the bus doesn't work—and besides the driver would have to stop the bus to even try. The solution is to do what Greyhound does. The driver puts a sign on the front of the bus saying where she is going and then goes there. That's called a commitment. If the passengers don't like the destination or the route they are welcome to leave, but leave or not, the driver is going where the sign says. The driver can only do this, of course, if she makes no deals with the passengers that they will keep out of sight if she drives where they say.

A final issue hasn't yet been described, but is also fundamental to this approach. People have a long history of engaging in formal analyses. They explain things and figure things out. They also have a long history of social reinforcement for the adequacy of such analyses. This is what is called "being right." Over time, being right becomes a very powerful reinforcer. People actively enlist members of the verbal community to support the analyses, so the reinforcement for this behavior is both pervasive and fairly rich.

The problem with this is that the social consequences of being right can override the natural consequences of the behavior. Thus, we will often work to maintain the apparent accuracy of our analyses even if the consequences are quite negative. For instance, if a husband has the view that his wife is screwing up the relationship, he may need to keep the relationship screwed up in order to keep his analysis correct. We actively work against our own interests because our interests are split between the social consequences for being right and the natural consequences for behaving effectively.

I deal with this issue by pointing out this system, and by asking the person to make a choice. If even one person knows the nature of the game, to some extent the game is up. For example, a client once came into a therapy session saying he was going to kill himself because his soon-to-be-ex-wife was now living with someone. I found myself angry. I said, "Look, if you are so interested in making your wife wrong and you right that you are willing to sacrifice your life to that end, go right ahead. But I want you to know that there will be one person left behind on this planet who will know the truth—who will know what you are doing. You may even fool your wife—she might even buy this crap—but you and I know what's really going on here." With that, he started to cry. The issue shifted quite quickly to what he was trying to defend himself against by being right. He gave me his bullets. Years later he was to tell me this was a turning point in his life. Had we not dealt with the right and wrong issue somewhat previously I would not have been able to take such a strong stand. He would have thought I was saying he was wrong—which I wasn't. I was just saying that what he was doing (trying to be right and make others wrong) wasn't working for him.

This gives the general strategy I follow when resistance emerges in therapy. I point it out, including the way in which it is being produced by old programming that has harmed the client in other ways. I get the client to focus on the costs, and cut off verbal avenues of escape. I make sure the client sees that I am not challenging him or her, but rather the system that runs him or her. Thus, the client is not wrong to be controlled by this, rather it simply has a cost. I try to make sure that the issue doesn't slip into that of me versus the client, because it is invariably the client's programming versus the client. Then I let the client choose. *Choose* might seem to be a strange word for a behaviorist to use, but I mean it simply descriptively. The client chooses. That is a behavior, not an explanation. We usually don't know the explanation. Personally, I like to use the language of choice with clients because it allows for no justification or explanation: We choose because we choose, we don't choose for reasons. We sometimes say, "It's a free choice." This may sound mentalistic, but actually it is a most behaviorally sound way to speak. If one can "choose freely," there are no reasons one can give for failing to follow through with choices. Thus, the word *free* in "free choice" keeps talk of choice at the level of description, since it incapacitates the ability to explain. Description is right where choice belongs. Parenthetically, this is an example of how words can literally conflict with behaviorism, and yet functionally support behaviorally sound moves with the client.

Generalization and Maintenance

The approach to therapy I am describing applies to many situations in people's lives. When you get right down to it, jobs, school, friends, relationships, health habits, and so on all suffer from our tendency to try to use mental way stations to explain and justify our actions. I have repeatedly found major areas of generalization simply emerge as the nature of the similarity becomes plain. For example, I recently concluded my work with an obsessive-compulsive who came to see me right after her second psychiatric hospitalization for her disorder. She was very afraid of hurting others, and had multiple checking rituals. For example, she would repeatedly retrace her route while driving to make sure she hadn't hit anyone with her car. She had received about every kind of therapy you could think of, from tranquilizers to electroshock therapy. After her treatment, her problem of 25 years cleared up (see Figure 2, Client 1). She stopped trying to fight with anxiety.

After I concluded therapy with her I asked her to talk to a graduate class I was teaching, which she did. She was asked by a student, "What was the most important thing Dr. Hayes did for you?" She replied, "The main thing, I think, was that I thought that in order to get well I had to somehow not even think that I could have done something to hurt somebody. I didn't think I could have those thoughts and live with them. I thought, you know, that 'the thought can't be there because I can't live with it, so I've got to act on it.' And right off the bat, Dr. Hayes said, 'It ain't gonna be like that. The thoughts will probably not get any less. You may not have them any less than you do now, but they don't have to push you around.' And he told me that the only things I could change were my willingness to be anxious and my behavior. I think it was when I decided that it was okay to be anxious and that it was preferable to practically killing myself to get rid of the anxiety that then sometimes I was anxious and sometimes I wasn't."

This kind of insight is the sort that naturally seems to generalize. For example, during therapy, as she became more willing to feel anxiety for what it really was, she suddenly also began to be much more assertive. She started taking broken things back to the stores, handling relationship problems at work, and in general showing a most impressive form of generalization. Yet we spent very little time directly on this in therapy. When I asked her how she was able to be so much more assertive, she explained that she was simply more willing to experience the thoughts that she shouldn't be assertive, the feelings that it would be disastrous to be assertive, *and* to behave in accordance with the reality that it works to be assertive.

I encourage this process in four ways. First, I deliberately expand the scope of therapy topics as therapy progresses. Old issues that may not have led to therapy in the first place but are nevertheless irksome are brought up and dealt with. Second, I allow connections to emerge in therapy, and am quite willing to wander off periodically into areas that are only loosely associated with the topic. For example, I am quite willing to talk about old memories, family issues, financial problems, or just about anything the client brings up. In the end, they usually are more related than they at first seem. In a sense, I am following Stokes and Baer's (1977) advice to "train loosely." Third, I try to show how each new issue is really the same thing: The same principles apply. As new issues emerge, it is sometimes hard for clients to see this, but after several issues have been dealt with in the same way, generalization becomes more likely. In a sense, they learn the strategy, not just the specific instance. Finally, I have many of my clients participate in a group toward the end of individual therapy. The group consists of former clients, and current clients late in therapy. It meets once each month, and tends to focus on ways to expand the progress they have made into other areas. Due to a move, I just recently had to terminate a group of this sort after 2½ years. The last year was not even spent directly on anxiety but on issues chosen by the group, such as friends, money, sex, jobs, intimate relationships, and so on. By seeing the relevance of this approach to general life issues, clients seem to become better able to generalize what they are learning in therapy to new topics.

Given the support from the mainstream culture for reasons and emotional struggle, one would think that maintenance would be very difficult in this approach. The reinforcement for normal rule following continues. In this approach the therapist can't just cover the major issues once. They have to be covered again and again. When clients finally break through, however, the issue seems to change. Maintenance continues to be an issue, but a surprisingly moderate one. Once the system is seen clearly, it is difficult to go back to it fully. It is hard to believe one's beliefs 100% after it is clear that beliefs are just more behavior. The two mechanisms I use for maintenance are the group I just mentioned and booster sessions as needed. About half of my clients will see me once or twice in the year following termination, just to clear up a sticking point. Usually this can be done quite rapidly, because they simply have to make contact with the repertoire established earlier in therapy. For example, an ex-agoraphobic client (over 2 years posttherapy) recently had a panic attack in a movie theater and then quickly began to slide into a struggle with anxiety. In three sessions compressed into 1 week we were able to reverse the slide and to find how the attack had been set up by some struggling that preceded it. Additional treatment was not necessary.

The Therapeutic Relationship

I have already explained why comprehensive distancing is not just something that can be presented as a set of stories. It is necessary to have the therapist there to shape the client directly. A therapeutic relationship seems very important. But to shape, we also need to have some social power. In my opinion, one of the quickest ways to gain this is to respect clients.

Humans have problems. When we handle our deficiency problems, we make up new problems called "challenges." It never stops, nor does it need to. In this context, there is no real difference between clients and therapists. It is not a matter of a whole person and a broken person. It is not a matter of those that know and those that don't. Rather, it is simply easier to see other's traps than our own. Sometimes I tell my clients a metaphor to make the point. I ask them to imagine a team climbing a mountain. Across a great ravine sits another member of the team, who is watching progress up the cliff. He can radio to the team to tell them about blocks in their way up the mountain. If he were on the mountain, he'd probably be having as much of a problem as the team members. Therapy is often like that.

The therapeutic relationship is thus established between two human beings, one of whom is supporting the other not out of a position of superiority, but out of a position of advantaged perspective. I respect my clients—love them really. I value them as human beings, and do not view their problems as deficiencies on their parts. The kind of relationship this naturally fosters is one that is supportive but task oriented—we're here for a purpose. One of my clients once called it "colleagial." I knew what she meant.

Ambivalence

The dictionary defines ambivalence as the existence of "mutually conflicting feelings about a person or thing." It is a common clinical issue in everything from marital difficulties to disorders such as schizophrenia or borderline personality. In a contextual approach, ambivalence is viewed as troublesome only because the context of literality makes the feelings seem literally conflicting. The goal is to allow the client to experience both of the feelings without having to have one win out over the other, and at the same time to choose a consistent course of action regardless of which side seems stronger at the moment.

When this works it can have dramatic effects. One of my students (Zamir Korn) successfully treated a client diagnosed as a borderline personality disorder. He had a long history of relationship problems and an inability to hold a job. He would alternate between wanting to be close to people and hating them. He would want to succeed at a job only to be totally bored with it a short time later. He had an extremely negative view of himself generally. The ambivalence can be thought of in terms of the chessboard analogy. It was as if sometimes he viewed things from the white pieces, and sometimes from the black—what is called "splitting."

The goal in therapy was to help him to see both sides from "board level", and then while holding both sides, to set a course of action. The client learned to make room for ambivalence *and* to set and keep commitments. Toward the end of therapy, for example, the client chose to remarry his ex-wife. He described his 4-hour drive to meet her as full of "ghosts and goblins" (thoughts and feelings about remarrying or not remarrying). Instead of trying to fight these off he acknowledged them and kept to his commitment. He did in fact remarry, and has kept his job for over three years. Six of the seven highly elevated MMPI scales that were present at the beginning of therapy decreased to the normal range by the end of treatment. Near the termination of therapy, the client read a poem he had written that described his therapeutic experience and that makes clear the relevance of this approach to ambivalence:

> I've been in this life for over 33 years
> I've seen the joy and I've experienced the tears
>
> I've lived with people and I've lived alone
> I've been lazy and I've put my fingers to the bone
>
> I've never much followed my intuition
> My life has been filled with indecision
>
> But now I think I've scratched the surface
> Into who I am and my whole purpose
>
> Hating myself isn't really a crime
> I feel happy and sad at the same time

Termination

The end of something implies a state of affairs that is permanent or settled. In therapy it doesn't usually work that way. When are our problems permanently handled? When are they settled? My goal is not to fix people, but to get them unstuck. The natural contingencies will move our lives forward. Thus, the "end" of therapy is a place in which a process of learning is established. The process will hopefully always continue.

I try to ease termination by making sure clients know they can come back if need be, by providing long-term resources like the group, and by increasing the intervals between therapy sessions over the last few months of therapy. Most of all, however, I try to make clear what the end of therapy is: It is a process, not an outcome.

Successes and Failures

At this point, my impression is that the approach is quite powerful with anxiety disorders and depression. I have also used it successfully with drug and other self-control problems. I have tried it in case management with schizophrenics, and while I do not pretend that it treats the psychosis itself, it has seemed to help the clients be a little less controlled by delusional thinking and hallucinations.

Not all clients will respond to this approach, of course. Clients who are not in considerable pain or otherwise ready for a major change will not give the therapist the room necessary for such a fundamental challenge to our normal perspective on things. For example, I was unable to treat a highly successful businessman who could not urinate in public. He viewed his own life in such a highly positive way that he had no interest in altering how he dealt with emotions more generally. I also failed, however, with a more traditional behavioral approach with this same client.

Although some of my most successful cases have been obsessive–compulsives, others seem to have a system of verbal control that is so tight that I could not "get through" enough to accomplish the job fully. I have, like most other clinicians, banged my head against the brick walls of personality disorders of all kinds with only a few successes, but the failure here seems more related to the power of the disorder than the poor fit with this approach.

People hearing about comprehensive distancing for the first time often believe that the approach could only be used with very intellectual clients. In fact, I have used it successfully with children as young as age 9 (although all the language has to be changed, they catch on very quickly), and with uneducated people with borderline IQs. The clients have to be willing to examine basic issues, but they do not seem to need unusual degrees of intelligence to do so. A few clients can't relate at all to the metaphors and with these I seem to have much more difficulty. I don't know exactly what distinguishes these people from others. I know it is not a matter of socioeconomic status or any other obvious demographic variable, since I have had successes with clients from a range of backgrounds. There seems to be a kind of rigidity to the thinking of these people that doesn't allow them to see the meaning of metaphors. It is as if everything has to be taken literally.

THE IMPACT OF COMPREHENSIVE DISTANCING

We have attempted to evaluate this approach in several ways. The majority of the data that exist in support of the position has already been reported, namely the variety of basic findings that seems to make the analysis plausible. We have spent some time evaluating the therapeutic approach specifically. Because these data have been relatively supportive, more of our research efforts continue to be put into developing the basic principles necessary to analyze verbal behavior in this way. As we have learned more about equivalence classes, rule-governed behavior, and so on, our therapeutic techniques have been modified.

We have developed outcome data of three types: analogue studies, clinical replication, and formal comparative outcome studies.

Analogue Studies

One of the first studies we attempted was a study on the tolerance of pain (Hayes, Korn, Zettle, Rosenfarb, & Cooper, 1982). This seemed like a good place to start because the behavioral measure is precise, pain tolerance studies can be done with analogue subjects, and it seemed as though pain is often given as a reason for various behavior. We tested out this latter assumption by presenting a description to several dozen undergraduates of several common situations in which pain was used as an excuse. For example, we described a situation in which someone has agreed to help clean up a shared dorm room, but fails to keep the commitment. The reason that is given is "I started to do the floors but my knees hurt." Subjects are asked to rate the validity of the reason given. We found that reasons of this sort were rated quite highly. This seems to fit the analysis of reasons given earlier and supports the use of pain tolerance as an analogue task.

We brought in 24 undergraduates, tested their pain tolerance on a cold pressor task, and then assigned them to three groups: an attention placebo group, a cognitive package, and a comprehensive distancing package. The cognitive package was a combination of procedures shown in the literature to have the greatest influence on pain tolerance (see Hayes *et al.*, 1982, for a more complete description). The distancing package included an analysis of reasons given, emotional control, and willingness. Clients were not asked to make a commitment regarding the tolerance task. The data for all subjects are shown in Figure 9-1. As can be seen, there was a

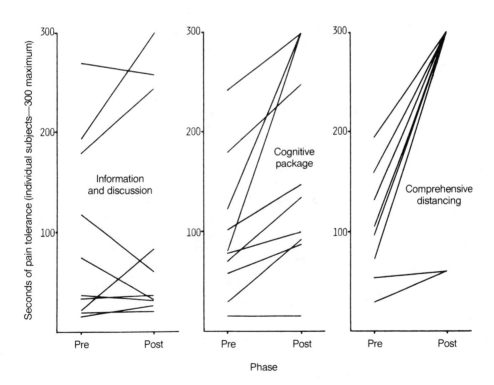

FIGURE 9-1. The pretest and posttest pain tolerance scores in seconds for each individual subject in each group.

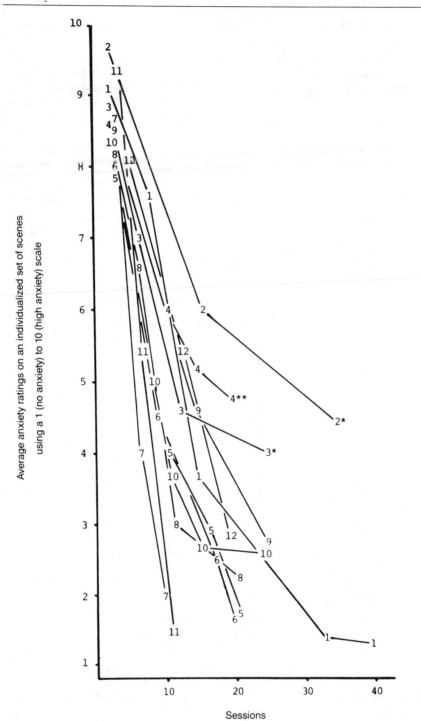

significant difference between the groups in the difference in pain tolerance from pre- to posttest. The cognitive package produced significantly
greater improvement than the attention placebo group, with the comprehensive distancing group significantly more improved than the other two
groups.

We later attempted to use comprehensive distancing in a large group
approach for treatment of studying problems, but without success. It
seems as though fairly close contact between the therapist (or experimenter) and the client may be required to keep the client from using verbal
defenses of the sort the approach attempts to undermine.

Clinical Replication

At the present time I have been using this approach primarily with anxiety
disorders, depression, and a few other disorders (e.g., bulimia, personality
disorders) in my private practice. Some of my students have also used the
approach with similar clients. In Figure 9-2 I have presented the first
twelve clients with anxiety disorders so treated. The data are average
ratings of anxiety felt toward several individualized scenes on a scale of 1
(no anxiety) to 10 (total anxiety). The characteristics of these patients are
shown in Table 9-1. The picture presented in Figure 9-2 closely parallels
the picture seen in the behavioral measures and measures of general
clinical outcome.

Comparative Clinical Outcome

To date, only one comparative clinical outcome study has been reported on
comprehensive distancing (Zettle & Hayes, 1984). In this study, 18 clinically depressed women were assigned to cognitive therapy (Beck, Rush,
Shaw, & Emery, 1979) or to comprehensive distancing. In addition, some
of the clients were given behavioral homework, and some were not. The
results were quite consistent. On most measures, comprehensive distancing was superior to Beck's approach. On none of the measures was
comprehensive distancing less effective. Figure 9-3, for example, shows
the data for the Hamilton Rating Scale—an interview-based rating scale of
depression. On this measure, comprehensive distancing was significantly
superior both at the end of a 12-week therapy period and at follow-up.
Also, when we compared the comprehensive distancing group to the
subjects' data in the well-known Rush, Beck, Kovacs, and Hollon (1977)
study, comprehensive distancing was shown to be superior.

FIGURE 9-2. The average amount of rated anxiety to individualized scenes (an average of
seven scenes per client) for each of the first 12 clients with anxiety disorders treated with
comprehensive distancing, plotted as a function of outpatient session. Clients marked with
one asterisk dropped out of therapy. The client marked with two transferred at my initiative
to another therapist. Client numbers are keyed to Table 9-1.

TABLE 9-1. The First Twelve Clients with an Anxiety Disorder Treated with Comprehensive Distancing

Client (see Figure 9-2)	Diagnosis	Age	Sex	Age at first therapy contact	Number of previous psychiatric hospitalizations	Previous kinds of therapy	Approximate length of current crisis condition
1	Obsessive–Compulsive	39	F	10	3	ECT, drugs (antianxiety, antidepressant, antipsychotic), relationship-oriented, insight-oriented	2 yr
2	Obsessive–Compulsive	60	F	38	6	ECT, insulin shock, drugs (antianxiety, antidepressant, antipsychotic), implosive therapy, *in vivo* exposure	1.5 yr
3	Obsessive–Compulsive	28	F	10	0	Cognitive therapy, insight-oriented, pastoral counseling	3 yr
4	Obsessive–Compulsive	36	F	26	4	Exposure, insight-oriented, humanistic, flooding, drugs (antianxiety, antidepressant, antipsychotic)	2 yr
5	Agoraphobia with panic attacks	38	F	22	3	Exposure, insight-oriented, group therapy, drugs (antianxiety, antidepressant, antipsychotic)	2 yr

6	Agoraphobia with panic attacks	29	F	21	0	Exposure, group therapy, relationship-oriented, drugs (antianxiety, antidepressant)	1.5 yr
7	Agoraphobia with panic attacks	29	F	20	1	Insight-oriented, drugs (antianxiety, antidepressant)	.5 yr
8	Social phobia	54	M	37	0	Biofeedback, insight-oriented, relaxation, drugs (antianxiety)	6 yr
9	Agoraphobia with panic attacks	38	M	28	0	Drugs (antianxiety)	3 yr
10	Agoraphobia with panic attacks	29	F	28	1	Drugs (antianxiety), exposure	1 yr
11	Social phobia	31	F	27	0	Insight-oriented, drugs (antianxiety)	.5 yr
12	Panic disorder	28	M	27	0	Family therapy, insight-oriented, drugs (antianxiety)	.5 yr

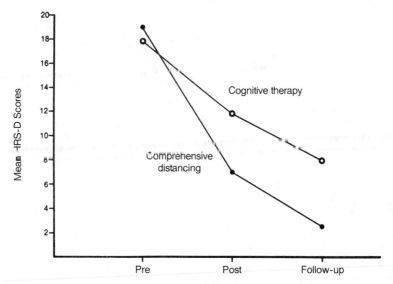

FIGURE 9-3. The average HRS-D scores for subjects in the two treatment groups at pretest, posttest, and at follow-up.

Naturally, much more remains to be done, but the data at the present time are sound enough so that I feel as though I am on the right track and that the analysis should continue to be tested and refined. Unfortunately, this is an approach that is very difficult to teach to others because its assumptions and techniques differ so much from the mainstream culture. For this reason, I have waited until I could give the analysis in a long-chapter format. Nevertheless, I am realistic about what is possible here. While someone reading this chapter may be able to get some good ideas, I do not pretend that a therapist will be able to use a comprehensive distancing approach based on this chapter alone. Nor do I believe that cautious therapists will necessarily be convinced either by the analysis or the data. I suppose what I hope for is that readers will consider the need for new approaches to therapy and the possible role radical behaviorism might play in organizing that search. These two considerations, in fact, guide my approach to therapy. Since this book is about what behavior therapists actually do in clinical practice, if I have shown readers how I am guided by these considerations, I have accomplished my goal.

REFERENCES

Adams, H. E. (1984). The pernicious effects of theoretical orientations in clinical psychology. *The Clinical Psychologist, 37*, 90–94.

Ader, R., & Tatum, R. (1961). Free-operant avoidance conditioning in human subjects. *Journal of the Experimental Analysis of Behavior, 4,* 275–276.

Anger, D. (1956). The dependence of interresponse times upon the relative reinforcement of different interresponse times. *Journal of Experimental Psychology, 52,* 145–161.

Assagioli, R. (1971). *Psychosynthesis: A manual of principles and techniques.* New York: Viking.

Azrin, R. D., & Hayes, S. C. (1984). The discrimination of interest within a heterosexual interaction: Training, generalization, and effects on social skills. *Behavior Therapy, 15,* 173–184.

Baron, A., & Galizio, M. (1983). Instructional control of human operant behavior. *The Psychological Record, 33,* 495–520.

Beck, A. T., & Emery, G. (1985). *Anxiety disorders and phobias.* New York: Basic Books.

Beck, A. T., Rush, A. J., Shaw, B., & Emery, G. (1979). *Cognitive therapy of depression.* New York: Guilford.

Devany, J. M., Hayes, S. C., & Nelson, R. O. (1986). Equivalence class formation in language-able and language-disabled children. *Journal of the Experimental Analysis of Behavior, 46,* 243–257.

Galizio, M. (1979). Contingency-shaped and rule-governed behavior: Instructional control of human loss avoidance. *Journal of the Experimental Analysis of Behavior, 31,* 53–70.

Harzem, P., Lowe, C., & Bagshaw, M. (1978). Verbal control in human operant behavior. *The Psychological Record, 28,* 405–423.

Hayes, S. C. (1984). Making sense of spirituality. *Behaviorism, 12,* 99–110.

Hayes, S. C. (1986). The case of the silent dog—Verbal reports and the analysis of rules: A review of Ericsson and Simon's "Protocol Analysis: Verbal Reports as Data." *Journal of the Experimental Analysis of Behavior, 45,* 351–363.

Hayes, S. C. (in press). *Rule-governed behavior: Cognition, contingencies, and instructional control.* New York: Plenum.

Hayes, S. C., & Brownstein, A. J. (1985, May). *Verbal behavior, equivalence classes, and rules: New definitions, data, and directions.* Invited address presented at the meeting of the Association for Behavior Analysis, Columbus, OH.

Hayes, S. C., & Brownstein, A. J. (1986a). Mentalism, behavior-behavior relations and a behavior analytic view of the purposes of science. *The Behavior Analyst, 9,* 175–190.

Hayes, S. C., & Brownstein, A. J. (1986b). Mentalism, private events, and scientific explanation: A defense of B. F. Skinner's view. In S. Modgil & C. Modgil (Eds.), *B. F. Skinner: Consensus and controversy.* Sussex, England: Falmer Press.

Hayes, S. C., Brownstein, A. J., Devany, J. M., Kohlenberg, B., & Shelby, J. (1985, October). *Stimulus equivalence and the transfer of functional control.* Paper presented at the meeting of the Southeastern Association for Behavior Analysis, Charleston, SC.

Hayes, S. C., Brownstein, A. J., Zettle, R. D., Rosenfarb, I., & Korn, Z. (1986a). Rule-governed behavior and sensitivity to changing consequences of responding. *Journal of the Experimental Analysis of Behavior, 45,* 237–256.

Hayes, S. C., Brownstein, A. J., Haas, J. R., & Greenway, D. E. (1986b). Instructions, multiple schedules, and extinction: Distinguishing rule-governed from schedule controlled behavior. *Journal of the Experimental Analysis of Behavior, 46,* 137–147.

Hayes, S. C., Korn, Z., Zettle, R. D., Rosenfarb, I., & Cooper, L. (1982, December). *Rule-governed behavior and cognitive behavior therapy: The effects of comprehensive distancing on pain tolerance.* Paper presented at the meeting of the Association for Advancement of Behavior Therapy, Los Angeles.

Hayes, S. C., Rosenfarb, I., Wulfert, E., Munt, E., Zettle, R. D., & Korn, Z. (1985). Self-reinforcement effects: An artifact of social standard setting? *Journal of Applied Behavior Analysis, 18,* 201–214.

Hayes, S. C., & Wolf, M. (1984). Cues, consequences, and therapeutic talk: Effects of social context and coping statements on pain. *Behaviour Research and Therapy, 22,* 385–392.

Herrnstein, R. J. (1970). On the law of effect. *Journal of the Experimental Analysis of Behavior, 13,* 243–266.

Killeen, P. (1984). Emergent behaviorism. *Behaviorism, 12,* 25–39.

Leander, J. D., Lippman, C. G., & Meyer, M. E. (1968). Fixed-interval performance as related to subjects' verbalization of the reinforcement contingency. *The Psychological Record, 18,* 469–474.

Lowe, C. F. (1983). Radical behaviorism and human psychology. In G. C. Davey (Ed.), *Animal models of human behavior.* Chichester, England: Wiley.

Lowe, C. F., Beasty, A., & Bentall, R. P. (1983). The role of verbal behavior in human learning: Infant performances on fixed-interval schedules. *Journal of the Experimental Analysis of Behavior, 39,* 157–164.

Lowe, C. F., Harzem, P., & Bagshaw, M. (1978). Species differences in temporal control of behavior II: Human performance. *Journal of the Experimental Analysis of Behavior, 29,* 351–361.

Lowe, C. F., Harzem, P., & Hughes, S. (1978). Determinants of operant behavior in humans: Some differences from animals. *Quarterly Journal of Experimental Psychology, 30,* 373–386.

Mahoney, M. J. (1974). *Cognition and behavior modification.* Cambridge, MA: Ballinger.

Matthews, B. A., Shimoff, E., Catania, A. C., & Sagvolden, T. (1977). Uninstructed human responding: Sensitivity to ratio and interval contingencies. *Journal of the Experimental Analysis of Behavior, 27,* 453–467.

Michael, J. (1982). Distinguishing between discriminative and motivational functions of stimuli. *Journal of the Experimental Analysis of Behavior, 37,* 149–155.

Moore, J. (1981). Mentalism, methodological behaviorism, and radical behaviorism. *Behaviorism, 9,* 55–78.

Rosenfarb, I., & Hayes, S. C. (1984). Social standard setting: The Achilles' heel of informational accounts of therapeutic change. *Behavior Therapy, 15,* 515–528.

Rush, A. J., Beck, A. T., Kovacs, M., & Hollon, S. (1977). Comparative efficacy of cognitive behavior therapy and pharmacotherapy in the treatment of depressed outpatients. *Cognitive Therapy and Research, 1,* 17–37.

Shimoff, E., Catania, A. C., & Matthews, B. A. (1981). Uninstructed human responding: Responsivity of low-rate performance to schedule contingencies. *Journal of the Experimental Analysis of Behavior, 36,* 207–220.

Shimoff, E., Matthews, B. A., & Catania, A. C. (1986). Human operant performance: Sensitivity and pseudosensitivity to contingencies. *Journal of the Experimental Analysis of Behavior, 46,* 149–158.

Sidman, M., Rouzin, R., Lazar, R., Cunningham, S., Tailby, W., & Carrigan, P. (1983). A search for symmetry in the conditional discrimination of rhesus monkeys, baboons, and children. *Journal of the Experimental Analysis of Behavior, 37,* 5–22.

Sidman, M., & Tailby, W. (1983). Conditional discrimination vs. matching to sample: An expansion of the testing paradigm. *Journal of the Experimental Analysis of Behavior, 37,* 23–44.

Skinner, B. F. (1945). The operational analysis of psychological terms. *Psychological Review, 52,* 270–277.

Skinner, B. F. (1957). *Verbal behavior.* New York: Appleton-Century-Crofts.

Skinner, B. F. (1966). An operant analysis of problem solving. In B. Kleinmuntz (Ed.), *Problem-solving: Research, method, and theory.* New York: Wiley.

Skinner, B. F. (1969). *Contingencies of reinforcement: A theoretical analysis.* Englewood Cliffs, NJ: Prentice-Hall.

Skinner, B. F. (1974). *About behaviorism.* New York: Knopf.

Stokes, T., & Baer, D. M. (1977). An implicit technology of generalization. *Journal of Applied Behavior Analysis, 10,* 349–367.

Weeks, G. R., & L'Abate, L. (1982). *Paradoxical psychotherapy.* New York: Brunner/Mazel.

Weiner, H. (1964). Conditioning history and human fixed-interval performance. *Journal of the Experimental Analysis of Behavior, 7,* 383–385.

Weiner, H. (1969). Controlling human fixed-internal performance. *Journal of the Experimental Analysis of Behavior, 12*, 349–373.

Zettle, R. D., & Hayes, S. C. (1980). Conceptual and empirical status of rational–emotive therapy. In M. Hersen, R. M. Eisler, & P. M. Miller (Eds.), *Progress in behavior modification* (Vol. 9). New York: Academic Press.

Zettle, R. D., & Hayes, S. C. (1982). Rule-governed behavior: A potential theoretical framework for cognitive–behavioral therapy. In P. C. Kendall (Ed.), *Advances in cognitive-behavioral research and therapy* (Vol. 1). New York: Academic Press.

Zettle, R. D., & Hayes, S. C. (1983). The effect of social context on the impact of coping self-statements. *Psychological Reports, 52*, 391–401.

Zettle, R. D., & Hayes, S. C. (1984, August). *Cognitive therapy of depression: A behavioral analysis of component and process issues.* Paper presented at the meeting of the American Psychological Association, Toronto.

CHAPTER 10

Functional Analytic Psychotherapy

Robert J. Kohlenberg
University of Washington

Mavis Tsai
Private Practice, Seattle, Washington

INTRODUCTION

"If I look back on those patients whom I have seen change a great deal, I know the heat was in the therapeutic relationship. . . . There was struggle and fear and closeness and love and terror. There was intimacy and outrage, concern and humiliation. . . . It was a journey of importance, more to the patient who had come seeking help, but in fact to both participants. It was a process which carried on throughout the course of therapy and left both patient and therapist altered by the experience. . . . The therapeutic relationship is at the absolute heart of psychotherapy, and is the vehicle whereby therapeutic change occurs. . . ." (Greben, 1981, pp. 453–454).

Most experienced clinicians, regardless of theoretical orientation, have had memorable clients who changed markedly in ways that far exceeded the stated goals of the therapy. For those clients, the above description seems to capture an aspect of what the therapeutic process was like, even if the treatment were based on a theory that is quite different from Greben's psychodynamic perspective. What is missing, however, from Greben's writing and from most systems of therapy that focus on the relationship betweeen therapist and client is a coherent conceptual system, with well-defined theoretical constructs, that leads to step-by-step therapy guidelines.

In this chapter we will describe a treatment, in its fledgling stage, that has a clear and concise conceptual framework and yet seems to produce the kind of treatment and change that Greben describes. We call our treatment "Functional Analytic Psychotherapy" (FAP). It is, perhaps unexpectedly, derived from a Skinnerian functional analysis of the typical psychotherapy environment, and its foundations are in radical behaviorism and applied behavior analysis. FAP leads the therapist into a caring, genuine, sensitive, involving, and emotional relationship with his or her client, while at the same time capitalizing on the clarity, logic, and precise definitions of radical behaviorism.

The term "radical behaviorism" refers to the conceptual framework described in the writings of B. F. Skinner (e.g., 1945, 1953, 1957, 1974). Its most general application to clinical problems has been that of providing a language and concept of human nature intended to clarify the interaction between an individual's behavior and the natural environment. For instance, it has been used to describe a wide range of therapeutic practices such as psychoanalysis and desensitization, as well as human experiences such as hallucinations, worrying, and anger.

The application of Skinnerian concepts, termed "applied behavior analysis," is a more narrow approach that uses analogies to operant conditioning procedures developed in the laboratory for solving real-life clinical problems. Applied behavior analysis is highly effective with clients such as residents of hospitals, students in classrooms, and young or severely disturbed children, for whom the therapist exerts a great deal of control over the client's daily life environment (Kazdin, 1975). Radical behaviorism and applied behavior analysis, with the exception of the work of Hayes (Chapter 9), has largely been overlooked as a source for clinical procedures in the treatment of problems that do not readily lend themselves to standard behavior therapy.

FAP is not intended to be another restatement of psychoanalysis in behavioral terms. Throughout the years, psychoanalytic psychotherapy has been analyzed from a variety of learning standpoints, including radical behaviorism (Ferster, 1972c; Skinner, 1953), as well as other nonradical behavioral learning theorists (Dollard & Miller, 1950). The main purpose of these learning theory explanations of psychoanalysis was to make psychodynamic principles more understandable to the behaviorally trained person. They were not intended to have implications for devising or selecting therapy techniques.

The radical behavioral analysis in this chapter leads to suggestions for therapeutic technique. Although it is a type of behavior therapy, FAP's procedures are different from traditional behavior therapy procedures such as social skills training, cognitive restructuring, desensitization, and sex therapy. FAP can be used in combination with other behavior therapy approaches, although there may be some theoretical incompatabilities to resolve. It can also, at times, be used by itself. The techniques are concordant with the expectations of clients who seek an intensive, emotional, in-depth therapy experience. It is also well suited for clients who have not improved adequately with behavior therapy, who have difficulties in establishing intimate relationships, or who have diffuse, pervasive, interpersonal problems typified by Axis II diagnoses in DSM-III.

This chapter is organized in the following manner: (1) the theoretical underpinnings of FAP are outlined; (2) clinical techniques and issues are discussed; (3) FAP is compared and contrasted with other behavior therapies and with psychoanalytically oriented therapies; and (4) professional and ethical issues are examined.

RADICAL BEHAVIORISM AS A MODEL FOR ADULT OUTPATIENT THERAPY

Our approach is based largely on our analysis of how to utilize applied behavior analytic procedures within the constraints of the typical office treatment setting. These constraints include: therapist–client contact limited to 1 or more therapy hours per week, the therapist not observing the client outside of the session, and lack of control over contingencies outside of the session. Within these constraints, we will examine the implications of using (1) reinforcement, (2) specification of clinically relevant behaviors, and (3) arrangement for generalization, all of which are the hallmarks of applied behavior analysis. Although behavior analysis consists of more than these components, they are major features of the approach. For more complete descriptions see Kazdin (1975), Lutzker and Martin (1981), and Reese (1966). In deriving the implications for therapy, we will also show why these procedures may have been overlooked as having relevance for adult outpatient therapy.

Reinforcement

The world of people's behavior, according to radical behaviorists, consists of respondents and operants. Although both are important, the traditional emphasis in clinical work has been on operants. The two main ways to influence the immediate operant behavior of a client are through discriminative control, as in giving instructions, or through contingencies. Ultimately, however, all behavior is contingency shaped. Typical office therapies such as relaxation training and cognitive restructuring rely primarily on some form of instruction. Hayes (Chapter 9, this volume) presents a radical behaviorally based therapy that emphasizes discriminative control. Instructions are a significant part of the therapeutic process and the FAP methods should enhance the effectiveness of these procedures. FAP techniques, however, are primarily based on the role of reinforcement in the office setting.

Time and Place of Reinforcement

Central to behavior analytic treatment is the direct shaping and strengthening of the required repertoires through reinforcement. A well-known aspect of reinforcement is that the closer in time and place the behavior is to its consequences, the greater will be the control. Anyone who has delivered food pellets to a rat in a Skinner box has seen the deleterious effects that delaying the reinforcer can have on the behavior of the animal. The shaping process is very effective, however, if the lever press and food pellet are close in time and place. Every behavior therapist has seen how easy it is to reinforce and thus strengthen a client's relaxation skills as they occur in the office, and how difficult it is to reinforce the same behavior occurring at home in between sessions.

The implication for office therapy is that the effects of treatment will be stronger if the client's problem behaviors and improvements occur during the session, where they are closest in time and place to the reinforcement. Thus, a major feature of FAP is that it is aimed at daily life problems that also occur during the therapeutic session. This occurs much more frequently than behavior therapists seem to believe. Examples of such problems can include behaviors manifested as intimacy difficulties, including fears of abandonment, rejection, engulfment; difficulties in expressing feelings; inappropriate affect, hostility, sensitivity to criticism, social anxiety, and obsessive–compulsiveness. These terms are not intended to refer to unobservable or inferred states. They are used as general descriptive terms to give the reader an idea of the range of observable client behavior that could be evoked and changed under the appropriate conditions during therapy.

Another major feature of FAP, and one that is more problematic, is that improvements in the client's behavior should be immediately reinforced. The reinforcement of behavior during the session is problematic because the therapist's very attempt to make it immediate and contingent also may inadvertently make it ineffective and perhaps even counterproductive. In the following discussion, the term reinforcement is used in its technical, generic sense and refers to all contingencies that affect behavior. Reward refers to the attempt by a therapist to obtain a behavior and the attempt may or may not be effective.

Arbitrary versus Natural Reinforcement

The problem in using reinforcement during treatment comes from emulating the methods of experimental behavior analysts. As a means of obtaining reinforcement that closely followed the response when doing clinical work, applied behavior analysts have used procedures that are metaphorically analogous to those used in operant animal laboratory experiments. These clinicians took the "Give the food pellet immediately after the response" and literally transposed it to clinical problems, as in "Deliver the M&M immediately after the child remains in his chair for 2 minutes." The purpose of the laboratory experiments, however, was to study the parameters of reinforcement. This was useful to the experimenter, but was not meant to benefit the subject or to obtain generalization to his or her daily life.

C. B. Ferster (1967, 1972b) has extensively discussed the clinical implications of using the type of reinforcement employed in laboratory settings and contrasted it to the type that occurs in the natural environment. He refers to these as arbitrary and natural reinforcers. Some of the formal characteristics of the two types of reinforcers are:

1. The performance that is specified is narrow for arbitrary reinforcement, whereas natural reinforcement is contingent on a larger response class.

2. Natural reinforcement begins with a performance already in the individual's repertoire, which is also reinforced by an event that occurs reliably in the individual's milieu. Arbitrary reinforcement does not take into account the client's existing repertoire to the same degree as does natural reinforcement.

3. Natural reinforcers are more fixed and stable parts of the natural milieu than are arbitrary ones.

4. Arbitrary reinforcement occurs in situations where the therapist has great discretion over the specific behavioral goals of the treatment.

The functional characteristics of arbitrary reinforcement are: (1) it produces behavior changes in the client that are reinforcing to the therapist, and (2) the reinforcing effects of the behavior changes on the therapist are independent of the benefits they provide for the client in his or her milieu. Reinforcing procedures used by therapists that are affected by the benefits for the client in his or her milieu are natural. Although natural reinforcement produces beneficial effects and arbitrary may not, it is possible for a therapist to use arbitrary methods that incidentally benefit the client.

Using the functional definitions of arbitrary and natural reinforcement, it may not be possible to determine whether a reinforcer is natural unless the history of the therapist is known, or until one can observe its effects on the client and the degree to which the improvements in the client's daily life in turn affect the therapist. However, formal characteristics or telltale signs of natural and positive reinforcers allow reasonable guesses about their nature without directly observing their reinforcing effects. This is particularly true when they are used for nonverbal behaviors that have natural environmental consequences, such as putting on a coat that avoids the cold. It is reasonable to assume that offering a child candy to put on a coat involves arbitrary reinforcement. One can spot the arbitrariness of candy by comparing it to the known natural consequences. It is obvious that generally people do not get candy for putting on their coats. A danger in using arbitrary reinforcement is that the child might only wear the coat when the parent is present or only when there is a disposition to eat candy and not use it as a means of keeping warm. This can happen because the arbitrary reinforcement can replace or interfere with natural ones gaining control over the behavior (Ferster, 1972b). In terms of what reinforces the parent for using the bribe method, it is possible that the parent may have long-term benefits in mind when the bribe is offered. The same bribe, however, could be used for less noble motives, such as being concerned about what the neighbors might think about their coatless child. In both cases, the parent receives immediate reinforcement, that is, the child puts on the coat.

Another illustration is that of a child being reinforced with candy for practicing the piano. If the naturally reinforcing effects of making music take over as the skill develops, the child has had a good experience with arbitrary reinforcement. The very same candy, however, can be used to make the child engage in sexual activities with the parent. Needless to say, in the long run the sexually used child has had a bad experience with arbitrary reinforcement. These two children would be expected to react very differently to subsequent attempts to use arbitrary reinforcement. A characteristic of arbitrary reinforcement is that it *can* be used to the detriment of the person being reinforced while uniquely benefiting the person doing the reinforcing. By definition, this cannot happen with natural reinforcement. The exploitation of others through misuse of arbitrary reinforcement does and will frequently occur. This happens because the contingencies involved in misusing arbitrary reinforcement are positively reinforcing to the controller. The classic warning "don't take candy from strangers" is a recognition of the dangers of arbitrary reinforcement.

Of particular importance in the adult therapy situation is the fact that the only natural reinforcers available are verbal behaviors consisting of the interpersonal actions and reactions between client and therapist. At times, it is also easy to spot arbitrary reinforcers involving verbal behaviors. For example, fining a client $5 for a lack of eye contact while speaking to the therapist is probably arbitrary, while the therapist's drifting attention and consequent inability to respond appropriately is probably natural. Drifting attention would be natural because it is more likely to result in improved eye contact that would generalize to the client's daily life. Eye contact reinforced by money is functionally different from eye contact reinforced by therapist attentiveness. Thus, there is no compelling reason for eye contact caused by money contingencies in therapy to be useful outside of the therapy situation. Arbitrary reinforcement, however, may be useful as a transition procedure. This is probably the intent of most therapeutic use of arbitrary reinforcement, but it is usually done without consideration of the difficulties inherent in the process. For example, it may be necessary for the therapist to take steps to ensure that natural reinforcers take over. These steps could include fading out the arbitrary reinforcer paced with the natural environment's reinforcement until the repertoire is totally sustained without the therapist's intervention. Although this procedure seems straightforward, it becomes complex in the adult therapy situation. The fading process, for instance, is complicated with a client who initiates social interactions to please the therapist and with whom the naturally occurring effects of social contacts are not gaining control.

It is also easy to see the arbitrariness of a tangible reward for overtly expressing feelings of warmth and affection; it is less clear how one would classify the stock therapist reaction "I'm glad you shared those feelings with me." A comparison to the natural environment suggests that expressions of warmth are reinforced by recirpocated warmth. If the client's expression of warmth is a target behavior and the therapist has a reciprocal reaction, the reinforcement is most likely natural.

Although there have been no direct comparisons of arbitrary and natural reinforcement, data that bear on this issue have been obtained from cognitively oriented research on the effects of external reward on intrinsic motivation. Deci (1971), in a study typical of this type of research, paid one group of subjects for correct solutions to a puzzle and compared them to an unpaid group given the same puzzle. When left alone for 8 minutes in a "free time" situation, the paid subjects spent less time playing with the puzzle than the unpaid subjects. After reviewing the literature, Levine and Fasnacht (1974) argue that "external rewards" are dangerous because they reduce resistance to extinction and interfere with generalization, thereby "undermining" the very behavior we are trying to strengthen. Operationally, "external rewards" and "intrinsic motivation" correspond to Ferster's notions of arbitrary and natural reinforcement. Although originally used to demonstrate deficiencies in the behavioral approach, the intrinsic motivation data can be seen alternatively as an instance in which arbitrary reinforcement has negative effects.

Problems Produced by Arbitrary Reinforcement

Ferster warns that many of the common rewards used by applied behavior analysts—food, tokens, and praise—may be arbitrary. He sees this as a serious clinical problem, since the arbitrarily reinforced behavior only occurs when the controller is present or if the client is interested in the particular reward being offered. He cites the case of a mute autistic, treated by behavior analysts, who ceased to speak when food was not present. In fact, Ferster (1972b) proposes that some of the successes of food or praise reinforcements are due to "the way they make the [client's] behavior more visible to the [therapist] and the [client] himself" (p. 6). Once this awareness has occurred, naturally reinforcing reactions on the part of the therapist would shape and prompt relevant repertoires and increase the natural collateral reactions that accompany the arbitrary reinforcers.

Another problem with arbitrary reinforcement is that it can be reacted to as coercive, and a power struggle can ensue (Ferster, 1972c). Indeed, the bad public image that behavior therapy has received is probably due to the public's perception of its procedures as involving arbitrary reinforcement and being manipulative or controlling. As such, the use of arbitrary reinforcement can be termed Machiavellian, since they appear to benefit the prince (the hospital, prison, or school) rather than the subject (the client). Resistance is likely to develop in those persons who have had considerable exposure and consequent bad experiences with arbitrary reinforcement. The development of resistance based upon arbitrary reinforcement during adult psychotherapy can easily result in the client leaving treatment or using up time to focus on this issue when other issues are more important.

A related issue concerns clients not improving or leaving treatment because they regard the therapist as phony or insincere due to the use of arbitrary reinforcement. This problem was alluded to by Wachtel (1977), who observed that behavior therapists were overly exuberant in their use of praise, which "cheapened" the interaction. This is probably what Ferster was referring to when he stated "natural reinforcers are sometimes puzzling because they seem to reinforce so much behavior and yet their effects appear to be evanescent when there is an attempt to use them deliberately" (1972a, p. 105).

Aversive Stimuli

Positive reinforcement is the mainstay of applied behavior analysis. Aversive stimuli are used only when positive reinforcement approaches are ineffective. The bias against therapeutic use of aversive stimuli is based on its problematic side effects: (1) it can lead to avoidance of the therapy, (2) it can lead to general aggressiveness, and (3) it substitutes avoidance and escape for productive behavior. Ferster points out that most aversive control that occurs between people is arbitrary in nature. Thus, it makes sense to avoid, whenever possible, the use of aversive control in the office treatment of adults.

Specification of Clinically Relevant Behavior

Second to reinforcement, behavior analysis is characterized by its attention to specification of the behaviors of interest. The term "clinically relevant behavior" (CRB) includes the problem as well as goal or target behaviors. We will discuss, in turn, the two components of the specification of CRBs—observation and behavioral definition—and the implications of specification for the adult therapy situation.

Observation

Observation is a precursor to behaviorally defining CRBs. Behaviorists assume that if the behaviors can be observed, they then can be specified and counted. Obviously, the client's problem behavior cannot be observed unless it occurs in the presence of the therapist. In order to meet this requirement, behavior analysts have either (1) treated clients who are restricted in movement, such as those who are in hospitals or prisons, or (2) treated problems that are severe, such as echolalia in an autist, which occurs with high frequency. Although it is convenient to use severe problems and restricted environments in order to directly observe the problem behavior, *any* environment or problem that can be directly observed is adequate for behavioral analysis. The therapeutic environment is therefore acceptable if the client's daily life problem is of such a nature that it also occurs during the session. A salient, although trivial example is a client who is seeking treatment for becoming tongue-tied when telling a doctor about problems, and who then actually becomes tongue-tied when telling the therapist about this problem. Thus, based on the observation requirement alone, a behavior analytic approach to therapy leads to a focus on those problems in the outside world that also occur during the session.

Behaviorally Defining CRBs

The selection and discriminability of CRBs by the therapist is greatly facilitated if the goal behavior is in his or her own repertoire. For example, the therapist who can speak English, that is, has English in his or her repertoire, can easily tell when the client has shown some improvement in speaking. Thus, behavior analysts have generally restricted themselves to goal behaviors that are present in their own repertoire.

Another factor restricting the range of selected target behaviors is the requirement of written descriptions of the behaviors, which refer only to observables and do not involve inferences. In practice, it is almost impossible to achieve such objectivity for applied problems (Hawkins & Dobes, 1977). A major function of the written description is to provide a basis for obtaining reliability as measured by interobserver agreement. Interobserver agreement is greatly assisted if the behavior being observed is highly discriminable and is in the repertoires of the observers. Since observers, as a matter of convenience, are usually such relatively inexperienced persons as undergraduates, the net result is that it is highly expedient if the client's target behaviors are in the repertoires of the therapist *and* in an almost random sample of briefly trained observers. Needless to say, this practice has severely limited the types of problems that have been studied and would rule out treatments involving goal behaviors that are absent from the observers' repertoires or that require considerable experience to detect. Examples of such client behaviors include more subtle interpersonal reactions such as those related to intimacy and taking interpersonal risks.

In summary, direct observation, defining problem and goal behaviors, and obtaining interobserver agreement for the more subtle types of problems that clients present in therapy can be accomplished if (1) the problem-related behaviors occur during the session and thus can be directly observed and, (2) the therapist and observers are carefully selected so that they have in their own repertoires the client's goal behaviors.

Arranging for Generalization

The best way to arrange for generalization is to do the therapy in the same environment where the problem occurs. Historically, behavior analysts have accomplished this by delivering immediate reinforcement in institutions, classrooms, homes or wherever else it was possible to provide treatment in the natural mileiux where the problem occurred. Although behavior analysis traditionally has not been done in the adult psychotherapy environment, it would be suitable if the therapy environment were functionally similar to the client's daily life environment. A functional similarity between the natural and the therapeutic environment is indicated if similar problem-related or clinically relevant behaviors occur in both settings. For example, a client whose presenting problem is a hostility that develops in close relationships would show that the therapy environment is functionally similar to the daily life environment if he or she became hostile towards the therapist as their relationship developed.

CLINICAL APPLICATION OF FAP

The clinical application of FAP is based on three types of client behavior and five types of therapist behavior that can occur during the therapy session. To begin with, we describe client problems and behaviors that are the focus of the therapeutic process. Then, clinical techniques or therapist behaviors are delineated. These consist of evoking, noticing, and reinforcing clinically relevant behavior during the session and describing the involved functional relationships. Next, ways of enhancing therapist awareness of clinically relevant behaviors in the client are discussed. Finally, the role of emotions, memories, and cognitions in behavior change is examined.

Client Problems and Clinically Relevant Behaviors

To reiterate, the most important characteristic of a problem that makes it suitable for FAP is that it can occur during the therapy session. This conclusion is based on the following assumptions: (1) the effect of therapy is a result of events occurring during the session, (2) the only controlling events that can occur during a session, regardless of the theoretical orientation of the therapist, are reinforcing, discriminative, and eliciting events and, (3) these events within the session will have their strongest effects on behavior that also occurs within the session.

In addition, improvements in the client must also occur during the session and be naturally reinforceable by the reinforcers present within the session. The vast majority of the potential reinforcers are the therapist's behaviors, mainly consisting of his or her reactions to the client. The type of client behavior that would be naturally reinforced by therapist reactions is interpersonal.

Three types of client behaviors that are of particular relevance can occur during the session. These CRBs are discussed below.

CRB1. Actual Instances of Behavior during the Therapeutic Session That Are Occurrences of the Clinical Problem

These behaviors decrease in frequency during the course of therapy, and they include operants as well as disruptions of operant behavior. Most typically, CRB1s are under the control of aversive stimuli and consist of avoidance. Disruptions of operant behavior are usually observed as negative emotional states. Examples of operants that are actual instances of presenting clinical problems include the following:

1. A client whose problem is that she has no friends and "does not know how to make friends" exhibits these behaviors: avoids eye contact, answers questions by talking at length in an unfocused and tangential manner, has one "crisis" after another and demands to be taken care of, gets angry at the therapist for not having all the answers, frequently complains that the world "shits" on her and that she gets an unfair deal.

2. A man whose main problem is that he avoids getting into love relationships always decides ahead of time what he is going to talk about during the therapy hour, watches the clock so he can end precisely on time, states that he can only come to therapy every other week because of tight finances (he makes $30,000 a year), and cancels the next session after making an important self-disclosure.

3. A self-described "hermit" who would like to develop a close relationship has been in therapy for 1½ years and continues to muse periodically that his therapist is only in this for the money and is secretly contemptuous of him.

4. A woman who has a pattern of getting into relationships with unattainable men develops a crush on her therapist.

5. A woman who has a history of people leaving because they "get tired" of her introduces new and involved topics at the end of the hour, frequently threatens to kill herself, and shows up drunk at her therapist's house in the middle of the night.

An example of a disruption of operant behavior is, for a client whose problem is speech anxiety, "freezing" and not being able to speak to the therapist during the session.

CRB2. Repertoires Whose Absence or Low Strength are Directly Related to the Presenting Problem

These behaviors increase in strength over the course of treatment. During the early stages of treatment, these repertoires typically are not observed, or are of low strength at those times when an actual instance of the clinical problem, (CRB1), has occurred. For example, consider a client whose problem is withdrawal and accompanying feelings of low self-esteem when "people don't pay attention" to him during conversations and in other social situations. This client may show similar withdrawal behaviors during a therapy hour in which the therapist does not attend to what the client is saying and instead interrupts before he has completed his sentence. Possible CRB2s for this situation include repertoires involving assertive behavior that would have directed the therapist back to what the client was saying, or the discrimination of the therapist's waning interest in what was being said before the therapist actually interrupted. The absence or low strength of these repertoires is most likely the result of a lack of experience throughout this client's life, which might have fostered the development of these types of behavior.

CRB3. The Client's Verbal Repertoires That Correspond to His or Her Own CRB and the Controlling Variables

CRB3 refers to clients talking about their own behavior and what seems to cause it. More specifically, this involves the observation of one's own behavior and its associated reinforcing, discriminative, and eliciting stimuli. This describing of functional connections can help in obtaining reinforcement in daily life.

CRB3 repertoires also include descriptions of functional equivalence that indicate similarities in the stimulus situation present during the session to those that happen outside treatment. For example, "I'm reacting to your suggestions to dress better in the same way I do to my lover criticizing me."

Therapists sometimes confuse CRB3 repertoires with the behavior to which they refer. A client stating that she withdraws whenever she becomes dependent in a relationship (CRB3) is very different from the behaviors emitted in actually withdrawing during the session because she feels dependent on the therapist (CRB1). It is also unfortunate that many therapists focus on those verbal repertoires that describe a problem behavior to the exclusion of observing the problem behaviors (CRB1) or improvements (CRB2) as they occur.

Assessment

Initially, the assessment procedures of FAP are no different from those routinely used by behavior therapists in clinical practice. The client is asked to report on problems and other conditions in his or her life. Interviews, self-reports, recorded material, questionnaires, and record keeping are used to define the problem, generate hypotheses about controlling variables, and monitor progress. Once the therapist has some idea about what the problem and its controlling variables are, an assessment as to whether these are also occurring during the session is initiated. First, the therapist hypothesizes about whether a CRB1 is occurring at any particular moment or presents a situation thought to be evocative of CRB1. These hypothesizing and evocative procedures are discussed in later sections. The primary technique of assessment then centers on one key question that the therapist continuously asks the client during treatment: "Is it happening now?" The "it" refers to CRB1. Variations are "How are you feeling about yourself right now," "Are you withdrawing right now," "Is what just happened the same as the problem that brought you into treatment," "Is the difficulty you have in expressing your feelings right now the same that you experience with your mother," and "What are you feeling right now . . . is it similar to the speech anxiety that brought you to therapy?"

FAP has no unique procedures for evaluating the validity of the client's self-report in response to the assessment question. On the one hand, the client's self-report is based on an event that just occurred—perhaps as little as 2 seconds before. It may, therefore, be less subject to distortions that time and distance can introduce into reported events that occurred in the past. On the other hand, the CRB1 is likely to have accompanying emotional responses that interfere with self-observation and also can be biased by the implied demand in the therapist's question. The advantage of assessment of ongoing behavior is that the therapist can directly observe the behavior that the client is describing. This allows for interobserver reliability assessments, the counting and recording of responses, and an opportunity to assess the correlation between verbal reports and the referent behavior.

Therapeutic Technique: The Five Rules

Given that psychotherapy is a complex interactional process involving multi-determined behaviors, our suggestions for therapeutic technique are not intended to be complete or to exclude the use of procedures not described here. Instead, the therapist's existing approach can be complemented and augmented by assisting him or her in taking advantage of therapeutic opportunities that otherwise may go unnoticed.

Our techniques are given in the form of rules. Rather than the rigid, threatening quality that is associated with common usage of this term, the rules we propose are based on Skinner's verbal behavior conception (1957, p. 339), in combination with an elaboration by Zettle and Hayes (1982). Within this context, the FAP rules are suggestions for therapist behavior that result in reinforcing effects for the therapist. It's more of a "Try it, you'll like it" than a "You'd better do it."

Further, the rules do not give therapists specific guidance to cover every situation or moment during the therapeutic hour. It is expected that therapists will act in ways that depend on their experience and other theories. At the beginning of therapy, the time is usually spent on history gathering and obtaining descriptions of presenting problems. This may be followed by explorations with the clients as to how they could act to improve their situation or the application of some specific behavior therapy procedure such as desensitization, social skills training, or contingency contracting. At any point during this process, the application of FAP rules can shift the focus of treatment to CRBs. The focus may be momentary or may dominate the therapy. Thus, there are no procedures that are ruled out, but at any moment, a FAP rule-governed technique could lead to the awareness and utilization of therapeutic opportunity.

Rule 1: Develop a Repertoire for Observing Possible Instances of CRBs Occurring during the Therapy Session

This rule forms the core of FAP. Our major hypothesis is that following this rule improves therapeutic outcome. The more proficient a therapist is at observing CRBs, the better will be the outcome. It is also hypothesized that following Rule 1 will lead to increased intensity during the session. Intensity refers to the emotional reactions of the therapist and client to each other.

During the session, the primary consequence of client behavior is the therapist's reaction. Without observation of the client's behavior by the therapist, reactions can be inconsistent or antitherapeutic and progress will be compromised. In other words, if the therapist is not aware of the client's clinically relevant behaviors that occur during the session, reinforcement of improvements at the time they occur will be a hit-or-miss proposition. Although awareness or observation does not guarantee that improvements will be reinforced and that unfavorable behaviors will be extinguished or punished, it does increase the likelihood of appropriate therapist reactions.

The use of Rule 1 in adult psychotherapy can be clarified by first looking at how it operates in the behavior analytic treatment of more disturbed clients. Although not explicitly stated, applied behavior analysts routinely use Rule 1 in their treatment programs for severely disturbed clients.

Consider the behavioral treatment of an autistic boy who is speech deficient. Let's say the therapy is aimed at improving speaking and at some point the focus is on the client tacting (labeling) his own nose. That is, the specific therapeutic task is the reinforcement of this tact. The therapist is instructed to "Point to the boy's nose and ask 'What's that?' When he says 'nose' make sure you respond in a way likely to be reinforcing because his response is an important instance of clinically relevant behavior. If you do it right, the child will improve."

The action referred to in the instructions given to the therapist has three parts. The first part—the therapist being requested to "Point to the boy's nose and ask 'What's that'"—consists of the therapist presenting the S^D or discriminative stimulus. This part corresponds to FAP Rule 2, arranging for the evocation of CRB.

The second part pertains to the behavior of the client and tells the therapist which behavior to watch for, that is, "When the client says 'nose'. . . ." This second part is the same as Rule 1. The therapist is requested to observe the occurrence of the CRB. In this case, the CRB is the utterance of "nose" after the client is asked, "What's that?" Before the therapist can observe the occurrence of the CRB, it must be specified. In this case, specification of the CRB is easy, that is, the utterance "nose." It is easy because the therapist is a member of the verbal community and is very familiar with the "nose" response. Further, the therapist probably also is familiar with the existing verbal repertoire of the child and the concept of shaping. Because of all these factors, an utterance of "nooss" during the early stages of therapy might be observed as a CRB2, an improvement, and appropriately reinforced. In the conduct of FAP with adults, observing CRB is usually not so easy.

The third part directs the therapist to reinforce the specified behavior. This corresponds to Rule 3 and is discussed below. As pointed out earlier, this third part is performed with caution in adult psychotherapy since it may lead to arbitrary reinforcement.

Needless to say, it is extremely unlikely that nose tacting will be reinforced if the therapist doesn't hear the child say "nose" or if the child's utterance is not identified as clinically relevant behavior. Fortunately, in such a child, appropriate speech is salient and is easily recognized as a CRB2.

Once recognition of improvement (CRB2) occurs, the therapist reacts by giving the arbitrary reinforcement. As discussed previously, the CRB can also evoke unplanned but significant collateral reactions that ideally will be naturally reinforcing along with any arbitrary reinforcement that may be given. This is likely to happen if clinical improvement in the child is reinforcing for the therapist. If improvement isn't reinforcing for the therapist, it is unlikely that the therapist's reaction to the utterance will be naturally reinforcing when the arbitrary reinforcement is delivered; therefore, the therapy probably will not be successful.

The countertherapeutic problem caused by a lack of awareness is familiar to those who have worked with severely disturbed children. The first author recalls the painstaking teaching of an inpatient child to put on his own socks—he had never done this before and it took about an hour a day for several weeks before this behavior was reliable. His parents came one morning to take him home for a visit and watched him get out of bed and put on his socks. The therapist was beaming with pride at the child's accomplishment. But as soon as he had finished putting on both socks, his parents scolded him for putting on two different colored socks and roughly pulled one off and replaced it with the right one. The client had a tantrum. Obviously, the parents did not observe the putting on of the socks (even though they didn't match) as a CRB2, a member of the repertoire whose absence or low strength was directly related to the presenting problem. If the parents had been present during the tedious weeks of training, their awareness probably would have changed and they instead would have naturally reinforced their son for having put on his socks. It is unfortunate that psychotherapists are all too often unaware of their clients' CRB occurring during the session and are prone to react in an antitherapeutic manner as did the autistic child's parents.

As stated previously, the therapist is most likely to appropriately reinforce CRB occurring in the therapy situation if he or she observes the occurrence of the relevant behavior. Consider a female client who is in treatment for lack of assertiveness. Let's say the client asks the therapist to call her physician so she can refill her prescription for tranquilizers. In making this request, the client may be emitting CRB. That is, the client is being assertive with the therapist and is showing an improvement. The therapist may or may not respond in a way that reinforces this behavior. If the therapist observes this behavior as being a CRB2, he or she can increase the probability that her response will be naturally reinforcing. On the other hand, if the therapist is not observant in this way, he or she might view the client's request as irritating or presumptuous, and correspondingly react in a naturally punitive way.

The importance of Rule 1 cannot be overemphasized. Theoretically, this rule by itself could be sufficient for successful treatment. That is, a therapist who is skilled at observing instances of CRB as they occur is also likely to naturally react to (reinforce, punish, extinguish) the client in a way that will foster the development of behavior useful in daily life.

Observing repertoires that include those specified by Rule 1 are highly developed in psychodynamic and eclectic therapists who are considered to be especially competent. This would be expected because those occurrences of CRB that are labeled "transference" serve as important discriminative stimuli in psychodynamically oriented treatment. In addition, most experienced therapists would be expected to show Rule 1 types of behavior because awareness of CRB facilitates clinical improvements that automatically reinforce the psychotherapist's Rule 1 behavior.

Rule 2. Construct a Therapeutic Environment That Will Enhance the Evocation of CRB

It was suggested above that the typical therapeutic situation is so constructed that certain CRBs are likely to occur, and that a major technical problem facing the therapist is increasing discrimination of CRBs that do occur. In some cases, however, it is difficult to get CRBs to occur during the hour. In such instances, the therapist can try to alter the environment to favor the appearance of CRBs. Examples include: (1) requesting that a spouse attend the sessions if repertoires relevant to the client's relationship problems only emerge when the spouse is present (couples counseling), (2) beginning a session with eating lunch if a bulimic's CRBs occur only after a meal has been eaten, and (3) withholding comments of client acceptance or approval for a period of time if the CRBs concern the client's difficulties relating to people who are not explicit about their approval and acceptance.

The last example given raises a problem that can occur when a therapist deliberately alters an aspect of his or her behavior in order to increase the chances of obtaining CRBs. The therapist can go too far in setting up conditions to evoke CRBs, and his or her credibility can become jeopardized due to such arbitrary reinforcement. For example, a therapist may feign anger in order to evoke CRBs in a client whose difficulties are provoked by people who get angry. Even though the feigned anger can result in an important therapeutic interaction, the client may come to recognize that the anger was not really anger but was instead performed for the benefit of the client. Subsequent therapist anger then could be viewed, justifiably, as a ruse and thereby not serve to evoke CRBs. Further, the client may come to distrust the reasons for other affective expression or statements from the therapist.[1] Needless to say, such an outcome would seriously hamper progress.

The above situation needs to be differentiated from that in which a client's presenting problem is a lack of trust that interferes with important relationships. This client's distrustfulness did not originate from interactions with the therapist as in the above example, but instead has a long history, and its occurrence in the therapeutic relationship is consistent with this history. In this case, the doubting of the sincerity of the thera-

---

1. The behavioral literature relating to this issue is found in Skinner's (1957) discussion of mands that have the appearance of tacts.

pist's reactions would constitute CRB and would be a focus of treatment. It would be particularly unfortunate if a therapist strengthened mistrust in such a client through a misguided attempt to set up conditions in order to provoke CRBs. A safeguard that might help prevent mistrust would be to explain to the client why the therapist is altering his or her behavior before actually doing so.

Rule 3. Arrange for the Positive Reinforcement of CRB2

Putting this rule into practice is problematic. On the one hand, reinforcement that is close in time and place to the goal behavior is the primary change agent available in the therapeutic situation. On the other hand, behaviorists who are aware of the importance of reinforcement are prone to use procedures that are arbitrary and thereby risk compromising their effectiveness.

Our suggestions for dealing with these problems involve both direct and indirect approaches. The direct approach concerns what the therapist can do at the moment that a reinforcer is called for. The direct approaches carry the largest risk of producing arbitrary reinforcement. The indirect approaches enhance the occurrence of natural reinforcement by manipulating variables other than what one does immediately after the behavior and carry the least risk of being arbitrary.

Direct Approaches

Quite clearly, a therapist who plans to say "good client" whenever a reinforcer is called for and displays exaggerated, overexuberant reactions risks being arbitrary. A deliberate attempt to reward an adult client that is guided by a rule such as "When the client shows an improvement, make a positive gesture or pay a compliment" could easily lead to arbitrary reinforcement. So, as a general guideline, it is advisable to avoid procedures that attempt to specify the form of the therapist reaction in advance. This seems to happen whenever one attempts to conjure up a reinforcing reaction without relating it to the specific client–therapist history. For example, if you were to try to think of what you could say to a client that would be reinforcing, such phrases as "That's terrific" or "Good" come to mind. These specific forms of response could easily be arbitrary because they were thought of outside the context of the client–therapist environment at the moment of reinforcer delivery.

One characteristic of natural reinforcement is that it occurs in the community. The therapist, as a member of the verbal community, has access to the natural reinforcers contingent on a particular client behavior occurring during the session. There are at least two ways for the therapist to access these natural reinforcers. First, one can ask oneself, "How would the community respond to this behavior?" And second, one can observe the spontaneous reactions that occur immediately in oneself after the client behavior occurs. Neither assure that the reinforcer accessed is natural or that it is therapeutic, but it is a starting point.

The private reactions of the therapist are an important source of information that can be used to provide natural reinforcement. Technically, the private reaction per se is not naturally reinforcing; rather, it is accompanied by dispositions to overtly act in ways that are naturally reinforcing. Two factors must be taken into account in determining whether the therapist's private reactions are likely to be naturally reinforcing: the degree of awareness on the part of the therapist of the current repertoire of the client and the therapist having the goal repertoires as part of his or her own behavior. For example, the spontaneous reactions of a therapist who has not developed intimate relationships probably will not be representative of the community that the client is trying to access, and this therapist is less likely to discriminate improvements (CRB2s) when they occur.

One of the ways in which the therapeutic environment differs from the daily life of the client involves the amplification of subtle or private therapist reactions that increase their saliency. Although the nature of the reinforcer is not fundamentally changed in this process, amplification can be therapeutically important. This is manifested in a therapist being especially careful in explaining his or her reactions to the client, as well as describing private or weak reactions that may not be immediately discernible. An example of the latter is a therapist describing out loud a private reaction such as "I feel especially close to you right now" to a client who has intimacy concerns and lacks friends. The client has emitted a response that has resulted in private, spontaneous reactions in the therapist, which included (1) predispositions to act in intimate and caring ways, and (2) private respondents that correspond to "feeling close." These have either not been discriminated by the client or have weak reinforcing effects. Thus, without amplification, this basic reaction would have diminished reinforcing effects on the client's behavior that caused it. Thus, FAP involves self-disclosure of the therapist's feelings if it is reasonable to assume that the self-disclosure is naturally reinforcing to the client.

In the above example, the behavioral process involved in the amplification of natural reinforcement is an autoclitic, self-editing one. Skinner (1957) describes the autoclitic as a verbal behavior that is partially under the control of stimuli that are products of one's own behavior as a speaker. The addition of the autoclitics "augment and sharpen the effect on the listener" (p. 369). The speaker also examines the potential effect on the listener and then either "rejects or releases the response," that is, either says it out loud or does not. In the case of amplification of naturally positively reinforcing therapist behavior, the therapist first has a basic reaction to the client and then adds in other verbal behavior to this reaction that enhances its effects on the client.

There are times when a therapist may want to use arbitrary reinforcement as a transition phase of treatment. This should be done with great caution. It is helpful to explain to the client why this is being done, and that it should be phased out and replaced with natural reinforcement. For example: A client has a high absenteeism rate at work and in therapy. Obviously, without contact it is difficult to get the therapeutic process going. Surprises in the form of tangible rewards have been offered as an inducement to regularly attend appointments. These rewards will be phased out as new repertoires are developed that will help in making the therapy itself sufficiently reinforcing.

Indirect Approaches

Indirect approaches are intended to aid in natural reinforcement by manipulating variables other than what one does immediately after noticing the CRB. The most important of these is methods of increasing awareness of what to reinforce—the behavior called for in Rule 1. The chances that a therapist's spontaneous reactions will be naturally reinforcing are improved if the client's behavior is discriminated as a clinical improvement. A second indirect approach involves a *post hoc* analysis, on a session by session basis, of potential reinforcing effects of the therapist's reactions on the client's behavior. This feedback can help to change the therapist's reactions in a favorable way (Rule 4).

Since natural reinforcement builds client repertoires that work in daily life, a third indirect method is simply selecting therapists who are reinforced by those improvements in clients that are functional in the clients' milieux. These therapists are not reinforced by clients who are just trying to please them. Thus, a therapist who is castigated by a client for being late would have a positively naturally reinforcing reaction to this behavior if it represented an improvement that is relevant to the client's problems. Such a therapist would not tell the client that he or she has no right to criticize the therapist for being late. On the other hand, if this type of angry behavior has caused a client problems in daily life, the therapist would then point out that it is a CRB1 and help the client decrease the likelihood of its occurrence. In other words, the therapist really cares about and wants what's best for the client.

The characteristics of a naturally reinforcing therapist are reminiscent of Carl Rogers's concepts of caring and genuineness. Rogers, known for his opposition to "using reinforcement" to control other people, would certainly not "try" to use it. Yet, a careful analysis of his reactions to clients indicates that contingencies exist (Truax, 1966) in that Rogers differentially reacted to certain classes of client behavior. The explanation is that Rogers's call for genuineness and caring is an indirect method of enhancing the occurrence of naturally reinforcing contingencies. A therapist who cares, according to the present formulation, is one who naturally reinforces or, is governed by what is best for the client Presumably, caring is a therapist trait and therapist selection is an important part of treatment.

The FAP position is that the occurrence of appropriate natural reinforcement depends on the presence of relevant therapist repertoires. One way to get a therapist with these repertoires would be to select one with a personal history that just happens to result in the natural reinforcers required for a particular client's problems. The other way is to specify more clearly the requisite repertoires so that they can be acquired. It is hoped that this chapter is a step in that direction.

Since FAP requires that the natural reinforcement extant in the therapy situation be relevant to the client's problem-related behaviors, a fourth approach that indirectly enhances the occurrence of natural reinforcement is the selection of clients who are likely (1) to have problems that occur during the session, and (2) to be affected by the therapist's reactions.

Aversive Control

Consistent with the radical behavioral bias against aversive controls, the emphasis in the preceding sections has been on positive reinforcement. There are instances, however, when the client's CRB1 consists of avoidance or escape behavior that precludes the occurrence of CRB2—the development of more effective positively reinforced repertoires. In such instances, the therapist might attempt to block the avoidance by re-presenting the aversive S^D that originally evoked the escape or avoidance.

Consider, for example, a simple question asked by the therapist such as "How did your relaxation practice go during the week?" after the client had agreed to practice daily. For some clients, the question would be an aversive S^D, which would evoke avoidance or escape such as changing the topic, lying, or giving an ambiguous response. If these reactions are related to the presenting problem, they would be CRB1s. These reactions, (e.g., not giving a "straight answer"), could be related to a wide range of presenting problems concerning ineffectiveness in interpersonal relationships. If the therapist dropped the topic and went on to something else, the avoidance CRB1 would be reinforced and a significant client repertoire with far-reaching ramifications, "be direct," would not be developed. The main technique for weakening avoidance CRB1s is to re-present the aversive S^D which, for the above example, means repeating the question "How did your relaxation practice go during the week?"

It is our impression that CRB1 avoidance behavior frequently occurs, perhaps during every session. The therapist can always ask oneself "what does the response avoid?" It is difficult to detect avoidance because the aversive S^D can be highly idiosyncratic and thereby obscure to the therapist. In the above example, for instance, the client might start the session by bringing up a crisis even before the therapist asks the question about relaxation. The crisis may or may not be avoidance of the relaxation homework issue. Unless the therapist had formulated hypotheses about CRB1s related to the assignment of homework, the crisis would be a successful avoidance. The notion of avoidance, incidentally, from a functional standpoint has nothing to do with the client's awareness and is primarily a contingency-shaped behavior.

It is not advisable to block each and every escape or avoidance response. Blocking is aversive control and carries all of the associated untoward effects. Correspondingly, it should be applied sparingly in the context of a primarily positive reinforcing environment and in accord with the client's current level of toleration for aversive stimulation. Toleration refers to a decreased reaction and disruptive effect of the aversive stimulation. Toleration is increased through the positive reinforcement resulting from new behavior that develops after the initial aversiveness associated with a blocked avoidance. A verbal repertoire corresponding to the controlling variables involved in the avoidance (Rule 5) may also help to increase tolerance, such as "I'm going to ask you again about the relaxation because you didn't answer. I'm doing this because I think your not answering is like what you do when your wife asks you about your day and you both end up feeling angry. This may be an opportunity to do something about that problem."

Rule 4. Develop a Repertoire for Observing the Potential Reinforcing Properties of the Therapist's Behavior that are Contingent on Occurrences of the Client's Clinically Relevant Behavior

Note the formal or topographical properties of therapist response as well as changes in client behavior after such an interaction. This rule is directly derived from behavioral analytic principles that stress the importance of the effects of the consequences of behavior on the future probabilities of that behavior. Rule 4 only specifies the therapist's *observation* of the reinforcing relationship between client and therapist behavior and does not suggest that the therapist intentionally alter his or her own behavior. This rule is an indirect method of enhancing natural reinforcement.

The observation of the reinforcing relation can have important effects on therapeutic outcome. For example, the therapist's observation that his or her reactions appear to be punishing the client's low-strength desirable behavior can lead to changes in the therapist's behavior that will be positively reinforcing. It is also possible, however, that the therapist will continue to punish favorable behavior even after observing the anti-therapeutic nature of the punishment. This, in turn, can result in a decision to refer the client to another therapist, or it can indicate personal therapy aimed at altering those particular behaviors for the therapist.

One result of the therapist self-observing his or her own reactions for their reinforcing effects on the client's behavior is that it helps develop similar behaviors in the client (i.e., CRB3). The most obvious way this occurs is when the therapist tells the client about the self-observation, as in, "I've noticed that each time you start talking about your spiritual beliefs I've changed the topic and you no longer bring it up."

Rule 4 can also lead the therapist to search for ways to enhance the effects of those reactions that could be reinforcing of CRBs but that are not noticed by the client. For example, consider a client who had trouble expressing feelings because of a history of being ridiculed or criticized when he did so. He did not increase these behaviors, even though the therapist listened intently with empathic facial reactions and softly spoken comments each time the client expressed a feeling. As it turned out, the therapist's reactions were not discerned by the client because the act of expressing feelings evoked such intense emotions (collateral private respondents) that outside stimulation was not noticed. The rate of feeling expression appeared to increase after the therapist amplified the empathetic reaction by speaking loudly and clearly.

It is advisable to avoid starting treatment if it seems likely that natural contingencies do not favor improvement for a particular client. This would be the case if: (1) Rule 4 leads the therapist to conclude that most of his or her reactions to a client will be punitive, (e.g., the therapist doesn't like the client for an enduring reason such as the client reminds the therapist of a cruel foster parent), and (2) these negative reactions are not related to the client's presenting problem such as "people react negatively to me."

Rule 5. Develop a Repertoire for Describing the Functional Relationships between Controlling Variables and the Client's Clinically Relevant Behavior

This rule is based on the notion that verbal repertoires enhance positive and negative reinforcement density (Ferster, 1979). An analogy from animal research can illustrate this principle. Rats were placed for a period of time in two distinctive shock chambers from which there was no escape. In one chamber, noncontingent shocks were delivered at random intervals. In the other chamber, the same number of noncontingent shocks were given but each shock was preceded by a warning light. When given a choice, rats invariably preferred the signaled shock chamber. The same holds true for signaled and unsignaled food.

A verbal repertoire similarly could "signal" events for clients. For example, a client learns during FAP that the therapist's attentiveness during the session is related to how harried or rushed the therapist appears at the beginning of the session. This verbal repertoire could significantly affect the client's experience of a lapse in the therapist's attentiveness.

Statements of Functional Relationships

The verbal repertoire to be developed involves statements by the therapist that relate events during the session to the relationships $S^D \cdot R \rightarrow SR$ and $CS \rightarrow CR$. For example, "When I asked you how you felt about me, you responded by talking about your jail experience, which is another topic that you know I'm interested in. I rewarded your avoidance by getting into discussing jail and not your feelings about me." Usually it is preferable to make the statement in everyday language but it could be argued that it is valuable to teach behavioral language to the client. Statements regarding parts of the functional relationships are better than none at all: "Whenever I ask about your feelings toward me, you change the topic."

Rule 5 repertoires that correspond to behavior occurring in the session are preferred to those corresponding to events occurring elsewhere. Generalization is aided, however, by those verbal repertoires that relate controlling variables occurring outside the session to those occurring in the session.

The following case gives a detailed illustration of Rule 5.[2] Andi, a 25-year-old black lesbian, had been in therapy on and off since junior high school, and had seen numerous therapists. She came into therapy with the

---

2. In a chapter such as this, illustrative clinical cases aid the explanation of concepts. Writers of a behavioral persuasion generally describe cases with more delimited problems and use terms that are popular in the behavior therapy literature, such as "speech anxiety," thereby specifying the problem behavior more precisely and minimizing reification of the descriptive term. The behaviorists' case examples tend to be less representative of the type of person actually seen in practice and are often less relevant to the practicing clinician. On the other hand, nonbehavioral writers describe clinical cases that have more pervasive repertoire disturbances and are more typical of the type of client that is actually seen in clinical practice. These nonbehavioral descriptions tend to suffer from less precision in identifying actual behaviors, as well as from imbuing the descriptive term with causal or ontological status. Although a term such as "low self-esteem" allows considerable room for interpretation as to which behaviors it refers, it can more or less quickly convey to a reader something about the nature of the client's problems. Since FAP is intended to be used with more pervasive repertoire disturbances, it would be useful to describe these cases without having to list all possible behaviors that can be found in the problem repertoire. It should therefore be understood that cases described with descriptive terms refer to specifiable repertoires for given clients that may include a very wide range of behaviors. The descriptive term does not have an existence on its own and is not causal of the behaviors in the repertoire.

second author wanting to "change old patterns that prevent me from getting close to people." She had difficulty in talking about her feelings and in showing any kind of affect during therapy and reported similar behavior elsewhere.

Andi spontaneously started writing notes with more affective expressions to the therapist in between sessions. Given Andi's paucity of expression during the sessions, the therapist was delighted, read the notes, and verbally responded to them. The notes increased in frequency and length. The therapist was aware (Rule 1) of the possibility that the notes were a step in the right direction in terms of developing intimate relating (CRB2) and that the content of the notes included descriptions of controlling variables (CRB3).

After about a year of therapy she wrote to the therapist, "I'm starting to feel scared about how dependent I'm getting. I can't imagine not having you in my life. It's one thing to become dependent on therapy, it's worse to become dependent on a particular person, a particular therapist. After all, there are lots of therapists out there, but not that many Third World feminists with left-of-liberal politics and an understanding of the lesbian community who like the way I write. . . ." The following conversation took place in the next session:

THERAPIST: Those are all true, but you left out that our relationship is special and unique and that I really care about you. [The therapist is aware that this is an S^D for the type of intimate relating behavior that the client lacks (CRB2) as well as one that elicits avoidance and consequent difficulties in maintaining close relationships (CRB1).]

ANDI: Lots of people care about me, but those characteristics set you apart. [Andi responded in such a way that the therapist felt discounted and was probably in the position that other would-be intimates had found themselves when they expressed caring—a CRB1.]

THERAPIST: I feel discounted when you say that. [Andi was visibly shaken by this reaction. The therapist then gave a description of the functional relationship.] Andi, when I told you that I really care about you and wanted you to acknowledge my feelings, you reacted in an impersonal way. This reaction made me feel like my feelings don't count, and punished my telling you that I care. I think that's why you reacted the way you did, that is, you don't want me to bring up my caring and positive feelings about you.

Andi elaborated on this and described how in general it was hard for her to hear messages from others that were caring, complimentary, or sensitive to her feelings—a pattern that interfered with her getting close to people.

General Case Illustration

Gary came into therapy with a history of personal relationships that began well but became superficial and unsatisfying, and ended because of "bad" feelings that developed. He also had a long-standing problem of depression that seemed to vary with the quality of current interpersonal relationships. He was now in an important relationship that appeared to be following the ill-fated course of previous ones.

Gary seemed to be warm and likable. He did not appear to have any difficulty in relating to the therapist during the early stages of treatment, which consisted of history taking and directive approaches involving RET, behavioral rehearsal, and couples therapy. The original therapy contract of 10 sessions was extended to 20 sessions over a 9-month period. During this first phase of therapy, discussions of Gary's problem centered on behavior occurring outside the session in the recent and distant past. The early childhood origins of his problem were also explored. These discussions helped him to piece together a reasonably plausible verbal repertoire corresponding to the relationship between his history and the currently operating controlling variables that related to his presenting problem.

Thus, at the end of the 20 sessions, Gary had learned that his relationships seemed to sour when he got angry or irritated at his partner and didn't discuss his concerns with her. He would become increasingly depressed, his partner would respond in kind with depression or anger, and then they would eventually split up. During the initial course of treatment, Gary had agreed to express his negative feelings to his woman friend. He made this agreement because he felt that not doing so led to a lack of openness, lingering bad feelings, and eventual deterioration of the relationship. Even though Gary had this awareness of the problem, and had gone through cognitive therapy, behavioral rehearsal, and conjoint therapy aimed at helping him with the problem behavior, he still did not adequately express negative feelings and the relationship ended as had previous ones.

With each successive session following the breakup, Gary grew more reticent and depressed. When asked about his growing depression, Gary attributed it to mourning over the lost relationship and his inadequacy. The therapist also observed within-session increases in severity of depression. The focus of the treatment shifted to the depression and negative self-thoughts and a loss of hope that he would ever have a successful relationship.

The therapist applied Rule 1 and hypothesized that Gary's problems were occurring in the session. When Gary was asked if he was angry at the therapist or had other negative feelings, he denied that any were present or that his reticence or depression had anything to do with the therapist. Although not completely convinced, the therapist dropped the topic of the client–therapist relationship for the moment and concentrated on behavior therapy for depression. The therapist was becoming less comfortable during the sessions, it was harder to keep the interaction going, and Gary seemed to become even more depressed. When it was suggested that Gary see a physician to try some antidepressant medication, Gary went into a virulent tirade about how doctors don't know what they are doing and that they cause more harm than they do good.

It was hypothesized that Gary's comments about doctors was stimulated by his reaction to the therapist. At this time, the following interaction occurred:

THERAPIST: It looks like it's happening now—your problem that is. Our relationship started out fine, it started out very relaxed and open. You had no trouble telling me about all your feelings and problems, and I looked forward to our sessions. The way our therapy started sounds like the way most of your past relationships started. Then things started going bad. You couldn't voice your negative feelings to Joyce even though we tried a variety of therapeutic approaches. Your relationship ended. You started getting depressed and became less open in our sessions. This gradually worsened to the present point—you have very little to say and I am finding the sessions frustrating because I don't know what to do that might help. [Rule 5]

GARY: It feels the same as times in the past. And I have been thinking about quitting.

THERAPIST: So our relationship is even headed for the final step that seems to have occurred so often in the past—it will end on a sour note.

GARY: And I feel depressed and lousy about it. This is what always happens and I feel frustrated too because I don't know what to do.

THERAPIST: Well, now you have a chance to make our relationship different and not feel lousy or frustrated. You can either let our relationship end like the others and you will continue to be unhappy and depressed, or you can be different and maybe feel better.

GARY: What do you mean be different—I don't know what to do.

THERAPIST: Based on your past pattern, there must be negative and/or angry feelings toward me.

GARY: All I know is that I'm depressed and I want some help because it feels lousy. [CRB1, avoidance]

THERAPIST: You didn't answer my question. I said that I thought you had negative or angry feelings toward me. [Rule 3, blocking avoidance]

GARY: I don't. Can't we get back to my depression? [CRB1, avoidance]

THERAPIST: I think you are avoiding something about me that bothers you. When you first started therapy, I said I would try to help. Right now you are asking for help and I am trying to direct you to a topic that you don't think is related and you try to change the topic. [Rule 2, presenting the evocative situation—the therapist is again trying to help right now, which has not worked previously; the failure of the therapist's previous interventions to help is hypothesized to evoke Gary's negative feelings and subsequent avoidance. Rule 3, blocking avoidance, and Rule 5, describing the interaction, are also demonstrated here.]

GARY: (*sobbing*) I did everything you asked me to do and Joyce still left me. [CRB2]

THERAPIST: You did what I asked and Joyce still left you and . . ."

GARY: And you didn't help like you said you would. [CRB2, the first complaint ever directly expressed to the therapist]

THERAPIST: I tried but it didn't come out well, and you did do everything that I asked. I feel bad about that and wonder what I should have done differently so that Joyce and you could have stayed together. I think it's important that you brought it up, and I want to see what can be done at this time. [Rule 3, natural reinforcement for a complaint is to take it seriously and try to do something about it]

The therapist observed an increase in subsequent expressions of dissatisfaction with therapy and the therapist (Rule 4).

The therapeutic relationship intensified after this point. As treatment went on, there were more and more open expressions of emotional reactions between therapist and client. The sessions almost exclusively focused on the relationship between Gary and the therapist. Gary went into more detail about his disappointment in the therapist and related issues of trust. Positive feelings of caring and warmth were also expressed. The original CRB1s of avoidance appeared less frequently, but whenever one was detected by the therapist, it was blocked and an opportunity was provided for the development of Gary's new repertoire of open expression of negative feelings involving trust, disappointment, and anger. Gary became skilled at noting CRBs as they occurred (CRB3), which in turn led to an even better therapeutic relationship. The repertoires developed in therapy readily transferred to the outside environment, and Gary later reported that he was in the most satisfying intimate relationship he had ever had.

Supplementation: Enhancing Therapist Awareness of CRB

Since the outcome of treatment is theoretically related to how skilled a therapist is at observing CRB, it is important to strengthen the therapist's awareness of such operants occurring during the hour.

Obvious ways to enhance the observing process include wearing glasses and/or a hearing aid if these would lead to improvements in hearing or seeing. Although such behaviors can be helpful or even necessary, they are not sufficient for the awareness required of a psychotherapist. The autistic child's parents in a previous example who got angry at him for putting on different colored socks would not have been helped by corrective lenses nor would the therapist who is put off by a nonassertive client requesting a scheduling change. Observation refers to the discrimination of CRBs, which means that merely noticing is not enough. Therapeutic value comes from noticing the client's behavior as an instance of CRB. Occurrences of CRB during the session, however, usually are less salient and serve as weak variables controlling the therapist's observations. Such weak variables usually require supplementation (Skinner, 1957) in order to increase their control. The following sections on shaping, analysis of verbal behavior, and therapeutic situations that evoke CRB, are aimed at providing supplementation for therapist skill or competence in observing CRB, sometimes called sensitivity or insightfulness.

Shaping

The concept of shaping can help the discrimination of CRB2s. The second author was seeing a client named Linda, diagnosed as "borderline" according to DSM-III, who was moody, explosive, and verbally abusive. Often, she would abruptly terminate therapy without prior notice and without any apparent provocation. These were the same problems Linda was having in her daily life and that had led to only short stints of previous therapy with multiple therapists, because they would find her intolerable. After the therapist showed an unusual amount of patience and tolerance for this behavior, Linda once again terminated the therapy, threatened suicide and stated she was doing this because the therapist didn't care about her needs because of the limited time she was willing to spend with her. Although this could have been viewed as the last straw, the concept of shaping helped in the discrimination of this event as a potential CRB2. Linda was for the first time describing external variables as the cause of her outburst before storming out of the office. The therapist reinforced this improvement by offering a compromise involving longer but fewer sessions.

Analyzing Client Verbal Behavior

Skinner's analysis of verbal behavior (1957) is a rich source of concepts that lends itself to application in the office setting and can help in the detection of CRB. Skinner's approach gives the therapist a method to hypothesize about the controlling variables responsible for each client utterance. Some of the hypothesized variables may, in turn, suggest that CRBs are present and thereby increase therapist awareness of them. Like Freud, Skinner believes everything the client says has meaning, even slips of the tongue. The meanings, however, may or may not be of clinical significance. Needless to say, even though the client is usually not aware of the variables controlling his or her statements, this is not taken as evidence for the existence of mental structures or apparatus such as the unconscious.

Hypotheses about CRBs are often suggested by analyzing a seemingly innocuous client utterance from a verbal behavior standpoint. The client, Betsy, was in treatment for stress-related somatic symptoms, excessive worrying, and anxiety. She had been receiving a typical cognitive-behavior therapy stress management treatment. For example, the following statement was made at the beginning of a session in response to the therapist's inquiry about the previous week: "Last week was really rotten, I got a $108 ticket (sigh) for expired license tabs."

The analysis of this comment starts with the therapist hypothesizing about the controlling variables that correspond to each of the cells in Figure 10-1.

In this figure, tact refers to a verbal operant that is under precise control of discriminative stimuli and reinforced by generalized secondary reinforcers. In its pure form, the mere presence of a stimulating environment and an audience are sufficient to produce tacting. A tact is the speech involved in naming, asserting, announcing, and describing. It is under tight control of the S^Ds present and is reinforced by conditioned generalized reinforcement such as "uh-huh," "right," "thank you," or an appropriate response indicating understanding of what was said. Based on the form of the client's statement, the most obvious hypothesis is that it is a tact that is controlled by the therapeutic environment consisting of the therapist's inquiry and the past reinforcement for talking about problems as well as the actual event referred to in the comment—getting a ticket. These are the variables that go in Cell 4 in the figure.

	Mand	Tact
Subtle	1	2
Obvious	3	4

FIGURE 10-1. A matrix of hypotheses about the causes of client statements.

The subtle and obvious columns refer to the degree of formal correspondence between the terms in the utterance and the hypothesized S^D that controls them. The subtle variables controlling the tact are supplemental to the obvious ones and account for why this particular comment is being made at this time when many others are also possible. Skinner refers to this process as response selection and proposes it as an alternative to saying the client has chosen the particular utterance from among those available. A myriad of such possible variables could go in Cell 2. Some of these would not be of clinical relevance, such as Betsy seeing a policeman in the waiting room right before the session or noticing an airplane ticket lying on the receptionist's desk as she passed by. Supplementary variables of potential clinical relevance would be those that indicate the client is reacting to the therapist in a way that resembles the clinical problems occurring in daily life. The therapist generates relevant hypotheses based on the particular client and past experience in this type of activity.

The list of evocative situations commonly present in therapy that are given in the next section can also contribute to generating hypotheses about clinically relevant subtle variables that may be determining the client utterance. Examples of Cell 2 variables are: the therapy is aversive and punitive, the client is worried about the cost of the treatment or that he or she is violating the rules of the therapeutic contract. Once the therapist hypothesizes about subtle variables, they can be checked out with the client. One way is to ask the client a direct question, such as "What about my fees?" There is, of course, no definitive way to assess the actual validity of the hypothesis even if it is supported by the client. Part of the problem is the bias of the therapist who both makes the hypotheses and then checks them for validation. The process is useful if it leads to detection of a CRB that might have been missed. It is important for the therapist to recognize the high probability that the hypothesis is wrong and not to pursue it if the client gives no corroborative information.

A mand is behavior followed by a characteristic reinforcer or reaction under functional control of relevant deprivation or aversive stimulation. The speech involved in commands, questions, and the imperative mode are mands. It may indirectly involve deprivation or aversive states, as in "Please take me for a ride" or "Love me" or "Don't abandon me." Behaviors on the part of a client that get sympathetic reactions and caring from the therapist may be mands. There is not necessarily any clinical significance to such behavior, although some forms are more effective than others and the client may not be very effective at evoking caring or sympathy. Referring to Figure 10-1, there is no obvious mand and Cell 3 is empty. If Betsy had said, "I got the ticket—please help me feel better about it," there would have been an obvious mand because the reinforcer is specified in the statement, that is, "feel better." Even though Betsy did not actually say, "Make me feel better," that is what she might have meant by the comment she did make. Her comment then would be a "mand in tact's clothing" (Zettle & Hayes, 1982, p. 2), and the hypothesized controlling variables would fit into the subtle cell. A relevant CRB might have been the indirect and ineffective nature of how she obtains help from people. A rather general but commonly occurring subtle mand occurs when the reinforcer is a change in topic and the offset or avoidance of an aversive stimulus. In Betsy's case, she may not have improved on a targeted behavior, and bringing up the ticket could have diverted attention from this topic.

As indicated in the transcript below, the therapist proceeded to check out the "money hypothesis" with Betsy. As it turned out, she was worried about the money owed to the therapist in much the same way she was worried about money owed to others. This particular problem had been the focus of previous cognitive restructuring and the client had avoided further therapeutic work on this topic by reporting that it was no longer a problem. By asking about hypothesized variables, however, the therapist discovered that Betsy's behavior in dealing with the bill was still a CRB1.

THERAPIST: "What about our bill, are you worried about that?"

BETSY: "No, because my insurance has a $100 deductible and I've used over that in drugs already so that covers my deductible, and they've assured me that the first ten visits would be covered. I don't know about after that but they've been really good."

THERAPIST: "The reason I'm bringing up my bill is I'm trying to find out what would bother you about owing me money."

BETSY: "I don't like owing anybody money."

THERAPIST: "I know, but let's get down to real specifics. What would bother you?"

BETSY: "I think about it, and dollar signs ring every time I walk in the door."

The last statement is supportive of the notion that Betsy's concern about fees influenced the selection of the ticket incident as the first item to talk about. After the CRB was identified, the remainder of the session focused on this problem. It is impossible to know if the same focus would have occurred if the therapist had not hypothesized about the variables influencing the client's initial comment, but this process does seem to hold promise.

Therapeutic Situations That Frequently Evoke CRB

The following suggestions are meant to supplement weaker discriminative functions of clinically relevant behavior that may occur during the session. Stimuli common to the therapeutic situation often precipitate client behavior that may be clinically relevant for a particular case. Calling attention to these situations increases the likelihood that they will be observed as they occur during the session.

Time Structure

Therapy hours are scheduled to start and end at a certain time. The client may come late, give excessive attention to arriving early, wish to leave early, or not leave on time. Coming late to an appointment can be related to general problem operants concerning the avoidance of emotionally laden discussions, the planning of time, or work problems produced by not being punctual. Having difficulty in leaving at the end of the hour can be related to behavior such as excessive dependence that has caused problems in other relationships. Inordinate attention paid to promptness can be related to such presenting problems as compulsiveness or extreme fear of disappointing others associated with a lack of self-worth. Coming late to appointments when therapeutic progress is occuring also may be an instance of the presenting problem for the client who had difficulty in completing tasks and who seems to "screw up" situations in which she or he could be successful. Coming late or leaving early can be instances of clinically relevant operants for a client who presents anxiety problems. In each case, the operant behavior observed during the session is evaluated for possible relevance to the particular client's presenting problems.

Therapist Vacations

Some clients, especially those with histories of rejection and abandonment, react strongly to aversiveness associated with disruptions in the pattern of contact with the therapist. For these clients, the therapist going away can elicit intense fear, anxiety, anger, and/or sadness with accompanying thoughts such as: "You won't come back," "You're trying to get away from me because I was 'bad'," "You'll be different and won't care about me when you get back," "How can you leave me right now when I need you so much," "I can't live without you," and "I can't take care of myself." Most behavior that accompanies such feelings (other than talking about them) is CRB1 (e.g., becoming withdrawn, breaking things, attempting suicide).

Termination

The most difficult type of termination is the ending of an incomplete treatment due to factors in the therapist's life, such as changing jobs, moving, or ending an internship. This can bring forth the feelings described in the section above in an even more intensified fashion. Mutually agreed-upon terminations are a time for the therapist to be vigilant for

CRB evoked by endings. Terminations can bring up concerns about self-reliance and independence, and grief about previous losses, separations, and deaths. It is a chance for the client to learn to say good-bye properly by expressing the range of feelings engendered by the ending of a special but transitional relationship. How the client reacts to termination is likely to be an indication of how she or he reacts to endings and beginnings in other areas of life.

Fees

How a client handles therapy fees can be representative of the way she or he deals with money elsewhere. Does the client pay on time, or does she or he manage bills and budgeting poorly? The fee issue can be brought into the treatment in numerous says:

1. It can lead to termination and withdrawal types of behavior that are associated with statements like "I don't deserve to be spending this money on me, other family members are more important and deserving of funds than me."

2. It can be used to avoid feelings of closeness toward the therapist (e.g., "You're being nice to me because I pay you and that's your job.")

3. It can be used to explore the behaviors and/or affect evoked by: making (or not making) a certain amount of money; feelings of success, inferiority, incompetence, insecurity, shame; competitiveness with or envy toward the therapist.

4. Rather than directly expressing negative feelings to the therapist about fees, avoidance of this may involve the client being late with payments.

5. The client may try to get the therapist to lower the fee by understating the amount of money earned.

6. If the client is in a financial crisis, can she or he accept the idea of carrying a balance, in essence, taking a loan from the therapist?

Critical behaviors around giving and taking in relationships, and not wanting to owe anybody anything, to the point of one's detriment, are often observed at these times.

"Mistakes" or Unintentional Therapist Behavior

The saying "It's grist for the therapy mill" applies here. The best of therapists may come late to the session, run overtime with the previous client, lapse into daydreams while the client is talking about something important, forget to make a phone call she or he promised the client she or he would make, or otherwise act in ways that result in the client feeling unimportant or misunderstood. How does your client react to a less than perfect therapist? Therapist errors are occasions in which CRB such as these can be evoked: avoidance of direct expression of anger and frustration, problems associated with feelings of lack of worth to oneself and to significant others, or extreme reactions to therapist mistakes associated with idealizing others so much that disillusionments are inevitable. Any of these behaviors can interfere with development of a stable relationship.

Silences and Lapses in the Conversation

The most salient feature of adult psychotherapy is that it consists of two people talking to each other. It is common for this conversation to run into dead ends and stop—both people seeming to have nothing to say. This situation can evoke CRB in the client, not to mention the therapist. A lapse in the conversation evokes anxiety and accompanying confusion, which in turn makes it even more difficult to start talking again. The anxiety, confusion, and difficulty in resuming the interaction is the problem. Learning to tolerate the silences more, extinguish anxiety, and/or develop stronger conversation-resuming behavior at the time that conversation stalls would constitute CRB2.

Expression of Affect

Expressing feelings such as sadness, need, vulnerability, anger, and caring facilitates the development and maintenance of close relationships. Most people have trouble crying in front of others and expressing anger appropriately. A client's discomfort with showing strong affect often hinders treatment, as discussed in a later section. Clients have said that showing their feelings would mean being "weak," "one down," "too vulnerable," "unable to stop," "out of control" or "laughed at." Avoidance behaviors associated with showing affect include: changing the subject, talking endlessly in great detail about tangential topics, not talking, focusing on an object in the office, counting backwards from 1000 to oneself. In rare instances, the CRB is the client's deliberate use of anger or tears to control the behavior of others.

Feeling Good, Doing Well

For some clients, feeling good or doing well serves as an aversive S^D. This then motivates avoidance behavior in the form of being and acting miserable and depressed. Clients report feeling afraid, anxious, out of control, and that they are "waiting for the other shoe to drop." Their histories reveal experiences in which they had been punished in some way for feeling good, thereby giving "doing well" its aversive controlling properties. For example, a jealous and psychologically disturbed parent might withdraw or otherwise punish a child for being successful. Doing well might also signal losing the therapist because therapy will have to end. Needless to say, CRB1 consisting of depression and misery as avoidance of doing well or termination of treatment would seriously compromise long-term reinforcement for the client.

Positive Feedback and Expressions of Caring by the Therapist

Some clients do not react well to positive expressions by the therapist. The positive feedback may be reacted to as an arbitrary reinforcer, as a signal for increasing demands, or as a prelude to withdrawal of positive reinforcement. Clients may then resist, avoid, ignore, or otherwise discount what the therapist has said. Their reactions may also be accompanied by feelings of embarrassment, unworthiness, discomfort, and thoughts such as "Now I'm going to have to live up to these expectations or you'll withdraw approval," "You don't really know me, and when you do, you'll leave," "You're just saying that to be nice and I don't believe you." All of these reactions can be acquired in families in which positive feedback has been associated with aversive consequences.

Feeling Close to the Therapist

These feelings normally accompany repertoires of maintaining contact, which can include spending more time with the person; physical closeness or contact; expressing positive feelings; and doing things to help or protect the person. These repertoires and the accompanying feelings can be evoked by the therapist showing caring, concern and understanding, staying with the client even though there have been rough times. The behavioral repertoires may have been punished in the past by loss, rejection, or abandonment. Further, the limitations of the therapeutic relationship also result in punishment of the "closeness repertoires." As a result, closeness is an aversive S^D that motivates client behavior to remove it. This avoidance can be difficult to detect because most of the closeness behaviors cannot occur in the session and the therapist must rely on the collateral feelings as a guide. When you are feeling close to the client, does she or he act in a way that facilitates closeness, or does she or he engage in behavior that decreases your feelings of closeness? A variety of avoidance reactions on the part of the client result in distance, including becoming critical, getting angry, getting numb inside and not feeling anything, saying she or he doesn't need to come in anymore, or making comments that devalue the meaning of the relationship because it's a professional one. A primary step in remediation involves the client learning to talk about the functional relationships (CRB3s) as in, "I'm feeling close to you right now and I feel like staying with you and know I can't. This upsets me, so I want to distance you."

Therapist Characteristics

Stable characteristics of the therapist such as age, gender, race, weight, physical attractiveness, and behavioral tendencies to be talkative or quiet, gentle or confrontive, self-disclosing or private, open-minded or opinionated can evoke CRB. An older male figure can be reminiscent of father; a confrontive or talkative therapist can evoke unassertiveness accompanied by feelings of intimidation and powerlessness; a thin therapist can bring forth envy, withdrawal, and comments from an overweight client such as "There's no way you'll understand my problem."

Unusual Events

Sometimes the most important clinically relevant operants can occur under less common conditions. Singular or uncommon events such as seeing the therapist with a partner outside of therapy, the therapist becoming pregnant, breaking a leg, or leaving town for a family emergency can serve as powerful aversive stimuli that provoke behavior and intense feelings associated with possessiveness, sibling rivalry, dependence, helplessness and mortality.

Feelings or Private States of the Therapist That Can Clue the Occurrence of CRB

The therapist's private reactions to the client can be a good source of information about clinically relevant behavior. Feelings of boredom, irritation, or anger in the therapist may highlight that the client is behaving in ways that are likely to elicit the same feelings in other people. For example, a client complains that she has trouble making friends and does not know why. The therapist notices that she or he easily becomes bored with her and her or his attention drifts because the client tends to talk in a monotone about trivial details for minutes at a time without checking to see whether the therapist is interested in what she is saying. Thus, self-observation can aid in the discrimination of the above problem behaviors as well as client target behaviors, such as talking in a more animated fashion, curtailing verbosity, and asking questions.

The Role of Emotions, Memories, and Cognitions in Behavior Change

Emotions, memories and cognitions have always occupied a central position in psychotherapy. Their utility is compelling, yet their definition and measurement elusive. The radical behavioral foundations of FAP bring a different perspective to these topics and to their relevance in clinical practice.

Emotions

As we have repeatedly stated, bringing clinically relevant behavior into the session is of highest priority to the FAP therapist. Sometimes, these CRBs do not occur because the client is not sufficiently in contact with controlling variables that are present. This lack of contact is often due to the client's avoidance of situations that evoke the expression of affect.

The therapist's task is to limit this avoidance, thereby enhancing contact with controlling variables and the occurrence of associated CRBs. When this happens, the affective expression will occur.

Emotions or feelings are "merely collateral products of the condition responsible for the behavior" (Skinner, 1974, p. 47). Thus, the expression of emotion during a session serves as a marker indicating to the therapist that the client is in contact with the controlling variables eliciting the emotion and associated CRB. It serves as a marker indicating contact in the same way that a person who gets close to a hot stove shows actual contact with the stove by crying out in pain and withdrawing from the hot surface. Crying out, the expression of affect, is an automatic effect of coming into contact with the stove. The associated feelings of pain are collateral products. The withdrawal is also evoked by the stimulus. If a client is not in contact with relevant controlling variables that would otherwise elicit an emotional response, the marker emotions and associated CRB will not occur.

For example, the second author had a client, Roxie, with a history of episodes of severe depressions, suicide attempts, and hallucinations. These intense episodes seemed to be provoked by interpersonal situations in which Roxie was criticized, rebuffed, or otherwise rejected. She would react very emotionally to these events, and engage in behaviors such as trying to stab herself with a knife or take an overdose of barbiturates. This was particularly true when the rejection occurred in a relationship that evoked attachment and dependency. After a 2-year course of therapy that involved many crises, the therapeutic relationship had developed to the point that it approximated the type of relationship that could evoke severe episodes if Roxie experienced a rejection by the therapist. From a FAP standpoint, such an occurrence would provide an invaluable opportunity for the development of more effective ways of dealing with the rejection (CRB2s) and increased self-understanding (CRB3s).

The therapist was anticipating just such an opportunity because she was about to tell Roxie that the number and type of evening and weekend phone calls were to be curtailed. When Roxie was told about this limitation, she appeared to be only minimally reacting to the information. She didn't cry or act angry but only seemed to be less talkative and changed the topic. It appeared that little contact was made with the situation at hand.

In an effort to bring Roxie into contact, the therapist brought the conversation back to the topic, stated the limitations again and asked Roxie to repeat what she understood about the phone call limitation. As Roxie spoke, she became more agitated. With further focusing on the topic and with the therapist's stating her observations of avoidance, Roxie began to sob and soon voiced a suicidal thought.

Over the next several months, Roxie gained a greater understanding of the controlling variables (CRB3)—a complex S^D involving her attachment to the therapist, the phone call limitation, and a history of rejection and abandonment. Also, in the give-and-take of the interaction, she learned a new way of reacting to a rejection. Rather than avoiding and engaging in suicidal behavior, she learned to discuss her dependency and fears of abandonment and to seek reassurance from the therapist. She was gently led to examine which of her behaviors pushed other people, including this therapist, away. Roxie was able to experience the therapist's caring even though her telephone privileges were curtailed. Although it took many months, the process of repeatedly bringing Roxie into contact with her true feelings about the phone call limitation proved to be a turning point in how she reacted to rejection, and set the stage for the development of improved interpersonal repertoires.

Degree of Contact with Controlling Variables

What is meant by degree or amount of contact is no more elaborate than the relationship between the salience of a S^D in a Skinner box and the control exercised by that stimulus. If a dim light is used to signal the availability of food for lever pressing and the light is turned on while the rat is facing away from it, it will have little or no effect on lever-pressing behavior. Another way of describing the weak relationship between the signal light and the lever press is that the rat is only partially, if at all, in contact with the stimulus. More control over behavior by the S^D would be seen during a subsequent presentation of the light if its intensity were increased and if the rat were oriented towards it.

As an analogy to the psychotherapeutic situation in which a client learns to react in a new way, let's say one wanted to change the behavior of the rat from the above example so that it scratched its head whenever the light came on instead of pressing the lever. The retraining procedure would involve reinforcing scratching only when the light was on. Needless to say, it would be impossible to try to bring scratching under the control of light and get rid of lever pressing at a time when the rat is not in contact with the light. There would be no training opportunities.

This situation is comparable to the difficulty that a client would have in learning new behaviors during a session when the relevant controlling stimuli are not present. For example, a client whose problem behaviors only are provoked by intimate situations, will have difficulty in learning new behaviors if the provocative intimate situation does not occur during the session. A few other analogies will help to illustrate the status of affect in FAP. Keep in mind that CRBs can only occur when controlling variables are contacted. Contacting a controlling variable during the session is analogous to having a training opportunity for the rat.

Contacting controlling variables can have two simultaneous effects. For example, the light in the Skinner box concomitantly can serve as a S^D

that controls the operant lever pressing and also as a conditioned stimulus that probably elicits salivation and other autonomic changes. Both the operant and respondent behavior are evoked by the same stimulus. The client who comes into contact with controlling variables could also show both operant and respondent behavior. For instance, the occurrence of an intimate interaction between the therapist and a client with intimacy problems could produce two simultaneous effects. One could be an affect involving tears and sadness (respondent), whereas the other could be a CRB involving an attempt to terminate the therapy (operant).

Depending on the degree of contact, the light will have more or less discriminative and eliciting effects and hence more or less effect on the behavior of the rat. Similarly, during FAP, a client can have more or less contact with controlling variables. Correspondingly, the client will show more or less of the associated CRB (operant) or affect (respondent).

For example, Karen's problems centered around forming and maintaining intimate relationships. She had been in FAP for several months and an increasingly close relationship with the therapist was developing. Although progress had occurred, some repertoire deficiencies still remained. One of these, as described by Karen, concerned a fear that the person she would become close to would disappear, never to return after being temporarily separated from her due to a trip or other such reason. She felt she would be devastated and would not be able to carry on her life. Karen saw these feelings as contributing to her past and present reluctance to become intimately involved. This problem also interfered with relationships as they were developing by causing her to feel intense sadness and to withdraw when threatened with separation. She could also relate her fears to having been left by a lover several years before.

Karen's account of how her fears relate to her relationship problems is a description of her problem behavior and possible controlling variables (CRB3). Her account, however, does not constitute an actual occurrence of the problem during the session (CRB1). From a FAP standpoint, the prospects of clinical improvement are enhanced if the fears and associated CRBs provoked by intimacy actually occur within the therapeutic relationship and thereby provide the client with an opportunity to learn new ways of responding. Further, a description of her problem behavior and controlling variables that is based on an event occurring during the session would be more beneficial than one based solely on behavior from the client's past.

The marker properties of affect were indicated as Karen began to cry when told about the therapist's upcoming 2-week vacation. She reported an overwhelming sadness. The client then attempted to minimize the event, tried to change the topic, and with a smile talked about not needing therapy any longer.

The therapist, governed by FAP rules, was aware that CRB1 possibly was occurring. He was empathic but brought the topic back to his upcoming departure. Karen again became tearful and an intense discussion followed involving the ongoing feelings of both client and therapist toward each other as well as possible solutions to the immediate problem caused by the vacation, such as having phone contact. A memory of an early, traumatic experience of being left at an aunt's was also recalled.

During the session after the therapist's return, Karen reported that she felt much better than she had anticipated during his absence. The interaction was good during that session, with both feeling closer to each other; this was different from the angry and resentful interactions that usually followed previous reunions with significant others, including this therapist. In the ensuing months, separations from the therapist became less disruptive and eventually, Karen reported that she was able to remain stable and not withdraw when anticipating a separation from a person she was becoming involved with. It appeared that new interpersonal repertoires concerning separation within an intimate relationship had been developed.

The expression of affect was important in the above interaction in two ways. Firstly, its presence was an indication that the therapeutic situation was functionally similar to the daily life situation involving intimacy and separation. They were similar in their eliciting properties because both resulted in sadness and associated affect. Discriminative similarities, evocative of operant behavior, were indicated by Karen's withdrawal from the interaction. These similarities are salient stimuli that can increase the discriminability, or therapist awareness, of CRBs. Secondly, the disappearance of affect along with the attempt to change the topic was an indication that the client was losing contact with controlling variables. The therapist intervened by bringing up the impending separation again, which helped to maintain contact with controlling variables. If contact is maintained, CRB can occur and provide the opportunity for learning improved repertoires.

The FAP view of emotions can be contrasted with prevalent mentalistic conceptions. Many psychotherapeutic systems and the general public view emotions as something that can be stored, repressed, and discharged. As appealing as these notions are, they leave us with the nagging questions as to where they are stored, where they go when they are discharged, and what is left in their place after discharge. Treating emotions as entities leads us to focus on these types of questions and steers us away from their context as part of a person's experience and behavior.

Memories

Rather than using the prevalent, up-to-date "cognitive-scientific" view of memory, FAP proceeds on the basis of Woodworth's 1921 notion as quoted in Catania (1984):

> Instead of "memory" we should say "remembering"; instead of "thought" we should say "thinking". . . . But, like other learned branches, psychology is prone to transform its verbs into nouns. Then what happens? We forget that our nouns are merely substitutes for verbs, and go hunting for the *things* denoted by the nouns; but there are no such things, there are only the activities that we started with . . . remembering. . . .

An extensive literature on state-dependent learning shows that memory is facilitated by having stimuli occur in the current situation that are similar to those present when the remembered event first occurred (Catania, 1984). Karen's recollection of a previously forgotten separation experience from childhood was probably the result of being in contact with controlling variables and the presence of their elicited affect. The separation stimuli, and perhaps the associated affect present in the session, were similar enough to the stimuli present at the aunt's house to evoke the recollection. Memory of the event had been inhibited because the client apparently did not maintain sufficient contact with the relevant controlling variables that could have elicited the affect and evoked the memory. From this standpoint, then, recollections of traumatic events are an automatic effect of contact and serve as an indicator or marker showing the presence of relevant controlling variables.

Within the FAP framework, affect and memories are primarily viewed as evidence that variables controlling the occurrence of certain CRBs have occurred, but are not directly responsible for clinical improvement. Instead, it is the occurrence of the CRBs that can lead to clinical improvement through opportunities for relearning.

Client Avoidance of Affect and Memories

The expression of affect is often aversive. This happens, according to Nichols and Efran (1985), because most cultures place substantial prohibitions on displays of emotion in adults. The reason for this cultural punishment is that the display means that the person is "off duty" and is not attending to the task at hand. This seems to hold true for a wide range of situations. A male grocery clerk who emotionally responds because a customer reminds him of his abusive mother would suffer negative consequences, as would an airline pilot who "breaks down" in an emergency. It is often in the best interests of the culture to limit the expression of affect.

The behavioral process involved in limiting affective expression is simple avoidance. Just as a rat avoids starting down one runway because it has ended in punishment and instead starts down another, people avoid attending to certain aspects of an evocative situation in favor of attending to others. The focus of clinical treatment often is on the client's most aversive affective experiences and memories—the very ones they would want to avoid because of the associated negative emotions.

Therapeutic techniques that help to bring the client into contact with controlling variables include: (1) being sensitive to when affect is avoided, (2) re-presenting the relevant stimuli, and (3) encouraging the expression of affect and the recollection of traumatic events. As with other FAP procedures, the encouragement of affective expression is not unique and is found in other therapeutic systems. Its ubiquity probably speaks to the usefulness of affective expression or, as it is commonly called, catharsis. Some characteristics, however, differentiate FAP from the other approaches. One is that the FAP therapist's explanation to the client would not involve appeals such as "Get it out," "It's good to release those bottled-up emotions," or "If you hold these emotions back, they will come out in some other way." Instead, the client would be told that the emotion is only an incidental product of dealing with the issues, or coming into contact with them, and that their absence indicates avoidance. Catharsis is not an end in itself but serves only as a marker.

The therapist's response to displays of emotion should ideally be naturally reinforcing. A therapist who has difficulty with affective expression is unlikely to offer such encouragement and may punish client affect. Someone with this type of deficient repertoire would not be the best therapist in such cases.

To reiterate: It is important that affect expression occur in the session. Such emotional expressions are not curative by themselves, but their avoidance is accomplished through reduced contact with controlling variables for CRB, which then diminishes the opportunity for the acquisition of new behavior.

Cognitions and Beliefs

When attempting to differentiate radical behaviorism from other approaches, most psychologists would first bring up its position on events beneath the skin, also known as private events. Contrary to popular belief, Skinner accepts the existence of private events and their relevance in the study of behavior. What does distinguish radical behaviorism from other approaches is that private events are not given any unique status other than their privacy. A client's private response can have as much or as little causal effect on subsequent behavior as a public response. The determination of causal effects is based on factors independent of the public–private distinction.

Private behavior also does not have unique status in terms of what it represents. It is cut from the same cloth as public behavior. The behavior of putting a coin in a candy vending machine is seen as behavior and not as a mere sign that indicates the presence of some other nonbehavioral entity such as drive, desire, expectancy, or a breakdown in ego functions. An explanation would focus on those variables affecting the behavior, such as the number of hours without eating, and not on the nonbehavioral entities. Similarly, a person thinking "I'll never get a job" is viewed as engaging in behavior, not as generating a sign of some nonbehavioral entity such as an assumption, belief, schema, or attitude that the person holds.

Rather than entities that exist within the person, the radical behavioral view is that "attitudes," "beliefs," and "assumptions" are terms invented by observers to describe behavior that is consistent under a wide range of conditions. Skinner states that the term "belief," as commonly used, refers to the probability that certain actions will occur. When seeking a therapist, it may be useful, for example, to know if he or she believes in behaviorism, primal scream therapy, medication, or psychosurgery. A therapist who says, "I believe primal scream therapy can cure anyone's problems" is also likely to use primal scream techniques during treatment, but these behavioral facts do not prove that one causes the other. It is also possible that the therapist's training and other experiences cause the belief statement as well the actual use of primal scream therapy. The occurrence of these two behaviors—the belief statement and the actual use of primal scream therapy—certainly do not prove that some cognitive structure actually exists within the therapist.

The patterns of behavior that constitute the actions associated with a particular belief are acquired in the same manner as any other behavior, namely, through the experiences known to influence operant and respondent behavior. From this perspective, beliefs are a summary statement of a person's experiences associated with the belief. A client who says, "I believe men can't be trusted" is giving a short descriptive statement that is a residue of her past experiences with men. Fraley (1984), in his radical behavioral analysis of belief, goes one step further in specifying the conditions that result in our use of the term belief. He differentiates between a belief statement, (e.g., "I believe in equal rights for women") and the true belief per se, which refers to the actual unconscious behavior of the client in situations where equality is an issue, and which may or may not correspond with the belief statement. Unconscious refers to a lack of awareness.

The following case compares cognitive–behavioral and FAP theories in terms of clinical technique: Harriet was asked to change her regular appointment time from 4:00 P.M. Mondays to 3:00 P.M. Tuesdays. She consented, but revealed several weeks later that it had caused a great deal of hardship in terms of rearranging her work and school schedule. When asked why she hadn't refused the therapist's request or point out it would be difficult, she said, "It wouldn't have done any good, because you wouldn't have kept the old appointment time just to save me from the trouble I would have in rearranging things. Besides not getting what I want, you'd also get angry and be irritated with me and I can't stand to have people get angry at me." The interaction was directly related to one of Harriet's presenting problems—not telling significant persons what she wants if she thinks they may get upset with her (CRB1).

Four of Harriet's behaviors are of particular interest. The first is the *telling*, at the present time, about what happened when the appointment change was originally requested. The second is *stating beliefs* at the present time such as "He will get angry." (For convenience, the discussion will focus on beliefs, but similar arguments apply to all cognitive constructs, such as assumptions and attitudes.) Harriet presumably was giving a description of the third behavior of interest—her *thinking*—that occurred at the time. That is, she had an inclination to say "no" and then thought something like "If I say 'no,' he will get angry and I can't stand that" and "Besides, he won't change his mind anyway." She then *acquiesced*, the fourth behavior of interest. She also had some bad feelings in the form of collateral respondents that accompanied her latent "no" and the thought "He will get angry." From the radical behavioral standpoint, all four behaviors are, above all, behavior. They are therefore to be explained and understood as one would explain any behavior.

This can be contrasted with cognitive approaches in which special theoretical and causal status are given two of these behaviors, the thinking and the stating of beliefs. The cognitive therapist assumes that Harriet's thinking is a manifestation of an underlying cognitive structure such as a belief or attitude (Ellis, 1962), or schemas made up of beliefs or assumptions (Beck, Rush, Shaw, & Emery, 1979). The identification of these structures is based on Harriet's description of her thoughts and what she says she believes to be true—mainly "I can't stand anger," "He will get angry," and "He won't change to accommodate me." When Harriet said that she "believed," "expected," and/or "thought" the therapist would get angry, the cognitive therapist takes this as evidence for the existence of a "belief" or "schema" in Harriet. It is then assumed that Harriet acquiesces because of her cognitions. Thus, the cognition is seen as more than just a term that describes a pattern of past behavior or the probability that Harriet will react in certain ways. It is an entity that has existence independent of behavior. Now, in order to account for Harriet's actions, the cognition needs to be accounted for in some other way than one would account for a behavior.

The FAP view is that Harriet's statement is a summary description and also a result of her past experiences concerning (1) people's anger when she inconvenienced them and (2) the likelihood they would accommodate her wishes. Harriet's account of her childhood was replete with instances of her parents not accommodating her and being punitive under these circumstances. Subsequent to these childhood experiences, Harriet has often behaved just as she did during the therapy session. Hence, it is not unreasonable for Harriet to think what she did when she did, nor would it be unexpected for her to acquiesce. Harriet's thoughts were also an indication of what to expect from her in the future should a similar situation arise.

In other words, Harriet's belief statement is a label or tact of past patterns of behavior. Viewed in this fashion, a belief statement is not an invention of the client but is instead an automatic description of the client's experiences. For Harriet "I can't stand anger" is derived from her past reactions to anger. It also follows that the belief statement will not change until her experiences have changed.

Entities aside, both the radical behaviorists and the cognitive therapists agree that thinking can precede an overt action. A central question has to do with the degree to which the behavioral process of "thinking" is a cause of subsequent behavior. In the case of Harriet, to what degree is her thinking "He will get angry", "I can't stand it," and "He won't accommodate me" responsible for her acquiescence? Answering the question is complicated by the fact that her private behavior was caused by the same history that accounts for her public behavior. Since her history is full of instances in which she was harshly punished by significant others when she made requests that inconvenienced them, her thoughts following the therapist's request are tacts that are the natural results of this history. Similarly, the acquiescence was a response shaped by the same past experience. She tacts (thinks) and acquiesces; each could be independent behaviors caused by the same stimulus conditions.

Clinical Procedures in Dealing with Beliefs
How do the theoretical positions of cognitive therapy and FAP influence what may happen during treatment? The most salient difference is that FAP, whenever possible, focuses on thinking, believing, and other relevant behavior that occurs during the session itself, whereas cognitive therapies emphasize behavior occurring elsewhere. For example, in a discussion of "technical problems" in doing cognitive therapy for depression, Beck *et al.* (1979) bring up the problem of a client who says, "You are more interested in doing research than in helping me." First, Beck wisely points out that even if such a statement were left unsaid, one who is involved in a clinical research project may be secretly harboring such thoughts. The reason such thoughts may occur, according to Beck, is that depressed clients might be distorting what the therapist does. He then suggests that the therapist inquire if any such notions are present and then put these worries to rest. If possible, Beck says, one should avoid such problems in the first place by anticipating their occurrence and giving complete explanations to the client.

The FAP analysis of the situation would be somewhat different. A depressed client who feels unimportant to the therapist highlights the fact that the therapeutic situation could be evoking the very problem that brought the client into treatment. This would not be viewed as a technical problem to be disposed of, but as a situation that provides a therapeutic opportunity. The FAP therapist would not assume that the client is distorting, just that the therapist is contacting different aspects of the current situation than the client. It is even possible that the research *is* more important to the therapist and, if so, the client would not be "distorting" at all. The notion that the client might be secretly harboring such ideas rather then telling the therapist about them is also suggestive of the occurrence of a clinical problem during the session.

Although Beck's theory may lead the therapist to overlook many situations that would be of interest to a FAP therapist, he does recognize that certain therapist–client interactions can provide therapeutic opportunity. For example, in discussing ways to strengthen collaboration, he points out that a client may react to a homework assignment as a test of self-worth, and that the therapist should try to sense this (FAP Rule 1) and use it as an opportunity to correct faulty cognitions. Beck gives however, no special significance to the fact that the therapeutic work is focusing on behavior as it is occurring. Instead, it is viewed as having the same effects as dealing with a cognition that occurs elsewhere.

Another technique used by cognitive therapists is that of trying to convince clients that their beliefs are illogical or incorrect by pointing out the logical fallacies or errors of fact. From a FAP perspective, getting Harriet to change her belief by rationally convincing her, à la Albert Ellis, that she *can* stand anger is not guaranteed to have a favorable result when she actually finds herself in the problem situation in the future. No guarantee exists, because it is unclear what behavior has changed due to the "convincing," other than her saying "Okay, I believe I can stand it." The client changes the belief statement because of the logical arguments of the therapist, but it loses its essential properties of being a description of past experiences or an indication of the likelihood of certain actions. It is therefore not surprising that many clients who have been "convinced" to change their beliefs, subsequently do not change their behavior in the problem situation. Such "failures" are usually accompanied by explanations such as "I intellectually believe it, but I don't accept it on an emotional level." The FAP therapist would not find such a state of affairs perplexing, since no necessary connection exists between "intellectual believing" behaviors and those behaviors contributing to the emotions. In fact, there is no reason to expect anything else.

On the other hand, changing a client's belief statements can at times affect subsequent "believing" and acting in the problem situation. These successes accrue from the premium that the culture places on being consistent: "One should practice what one preaches," not "say one thing and do another." Thus, some inclination exists for clients to act in accordance with a "belief" that a therapist has directly instructed a client to hold. The strength of such inclinations, however, are generally weak and are dependent on the emphasis placed on consistency by a client's subculture. This consistency effect is strongest in scientific subcultures such as psychology. For example, during classroom instruction at certain universities, fledgling psychologists acquire verbal repertoires such as "Clients wanted to have sex with their parents." At other institutions, it may instead be "Behavior is affected by its consequences." After graduating, they become members of their respective scientific groups, such as APA's divisions for psychoanalysis and for the experimental analysis of behavior. The same repertoires are reinforced at professional meetings and over cocktails with colleagues who have been trained under similar conditions. They may then incorrectly "see" such phenomena while doing therapy because the control over what is seen through contact with their clients' behavior (reality) may be overwhelmed by the social control to be consistent with one's theory. Or, in the language of the cognitive psychologists, one's beliefs influences one's perceptions.

In addition to the effects of consistency, there are other ways to account for instances in which cognitive therapy is effective without relying on a presumed ontological status of beliefs. For instance, an unintended effect of rationally convincing Harriet that she can stand anger is the therapist's covert demand or implied instructions for Harriet to act differently. Changes in Harriet's behavior would then be the result of her instruction following or "rule governed behavior" (Zettle & Hayes, 1982). Significant clinical improvement will occur if her new behavior is naturally reinforced in her daily life. However, cognitive therapy also often involves explicit, overt instructions to the client for behavior change. For example, Beck et al. (1979) encourage clients to act against their assumptions because it is ". . . the most powerful way to change it" (p. 264). This emphasis on building in new behavior is consistent with FAP. For the FAP therapist, however, the behavior change is the goal, whereas at least for some cognitive therapists (Beck et al., 1979), it is merely a means to change cognitions.

FAP is aimed at developing new adaptive behavior while simultaneously producing "improved" beliefs. A FAP therapist thus would not depend on logic to convince a "worthless" client that her belief is incorrect and thereby change her into a "worthwhile" person. Instead, FAP would focus on strengthening those repertoires that are characteristic of a "worthwhile" person. This would entail reacting to the client as a "worthwhile" person. The client's expression of opinions and negative feelings would be reinforced if the therapist seriously considered and reacted to all of the client's thoughts and ideas during the course of treatment.

Interventions along the lines of cognitive therapies may also be used, such as using logical arguments, appeals to reason, or telling the client that a particular belief doesn't match the therapist's observations. For example, the therapist might say, "You are worthwhile to me" or "Since

I find you an attractive person, you cannot logically say you are unattractive to others." These statements, however, are viewed as single occurrences of an extensive repertoire involving the therapist's regard for the client as attractive and worthwhile. Above all, the client would not be expected to say "Okay, I now believe I am worthwhile and attractive" just because the therapist gave his or her opinion. The intervention probably would have minimal therapeutic benefit other than that provided by the client attempting to be "consistent." That is, the client would try to act and feel in a manner consistent with the "logic" the therapist is asking for. Most likely, many other occurrences are required of the therapist repertoire of "reacting to the client as worthwhile" over the course of treatment in order to obtain therapeutic benefit.

Although FAP therapists may use appeals to reason, theoretical differences between FAP and cognitive therapies lead to different therapist behaviors when such interventions are not successful. The cognitive therapist probably would try additional ways of pointing out to the client why his or her thoughts are incorrect. The FAP therapist would instead accept the client's "inconsistencies" and try to identify variables that account for behaviors such as (1) espousing belief A and acting belief B, (2) trying to be consistent in espousing and acting, or (3) trying to please the therapist by being rational.

In summary, the use of appeals to rationality in FAP are seen as one small part of a larger set of therapeutic interactions that will help develop a new set of client experiences and behaviors, and produce a favorable change in associated believing.

SO WHAT'S NEW

It can be argued that FAP treatment techniques are already advocated by existing systems of therapy. Given the marked differences between radical behaviorism and other theories on which treatment is based, such similarities are of interest in their own right. Commonalities can also aid in integration and in underscoring procedures that can be especially important in producing therapeutic change. Similarities notwithstanding, FAP has implications for treatment that differentiate it from other systems.

FAP Contrasted with Psychodynamic Approaches

Although both psychodynamic approaches and FAP point to the importance of the occurrence of the client's problem in the session, the difference between the two is highlighted by the FAP position that the problem behaviors that occur during the session are instances of the same operant that encompasses the presenting problem, and not the result of a misperception or other "transference" phenomena. As an operant, there is no guarantee that the problem will occur during the session, and whether it does or not depends on the discriminative stimuli that are present, as well as on other conditions that are known to influence the occurrence of any behavior. This can be contrasted with the psychodynamic assumption that problem-related behavior, or transference, will almost always occur. Furthermore, clinical improvement would depend on the consequences or the reinforcing properties of the therapist's reactions to the problem behavior and not as a result of its mere occurrence as implied by psychodynamic theory.

The psychodynamic conception of the therapist's role is that of a teacher who creates the conditions during treatment that bring about change in the client (Waterhouse & Strupp, 1984). This notion is similar to the radical behavioral position. The two differ, however, with respect to the teaching process itself. The psychodynamic view is that the therapist should "disengage from the emotional climate presented by the client" in order to avoid responding to the client with reactions that might occur naturally in the social environment. The radical behavioral view is that natural therapist reactions are the primary change agent. Many other differences exist between the two approaches—for instance, regarding the concepts of drive and energy, psychic structures, developmental stages, and how behavior is acquired. It is beyond the scope of this chapter to delineate the treatment implications of these differences.

FAP Contrasted with Current Behavior Therapies

FAP differs from other behavior therapies primarily in the core significance given to certain aspects of the therapeutic relationship. Specifically, the therapeutic relationship is an environment that can evoke and immediately reinforce clinically relevant behavior. This aspect of the relationship rarely has been mentioned by behavior therapists, and when it is mentioned, it occupies a minor role in the overall treatment plan (e.g., Goldfried & Davison, 1976) and seems to have had little impact on the field. Instead, when behavior therapists talk about the therapeutic relationship and recognize its importance, they typically refer to such factors as "nonspecific effects," "the using of a 'good relationship' as the basis for obtaining cooperation during treatment," or "using the therapist's social reinforcement value to motivate or maintain changes in daily life." As important as such variables are, they do not direct attention, as does FAP, to the clinically relevant behaviors occurring during the session.

For example, Sweet's (1984) review of therapeutic relationship issues attended to by behavior therapists included such factors as the impact of the relationship, therapist time, and social reinforcement. None of the reviewed studies had mentioned the importance of the client's presenting problem behaviors occurring during the session. At times, these behaviors were ignored even though they attracted the attention of the therapist, as in the following case example given by Sweet. A client was frightened of making progress in treatment, which was manifested, in part, by her negative reactions to the therapist's praise (social reinforcement was the therapeutic procedure being employed). The therapist used flooding to "overcome this impasse." In citing this case as an example of overcoming a technical difficulty—"fear of success"—in doing the therapy, Sweet overlooked the potential importance of the "fear of success" in the therapeutic relationship as an occurrence of a problem that has significant impact in other areas of this client's life. Further, no consideration was given to the potential benefits that the "overcoming of a technical difficulty" may have had for the client in her daily life.

FAP is similar to social skills training (SST) in that both emphasize deficits in interpersonal repertoires as the cause of the client's problems and view treatment as a means of remediating the deficits. They differ markedly, however, in how the skill deficits are supposed to be detected and in the remediation process itself.

In FAP, the therapist is supposed to observe directly, during the session, presenting symptoms and the variables controlling them. The type and amount of behavioral improvement is based on the particular client's existing repertoire. The target behaviors might be subtle and difficult to recognize without this direct observation, such as the client (Linda) discussed earlier whose improvement consisted of giving reasons for quitting therapy before actually doing it. Perhaps most importantly, an improvement is a behavioral change that occurs under the stimulus conditions that bring about the symptoms. The functional equivalence between the therapeutic situation and the natural environment is a precondition for FAP. If the therapeutic situation doesn't evoke the symptoms, FAP can't be done. Thus, symptoms and improvements are functionally defined.

In contrast, social skills training rarely involves the direct observation of the symptoms or the conditions that bring them about. Further, the skills are acquired under conditions that are obviously different than the conditions that bring about the symptoms. Behavior acquired via coaching, modeling, role playing, and behavioral rehearsal during the session is functionally different than the behavior that is supposed to occur in daily life, even though they might look the same. Ignoring the functional aspects of the behavior is like ignoring the difference between the rote learning of the sounds that compose a sentence in French and learning the same sounds but with an understanding of their meaning. The sentences may sound exactly the same to a listener but they are functionally very different. This problem was alluded to in a review of the literature on SST generalization by Scott, Himadi, & Keane (1983). They concluded that the lack of demonstrable generalization is responsible for SST's limited acceptability as a viable treatment. Given the lack of functional similarity between training and natural environments, there is no guarantee that SST behavior will transfer, and explanations are needed to account for those instances in which it does.

Differences notwithstanding, it should be emphasized that FAP complements and overlaps with other behavior therapies (BT). BT is still the treatment of choice for the initial intervention in most situations. Above all, empirical data to support the efficacy of FAP have not yet been gathered, whereas BT has demonstrated effectiveness. For this reason alone, it makes sense to try BT as the first intervention and then to complement it with FAP as the occasion or need arises.

FAP was developed in the context of on-going behavior therapy. At first, it was used when BT did not appear to be effective. Now, we use FAP in conjunction with BT from the very beginning, and at times, it becomes the primary mode of treatment. FAP integrates easily with BT because many of the methods of behavior therapy are evocative of CRB. For example, specific homework instructions are often assigned during BT. For clients whose problems involve excessive compliance, rebelliousness, or guilt or anxiety for not meeting expectations, BT naturally provides the opportunity for FAP.

PROFESSIONAL AND ETHICAL ISSUES

Precautions

In our experience, FAP procedures are powerful in that they tend to evoke intense emotional reactions and reinforcing effects that are associated with intimate relationships. Because of this, FAP can be very beneficial to the client by affecting large repertoires. These same factors, however, can produce harmful effects due to intense negative affect and associated avoidance and escape repertoires. The following factors should be kept in mind when following FAP procedures.

First, because the controlling variables during the session are the most potent ones, they have the potential of being extremely aversive. Since it is common for CRB1 to be aversively controlled behavior, an optimal level of aversiveness must be present in order for therapy to occur. Too little aversiveness means that the client's avoidance is successfully reinforced in the session and this will stagnate progress; too much aversiveness can overwhelm and immobilize. Those clients who have histories in which their behavior is frequently disrupted by reactions to aversive stimuli should be exposed to FAP procedures with caution. Generally, it is a good idea to start treatment with a focus on problems occuring outside the session, using standard BT procedures before doing anything about CRB, that is, before focusing on the therapist–client relationship. This will help to develop the task orientation of treatment and give both client and therapist a chance to establish a general method of working together which is not complicated by disruptive emotional reactions.

Second, it is important to remember that clinically relevant behaviors are hypotheses to be explored, and their actual clinical relevance needs to be demonstrated, not assumed.

Third, focusing on behavior occurring during the session intensifies the feelings between client and therapist. This can enhance sexual attraction between the two individuals. While discussion of such feelings can provide opportunities for therapeutic progress, acting on them is untherapeutic and unethical. A variant of this issue is a client who has sexual problems. A naive or self-serving therapist may point to the tenets of FAP and state that the best intervention would be to become sexual with the client, since the clinically relevant behaviors would only come up in a sexual relationship. In such a situation, sex therapy with the client and a significant other would be the best intervention. Sexual activity in these circumstances seems to be arbitrarily reinforced by the therapist, and the client sooner or later feels exploited and betrayed, as evidenced by the increasing number of malpractice suits brought by clients against therapists who have had sex with them.

Fourth, the basic FAP notion that CRB occurs within the therapeutic relationship may result in the continuation of a nonbeneficial treatment. For example, a client whose problems center on not being able to terminate destructive relationships may also show similar behavior during therapy. Therefore, a client may stay in therapy when it would be better if treatment were terminated or if the client were referred to another therapist. The role of the therapist as expert/authority figure decreases the likelihood that the client will take the initiative to terminate, particularly when he or she has been cautioned against leaving treatment prematurely.

And finally, as is elaborated in the next section, therapists must be well-trained, clinically aware, and sensitive individuals with the client's requisite behaviors in their own repertoires.

Suitable Therapists

A suitable therapist is one who is differentially reinforced by client improvements. According to our analysis, clinical improvement is achieved through the shaping and reinforcement of the client's behavior during the session. This can happen only if clinically relevant behaviors occur, and if there are therapist repertoires that will be likely to provide natural reinforcement for improvements as they occur. A suitable therapist, therefore, must have the requisite repertoires for a particular client. The main point, however, is that not all therapists are therapeutic for all clients, and awareness of the nuances of interpersonal interactions related to the particular presenting problem is required for successful treatment. The assumption that matching is necessary between therapist and client is, of course, not new. The present analysis, however, suggests that a determination of the match depends on a detailed assessment of therapist reactions and associated reinforcing effects. This can be contrasted with the previous research on this issue that has studied macro variables such as age, sex, and social class.

FAP's Position on Sexism and Racism

Two aspects of FAP have relevance to the issues of sexism, racism, and other forms of discrimination. First, because of its radical behavioral foundations, FAP does not have any sexist or racist assumptions. There are no models of what a healthy person should be like or what kinds of goal behaviors should be in the repertoire, other than a favoring of positively reinforced repertoires and an eschewing of aversive controls. There is, therefore, no theoretical basis for deciding what specific behaviors should be in the repertoires of a person based on his or her membership in racial, sexual, or any other groups. The theory is neutral with respect to these issues.

A second aspect of FAP that relates to sexism and racism is based on the powerful reinforcing effects that are assigned to the therapist reactions to client behavior occurring during the session. The therapist, as a member of the culture that supports subtle, and sometimes not so subtle, racism and sexism could have values consistent with the culture. Values refer to a person's reinforcers; a sexist or racist therapist would continue to reinforce those client behaviors that have been shaped by a racist or sexist culture. Racism and sexism limit access to reinforcers. Thus, a therapist who reinforces on the basis of sexism or racism would be interfering with repertoires that could increase long-term positive reinforcement and thereby compromise the goals of FAP. This problem is compounded by the fact that the bias may be subtle and not self-observable by the therapist. As a precaution against such bias and as a general aid in following the five rules, it is helpful to have sessions regularly videotaped and observed by individuals who are sensitive to such issues.

Evaluation

FAP predicts that a number of variables are important to the conduct and outcome of therapy in general: (1) the occurrence during the session of the client's clinically relevant behavior, (2) the discrimination and specification by the therapist of the client's problem-relevant and goal-related behaviors, (3) the availability of goal-related repertoires in the therapist, and (4) the presence of therapist reactions that shape and naturally reinforce client improvements. The prediction of outcome based on the above variables, however, requires fine-grain analyses examining the interactions of therapist–client pairs over a number of sessions.

Before such research can be done, the therapeutic system must be further developed and skilled therapists must be available. Further development is needed so that additional guidance can be given to therapists to detect and appropriately reinforce CRB. In the meantime, evaluation will be based on the outcome of case studies, process research, and the prediction of psychotherapy outcome in general. Our hope is that the theory and procedures of FAP will influence therapists to adopt this approach.

ACKNOWLEDGMENT

Thanks to Barbara Kohlenberg for reigniting a burnt out radical behaviorist.

REFERENCES

Beck, A., Rush, A., Shaw, B., & Emery, G. (1979). *Cognitive therapy of depression*. New York: Guilford.

Catania, A. C. (1984). *Learning*. Englewood Cliffs, NJ: Prentice-Hall.

Deci, E. L. (1971). Effects of externally mediated rewards on intrinsic motivation. *Journal of Personality and Social Psychology, 55*, 467–517.

Dollard, J., & Miller, N. E. (1950). *Personality and psychotherapy*. New York: McGraw-Hill.

Ellis, A. (1962). *Reason and emotion in psychotherapy*. New York: Lyle Stuart.

Ferster, C. B. (1967). Arbitrary and natural reinforcement. *Psychological Record, 22*, 1–16.

Ferster, C. B. (1972a). Clinical reinforcement. *Seminars in Psychiatry, 4*(2), 101–111.

Ferster, C. B. (1972b). An experimental analysis of clinical phenomena. *Psychological Record, 22*, 1–16.

Ferster, C. B. (1972c). Psychotherapy from the standpoint of a behaviorist. In J. D. Keehn (Ed.), *Psychopathology in animals: Research and clinical implications*. New York: Academic Press.

Ferster, C. B. (1979). A laboratory model of psychotherapy. In P. Sjoden (Ed.), *Trends in behavior therapy*. New York: Academic Press.

Fraley, L. E. (1984). Belief, its inconsistency, and the implications for the teaching faculty. *The Behavior Analyst, 7*(1), 17–28.

Goldfried, M. R., & Davison, G. C. (1976). *Clinical Behavior Therapy*. New York: Holt, Rinehart, & Winston.

Greben, S. E. (1981). The essence of psychotherapy. *British Journal of Psychiatry, 138*, 449–455.

Hawkins, R. P., & Dobes, R. W. (1977). Behavioral definitions in applied behavior analysis: Explicit or implicit? In B. C. Etzel, J. M. LeBlanc, & D. M. Baer (Eds.), *New developments in behavioral research*. Hillsdale, NJ: Erlbaum.

Kazdin, A. E. (1975). *Behavior modification in applied settings*. Homewood, IL: Dorsey Press.

Levine, F. M., & Fasnacht, G. (1974). Token rewards may lead to token learning. *American Psychologist, 29,* 816–820.

Lutzker, J. R., & Martin, J. A. (1981). *Behavior change.* Monterey, CA: Brooks/Cole.

Nichols, M. P., & Efran, J. (1985). Catharsis in psychotherapy: A new perspective. *Psychotherapy: Theory, Research and Practice, 22*(1), 46–58.

Reese, E. P. (1966). *The analysis of human operant behavior.* Dubuque, IA: Wm. C. Brown Company Publishers.

Scott, R., Himadi, W., & Keane, T. (1983). Generalization of social skills. In M. Hersen, R. Eisler, & P. Miller (Eds.), *Progress in behavior modification.* New York: Academic Press.

Skinner, B. F. (1945). The operational analysis of psychological terms. *Psychological Review, 52,* 270–277.

Skinner, B. F. (1953). *Science and human behavior.* New York: Macmillan.

Skinner, B. F. (1957). *Verbal behavior.* New York: Appleton-Century-Crofts.

Skinner, B. F. (1974). *About behaviorism.* New York: Knopf.

Sweet, A. A. (1984). The therapeutic relationship in behavior therapy. *Clinical Psychology Review, 4,* 253–272.

Truax, C. B. (1966). Reinforcement and nonreinforcement in Rogerian psychotherapy. *Journal of Abnormal Psychology, 21*(1), 1–9.

Wachtel, P. L. (1977). *Psychoanalysis and behavior therapy: Toward an integration.* New York: Basic Books.

Waterhouse, G., & Strupp, H. (1984). The patient–therapist relationship: Research from the psychodynamic perspective. *Clinical Psychology Review, 4,* 77–92.

Zettle, R. D., & Hayes, S. C. (1982). Rule-governed behavior: A potential theoretical framework for cognitive-behavioral therapy. In P. C. Kendall (Ed.), *Advances in cognitive-behavioral research and therapy* (Vol. 1). New York: Academic Press.

INDEX